CORAL REEFS OF THE INDIAN OCEAN

CORAL REEFS OF
THE INDIAN OCEAN

Their Ecology and Conservation

Edited by
T.R. McClanahan
C.R.C. Sheppard
D.O. Obura

OXFORD
UNIVERSITY PRESS
2000

OXFORD

UNIVERSITY PRESS

Oxford   New York
Athens   Auckland   Bangkok   Bogotá   Buenos Aires   Calcutta
Cape Town   Chennai   Dar es Salaam   Delhi   Florence   Hong Kong   Istanbul
Karachi   Kuala Lumpur   Madrid   Melbourne   Mexico City   Mumbai
Nairobi   Paris   São Paulo   Shanghai   Singapore   Taipei   Tokyo   Toronto   Warsaw

and associated companies in
Berlin   Ibadan

Copyright ©2000 by Oxford University Press, Inc.

Published by Oxford University Press, Inc.
198 Madison Avenue, New York, New York 10016

Oxford is a registered trademark of Oxford University Press.

Library of Congress Cataloging-in-Publication Data
Coral reefs of the Indian Ocean : their ecology and conservation /
edited by T. R. McClanahan, C. R. C. Sheppard & D. O. Obura.
p.   cm.
Developed from a workshop, Coral Reefs of Western Indian Ocean,
held in Mombasa, Kenya in March 1997.
Includes bibliographical references.
ISBN 0-19-512596-7
1. Coral reef ecology — Indian Ocean.   2. Coral reef conservation — Indian Ocean
I. McClanahan, T. R. II. Sheppard, Charles (Charles R. C.)   III. Obura, David O.
QH94 .C67   2000
577.7'895 — dc21   99-040236

1 3 5 7 9 8 6 4 2

Printed in the United States of America
on acid-free paper

Introduction

This book was written for students, teachers, naturalists, ecotourists, researchers and managers learning or working in the marine environment who would like a recent review of the status of coral reefs and reef science and conservation in the Indian Ocean. It is focused on the western Indian Ocean as this represents a distinct biogeographic unit (see Chapter 1) that shares many of the same species and has many common processes and responses to environmental or human disturbances. The scientific literature from this region is scattered and much of it is not published in the standard journals or difficult to access. This book will therefore make it easy for the reader to become current with existing information as well as with current thinking and foci of reef investigations.

This book was developed from a workshop organized by The Wildlife Conservation Society's Coral Reef Conservation Project as part of the 1997 International Year of the Reef (IYOR) activities. One of the primary focuses of IYOR was to assess the status of coral reefs worldwide and the workshop and book represent part of this continuing effort. The authors of the following chapters focus on introducing the reader to the coral reefs of the region through past surveys, scientific research and conservation work. Environmental descriptions are not, however, restricted to the physicochemical and biological environment but also incorporate the human environment including the use of resources, the structures and mandates of national government and nongovernment organizations and their successes and failures in conserving marine resources.

Each chapter discusses the physical environment, the distribution of coral reefs, factors which are important for ecological processes and species diversity, and discuss how these ecological factors can be affected by present and projected human influences. Human influences over different time and spatial scales are considered and include harvesting, aquaculture, dynamite blasting, coral mining, pollution and poisons, global warming and species losses. The causes of ecological changes are discussed as well as the way reefs could be used in a sustainable way. The book also contains a number of case studies both in the text and in boxes which describe important concepts, problems or reef sites, such as the status of coral-eating starfish, coral disesases or the effects of aquaculture on reef resources. Authors have made an effort to keep the reviews and language simple and easy to understand. Readers may want to read the first two introductory chapters and then move to subsequent chapters as their interest dictates. Consequently, we have kept some redundancy among chapters.

The workshop and book were also an attempt to coordinate methods and activities of coral reef investigators and investigations in this region which is known to have poor scientific societal organization. Consequently, we held the workshop adjacent to the recently created Mombasa Marine National Park so that participants could undertake comparative field studies on the coral-reef parks and reserves of Kenya during the meeting. This workshop, the presentations of regional organizations, and the book's chapters suggest that the level of information and human capacity to collect and disseminate this information has increased greatly in the last decade. The presentations also demonstrate, however, that reefs are threatened by a number of environmental problems that are only moderately documented and understood. Nonetheless, these chapters do reveal the underlying causes of reef degradation and suggest ways to prevent it. Finding successful conservation, restoration or mitigation methods may increase the rate at which the elusive goal of sustainable resource use in this region can be reached. We hope this book helps to make the next step in assessing and ultimately managing this precious and biologically diverse tropical ecosystem.

McClanahan, T.R., Sheppard, C.R.C. & Obura, D.O.
Mombasa, Kenya and Warwick, United Kingdom

Acknowledgments

This book developed from a workshop *Coral Reefs of the Western Indian Ocean* held in Mombasa, Kenya in March 1997. We are grateful for the financial support for the workshop provided by an award (Pew Fellows Program in Conservation and Environment) to T.R. McClanahan by The Pew Charitable Trust. Numerous people assisted with the many aspects of collecting and providing information and reading and commenting on the various chapters. For their assistance we thank R. Abrea, Bill Allison, Jim Bohnsack, David Boullé, J. Brodie, Eleanor Carter, P. Chabanet, A. Cooke, D. Choussy, John Collie, I. Dutton, Gérard Faure, W. Gladstone, Dr. Hansa, M. Hatchwell, M. Hedrick, B. Lassig, Cam Lewis, T. Lison de Loma, Robert Lucking, J. Makkar, R. Mau, R. Melchers, N. Mohan, P. Moran, Jeanne Mortimer, Omari Nyange, Yussuf Said, Hassan Shakeel, Ahmed Shakeel, Aishath Shaan Shakir, J. Stoddart, Bevan Vidot, C. Wallace and S. Wells. Special thanks goes to R.N. Ginsburg for his desire and efforts to determine the ecological status of Earth's coral reefs.

In addition, numerous organizations assisted with financial support for the authors and their research. For this assistance we thank the American Association for the Advancement of Science, American Museum of Natural History, Finnish International Aid Agency (FINNIDA), French National Program on Coral Reefs (PNRCO), French Departments of Education and Research, and Environment, International Centre for Ocean Development (ICOD), John G. Shedd Aquarium, Kenya-Dutch Wetland Program of the Dutch Embassy, Lerner Gray Fund for Marine Research, The MacArthur Foundation, Maldives Marine Research Section of the Ministry of Fisheries and Agriculture, Mission of Cooperation and Cultural Action of the French Embassy in Madagascar, National Geographic Society, Natural Sciences and Engineering Research Council of Canada (NSERC), NORAD, Oceanographic Society of Maldives, Regional Council of Reunion, Rockefeller Foundation, Dr. Scholl Foundation, Seychelles Fishing Authority, Seychelles Marine Parks Authority, Swedish International Development Agency (Sida), Society for Environmental Exploration, South African Association for Marine Biological Research, United Nations Development Program, Food and Agricultural Organization, and Regional Seas Program, The Wildlife Conservation Society, The World Bank, World Conservation Union (IUCN).

List of Contributors

Rohan Arthur, Center for Ecological Research and Conservation, 3076/5, Mysore, India

P. Bachelery, Laboratoire de Géologie, Université de la Réunion. 15, avenue René Cassin, 97715 Saint-Denis Messag Cedex 9, France

Gerry Bakus, Department of Biological Sciences, University of Southern California, University Park, Los Angeles, CA 90089-0371, USA

Chantal Conand, Laboratoire d'Ecologie Marine, Université de la Réunion, BP 9751, 97715 Saint-Denis, La Réunion, France

Julie Church, World Wide Fund for Nature, P.O. Box 99, Lamu, Kenya

Pascale Cuet, Laboratoire d'Ecologie Marine, Université de la Réunion, BP 9751, 97715 Saint-Denis, La Réunion, France

Will Darwall, GEF Lake Malawi Biodiversity Project, P.O.BOX 311, Salima, Malawi

David Dixon, 34 Thornbury Park Ave., Peverall, Plymouth, PL3 4NJ, UK

Catherine Gabrie, Consultant in Tropical Marine and Coastal Environment - 4, villa Juliette de Wills, 92170, Vanves, France

J. Gascoigne, MacAlister Elliot & Partners, 56 High Street, Lymington, Hampshire, SO41 9AH, UK

Heidi Glaesel, Elon College, Department of History, Burlington, North Carolina, 27215, USA

Martin Guard, Frontiers-Tanzania, P.O. Box 9473, Dar es Salaam, Tanzania

Chris Horrill, IUCN, Tanga Coastal Conservation Project, P.O. Box 5036, Tanga, Tanzania

Chia-I Hsieh, Tropical Marine Research Unit, Department of Biology, University of York, York YO10 5ES, UK

Simon Jennings, School of Biological Sciences, University of East Anglia, Norwich, NR4 7TJ, UK

Albogast T. Kamukuru, Kunduchi Fisheries and Training Institute, P.O. Box 60091, Dar es Salaam, Tanzania

Jerry Kemp, Department of Biology, University of York, York, YO1 5YW, UK

Jan L. Korrubel, Invertebrate Conservation Research Center, Department of Zoology and Entomology, University of Natal, Private Bag X01, 3209 Scottsville, Pietermaritzburg, South Africa

Vijay Mangar, Albion Fisheries Center, Ministry of Co-operatives, Fisheries and Marine Resource Development, Mauritius

Suzanne Marshall, Division of Environment, Ministry of Foreign Affairs, Planning and Environment, PO Box 445, Victoria, Mahé, Seychelles and Scottish Agricultural College, University of Edinburgh, Edinburgh, EH9 3JG, UK

Jean Maharavo, Centre National de Recherche Oceanographique, Nosy-Be, Madagascar

Judy Mann-Lang, Oceanographic Research Institute, P.O. Box 10712, Marine Parade, Durban 4056, South Africa

E. Mara, Institut Halieutique et des Sciences Marines, University of Tulear, Madagascar

David Medio, Tropical Marine Research Unit, Department of Biology, University of York, York YO10 5ES, UK

Yunus Mgaya, Department of Zoology and Marine Biology, University of Dar es Salaam, Dar es Salaam, Tanzania

Helena Motta, Ministry for the Coordination of Environmental Affairs, P.O.Box 2020, Maputo, Mozambique.

Timothy R. McClanahan, The Wildlife Conservation Society, Coral Reef Conservation Project, P.O. Box 99470, Mombasa, Kenya

T. Munbodh, Albion Fisheries Center, Ministry of Co-operatives, Fisheries and Marine Resource Development, Mauritius

Nyawira A. Muthiga, Kenya Wildlife Service, P.O. Box 82144, Mombasa, Kenya

Odile Naim, Laboratoire d'Ecologie Marine, Université de la Réunion, BP 9751, 97715 Saint-Denis, La Réunion

Flower Msuya, Institute of Marine Sciences, University of Dar es Salaam, P.O. Box 668, Zanzibar

David Obura, Coral Reef Degradation in the Indian Ocean, P.O.Box 10135, Bamburi, Mombasa, Kenya

Rupert Ormond, Tropical Marine Research Unit, Department of Biology, University of York, York YO10 5ES, UK

H. D. Rabesandratana, Département Muséologie/Aquariologie, Institute Halieutique et des Sciences Marines, Université de Tuléar, Madagascar

H. Randriamiarana, National Coordination for Marine and Coastal Program, ONE, Antananarivo, Madagascar

Sibylle Riedmiller, Chumbe Island Coral Reef Marine Park, P.O. Box 3023, Zanzibar, Tanzania

Mike Risk, Department of Geology, McMaster University, 1280 Main Street West, Hamilton, Canada

Maria-João Rodrigues, Institute for Fisheries Research, P.O.Box 4603, Maputo, Mozambique

Rodney V. Salm, IUCN, East African Regional Programme, 68200, Nairobi

Charles R.C. Sheppard, Department of Biological Sciences, University of Warwick, Coventry, CV4 7AL, Warwick, UK

Michael Schleyer, Oceanographic Research Institute, P.O. Box 10712, Marine Parade, Durban 4056, South Africa

P. Vasseur, Ecologie des Récifs Coralliens et Environnement Littoral, Université de Provence, Marseille, France

Mark W. Whittington, Society for Environmental Exploration, 77 Leonard Street, London, United Kingdom

Simon C. Wilson, P.O. Box 2531, CPO 111, Seeb, Oman

Leon P. Zann, Southern Cross University, Box 157, Lismore, New South Wales, Australia

Rudy van der Elst, Oceanographic Research Institute, P.O. Box 10712, Marine Parade, Durban 4056, South Africa

Contents in Brief

Contents

Section II: Country Profiles   81

Chapter 5. *Southern Tanzania* 131
W.R.T. Darwall & M. Guard

Chapter 6. *Northern Tanzania, Zanzibar and Pemba*   167
J.C. Horrill, A.T. Kamukuru, Y.D. Mgaya & M. Risk

Chapter 7. *Kenya*   199
D.O. Obura, N.A. Muthiga, & M. Watson

Chapter 11. *The Maldives: A Nation of Atolls* 325
M.J. Risk & R. Sluka.

Section I

Coral Reefs and Conservation in the Wester Indian Ocean: An Overview

Chapter 1

Coral Reefs of the Western Indian Ocean: An Overview

Charles R.C. Sheppard

Coral reefs of the Indian Ocean exist in a very wide range of environments. Good examples exist of classic, oceanic atolls in clear water, and also of extensive fringing and patch reefs which grow in conditions of high environmental stress, where corals mix with other major benthic groups. Reefs develop best where sea surface temperatures remain above about 22°C, and classically, the reef province has previously been defined as that where temperatures rarely fall below about 18°C (40,47). The relationship between reef distribution and sea surface temperature has, however, turned out to be much too simplistic. Many reef species tolerate much lower water temperatures, and thriving coral communities may occur in conditions which are too cool, or perhaps too rich in nutrients, for reef construction to occur. The Indian Ocean is particularly rich in these examples, which will be discussed later.

As well as containing many clearly defined reef areas, the periphery of the ocean also contains extended mosaics of a wide range of benthic habitats. In these areas, reefs are but one integrated component of the shallow oceanic system. Research which has focused, not only on the reefs but on their links with adjacent habitats, has led to greater understanding of crucial processes that drive the Indian Ocean system. Knowledge of the energy, productivity, and mineral linkages between the different ecosystems may also be used to help manage and reduce the continuing damage that is being done to reefs in this region.

The Western Indian Ocean

The western ndian Ocean forms a coherent subdivision of the world's largest biogeographic province - the tropical Indo-Pacific (54). Yet, at first site it does not seem to be a particularly well-defined biogeographical area. The Indian Ocean as a whole is a more understandable sub-region, being bounded by great continental land masses, but even this is illusory as on its eastern side tropical water flows continuously through to the Pacific Ocean. Indeed, many shallow-water species of the Indian Ocean occur continuously along an equatorial band which stretches around nearly three quarters of the Earth's circumference. Within this realm, however, several sub-divisions are identifiable by groupings or associations of species. These groupings may be well defined and contained within boundaries, clearly marked by land masses, or they may be constrained by currents or by oceanic expanses which lack suitable shallow habitat.

The western Indian Ocean grouping may be determined in part by its distance from the high diversity locus in south-eastern Asia. The origin and maintenance of this high-diversity locus is not well understood but is central to much of the biogeographical debate about sub-regional areas within the Indo-Pacific. In the case of corals, diversity contour lines have been drawn since as early as 1971 using genera (65), and the early 1980s using species (53). Diversity is highest in the Indonesian region, falling in a regular way eastwards across the Pacific. However, diversity does not fall in a regular way, or at all, westwards across the Indian Ocean. Instead, species richness stays high along the equatorial belt across the whole width of the ocean. Species identity does tend to change from east to west, along with a decline in Asian species, but this species loss is made up for by Indian Ocean endemics. As a consequence, contours of coral species richness, when drawn for the Indian Ocean, tend to remain similarly high roughly between the Tropics of Capricorn and Cancer, then collapse over very short latitudinal distances to the north and south. The Indian Ocean as a whole is, thus, unlike the Pacific, and there are no simple diversity clines expanding outwards neatly from the highest diversity center around Indonesia.

Nevertheless, there is a drop in coral diversity immediately west of Indonesia. This is because there is a lack of land and shallow water suitable for reef development for a considerable distance. Islands which do exist are tiny and, for reasons connected with small size, support a greatly reduced biotic diversity. Shallow continental substrate around the Bay of Bengal and along eastern India is too muddy for reef growth, and with only rare and small exceptions, is devoid of any corals (1). Substantial quantities of substrate suitable for reefs do not occur westwards until the Lakshadweep - Chagos chain of atolls.

The distribution of substrate in the western part of this ocean which is capable of supporting reefs is shown in Figure 1.1. Suitability is determined, partly by depth, but is also affected greatly by a range of other controls which preclude reef development. Westwards from the Lakshadweep - Chagos ridge lie the numerous islands and shallow platforms of the Seychelles territories, the Mascarene group and their outliers. Also, and probably most importantly, there is the vast range of shoals and shallow waters which stretch discontinuously between the Seychelles and Mascarenes; these include the Nazareth Bank, Saya de Malha Bank and Cargados Carajos Shoals. The potential reef substrate on this mainly submerged limestone chain is at least as great as that of all other islanded and inhabited groups, and is greater than that along the continental rim of the ocean. Yet, apart from limited and tantalizing anecdotes suggesting that this platform supports reefs with enormous algal ridges (63), it is still largely unknown territory. All shallow areas combined in the western Indian Ocean contain almost as much potentially reefal area as does the oceanic Pacific, and several times more than that which exists in the Atlantic province.

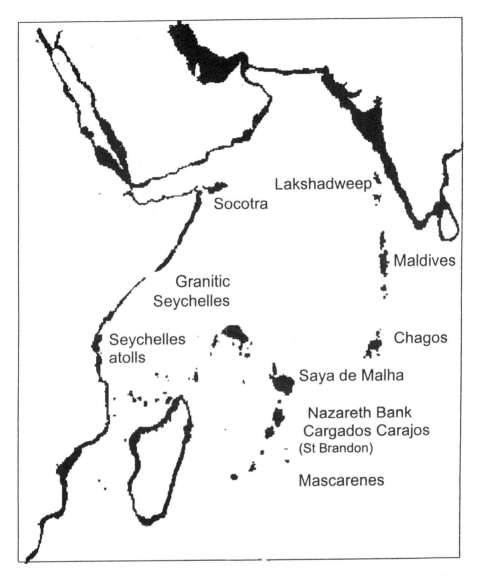

Figure 1.1. Potential reef substrate in the western Indian Ocean. Shaded areas are those where water is shallow enough for reef development. Based on GEBCO Digital Map of the Oceans, from 200 m contours with modifications. Not all shaded areas actually support reefs for reasons described in the text.

Reefal areas of the western Indian Ocean are thus separated by substantial distances of deep ocean or muddy shallow water from the richer areas to the east. Although boundaries defined by an absence of anything, like lack of suitable substrate, may be vague, they are nonetheless important, and geographically there is a marked contiguity about the western side of the Ocean and a validity to its definition as a 'region'. This is amplified in more detail later from the viewpoint of the reef-building corals themselves.

Present Knowledge of Western Indian Ocean Reefs

Thirty years ago researchers noted that the Indian Ocean was the least known and understood of the tropical oceans (3,74). Since then, considerable work has clarified our understanding of its biological systems and processes, but much less than for other tropical oceans, leaving this still very much the least known of the tropical oceans. For example, it is surprising that the Seychelles, which is spread out over such a large fraction of the Indian Ocean, is the source of so few marine science publications. There are very few established research institutions located in the area, unlike the case in the other tropical oceans, so that although notable work has come from some local research stations, most of our knowledge has come from occasional expeditions originating outside the region.

Scarce knowledge does not mean that human influences on the coastal and marine habitats are equally limited, however. Human pressure on marine habitats is increasing to the point, in some cases, where serious concerns exist as to their continued integrity. These concerns are not limited to the immediate proximity to areas of dense human populations since it is becoming clear, for example, that wide-ranging fishing fleets have caused fish stocks on some of the unstudied areas to become depleted in similar manner to reefs closer to home.

Our understanding of marine systems is often couched in terms of three broad features: biodiversity, productivity and system integrity (57), all of which require priority attention when habitats are under pressure. The first two of these, diversity and productivity may, in some cases, exhibit a reciprocal relationship. In the tropical Indian Ocean, biodiversity patterns are now becoming slightly better known, while productivity of the marine systems is similarly becoming better known from an increasing number of studies scattered across the region, from the Arabian peninsula to the Mascarenes. The third feature, system integrity, is an emergent one, derived in part from the first two. The need to determine the system integrity of Indian Ocean habitats remains a priority, as does the need to maintain it.

The main function of this chapter is to place coral reefs of the Indian Ocean into a wider ecological context. Many of the main controls which act on reefs of the region, such as currents, tides and other oceanographic conditions, are described for each area of the Indian Ocean in the relevant chapters of this volume. Box 1.1 provides an overview of salient features of marine climate which connect, separate or otherwise interact with the major marine habitats on an oceanic scale. This chapter also presents a large-scale perspective of all Indian Ocean shallow habitats, including those areas where corals and reefs are not necessarily at their most abundant or profuse. Such areas are generally much less studied than are 'good' reef areas, and by understanding the environment in which they live, marginal areas tell us a great deal about the limits which reefs can tolerate before being extinguished.

Box 1.1. Marine Climate: Ocean-Scale Effects

The main climatic control on the northern Indian Ocean's reefs is the monsoon cycle. In January the Intertropical Convergence Zone (ITCZ) lies south of the equator where the southeast trades winds blow, while in the north the northeast monsoon is fully developed. In the second quarter, the ITCZ moves north reaching southern India in late April. From then, the southeast trades occupy the whole of the southern ocean, while in the north, rainfall become frequent and a few systems develop into cyclones. In the third quarter the southwest monsoon holds sway over the north where mean wind speeds and rainfall reach their maximum, and in the southern ocean, the southeast trades reach a mean speed of 9 m/sec - the world's most vigorous trade winds. Finally, in the fourth quarter, the southwest monsoon diminishes, winds change to north-easterly, and the ITCZ migrates south again (2,4). The currents driven by this create one of the world's five major upwelling systems, whose nutrient enriching properties have profound effect in the north-west, generating most of the pelagic productivity of the Indian Ocean (3). The Arabian upwelling (see Fig. 1.10), which has varied in intensity through the Holocene (5), offers a significant, selective barrier to the migration of species (6).

Storms and cyclones are equally important to some reefal areas. They generally track northwest and southwest from the equatorial belt between 5°N and 5°S. The southwest Indian Ocean experiences the most, peaking in January, but affected land is relatively sparse. The northern Indian Ocean has fewer cyclones than the south, but many more reach populous areas, especially in May and November. Generally, soft substrate habitats are affected more than reefs. Arabian areas experience cyclone strength winds only rarely, but strong thermally generated winds are very common, causing desiccation of shallow habitats in summer and chilling in winter.

Currents close to shore are well mapped, but those in mid ocean are sometimes only vaguely sketched and sometimes even contradictory. Most major currents are seasonal and follow the monsoons, but the west-flowing South Equatorial current in the southern Indian Ocean exists all year. These have significant larval mixing consequences on an ocean-wide scale, and some major currents are shown in Figure 1.11 in connection with productivity patterns. Deep currents are also important. From principal water sources in the Antarctic region, at least two northerly streams flow up both sides of the Indian Ocean and are deflected back towards the central Indian Ocean near or north of the equator. The western stream is deflected off Arabia where nutrient rich upwelling occurs. Another important deep current arises from evaporation and increased salinity in the Red Sea and Arabian Gulf; dense water flows into the Arabian Sea and Indian Ocean where it is detectable as far east as India.

Sea surface temperature is the one limiting factor for reefs and corals. In the extreme north of the Bay of Bengal and Arabian Sea, as well as in the semi-enclosed Red Sea and Gulf, temperatures rarely have extreme values or greater seasonal ranges than can be tolerated by most corals, but in many cases other factors combine to restrict reefs, such as turbidity, unsuitable substrate, and high nutrients. Off many of the oceanic islands in particular, thermoclines may exist shallower than 50 m, below which temperatures may drop 2 to 4°C, but in these areas surface temperatures have low seasonal variation. In the region of present interest, coral distribution is restricted by low temperatures only on the southern African coast. High temperatures may restrict corals in local areas throughout the region, particularly the north-west.

Oceanic surface salinity shows a clear gradient from greatest in the west and Arabian Sea (36 to 37 ppt) to lowest in the east and Bay of Bengal (<33 ppt). Except in embayments, extreme levels seldom impact any of the coastal marine habitats. In the Red Sea and Arabian Gulf, salinity rises gradually to over 41 ppt apparently without affecting corals or other habitats which appear to be well adjusted to these elevations, until levels exceeding 45 or even 48 ppt are reached.

Throughout the ocean where reefs occur, tidal ranges are usually 2 m or less, though in the far north, tidal ranges increase gradually to 5 m. In the northerly coral bearing Gulf of Kutch, tides reach 6 m and generate sediment laden currents of 2.5 m/s (1).

Charles R. C. Sheppard

References

1. Bakus, G.J. 1994. *Coral Reef Ecosystems*. New Delhi: Oxford & IBH Ltd.
2. Couper, A. 1983. *Times Atlas of the Oceans*. London: Times Books Ltd.
3. Fagoonee, I. 1983. Why is the Indian Ocean considered less productive? Unpublished manuscript. Gland: IUCN
4. Pathmarajah, M. 1982. *Pollution and the Marine Environment in the Indian Ocean*. UNEP Regional Seas Reports and Studies No 13
5. Prell, W.L., Kutzbach, J.E. 1987. Monsoon variability over the past 150,000 years. *Journal of Geophysical Research* 92: 8411-8425
6. Sheppard, C.R.C., Price, A.R.G., Roberts, C.J. 1992. *Marine Ecology of the Arabian Area. Patterns and Processes in Extreme Environments*. London: Academic Press

Western Indian Ocean Tropical Marine Habitats

The tropical Indian Ocean, like other tropical oceans, is only 'tropical' in its uppermost 50 or 100 meters of water (56). Below this depth, rapidly falling temperatures provide conditions which are similar to temperate and Arctic seas. Tropical benthic habitats occur only where this relatively thin film of warm water spills over continental shelves. Tropical habitats are disrupted where this thin film is displaced by permanent, seasonal or even apparently random episodes of cool currents, extreme salinity or nutrient enrichment. Such factors are important for controlling the distribution of the habitats themselves, and for determining levels and origins of productivity. There are very few areas of the Indian Ocean where the cold-water layer is much deeper than the limits of the photic zone, one unusual example where this is the case is the Red Sea. It is as common for the vertical extent of so-called tropical communities to be controlled by temperature drop as much as by loss of illumination. Horizontal mixing of water is 100 to a 1000 times greater than vertical mixing (32) for physical reasons connected with properties of water and the Earth's rotation. Productivity is greatest where vertical and horizontal mixing are both greatest.

Indian Ocean Reefs and Corals

Work on Indian Ocean reefs increased during a period which saw the start of analytical rather than descriptive work (50,63,67,68). Coral reef structure, profile and zonation has been described more than adequately (40) and is not repeated here. Indeed, there may have been a preoccupation with describing reefs which has led to too simplistic a view that there are only a few discrete kinds or shapes of reefs, including those initially described by Darwin, and this has sometimes concealed the vast array of reef shapes and 'types' that actually exists. A continuum exists not only between reef 'types' themselves but, as importantly, between reef habitats of all forms and non-reefal habitats, especially in marginal areas in the Indian Ocean.

Coral reefs fringe less than one half of the continental shorelines of the tropical Indian Ocean. Reefs are limited in the north by the lack of firm substrate, massive fresh water and sedimentary inputs from the Indus, Ganges and other smaller rivers (Fig. 1.2). Therefore, Pakistan and much of India and Bangladesh have no significant reefs. In the northwest, Oman, South Yemen and Somalia have very restricted reef development due to cold-water upwelling, and reefs there exist mostly in conjunction with macro-algal communities. The Red Sea has extensive fringing and barrier reefs in the north and central regions but has much less reef development in the south. Reefs fringe only a relatively small part of Indian and about half of the Sri Lankan coastlines, partly due to turbid conditions, and partly due to seasonal monsoon changes which drive massive quantities of sand causing severe scouring. In East Africa, substantial fringing reefs are found discontinuously between 5° North and 20° South, along with numerous forms of 'shelf' or 'patch' reefs arising from the continental shelf.

Atolls are abundant on the Lakshadweep - Chagos ridge, in several Seychelles groups and on other limestone plateaux in mid ocean. High islands may have good reef development (Rodrigues, Andamans, Nicobars), but many of the tropical high islands have relatively poor reefs or even no reefs at all (Reunion, Mahé). Notable features include the Mayotte double barrier reef and numerous exceptionally large algal ridges, notably those on the Cargados Carajos shoals and Chagos. The range of atoll size is also striking. Some are enormous (Great Chagos Bank) or have a nearly continuous island rim (Diego Garcia). Several atolls of the Seychelles have extremely shallow lagoons (Farquhar), while many have very deep lagoons or wholly drowned rims as well. The relationship of lagoon depth with atoll size is tenuous at best (66) though past sea level is known to be an important controlling factor on many aspects of reef structure (see Box 1.2).

Coral Biogeography of the Western Indian Ocean. Strong underpinning for the concept of a western Indian Ocean region comes from the biogeographic pattern of corals. A new database of Indian Ocean corals has been compiled and reanalyzed (58), building on work done 15 years earlier

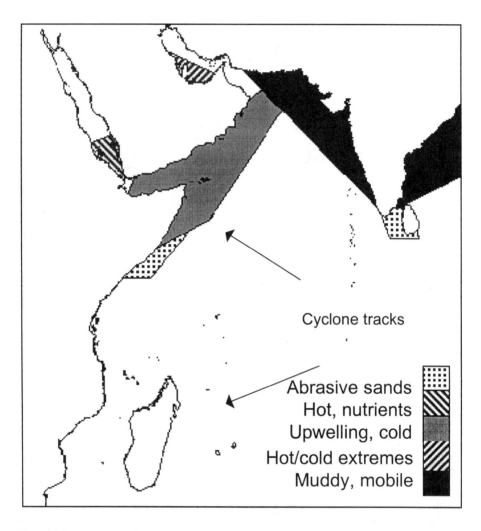

Figure 1.2. Generalized distribution of conditions which are hostile to the establishment of reefs. The annual mean 20°C contour which conventionally defines the limits to reef growth is not drawn though it roughly coincides with the bottom of the map. There is no equivalent temperature contour in the north of the ocean. Arrows show cyclone tracks in the ocean.

(54). Table 1.1 summarizes generic and species data from sites across the whole Indian Ocean. In the data matrix of 26 sites and 491 coral species, about 5000 of the cells, or 40%, are 'filled', nearly double that recorded in the compilation of 15 years ago. Cluster analysis has confirmed that, from the viewpoint of corals, there is a clear biogeographic separation of the region west of the Sri Lanka to Chagos line (Fig. 1.3). A sub-regional structure is also evident. Reinforcing the validity of the cluster analyses is the fact that tests for the effects of error in the taxonomic database show that considerably more error can be contained in the species lists before these patterns disappear. The

Box 1.2. Reefs and Sea Level Changes

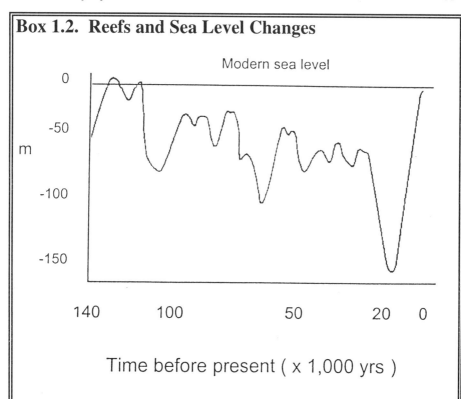

Figure. Sea level changes, based mainly from reef studies using a combination of dating and the relative locations of micro-atolls.

At the start of the Holocene, sea level was approximately 130 m or more below present (5) following a long period of major fluctuations (Fig. 1.1). Then sea level rose rapidly to near its present day level during the last 7000 years.

For the Red Sea, minimum water level lay close to the depth of the sill at its entrance. Complete "drying out" of the Red Sea was unlikely, but outward flows of highly saline water could not be supported, and salinity increased to >50 ppt and even 70 ppt (7,8) enough to kill most biota (3,4), though episodes of new inflows of Indian Ocean water occurred (1). Elsewhere, shallow, coastal areas including the Arabian Gulf dried out, and the limits of drying approximately match the shaded area in Figure 1.1. Recruitment of macroscopic marine life into all such areas commenced anew about 6000 years B.P.

Because the lagoons of most atolls are shallower than 130 m, sea level changes had profound effects on the amount of land and shallow reef flat that was exposed. Apart from islands about 2 to 3 meters above high tide, a typical atoll top is a vast reef flat near low water level. Seaward of atolls, reef slopes are generally steep, plunging in steps or continuously to depths of hundreds of meters. Within atoll rims, lagoons are most commonly 10 to 200 m deep, depth bearing only a loose relationship to atoll diameter (9). Thus even modest falls in sea level will expose reef flats and some lagoon floors as well, greatly increasing the dry land area. At lower still stands, new 'benchmarks' developed, evidenced by shelves, relict spurs and erosion caves seen in many reefs 20 to 60 m below present sea level.

Sea level fall is likely to have had little effect on the quantity of steep seaward reef slope habitat; the sea level merely sliding up and down seaward slopes at rates sufficiently slow to permit more than adequate time for coral and other species to 'relocate' vertically. A great reduction of lagoonal habitat may have occurred, where existing lagoons emerged. Current ideas of lagoon formation suggest, however, that exposed limestone subjected to rain erodes into dish-shaped lagoons cut by channels whose depth equals the deepest part of the lagoon floor, a condition actually observed in most atolls. In this manner, rain tends to erode atolls back down to sea level, maintaining an atoll shape. Conversely, sea level rises are generally thought to be balanced by upward reef growth, whose rate is usually, but not always, capable of keeping up with sea level rise (6).

On continental shelves, sea level change has complex effects caused by extensive lateral movement of the waterline, the slopes being very gradual in comparison to atoll slopes. In several continental areas, tectonic rise or fall of the shore also modifies the pattern greatly - elevated fringing reefs line much of the Red Sea and African shores, for example. Many patch reefs located mid way on shelves probably owe their origins to patches of ground which lay in water much shallower than today, their growth matching subsequent sea level rise. Chains of present-day patch reefs are located on top of old reefs which used to line palaeo shores; excellent examples being seen in Somalia (2) and in the 'Little Barrier Reef' off Saudi Arabia (8).

Charles R.C. Sheppard

References

1.   Braithwaite, C.J.R. 1987. Geology and palaeogeography of the Red Sea region. In *Red Sea*. eds. Edwards, A.J., Head, S.M. pp 22-44 Oxford: Pergamon Press
2.   Carbone, F., Matteucci, R., Rosen, B.R., Russo, A. 1994. Recent coral facies of the Indian Ocean coast of Somalia with an interim check list of corals. *Facies* 30: 1-14
3.   Friedman, G.M. 1972. Significance of Red Sea in problems of evaporites and basinal limestones. *American Association of Petroleum Geologists* 56: 1072-1086
4.   Friedman G.M., Krumbein, W.E. eds. 1985. *Hypersaline Ecosystems. The Gavish Sabkha.* Springer Verlag
5.   Hopley, D. 1982. *The Geomorphology of the Great Barrier Reef. Quaternary Development of coral reefs.* New York: Wiley Interscience
6.   Kinsey, D.W., Hopley, D. 1991. The significance of coral reefs as global carbon sinks - response to Greenhouse *Palaeogeography, Palaeoclimatology, Palaeoecology*, 89: 363-377
7.   Reiss, Z., Luz, B., Almogi-Labin, A., Halicz, E., Winter, A., Wulf, M. 1980. Late Quaternary paleo-oceanography of the Gulf of Aqaba (Eilat) Red Sea. *Quaternary Research* 14: 294-308

8.   Sheppard, C.R.C., Price, A.R.G., Roberts, C.J. 1992. *Marine Ecology of the Arabian Area. Patterns and Processes in Extreme Environments.* London: Academic Press
9.   Stoddart, D.R. 1965. The shape of atolls. *Marine Geology* 3:369-383

general pattern is, therefore, robust, although further sampling in several sites may influence details.

Several of the most distinct clusters are the subject of separate chapters in this volume. The Red Sea is a relatively homogeneous basin in terms of species presence, though it contains marked environmental gradients along its length (59). The Arabian Gulf, Gulf of Oman, and Arabian Sea is out on a limb, like the Red Sea only more so, as is reflected by its lower diversity. Due to the different kinds of environmental extremes in this area (Fig. 1.2 and see later Table 1.5) the Arabian Gulf is rather dissimilar to that of the Red Sea despite being geographically closest. Its ecological constraints have been more severe since the start of the Holocene (60).

The oceanic island groups of the central and western Indian Ocean similarly reveal a diversity and species substructure which has important consequences. Firstly, it shows that the Indian Ocean is not a thoroughly well-mixed basin. Distances are great, which undoubtedly is important, but sub-regional differences in the environment almost certainly are important as well. Of all the coral species in the Indian Ocean, about one third are very widespread and one third are restricted to less than three or four sites, almost always geographically adjacent ones.

In support of the view that the western Indian Ocean is a sub-province, at generic level eight genera appear only to the west of the central line. This has long been recognized (46), but is strengthened with subsequent records (Table 1.2). All these genera are monospecific and may be described as western Indian Ocean genera. Also shown in Table 1.2 are genera which occur in the eastern but not western Indian Ocean. These too are monospecific genera. There are of course, several other genera of the Indo-Pacific realm which do not occur in any part of the Indian Ocean at all.

A total of about 400 different species have been recorded for the western Indian Ocean, 80% of the number for the whole ocean. Figure 1.4 shows the patterns of species and generic diversity with both latitude and longitude in the 21 western Indian Ocean sites for which adequate data are available. R^2 values and lines of fit are added for the species distributions. These are not very strong, and those for genera are very weak. Scatter is considerable, but there is a tendency for a decline with increasing latitude both north and south, and there is a richer fauna in the extreme east and west. Using these data it is safest to assume that there is no developed diversity trend in any direction, and certainly not a very significant gradient. Decline in diversity with high latitude is abrupt when it occurs.

Distributions and Environmental Constraints. The coral diversity pattern noted is only very loosely correlated with the abundance or even with the existence of reefs over this oceanic scale. Areas with high coral diversity may contain well developed reefs, marginal and weakly developed reefs, or even no true reefs at all but which instead support rich coral

Table 1.1. Summary of number of species and genera in 26 relatively well-sampled sites in the Indian Ocean region. Sites from the eastern Indian Ocean are included since these are pertinent to determination of a western Indian Ocean province. Sources are exactly those discussed extensively in (58) and used in the cluster analyses described in the text. Newer work, for example (31) and Veron (unpublished data for East Africa), as well as new personal observations for East Africa are not included to remain consistent with the figures.

Site	Latitude at center	Longitude at center	No Species	No Genera
All sites			491	87
Gulf of Aqaba, Gulf of Suez	27	34	138	54
Central Red Sea (Yanbu)	23	37	150	50
South Red Sea Jeddah-Jizan, Sudan	16	41	115	49
Arabian Gulf	26	51	62	27
Gulf of Oman	24	59	77	34
South Oman, Gulf of Aden, Socotra	14	53	101	43
Gulf of Kutch	23	69	37	20
Somalia	5	49	52	22
Kenya / Tanzania	-5	40	112	50
Mozambique	-20	35	110	44
Tulear Madagascar	-24	43	112	57
South Africa	-28	32	89	39
Aldabra, Cosmoledo, Farquhar	-9	46	95	40
Granitic Seychelles, Amirantes	-4	55	174	55
SE India, Sri Lanka	8	79	182	55
Lakshadweep	11	73	95	34
Maldives	5	73	187	57
Chagos	-7	72	220	58
Reunion	-21	56	124	43
Mauritius	-20	58	133	47
Rodriguez	-20	64	84	36
Cocos Keeling	-12	97	94	29
Nicobars, Andamans	10	92	131	50
Thailand, Mergui Archipelago	10	98	214	64
Northwest Australia	-18	116	311	71
Southwest Australia	-30	115	192	47

communities on non-reefal substrates. Conversely, areas with relatively low diversity may contain well-developed reefs. There is no strong relationship between coral diversity and degree of reef development. Many areas contain moderate coral diversity but do not form reefs, the corals growing on a wide variety of non-limestone substrates and old limestone platforms which currently do not accrete (60).

For example, in the Arabian Gulf as a whole, diversity is fairly low, probably more because of barriers to recruitment provided by upwelling and muddy substrate (Fig. 1.2, and see Fig. 1.10 later) rather than to conditions in most of the Gulf, yet substantial coral reefs exist there. Conversely, the Oman and Somalia coasts which are subjected to seasonal upwelling, have more than double the number of coral species, but contain very poor reef development. The identity of the species are similar, though there are more of them, but over wide expanses they do not develop into reefs. Commonly they exist mixed with macroalgae. Similar accounts can be drawn for several areas, from the Mascarenes where reef development is poor in several parts (39), to Sri Lanka (61). Table 1.3 shows that the considerable influence of adverse conditions in the north-western part of the Indian Ocean extends to several other

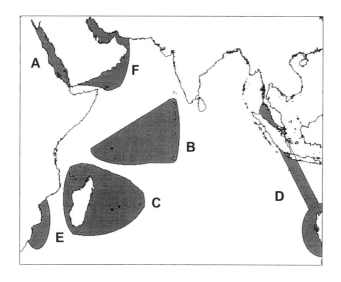

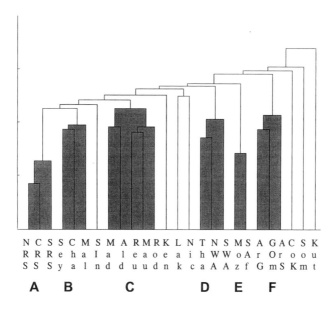

N	C	S	S	C	M	S	M	A	R	M	R	K	L	N	T	N	S	M	S	A	G	A	C	S	K
R	R	R	e	h	a	I	a	l	e	a	o	e	a	i	h	W	W	o	A	r	O	r	o	o	u
S	S	S	y	a	l	n	d	d	u	u	d	n	k	c	a	A	A	z	f	G	m	S	K	m	t

A   B   C   D   E   F

Figure 1.3. Cluster analysis of coral species records. The Jaccard similarity coefficient was used, with weighted clustering. Clusters are shaded, both on the map and dendrogram: the clusters marked A to E on the dendrogram correspond to the same letters on the map. Site codes on dendrogram: NRS= Northern Red Sea, CRS= Central Red Sea, SRS= South Red Sea , ArG= Arabian Gulf, Gom= Gulf of Oman, ArS= Arabian Sea, Kut= Gulf of Kutch, Som= Somalia, Ken= Kenya + Tanzania, Moz= Mozambique, Mad= Tulear Madagascar, SAf= South Africa, Ald= Aldabra + Cosmoledo + Faarquhar, Sey= Granitic Seychelles + Amirantes, Sin= SE India + Sri Lanka, Lak= Lakshadweep, Mal= Maldives, Cha= Chagos, Reu= Reunion, Mau= Mauritius, Rod= Rodriguez, CoK= Cocos Keeling, Nic= Nicobars + Andamans, Tha= Thailand + Mergui Archipelago, NWA= Northwest Australia, SWA= Southwest Australia.

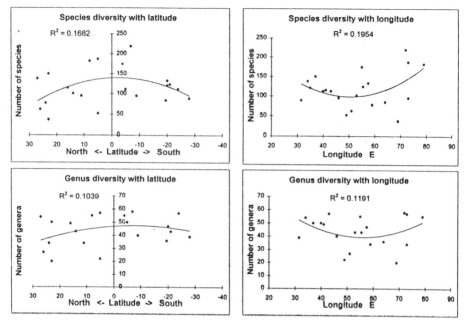

Figure 1.4. Plots of species (top) and genera (bottom) against latitude (left) and longitude (right) in the 21 western Indian Ocean sites.

major biotic groups as well. All fall in diversity from east to west in these sites. The Red Sea is a special case. Characteristics such as higher than oceanic rates of speciation, forcing by currents which makes the Red Sea act like a large catchment, and a reasonably equitable environment, all mean that diversity in the Red Sea, for many groups, rises again to levels higher than in many other parts of the Indian Ocean.

Questions have sometimes been raised about the validity of phrases like 'stressful environment' or 'increasing stress' (or 'equitable environment' used above) since stress for one group may be inconsequential or even desirable to another. From the viewpoint of the corals and reefs, however, the use is clear: increasing stress refers to an environmental gradient along which, at some point, corals can no longer live. Examples include elevated salinity, low or high water temperature, and elevated nutrients and sediments.

There is of course no doubt that environmental conditions of increasing severity do eventually kill off both reef development and coral diversity. Figure 1.5 shows a decline in diversity with increasing salinity in the northwest of this region, while Table 1.4 presents data showing the rate at which diversity is lost with increasing seasonal temperature fluctuation rather than just with high or low temperature.

It is clear that the demise of reef growth may take place at quite different points along an environmental gradient than the demise of corals. The reasons for this have been discussed, but are still not explained (60). While it is now understood that reefs do not simply develop because corals grow on top of other corals, other so far undetermined causes of reef construction require explaining possibly incorporating microbial or micro-chemical processes (60). The 'corals-

Table 1.2. Zooxanthellate coral genera restricted to the western and central Indian Ocean, and those found in the eastern Indian Ocean which do not occur in the western region. Several additional genera of the South East Asian region do not occur in any part of the Indian Ocean.

Genus	Family	Where recorded
Western Indian Ocean		
Anomastrea	Siderastreidae	Arabia, Africa, Seychelles
Astraeosmilia	Faviidae	Africa, Chagos
Craterastrea	Siderastreidae	Arabia, Chagos
Ctenella	Meandrinidae	Chagos
Erythrastrea	Faviidae	Arabia
Gyrosmilia	Caryophylliidae	Arabia, Africa, Aldabra, Mascarenes
Horastrea	Siderastreidae	Africa, Madagascar, Mascarenes
Parasimplastrea	Faviidae	Arabia
Eastern Indian Ocean		
Palauastrea	Pocilloporiidae	
Lithophyllon	Fungiidae	
Moseleya	Faviidae	
Acrhelia	Oculinidae	
Scapophyllia	Merulinidae	
Physophyllia	Pectinidae	
Montigyra	Caryophylliidae	
Duncanopsammia	Dendrophylliidae	

Table 1.3. Gradients in the number of species in six groups in three broad locations of the Indian Ocean. Western and 'central' Indian Ocean refers to the main body of the Ocean excluding peripheral seas.

Taxonomic group	Arabian Gulf	Arabian Sea	Western and 'central' Indian Ocean
Dinoflagellates	~50	130	452
Corals	~50	~80	300+
Non-reef fishes	300	300-500	600+
Reef fishes	190	200-300	1,400
Mangroves	1	3-10	50+
Seagrasses	3	11	~20

Table 1.4. Temperature extremes recorded in reef areas in embayments in peripheral parts of the Indian Ocean (60), and numbers of coral species.

Location	Latitude (^{0}N)	Min (^{0}C)	Max (^{0}C)	Range	Coral diversity
Saudi Gulf	27	11.4	36.2	24.8	60
Qatar Gulf	24	14.1	36.0	21.9	40-60
Abu Dhabi Gulf	25	16.0	36.0	20.0	40-60
Kuwait	29	13.2	31.5	18.3	40
Gulf of Suez	29.5	17.5	30.0	12.5	100
Gulf of Aqaba	29	20.0	28.0	8.0	150+

on-corals' scenario for reef development does exist, but it is not particularly common. Examples include the huge *Porites* clusters which develop in many sheltered embayments throughout the Indian Ocean. Few other corals can form reefs in this way. Equally dense cover of *Acropora*, *Pocillopora* or even *Montipora* exist, but these do not necessarily consolidate into anything more than a tangle of friable limestone branches. The test of reef durability will come only when their survival is seen following a cyclone, or with a glacial-

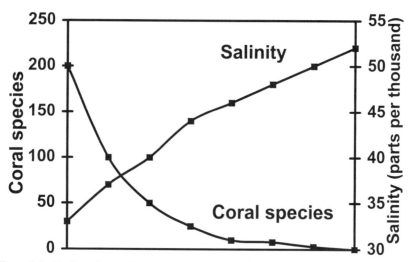

Figure 1.5. Decline of coral diversity with increasing salinity in the Indian Ocean. The decreasing line is coral diversity (left axis), increasing line is salinity (right axis). Sampled sites are all from the Arabian region where sufficient measurements exist. In many sites with oceanic conditions (about 33 ppt salinity) diversity exceeds 200 species of corals.

scale fall in sea level. Observation of pre-Holocene structures suggests that only those with a substantial cementing matrix, in addition to coral skeletons, survive (20).

In the Indian Ocean there is an abundance of habitats which, for any of several reasons, is marginal for both reefs and corals. These may be found over two scales. Firstly there is a 'macro-scale' as has just been mentioned, of hundreds or a few thousand kilometers, over which increasing stress gradually eliminates the ability of reefs to develop, causing the sequence: corals and accreting reefs > corals without reef formation, commonly with macro-algae > algal communities on non-coral reef substrates. An example, apart from the Arabian Sea already noted, is the Red Sea which shows this sequence in a southerly direction (59). Secondly, there is a 'meso-scale' at which reefs and corals habitat disappears over a distance of tens of meters to a few kilometers at most, as they grade into adjacent habitats dominated by, for example, seagrasses or mangroves.

Together, both conditions account for substantial expanses of gradually grading or mosaic habitats. The area is certainly substantial but it cannot at present be estimated with any degree of certainty, perhaps a reflection in part of the species-group approach of most marine ecologists to date. Table 1.5 summarizes physical characteristics in several such areas. There is very little indication to suggest that any one variable is present consistently or is essential in driving a coral-based system towards an algal based one, though elevated nutrients is a likely common characteristic. For any one species of coral there are clear inhibiting variables, as shown by the fact that corals drop out in a fairly consistent sequence along the transects shown earlier in Figure 1.5 and Table 1.4. At the level of the coral community, however, any consistency has yet to be discovered.

Table 1.5. Physical characteristics of reef and other hard substrate areas where corals live but where reefs do not develop and where fleshy macroalgae dominate some or all of the shallow substrate. This excludes coralline algal ridges and reef crests made mainly from encrusting reds.

Reef/Algal Characteristics	Salinity	Temperature			Sedim.	Nutr.	Areas
		Summer		Winter			
	High	High	Low	Low	High	High	
Red algal patch reefs covered with *Sargassum*, very low coral cover	No	Yes	No	No	Yes	Yes	Southern Red Sea
High to moderate coral cover, *Sargassum* dominated reef crest but coral domination on reef slope	slight, 36 to 40 ppt	Yes	No	No	No	Yes	Central, Southern Red Sea
Limestone domes, mainly devoid of corals, in 1 to 5 m deep	Yes, > 40 ppt	Yes	No	Yes	Yes	No	Central and eastern Arabian Gulf
Reef flats at 0 to 1 m below low water springs, high energy areas, abundant algae on reef flats, but high coral diversity deeper	No	No	No	No	Yes some areas	Yes some areas	for example Western Sri Lanka
Upwelling areas, mainly dominated by Fucales but including *Ecklonia*	No	No	Yes	No	No	Yes	Oman to Somalia, *Ecklonia* in southern Oman, possibly also Yemen.
Simplest 'corals-on-corals' mode of reef development	No	No	No	No	Yes	Yes some areas	Embayments, these are notably formed by *Porites*

Productivity The overall high production that occurs on reef slopes with good coral and turf algal cover is well established and has been reviewed more than once (29,40). It should be recognized, however, that the many different components of reefs, such as reef flats, shallow slopes and lagoon floors, have widely different productivity. The variation in 'average reef' values, some established long ago, arises partly because of the different ways of extrapolating from the experimental glass jar on a patch of reef to the whole reef. The inclusion of sandy patches, 'bare' patches, and the different estimates of planar surface area or the inclusion of a three-dimensional aspect, all affect calculations greatly and probably none, by themselves, are either 'right' or 'wrong'. Listing 'typical values' should only be done with recognition of these limitations. Table 1.6 lists a selection of values of comparative levels of production for coral reefs and their components. It also includes comparative values for all non-reef groups discussed later in this chapter. Other than the difficulties already noted, the real differences in production, seen in different parts of reefs, are partly a consequence of the different light, sediment, and exposure regimes. Productivity, in turn, is probably important in driving differences in diversity and consumer biomass in each zone. It remains reasonable to state that the reefs of the Indian Ocean are highly productive. Also, as we see later, their productivity is of a very similar order to most other benthic habitats with which they might be compared.

Seagrasses of the Western Indian Ocean

Seagrasses are widespread in the Indian Ocean where they are commonly associated with coral reefs, although areas such as bays where they develop their largest stands generally contain only weakly developed reefs or scattered corals. Seagrasses are supported on continental reefs flats, but more rarely on those of oceanic atolls. World wide there are about 50 species of twelve genera, of which about half are tropical. The western Indian Ocean contains 13 species of nine genera (38). Currently known geographical distributions of these are mapped in Figure 1.6. It is apparent that several seagrasses are likely to be found in areas where they are not yet formally recorded, and it is also the case that their diversity has no correlation with their cover. For example, the Arabian Gulf has only three species which form vast, unbroken expanses in shallow water, while less enclosed sites may have more species which grow in smaller, ecologically less important quantities. Biogeographical patterns of seagrasses show several similarities in distribution to those of corals. The Arabian Sea region (25) is similar to the Arabian Gulf but dissimilar to the Red Sea. The central atolls are insufficiently studied, but appear to be relatively poor in both abundance and diversity.

Stands of several species may be monospecific, though mixing of several species is common, in which case zonation from low intertidal to about 10 m deep may be seen (25). Dense stands are generally found in shallow, sheltered water, including bays and reef flats, and although seagrasses may occur in deep water they generally are sparse below about 10 to 20 meters, unlike the case for the Caribbean, or Mediterranean for example, where dense beds extend to over 30 m depth. Most stands are fairly dynamic, their position being determined by frequency of exposure, sediment grain size and sediment movement.. Curiously, the scattered seagrasses on reef flats which are sheltered by the reef crest may persist more readily than do dense beds in deeper water further offshore which are not protected.

In the Red Sea, seagrasses show a marked and significant increase in abundance southwards, at least along the northern shore, which is the reciprocal of the diversity and abundance of coral reefs (60). Overlap of reefs and seagrass communities extends over hundreds of kilometers. In the north, dense beds of seagrasses are limited to sheltered shallow sites and to scattered patches on reef flats. As shallow shelf conditions increase towards the south, reef development declines and seagrasses (with macroalgae) increase. Sites along the coast of Africa, India and Sri Lanka similarly have mixtures of both corals and seagrasses (38). Commonly an abrupt transition in dominant species takes place which can be ascribed to a sudden deepening of the substrate on a reef flat, for example.

In particularly dense seagrass beds, such as in sheltered, saline areas in the Arabian Gulf, seagrasses are mixed with algae. While it is commonly held that seagrasses occur in soft substrates and algae are attached to hard substrates, in very sheltered sites mixtures of both groups occur together over many hundreds of km^2. Substrates may be coarse and shelly, to muddy, but if the shelter is sufficient, both seagrasses and algae up to 30 cm tall occur profusely.

Productivity. Seagrass areas are extremely productive (Table 1.6). Their roots add to the stability of otherwise dynamic substrates, encouraging algal

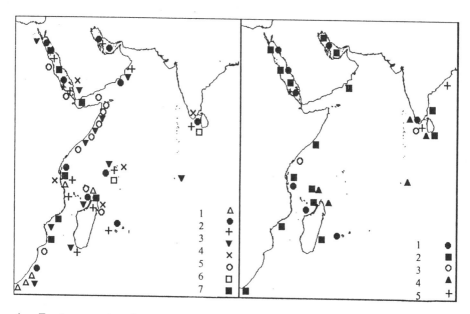

1. Zostera capiensis
2. Halodule uninervis
3. Syringodium isoetifolium
4. Enhalus acoroides
5. Thalassia hemprichii
6. Cymodocea serrulata
7. C. rotundata + serrulata

1. Halophila stipulacea
2. Halophila ovalis
3. Halophila minor
4. Halophila decipiens
5. Halophila beccarii

Figure 1.6. Seagrass distribution in the western Indian Ocean. Based on Phillips and Menez (38) with later additions for East Africa and atoll groups in central Indian Ocean.

settlement in sheltered areas. Seagrass blades are generally covered with epibiota, and it has been suggested that the high productivity of seagrasses is partly because each 1 m^2 of seagrass bed provides up to 12 m^2 of attachment substratum. Average leaf turnover or renewal time is about 35 days. Epiphytes are dominated by nitrogen-fixing cyanophytes and diatoms, and the amount of nutrient transfer between epiphytes and host plants suggests that these attachments might be symbiotic rather than merely mechanical. Fauna associated with seagrass beds is commonly extremely abundant, with organism densities of 2000 and even 52 000 per m^2 of seagrass being recorded (6,72), in the latter case these being mainly gastropods, bivalves and polychaetes (nematodes which might be expected to occur in still greater number were not, apparently, recorded). Seagrasses are also important food for several vertebrates, including rabbitfish and parrotfish (33), as well as for turtles and dugong.

Migratory and other animals provide a major link between seagrasses and other ecosystems, for example, shrimp between seagrasses and algae, snappers and turtles between seagrasses and reefs. 'Halos' around outcrops of hard substrate projecting above seagrass beds also reflect the intensity of foraging

Table 1.6. Values for productivity of Indian Ocean systems, from numerous sources (40,56,60). Some of the generalized data are from outside the Indian Ocean, for which much less data exists than for the Pacific and Caribbean. Values are g C /m^2 /d unless otherwise stated.

System	Common or average values (g C /m^2/ d)	Extreme records (g C /m^2 /d)	P/R ratio
Reefs			
Whole reef systems	3.2-4.0	2.3-6.0	Usually ~ 1
Outer slopes	2.0-7.1		0.7-1.1
"High activity areas"	9.0-14.0	8.0-23.0	0.6-1.7
Reef flats, lagoons	3.0-7.0	2.9-19	0.7-2.5
Corals with zooxanthellae	2.63		
Sandy reef areas	0.9-1.5	0.6-2.7	0.6-1.1
Mangroves			
Global averages	6.0-15.0		1.2
"Dwarf" in Red Sea	<6.0		
Seagrasses			
Global averages	6.0-15.0		1.2
Thalassia, Syringodium, Lakshadweep	5.8		
Northwest Indian Ocean	3.0		
Algae			
Turfs and pavement	2.0-7.0	1.0-14.0	0.5-13.7
Coralline algae	0.8-1.0	7.0	1.3-1.4
Sargassum belts	60	(dry organic wt)	
Tropical kelp (Oman)	4.0	(dry organic wt)	
Halimeda beds	0.2-6.0		
"Mixed algae" Lakshadweep	1.9		
Cyanophytes	0.62-1.39		
Endolithic algae (*Ostrobium*)	0.4-0.6		
Benthic diatoms (sand, 5m)	0.41		
Bacterial			
pelagic	0.007-.11		
in sediments	1.2		
on coral rubble	0.01-0.1		
Planktonic			
Open ocean	0.04-0.06	.003-.4	0.3-1.4
Arabian upwelling southwest monsoon	1.16		
Arabian upwelling northeast monsoon	0.23		
Arabian Sea, central	0.12-0.76		
East Africa, aouthwest monsoon	0.83		
East Africa, northeast monsoon	0.42		
Bay of Bengal	0.21		
Atoll Lagoons	0.10-0.42		
near shore or reefs	0.2-0.9	0.1-1.0	
North Red Sea	0.21-0.50		
Central Red Sea	0.39		
Southern Red Sea	1.60		

and grazing in such boundary areas. The net effect is transfer of nutrients and biomass between the habitats. Seagrass detritus itself becomes widely scattered throughout the continental shelf area.

Productivity of dense seagrass beds is as high as that recorded for reefs (Table 1.6) but difficulties arise when scattered seagrasses or sparse beds are included in the records. Areas suffering disturbance may always contain seagrass beds whose densities are very sub-optimal, a consequence of the dynamic substrate on which they occur. Many inlets and indeed 'inlets' the

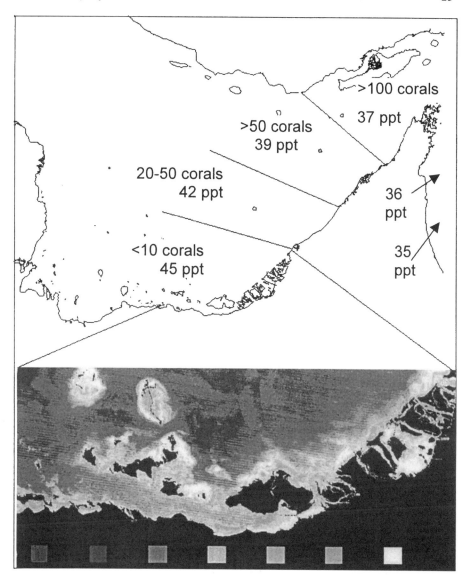

Figure 1.7. Section of coast with extensive seagrass and mixed seagrass and algal beds (Abu Dhabi). Remote sensed scene is Landsat TM, brightest areas being 100% cover of substrate, mid range grays being 40 to 60% cover, darkest shades being 0 to 10% benthic plant cover. Land is black. Numbers and contours show mean salinity and coral diversity.

size of the entire Arabian Gulf show high productivity. One such area (Fig. 1.7) from the Arabian Gulf is typical of many examples found throughout the Indian Ocean's continental shelf. Seagrasses are thoroughly mixed with algae, so that separation of algal production from that of seagrass is virtually impossible. The highest production comes from substrate completely and densely packed with a mixture of seagrasses and algae (Sheppard, C. personal observations). From literature values, production is in the order of >10g $C/m^2/d$. The lowest shading in Figure 1.7, representing areas with <10% vegetative cover, is likely to have production values of closer to 1g C /m^2/d.

Mangroves of the Western Indian Ocean

Mangroves form important ecological transition zones between terrestrial and marine habitats, and form effective sediment traps between land and reefs, the latter becoming increasingly important in view of wide scale-soil erosion in many countries. Partly because they, too, are threatened and declining habitats they have been extensively studied in the past decade (22). Additionally, a new atlas of mangrove distribution shows the current extent in the Indian Ocean in some detail (64). These details are not repeated here; instead, the association and interactions of mangal communities with coral reefs are examined.

Mangrove stands are greatest in shallow estuaries and bays of the continental rim of the Indian Ocean. In such areas, corals generally do not exist at all. Unlike seagrasses which can exist abundantly in conjunction with corals, the environmental demands made by developed mangrove stands, preclude all but occasional hardy corals. Mangroves trap mud efficiently and, unless human destruction occurs, this process extends the muddy habitat seaward at rates of many meters each year, which prevents coral reefs from developing. However, sparse mangroves or the edges of developed mangrove stands may happily coexist with corals over distances of a few hundred meters or less. Such areas are widespread. More widespread still are regions where mangroves occupy a shoreline area of shallow embayments, and well developed reefs extend seawards of them.

Over 40 species of mangrove tree exist on the northern continental rim of the Indian Ocean, reducing to ten or less in the eastern and north-eastern sides, to one or two in the peripheral Red Sea and Arabian Gulf (Table 1.3). *Avicennia marina* is the most widespread and hardy species. All species are restricted to warm waters of salinity ranging from brackish to slightly elevated. Rising salinity probably keeps diversity low in the Red Sea, but the final extinction in the north-west corner of the Indian Ocean is due to cold winter temperatures rather than either high salinity or hot summer temperatures. Possibly the broadest stands in the world today are the Bangladesh Sundabans (34), though stands in parts of north-western India may have been substantial until this century. In many parts of the Indian and Sri Lankan shore, for example, a recent sudden surge in mangrove destruction has taken place due to development of shrimp farms, which themselves tend to last only a few years until diseases or chemical changes in the soils render them unworkable, requiring more new mangrove conversion (34,61).

Of particular interest in the present context of reefs are the 'hard substrate' or 'reef' mangals (41) which are common in many parts, notably in the Red Sea but also as far east as Sri Lanka. These trees, mostly the species *Avicennia marina*, have shallow, spreading root systems and develop dense stands of many hectares at landward sides of reef flats (Fig. 1.8). Their substrate is extremely thin, may be sandy rather than muddy, and the stands may be independent of any larger, adjacent muddy mangrove stands. Indeed in the more arid regions of the north of the western Indian Ocean they might often be the only trees for

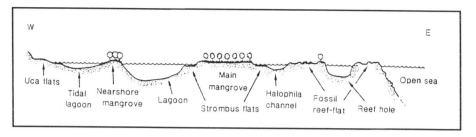

Figure 1.8. Cross section through a typical 'hard substrate mangrove stand. Evident in this illustration are depressions containing substrate suitable for seagrasses. The open sea at the right of the illustration is typically a steep reef slope. These hard substrate mangrove profiles are common in the western Indian Ocean from the Red Sea to Sri Lanka, though much less common than the typical mangrove-filled muddy embayments.

hundreds of kilometers. The fauna associated with them is similar to that of soft substrates (60) though being on reef flats, there is a much greater abundance of typical reef species, including corals, sponges and echinoderms, groups not usually associated with mangroves. The corals may even grow attached to mangrove roots in these areas.

Productivity. Table 1.6 provides typical examples of mangrove production. The main marine biota associated with mangroves is generally similar in species composition to that found over adjacent soft substrates not colonized by mangroves (41,56) though relative abundance of the component species may differ. For most species, the benefit of the mangroves are physical attachment and shelter, as much as the organically rich muds trapped by the tree roots. Densities of small invertebrates may be enormous, exceeding $5000/m^2$ in the case of polychaetes and small gastropods. Of the total production of a typical mangrove stand in the northern Red Sea, 86% may come from the mangrove trees themselves, with 12% from benthic macroalgae, leaving less than 1% coming from microalgae and phytoplankton (9). This is in undisturbed conditions. Disturbance, such as occurred in an adjacent site covering many hectares where chlorinated water from a power station discharged through the mangroves, benthic grazers were killed and algae formed a thick mat within a few weeks, eventually causing the demise of some of the trees themselves (52), demonstrating the dynamic nature of these systems.

Cyanophyte Flats and Salt Marshes

Almost as much shoreline in the Indian Ocean is dominated by mud or saline flats as by any other habitat, though being much less commonly studied, there is a relatively poor literature on these habitats. Generally, but not always, corals are seldom found in such areas, though reefs and mud flats commonly form mosaics in which reefal areas provide the protection behind which muddy areas can develop. In the Indian Ocean, mud flats remain bare of larger plants to a degree rarely seen in higher latitudes, or even in tropical parts of the Atlantic. These apparently bare flats extend from the high intertidal regions and above, down to the lowest tidal areas where seagrasses generally colonize. High salinity resulting from high evaporative rates, as well as high temperatures, are usually associated with flats devoid of macro-biota. Surface water temperatures of well over 40°C and salinity exceeding 80 ppt often arise in tidal water, especially in the northern parts of the Indian Ocean, in embayments in Arabia, northern India, Pakistan and Sri Lanka. In ponded areas salinity of double this value are common (60).

Mud flats which are inundated at least daily and which have salinity of below about 70 ppt support abundant invertebrates, and commonly spectacular bird life. As salinity rises, very high productivity is maintained by the development of 'algal mats', based on a micro-flora, including diatoms, filamentous algae, and most importantly, 'blue-green algae' (also termed cyanophytes or cyanobacteria). The most salt-resistant diatoms ever recorded are from the Sinai, which tolerate up to 180 ppt, but cyanophytes can grow in water with up to 300 ppt salinity, and halophilic bacteria may thrive in salinity up to 400 ppt in hypersaline lakes in Somalia (11,14). As salinity increases, the amount of dissolved oxygen falls to less than a quarter that of the open sea at the same temperature. Consequently, primary producing biota in high salinity regions often are those which use hydrogen sulfide anaerobically as a hydrogen donor rather than water, resulting in the release of sulfur instead of oxygen. These mats are commonly called 'sabkha', a word from the Arabian region where this community occupies tens of thousands of square kilometers, and where single continuous sabkha may cover areas 32 by 300 kilometers in size (26,27).

, The upper surface of the sabkha community is a mixture, possibly symbiotic or commensal in part, of cyanophytes and a varying composition of algae, the latter depending on exact conditions. The mats which develop have a vertical thickness of 1 to 3 cm, and vertical stratification of the community is pronounced. The lower side has a clear sulfur odor, is anoxic, and composed mainly of bacteria (Fig. 1.9). In times of desiccation, the whole community cracks into easily recognizable polygons and may sparkle from large surface crystals of gypsum as well as common salt. When hydrated sufficiently the mats form a continuous slippery sheet. Cyanophytes' ability to withstand severe desiccation comes not only from physiological adaptation, which is extremely developed and which includes secretion of mucilaginous jackets, but also from wicking and capillary action of water, assisted by hygroscopic salts which can attract water from relative humidities as low as 10%.

Sabkha systems may expand seaward and have a role in dissolving and re-precipitating aragonite, the form of limestone also deposited by corals (26,27). The exact composition of the mats depends partly on the precise elevation, allowing some use to be made of the community as palaeographic markers (42,43). Over sufficient time, the shoreline may be considerably modified by seaward extension. One important feature of the mats is the ability of the cyanophyte component to fix nitrogen. Most areas experience at least seasonal tidal flushing, and fertilization of surrounding areas is one possible, little researched, consequence of these communities.

Coastal Marshes. In past centuries, salt marshes growing in extensive stands of over seven meters tall formed a much more significant component of the northern Indian Ocean coastal environment than is the case today. Possibly no tropical coastal habitat has been as severely affected by man. Once

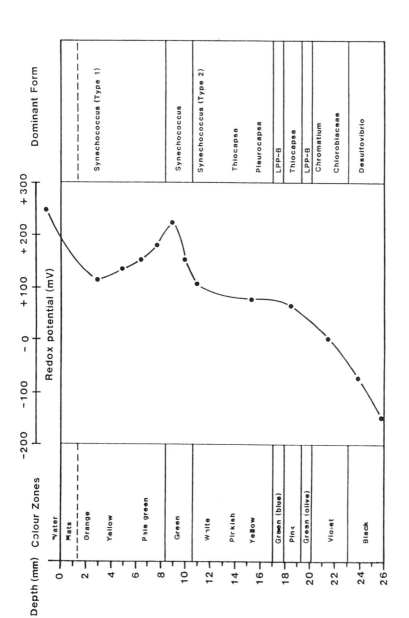

Figure 1.9. Cyanophyte algal mats. Chemical and physical details through a typical algal mat on a Sabkha (composite) (14). Thickness of mat (mm) is shown on left, with color of the various 'sub-layers'. Redox potential shows anoxic conditions below about 2 cm deep. Main microorganism groups at each depth point are indicated on right.

widespread, it is clear that impressive areas grew in the Arabian Gulf, Gulf of Suez, probably southern Red Sea and many other arid parts of the north-western Indian Ocean region; indeed in 1792 Niebuhr suggested that one contender for the name Red Sea is *Jam Suf* meaning Reed Sea (35), though there is no remnant left now of the vast marshes and fens reported by Strabo in 5 B.C. Ironically, today, there is a possibility of a recovery of reed beds in some areas in the vicinity of cities where sewage has led to enrichment of coastal waters (60). In Bahrain in the Arabian Gulf, and Jeddah in the Red Sea, salt marshes now show up on remote sensed images more strongly than mangrove stands.

Phragmites and *Typha* dominate reed swamp vegetation in many *wadis* on the African side of the southern Red Sea (37) where up to twenty community types of salt marsh vegetation can be classified, identified by their dominant species. Apart from the above, most of these community types are those of *Halocnemum, Limonium, Nitraria* and allied forms, which appear to form some of the most productive zones in these regions. These areas are not well studied, beyond description of the bird communities and general plant zonation patterns. While the term salt marsh is appropriate, they may more simply be termed eutrophic and mesotrophic zones.

Where conditions are appropriate, notably near a tropical river estuary, true marshes and reed beds develop. These occur nowhere more extensively than in the Shatt al Arab waterway, a large deltaic plain of the Euphrates, Tigris and Karun rivers covering an area of about 18 500 km^2 in the late 1980s (18). Eleven halophytic community types occur in northern Kuwait, the most important being dominated by *Juncus* and *Phragmites*, which reach 1.3 and 2.5 m tall respectively. The latter especially covers thousands of km^2. The woody stems float, and are extensively used by the 'Marsh Arabs' for rafts from which they fish and on which many live. However, because the local population opposes the Iraqi government, in the past five years this area has been systematically drained to allow access for military vehicles (imposition of a 'no-fly' zone in the region precluded aerial attack). By 1996, in the first three years of the drainage program, 50% of this vast, last remaining marsh of the Indian Ocean province had already been destroyed (36).

Along the African coast detailed descriptions of marsh plants show some extensive patches (21), though here also, the utility of the plants have led to their extensive over-exploitation. No data is available for marshlands along the Indian coast, though conditions would seem to be similarly favorable as in Africa. The islands of the Indian Ocean contain little or no habitat suitable for such communities.

Macroalgae Communities

Raised levels of nutrients encourage increased growth of macroalgae. In areas where nutrients are raised above oceanic levels, corals decline in diversity, even though some species may remain abundant and provide high coral cover. This is a common feature of 'marginal' reef conditions, a term commonly taken to mean conditions found in high latitude locations, although in several parts of the Indian Ocean marginal conditions increase towards the equator rather than away from it due to the Arabian upwelling. The condition of high latitude is not essential, neither are those of large temperature fluctuations or elevated salinity, though all these factors are commonly associated with algal dominance. Elevated nutrients is essential in most cases (Table 1.5) though the complete reason for strong development of algal communities is likely to be more complex and involve several variables. Where coral dominated communities grade into algal dominated ones, there is debate over whether the gradual change from coral domination to algal domination is a simple consequence of conditions being favorable to algal growth and unfavorable to corals, or whether competition between the two groups plays a major role (4,5,60). Probably both factors are important. Such areas are common throughout the Indian Ocean, and also on the eastern side of the ocean along Australia.

The most important macroalgal group is the Fucales which includes *Sargassum, Sargassopsis, Cystoseira*, and *Hormophysa*. In the Red Sea an increase in *Sargassum* dominance on the seaward edges of reef flats leads to the formation of nearly impenetrable barriers up to 40 to 50 m wide. These develop from the center of the Red Sea southwards, to a point at which fringing coral reefs literally disappear, grading into reefs composed entirely of red coralline algae covered in *Sargassum*. *Halimeda* may be locally abundant also, as is the case in numerous patches throughout the Indian Ocean. In areas with seasonal stress and high nutrients, low cover of corals correlates with raised algal cover (55), and areas suffering substantial abrasion affected by the southwest monsoon likewise have Fucales domination.

Kelp communities of southern Oman are notable for their curiosity value as much as for extended abundance. These may extend into Yemen also. The genus concerned, *Ecklonia*, is otherwise restricted to the southern hemisphere (2) where it grows in southern Africa, Australia and New Zealand. This kelp co-occurs with *Sargassopsis*, and unlike the *Sargassum* communities more common on reefs, has a marked seasonal cycle. The flora beneath the canopy has a particularly high diversity of at least 90 other algal species. Remarkably, corals of modest diversity (about 100 species) may be found scattered among the algae and beneath the canopy, though these rarely develop true coral reefs (49,62).

Other notable algal genera which are associated with reefs include *Turbinaria*, sometimes quantitatively important and an easily recognizable genus particularly in shallow water and reef flats (although it is confusing that this genus name is shared with a coral, beside which the alga commonly grows, especially on reef flats). A most important algal genus is *Halimeda* which is important for its production of copious quantities of calcareous disks. Although, to date, no huge bioherms of the genus appear to have been found in the Indian Ocean as they have in the Caribbean and eastern Australia, the density of coverage by members of the genus in sheltered areas such as central oceanic lagoons is such that it provides much of the sediment in such places.

Plankton

The plankton of the Indian Ocean have been divided into eight geographical regions, determined by the relative ratios of diatoms, dinoflagellates and cyanophytes, itself influenced by whether there is annual stability or strong seasonality induced by upwelling (30). These regions are not necessarily continuous: for example the Arabian Sea is grouped with upwelling areas off Australia and Indonesia. All regions may be viewed as components of a 'basic

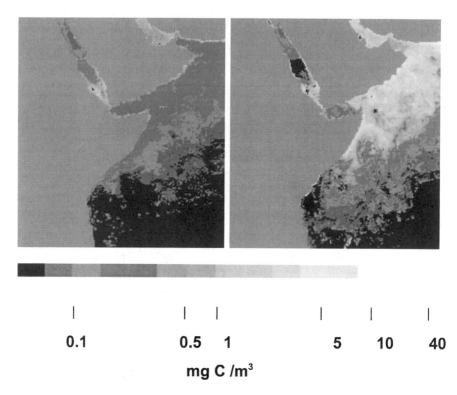

0.1   0.5   1   5   10   40

mg C /m³

Figure 1.10. Arabian Sea upwelling. Images derived from Coastal Zone Color Scanner of the Arabian region showing (left) northern winter and (right) northern summer upwelling values of chlorophyll in surface waters. Data from several overpasses were used to form monthly average composites (in 1979) on a grid of nominal size 20 x 20 km. Top scale on color bar is a linear mapping interval, lower scale is chlorophyll in C mg /m³, on log10 scale. (Images adapted from UNESCO TredMar remote sensing lessons series with permission from the author.)

Indo-oceanic complex' in which several dinoflagellates and diatoms are an outstanding feature of the whole Indian Ocean (28). In terms of diversity there is a general and marked decline from east to west. For example, of 452 known Indian Ocean dinoflagellates, only 130 are recorded from the Arabian Sea and only 88 and about 50 recorded from the western enclaves of the Red Sea and Gulf respectively (see Table 1.3).

Diversity, of course, commonly has no simple correlation with productivity. In fact the two variables may act in opposition, something demonstrated in terrestrial systems (24) but not so far in the sea (57). The most productive parts of the Indian Ocean in large scale terms is the Arabian upwelling (Fig. 1.10). This Coastal Zone Color Scanner image (CZCS) shows January (non-upwelling) and July (upwelling) conditions in the Arabian Sea, the upwelling causing increased pelagic production by a factor of 10 to 20. This upwelling is fundamental to the fishery of several adjacent countries (16). Also regionally important is the continuously raised pelagic productivity in the southern Red Sea. This is caused by wind driven forcing. Although the plankton entering the Red Sea do not survive, the quantities are sufficient to drive the general system

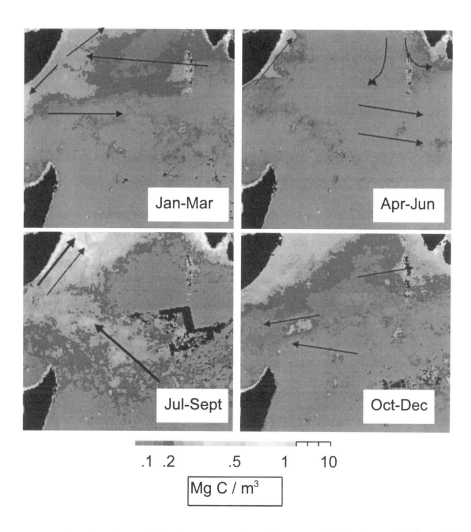

Figure 1.11. Coastal Zone Color Scanner composite of the western Indian Ocean, showing 'halos' or plumes of increased production around atolls. Arrows indicate some of the major ocean currents.

in the southern Red Sea to one based around macroalgae and seagrass instead of the reefs.

On a smaller scale many smaller bays throughout the region may be equally productive, where local conditions and mixing with benthic sediments liberate and continually recycle nutrients (Fig. 1.10). Indeed the entire Arabian Gulf shows high production too, but it must be emphasized that, where water is very shallow, the raised production, as determined by remote sensing techniques, almost certainly comes mainly from benthic production.

A further CZCS image (Fig. 1.11) shows an enhancement of part of the Indian Ocean containing islands and submerged reefs. Features of importance here are the 'haloes' of raised production around the oceanic atolls. Haloes have been noted around some Seychelles atolls (10), where they have been assumed to represent 'leaking' of nutrients into the nutrient poor ocean from the reefs and associated systems. The haloes appear to be a common occurrence around Indian Ocean atolls, and remain poorly understood. As likely as the leakage hypothesis, is the possibility that it represents a moderate enrichment caused by very mild but sustained upwelling. Noting especially the Maldives in composite 1 (January to March) and 4 (October to December) there is a distinct, large plume westwards in the first case and eastwards right up to the Indian coast in the second case, both of which fit the oceanic current pattern prevailing at these times. Similar though less visually dramatic events may be seen around the Chagos atolls and the main Seychelles group at certain times too.

Atolls in this ocean arise rapidly from abyssal depths, and ocean currents, though not necessarily very strong, impinge on undersea mountains of several kilometers high in many cases. Modest enrichment of the surface from deeper water is at least a possibility. The dramatic increase in surface production in the central region between Chagos and the Seychelles in Figure 1.11 (composite 3, July to September) is not a plume traveling south-east from the main Arabian upwelling region; winds and currents at this time flow towards Arabia. The enrichment matches the strong and persistent Southeast trades in the southern ocean which cause severe sea states, and possibly is the consequence of greater mixing with deeper layers. The consequences of such upwelling enrichment (or indeed of leakage if the latter is the main cause of the halos) are likely to be profound, and may bear on current views on the alleged essential nature of tight nutrient recycling in reefs, as well as on fishery potential around them (51,73).

Although plankton generally has a density of only 0.1 to 1/mm^3 of living material in each liter of sea water (56), it is the level where the food chains of most of the aerial extent of the Indian Ocean start. Except near land, and except when events such as red tides occur, oceanic productivity is low. In the central and nutrient poor parts of the ocean, average planktonic productivity is <0.15 g C/m^2/d which rises to 0.25 to 0.5 g C/m^2/d on the limestone plateau and to over 0.5 g C/m^2/d on much of the continental shelf. Zooplankton abundance in the south is <50 mg/m^3 which rises to 200 mg/m^3 in the north. Only on the west Indian continental shelf is this exceeded, where values approach 500 mg /m^3 (1,8). However, because of the upwelling, on average the tropical Indian Ocean is not less productive than the other two tropical oceans (12).

It is commonplace to remark that oceanic production is much lower than benthic production so is of less consequence. This of course overlooks the vastly greater area over which this 'lesser' production takes place, raising its importance in quantitative terms in the Indian Ocean to at least as great as the benthic systems. It also distracts from the main issue, which is not which system is more productive, but rather how the oceanic and benthic systems are linked together. The plankton are "something more than a diluted suspension of life" (32).

Environmental Concerns

Human use of Indian Ocean reefs has increased dramatically in the last few decades for reasons of both commerce and subsistence living. Noticeable declines of many Indian Ocean reefs go back at least as far as Gardiner who in 1936 expressed worry about the degree to which reefs near habitation had deteriorated since 1905 (15). In the 1960's Ray (45) said in connection with one East African coastal country "It is fashionable to say that traditional (mostly subsistence) fishing is centuries old, implying no measurable effect. This is a delusion. Subsistence fishing is no less destructive of marine habitat than subsistence farming is to land." Since then, the pressures on the reefs of populous areas have increased enormously. Of Tanzania, Salm (48) said 15 years ago that many of its reefs, including those in six out of eight proposed National Parks, had been reduced to rubble as a result of dynamiting for fish. Dynamiting continues there (17).

At the end of this century, very few Indian Ocean reefs will have received no impact at all, most have received some, and a few have been severely affected. Other chapters in this volume attest to this. Some reefs have even been completely removed, either inadvertently or by intentional activity such as limestone mining. Two generalizations may be made. Firstly, the degree of reef degradation in populous areas of the Indian Ocean is alarming, and indeed, may be surprising to anyone who has previously been concerned only with reefs such as those commonly used in connection with research or tourism. Conventional literature does not yet contain much reference to the worst affected areas. The second is that the degradation of coral reefs is only one manifestation of a much wider and more intractable problem that currently afflicts many of the countries of the Indian Ocean. This is that the main cause of reef degradation in many areas comes from agricultural malpractice (44). The extent of terrestrial runoff was summarized nearly two decades ago (13,49,69,70,71) when it was shown that soil destabilization resulting from vegetative denudation of the interiors of many countries causes the loss of up to 250 tons of topsoil per hectare each year. The total terrigenous load reaching the western Indian Ocean was, at that time, 500 million m^3/y. Aside from the obvious impact on agricultural productivity, this has severe consequences to the estuarine and coastal fisheries and habitats, and has caused the obliteration of substantial tracts of fringing reefs. Finn (13) stated: "This is not a pretty picture. It will be extremely difficult for the Region's governments to confront such large scale and diffuse problems. A major financial and organizational commitment will be required to avert disaster."

It may be argued that the disaster did not happen, or it may be argued that it is indeed happening. Whichever point of view prevails, there has continued to be a fast deterioration of the reef ecosystem generally, manifested for example by worsening problems such as intractable poverty. The creation of policies which are locally acceptable, of course, was one of the themes at least as far back as 1980 in the *World Conservation Strategy* (23). Warnings are not new but, as expressed by some authorities, the failure to implement effective solutions means that ecosystems, including coral reefs, are collapsing in several Indian Ocean countries, and some of those countries are "no longer part of the 'Third World' as it is usually defined. Rather these impoverished and deteriorating countries are forming a sort of Fourth World of their own." (19). Since then, there are few stories of major improvements except in some localized and, it has to be said, often trivial examples, in any of the four major 'regions' as defined by the Regional Seas Programme of UNEP that cover the western Indian Ocean. Possibly the over-arching problem is that, even in a world as dominated by accountants as ours is, there remains no widely accepted way of putting value to coral reefs and habitats, although one recent estimate put the price benefit of coral reefs at over US $6000 /ha/y, mangroves at $10 000 /ha/y, and seagrass beds at nearly double the latter (7).

Accounts of specific impacts are contained in several of the chapters of this volume. What is emphasized here is that the interdependence of habitats is increasingly seen to be important. Destruction of mangroves as well as reef damage causes flooding in low lying areas and destabilization of sediments with consequences to mangroves. Seagrasses also have usually been overlooked in priorities for protection in the countries of this region, and have been the subject of much less research although they are a highly productive and economically valuable resource. Estuarine disturbances, as well as agriculture inland are all known to have affected areas of reef and caused the destabilization of reefal and adjacent sediments. It might be concluded that not only was the shift in the 1980s from species to habitat conservation by environmental scientists welcome, if overdue, but that this perspective should be shifted one step further. The habitats themselves in Indian Ocean nations are interdependent to such a degree that management of coral reefs cannot be considered in isolation from that of other habitats.

References

1. Bakus, G.J. 1994. *Coral Reef Ecosystems.* Oxford & IBH Ltd New Delhi
2. Barratt, L., Ormond, R.F.G., Wrathall, T. 1986. Ecology and productivity of the sublittoral algae *Ecklonia radiata* and *Sargassopsis zanardini.* Part 1. *Ecological Studies of Southern Oman Kelp Communities.* Council for the Conservation of the Environment and Water Resources, Muscat, Oman, and Regional Organization for the Protection of the Marine Environment, Kuwait, pp 2.1-2.2
3. Behrman, D. 1981. *Assault on the Largest Unknown. The International Indian Ocean Expedition.* UNESCO
4. Coles, S.L. 1988. Limitations on reef coral development in the Arabian Gulf: Temperature or algal competition? *Proceedings of 6th International Coral Reef Symposium*, Townsville, Australia. 3: 211-216
5. Coles, S.L., Fadlallah, Y.H. 1991. Reef coral survival and mortality at low temperatures in the Arabian Gulf: new species-specific lower temperature limits. *Coral Reefs* 9:231-237
6. Coles, S.L., McCain, J.C. 1990. Environmental factors affecting benthic communities of the western Arabian Gulf. *Marine Environmental Research* 29: 289-315

7. Costanza, R and twelve others. 1997. The value of the world's ecosystem services and natural capital. *Nature*, London, 387:25-260
8. Couper, A. 1983. *Times Atlas of the Oceans*. Times Books Ltd, London
9. Dor, I., Levy, I. 1984. Primary productivity of the benthic algae in the hard bottom mangal of Sinai. In *Hydrobiology of the Mangal*. eds Por, F.D., Dor, I.. pp 179-191. The Hague: Dr Munk Publishers
10. Dustan, P. 1992. Estimates of Indian Ocean Productivity using natural fluorescence. *Atoll Research Bulletin* 378:1-13
11. Ehrlich, A., Dor, I. 1985. Photosynthetic microorganisms of the Gavish Sabkha. In *Hypersaline Ecosystems. The Gavish Sabkha*. eds. Friedman G.M., Krumbein W.E. pp 296-321. Springer Verlag
12. Fagoonee, I. 1983. Why is the Indian Ocean considered less productive? Unpublished manuscript. IUCN, Gland
13. Finn, D. 1983. Land use and abuse in the East African region. *Ambio* 12: 296-301
14. Friedman, G.M., Krumbein, W.E. eds. 1985. *Hypersaline Ecosystems. The Gavish Sabkha*. Springer Verlag
15. Gardiner, J.S. 1936. The reefs of the Western Indian Ocean. I. Chagos Archipelago. II. The Mascarene region. *Transactions of Linnean Society, London* Vol 19 pp 393-436
16. Gjøsaeter, J. 1984. Mesopelagic fish, a large potential resource in the Arabian sea. *Deep Sea Research* 31:1019-1035
17. Guard, M., Masaiganab, M. 1997. Dynamite fishing in southern Tanzania, geographical variation, intensity of use and possible solutions. *Marine Pollution Bulletin* 34:758-762
18. Halwagy, R., Clayton, D., Behbehani, M. eds. 1986. *Marine Environment and Pollution*. Proceedings of First Arabian Gulf Conference on Environment and Pollution. Kuwait, 7-9 February 1982
19. Hilary, Sir E. ed. 1984. *Ecology 2000*. Michael Joseph, London
20. Hopley, D. 1982. *The Geomorphology of the Great Barrier Reef. Quaternary Development of Coral Reefs*. Wiley Interscience New York
21. Hughes, R.H., Hughes, J.S. 1992. *A Directory of African Wetlands*. IUCN, Gland
22. Hutchings, P.A., Saenger, P. 1987. *Ecology of Mangroves*. University of Queensland Press, Queensland
23. IUCN 1980. *World Conservation Strategy: Living Resource Conservation for Sustainable Development*. IUCN, Gland
24. Johnson, K., Vogt, K.A., Clark, H.J., Schmitz, O.J., Vogt, D.J. 1996. Biodiversity and the productivity and stability of ecosystems. *Trends in Ecology and Evolution*, 11372-377
25. Jupp, B.P., Durako, M.J., Kenworthy, W.J., Thayer, G.W., Schillak, L. 1996. Distribution, abundance and species composition of seagrasses at several sites in Oman. *Aquatic Botany* 53: 199-213
26. Kendall C.G. St. C., Skipwith, P.A.d'E. 1968. Recent algal mats of a Persian Gulf lagoon. *Journal of Sedimentary Petrology* 38:1040-1059
27. Kendall C.G. St.C., Skipwith, P.A. d'E. 1969. Holocene shallow water carbonate and evaporite sediments of Khor al Bazam, Abu Dhabi, southwest Persian Gulf. *Bulletin of American Association of Petroleum Geologists* 53:841-869

28. Kimor, B. 1973. Plankton relations of the Red Sea, Persian Gulf and Arabian Sea. In *The Biology of the Indian Ocean.* ed Zeitschel, B., pp 221- 232. New York: Springer Verlag

29. Kinsey, D.W. 1991. The coral reef: an over-built, high density, fully-serviced, self-sufficient housing estate in the desert - or is it? *Symbiosis* 10:1-22

30. Krey, J. 1973. Primary production in the Indian Ocean. In *The Biology of the Indian Ocean.* ed. Zeitschel, B. pp 115-126. New York: Springer Verlag

31. Lemmens, J.W.T. 1993. Reef-building corals (Cnidaria: Scleractinia) from the Watamu marine national reserve, Kenya; an annotated species list. *Zoologische Mededelingen* 67:453-465

32. Margalef, R. 1997. *Our Biosphere.* Vol 10 *Excellence in Ecology.* ed. Kinne, O. Ecology Institute, Germany.

33. McClanahan, T. R., Nugues, M., Mwachireya, S. 1994. Fish and sea urchin herbivory and competition in Kenyan coral reef lagoons: the role of reef management. *Journal of Experimental Marine Biology and Ecology* 184: 237-254

34. Mukherjee, A.K., Tiwari, K.K. 1984. Mangrove ecosystem changes under induced stress: the case history of the Sundaban, West Bengal, India. In *Proceedings of Asian Symposium on Mangrove Environmental Research and Management.* eds. Soepadmo, A.N., Rao, A,N. Macintosh, D.J. pp 633-643

35. Niebuhr, C. 1792. *Travels Through Arabia, and Other Countries in the Far East, Performed by M. Niebuhr, now a Captain of Engineers in the Service of the King of Denmark. (Translated into English by Robert Heron, with notes from the Translator, and illustrated with gravings and Maps.)* Two volumes. Libraire du Liban, Beirut, reprint (no date)

36. North, A. 1993. Saddam's water war. *Geographical Magazine*, July 1993. pp 10-14

37. Orme, A.R. 1982. Africa: Coastal Ecology. In *Encyclopedia of Beaches and Coastal Environments.* ed. Schwartz, M.L. pp 3-16. Stroudsburg: Hutchinson Ross

38. Phillips, R.C., Menez, E.G. 1988. Seagrasses. Smithsonian Contributions to the Marine Sciences, No 34

39. Pichon, M. 1971. Comparative study of the main features of some coral reefs of Madagascar, La Reunion and Mauritius. In *Regional Variation in Indian Ocean Reefs.* eds. Stoddart, D.R, Yonge, C.M. pp 185-216. Symposium of the Zoological Society of London, 28. Academic Press

40. Pichon, M. 1995. Coral reef ecosystems. In *Environmental Biology.* ed. Nierenberg W.A. pp 425-447. Academic Press. Volume 1

41. Por, F.D., Dor, I., Amir, A. 1977. The mangal of Sinai: limits of an ecosystem. *Helgolander. Wiss. Meeresuntersuchungen* 30:295-314

42. Purser, B.H. 1985. Coastal evaporite systems. In *Hypersaline Ecosystems: The Gavish Sabkha.* eds. Friedman G.M., Krumbein W.E. pp 72-102. Springer Verlag

43. Purser, B.H. 1973. *The Persian Gulf.* New York: Springer Verlag

44. Randrianarijaona, P. 1983. The erosion of Madagascar. *Ambio* 12:308-311

45. Ray, C. 1969. Marine Parks for Tanzania. Conservation Foundation and New York Zoological Society

46. Rosen, B.R. 1971. The distribution of reef coral genera in the Indian Ocean. In *Regional Variation in Indian Ocean Coral Reefs.* eds. Stoddart, D.R., Yonge, C.M. pp 263-299. Symposium Zoological Society of London, 28. London: Academic Press

47. Rosen, B.R. 1981. The tropical high diversity enigma - the corals eye view. In *Chance, Change and Challenge. The Evolving Biosphere.* ed. Forey, P.L. pp 103-129. BM(NH) and Cambridge University Press

48. Salm, R. 1983. Coral reefs of the Western Indian Ocean: a threatened heritage. *Ambio* 12:349-354.

49. Salm, R. 1993. Coral reefs of the Sultanate of Oman. *Atoll Research Bulletin* 380: pp 1-84

50. Scheer, G. 1984. The distribution of reef corals in the Indian Ocean with a historical review of its investigation. *Deep Sea Research* 31: 885-900

51. Shashar, N., Feldstein, T., Cohen, Y., Loya, Y. 1994. Nitrogen fixation (acetylene reduction) on a coral reef. *Coral Reefs* 13:171-174

52. Sheppard, C.R.C. 1982. Overview and status report of the mangroves at Madinat Yanbu al Sinaiyah. Report for Royal Commission for Jubail and Yanbu. E&E Buffalo

53. Sheppard, C.R.C. 1983. *A Natural History of the Coral Reef.* Blandford Press

54. Sheppard, C.R.C. 1987. Coral species of the Indian Ocean and adjacent seas: a synonymised compilation and some regional distribution patterns. *Atoll Research Bulletin* 307: 1-32

55. Sheppard, C.R.C. 1988. Similar trends, different causes: Responses of corals to stressed environments in Arabian seas. *Proceedings of the 6th International Coral Reef Symposium,* Townsville: Australia 3: 297-302

56. Sheppard, C.R.C. 1995. Biological communities of tropical oceans. In *Environmental Biology.* ed. Nierenberg, W.A. pp 277-289. Academic Press

57. Sheppard, C.R.C. 1997. Biodiversity, productivity and system integrity. *Marine Pollution Bulletin* 34: 680-681

58. Sheppard, C.R.C. in press. Biodiversity patterns in Indian Ocean corals, and effects of taxonomic error in data. *Biodiversity and Conservation*

59. Sheppard C.R.C., Sheppard, A.L.S. 1991. Corals and Coral Communities of Arabia. *Fauna of Saudi Arabia,* Vol. 12

60. Sheppard, C.R.C., Price, A.R.G., Roberts, C.J. 1992. Marine Ecology of the *Arabian Area. Patterns and Processes in Extreme Environments.* London: Academic Press

61. Sheppard, C.R.C., Premeratne, A., Klaus, R., Caulfield, N. 1997. Coastal Zone Habitat Atlas of Southern and Western Sri Lanka. 55 pp large format and GIS digital format. London: Dept of Environment

62. Sheppard, C.R.C., Salm, R.V. 1988. Reef and coral communities of Oman, with a description of a new coral species (Order Scleractinia, genus *Acanthastrea*). *Journal of Natural History* 22:263-279

63. Sheppard, C.R.C., Wells, S.M. 1988. *Coral Reefs of the World. Volume 2: Indian Ocean, Red Sea and Gulf.* UNEP Regional Seas Directories and Bibliographies. IUCN, Gland, Switzerland and UNEP Nairobi

64. Spalding, M.D. and others. 1997. *World Mangrove Atlas.* International Society for Mangrove Ecosystems, Japan and IUCN , Cambridge, UK

65. Stehli F.G., Wells J.W. 1971. Diversity and age patterns in hermatypic corals. *Systematic Zoology.* 20:115-126
66. Stoddart, D.R. 1965. The shape of atolls. *Marine Geology* 3: 369-383
67. Stoddart, D.R. 1973. Coral reefs of the Indian Ocean. In *Biology and Geology of Coral Reefs.* eds. Jones, O.A., Endean, R. pp 51-91. London: Academic Press
68. Stoddart, D.R., Yonge, C.M. eds. 1971. *Regional Variation in Indian Ocean Coral Reefs.* Symposium of the Zoolgocal Society of London 28. London: Academic Press
69. UNEP 1982. Conservation of the coastal and marine ecosystems and living resources of the East African region. *UNEP Regional Seas Reports and Studies No 11.*
70. UNEP 1982. Environmental problems of the East African region. *UNEP Regional Seas Reports and Studies No 12.*
71. UNEP 1982. Marine and coastal area development in the East Africa region. *UNEP Regional Seas Reports and Studies No 6.*
72. Wahbeh, M.I. 1981. Distribution, biomass, biometry and some associated fauna of the seagrass community in the Jordan Gulf of Aqaba. *Proceedings of the 4th International Coral Reef Symposium* 2: 453-459
73. Wilkinson, C.R., Williams, D.M., Sammarco, P.W., Hogg, R.W., Trott, L.A. 1984. Rates of nitrogen fixation on coral reefs across the continental shelf of the central Great Barrier Reef. Marine Biology 80: 255-262
74. Zeitzschel, B. ed. 1973. *The Biology of the Indian Ocean.* New York: Springer Verlag

Chapter 2

Coral Reef Use and Conservation

Timothy R. McClanahan

Conservation of coral reefs is primarily concerned with controlling or reducing the levels of fishing or resource extraction and marine pollution. These two factors are considered, by coral reef scientists, to be the main human influences on coral reefs (25). There are, however, a number of other threats to the diversity and function of coral reefs (Table 2.1) but they are less well understood and often uncontrollable at the local or regional level and therefore not amenable to management. For instance, warming of the earth by the burning of fossil and wood fuels may cause the temperature of the oceans to increase beyond a maximum threshold tolerable to corals (10,27) and is, therefore, arguably one of the major threats to the survival of coral reefs. This warming is, however, largely caused by waste emissions from developed countries that do not have coral reefs and is largely ignored or beyond the control of local managers of coral reefs. In contrast, there is mounting evidence that local small-scale fishers are having a major influence on coral reef ecology throughout the tropical oceans and that some of these detrimental effects could be managed or reduced (33). This problem of the scale of threats, their interactions and boundaries, and our recognition of important and manageable threats is an important theme for understanding reef management.

In the western Indian Ocean region the most wide-spread and manageable threat to reef conservation is fishing although there are localized pollution problems (25). While coral reefs only contribute about 1% of the world's total fish catch, a large human population depends on this catch for survival, and it comes from one the Earth's most diverse marine ecosystem. Reef fisheries have not been well studied and managed and this lack of understanding, recognition of the problems, and management is perhaps the greatest threat to reef species diversity and the people that depend on reefs for their livelihood. Below I will review conservation-related research and attempts to conserve coral reefs in this region with special emphasis on marine protected areas.

Table 2.1. List of important hazards to coral reefs in the Indian Ocean developed from a workshop of reef investigators working in the Indian Ocean (25). Far right column includes factors listed in other regions, but not by the Indian Ocean study group.

High Concern	Medium Concern	Low Concern	Listed for Other Regions
Nutrient enrichment	Hurricane/Storm Damage	Coral Mining/Collection	Herbicides & Pesticides
Fishing (Overfishing)	Tourism (coral contact)	Acanthaster predation	Salinity changes (Natural)
Sediments/Turbidity	Industrial/Urban Pollution	Rising sea level	Coral diseases
Habitat destructive fishing	Vessel anchoring	Vessel grounding	Bleaching
	Global warming	Cold water exposure	Oil pollution
		Algal competition	Human population growth
		Drupella predation	Salinity changes
		Urchin grazing	Ultraviolet exposure
			Lack of education
			Laws/Regulations/ Enforcement
			El Nino
			Sea Urchin die off
			Xenobiotics
			Volcanoes/ Earthquakes
			Warm water exposure
			Scientific research

Traditional Forms of Social Organization and Resource Management

Fisheries have been a notoriously difficult system to manage because the resource is frequently viewed as a common-property resource and fishers are often allowed uncontrolled or open access (5,63). If fishers act independently and selfishly and the resource is open to any user then overexploitation of the fishery is a common problem for management. Nonetheless, common property does not always mean that access is open to all and traditional and modern management have produced numerous mechanisms to avoid open access. Modern fisheries management has, therefore, largely developed to decrease the level of fisher independence, selfish behavior, unrestrained growth, and open access to common property. The concept of open access or 'freedom of the seas' was largely a western concept developed before the turn of this century and, although this freedom of the seas concept is still professed by some nations, it is largely being replaced by more restraining concepts and activities such as the 200 mile limit, Exclusive Economic Zone, and the highly structured coastal area management systems (38). Many traditional cultures also had a number of restraining mechanisms (35,61,86), but many did not, and only low human populations allowed ecosystems to persist relatively undisturbed until now.

Studies of traditional coastal fishing communities indicate that they have a number of cultural practices comparable to modern fisheries management activities in that they regulate fishing people, places, times, and gear (35,76). Traditional forms of management still exist but they are often being replaced or modified by changes in culture with the increasing influence of national and international governance and religious organizations (61,88). These organizations often have different concepts of land ownership and tenure than traditional social or economic organization (78).

The Case of the Mijikenda, Kenya

In much of Africa it was recognized that the use of land or resources gave the user certain rights and privileges to the area or resources. The rights were most often recognized or formalized within the lineage, clan, or chiefdom. If the resource was used until death then it would transfer to an oldest or youngest son while other sons would develop access to resources by a lineage or central authority which would allocate unused resources (24). If one did not use the resource, however, the chance of losing it, at the decision of a central authority, was high. Now that resources are scarcer and ethnic leaders are most often subservient to national leaders, the western ideal of individual ownership is competing with traditional tenure and management of resources. Interestingly, even in African countries that have legally and technically adopted private ownership there has been a poor compliance with this system and many of the traditional forms of ownership still persist (24).

The Mijikenda people are a loose association of nine closely-related ethnic groups that inhabit Kenya's coastline. The oldest of these ethnic groups, the Digo, migrated to their present location in southern Kenya during the 16th century from an area near the Tana River, where they were in conflict with the Oromo people (79). The Digo settled in forests, called *kaya*, that acted as centers of defense against Oromo warriors. Deceased Digo elders were buried in these *kaya*. *Kaya* are still considered sacred forests where prayers and rites of sacrifice are performed.

The Digo's oldest coastal settlements also have similar sacred sites on the beach and at sea called *mzimu* but they differ from *kaya* in being smaller and not used as burial sites (Fig. 2.1, 61). *Mzimu* are frequently unusual features on the beach or water that are believed to house spirits. Annual sacrifices, usually performed at the end of the year, begin at a forest *kaya*, move to a beach *mzimu*, and then end at a *mzimu* in the sea. These sacrifices are lead by two *kaya* elders, a leader and his assistant, who inherit their positions from their fathers by virtue of being the eldest sons. The prayers and sacrifices of this area are among the most elaborate of the Kenyan coast and include specific clothing, times of day, and specific sacrificial items (26). Elders commonly lead prayers and sacrifices at these sites to request favors from the spirits that inhabit them. *Mzimu* were avoided during other times of the year for fear of upsetting the spirits. How widespread these cultural forms of sacred sites and sacrifice are is unknown but fishers from southern Kenya claim that they are very widespread. Sacred sites on the beach and sea also occur in eastern Madagascar (69) and similar cultural systems are common in Asia (88).

Traditional View of Management. Marine resources were traditionally seen to fluctuate independently of fisher numbers and catches, and were seen to reflect adherence to tradition and the fishers relationships with spirits, ancestors, and each other (see Box 2.1). Many traditional fishers believe that catches

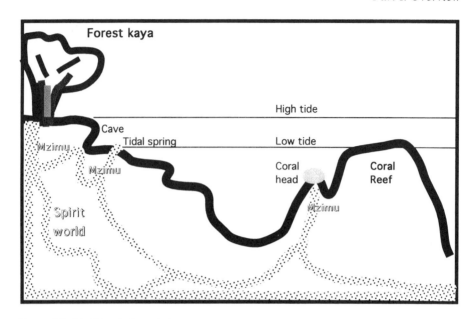

Figure 2.1. Traditional view of the Mijikenda land and seascape based on interviews with elders from the Chale-Kinondo area of Southern Kenya. Unusual features in the physical world are often seen as a link of communication between the physical and spiritual world. *Kaya* forests are traditional sacred grounds where ancestors were buried (see 61 for more details).

reflect the moral characters of the fishers and their daily practices and ceremonial performances. Consequently, if catches have been poor a meeting is called and the likely outcomes are to perform a sacrifice and prayer or to ask a troublesome fisher to leave, stop fishing, or make an offering to the community. Some fishers will also blame poor fish catches on the influx of tourists or fishers from other ethnic groups or occupations who are not trained in their traditional methods of fishing. Despite the lack of recognition of the relationship between fishing effort and fish catches, it is common practice for the leaders of Digo fishing communities to ask for a payment, called *ubani*, from outsiders to use their fishing grounds. This payment reflects the recognition that active fishers have rights to the fishing grounds and outsiders using it must pay. This custom is, therefore, not necessarily a means to reduce fishing effort.

Many of these beliefs and practices exclude outsiders, foreign gear, or reduce the number of fishers or their time spent fishing and may, therefore, be seen as management. The difference is that the traditional view rarely explicitly admits that the number of people and their off take or imbalance of the resource are the causes of declines in catches. Consequently, the western concepts of managing human effort, manipulating food webs, and protecting habitat are often viewed with skepticism by traditional fishers who are less likely to admit that these factors are contributing to poor catches. Sacred sites may seem similar to marine protected areas, but sacred sites are traditionally avoided for fear of the spirits and are not viewed as places to be visited regularly, especially by foreigners, who do not respect these spirits. Regardless,

Box 2.1. Fisher Folklore: A Basis for Flexible Marine Management Plans of the Future

How, where, and when fishers use the sea has long been affected by their belief in the existence of potentially evil spirits (1). That fishers should harbor such beliefs is hardly surprising given the unpredictable and dangerous nature of their work (2). Belief in spirits can help allay fears of death and injury by providing people with reasons for individual and communal misfortune. Belief in an active spirit world influenced by human actions not only comforts individuals but also gives community leaders, generally elders, a level of social control over members' access to and use of community resources, through dissemination of information about which actions will satisfy or anger spirits (3).

Contented sea and coastal spirits are presumed not only to ensure a plentiful supply of fish and marine organisms but to protect fishers and their entire community from misfortune including drowning, inundation by flood, and being turned into non-human form such as human size seaside rocks, dolphins, manatees, or mermaids (6). Individuals generally police their own behavior so as not to be viewed as a liability to the entire community. Sanctions for breaking with local norms tend to be minor in terms of cash sums or goods, but more significant in terms of appearances and social standing. As such spirit-informed marine management remains most effective in closer-knit, single ethnicity communities where younger generations continue to rely on fishing for a livelihood (3).

Elder fishers generally determine which activities or actions at sea are taboo. They may protect critical resources from overuse by labeling them sacred or as homes to dangerous spirits (8). Taboo times and places keep fishers from using particularly dangerous waters such as surge channels near coral reefs or non-lagoonal waters on a seasonal basis, fishing further from shore at night, and so forth. In addition to promoting fisher safety, taboos may have the effect of conserving fish stocks. For example, it might be taboo to put excessive effort into fishing, use fish poisons, kill juvenile fish, or fish on holy days (3). In addition, by making alliances or pacts with powerful local spirits elders can restrict outsider access to the fishery, having a conservation effect.

Types of spirits of the sea and the actions said to appease them are similar across continents (1). Elders lead ceremonies of offerings of food, blood, and praise to appease sea spirits. Slaughtering animals and letting the blood into the sea is intended to reduce the number of drownings by curbing sea spirits appetite for blood and is the basis of a shared meal among spirits and fishers who consume the meat of the slaughtered animal (8). Good and bad omens which are predictive of fish catch influence fisher effort and days and times fishing occurs. Globally, two of the most commonly recognized spirits include a spirit which causes people to drown and a spirit whose movement is observed as flashing or blinking lights in the night sky (1). Frequently associated with electrical storms, spirits which appear as blinking lights are considered malicious, dangerous, or simply playful in different world regions. The appearance of some water spirits is considered a good sign and associated with sudden riches or bumper harvests. Conversely, the cause of a spirit-induced death varies among communities but is often attributed to the victim's morally dubious actions or manipulation of the spirit world by an envious, malicious being (6).

Elders, more than younger fishers, often use the oldest forms of fishing such as fish weirs and basket traps (4). Fish traps and weirs have long been associated with high catches, but require few hours at sea relative to other methods of fish capture. Elders put offerings to spirits in weirs during annual fishing ceremonies in the hope of maintaining the favor of the sea spirits able to guide shoaling fish toward or away from fishing grounds (3). In some areas weirs were considered homes to spirits who protected elders' catch from theft. As nearshore stocks become depleted, many elders abandon shoreline weir fishing. Whenever fewer elders construct fish weirs their knowledge of sea spirits may be questioned by younger fishers.

Technological changes in nearshore marine fisheries have contributed to recent challenges to elder authority. For example, in addition to knowing the most about human-sea spirit relations and what constitutes wise use of the sea, local elders once passed down knowledge of which shrubs and tree parts to collect for weaving basket traps and building weirs, but also which barks, leafy materials or resins were most effective for preserving or tanning fishing lines and nets constructed from natural fibers (3). Before widespread use of radio and television elders served as prime information sources and story tellers. Furthermore, prior to widespread access to hospitals and clinics, elders also served as reserves of medicinal knowledge when fishers sustained minor injuries from contact with corals, rays, stone fish, eels, or sea urchins (3).

Challenges to elders' powers have occurred in fishing communities sporadically for centuries and are hardly a present-day phenomenon. Faith in elders' ability to maintain the favor of sea spirits wanes in fishing communities when stocks of fish and marine organisms decline, new religious ideas are introduced, or outsiders, not observing local taboos, obtain larger catches than locals (1,3). Belief among fishers in the existence of sea spirits remains widespread if not openly discussed (2). What is of frequent issue in the present-day is who is best able to communicate with spirits, what form praise or offerings to them should take, and to what extent actions with origins in local religions, have in the modern world (3). Younger men may claim superior ability to address spirits based on their literacy and ability to read the Bible or Koran or the obvious failure of elders to ensure an acceptable level of fish catch.

It appears that multiple challenges to elder authority are converging in the present day posing a great threat to elder power. For example, more permanent broad-scale declines in fish stocks, marine turtles, dugong and select shellfish in the twentieth century have often been coupled with a massive influx of non-locals to coastal areas for tourism and permanent residence (7). Under such conditions younger community members may abandon fishing in favor of wage labor potentially earning more than elders. In addition, with a rise in tourism there is often increasing state regulation of the seas through the burgeoning of marine parks. Tourist presence also increases demand for marine life which lives in deeper, more dangerous waters that elders would like fishers to avoid (3). As beach-front tourist hotels flourish fishing communities are often pushed to the interior, decreasing the involvement of very young family members in fishing (3). Furthermore, tourists recreational use of destructive fishing techniques including spearguns has been copied by unemployed youths adding fishing pressure and contributing to a more widespread failure to observe local fishing taboos as well as intergenerational strife in fishing communities (3).

Elders increasingly are seeking new allies and means of maintaining social control. It has been to their advantage that waters considered sacred or taboo are frequently more fish-rich and biodiverse than areas not labeled as such (8). Thus, there have been some recent attempts by governments to embrace indigenous marine management practices and incorporate them into official management plans. Results have been mixed. For example, in some cases locals do not wish to reveal the location of sacred or taboo waters as they are often meaningful places associated with unfortunate deaths of loved ones, burial grounds, or locations where founding peoples took refuge from past invaders (see Figure). In addition, sacred spaces can lose local meaning when they are patrolled and controlled by state officials. Indeed many areas locals consider sacred include unusual or spectacular environmental features (caves, cliffs, large coral heads, waterfalls) that have been partially or completely coopted by states for touristic purposes (2). In such cases, the state, not local people receive the financial rewards of environmental protection.

Elders are commonly recognized within their own communities as joint managers of the sea with state officials but government officials rarely recognize local elders as marine managers. More effective hybrid management plans would give locals as well as the government recognized enforcement rights over marine areas, and include rules which are locally known but malleable and changeable without state approval or involvement. The strength and persistence of fishers' marine management systems lie precisely in their flexibility to add new rules and abandon others as needed (3). For example, elders' ability to define new fishing methods as against existing local sea codes can limit the number of local, if not non-local fishers, from using environmentally-destructive fishing techniques such as spear guns or pull seines (3). Although fewer taboos or codes of behavior at sea are presently observed most fishing communities still recognize informal territorial boundaries at sea between fishing communities and maintain informal mechanisms for restricting outsider access to local waters. Territorial boundaries at sea represent another aspect of local management which could be used to inform community-state marine management plans. Where joint management is desirable, state officials may facilitate dialogue by acknowledging the belief in spirits or that "modern" and spirit-informed fisheries management are not mutually exclusive.

Heidi Glaesel

References

1. Anson, P. F. 1965. *Fisher Folk-Lore*. London: The Faith Press
2. Carmichael, D.L., Hubert, J., Reeves, B., Schanche, A. eds. 1994. *Sacred Sites, Sacred Places*. London: Routledge
3. Glaesel, H. 1997. *Fishers, Parks, and Power: The Socio-Environmental Dimensions of Marine Resource Decline and Protection on the Kenya Coast*. PhD Dissertation, University of Wisconsin-Madison
4. Johannes, R.E. 1981. *Words of the Lagoon*. Berkeley: University of California Press

5.   McGoodwin, J.R. 1990. *Crisis in the World's Fisheries: People, Problems, and Policies.* Stanford: Stanford University Press
6.   Smith, N. 1981. *Man, Fishes, and the Amazon.* New York: Columbia University Press
7.   Weber, P. 1993. *Abandoned Seas: Reversing the Decline of the Oceans.* Washington: World Watch paper #116
8.   Western, D., Wright, R.M., Strum, S.C. eds. 1994. *Natural Connections: Perspectives in Community-Based Conservation.* Washington: Island Press

traditional beliefs can inadvertently promote conservation of resources (Box 2.1).

The Effectiveness of Traditional Management. Investigations into the effectiveness of traditional management of Digo fishers on fish catches and the ecology of fishing grounds were recently undertaken in the Digo area of southern Kenya (61). This included one of the major environmental problems facing coral reef ecosystems in East Africa, the proliferation of beach seines since the 1960s.

Beach seines are large nets (150 m long and 5 m high) with small mesh sizes of around 3 cm that have been introduced into Kenya and mainland Tanzania. Fishing crews are, however, a mixture of local Kenyan and Tanzanian citizens. Beach seines are an environmental problem because they catch very small and immature fish (Fig. 2.2) and they are dragged across the bottom, which abrades the bottom, breaking corals and other bottom-attached organisms. Dragging reduces the topographic complexity of the substrate, which is important for maintaining fish habitat (3,30,43). Beach seines are not considered a traditional fishing method by the park service (Kenya Wildlife Service) and some traditional fishing communities. Some fishing community leaders say that nets made from the bark of trees were used by tradition and that beach seines are simply a modification of this traditional fishing method (61). Beach seines have probably proliferated because they catch smaller fish than the traditional gear of traps and lines and are, therefore, more 'competitive'. Beach seines are arguably a gear arising from and further causing low fish abundance. Investigators examined the adaptations of eight fishing communities to the introduction of beach seines.

Two of the eight communities discouraged the use of beach seines in 'their waters' and did not adopt beach seines at their landing for over 25 years, claiming that beach seines were not a traditional gear. These two adjacent landing sites had *kaya* elders who had strong opinions about adherence to 'correct tradition'. The communities were able to deter beach seiners by refusing to buy their landed catch or to accept the traditional payment of *ubani*. Additionally, when beach seine crews arrived at the landing, the local community, of around 50 people, would push their boats past the high tide mark making it difficult for the seiners to return to the water. This stopped beach seiners from landing and selling fish at these two communities. They did, however, continue to fish in this area and transport the fish to other landings. This lead to physical conflict between traditional fishers and beach seine crews which was partially resolved when the Kenya police told the traditional fishers

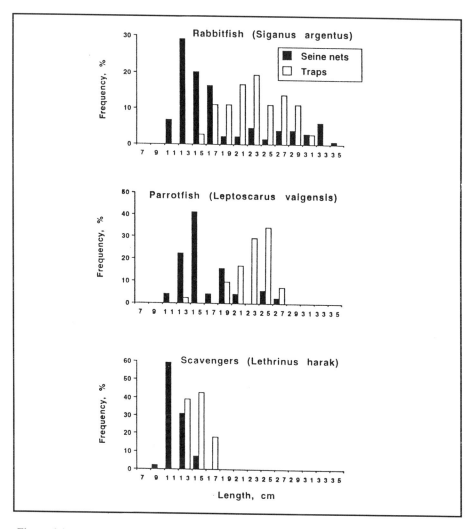

Figure 2.2. The relative size-frequency distribution of catches of three major fisheries species caught by beach seines and traps in the Diani-Kinondo area of southern Kenya. Data from (75).

that they had no authority to stop beach seining and would be arrested if they used physical violence. The traditional community leaders continued to talk to the beach seine crews to dissuade them from seining. The net effect was that beach seining continued particularly on the edges of the traditional fishers waters and at night but fishing effort by this method was probably reduced significantly compared to beach-seine-friendly landing sites.

Comparisons of the fish catches of these same eight landing sites, grouped by sublocations, show that the two landing sites that restrained beach seiners had higher per capita and per area fish catches as well as larger fish (Table 2.2). This does not account for the catch lost to these two sites by beach seiners who fished in these waters but landed their catch elsewhere. Consequently, the

Table 2.2. Fisheries catches and ecological parameters in areas with and without beach seining in the Diani-Kinondo area of southern Kenya (61). NS = not significant.

Catch and field measurements	Seine landing		No-seine landing			ANOVA	
	Mean	S.D.	Mean	S.D.	Diff, %	F-Value	p
Resource extraction							
Fish catch, kg/ha/y/man	12.4	1.9	17.5	2.0	41.1	14.7	0.0002
Fish catch, kg/ha/y	115.2	12.8	131.4	9.8	14.1		
Ecological parameters							
Hard coral	6.1	5.9	6.6	3.8	7.1	0.0	NS
Fleshy algae	9.6	8.9	9.9	5.0	3.3	0.0	NS
Sea urchins, #/10m^2	123.2	15.3	152.9	54.6	24.1	1.1	NS
wet weight, kg/ha	5696.3		5616.1		-1.4	0.0	NS
Fish wet weight, kg/ha	65.2	34.6	72.9	15.7	11.8	0.1	NS
Fish species, #/transect	23.2	5.6	19.8	1.8	-14.7	0.6	NS

differences are probably larger in favor of traditional fisherfolk management. In contrast to the fisheries productivity result, there was no indication that biological diversity or ecological condition of the reef in front of the traditional landing sites was better than the other landing sites. All areas were dominated by large numbers of sea urchins and had low coral cover and fish diversity and abundance (Table 2.2).

This study shows that the lack of correspondence between local and national policies and enforcement prevented these two local communities from achieving their management objectives. These two communities were unique in their ability to partially resist a competitive and destructive fishing gear whereas most fishing communities adopted or permitted beach seines. We can conclude that traditional management is now weak at resisting the degradation of the environment, particularly when these communities are not allowed to enforce their management, which is frequently seen as a role of national governments. The chances for success should, however, be improved if local management is compatible with national policies and enforcement. More recently, beach seining has been excluded from many areas in Kenya through the district-level initiatives involving District Officers and government-appointed chiefs. The district level may be the most appropriate level for management because this scale of governance has the greatest potential to integrate local ethnic culture and management with the national culture and management policies.

Role of National Governments

During the colonial period and national independence movements since the 1950s the conservation of marine resources has increasingly become a national concern. Economic development is a priority of these emerging nations. Therefore, maximizing the benefits of tourism and resource extraction while protecting the environment are the primary objectives and, clearly, require trade offs between extraction and preservation of resources. One of the most fundamental ways that these governments have dealt with tourist development

Table 2.3. Summary of marine protected areas of the region by region and biogeographic zone (37).

Marine Region	Number of Existing MPAs	Percentage of Region	Percentage of World	Number of BioZones with 1 MPA	Number of BioZones with no MPAs	Percentage of Protected BioZones
Central Indian Ocean	15	16.7	1.1	4	2	66.7
Arabian Seas	21	23.3	1.4	8	5	61.5
East Africa	54	60.0	4.1	3	2	60.0
Western IO Region	90		6.9			
World	1306			118	32	78.7

and conservation is through the establishment of nationally-recognized marine protected areas (MPAs) which prevent or limit resource extraction.

Existing and Planned Legislation

National and international organizations have been prolific in designating marine protected areas in the region since the 1960s (Table 2.3, 37,82). A recent compilation of MPAs in the central and western Indian Ocean and Red Sea area indicates that there were 90 existing MPAs and somewhere between 59 and 160 proposed MPAs in 1994. This represents about 7% of the world's total of 1306 MPAs. Despite this large number, about 40% of the biogeographic zones for each subregion did not have a single MPA in 1994.

The different estimates for the proposed MPAs occurs because, in many cases, there is a lack of coordination between international and national organizations in deciding which and how many areas should be protected. It is common to have international consultants and agencies develop MPAs from survey work but these plans are not considered, accepted, or implemented by the national governments. Many of the World Bank and IUCN compilations include such areas.

Effectiveness of Legislation. The existence of MPAs means that legislation has or will shortly occur to designate areas as protected, but it does not mean that these areas receive protective or restrictive management. For instance the seven MPAs of Tanzania were gazetted by the government in the 1970s but protective management did not follow and fisher densities in the near shore areas range between 2 and 5 fishers/km^2 (80). These MPAs are, therefore, heavily fished and fishing gear include destructive methods such as dynamite fishing and beach seines (Chapters 5 and 6). In addition, many of the listed MPAs are primarily terrestrial or estuarine parks. MPAs have a shoreline or border extension into the sea but the management of the park may seldom extend into the sea. This is the case for most of the MPAs of India (Chapter 10).

A large number of the MPAs listed receive only partial management, depending on their designation as parks or reserves, and may be severely impacted by fishing or other human disturbances. For instance most of the 15 MPAs of the Seychelles are regularly fished with fisher densities ranging from

3.5 to 20 boats/km² (32). The one fully protected area is the Seychelles Cousin Island Nature Reserve which has an area of only 1.5 km² with a reef area of only 0.4 km² (31,34). Similarly the only presently effective protected area in Tanzania is the privately owned Chumbe Island Reserve off Zanzibar with an area of less than 0.5 km² (Chapter 16).

Kenya provides the best protective management of MPAs in the region, but only four of the 10 listed MPAs are parks and fully protected from fishing. The park area represents less than 40 km² or less than 6% of the nearshore waters. The other Kenyan MPAs are reserves which allow 'traditional fishing'. The interpretation of tradition is often dependent on the particular warden and some areas receive little or no management for a variety of reasons. Consequently, the effectiveness of conservation derived from the large number of designated MPAs in the region needs to be viewed with skepticism as their present effectiveness in protecting species and ecosystems is probably poor.

Given that many of the existing MPAs are not functioning and that the biogeographic zones suggested by the World Bank report (37) are largely based on subjective boundaries and data (Chapter 1), the identification of gaps between existing MPAs and biogeographic zones is probably not a good means to develop priorities for conservation. A higher priority would be to redesign or rehabilitate existing MPAs in order to make them economically viable and socially acceptable, such that they and their conservation objectives are sustained into the future. It is much cheaper and easier to survey and designate MPAs than it is to manage and financially sustain them. Additionally, it may be important to reexamine the biogeographic provinces in order to identify gaps in ecological conditions or important habitats that are not being sufficiently protected to insure that most of the major marine habitats and species of the region are protected.

Economics of Conservation. One reason for the poor performance of MPAs may be that they are not financially competitive with alternate economic uses such as fishing (Fig. 2.3). Their competitiveness depends on the number of park visitors, their boat and entry fee expenditures, and the park's assurance of providing a better nature experience than unprotected areas that might be less expensive to visit. These factors were included in a simple economic model that compares the gross per area incomes by the designation of the area as a park or fishing ground under two conditions of visitation and a expenditure of US $20 per day. The model presents a range between 50 000 and 100 000 visitors per year as this reflects the current range of park visitation in the Seychelles and Kenya.

The model suggests that parks are more competitive than fishing for small areas but, even under moderate-visitation conditions, fishing becomes competitive above 40 km². This model assumes a maximum fisheries yield, but if fisheries were either under or over utilized the area for which parks are competitive would increase. It is interesting to note that the area in Kenya's fully protected parks is around 40 km². Because some of Kenya's reefs are heavily overfished and near tourist beaches, a continued increase in total park area would be economically sensible at a national scale, but less so at the local scale because local fishers may not necessarily benefit from improvements in the nation's economy.

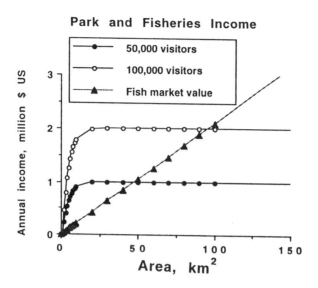

Figure 2.3. Graph of the projected gross income of the nearshore for fishing and marine protected areas for different numbers of visitors (visitors pay = U.S. $20 dollars/person and fish valued at $1.5 per kilogram). The model assumes that visitors are less willing to pay this amount as the park size is reduced.

Park expansion in Kenya is in progress but is encountering resistance from local fishers who feel they may be displaced while lacking alternative fishing grounds and incomes (Chapter 7, Box 7.2). Clearly, the resolution and harmonization of local and national economics is an important step towards the success of marine protected areas. Future designation and maintenance of marine protected areas need to consider the economic constraints on the use of marine resources as well as who is benefiting from these resources. Many of the 'paper parks' of this region are the result of uneconomic or wishful thinking or poor social acceptance of MPAs. Recent studies show that many reefs have a capacity to recover quickly, and, even after a few years, once-fished areas can provide nearly the equivalent biological diversity of older parks (58,60). Poor people will, however, not be interested in long-term benefits if they have too much short-term hardship to endure, and, therefore, revenue sharing and alternative sources of income for displaced fishers needs to be considered when establishing MPAs.

The value of protected areas should not be based solely on the income and their competitiveness in the use of resources. Protected areas provide numerous values difficult to assess monetarily. These include aesthetic pleasure, preservation of breeding stocks, species and their genetic diversity, and ecological functions such as the calcium-carbonate balance and protection of the shoreline. Preserving these functions can help both avoid disasters and the economic costs of replacing these functions artificially. The greatest value of MPAs is probably to increase the resiliency and recovery ability of disturbed areas outside of protected areas. Consequently, it is probably good national policy to have more areas under protection than is economically competitive although competitiveness will increase the chances of a park's sustainability, particularly in the developing world.

Effectiveness of National Parks

Studies undertaken in the few areas that have been successful in reducing or eliminating resource extraction show that functioning MPAs have been effective in providing refuges for species and their ecological functions. The implication of these studies is that protected areas have provided an effective refuge from human influences.

Protection from Fishing

Fishing has produced a large number of changes to the biology and ecology of nearshore species, habitats and ecosystems. Numbers of fish, wet weights, biomass, and number of species are all affected by fishing. More surprising is the consequences of these changes on other members of the food web as well as changes in the life-history characteristics of harvested species. Published comparisons between protected and exploited areas support these contentions for South Africa (4,11,12), northern Tanzania (50), Kenya (43,55,83,84,85), Seychelles (31,34), and Sri Lanka (70). Low or no replication of marine protected areas in each of these sites and studies often weakens the conclusions of the individual studies. Taken together, however, the studies often strengthen the composite findings and conclusions, although the response to fishing is not uniform, as described below.

Abundance and numbers of species can be influenced by heavy fishing. Studies in Kenya, northern Tanzania, the Seychelles and Sri Lanka have shown that the wet weight or numbers of fish in these heavily fished reefs are between one tenth and one half the estimates from fully protected areas. A study in the Seychelles estimated fish abundance over a range of fishing effort and found that there was around a 50% initial drop in fish biomass at low levels of fishing which was largely maintained over the full range of fishing effort (31, Chapter 13). The implications of this study are that many of the changes in the fish fauna can occur for even very low levels of fishing effort (< 5 boats per km^2) and that there is probably some compensatory response of the fish fauna to fishing beyond an initial fishing effort that maintains fish abundance under heavy fishing conditions. This compensatory response may be a shift in the species composition of the fishes such that fishes with higher net production or different feeding habits dominate or may be due to a constant migration of fish from deep water into nearshore fishing grounds. This and another study (58) did not, however, find large differences in the feeding characteristics between exploited and unexploited fish communities. Perhaps a species' susceptibility to fishing is affected more by its body size or range of movement than feeding characteristics. It may be that resident or site-attached species are quickly eliminated by fishing while the more vagile and fast-growing species are able to maintain populations under heavy fishing (46).

The effects of resource extraction on numbers of species have been somewhat more variable. Studies in Kenya (43) and Sri Lanka (70) suggest that heavy fishing reduced the number of species by as much as one half at the scale of individual transects (around 500 m²), and this reduction was still evident in the Kenyan study at the scale of 1 ha. Studies in Kenya and the Seychelles also indicate that the level of management and its duration can influence the numbers of fish species (34,43). In these studies the number of species increased with the increasing level of protection and length of time since protection.

In some cases, some species assemblages or guilds increase in diversity while others lose diversity with increasing exploitation. For example, two studies in East Africa (50,85) did not find large differences in the total number of species between exploited and unexploited populations. The northern Tanzania study found, however, that there were more species among the speciose small-bodied damselfish and wrasses families in the exploited reefs while some fish families including butterflyfish, parrotfish, surgeonfish, and triggerfish were more speciose in the protected reef (50). The Seychelles study found losses in species among predatory groups such as scavengers and groupers but fewer losses for other groups such as parrotfish and goatfishes.

Many studies have shown that habitat and the structural complexity of the reef can influence fish abundance and diversity (32,40,43,70) and the effect of fishing may depend as much on the direct removal of fish as the indirect effect of the fishing gear on the reef's structural and habitat complexity. Fishing methods, intensity, the targeted species, as well as the indirect influences on the habitat and unexploited species in the food web may all interact to create the variable responses to fishing described above. Destructive fishing methods such as pull seines and dynamite fishing will reduce the reef's structural complexity with long-term consequences to the fishery. Future research will need to tease apart the influences of these various factors in order to determine the most ecologically benign and sustainable forms of fishing.

Protection of Rare Species. The exploitation of reefs can lead to localized species losses. There is, therefore, an immediate need to determine if some species are vulnerable to local or global extinction. Extinction is most likely to occur to endemic species with restricted distributions, though there are numerous cases of extinction among once wide-spread species. There is little evidence for sub-regional endemism for corals (Chapter 1) but there is somewhat higher endemism of fishes in the Red Sea, Madagascar and Mascarene Islands (1) and efforts to secure these endemics from extinction are a conservation priority. Unfortunately, nearly nothing is known about the status of these endemic populations nor about other coral-reef species that may be susceptible to extinction.

One study, in East Africa, found that the endemic clown fish (*Amphiprion allardi*) was actually more abundant in exploited reefs than no-take reserves but that a second recently-named damselfish (*Pomacentrus baenschi*, 1) was not found outside of the protected areas in this survey (44). The extent of this survey was small, and *P. baenschi* does occur outside protected areas, but its distribution is patchy and numbers are often low (McClanahan, T. personal observation). More studies are required to identify vulnerable species.

Preservation of Life-History Characteristics. Research on two endemic, long-lived, sex-changing species of harvested sparid fishes

(*Chrysoblephus laticeps* and *C. cristiceps*) of South Africa found a number of differences in their growth and reproduction that could be attributed to exploitation (Chapter 16, 11). One of them, *C. cristiceps*, had a faster growth rate and also changed into males at a larger size in the protected marine park compared to fished sites. Fast growth in the protected area was surprising because it was hypothesized that the loss of conspecific competitors, through fishing, should produce higher growth rates in exploited areas. Consequently, other aspects of this species feeding or prey abundance may have been disrupted by exploitation.

Both species had sex ratios skewed towards more males in the protected areas (11). The loss of larger reproductive females and fewer males in fished sites could potentially interfere with the reproduction and recruitment of these valuable fisheries species (Chapter 16). Consequently, by preserving the number of reproductively mature individuals and the balance of sexes found in unexploited populations no-take reserves could offer protection from recruitment failures that often plague fisheries. Similar studies have not been carried out on coral-reef fishes in this region but species, such as groupers, wrasses and parrotfish, are sex changing so may also experience changes in life-history characteristics with exploitation. The long-term consequences of these changes on the species and fisheries require further investigations (Chapter 16).

Protection of Keystone Species. Identifying and protecting species that contribute little directly to fish abundance and catch, but which have important controlling effects on diversity and ecology of coral reefs, is important (73). There is accumulating evidence that the red-lined triggerfish (*Balistapus undulatus*) may be a keystone predator in East Africa and that characteristics that make it a keystone predator also make it highly susceptible to exploitation.

Balistapus undulatus is a dominant predator of sea urchins. Comparative studies of protected and unprotected reefs and a reef where fishers were excluded to make a marine park found that sea urchin populations were being controlled by predators and, therefore, indirectly through the removal of their predators by fishers (Fig. 2.4 and 2.5, 46,54). Some sea urchin populations such as that of the common rock-boring sea urchin, *Echinometra mathaei*, have increased in many exploited reefs to such high levels that they have become pests which erode the coral substrate through their intense and destructive feeding. *B. undulatus* is frequently the dominant predator of this and other sea urchin species in shallow-water reefs.

Other species of wrasse and scavengers feed on sea urchins but behavioral studies show that *B. undulatus* is an agonistic and territorial species that dominates these other species. This same competitive behavior also makes this species very vulnerable to fishing as it is often among the first species to take bait or enter baited traps. This triggerfish is, therefore, often among the first species to be extirpated by fishing and is seldom an important fisheries species in reefs with a history of exploitation. When *B. undulatus* is absent or at low population levels, other species like the triple-lobed wrass (*Cheilinus trilobatus*) and some scavengers (Lethrinidae) will feed on sea urchins and partially compensate for the lost predatory effect of this triggerfish (46). Many of these wrasses and scavengers are more opportunistic and less specialized for feeding on sea urchins and it is likely that they are less effective predators than *B. undulatus* in controlling sea urchin populations.

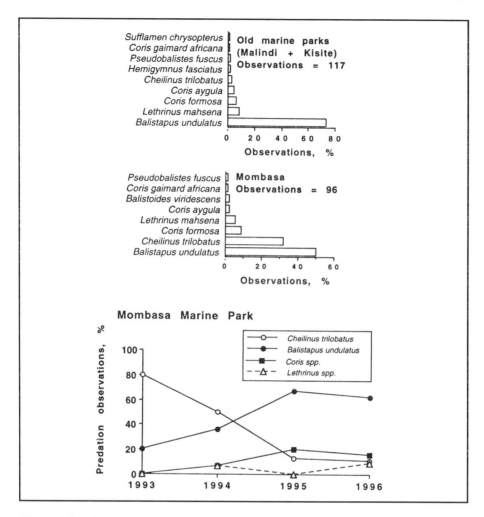

Figure 2.4. Direct observations on predators of sea urchins in (top) Kenya's older marine parks (Kisite and Malindi) and (middle) in a recently created park, the Mombasa MNP. (Bottom) Change in the frequency of observations of predators in the Mombasa MNP over a four-year period. Studies indicate the importance of the red-lined triggerfish (*Balistapus undulatus*) as a competitive dominant and in controlling sea urchin abundance.

Ecological Release of Pest Species

Field studies and subsequent modelling efforts both suggest that the loss or severe depletion of predatory fishes can result in increases in prey populations which can often greatly modify the ecological structure and processes of reefs. These prey can become pests if they significantly modify the ecology of the reef such as reducing living coral which is responsible for a good portion of the reef's growth. In many cases the environmental conditions of physical disturbance due to waves and currents, light, temperature, and nutrients modify the outcome of interactions of fishing on predators and the response of the prey to lost predators.

56

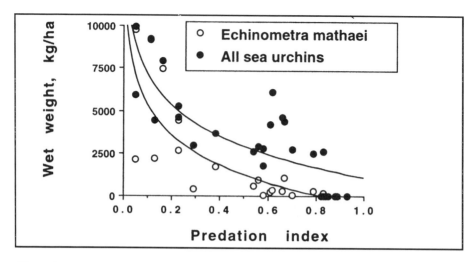

Figure 2.5. The abundance of all sea urchins and the rock-boring sea urchin (*Echinometra mathaei*) as a function of predation rates on a tethered sea urchin (*E. mathaei*) in Kenyan coral reef lagoons.

There is, therefore, significant between-site variation in coral reefs which has made the creation of simple ecological and management models difficult. Below are two examples in which predator losses appear to be affecting prey that are potential pests that detrimentally affect reef ecology.

Sea Urchins. Studies in both Kenya and northern Tanzania suggest that an increase in sea urchin populations is one of the most pervasive effects of heavy fishing (Fig. 2.6, 50). Grazing sea urchins are different from grazing herbivorous fishes in that they graze more intensely and can reduce and tolerate low levels of resources (47). Sea urchins are also able to erode the reef substrate at rates nearly ten times higher than herbivorous fishes (7). At low population densities sea urchins may be seen as a beneficial part of the reefs, as they eat some of the unpalatable algae and their feeding may increase both net productivity (13) and topographic complexity. At high population densities, however, sea urchins can eat nearly all of the algae and plant species and their erosion of substrate can greatly reduce topographic complexity. Reefs dominated by sea urchins are usually decaying rather than growing because of their high rates of substrate erosion and their lower coral and coralline algal cover (56). Additionally, there is good evidence from experimental reductions of sea urchins that they suppress many fish groups including parrotfishes, wrasses, and scavengers (51,57,59).

Coral-eating Snails and Starfish. A number of species of prosobranch snails feed on living coral. The two most common coral-eating species in this region are *Coralliophila neritoides* (=*C. violacea*) and *Drupella cornus*. *C. neritoides* is almost always found living in the crevices or indentations of massive *Porites*. The area of damaged coral around their home crevices is small and suggests that their effect on living coral is small. In contrast, *D. cornus*, when found at high population densities, has been reported to destroy living corals over large areas (65,81). In particular many of the reefs of western

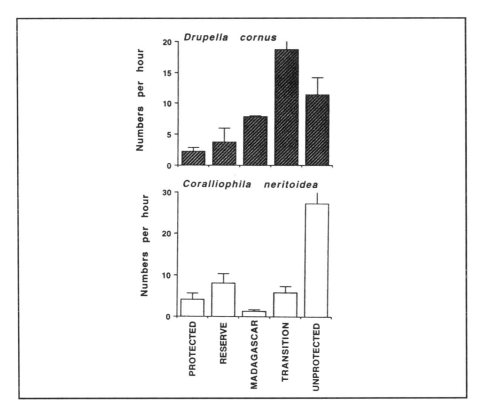

Figure 2.6. Abundance of coral-eating snails (top) *Drupella cornus* and (bottom) *Coralliophila neritoidea* along a gradient of fishing intensity.

Australia have been plagued by *D. cornus* populations reducing coral cover over large areas of reef. The cause of high population densities of *D. cornus* is, however, uncertain (81). It has been common to find high population densities associated with certain genera of coral such as *Acropora*, *Montipora*, *Seriatopora* and *Pocillopora*, which have been suggested to be their preferred prey (8,65).

A study of *D. cornus* populations in four MPAs and four fished reefs in Kenya over an eight-year period lends some insight into the complexity of these population dynamics (45,52). During the initial part of this survey *D. cornus* was a rare species in all visited reefs but increased to the second most commonly observed snail by the end of the survey in 1995. Population increases were found in nearly all reefs but the greatest increases were in the heavily fished reef, and one reef which recently excluded fishers (Fig. 2.6). The abundance of this snail was low to moderate in all of the studied MPAs, with intermediate levels in the Mpunguti fishing reserve which had restricted fishing. Curiously, *D. cornus* was mostly found associated with a supposedly unpreferred prey species of *Porites* having slender branchings (mostly *Porites nigrescens*) in these heavily fished reefs but largely found on *Acropora* in the MPAs (52). *Acropora* is uncommon in the heavily fished reefs and it therefore appears quite capable of switching its preference to other abundant branching species in the absence of its preferred prey. The most likely explanation for these observations is that some oceanographic factors created good conditions for the survival and dispersal of *D. cornus* and that they have increased greatly throughout the region during the late 1980s. Their post-settlement success and adult population abundance may, however, be an interaction between the abundance of fish predators, such as triggerfish, and the existence of other competitors, such as *C. neritoides*, and the existence or abundance of branching coral species. This may be true for a number of species of coral reef associated snails (42).

The crown-of-thorns starfish (*Acanthaster planci*) is an additional coral-eating reef pest common to this region (Box 2.2). Plague or 'outbreak' populations, like those reported in the Pacific (71), have, however, not been as commonly reported in the western Indian Ocean as the central Pacific. Ormond and his collaborators compared *A. planci* populations and their predators in the Red Sea and the Great Barrier reef (71). They suggested that the greater abundance of *A. planci* in the Great Barrier Reef was due to a lower abundance of scavengerous fish, triggerfish, pufferfish, and large wrasses than found in the Red Sea. Other models have emphasized the abundance of coral prey as an important factor in determining the success of *A. planci* (9,22) while others have argued that factors that favor larval success are important in determining adult populations (6). There has also been less thorough survey work in the Indian Ocean, but the existing data suggest that oceanographic conditions, perhaps affected by the Southern Oscillation (El-Niño) may influence larval settlement and subsequent adult populations (Box 2.2).

Despite extensive research the causes of *A. planci* population outbreaks remains obscure (64) and is unlikely to be attributable to a single factor. It is likely that many pests such as sea urchins and coral-eating snails and starfish respond synergistically to reductions in their predators, often associated with heavy fishing, the availability of their coral prey, and oceanographic conditions that are beneficial to their larval success. Fishing may, therefore, increase the variability and extent of population oscillations that would otherwise occur but less intensely.

The 'Spillover Effect'

From the perspective of fisheries sustainability and yields, MPAs are a way to preserve the breeding stocks of commercial species, increase fish catches through the emigration of adults from the MPAs, or by enhancing larval recruitment in fishing grounds adjacent to them. MPAs may also decrease the variability in catches by insuring a steady supply of larvae and by buffering against disastrous losses of breeding stocks that might occur through large-scale overfishing (39). As described above there is ample evidence that fish and breeding stocks are higher in MPAs than in heavily fished reefs but the evidence for a spillover of adults and their offspring is more equivocal.

Two studies in Kenya's MPAs have shown that the spillover effect may depend on the distance between the fishing grounds and the MPAs and also on the fisheries management in the adjacent fisheries grounds. One study was undertaken in the Kisite-Mpunguti MNP and Reserve in which fish were tagged in the Park and fishers fishing in the Reserve were asked to report the tagged

Box 2.2. Status of the Crown-of-Thorns Starfish in the Indian Ocean

Acanthaster planci is a large starfish with a diameter averaging 30 to 40 cm and 15 to 18 arms covered on its arboral side with hundreds of sharp, venomous spines. Adults predate on stony corals and other benthic organisms by everting their stomach onto the coral and digesting the soft parts. *A. planci* reaches sexual maturity at around three years and is highly fecund, releasing tens of millions of eggs during mid-summer mass spawning. Larvae remain in the plankton for two to three weeks and consume phytoplankton and possibly dissolved organic material (3,5). Larvae settle onto coral reefs and metamorphosed juveniles live within cryptic habitats along reef fronts and feed on coralline algae such as *Porolithon*. At 8 to 16 months of age they begin feeding on live coral. At around 18 to 24 months they leave their cryptic habitats (11,12) and, in high population density situations, they form feeding aggregations. These become the 'sudden outbreaks' witnessed by divers that have caused widespread damage to many Indo-Pacific coral reefs over the past three decades (3,5).

A. *planci* population densities are usually low (5 to 20 per km^2) and recolonisation of coral can often keep pace with mortality by *A. planci*. During 'massive outbreaks', however, there may be many thousands or even millions of starfish and most of the corals are killed in several months to a year (5). In some cases, termed 'spot outbreaks', starfish may be densely aggregated on a small part of the reef, and damage is only localized. In other situations, termed 'chronic outbreaks', starfish abundances and coral cover may both be low to moderate over many years and the coral never fully recovers. Outbreaks may be classified as 'primary events' which result from increased larval or juvenile survivorship or 'secondary events' when successive generations of starfish increase.

Outbreaks have been reported in many parts of the Indo-Pacific since the 1950s and 1960s. Reefs in southern Japan suffered several massive episodes in the 1950s to 1970s, and are now in a chronic situation (10, Yamaguchi, M. personal communication). The Great Barrier Reef has experienced three outbreak episodes during the past three decades. The first two outbreaks slowly progressed southwards over 10 to 15 years as successive generations of larvae were carried on the prevailing currents. During the 1979 to 1990 episode, around 20% of the GBR's 2000 reefs were affected and on some reefs over 90% of coral was killed (5,7).

The causes of the outbreaks are still unknown despite numerous investigations (4). The large size of *A. planci*, its high fecundity, coral diet, and life-history strategy naturally predispose it to population fluctuations. Geological evidence and oral histories of fisherfolk indicate outbreaks have occurred in the past. A correlative study suggested that outbreak episodes may be related to unusually high rainfall events which may produce nutrient pulses, thereby increasing plankton productivity and larval survivorship (3), but much of this evidence remains equivocal. Humans may influence these outbreaks by increasing   larval   survivorship   through   eutrophication   or

Photo. A feeding front of adult *Acanthaster planci*.

increasing juvenile survival through the removal of their predators.   Firm
scientific evidence for any of these claims remains weak (4).

Outbreaks in the Indian Ocean

The status of *A. planci* on Indian Ocean reefs is poorly documented but below is
a summary for the western Indian Ocean organized from published and
unpublished reports and questionnaire surveys circulated among reef scientists,
government agencies, dive operators, and sports divers between 1986 and 1997.

Andaman and Nicobar Islands. *A. planci* were reported in the Andamans in low
numbers between the 1960s to late 1980s. A rapid increase in abundance
began in 1988. Surveys in 1989 indicated that outbreaks were patchy, but coral
damage was locally severe. This outbreak may have been a secondary outbreak
from the episode in western Thai reefs in 1984.

Cocos Keeling. On Cocos Keeling Atoll, there were reports of fairly large
numbers and high coral mortality in 1977, and another significantly increase in
numbers in 1994.

Maldives. In the early 1970s, *A. planci* were reported to be common around
Male, Kurumba and Bandos but few details are known (9). A major outbreak
was first reported at Hembaddu in North Male atoll in mid 1986, and became
abundant in 1987 and 1988. Surveys of 111 sites throughout the group in 1990
found that Male was worst affected. During 1990, 30 500 starfish were
eradicated off four North Male resorts. A monitoring program, established in
1990 on 64 reefs, indicated that outbreaks continued during the early 1990s and
declined on most reefs in 1995. Only one reef, namely Kurumba, was still
affected in 1996. A survey of 34 reef sites on Laamu Atoll during 1997 found

the starfish in only 5 sites and the highest density was about three individuals per hour (8).

Sri Lanka. In Sri Lanka there was a major outbreak which caused serious damage to corals in the early 1970s (9), but no reports have been made since then.

Central and Western Islands. In the Chagos group there was massive destruction of corals in one area of Speakers Bank in the 1970s (Sheppard, C. personal communication). There have been no reports of outbreaks on Reunion or Seychelles. In Mauritius *A. planci* were quite common in the 1970s and their abundances greatly increased around 1985 (9), but there were no reports of major damage. Off Madagascar there have been no reports of outbreaks. In the Comoros, aggregations were reported in Moroni Harbor on Grande Comoro in 1971 and on the fringing reef off Lac-Sale, north-eastern Grande Comoro in 1973 (9).

East Africa. There have been no reports of outbreaks from Mozambique. There were unconfirmed reports of population increases off Dar es Salaam, Tanzania in 1970, and on Kenya reefs in 1973 (9). They have been present to common on Tanzanian and Kenyan reefs in the past two decades but there have been no reports of large aggregations but there may be a slow rise in abundance of dispersed populations (McClanahan, T. personal communication). An aggregation (20 to 30 per dive) was reported off Changuu Island off Zanzibar in 1997. There have been no reports from Somalia but there are reports from northern South Africa beginning in 1994.

Red and Arabian Seas and Arabian Gulf. In Oman, spot outbreaks occurred in the early 1970s but with little damage to corals. An outbreak occurred in the Muscat area and Jaza'ir in 1978 to 1979 where *Acropora*-dominated reefs suffered almost 100% mortality (9). In Egypt, an outbreak began in the Ras Mohammed Park in 1992, and aging of the spines indicated these individuals recruited in 1990. Abundances were low, however, in the adjacent Sharm el Sheikh area in 1995. A massive outbreak was also reported by dive tour operators off Eastern Sinai in the early 1990s, but there had been no reports from Aqaba (Jordan) over this period. In Saudi Arabia abundances were low during surveys of the Farasan Islands and Jiddah between 1993 and 1995, and local divers reported not seeing elevated numbers over the previous decade. In southern Yemen, surveys in 1995 to 1997 found that starfish were present in low numbers, but that the outer reefs have a very high proportion of dead *Acropora* and surviving *Porites*, consistent with outbreaks several years before between 1991 to 1993. There have been no reports of outbreaks from the Arabian Gulf.

Spatial and Temporal Trends

Although information on the status of *A. planci* from the Indian Ocean is limited and patchy, there have not been massive and widespread outbreak episodes, as has occurred in parts of the Western Pacific.

The close proximity of some areas affected at similar times suggests that larval dispersal may occur between reefs (for example Malaysia and Indonesia

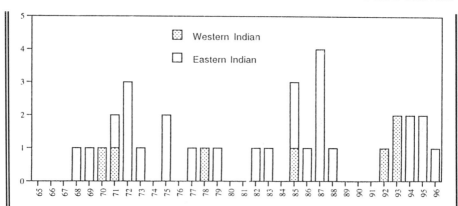

Figure. Frequency of reported *Acanthaster planci* outbreaks in the western and eastern Indian Ocean. from 1965 to 1996.

both had outbreaks in the early 1980s). Many other reefs affected around the same times are, however, widely separated and unconnected by currents (for example Western Australia, Philippines and Maldives all experienced outbreaks in 1987). This precludes the possibility of basin-wide dispersal of larvae which is supported by genetic studies in the Pacific (1).

Temporal trends are less clear because of the small number of reports, lack of scientific surveys, the variable natures of the outbreaks (elevated numbers, spot outbreaks, massive outbreaks) and uncertainties in the first year of an outbreak. While outbreaks averaged one per year between 1966 and 1996, outbreaks are not random, and may occur in widespread episodes (see Figure). The major episodes began in 1968, 1985, and 1992, and there may have been minor episodes beginning in 1975, 1977, and 1982. This suggests major episodes of larval settlement three years prior to these outbreaks (12).

Studies on the chronology of outbreaks in the Pacific suggests that oceanographic influences associated with the El Niño Southern Oscillation (ENSO, 6) may have contributed to these outbreaks (Zann, unpublished data). Such a correlation may also occur in the Indian Ocean as the years of recruitment of the three main outbreak episodes occurred around the time of the ENSO. In contrast, only one of the three minor episodes coincided with the ENSO. Major changes in ocean winds and currents, temperatures, rainfall and nutrient upwellings associated with the Southern Oscillation may enhance the survivorship of *A. planci* larvae.

Leon P. Zann

References

1.   Benzie, J.A.H. 1992. Review of the genetics, dispersal and recruitment of crown-of-thorns starfish (*Acanthaster planci*). *Australian Journal of Marine and Freshwater Research* 43: 597-610
2.   Birkeland C. 1982. Terrestrial runoff as a cause of outbreaks of *Acanthaster planci* (Echinodermata: Asteroidea). *Marine Biology* 69:175-185

3.   Birkeland, C., Lucas, J. L. 1990. Acanthaster planci: *Major Management Problem of Coral Reefs.* Boca Raton: CRC Press
4.   Engelhardt, U., Lassig, B. R. 1996. A review of the possible causes and consequences of outbreaks of the crown-of-thorns starfish on the Great Barrier reef - an Australian perspective. *The Great Barrier Reef, Science, Use and Management* 1: 243-259
5.   Moran, P.J. 1986. The *Acanthaster* phenomenon. *Oceanography and Marine Biology Annual Review* 24: 374-480
6.   NOAA 1998. El Nino/Southern Oscillation (ENSO). http://nic.fb4.noaa.gov: 80/products/analysis_monitoring/ensostuff/index.html
7.   Reichelt, R.E., Bradbury, R.H., Moran, P.J. 1990. Distribution of *Acanthaster* outbreaks on the Great Barrier Reef between 1966 and 1989. *Coral Reefs* 9: 97-104
8.   Sluka, R.D. 1997. The biology and ecology of Grouper in Laamu Atoll, Republic of Maldives. Oceanographic Society of Maldives, Male, Maldives
9.   UNEP/IUCN 1988. *Coral Reefs of the World. Volume 2. Indian Ocean, Red Sea and Gulf.* Gland: IUCN
10.   Yamaguchi, M. 1986. *Acanthaster planci* infestations of reefs and coral assemblages in Japan: retrospective analysis of control efforts. *Coral Reefs* 5:23-30
11.   Zann, L.P., Brodie, J., Berryman, C., Naqasima, M. 1987. Recruitment, ecology, growth and behaviour of juvenile *Acanthaster planci* (L.) (Echinodermata: Asteroidea). *Bulletin of Marine Science* 41: 561-575
12.   Zann, L.P., Brodie, J., Vuki, V. 1990. History and dynamics of the crown-of-thorns starfish *Acanthaster planci* (L.) in the Suva Reef area, Fiji. *Coral Reefs* 9: 135-144

fish (83). Watson (83) also studied the movements of these tagged and other coral reef fishes in the Kisite MNP. No tagged fish were reported in the catches and most of the studied species had limited movements usually less than a few hundred meters. She, therefore, concluded that the emigration of adults from MPAs is less likely to affect fisheries adjacent MPAs than the spillover of eggs and larvae. In this study the distance between the Kisite MNP and the fishing grounds was several kilometers and this may have affected her results and conclusions. A similar tagging study of the galjoen, a popular sportfish in South Africa, also found that most tagged individuals did not move far, but a few individuals traveled over a 1000 km, and there was some evidence that the population in the MPA was restocking the adjacent fishing grounds (2).

A second study in Kenya was undertaken in the Mombasa MNP which is a MPA that protects a section of continuous fringing reef (McClanahan, T. and Mangi, S. unpublished data). In this study the investigators placed traditional traps in transects at different distances from both the northern and southern edges of the park. The southern side of the park is also a Reserve and restricts fishing to traps, lines, and gillnets. On the northern side of the park the fishing is unregulated and dominated by beach or pull seiners using nets with small mesh sizes. The study showed that there were higher catches near the park boundaries on both sides of the park. The spillover was, however, negligible on the northern unregulated fishing side but probably extended for a few kilometers

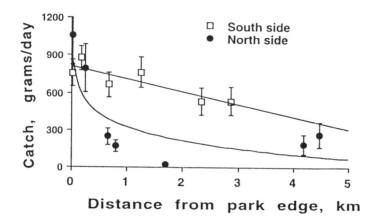

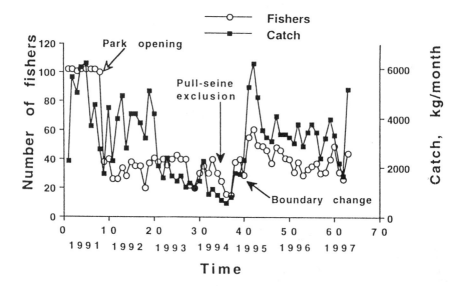

Figure 2.7. (Top) Fish catches of traditional traps located at different distances from two sides of the Mombasa MNP where the southern side had excluded beach seines but beach seines were used on the northern side which lacked gear restrictions. (Bottom) Reported fish catches at the Kenyatta Beach landing site on the southern side of the marine park before and after the creation of the Park. The adjacent fishing grounds had two changes in post-park management, beach-seine exclusion and a reduction in the size of the park, which caused increases in fish catches.

on the southern regulated fishing side (Fig. 2.7a). It may be that beach seines are so effective at catching all fish that the spillover effect is restricted to a very small area immediately adjacent to the Park. Greater spillover in Mombasa compared to Kisite may be attributable to nature of the reefs, Kisite being an isolated patch or rock-island reef and Mombasa being a continuous fringing reef. The isolated reef in Kisite is separated from other reefs by a bare sand plain that may not offer enough cover for fishes to safely disperse while a continuous fringing reef, with abundant coral and seagrass cover, should offer more protection for dispersing fishes.

The catch of fish at the landing site on the southern side of the Mombasa MNP was studied for eight months before and for approximately six years after the Park policy was initiated. This study also suggested that beach-seine exclusion, and perhaps the size and length of the Park area influenced the catch of fish adjacent the MPA (Fig. 2.7b). The establishment of the park area and the total protection policy caused approximately 60 of the 110 fishers to leave the fishing grounds (58). This resulted in a 35% loss of the total fish landed but a 110% increase in the catch per fisher during the first two years after the Park's creation.

The policy of eliminating beach seining was achieved about 3.3 years after the park creation. Additionally the park was reduced in size from 8.2 to 6.2 km^2 approximately 3.9 years after the Park's creation, due to political pressure from the fishers and a coastal zone management program for the area (18). Immediately after the reduction in the Park's size the fish catch increased two to three times above the previous years' catch rate, persisted for four months, and then dropped and leveled for nearly two years (Fig. 2.7b). The total catch during the last two years was as high as the total catch before the creation of the Park even though a moderate area was removed from the fishing ground.

The proximity of the two events of beach seine exclusion and the reduction in the park's size makes it difficult to determine the relative contributions of each policy to improving fish catches. An additional factor suggested by population modelling studies (68) is that it takes a number of years for fish populations to build up in the park. Additionally, the smaller the park area the longer it will take for fish populations to increase and achieve the spillover effect. These field studies and theoretical models suggests that some combination of park design and fisheries management can help to maintain fish catches while converting fishing grounds into protected areas. The greatest economic difficulty for establishing parks may be the transition period between the park's establishment and achieving the long-term gains. The success of marine parks as a tool for conservation will be increased by finding ways to bridge this transition period.

Interaction Between Fishing, Sediments, and Eutrophication

Fishing and eutrophication are the two major human influences on nearshore coral reefs (Table 2.1, 25). There is accumulating evidence that these two influences may interact to produce unexpected responses (Fig. 2.8). The reef's response to these human influences may largely depend on the influence of these factors to the growth and mortality of algae and heterotrophic organisms such as sponges and soft corals. Eutrophication has the potential to increase the growth rates of fast-growing algae and heterotrophic invertebrates relative to the growth of hard corals. In practice, however, there are a number of disturbances, particularly affecting algae, that prevent this from happening.

Disturbances are principally due to herbivores, usually sea urchins and a variety of fishes, water movement, such as waves and currents, and sediments.

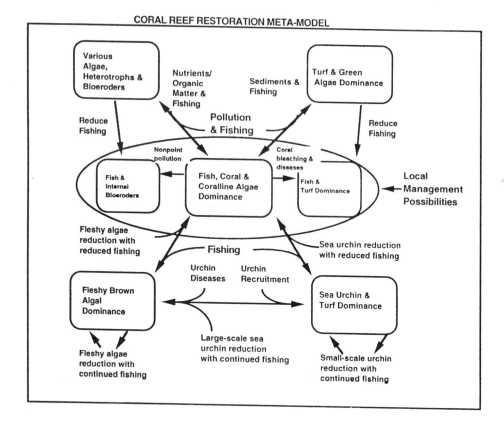

Figure 2.8. A metamodel describing some of the hypothesized dominant ecological states of the coral reef as influenced by fishing, sediments, eutrophication. and coral bleaching and diseases. Boxes represent states and arrows indicate the cause and direction of changes of those states.

Fishing can reduce the level of herbivorous fishes but it can, as described above, also promote sea urchin populations (29,55). Consequently, the corals (21,41). All other variables being equal this increase in algal growth should result in a reef dominated by late-successional fleshy algae, sponges and combination of fishing and pollution has a great potential to shift reefs from dominance by corals and early successional algae to one dominated by late-successional algae. In three cases, however, this is unlikely. In the first case fishing can promote the abundance of sea urchins which graze intensely and reduce the abundance of algae to levels even lower than when fish are the dominant grazer (47,53). In the second case, eutrophication is associated with sediments, usually from a river or dredging of marine sediments that can physical disturb algae and retard the successional development of algae (53,60). Lastly, in areas with high wave or current energy algae may be constantly disturbed and unable to reach high abundance (59).

Studies on the effects of eutrophication in this region indicate the importance of the above multiple factors in determining the outcome of cultural eutrophication. For example, some watersheds in Reunion were urbanized in the 1970s without the coincident development of sewage-treatment facilities (Chapter 12, 20). This resulted in sediment-free nutrient enrichment of the submarine groundwater which discharged onto the nearshore reefs (19). It was found that during the warm and calm northeast monsoon season there was a large increase in fleshy algae, particularly the rhodophyte *Gracilaria crasa*, and a subsequent loss of corals (66). With the onset of the southeast monsoon this algae was removed. This seasonal change did not, however, occur in a site that was less eutrophied and had many grazing sea urchins.

A second study in the Malindi-Watamu Marine National Park of Kenya explored the effects of sediments and associated nutrients on the coral and algae species on reefs fully protected from fishing (62). The study indicated that the section of the reef which experienced the heaviest sediment influence did not experience increases in fleshy algae but, during the times of the heaviest sediments, the substrate was dominated by early successional turf-forming algae which covered over coralline algae, but left corals undisturbed (53,62). The total cover of coral was unchanged by the sediment but there was a shift in the species composition of corals towards those species presumably more tolerant of sediments. They also found that soft corals only responded positively to sedimentation/ eutrophication when there was good water movement, on their wave-exposed reef edge site. The inability of algae to colonize and dominate under eutrophic conditions may be attributable to the two disturbances of fish grazing and sediments. An observation suggesting that sediment was the main influence is that the control site experienced a moderate increase in fleshy algae over the nine-year study period. This site had reasonably high nutrient levels, high herbivorous fish levels, but little sediment or sea urchin influences.

A curious and perhaps counter-intuitive finding of two studies of fish communities inhabiting algal-dominated reefs is that there is a considerably lower abundance of fish, even herbivorous fish, on reefs dominated by fleshy algae (Fig. 2.9). This is surprising because algae is typically more palatable and more productive than corals. Nonetheless, Chabanet and her investigators, working on the back reefs of Reunion, found that, of the 32 species of fish they studied, 14 had reduced population abundance on reefs with large fleshy algae (14). A study in the Watamu MNP of Kenya experimentally reduced the abundance of fleshy algae and found a doubling in the abundance of herbivorous fishes in the algal-reduction plots (Fig. 2.9; McClanahan, T. unpublished data). This manipulation removed the large canopy fleshy algae and exposed more of the early successional turfs. Turf-forming algae are generally the preferred food of most fish grazers (16) and fleshy algae is often less palatable. The implication of these studies is that a high abundance of unpalatable fleshy algae on reefs, which is often caused by cultural eutrophication, can reduce the abundance of fish and perhaps the productivity of coral reef fisheries.

Ecological States and Processes

Many of the studies described above suggest that the reef community can change with single and combined human influences of fishing, sediments, and eutrophication which often interact with natural environmental changes and disturbances (Fig. 2.8). The scientific study of these effects and their various permutations and subtleties is far from complete. Nonetheless, it is helpful for

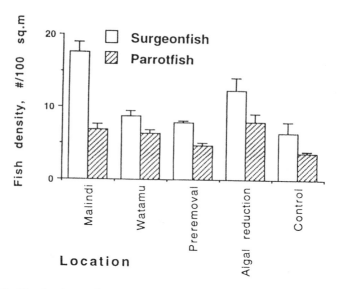

Figure 2.9. The abundance of two groups of herbivorous fishes (surgeonfish = Acanthuridae and parrotfish = Scaridae) in two older marine protected areas (Malindi and Watamu) and a site in the Watamu MNP which had a high abundance of fleshy algae. In the Watamu area dominated by fleshy algae an algal reduction experiment was completed and data presented are for fish abundance before, for 4 months after the reduction, and in control plots.

scientists and managers to develop simple conceptual or metamodels that attempt to predict the outcome of different human influences and management on the reef community. These simple models can help focus scientific inquiry and give managers a means to make decisions based on a current understanding of reef ecology and more detailed mathematical simulation models (48). As management and ecological science accumulate knowledge, models will change and become more sophisticated.

The model predicts a variety of ecological states depending on the combination of pollution, fishing, sediments, diseases, and human management. Because reefs often experience a combination of human and natural influences individual reefs may be an amalgamation of many of these states. In order to achieve the conservation objective of increasing the abundance and diversity of corals and fishes, managers have the option of trying to reduce fishing and pollution as well as reducing pest species or groups such as sea urchins and unpalatable fleshy algae. In many cases it is important to attempt a combination of these management options as the outcome will often depend on an interaction of two or more factors.

Role of Protected Areas in Reef Restoration

Multiple influences and their interactions make it difficult to develop simple or singular means to restore degraded reefs. For instance, the outcome of reducing a pest species may depend on the fisheries management of the reef (57,59) and even the total protection of reefs from resource extraction will not always lead to the rapid recovery of reefs (51).

Sea Urchin Reduction Studies

Sea urchin reduction experiments were undertaken in a reef that had recently been protected from fishing and two reefs that were moderate to heavily fished (57,59). The outcome of the reduction depended on the level of fishing. On the unfished reef the abundance and number of species of fish increased greatly while the increase on the fished reefs was more modest and usually attributable to small-bodied species such as the damselfish and wrasses. Algae increased on all reefs but the increase was greater on the fished reefs and resulted in a 30% loss of coral cover over the one-year study period. In contrast, the unfished reefs displayed a slight suppression in coral cover but by the end of the experiment the coral cover was the same in control and experimental reduction plots. In the unfished reef, coral cover increased in all plots and was attributed to the elimination of destructive drag nets from this reef. Reducing sea urchin populations in the unfished reefs resulted in an increase in herbivorous parrotfish populations that were able to keep algal abundance below the levels at which algae outcompete corals. Presumably these parrotfish populations did not recover in the fished reefs and the result was an excess of fleshy algae. Consequently, the investigators suggested that sea urchin reductions would need to be done in conjunction with fisheries management in order to achieve the goal of increasing fish and coral populations on these degraded reefs.

Coral Transplantation

A number of investigators have looked into the possibility of planting or transplanting bits of corals onto degraded reefs as a means to increase coral cover and restore reefs (17,28). These studies have shown that transplanted corals will attach and grow, at least on the short term. The long-term consequences of this restoration method may, however, depend on the causes of the coral death or reef degradation. If the cause is destructive fishing methods, such as dynamite fishing or the use of drag nets, it is unlikely that these corals will survive and restore reefs in the continued presence of these fishing methods. It is also unlikely that transplanted corals will survive if the cause of coral death is coral bleaching, diseases, algal overgrowth due to eutrophication, or the loss of herbivores by heavy fishing.

An experimental manipulation which physically removed the fleshy macroalgae from a polluted reef in Reunion (67) found that the algae had poor recovery after many months. A similar study in Kenya found that fleshy macroalgae began to recover but after a year it was still nearly half of the original abundance (McClanahan, T. unpublished data). The Kenyan study found that herbivores and their rate of herbivory increased in the algal reduction plot, which may explain the slow recovery of the algae. To restore reefs it may be necessary to attempt coral transplantation with some algal reduction techniques as well as fishing or nutrient reduction programs. These multiple management techniques are, perhaps, the only solution for restoring reefs that are typically degraded by numerous often interacting factors. Unfortunately, it

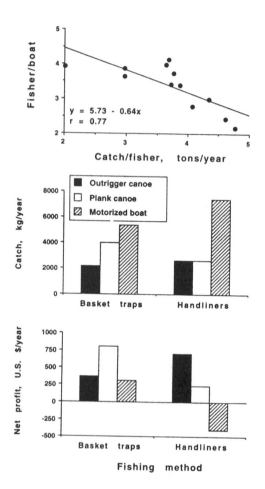

Figure. 2.10. Plot of the (top) number of fishers per boat as a function of the fish catch per person in Tanzania using data for the 1977 to 1991 period, (middle) the annual catch of different boat types and (bottom) their net profits in the Dar es Salaam area. Data from (36,80).

may be only economically practical to undertake these restoration methods on a fairly small scale, such as favorite snorkeling spot.

Effectiveness of Management

Fisheries Management

Management of fisheries in the region, during the last several decades, has largely focused on means to increase fish catches and much less on restricting gear or protecting fish stocks and their habitat. This strategy is fostered by the increasing human population, a common political ideology that promotes short-term economic and national development, the willingness of international donors to supply the required technology and expertise, and the increasing globalization of trade. The interaction of these factors has been successful such that nearly all of the countries of this region have fish capture near or beyond the estimated maximum sustained yields (77). The few exceptions are countries, such as Somalia and Eritrea, that have historically been politically unstable (49). Consequently, any future efforts to increase yields are unlikely to succeed or the costs will seldom be recuperable.

The above conditions create impoverished fishers who compete for dwindling fish stocks. Competition will often result in systems of fishing that 1) reduces the capital investments of fishing, 2) uses methods that are more effective, and often more destructive, than existing fisheries methods, and 3) subsidizes the fishing industry or particular methods of extraction, or by combining these three strategies. An example of the first adaptation, taken from mainland Tanzania's country-wide statistics (Fig. 2.10), indicate that the number of fishers sharing boats increases as the catch per fisher decreases. A second example compares the costs and benefits of motorized versus wind and hand-powered boats in the nearshore fishery of Dar es Salaam (36). Motorized boats had considerably higher total catches and sales than the nonmotorized boats but their costs were also substantially higher (for the capital costs of an engine and increased operational expenses such as petrol and repairs) such that they had the lowest rates of return and, therefore, longest pay-back periods on their investment. Motorized boats often persist in nearshore areas because a wealthy donor or individual subsidizes this form of fishing.

The poverty associated with competition for fish often leads to the use of gear that catches fishes that are small or otherwise hard to extract (Fig. 2.2). The proliferation of the small-meshed beach seines in East Africa described earlier is one good example. These beach seines catch fish that are considerably smaller than those caught by traditional traps (Fig. 2.2) but studies from areas which have excluded these beach seines suggest that they actually reduce the total catch of the area and per person (Table 2.2, 61). Despite reducing the total catch of the nearshore area, beach seines proliferate because they outcompete other methods that catch larger fish and not because they catch more fish on a per area basis.

Subsidizing fishing gear or particular methods is common for national governments and international donors hoping to improve the condition of poor fishers, but can also be supported by naive private investors, or unknowingly through the black market. Dynamite fishing is one example of a subsidy because most of the explosives used in this fishery are not actually purchased at the market rate, but are more frequently stolen from mining and construction companies. Paying the market rate for explosives would certainly make this method of fishing less profitable and attractive. There are many examples of subsidies including the purchase or swapping of gear or associated costs of fishing, storing, and transporting fish. Even low or no taxation on fishing equipment or products is a form of subsidy. Subsidies are a tempting form of aid, but they can often result in further depletion of fish stocks, environmental degradation, and the persistence of uneconomical resource use.

In conclusion, the existing systems of fisheries management in most countries are largely based on a policy to increase fishing yields through lax regulations or restrictions, and through donations or subsidies. Because most yields are near the maximum levels this regulatory system has, in most

Box 2.3. Coral Bleaching in the Indian Ocean and the El Niño Southern Oscillation

In the last 20 years there have been increasingly frequent reports of extensive coral bleaching events, often associated with high mortality. Bleaching occurs when corals lose their endosymbiotic algae (zooxanthellae), and/or photosynthetic pigments are lost from the zooxanthellae, thus the white skeleton becomes visible through the transparent host tissue. Under conditions of mild bleaching, and at early stages during a bleaching event, coral polyps may still be extended and actively feeding. Corals appear able to recover from short-term bleaching events in about 6 to 8 weeks (8). However if stressful conditions persist, or if the stress event was severe, then the corals die (4). Most bleaching occurs on the upper part of the reef where water temperatures are warmer and light and UV levels higher.

Bleaching was first noted in the Caribbean, but attracted particular attention after 1982-3 when widespread bleaching was reported widely both in the Caribbean and in the Indo-Pacific. Coral bleaching may be triggered by various stressful stimuli such as sedimentation, pollution and disease, however the most extensive bleaching events are related to raised sea-surface temperatures (SSTs), either briefly by 3 to 4°C for a few days, or by prolonged elevations of 1 to 2°C during seasonal summer maxima (6,7,9). High levels of UV irradiation are also implicated in temperature-related bleaching events. Controlled experiments duplicating conditions recorded in the Eastern Pacific in 1983 demonstrated that coral bleaching and mortality can be caused by temperature elevation alone (5,11).

Sustained abnormally high SSTs associated with widespread coral bleaching have been related to El Niño events. El Niño, which historically referred to the warming of surface waters that occurs off South America's west coast every 3 to 7 years, is now recognized as a component of a global climate phenomenon, the El Niño Southern Oscillation (ENSO). The term 'southern oscillation' refers to multi-year cycles in wind systems that drive ocean currents, which affect the transport of cool or warm water across the ocean surface. During El Niño events pools of warm surface waters are displaced from one side of equatorial oceans to the other, generating ocean 'hot spots' that last much longer (a few months) than during more typical warm conditions . In the eastern Pacific, in April to June 1997 an El Niño event began with the strongest SST anomalies in over 50 years, climbing to 4°C above normal in September, and persisting until June 1998. Following in phase behind this, high temperature anomalies occurred in the Indian Ocean in the first half of 1998, followed by the Caribbean in the northern summer of 1998.

Almost all reported bleaching events, from 13 different countries in the Indian Ocean, coincided with the occurrence of ENSO-related oceanic 'hot spots' as derived by NOAA from satellite data, although bleaching has not been reported from all areas affected by 'hot spots'. Significant bleaching occurred in the central Arabian Gulf during 1995, 1996, and 1998, and in the central and southern Red Sea in the summer of 1997. Bleaching also occurred in the Maldives in mid-1997, and again in 1998, after which it became widespread all over western Indian Ocean, including the Seychelles, La Reunion, Comoros and East Africa. In almost all cases bleaching was associated with SSTs

Table. Percent frequency of bleaching and mortality in corals surveyed during May to June 1998 in Kenya and Madagascar. Genera are ordered from highest to lowest frequency of bleached colonies.

Genus	Number of colonies	Normal %	Bleached %	Partial Mortality %	Full Mortality %
Montipora	93	19	**74**	3	2
Favia	82	23	**72**	2	2
Pocillopora	159	11	**64**	11	7
Porites	604	22	**50**	13	6
Stylophora	132	19	**44**	16	16
Galaxea	199	43	**42**	4	3
Acropora	350	37	**31**	14	12
Millepora	124	76	**16**	5	3

that were significantly above the normal maxima for each area. The number of bleaching observations since 1997 in the Indian Ocean represents a marked increase over previous reports from the region, and it is clear that the intensity of the most recent bleaching event is higher than previous reports at both local and regional levels. The apparent dramatic increase in bleaching in the Indian Ocean is consistent with a statistically significant long-term trend of increasing SSTs in the Indian Ocean, as well as in tropical oceans as a whole (2,3,10).

Some species are more susceptible to bleaching than others. In general branching corals such as *Acropora* and *Seriatopora* appear to be the most susceptible (1). Surveys of coral species bleaching responses in Kenya and Madagascar during this bleaching event showed both differential frequency of bleaching among species, and subsequent mortality (Table). Thus while *Montipora* and *Favia* showed high susceptibility to bleaching, they had low mortality rates, as compared to the branching corals *Acropora* and *Stylophora*, which had the highest frequencies of mortality. Since the data was collected during the bleaching event, final morality rates are likely to be higher. The balance of surviving species on a reef will have important implications for recovery following the bleaching event. With El Niño/ENSO events apparently becoming more frequent and severe, a trend that may be linked to climate change, coral reefs may be one of the first conspicuous casualties of global climate change (11).

Chia-I Hsieh, Rupert Ormond & David Obura

References

1. Birkeland, C. 1997. Disturbances to reefs in recent times. In *Life and Death of Coral Reefs*. ed. Birkeland, C. pp 365-367. New York: Chapman and Hall
2. Bottomley, M., Folland, C.K., Hsiung, J., Newell, R.E., Parker, D.E. 1990. *Global Ocean Surface Temperature Atlas*. London: Her Majesty's Stationary Office

3.   Brown, B.E., Dunne, R.P., Chansang 1996. Coral bleaching relative to
      elevated seawater temperature in the Andaman Sea (Indian Ocean)
      over the last 50 years. *Coral Reefs* 15: 151-152
4.   Gladfelter, E.H. 1988. The physiological basis of coral bleaching. In *Mass
      Bleaching of Coral Reefs in the Caribbean: a Research Strategy*. eds.
      Ogden J.C., Wicklund, R.I. pp 15-18. NOAA Research Report 88-2: 51
5.   Glynn, P. W., D'Croz, L. 1990. Experimental evidence for high temperature
      stress as the cause of El Nino-coincident coral mortality. *Coral Reefs* 8:
      181-191
6.   Glynn, P.W. 1993. Coral reef bleaching: ecological perspectives. *Coral
      Reefs* 12: 1-17
7.   Goreau, T.J., Hayes, R.L. 1994. Coral bleaching and ocean hot spots. *Ambio*
      23: 176-180
8.   Jaap, W.C. 1988. The 1987 zooxanthellae expulsion event at Florida reefs,
      In *Mass Bleaching of Coral Reefs in the Caribbean: a Research Strategy*.
      Ogden, J.C., Wicklund, R.I. pp 24-19. NOAA Research Report 88-2: 51
9.   Jokiel, P.L., Coles, S.L. 1977. Effects of temperature on the mortality and
      growth of Hawaiian reef corals. *Marine Biology* 43: 201-208
10.   Parker, D.E., Folland, C.K., Jackson, M. 1995. Marine surface temperature:
      observed variations and data requirements. *Climate Change* 31: 559-600
11.   Williams, E.H., Bunkley-Williams, L. 1990. The world-wide coral reef
      bleaching cycle and related sources of coral mortality. *Atoll Research
      Bulletin* 335: 1-71

countries, led to a competition for dwindling resources that will eventually
erode the present level of catches. Consequently, in order to prevent future
stock collapses, a regulation system that considers the importance of
maintaining stocks and habitat will be required. Future regulations that place
and enforce restrictions on gear, places, and times of fishing will become
increasingly important to maintaining fish populations (49).

Pollution Management

Very few water-treatment plants have been built in coastal communities along
the coast and many of those which have been built frequently suffer from break
downs, a lack of spare parts, and trained personnel. For example, in 1983 it was
estimated that only 17% of the region's population used sewers (72). An even
smaller percentage would have this sewage treated beyond the primary stage
before discharging it into rivers or the ocean. Consequently, the majority of the
human population relies on septic tanks, pit toilets, or direct discharge into the
watershed. Waste mixes with groundwater and eventually finds its way to the
sea. Under these conditions groundwater is frequently nutrient rich and can
result in increased algal growth, as described above for Reunion, and increased
erosion of reef substrates by boring organisms (74).
      Soil erosion from land increases as land use changes from forest, to shifting
agriculture, to intensive agriculture, to grazing (23). Consequently, with
increasing human population density and intensification of land use there is
frequently reduced retention of rainfall and increased soil erosion (87). This
eroded soil enters the sea and changes reef and marine ecosystems (62). There

is also increased irrigation and intensive farming along rivers which adds to the soil content of rivers. The addition of dams to rivers can retain some of the sediments but the detriment is that this sediment blocks electricity generating turbines, water pumps, and fills dams such that they no longer effective in storing water or generating electricity. Increased efforts to protect and restore riparian and estuarine vegetation, the use of sediment retention ponds, and the creation of artificial wetlands will help to reduce the problems associated with high sediment loads. Additionally, increased use of sewage and its treatment can reduce pollution of the groundwater. Many of the countries of this region are fortunate in having high wave, current, and tidal energy which disperses and dilutes polluted water. Without this coastal water would be far worse than at present.

Conclusions

There are a number of ways of improving scientific understanding of coral reef ecology and management. Fisheries management to date suffers a number of problems that are jeopardizing the long-term sustainability of existing fisheries yields. These are 1) policies that assume there are additional fish resources (such as subsidizing fishing gear and the lack of gear, fish size, area, or time restrictions), 2) the lack of fully protected areas in most countries, 3) the use of fishing gear destructive to marine habitats (such as explosives, poisons and drag nets), 4) the lack of protection of keystone species (such as the red-lined triggerfish), and 5) the lack of coherent policies and comanagement between local and national governments, and 6) the lack of greater efforts to reduce soil erosion and human waste.

Future research and management will need to develop means to rectify these problems. In addition, increased efforts to maintain water quality such as increased treatment of sewage and other wastes as well as protection of marine and freshwater wetland habitats will be required to maintain clean nearshore waters. The present level of human populations and resource-use is such that sustainability and maintenance of reef resources will now depend more on increased conservation rather than exploitation.

References

1. Allen, G. R. 1991. *Damselfishes of the World.* Melle: Hans A. Baensch
2. Attwood, C.G., Bennett, B.A. 1994. Variation in dispersal of Galjoen (*Coracinus capensis*) from a marine reserve. *Canadian Journal of Fisheries and Aquatic Science* 51: 1247-1257
3. Beets, J., Hixon, M.A. 1994. Distribution, persistence, and growth of groupers (Pisces: Serranidae) on artificial and natural patch reefs in the Virgin Islands. *Bulletin of Marine Science* 55: 470-483
4. Bennett, B.A., Attwood, C.G. 1991. Evidence for the recovery of a surf-zone fish assemblage following following the establishment of a marine reserve on the southern coast of South Africa. *Marine Ecology Progress Series* 75: 173-181

5. Berkes, F. 1985. Fishermen and the Tragedy of the Commons. *Environmental Conservation* 12: 199-206 276
6. Birkeland, C. 1982. Terrestrial runoff as a cause of outbreaks of *Acanthaster planci* (Echinodermata: Asteroidea). *Marine Biology* 69: 175-185
7. Birkeland, C. 1988. The influence of echinoderms on coral-reef communities. *Echinoderm Studies* 3: 1-79
8. Boucher, L.M. 1986. Coral predation by muricid gastropods of the genus *Drupella* at Enewetak, Marshall Islands. *Bulletin of Marine Science* 38: 9-11
9. Bradbury, R.H., Hammond, L.S., Moran, P.J., Reichelt, R.E. 1985. Coral reef communities and the crown-of-thorns starfish: Evidence for qualitatively stable cycles. *Journal Theoretical Biology* 113: 69 - 80
10. Brown, B.E. 1997. Coral bleaching: causes and consequences. *Coral Reefs* 16 (Supplement): 129-138.
11. Buxton, C.D. 1993. Life-history changes in exploited reef fishes on the east coast of South Africa. *Environmental Biology of Fishes* 36: 47-63
12. Buxton, C.D., Smale, M.J. 1989. Abundance and distribution patterns of three temperate marine reef fish (Teleostei: Sparidae) in exploited and unexploited areas off the Southern Cape Coast. *Journal of Applied Ecology* 26: 441-451
13. Carpenter, R.C. 1988. Mass-mortality of a Caribbean sea urchin: immediate effects on community metabolism and other herbivores. *Proceedings of the National Academey of Sciences* 85: 511-514 796
14. Chabanet, P., Dufour, V., Galzin, R. 1995. Disturbance impact on reef fish communities in Reunion Island (Indian Ocean). *Journal of Experimental Marine Biology and Ecology* 188: 29-48
15. Chabanet, P., Letourneur, Y. 1995. Spatial pattern of size distribution of four fish species on Reunion coral reef flats. *Hydrobiologia* 300-301: 299-308
16. Choat, J.H. 1991. The biology of herbivorous fishes on coral reefs. In *The Ecology of Fishes on Coral Reefs*, ed. Sale, P.F. pp. 120-155. New York: Academic Press.
17. Clark, S., Edwards, A.J. 1995. Coral transplantation as an aid to reef rehabilitation: evaluation of a case study in the Maldive Islands. *Coral Reefs* 14: 201-214
18. Coast Development Authority. 1996. *Towards Intergrated Management and Sustainable Development of Kenya's Coast*. The University of Rhode Island's Coastal Resources Center, Communications Unit, The University of Rhode Island
19. Cuet, P., Naim, O. 1992. Analysis of a Blantant reef flat degradation in La Reunion Island (I'Etang-Sale Fringing Reef). *Proceedings of the Seventh International Coral Reef Symposium* 2: 313-322
20. Cuet, P., Naim, O., Faure, G., Conan, J.Y. 1988. Nutrient-Rich groundwater impact on benthic communities of La salina fringing reef (Reunion Island, Indian Ocean): Preliminary results. *Proceedings of the Sixth International Coral Reef Symposium* 2: 207-212
21. Delgado, O., Lapointe, B.E. 1994. Nutrient-limited productivity of calcareous versus fleshy macroalgae in a eutrophic, carbonate-rich tropical marine environment. *Coral Reefs* 13: 151-159

22. Done, T.J. 1987. Simulation of the effects of *Acanthaster planci* on the population structure of massive corals in the genus *Porites*: evidence of population resilience? *Coral Reefs* 6: 75-90

23. Dunne, T. 1979. Sediment yield and land use in tropical catchments. *Journal of Hydrology* 42: 281-300

24. Ensminger, J. 1996. Culture and property rights. In *Rights to Nature*, eds. Hanna, S.S., Folke, C., Maler, K.G. pp. 179-203. Washington, D.C.: Island Press

25. Ginsburg, N.R. 1994. *Proceedings of the Colloquium on Global Aspects of Coral Reefs: Health, Hazards and History*. Rosenstiel School of Marine and Atmospheric Science, University of Miami, Miami

26. Glaesel, H. 1997. *Fishers, Parks, and Power: The Socio-Environmental Dimensions of Marine Resource Decline and Protection on the Kenya Coast*. PhD Dissertation, Madison: University of Wisconsin

27. Glynn, P.W. 1993. Coral reef bleaching: ecological perspectives. *Coral Reefs* 12: 1-17

28. Harriott, V.J., Fisk, D.A. 1988. Coral transplantation as a management option. *Proceedings of the Sixth International Coral Reef Symposium* 2: 375-379

29. Hay, M.E. 1984. Patterns of fish and urchin grazing on Caribbean coral reefs: are previous results typical? *Ecology* 65: 446-454

30. Hixon, M.A., Beets, J.P. 1989. Shelter characteristics and Caribbean fish assemblages: Experiments with artificial reefs. *Bulletin of Marine Science* 44: 666 - 680

31. Jennings, S., Grandcourt, E.M., Polunin, N.V.C. 1995. The effects of fishing on the diversity, biomass and trophic structure of Seychelles' reef fish communities. *Coral Reefs* 14: 225-235

32. Jennings, S., Boulle, D.P., Polunin, N.V.C. 1996. Habitat correlates of the distribution and biomass of Seychelles' reef fishes. *Environmental Biology and Fishes* 46: 15-25

33. Jennings, S., Lock, J.M. 1996. Population and ecosystem effects of fishing. In *Tropical Reef Fisheries*, eds. Polunin, N.V.C., Roberts, C.M. pp. 193-218. London: Chapman and Hall

34. Jennings, S., Marshall, S.S., Polunin, N.V.C. 1996. Seychelles' marine protected areas: comparative structure and status of reef fish communities. *Biology Conservation* 75: 201-209

35. Johannes, R.E. 1978. Traditional marine conservation methods in oceania and their demise. *Annual Review of Ecology and Systematics* 9: 349-364

36. Kamukuru, A.T. 1992. *Costs and Earnings of Basket Trap and Handline Fishery in the Dar-es-Salaam Region of Tanzania*. Msc Thesis, University of Kuopio, Finland

37. Kelleher, G., Bleakley, C., Wells, S. 1995. *A Global Representative System of Marine Protected Areas*. Washington, D.C.: The World Bank

38. Kenchington, R.A. 1990. *Managing Marine Environments*. Washington, D.C.: Taylor & Francis

39. Lauck, T., Clark, C. W., Mangel, M., Munro, G. R. 1998. Implementing the precautionary principle in fisheries management through marine reserves. *Ecological Applications* 8: S72-S78

40. Letourneur, Y. 1996. Dynamics of fish communities on Reunion fringing reefs, Indian Ocean. I. Patterns of spatial distribution. *Journal of Experimental Marine Biology and Ecololgy* 195: 1-30
41. Littler, M. M., Littler, D. S., Titlyanov, E. A. 1991. Comparisons of N- and P- limited productivity between high granitic islands versus low carbonate atolls in the Seychelles Archipelago: A test of the relative-dominance paradigm. *Coral Reefs* 10: 199-209
42. McClanahan, T.R. 1990. Kenyan coral reef-associated gastropod assemblages: distribution and diversity patterns. *Coral Reefs* 9: 63-74
43. McClanahan, T.R. 1994. Kenyan coral reef lagoon fish: effects of fishing, substrate complexity, and sea urchins. *Coral Reefs* 13: 231-241
44. McClanahan, T.R. 1994. Endemic survives adversity. *Coral Reefs* 13: 104
45. McClanahan, T.R. 1994. Coral-eating snail *Drupella cornus* population increases in Kenyan coral reef lagoons. *Marine Ecology Progress Series* 115: 131-137
46. McClanahan, T.R. 1995. Fish predators and scavengers of the sea urchin *Echinometra mathaei* in Kenyan coral-reef marine parks. *Environmental Biology of Fishes* 43: 187-193
47. McClanahan, T.R. 1995. Harvesting in an uncertain world: impact of resource competition on harvesting dynamics. *Ecological Modelling* 80: 21-26
48. McClanahan, T.R. 1995. A coral reef ecosystem-fisheries model: impacts of fishing intensity and catch selection on reef structure and processes. *Ecological Modelling* 80: 1-19
49. McClanahan, T.R. 1996. Oceanic ecosystems and pelagic fisheries. In *East African Ecosystems and their Conservation*, eds. McClanahan T.R., Young, T.P. pp. 37-64. New York: Oxford University Press
50. McClanahan, T.R. 1997. Effects of fishing and reef structure on East Africa coral reefs. *Proceedings of the 8th International Coral Reef Symposium* 2: 1533-1538
51. McClanahan, T.R. 1997. Recovery of fish populations from heavy fishing: does time heal all? *Proceedings of the 8th International Coral Reef Symposium* 2: 2033-2038
52. McClanahan, T.R. 1997. Dynamics of *Drupella cornus* populations on Kenyan coral reefs. *Proceedings of the 8th International Coral Reef Symposium* 1: 633-638
53. McClanahan, T.R. 1997. Primary succession of coral-reef algae: differing patterns on fished versus unfished reefs. *Journal of Experimental Marine Biology and Ecology* 218: 77-102
54. McClanahan, T.R., Muthiga, N. A. 1989. Patterns of predation on a sea urchin, *Echinometra mathaei* (de Blainville), on Kenyan coral reefs. *Journal of Experimental Marine Biology and Ecology* 126: 77-94
55. McClanahan, T.R., Shafir, S.H. 1990. Causes and consequences of sea urchin abundance and diversity in Kenyan coral reef lagoons. *Oecologia* 83: 362-370
56. McClanahan, T.R., Mutere, J.C. 1994. Coral and sea urchin assemblage structure and interrelationships in Kenyan reef lagoons. *Hydrobiologia* 286: 109-124

57. McClanahan, T.R., Nugues, M., Mwachireya, S. 1994. Fish and sea urchin herbivory and competition in Kenyan coral reef lagoons: the role of reef management. *Journal of Experimental Marine Biology and Ecology* 184: 237-254

58. McClanahan, T.R., Kaunda-Arara, B. 1996. Creation of a coral-reef marine park: Recovery of fishes and its effect on the adjacent fishery. *Conservation Biology* 10: 1187-1199

59. McClanahan, T.R., Kamukuru, A.T., Muthiga, N.A., Gilagabher Yebio, M., Obura, D. 1995. Effect of sea urchin reductions on algae, coral and fish populations. *Conservation Biology* 10: 136-154

60. McClanahan, T. R., Obura, D. 1995. Status of Kenyan coral reefs. *Coastal Management* 23: 57-76

61. McClanahan, T.R., Glaesel, H., Rubens, J., Kiambo, R. 1997. The effects of traditional fisheries management on fisheries yields and the coral-reef ecosystems of southern Kenya. *Environmental Conservation* 24: 105-120

62. McClanahan, T.R., Obura, D. 1997. Sediment effects on shallow coral communities in Kenya. *Journal of Experimental Marine Biology and Ecology* 209: 103-122

63. McGoodwin, J.R. 1990. *Crisis in the World's Fisheries: People, Problems, and Policies.* Palo Alto: Stanford University Press

64. Moran, P.J. 1986. The *Acanthaster* Phenomenon. *Annual Review of Oceanography and Marine Biology* 24: 379-480

65. Moyer, J.T., Higuchi, H., Matsuda, K., Hasegawa, M. 1985. Threat to unique terrestrial and marine environments and biota in a Japanese National Park. *Environmental Conservation* 12: 293-301

66. Naim, O. 1993. Seasonal responses of a fringing reef community to eutrophication (Reunion Island, Western Indian Ocean). *Marine Ecology Progress Series* 99: 137-151

67. Naim, O., Cuet, P., Letourner, Y. 1997. Experimental shift in benthic community structure. *Proceedings of the 8th International Coral Reef Symposium* 2: 1873-1878

68. Nowlis, J.S., Roberts, C.M. 1997. You can have your fish and eat it too: theoretical approaches to marine reserve design. *Proceedings of the 8th International Coral Reef Symposium*

69. Odendaal, F.J., Kroese, M., Jaomanana. 1995. *The Strategic Plan for the Management of the Coastal Zone of the Masoala Peninsula, Madagascar.* Eco-Africa Environmental Consultants, Observatory, South Africa

70. Ohman, M.C., Rajasuriya, A., Olafsson, E. 1997. Reef fish assemblages in north-western Sri Lanka: distribution patterns and influences of fishing practises. *Environmental Biology of Fishes* 49: 45-61

71. Ormond, R., Bradbury, R., Bainbridge, S., Fabricus, K., Kcesing, J., DeVantier, L., Medlay, P., Steven, A. 1988. Test of a model of regulation of Crown-of-Thorns starfish by fish predators. In *Acanthaster and the Coral Reef: A Theoretical Perspective*, ed. Bradbury, R.H. pp. 190-207. Townsville: Springer-Verlag

72. Osore, H. 1983. Pollution and public health in East Africa. *Ambio* 12: 316-321

73. Powers, M.E., Tilman, D., Estes, J.A., Menge, B.A., Bond, W.J., Scott Mills, L., Daily, G., Castilla, J.C., Lubchenco, J., Paine, R.T. 1996. Challenges in the quest for keystones. *Bioscience* 46: 609-620

74. Risk, M.J., Sammarco, P.W., Edinger, E.N. 1995. Bioerosion in *Acropora* across the continental shelf of the Great Barrier Reef. *Coral Reefs* 14: 79-86

75. Rubens, J. 1996. *An Analysis of the Benefits and Costs of Marine Reserve Regulations at Diani, Kenya.* Msc Thesis, Univerisity of New castle upon Tyne, New castle upon Tyne

76. Ruddle, K. 1996. Traditional management of reef fishing. In *Reef Fisheries*, eds. Polunin, N.V.C., Roberts, C.M. pp. 315-335. London: Chapman and Hall

77. Sanders, M.J., Sparre, P.,Venema, S.C. 1988. *Proceedings of the Workshop on the Assessment of the Fishery Resources in the Southwest Indian Ocean.* FAO Report # RAF/79/065/WP/41/88/E

78. Shipton, P. 1994. Land and culture in tropical africa: soils, symbols, and the metaphysics of the Mundane. *Annual Review of Anthropology* 23: 347-77

79. Spear, T.T. 1978. *The Kaya Complex: A History of the Mijikenda Peoples of the Kenya Coast to 1900.* Nairobi: Kenya Literature Bureau

80. Tanzanian Fisheries Department Statistics, Fisheries Department, Dar es Salaam, Tanzania

81. Turner, S. 1992. *Drupella cornus: A Synopsis.* Department of Conservation and Land Management Occasional Paper 3/92. Como: Western Australia

82. UNEP/IUCN. 1988. *Coral Reefs of the World.* Gland, Switzerland: IUCN/UNEP

83. Watson, M. 1996. *The Role of Protected Areas in the Management of Kenyan Reef Fish Stocks.* PhD Dissertation, York: University of York

84. Watson, M., Ormond, R.F.G. 1994. Effect of an artisanal fishery on the fish and urchin populations of a Kenyan coral reef. *Marine Ecology Progress Series* 109: 115-129

85. Watson, M., Righton, D., Austin, T., Ormond, R. 1996. The effects of fishing on coral reef fish abundance and diversity. *Journal of the Marine Biological Association of the United Kingdom* 76: 229-233

86. White, A.T., Hale, L.Z., Renard, Y., Cortesi, L. eds. 1996. *Collaborative and Community-Based Management of Coral Reefs: Lessons from Experience.* West Hartford: Kumarian Press

87. Young, T.P. 1996. High Montane Forest and Afroalpine Ecosystems. In *East African Ecosystems and their Conservation*, eds. McClanahan, T.R., Young, T.P. pp. 401-424. New York: Oxford University Press

88. Zerner, C. 1994. Tracking sasi: the transformation of a central Moluccan reef management institution in Indonesia. In *Collaborative and Community-Based Management of Coral Reefs: Lessons from Experience*, eds. White, A.T., Hale, L.Z., Renard, Y., Cortesi, L. pp. 19-32. West Hartford: Kumarian Press

Section II

Country Profiles

Chapter 3

South African Coral Communities

Michael H. Schleyer

South African coral communities are found in their greatest abundance in marine reserves in northern KwaZulu-Natal (Maputaland) where sub-tropical conditions prevail. They constitute the southernmost African distribution of this fauna and are limited in extent by the availability of reef habitat. They were thus not accorded much attention by the research community until the early 1990s. Despite this, *Coral Reefs of the World* (22) included information on the area, obtained to some extent from correspondence with local scientists.

There is a long history of game-fishing on the reefs and sport-diving has increased exponentially in recent years. This has lead to some user-conflict and a commensurate increase of interest in the reefs; reserve managers require information on matters such as the biodiversity, sensitivity and diver carrying capacity of the reefs to ensure their sustainable use. They are now considered a valuable and important ecosystem and are thus receiving more attention in South Africa. Research has lead to a number of advances which have been largely covered in recent reviews (86,92). The following chapter provides an update of this information.

Description and Distribution of the Reefs

Maputaland Reefs

The major coral-inhabited reefs in KwaZulu-Natal occur adjacent to the coast from 26° 50'S to 27° 55'S (Fig. 3.1a). They are thus some of the southernmost coral reefs in the world but are not typical of coral reefs resulting from biogenic accretion. Corals in South Africa consist rather of a veneer of this life-form on late Pleistocene sandstone, originating from submerged coastal sand dunes (59,61). As a result, the reefs run parallel to the coastline and are confined to the narrow continental shelf (2 to 7 km, 36). They are conveniently grouped into a northern, central and southern complex (69), these being respectively

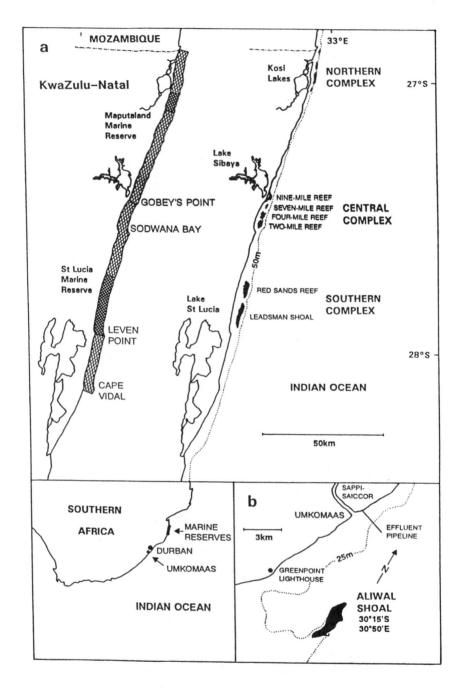

Figure 3.1. Location of the major coral-inhabited reefs in KwaZulu-Natal (86): a) The Maputaland reefs fall in reserve (light shading) and sanctuary areas (dark shading) within the Maputaland Marine Reserve (north of Gobey's Point) and the St. Lucia Marine Reserve (to the south, 9,61,69); b) Aliwal Shoal (12,17).

found at Kosi Bay, between Sodwana Bay and Lake Sibaya, and north of Lake St. Lucia (Fig. 3.1a).

The central complex has received the most attention, being the most accessible, but the reefs are basically all the same in structure. They lack the well-defined zonation of true coral reefs and conform to the topography of the base substratum. They thus tend to be flat with relatively few features comprising low pinnacles and shallow drop-offs and gullies. Nevertheless, eight separate zones based on physiographic and biological characteristics exist (61) which can be reduced to two (69) on purely biological grounds, comprising reef top and gully communities (Fig. 3.2). The former are dominated by soft corals while hard corals attain a greater abundance in the latter.

The reefs range in depth from 8 m to just over 35 m, with only a few peaks approaching the surface. The coastline is straight and exposed (Fig. 3.1a) and, as the prevailing north-easterly and southerly to south-westerly winds blow parallel to the coast, they give rise to substantial swells (Fig. 3.3a). The warm Agulhas Current, which has a mean peak velocity of 1.4 m/s (35), generates the sub-tropical conditions in the area. The mean seasonal sea surface temperatures (SST) range from 22°C in winter to 26°C in summer (based on data from 1960-1995), with the salinity varying between 35.0 and 35.5 ppt (98). Recent measurements of temperature recorded at a fixed station on one of the reefs are presented in Figure 3.4. These manifest an upward trend which will be discussed later. The maximum tidal flux is 2 m during spring tides, dropping to 1 m during neap tides.

A consequence of the conditions described above is substantial water movement on the reefs, both in terms of a current, usually north to south, and considerable surge from the swell. As no major rivers empty into the sea in the area, the sediments are devoid of terrestrial input and are coarse and bioclastic in origin (61). Visibility is thus generally good, normally being 10 to 15 m and occasionally reaching 35 m (Schleyer, M. personal observation).

Conditions on the reefs appear to be conducive to coral growth in spite of the latitudinal extremes at which they occur, so the question arises as to why the reefs are not more extensive or better developed. A geological study of *Porites lutea* growth at Sodwana Bay indicated that it is only slightly lower than that measured at a site on the Great Barrier Reef, being 9.4 mm/y as opposed to 10.3 mm/y (60). Observations on rapidly growing species such as *Acropora austera* also indicate a more than adequate growth rate (Schleyer, M. personal observation). Coral accretion on the reefs thus appears to be thin because of a relative paucity of hermatypic scleractinia rather than a slow rate of calcification among the reef building corals. In addition, unspecified physico-chemical factors may also be involved in limiting reef formation (59). Consequently, this chapter is entitled and focuses on "South African coral communities" rather than "South African coral reefs" because of the poor level of coral accretion; this must be borne in mind when the term coral reef is occasionally used here.

Aliwal Shoal

Aliwal Shoal is a reef similar in origin and structure to the Maputaland reefs, some 350 km to the south at 30° 15'S, 30° 50'E (Fig. 3.1b). It is located 4 km out to sea between Umkomaas and Scottburgh in 25 to 30 m of water. The

Figure 3.2. Reef top (left) and gully (right) communities, in which soft and hard corals are respectively more common. Photo credit: P. Ramsay

reef is 3 km long and 10 to 15 m deep along most of its length, except at its northern pinnacles which rise to within a few meters of the surface. Unlike the Maputaland reefs, Aliwal Shoal is in an area of substantial riverine input and is subject to greater turbidity from terrigenous material, algal blooms and, possibly, industrial effluent discharged from a pipeline in its vicinity (12). As it is further south, sea temperatures are also reduced; mean seasonal sea surface temperatures range from 20°C in winter to 25°C in summer. Aliwal Shoal is nevertheless occupied by a variety of Scleractinia, apparently the southernmost concentration of these organisms in the SW Indian Ocean. However, their abundance is limited by the conditions described above and alcyonaceans, sponges and antipatharians are conspicuous on the reef. A photographic record of life on the reef (12) shows that most of it is found on its sheltered landward side; the turbulence created by wind-generated swells of up to 5 m (Fig. 3.3) prevent much growth other than algae and sponges on the shallow reef top or seaward slope. The shallow depth at which the sponges and antipatharians are found on Aliwal Shoal relative to their occurrence on the Maputaland reefs lends credence to the theory that both light and temperature influence their distribution. A new alcyonacean genus (56), narrowly endemic to the area, also attests to the marginal and specialized conditions on Aliwal Shoal. The community structure of the fauna on the reef is presently under investigation.

Reef Community Structure

Corals are the dominant life form on the reefs and 43 scleractinian (hard coral) genera have been found in the area as well as one member of the fire coral genus *Millepora* (62,63,64,66,69). This exceeds the figures of 20 and 30 genera predicted earlier (1,105). Among the alcyonacean soft corals, 11 genera are listed for Sodwana Bay (central complex), with the family Nephtheidae, comprising at least four additional genera, still under examination (2,4). The combined checklist of material identified thus far constitutes 132 species of mainly Indo-Pacific corals but includes both new and endemic species (Table 3.1). Gorgonians and other alcyonaceans are found to a lesser extent in northern KwaZulu-Natal (106,107). Further taxonomic work on these groups is under way at the Oceanographic Research Institute (ORI), Durban.

Sponges and tunicates are also prominent in the sessile fauna on the reefs and are similarly being studied at ORI. Extensive collections have been made and, to date, over 20 species of sponges and eight tunicates have been identified in a collaborative exercise involving both ORI and the Tel Aviv University (Schleyer M. and Benayahu, Y. unpublished data).

The species richness of KwaZulu-Natal coral reefs is thus quite remarkable (85), but they are rendered unique by their community structure. Whereas hard corals are frequently dominant in a coral reef community, this is not so in the case of the South African reefs. Corals cover 31 to 63% of Two-mile reef at Sodwana Bay (3), with scleractinia providing 13 to 36% cover, peaking at 15 to 16 m, and alcyonacea providing 17 to 34% cover, reaching their maximum at 16 to 18 m. In a comprehensive study (69) soft corals were found to be dominant on the shallower reef tops while hard corals were more abundant in the reef gullies and on the deeper reefs studied. The three most abundant genera, in order, were *Lobophytum*, *Sinularia* and *Acropora*. Corals are

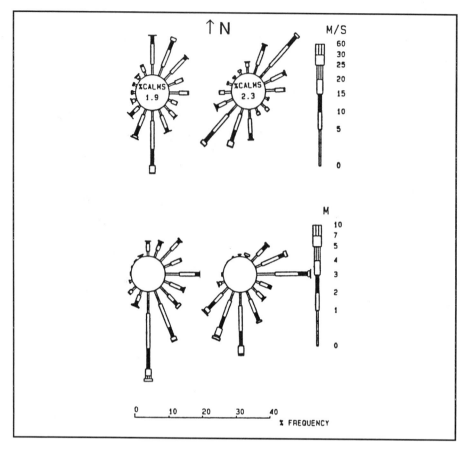

Figure 3.3. Wind (top) and swell (bottom) roses for Sodwana Bay (SADCO data 1960-1995, left), and Aliwal Shoal (SADCO data 1960-1996, right).

sparse beyond a depth of 27 m and the reefs are occupied almost exclusively by a low density of gorgonians, sponges and tunicates (86), characterizing a zone (61).

The fish fauna on the reefs is also notably rich; 399 species in 74 families have been recorded in the area, including 25 species of elasmobranchs (9). These ranged from the spectacular whale shark and manta ray through gamefish and brightly-colored coral fish to cryptic species and pearlfish. Endemic teleost species are *Gymnothorax johnsoni, Diplodus cervinus hottentotus, Rhabdosargus holubi, Apolemichthys kingi, Chaetodon marleyi, Chirodactylus jessicalenorum* and *Anchichoerops natalensis*. Of the fish found, 96% have an Indian Ocean or Indo-Pacific distribution and the balance are the endemics mentioned or are cosmopolitan species. More fish anticipated on the Maputaland reefs on the basis of collections and distribution records (9,100) and they thus expect the checklist should be expanded as the area becomes better known.

Two fixed line transects for regular fish counts which could prove useful in monitoring reef condition using fish indicator species (9). One is in a sanctuary

3. South Africa   *89*

Table 3.1. Corals found on the Maputaland reefs (2,4,5,63,62,64,66,69). Notes: hermatypic scleractinian corals unmarked; (a) ahermatypic; (h) hermatypic non-scleractinian corals; (n) new and (e) endemic species are also marked.

Order Alcyonacea:	Order Scleractinia:	
Anthelia flava	*Acanthastrea echinata*	
A. glauca	*A. simplex*	*Fungia (Pleuractis) scutaria*
Cladiella australis	*Acropora aculeus*	*Galaxea fascicularis*
C. kashmani (e,n)	*A. anthocercis*	*Gardineroseris planulata*
C. krempfii	*A. austera*	*Goniastrea edwardsi*
Efflatounaria sodwanae (e,n)	*A. clathratha*	*G. pectinata*
Eleutherobia aurea (e,n)	*A. danai*	*G. retiformis*
Heteroxenia fuscescens	*A. florida*	*Goniopora djiboutensis*
Lobophytum crassum	*A. horrida*	*G. somaliensis*
L. depressum	*A. humilis*	*Gyrosmilia interrupta*
L. latilobatum	*A. hyacinthus*	*Horastrea indica*
L. patulum	*A. latistella*	*Hydnophora exesa*
L. venustum	*A. millepora*	*H. microconos*
Sarcophyton crassum	*A. nasuta*	*Leptastrea purpurea*
S. ehrenbergi	*A. natalensis* (n)	*Leptoseris explanata*
S. flexuosum	*A. palifera*	*Montastrea annuligera*
S. glaucum	*A. sordiensis* (e,n)	*Montipora aequituberculata*
S. infundibuliforme	*A. tenuis*	*M. danae*
S. trochelipohorum	*Alveopora allingi*	*M. monasteriata*
Sinularia abrupta	*A. spongiosa*	*M. spongodes*
S. brassica	*Anomastrea irregularis*	*M. tuberculosa*
S. dura	*Astreopora myriophthalma*	*M. turgescens*
S. erecta	*Blastomussa merleti*	*M. venosa*
S. firma	*Coeloseris mayeri*	*M.verrucosa*
S. gardineri	*Coscinaraea cf. columna*	*Oulophyllia crispa*
S. gyrosa	*C. monnile*	*Pachyseris speciosa*
S. heterospiculata	*Cycloseris costulata*	*Pavona clavus*
S. hirta	*C. cyclolites*	*P. minuta*
S. leptoclados	*C. cf. marginata*	*Platygyra daedalea*
S. muralis	*Cyphastrea chalcidicum*	*Plesiastrea versipora*
S. notanda	*Dendrophyllia cf. robusta* (a)	*Pocillopora damicornis*
S. querciformis	*Diaseris distorta*	*P. eydouxi*
S. schleyeri (e,n)	*Echinophyllia aspera*	*P. verrucosa*
S. triangula	*Echinopora gemmacea*	*Podabacia crustacea*
S. variabilis	*E. hirsutissima*	*Porites lichen*
Sympodium caeruleum	*Favia favus*	*P. lutea*
Tubipora musica (h)	*F. laxa*	*P. solida*
Xenia crassa	*F. matthaii*	*Psammocora haimeana*
X. garciae	*F. pallida*	*Seriatopora caliendrum*
X. kükenthali	*F. rotumana*	*Scolymia cf. vitiensis*
	F. speciosa	*Stylophora pistillata*
Order Milleporina:	*F. stelligera*	*Symphyllia valenciennesi*
Millepora platyphylla (h)	*Favites abdita*	*Turbinaria mesenterina*
	F. complanata	*Tubastrea micranthus* (a)
	F. flexuosa	
	F. halicora	
	F. pentagona	
	F. peresi	

area and the other is on the most heavily dived reef in the central complex. The results thus far indicate that sport diving has not had a negative affect on the fish population on the latter reef. Matters pertaining to the harvest of certain of these fish stocks and their fisheries-related biology are dealt with below.

Although not common, turtles are also a feature of the local fauna and these have been extensively studied (19,20,21). Leatherback and loggerhead turtles

(*Dermochelys coriacea* and *Caretta caretta*) nest on beaches in the area while the olive ridley (*Lepidochelys olivacea*), green (*Chelonia mydas*) and hawksbill (*Eretmochelys imbricata*) turtles are also observed on the reefs.

Mollusks are a fairly conspicuous component on the reefs but have not been the subject of a specific study. They are, however, covered in a treatment of this group along the coast of the subcontinent (25). Massive forms such as the bivalves *Tridacna squamosa, Hyotissa hyotis, Lopha cristagalli* and *Pinctada margaritifera* are readily observed as well as some of the more nocturnal cowries (M. Schleyer, M. personal observation). Coral-eating gastropods (*Drupella* spp.) have been noted and their incidence is being monitored as part of the ORI coral reef program. At this stage, their numbers do not appear to be a cause for concern.

Echinodermsare relatively scarce except for brittle and feather stars (Echiuroidea and Crinoidea) and starfish such as *Fromia* and *Linckia* spp. However, substantial but isolated aggregations of the crown-of-thorns starfish (COTS; *Acanthaster planci*) have been encountered on Two-mile Reef in the central complex in recent years (90). These have been difficult to count in the often turbulent conditions but have typically attained population densities of, for example, 93 per 150 m^2. The COTS appear to aggregate in spring and disperse after spawning in summer, suggesting that the purpose of the local aggregations is for reproduction rather than feeding (90).

COTS sites manifested the highest levels of reef damage in an ORI survey on this subject, most of the corals being totally destroyed (97). The starfish are nevertheless being treated as a natural component of the environment rather than as a threat by the KwaZulu-Natal Nature Conservation Service, the conservation authority. They have adopted a policy of "cosmetic" removal of the COTS at popular dive sites at this stage, and only research material has been removed (90).

Of the other marine invertebrates, the palinurid lobsters include four species in the area on near-subtidal reefs (7,8). Only *Panulirus versicolor* has been observed on the deeper, coral encrusted reefs (Schleyer, M. personal observation). The other crustacea have not received specific attention.

Lastly, seaweeds are not conspicuous on the reefs but a checklist of those found in the area has been compiled (99), and additional records have been made by various authors (37 to 53).

Factors Influencing Reef Community Structure

Of the general environmental factors described earlier, the Agulhas Current and swell-generated turbulence, with its concomitant sediment transport and turbidity, exert the greatest influence on life on the Maputaland reefs. The extension of the distribution of many tropical Indo-Pacific organisms to northern KwaZulu-Natal is mediated by the Agulhas Current, which also maintains the tropical temperatures in the area. The balance of the conditions mentioned earlier clearly determine the community structure on the reefs, favoring the unusually high abundance of soft corals and preventing the development of a true (accretive) coral reef (3,69).

It would appear that soft corals can withstand turbulence in shallow water better than hard corals, hence their preponderance on shallow, flat reef tops. Simple laboratory experiments in aquaria (65), showed that local soft corals were less tolerant than the hard to sedimentation. Gullies are subject to considerable sediment movement and this was thought to be the reason they are occupied to a greater extent by sediment-resistant hard corals (*Montipora* spp. and the Faviidae, 64). However, the experimental approach appears to have been simplistic as a sediment-resistant soft coral community has been detected at the reef-sediment interface and is presently being quantified (91). Another factor, possibly reduced turbulence in the gullies, allows the hard corals to compete more successfully with the soft in this environmental niche. Branching and tabular *Acropora* spp. only become dominant on deeper reefs of low turbulence and sediment stress.

Light attenuation has not been extensively measured on the Maputaland reefs. However the near absence of hermatypic corals in depths greater than 27 m indicates that this is also a limiting factor. This is corroborated by the abundance of the azooxanthellate soft coral *Dendronephthya* on the top of some mid-depth (18 m) pinnacles in relatively turbid situations. Further work is to be undertaken on this parameter at ORI, as well as on temperature, as cooler water is regularly encountered on the deeper reefs. Both parameters thus appear to influence the distribution of the deeper water fauna.

Reference has already been made to sea temperatures (Fig. 3.4) and coral growth. Periodicity of oxygen and carbon isotope ratios and fluorescent banding in a *Porites lutea* core from Sodwana Bay (60), shows a correlation between extreme rainfall flood events and the fluorescent banding. The $\partial^{13}O$ values were correlated with the temperature records in Figure 3.4, indicating that the core provides a geological record of the SST (60). More importantly, sclerochronology indicated an increase in the width of the annual banding over the period studied, amounting to an increase in the coral growth rate of 9×10^{-3} mm per year. The recent temperature records indicate that the current increase in temperature is 0.25°C per year (Fig. 3.4).

Further temperature monitoring is needed to establish whether the increase in temperature is due to global warming or merely indicative of a macro-cyclical fluctuation in climate. A change in the coral community structure is anticipated if the former is the case and ORI has established a long-term monitoring site at which the temperature records are being made. Species diversity is also expected to change as the coral community is at the limit of its distribution. Fixed quadrats of the reef are being photographed annually at the site and the record of the first five years is presently being subjected to image analysis (94).

Current Research

Although little studied in the past, South African coral reefs are presently undergoing intensive investigation. It is thus difficult to comment fully on their research and management requirements. The present level of research is warranted in view of the multi-million rand sport-diving industry which the reefs support. It is further warranted in view of their biodiversity and the contribution they must make to adjacent environments, such as a nursery and feeding ground

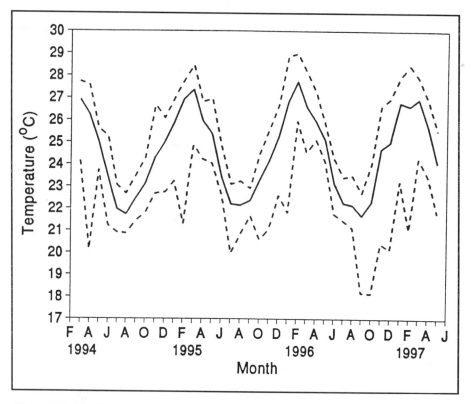

Figure 3.4. Monthly mean temperatures (solid line) with maxima and minima (broken lines) recorded since March 1994 at 18 m depth at the ORI fixed station on Nine-mile Reef at Sodwana Bay.

for pelagic fish. Their benefits and importance to man are clearly manifest. ORI is currently involved in an extensive coral reef program in the SW Indian Ocean over and above the aforementioned research. This has broadly focused objectives intended to meet the presently perceived needs of local reef management. In their broadest context, the objectives are to determine: a) the species composition of the corals, sponges and tunicates on the reefs, b) the community structure of corals and associated organisms on representative reefs, c) the condition of the reefs in terms of human and other disturbance, and d) the most effective management plan to ensure sustainable use of the reefs.

Part of the KwaZulu-Natal component of this program has been concluded in collaboration with the University of Cape Town and several aspects are being conducted in collaboration with the University of Tel Aviv. The following account outlines current and recently published work not covered above.

Coral Reproduction. Coral reproductionwas studied to establish whether the local communities are self-perpetuating or dependent on recruitment from reefs further north, the former being at the limits of their distribution. Seven coral species, manifesting the full range of reproductive strategies, were thus examined histologically and normal reproduction was encountered (6,28 to 32,93,95,96). The species studied were *Anthelia glauca, Pocillopora verrucosa, Sarcophyton glaucum, Lobophytum crassum, L. depressum, Sinularia dura* and *S. gyrosa*. The results are summarized in Table 3.2.'

Toxins and Interactions. Sessile reef organisms are being screened for toxic secondary metabolites as a study of their powerful chemical weaponry, used to secure and defend territory on the reefs. This will help elucidate the functioning of reef communities. A consequence of these studies has been the discovery and elucidation of marine natural products new to science which may have therapeutic applications in human medicine, for example in the treatment of cancer and AIDS. Information on some of these findings has been published (11,14,18,23,24,26,27,71-81,102). The natural products have ranged from amino acids and peptides to quinols; most have been terpenes. A correlation was anticipated between the toxin production and gametogenesis during the reproductive cycle in soft corals as these natural products are known to have a number of functions in coral reproduction, such as sperm attraction and larval defense. No such correlation was found in the South African corals (23).

Conservation Status, Threats and Management

Maputaland Reefs

The Maputaland reefs all fall in the St. Lucia and Maputaland Marine Reserves, with the southern complex lying in a sanctuary area (Fig. 3.1a). These reserves fall under the jurisdiction of the KwaZulu-Natal Nature Conservation Service. The reefs thus receive protection from all forms of extractive exploitation other than the capture of bait and gamefish, and even this is not allowed in the southern complex, being a sanctuary area. Sport-diving is allowed on the other reefs and this is the only obvious human interference at this stage. User conflict between the divers and fishermen has necessitated some zonation of the reefs for these activities.

Fisheries. A substantial harvest of bait and gamefish is taken, particularly during fishing competitions which are permitted despite the conservation status of the reefs. Comprehensive statistics are kept for analysis by ORI to monitor the catches, which includes the number of outings, fishing effort and the catch size and composition (54,55). Cape Vidal and Sodwana Bay (Fig. 3.1a) are the centers of these activities and representative results of the data collected for the latter in 1995 are presented in Figure 3.5. The total catch for the whole area in 1995 amounted to 5063 fish weighing 41 tons. The catch consisted of 38 species and included billfish, some of which were tagged and released. The fishery is tightly controlled and over-exploitation is not considered to be an issue, especially in view of the migratory nature of the gamefish.

Endemic sparids comprise an important catch in bottom fisheries on reefs outside the conservation areas (for example Aliwal Shoal) in KwaZulu-Natal (15). The extent to which these fish have been exploited has given cause for

Table 3.2. Summary of the reproductive strategies found in the corals studied on the Maputaland coral reefs (6,28-32,93,95,96).

Species	Sex	Reproductive mode	Periodicity
Anthelia glauca	gonochoric	brooder	repetitive
Lobophytum crassum, L. depressum	gonochoric	spawner	seasonal
Sarcophyton glaucum	gonochoric	spawner	seasonal
Sinularia dura, S. gyrosa	gonochoric	spawner	seasonal
Pocillopora verrucosa	hermaphroditic	spawner	seasonal

concern (16). They incorporate a sex change in their life cycle (protandrous and protogynous hermaphroditism), which complicates their management (15,16, and see Chapter 2). The principle most relevant to the conservation management of these fish is that the size at capture must exceed the size of sex change to ensure that sufficient mature specimens of both sex are available for reproduction. Protected stocks in the breeding refugia of the marine reserves provided valuable comparative data for studies on a representative species, the slinger (*Chrysoblephus puniceus*). These included growth and population modelling (16,58) in developing management recommendations on minimum catch sizes and bag limits. No change to the existing limits was needed (5 fish >250 mm per day) but monitoring was recommended for the timely detection of stock depletion (58).

Only limited, shore-based bait harvesting by subsistence collectors is permitted in the marine reserves (13,33,34,103). Mussels, oysters, limpets and sea squirts are collected intertidally on the rocks, while ghost and mole crabs are caught on the beaches. Most of the harvest is consumed and little is sold or used as bait. This traditional practice has been exercised for generations and is considered sustainable (13,33,34,103).

Diving Activities. Most diving takes place at Sodwana Bay in the central complex, with the maximum recorded number of SCUBA dives reaching 118 389 in 1996. This constitutes a nearly six-fold increase in this activity since 1987. The diving is strictly controlled; no anchoring or mooring is allowed and the dive boats remain manned at the dive sites. The regulations also stipulate that nothing be touched or removed from the reefs. Most divers are fairly responsible in this regard and many dive operators maintain a standard of diver buoyancy-control and non-interference with the reefs, but the regulations are difficult to police and enforce.

Reef Damage. While some information on the condition of South African coral reefs can be extracted from community structure data (68,69), a more intensive study undertaken (97) in the central reef complex at Sodwana Bay. A rapid reef survey technique was employed. Regression analysis on the divers damage data indicated that, apart from the COTS damage described above, and discarded fishing tackle were having a significantly deleterious effect on the reefs. Recommendations on the diver carrying capacity of the reefs were thus made to the conservation authorities. Probability estimates indicated that diver damage would exceed acceptable levels above a diving intensity of 7000 dives per site per year; this has been recommended as the maximum carrying capacity for most localities in the central complex.

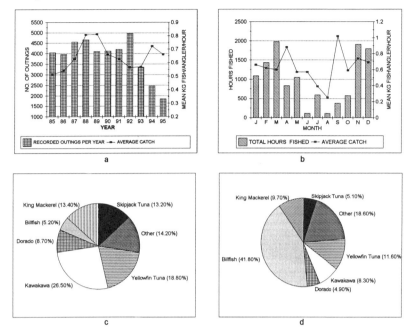

Figure 3.5. (a) Annual record of the number of outings undertaken by ski boat anglers from Sodwana Bay up to 1995, (b) with the time spent fishing each month, and the catch composition by number (c) and weight (d) for that year. The annual and monthly catch per unit effort are included in (a) and (b) (54,55).

The fouling of branching corals with fishing tackle which becomes overgrown with algae was a conspicuous manifestation of human interference on the reefs. Education of ski-boat anglers to stop this form of pollution is essential as it usually results in the death of the coral. No evidence of other problems such as coral bleaching and disease or conspicuous numbers of corallivorous *Drupella* spp. have been encountered up till 1998.

Pollution. Oil pollution poses a danger to intertidal life along the Maputaland coast. It is the first stretch of relatively uninhabited coast north of Durban and Richards Bay and in the past has been subject to the discharge of tank-washings by passing tankers. Historically, this problem reached a peak during the closure of the Suez Canal when tankers from the Gulf area were forced to use the Cape Route to Europe and America. A considerable amount of oil pollution resulted from the more recent sinking of the *Katina P* in the Mozambique Channel. However, damage to the Maputaland reefs appears to have been precluded by their depth.

In conclusion, the Maputaland reefs and associated marine reserves offer vast potential for ecotourism. Herein lies their greatest threat, as well as the reason for their protection. Tourism is expected to increase in South Africa as it re-enters the international community. The rich biodiversity and unique community structure of the Maputaland reefs is bound to make them a major attraction. Development will be necessary to derive the maximum sustainable economic benefit from the reefs, but it must be limited and undertaken in a disciplined manner to avoid exposing the area to a visitor density that could be deleterious. Press releases on proposed developments indicate that the threat of unrestrained development is neither distant nor imaginary.

Aliwal Shoal

Whereas the present condition of the Maputaland reefs is satisfactory, the same cannot be said of Aliwal Shoal. Its popularity as a diving venue is growing; although it is not as attractive as the Sodwana reefs, it is closer to the metropolis of Durban. Controversy surrounds its condition as the popular press frequently publicizes lay concerns over the harmful effects on reef life of the industrial discharge (lignosulphonates) from the nearby Sappi Saiccor pipeline. Divers with an interest in the shoal, both public and professional, are at the heart of this green movement. However, their concerns are not supported by pollution monitoring and research on the pipeline (12). Heavy fishing pressure with concomitant fouling of the reef with fishing line is also a concern and user conflict has developed between the fishermen and divers. All these factors lead one to the conclusion that Aliwal Shoal is a deteriorating resource which deserves better protection.

Two approaches have been used to resolve the matter. First, a public workshop was convened to deal with the issues of user conflict (88), giving rise to a public forum which formulated an interim management plan for the shoal (104). Moves are being made for its implementation through proclamation of Aliwal Shoal as a "protected seascape" in terms of current legislation. Features of the management plan are: a) sustainable use of Aliwal Shoal will be attained through user management, b) use of Aliwal Shoal will be self-regulated by the users, c) the plan will be self-administered by a voluntary Board of Trustees, d) its implementation will be self-funded on the basis of "the user pays", and e) it will engender a feeling of resource ownership through user participation in its implementation. Second, ORI was commissioned to conduct research on Aliwal Shoal to provide the refinements needed for the final management plan and attempt to assess what effects, if any, Sappi Saiccor effluent is having on its biota. A mapping and biological survey of the shoal is presently being undertaken.

Management Recommendations and Future Research

As the Maputaland reefs fall within a conservation area, the KwaZulu-Natal Nature Conservation Service (which manages them) particularly requires information on levels to which they can tolerate human activity with no long-term deleterious effects, and steps which may be required for their conservation in the event of a natural disaster, such as an outbreak of coral-eating pests or cyclonic damage.

The present research and monitoring programs will go a long way in providing this information and interim management recommendations are being formulated. Riegl (62), for example, has recommended that the number of dives on Four-mile Reef in the central complex be restricted, as the reef has many branching *Acropora* colonies which would be susceptible to breakage. He further recommends that the northern complex be closed to diving, thereby ensuring the provision of larval recruits for southward transport by the Agulhas Current to the lower complexes. The southern complex presently enjoys such protection but this is deemed unnecessary (62).

These recommendations are correct in principle but are in some respects impractical. The number of visitors to Maputaland is bound to increase (see Conservation Status and Threats) and the KwaZulu-Natal Nature Conservation Service, which has jurisdiction over the area, is planning the development of visitor facilities to take advantage of this location. This will probably become another center for sport-diving. The southern complex, although protected, is already accessible from visitor facilities at Cape Vidal (Fig. 3.1a) and pressure will mount to open this area as well. A greater dispersal of visitor pressure would seem advisable; the launching site at Sodwana Bay cannot handle a further increase in boat and vehicle traffic and the extent of diving in some areas of the central complex is intense. A more realistic approach would be to open all three complexes to regulated diving, with restricted diving at all sites similar to Four-mile Reef, and a protected area at the northern end of each complex as a breeding refuge.

The last-mentioned recommendation would provide a more secure safeguard to ensure recruitment success in view of the distances between the northern, central and southern reef complexes, these being 20 and 45 km respectively (Fig. 3.1a). Modern findings indicate that invertebrate larvae do not necessarily jump the enormous gaps originally anticipated (57). This is particularly true of corals (82,83), most larvae settling on or within 300 m of a reef (83). The Maputaland reefs are close to the shore (Fig. 3.1a) and the predominant incidence of waves from the south (Fig. 3.3) would generate a measure of closed-cell circulation around the reefs (101). Southerly currents are, however, most frequently encountered on the reefs (Schleyer, M. unpublished data) and the Agulhas Current would provide transport for the planktonic larvae produced by broadcast spawning corals. The majority of the corals on the Maputaland reefs employ this reproductive strategy and the protection of a northern breeding refuge in each reef complex would thus constitute a precautionary management approach.

With regard to this, recommendations were made to the KwaZulu-Natal Nature Conservation Service some time ago for the closure of Nine-mile reef (84, Schleyer, correspondence). This is the northernmost reef in the central complex and negotiations are still under way to close at least its northern half. The ORI long-term monitoring site is located here and warrants protection in its own right and as a reference site in assessing the effects of human activity on the other reefs. It will thus provide a control for further studies on the damage at heavily dived sites. The intention is thus to monitor both natural and man-made changes on the reefs.

Individual reef classification and zonation for use is recommended and options have been presented at KwaZulu-Natal Nature Conservation Service workshops (85,86,87,97) (Schleyer, M. unpublished data). It was proposed that diving at any particular site be limited to the recommended carrying capacity of 7000 dives per year and that the reefs be zoned in terms of the abundance of corals sensitive to damage (such as *Acropora* compared to more resilient soft corals). Diving on deep reefs (>18 m) should be restricted to divers of advanced qualification as this is where sensitive corals are more common. This would prevent considerable damage caused by poor buoyancy compensation and might improve diver safety. A ban should be placed on the use of diving gloves to reduce handling of the reefs and a program of diver education was recommended. The current research program has been largely focused on the central complex, where the need has been greatest, but further reef surveys in the northern and southern complexes have been proposed for their zonation.

The management requirements of Aliwal Shoal are perceived to be a matter of greater urgency. It is not in a conservation area and enjoys no protection other than that provided by normal fisheries legislation. The impending implementation of an interim management plan (104) will be refined through current research.

Conclusions

Coral-inhabited reefs occur mainly in conservation areas in northern KwaZulu-Natal. Information is presented on their extent and on local conditions. Recent investigations indicate that they are rich in biodiversity, have unique features, and include coral communities which extend unusually far south. Factors influencing reef community structure are discussed and a review of current research is presented. This ranges from studies on coral taxonomy and reproduction to long-term monitoring of coral predators and responses in reef community structure to climate change. The reefs are well-conserved with the exception of Aliwal Shoal which enjoys minimum protection. Most of the accessible reefs are used for recreational fishing and diving. Recommendations have been made for a cohesive approach in reef management incorporating zonation into open, restricted and protected diving areas. Whereas the present level of conservation of most of the reefs is satisfactory, they represent tremendous opportunities for ecotourism and a system of classification and zonation has been recommended for their sustainable use and conservation.

References

1.   Achituv, Y., Dubinsky, Z. 1990. Evolution and zoogeography of coral reefs. In *Ecosystems of the World*, Vol. 25: Coral reefs. ed. Dubinsky, Z. pp. 1-8. Amsterdam: Elsevier
2.   Benayahu, Y. 1993. Corals of the south-west Indian Ocean I. Alcyonacea from Sodwana Bay, South Africa. *Investigational Report. Oceanographic Research Institute* 67: 1-16
3.   Benayahu, Y., Shafir, A., Ben-hillel, R., Field, J.G. 1993. Soft corals and stony corals of Sodwana Bay, South Africa: Communities at the boundaries of reefs distribution. *First European Regional Meeting, International Society for Reef Studies*, Vienna, December 1993. Unpublished paper
4.   Benayahu, Y., Schleyer, M.H. 1995. Corals of the south-west Indian Ocean II. *Eleutherobia aurea* spec. nov. (Cnidaria, Alcyonacea) from deep reefs on the KwaZulu-Natal coast, South Africa. *Oceanographic Research Institute. Investigational Report* 68: 1-12

5. Benayahu, Y., Schleyer, M.H. 1996. Corals of the south-west Indian Ocean III. Alcyonacea (Octocorallia) from Bazaruto Island, Mozambique, with a redescription of *Cladiella australis* (Macfayden 1936) and description of *Cladiella kashmani* spec. nov. *Oceanographic Research Institute. Investigational Report* 69: 1-21

6. Benayahu, Y., Schleyer, M.H. 1998. Reproduction in *Anthelia glauca* (Octocorallia, Xeniidae). II: Transmission of algal symbionts during brooding of planulae. *Marine Biology* 131: 433-442

7. Berry, P.F. 1971. The spiny lobsters (Palinuridae) of the East Coast of Southern Africa: Distribution and ecological notes. *Oceanographic Research Institute. Investigational Report* 27: 1-23

8. Berry, P.F. 1974. A revision of the *Panulirus homarus* group of spiny lobsters (Decapoda, Palinuridae). *Crustaceana* 27: 31-42

9. Chater, S.A., Beckley, L.E., Garratt, P.A., Ballard, J.A., van der Elst, R.P. 1993. Fishes from offshore reefs in the St Lucia and Maputaland Marine Reserves, South Africa. *Lammergeyer* 42: 1-17

10. Chater, S.A., Beckley, L.E., van der Elst, R.P., Garratt, P.A. 1995. Underwater visual census of fishes in the St Lucia Marine Reserve, South Africa. *Lammergeyer* 43: 15-23

11. Chill, L., Kashman, Y., Schleyer, M. 1997. Oriamide, a new cytotoxic cyclic peptide containing a novel amino acid from the marine sponge *Theonella* sp. *Tetrahedron Letters*

12. Connell, A.D. 1988. *A Photographic Survey of reefs in the Vicinity of the SAICCOR Pipeline at Umkomaas*, Natal. Durban, National Research Institute for Oceanology

13. Fielding, P.J., Schleyer, M.H. 1992. Utilisation of marine resources along the Natal coast. *Workshop on the Establishment and Management of Marine Reserves along the South African Coast*, Cape Town, July 1992, Paper

14. Fridkovsky, E., Rudi, A., Benayahu, Y., Kashman, Y., Schleyer, M. 1996. Sarcoglane, a new cytotoxic diterpene from *Sarcophyton glaucum*. *Tetrahedron Letters* 37: 6909-6910

15. Garratt, P.A. 1991. Spawning behaviour of *Cheimerius nufar* in captivity. *Environmental Biology of Fishes* 31:345-353

16. Garratt, P.A., Govender, A., Punt, E. 1993. Growth acceleration at sex change in the protogynous hermaphrodite *Chrysoblephus puniceus* (Pisces: Sparidae). *South African Journal of Marine Science* 13: 187-193

17. Hattingh, D. 1992. *The Aliwal Shoal - Natal. Underwater* (20): Map supplement

18. Hooper, G.J., Davies-coleman, M.T., Schleyer, M.H. 1997. New diterpenes from the South African soft coral *Eleutherobia aurea*. *Journal of Natural Products* 60: 889-893

19. Hughes, G.R. 1974. The Sea Turtles of South-East Africa. I. Status, morphology and distributions. *Oceanographic Research Institute. Investigational Report* 35: 1-144

20. Hughes, G.R. 1974. The sea turtles of South-East Africa. II. The biology of the Tongaland loggerhead turtle *Caretta caretta L.* with comments on the leatherback turtle *Dermochelys coriacea L.* and the green turtle *Chelonia mydas L.* in the study region. *Oceanographic Research Institute. Investigational Report* 36: 1-96

21. Hughes, G.R. 1980. *Sea turtle research in Maputaland. In Studies on the Ecology of Maputaland.* eds. Bruton, M.N., Cooper, K.H.. pp. 288-292. Grahamstown, Rhodes University

22. IUCN/UNEP. 1988. *Coral Reefs of the World.* Vol. 2: *Indian Ocean, Red Sea and Gulf.* United Nations Environment Programme

23. Ketzinal, S. 1997. Variation in natural products in populations of two soft corals, *Eleutherobia aurea* and *Lobophytum crassum.* Unpublished MSc. Thesis, Tel Aviv University

24. Ketzinal, S., Rudi, A., Schleyer, M., Benayahu, Y., Kashman, Y. 1996. Sarcodictyn A and two novel diterpenoid glycosides, Eleuthosides A and B, from the soft coral, *Eleutherobia aurea. Journal of Natural Products* 59: 873-875

25. Kilburn, R., Rippey, E. 1982. *Sea Shells of Southern Africa.* Johannesburg: Macmillan

26. Koren-goldshlager, G., Kashman, Y., Schleyer, M. in press. Haliclorensin, a novel diamino alkaloid from the marine sponge *Haliclona tulearensis. Journal of Natural Products*

27. Koren-goldshlager, G., Klein, P., Rudi, A., Benayahu, Y., Schleyer, M., Kashman, Y. 1996. Sindurol and Nephtoside: New tetraprenyltoluquinols from the soft corals *Sinularia dura* and *Nephthea* sp. *Journal of Natural Products* 59: 262-266

28. Kruger, A. 1995. *Reproductive Strategies of Three South African Corals.* MSc. Thesis, University of Natal, Durban

29. Kruger, A., Schleyer, M.H. in press. Reproduction in *Pocillopora verrucosa* (Scleractinia, Pocilloporidae) in KwaZulu-Natal, South Africa. *Marine Biology*

30. Kruger, A., Schleyer, M.H., Benayahu, Y. 1994. *Coral Reproduction at Sodwana Bay, Natal.* Zoological Society of Southern Africa Symposium, Pietermaritzburg, 11-14 July, 1994. Unpublished paper

31. Kruger, A., Schleyer, M.H., Benayahu, Y. 1996. *Histological Analysis of Reproduction in Three Species of Coral.* Microscopy Society of Southern Africa, Symposium. University of Natal, Durban, 4-6 December 1996. Paper

32. Kruger, A., Schleyer, M.H., Benayahu, Y. 1998. Reproduction in *Anthelia glauca* (Octocorallia, Xeniidae). I: Gametogenesis and larval brooding. *Marine Biology* 131: 423-432

33. Kyle, R., Pearson, B., Fielding, P.J., Robertson, W.D., Birnie, S.L. 1997. Subsistence shellfish harvesting in the Maputaland marine reserve in northern KwaZulu-Natal, South Africa: Rocky Shore organisms. *Biological Conservation* 82: 183-192

34. Kyle, R., Robertson, W.D., Birnie, S.L. 1997. Subsistence shellfish harvesting in the Maputaland marine reserve in northern KwaZulu-Natal, South Africa: Sandy beach organisms. *Biological Conservation* 82: 173-182

35. Lutjeharms, J.R.E., de Ruijter, W.P.M. 1996. The influence of the Agulhas Current on the adjacent coastal ocean: possible impacts of climate change. *Journal of Marine Systems* 7: 321-336

36. Martin, A.K., Flemming, B.W. 1988. Physiography, structure and geological evolution of the Natal Continental Shelf. In *Lecture Notes on*

Coastal and Estuarine Studies, Vol. 26: Coastal Ocean Studies off Natal, South Africa. ed. Schumann, E.H. pp 11-46. New York: Springer

37. Norris, R.E. 1986. *Coelarthrum* (Rhodymeniaceae Rhodophyceae), a genus new to Southern Africa. *South African Journal of Botany* 52: 537-540

38. Norris, R.E. 1986. Studies on *Crouania franciscii* (Ceramiaceae, Rhodophyta) from South Africa and *C. Willae* sp. nov. from New Zealand. *Phycologia* 25: 133-143

39. Norris, R.E. 1987. Species of *Antithamnion* (Rhodophyceae, Ceramiaceae) occuring on the South East African Coast (Natal). *Journal of Phycology* 23: 18-36

40. Norris, R.E. 1987. Structure and reproduction in *Lenormandiopsis nozawae* (Rhodomelaceae, Rhodophyta). *Cryptogamie Algologie* 8: 211-221

41. Norris, R.E. 1987. *Lenormandiopsis* (Rhodomelaceae), newly recorded from Africa, with a description of *L. nozawae* sp. nov. and comparison with other species. *Japanese Journal of Phycology* (Sorui) 35: 81-90

42. Norris, R.E. 1987. The first confirmed records of *Lomentaria*, (Lomentariaceae, Rhodophyceae) in South Africa, with a description of *L. amplexans* sp. nov. *South African Journal of Botany* 53: 35-38

43. Norris, R.E. 1987. The systematic position of *Gelidiopsis* and *Ceratodictyon* (Gigartinales, Rhodophyceae), genera new to South Africa. *South African Journal of Botany* 53 239-246

44. Norris, R.E. 1987. *Claudea elegans* (Delesseriaceae, Rhodophyceae) in Natal, its first record in the western Indian Ocean and Africa. *South African Journal of Botany* 53: 311-315

45. Norris, R.E. 1988. Structure and reproduction of *Amansia* and *Melanamansia* gen. nov. (Rhodophyta, Rhodomelaceae) on the South Eastern African Coast. *Journal of Phycology* 24: 209-223

46. Norris, R.E. 1988. A review of Natalian Solieriaceae (Gigartinales, Rhodophyta), including the first South African records of *Solieria* and *Meristotheca*, and an investigation of *Erythroclonium corallinum*. *South African Journal of Botany* 54: 103-108

47. Norris, R.E. 1988. A review of *Colacopsis* and *Melanocolax*, red algal parasites on South African Rhodomelaceae (Rhodophyta). British *Phycological Journal* 23: 229-237

48. Norris, R.E. 1988. The specific identity of *Neurymenia* (Rhodophyceae Rhodomelaceae) in south eastern Africa. *Japanese Journal of Phycology* (Sorui) 36: 271-276

49. Norris, R.E. 1988. Structure and tetrasporangial reproduction in *Acrocystis* (Rhodomelaceae, Rhodophyta), newly reported for South Africa. *South African Journal of Botany* 54: 633-635

50. Norris, R.E. 1989. Natalian *Botryocladia* (Rhodomeniales, Rhodymeniales, Rhodophyceae) including description of a new, long axis-forming species. *Botanica Marina* 32: 131-148

51. Norris, R.E. 1990. *Ptilophora hilderbrandtii* (Hauck) comb. nov. (Gelidiales, Rhodophyceae), its range extended to South Africa. *South African Journal of Botany* 56: 133-135

52. Norris, R.E., Aken M.E. 1985. Marine benthic algae new to South Africa. *South African Journal of Botany* 51: 55-65

53. Norris, R.E., Wynne M.J. 1987. *Myriogramme marginifructa* sp. nov. (Delesseriaceae, Rhodophyceae) from Natal. *South African Journal of Botany* 53: 381-386

54. Oceanographic Research Institute. 1996. Cape Vidal recreational angling. Oceanographic Research Institute. *NMLS Angling Information Series* 8: 1-2

55. Oceanographic Research Institute. 1996. Sodwana Bay recreational skiboat angling. Oceanographic Research Institute. *NMLS Angling Information Series* 8: 1-2

56. Ofwegen, L.P. van, Schleyer, M.H. 1997. Corals of the south-west Indian Ocean V. *Leptophyton benayahui* gen. nov. & spec. nov. (Cnidaria, Alcyonacea) from deep reefs at Durban and off the KwaZulu-Natal south coast, South Africa. *Oceanographic Research Institute. Investigational Report* 71: 1-12

57. Philips, T.E. 1994. Dispersal, settlement and recruitment: their influence on the population dynamics of intertidal mussels. Unpublished Ph.D Thesis, Rhodes University

58. Punt, A.E., Garratt, P.A., Govender, A. 1993. On an approach for applying per-recruit methods to a protogynous hermaphrodite with an illustration for the slinger *Chrysoblephus puniceus* (Pisces: Sparidae). *South African Journal of Marine Science* 13: 109-119

59. Ramsay, P.J. 1996. Quaternary marine geology of the Sodwana Bay continental shelf, Northern KwaZulu-Natal. *Bulletin of the Geological Survey of South Africa* 117: 1-86

60. Ramsay, P.J., Cohen, A.L. 1997. Coral palaeoclimatology research on the southeast African shelf. In *Proceedings of the 8th International Coral Reef Symposium*. Panama City, Panama 2: 1731-1734

61. Ramsay, P.J., Mason, T.R. 1990. Development of a type zoning model for Zululand coral reefs, Sodwana Bay, South Africa, *Journal of Coastal Research* 6: 829-852

62. Riegl, B. 1993. *Taxonomy and Ecology of South African Reef Corals*. PhD Thesis, University of Cape Town

63. Riegl, B. 1995. Description of four new species in the hard coral genus *Acropora* Oken, 1815 (Scleractina: Astrocoeniina: Acroporidae) from SE Africa. *Zoological Journal of the Linnean Society* 113: 229-247

64. Riegl, B. 1995. A revision of the hard coral genus *Acropora* Oken, 1815 (Scleractina: Astrocoeniina: Acroporidae) in south-east Africa. *Zoological Journal of the Linnean Society* 113: 249-288

65. Riegl, B. 1995. Effects of sand deposition on scleractinian and alcyonacean corals. *Marine Biology* 121: 517-526

66. Riegl, B. 1996. Corals of the south-west Indian Ocean IV. The hard coral family Faviidae (Scleractinia: Faviina) in south-east Africa. *Oceanographic Research Institute. Investigational Report* 70: 1-47

67. Riegl, B., Branch, G.M. 1995. Effects of sediment on the energy budgets of four scleractinian (Bourne 1900) and five alcyonacean (Lamouroux 1816) corals. *Journal of Experimental Marine Biology and Ecology* 186: 259-275

68. Riegl, B., Cook, P.A. 1995. Is damage susceptibility linked to coral community structure? A case study from South Africa. *Beiträge zur Paläontologie* 20: 65-73

69. Riegl, B., Schleyer, M.H., Cook, P.J., Branch, G.M. 1995. Structure of Africa's southernmost coral communities. *Bulletin of Marine Science* 56: 676-691

70. Robertson, W.D., Schleyer, M.H., Fielding, P.J., Tomalin, B.J., Beckley, L.E., Fennessy, S.T., van der Elst, R.P., Bandeira, S., Macia, A., Gove, D. 1996. *Inshore Marine Resources and Associated Opportunities for Development of the Coast of Southern Mozambique: Ponto Do Oura to Cabo de Santa Maria.* Oceanographic Research Institute. Unpublished Report 130: 1-51

71. Rudi, A., Goldberg, I., Stein, Z., Benayahu, Y., Schleyer, M.H., Kashman, Y. 1993. Sodwanones A-C, three new triterpenoids from a marine sponge. *Tetrahedron letters* 34: 3943-3944

72. Rudi, A., Goldberg, I., Stein, Z., Frolow, F., Benayahu, Y., Schleyer, M.H., Kashman, Y. 1994. Polycitone A and Polycitone B; New Alkaloids from the marine ascidian *Polycitor* sp. *Journal of Organic Chemical* 59: 999-1003

73. Rudi, A., Green, S., Goldberg, I., Kashman, Y., Benayahu, Y., Schleyer, M.H. 1994. Phorbazoles A-D, novel chlorinated phenylpyrrolyl-oxazoles from the marine sponge *Phorbas* aff *clathrata*. *Tetrahedron letters* 35: 2589-2592

74. Rudi, A., Green, S., Goldberg, I., Kashman, Y., Benayahu, Y., Schleyer, M.H. 1994. Amino acid derivatives from the marine sponge *Jaspis digonoxea Journal of Natural Products* 57: 829-832

75. Rudi, A., Goldberg, I., Stein, Z., Kashman, Y., Benayahu, Y., Schleyer, M.H. 1995. Sodwanone G, H., and I; new cytotoxic triterpenes from a marine sponge. *Journal of Natural Products* 38: 1702-1712

76. Rudi, A., Kashman, Y., Benayahu, Y., Schleyer, M.H. 1994. Sodwanones A-F, new triterpenoids from the marine sponge *Axinella weltneri. Journal of Natural Products* 57: 1416-1423

77. Rudi, A., Kashman, Y., Benayahu, Y., Schleyer, M.H. 1995. Durbinal A, B and C: Three cytotoxic sponge metabolites. *Tetrahedron letters*

78. Rudi, A., Kashman, Y., Benayahu, Y., Schleyer, M.H. in press. Two new prenylated quinoids from *Nephthea* sp. and *Sinularia dura. Journal of Natural Products*

79. Rudi, A., Kashman, Y., Benayahu, Y., Schleyer, M.H. submitted.. Lobocrasolide, a new cytotoxic cembranoide from the Indo-Pacific soft coral *Lobophytum crassum*

80. Rudi, A., Ketzinel, S., Goldberg, I., Stein, Z., Kashman, Y., Benayahu, Y., Schleyer, M.H. 1995. Antheliatin, Zahavin A and Zahavin B; three new cytotoxic, xenicane diterpenoids from two soft corals. *Journal of Natural Products* 38: 1581

81. Rudi, A., Talpir, R, Kashman, Y., Benayahu, Y., Schleyer, M.H. 1993. Four new cytotoxic C^{16} 1,2-Dioxene-polyketides from the sponge *Plakortis* aff *simplex. Journal of Natural Products* 56: 2178-2182

82. Sammarco, P.W., Andrews, J.C. 1988. Localized dispersal and recruitment patterns in Great Barrier Reef corals: The Helix experiment. *Science* 239: 1422-1424

83. Sammarco, P.W., Andrews, J.C. 1989. The Helix experiment: Differential localized dispersal and recruitment patterns in Great Barrier Reef corals. *Limnology and Oceanography* 34: 896-912

84. Schleyer, M.H. 1991. *Report on Visit to ORI by Dr. Y. Benayahu to Study the Soft Corals of Sodwana Bay, with Subsequent Recommendations.* Oceanographic Research Institute. Unpublished Report 71: 1-7

85. Schleyer, M.H. 1994. The Maputaland Coral reefs: A review on current research and outline of management principles. Zoological Society of Southern Africa Symposium, Pietermaritzburg, 11-14 July, 1994. Paper

86. Schleyer, M.H. 1995. South African coral reef communities. In *Wetlands of South Africa.* ed. Cowan, G.I. pp 137-146. Department of Environmental Affairs and Tourism, Pretoria

87. Schleyer, M.H. 1995. *Biodiversity Value of Maputaland's Coral Reefs:* Natal Parks Board Annual Research Symposium, Queen Elizabeth Park, Pietermaritzburg, 19-21 September, 1995

88. Schleyer, M.H. 1995. Proceedings of the Aliwal Shoal Workshop held at the Amanzimtoti Town Hall on 8th June 1995. Oceanographic Research Institute. Unpublished Report 117: 1-47

89. Schleyer, M.H. 1996. *Resolution of Conflict in the Use of Aliwal Shoal. Ninth Southern Africa* Marine Science Symposium. University of Cape Town, South Africa, 21-23 November 1996

90. Schleyer, M.H. 1998. Observations on the incidence of crown-of-thorns starfish in the Western Indian Ocean. *Reef Encounter* 23: 25-27

91. Schleyer, M.H. in prep. Community structure of sediment-tolerant corals at the reef-sediment interface of marginal reefs in KwaZulu-Natal.

92. Schleyer, M.H., Beckley, L.E., Fennessy, S.T., Fielding, P.J., Govender, A., Mann, B.Q., Robertson, W.D., Tomalin, B.J., Van Der Elst, R.P. in press. Marine and estuarine resources: Status, trends and future potential. In *Back from the Brink: Pathways to Sustainability in South Africa.* ed. Preston-Whyte, R.A. Oxford University Press

93. Schleyer, M.H., Kruger, A., Benayahu, Y. 1997. Reproductive strategies of South African corals. In *Proceedings of the 6th International Conference on Colenterate Biology.* ed. Den Hartog, J.C. pp 429-435. The Leeuwvenhorst-Noordwijkerhout, 16-21 July 1995. The Netherlands, National Natuurhistorisch Museum

94. Schleyer, M.h., Kruger, A., Benayahu, Y. in prep. Long-term changes in coral community structure on marginal reefs at Sodwana Bay, South Africa

95. Schleyer, M.H., Kruger, A., Benayahu, Y. in prep. Reproduction in *Sarcophyton glaucum* (Octocorallia, Alcyoniidae) in KwaZulu-Natal, South Africa

96. Schleyer, M.H., Kruger, A., Riegl, B., Benayahu, Y. 1993. Natal coral reefs: A case for monitoring climate change. Eighth Southern African Marine Science Symposium, Club Mykonos, Langebaan, South Africa, 17-22 October 1993. Paper

97. Schleyer, M.H., Tomalin, B.J. submitted. Ecotourism and damage on South African coral reefs with an assessment of their diver carrying capacity

98. Schumann, E.H., Orren, M.J. 1980. The physico-chemical characteristics of the South-West Indian Ocean in relation to Maputaland. In *Studies on the Ecology of Maputaland.* eds. Bruton, M.N., Cooper, K.H. pp. 8-11. Grahamstown: Rhodes University

99. Seagrief, S.C. 1980. Seaweeds of Maputaland. In *Studies on the Ecology of Maputaland.* eds. Bruton, M.N., Cooper, K.H. pp 18-41. Grahamstown: Rhodes University: 18-41

100. Smith, M.M. 1980. Marine fishes of Maputaland. In *Studies on the Ecology of Maputaland.* eds. Bruton, M.N., Cooper, K.H. pp 164-187. Grahamstown: Rhodes University

101. Swart, D.H. 1983. Physical aspects of sandy beaches. In *Sandy Beaches as Ecosystems.* eds. Mclachlan, A., Erasmus, T. pp 5-44. Developments in Hydrobiology 19, The Hague: Dr W. Junk Publishers

102. Talpir, R., Kashman, Y., Benayahu, Y., Pannell, L., Schleyer M. 1994. Hemiasterlin and Geodiamolide TAI: Two new cytotoxic peptides from the marine sponge *Hemiasterella minor* (Kirkpatrick). *Tetrahedron letters* 35: 4453-4456

103. Tomalin, B.J., Kyle, R. 1998 Subsistence and recreational mussel (*Perna perna*) collecting in KwaZulu-Natal, South Africa: Fishing mortality and precautionary management. *South African Journal of Zoology* 33: 12-22

104. Trebble, G.W., Schleyer, M.H., and others 1996. *Aliwal Shoal Protected Seascape Management and Development Plan.* Unpublished Report

105. Veron, J.E.N. 1986. *Corals of Australia and the Indo-Pacific.* Honolulu: University of Hawaii Press

106. Williams, G.C. 1992. The Alcyonacea of Southern Africa. Gorgonian octocorals (Coelenterata, Anthozoa). *Annals of the South African Museum* 101: 181-296

107. Williams, G.C. 1992. The Alcyonacea of Southern Africa. Stoloniferous octocorals and soft corals (Coelenterata, Anthozoa). *Annals of the South African Museum* 100: 249-358

Chapter 4

Coral Reefs of Mozambique

Maria-Joao Rodrigues, Helena Motta, Mark W. Whittington & Michael Schleyer

Mozambique lies on the east coast of Africa between latitudes 10°20' to 26°50' South (Fig. 4.1) and possesses the third longest coastline in the Western Indian Ocean at 2700 km. The coastline is characterized by a variety of habitats including; delta estuaries, sand beaches, mangroves, island archipelagos and coral reefs. The continental shelf (down to a depth of 200 m) is very narrow along much of the coastline, typically less than 20 km wide, although this widens in the central part of the country to 130 km.

Much of the coast is bordered by fringing coral reefs, especially in the north of the country. With the exception of a few localized areas which have been the focus of limited research, little is known about the coral reefs in Mozambique. According to IUCN/UNEP (15), Mozambique's coral reefs occupy an area of 2500 km². However, there is little information to support this and it is possibly an overestimation that needs revision.

The coast of Mozambique is one of the country's most valuable natural assets but is also subject to considerable pressures from resource exploitation and coastal development. Exploitation of coastal resources in the form of fisheries, agriculture, tourism and forestry contribute significantly to the national income as well as providing social and economic benefits to the population that lives in this area. However, in many of the locations where resource use and development are greatest, significant coastal degradation has taken place (20).

Geographical Background

Coastal Climate

Rainfall. Mozambique has a tropical humid to sub-humid climate with a relatively dry winter season. Precipitation is affected by two climatic systems: north of the Zambezi, it is strongly influenced by the southern end of the East African Monsoon System, and south of the Zambezi it is influenced by the Indian Ocean Sub-tropical Anticyclone System of the Southeast Trade Wind Zone (30). The coast experiences rainfall in all months with a maximum in the

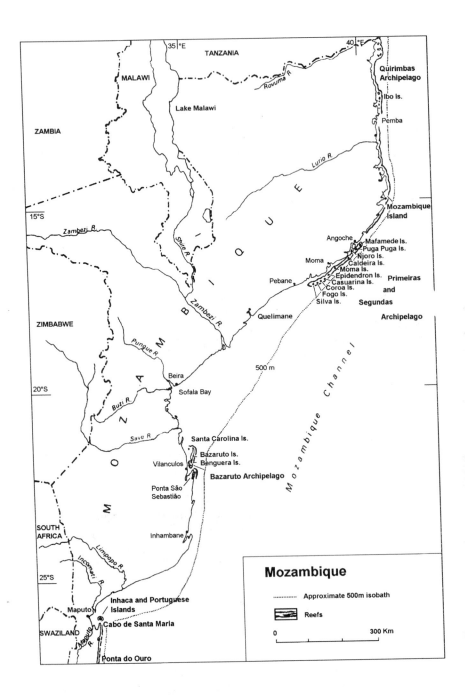

Figure 4.1. Map of Mozambique showing coral reef distribution.

summer months (November to April) and a minimum in winter months (May to October). Monthly average rainfall for the coast is given in Table 4.1.

Wind Patterns and Cyclones. Northern Mozambique is affected by the southern extension of the East African Monsoon System with winds blowing from north to northeast during the southern summer and from south to southwest during the southern winter. Central and southern Mozambique is affected by the Southeast Trade Wind System and receives easterly prevailing winds throughout the year (30).

The Mozambique coast is periodically subject to cyclones, especially during the southern summer. There is an average of 3.1 tropical storms annually in Mozambique channel, with most along the west coast of Madagascar. These hurricanes affect Mozambique as they cross from Madagascar. Twelve high-intensity hurricanes and 38 near-hurricanes to medium-intensity tropical storms have occurred over the last 50 years (30).

Coastal Population

The current population of Mozambique is estimated at more than 16.5 million, and expected to grow at an annual rate of 3%. About 40% of the population now live on the coastal strip (18) and consequently the mangroves, islands, dunes and coral reefs ecosystems are under increasing human pressure. During the country's civil war (1976-1992), most of the population migrated to urban and peri-urban areas as well as coastal areas for protection and access to natural resources.

About 23% of the total surface area of the country falls within the 42 coastal administrative districts. The population density in these coastal districts was 28 persons/km^2 in 1994. However, as most of the population tends to be crowded in the cities, particularly the coastal cities, densities can be as high as 1525 persons/km^2 in Maputo, 625 persons/km^2 in Beira and 409 persons/km^2 in Nacala (18).

Most of the islands found along the coast are inhabited. The exception are the Primeiras and Segundas Islands which are far from the mainland and consequently less accessible to the people. In contrast, Mozambique Island is the most populated island with 13 000 people in an area of 1 km^2 (12).

Coastal Geomorphology

The coast from Ponta do Ouro (26°51' S) to immediately north of Angoche (16°S) is composed of unconsolidated Quaternary to Recent sediments, mostly sand (dunes and sandy plains), but interspersed with heavier textured soils (alluviums) at the larger river mouths. Around 16°S and at Mocambo, Nacala and Memba Bays, small areas of Tertiary Basalt occur. Heavily-faulted Cretaceous to Tertiary sediments line the coast from Angoche northwards (30).

The coastal region is generally characterized by sandy soils, including riverine and deltaic-alluvial soils and compacted sands. There is considerable deposition and longshore transport of river-derived sediments (33) which in central Mozambique, has resulted in the seaward growth of the shoreline.

Table 4.1. Monthly average rainfall for selected coastal sites (INAM, 1958-1997).

Location	Coordinates	Monthly Average (mm)											
		Jan	Feb	Mar	Apr	May	Jun	Jul	Aug	Sep	Oct	Nov	Dec
Pemba	13°00'S, 40°38'E	147	162	207	112	33	17	13	7	2	10	38	118
Pebane	17°16'S, 38°09'E	236	207	229	136	99	80	70	37	13	16	52	153
Beira	19°50'S, 34°51'E	259	301	260	129	73	47	47	40	27	33	108	225
Vilanculos	22°00'S, 35°20'E	158	157	80	41	36	24	18	25	15	36	63	130
Maputo	25°50'S, 32°36'E	153	131	94	54	35	18	18	16	43	55	80	96

Physical Oceanography

Madagascar protects Mozambique from the full influence of the open ocean except in the extreme south (south of latitude 25°S) and the extreme north (north of latitude 12°S). The Mozambique Channel is 400 km wide at its narrowest point. The South Equatorial Current has its dividing point in the extreme north of the country. The warm southward-flowing branch of this current, known as the Mozambique Current (and further south as the Agulhas Current), has far-reaching influences on the climate and biogeography of Southern Africa (30).

Surface water temperature vary seasonally along the coast. In general, high surface water temperatures (26°C to 30°C) are observed from November to May, while lower values (21°C to 26°C) occur from June to October (SADCO data, 1960 to 1997). The surface water temperatures along the northern coast are normally 1 to 2°C higher than those on the southern coast. Seasonal patterns of the surface water temperature along selected sites are shown in Figure 4.2.

Surface salinity along the coast varies between 34.3 ppt and 35.5 ppt, is influenced primarily by the freshwater river drainage and varies with seasonal rainfall patterns. This is most evident along the central coast where the Zambezi River, one of Africa's largest rivers, drains a catchment area of some 1 250 000 km² and discharges about 15 000 to 20 000 m³/s into the Bight of Sofala. The seasonal variations in salinity are far less marked along the northern and southern coasts, although in the south, pulses of low salinity can be detected due to the southward transport of water from the Sofala Bank (25).

Low-intensity upwelling occurs seasonally in Mozambique waters, mainly in the vicinity of Angoche, Bazaruto and Maputo Bay, although it is thought that in Maputo Bay the upwelling may be a permanent phenomenon (25). Tidal range averages 3 m with the greatest range along the entire African coast found at Beira (6.3m) caused by the broad, shallow continental shelf (30).

Distribution of Coral Reefs

The coast of Mozambique is a compound shoreline produced by a succession of emergences and submergences (30) and in relation to the distribution of coral reefs can be divided into three regions (Fig. 4.1):

Northern Coast. The northernmost section of the coast extends for 770 km from the Rovuma River in the north to Pebane in the south (17°20'S). It is essentially a coral coast and is characterized by numerous small islands that form the Primeiras and Segundas and the Quirimbas archipelagos. An almost

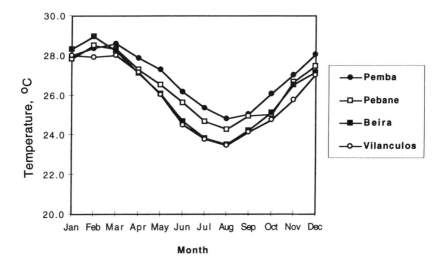

Figure 4.2. Seasonal patterns of the water surface temperatures of selected coastal sites of the Mozambican coast (SADCO data from 1960-1997).

continuous fringing reef exists along the eastern shorelines of the islands and the more exposed sections of the mainland coast.

Central Coast. The central section of the coast between Pebane (17°20'S) and Bazaruto Island (21°10'S), a distance of about 950 km, is classified as a swamp coast (30). Twenty-four rivers discharge into the Indian Ocean along this section, each with an estuary supporting well-established mangrove stands. The coastal waters are shallow and combine with the sediment loading from the rivers to cause typically high turbidity levels. Consequently, coral reef formation in this area is severely limited.

Southern Coast. This section stretches for 850 km from Bazaruto Island southwards to Ponta do Ouro (26°50'S). The coastline is characterized by high parabolic dunes, north-trending capes and barrier lakes. These dune systems attaining heights of 120 m are considered to be the tallest vegetated dunes in the world (30). The distribution of reefs along the coast and near-coast islands is patchy and are typically rock reefs with scattered corals.

Coral Reef Areas

The following section describes in detail the main areas of coral reefs along the coast of Mozambique, highlighting the physical and biological features, socio-economic importance and the current management status. The location of each area is illustrated in Fig. 4.1.

Quirimbas Archipelago

Physical Description. The Archipelago comprises an almost continuous chain of 32 islands and numerous reef complexes which stretch for 200 km (10°45'-12°42'S) close to the coast of Cabo Delgado Province, northern Mozambique. The islands range in size from less than 1 km² to 25 km² and support a variety of coastal scrub, grassland and mangrove (Whittington, M. personal observation). Many of the islands are permanently inhabited although only five have freshwater. The waters to the west of the islands are generally shallow and relatively sheltered in comparison to the deep oceanic waters of the Mozambique Channel that run alongside the islands to the east.

Reef Description and Status. To the west of the islands, small patch reefs are common in places although the large number of rivers entering the sea in this area inhibits reef development. Extensive seagrass beds cover most of the seabed and large stands of mangrove fringe both the coastline and the western shores of many of the islands (37). The major reefs of the archipelago are located along the western shores of the islands, commonly bordering large lagoon and littoral zone coral platform areas.

The exposed aspect of the islands to the seasonal monsoon winds and their close proximity to the edge of the continental shelf has largely determined the structure of the reefs. The devastating effects of periodic cyclones (6) and inundation by freshwater (Gessner, personal communication) has also had long-lasting effects on some reef areas. Recent studies (24,37) have recorded large areas of highly-developed coral growth with an associated high diversity and abundance of reef flora and fauna.

Hard corals commonly dominate the biotic cover with over 50 genera recorded and the genera *Acropora* and *Porites* widespread (24,37, Sheppard, C. personal communication). Over 300 species of reef-associated fish have been recorded (37, Planes and Bailly, personal communication), including; triggerfish (Balistidae) 11 species, butterflyfish (Chaetodontidae) 21 species and angelfish (Pomacanthidae) 11 species. On the exposed reefs, where the fishing pressure is typically minimal, the larger predatory fish are also abundant, particularly snappers (Lutjanidae) and groupers (Serranidae).

Socio-Economic Importance. The local inhabitants of the islands are highly dependent on the natural resources of the islands, particularly the finfish and marine invertebrate populations which form the primary protein source, and the mangrove wood which is used for building and firewood (1,9,37). The majority of finfishing activity is concentrated in the sheltered waters to the west of the islands, where seine netting, hand-lining and trap fishing are the preferred fishing methods. The reef-based fishery is relatively small due to the hazardous conditions that occur on the exposed outer reef.

Increasingly large numbers of migrant fishermen come to the islands during the dry season from Nampula Province to the south to catch finfish and collect gastropods for the curio trade, and illegally from Tanzania to collect sea cucumbers (Holothuria) in large numbers. Table 4.2 shows a list of the resource use and associated problems in the Quirimbas Archipelago (34).

Management and Research Developments. No management plan yet exists for the Quirimbas although the islands have long been recognized as nationally important and recommended for designation as a protected area (31). Currently, the Ministry for the Coordination of Environmental Affairs (MICOA, Maputo) is coordinating the gathering of information for the formulation of a management plan for the islands. Frontier-Moçambique (Anglo-Mozambican NGO) is collecting baseline biological and resource use information throughout the archipelago to support this initiative (1,9,36,37).

Mozambique Island

Physical Description. Mozambique island is situated at approximately 15°02'S; 40°41'E in the entrance of Mozambique Bay and is 4 km off the mainland. The district called Mozambique Island is formed by Lumbo on the continent and Mozambique, Goa and Cobras Islands (the latter also named as Sena island).

Reef Description and Status. The best coral reefs of the region are found around Goa and Cobras Islands (8). Coral aggregations of recent formation occur on rocky platforms in depths of 5 to 20 m close to the islands and within bays on the adjacent mainland. A comprehensive survey has been completed on the shores of Mozambique Island (16) and the following reef descriptions are taken from this study unless otherwise stated.

There is a well-developed submerged reef along the east coast of Mozambique Island, about 5 km in length, and abundant coral growth within the adjacent shallow bay. Within the lagoon areas coral formations enclose shallow water pools and the following genera were found: *Pavona*, *Platygyra*, *Porites*, *Pocillopora*, *Stylophora, Montipora* and *Favia*. Outside the lagoon, coral was observed growing in 1 to 10 m of water at various points northeast of the island and was similar to that found within the coral pools.

Reef-associated fauna found in the coral pools was characteristic of a fully developed subtidal reef and included anemones, soft corals, gorgonians, sponges and tridacnid clams. Few echinoderms were observed. Two species of sea cucumbers were found on the reefs, the mammy cucumber (*Holothuria nobilis*) and grey cucumber (*H. scabra*) (8).

Initial assessments of the reef-associated fish recorded a high species richness including numerous damselfish (Pomacentridae), butterflyfish (Chaetodontidae), gobies (Gobiidae), blennies (Blennidae) and wrasses (Labridae). A large diversity of fishes, in particular parrotfishes (Scaridae), triggerfishes (Balistidae), snappers (Lutjanidae), rabbitfish (Siganidae) and groupers (Serranidae) have been reported more recently (8).

Five species of turtles are found in these waters: Loggerhead turtle (*Caretta caretta gigas*), Green turtle (*Chelonia mydas*), Leatherback turtle (*Dermochelys coriacea*), Ridley turtle (*Lepidochelys olivacea*) and the Hawksbill turtle (*Eretmochelys imbricata*). All these species are known to nest on the beaches of this area (8).

Table 4.2. A summary of resource use in the Quirimbass Archipelago (34).

Resource Use	Method and Scale	Associated Problems
Mangrove cutting	SITES: Evidence of cutting within all stands, although concentrated around population centers. SCALE: For local building material and firewood. METHODS: Hand tools only.	PROBLEMS: Localized intensive cutting causing substratum destabilization. SUSTAINABILITY: Generally sustainable although habitat degradation expected in areas of intensive cutting.
Finfish fishery	SITES: Conducted throughout the islands but concentrated within the shallow, sheltered seagrass beds. SCALE: Artisanal subsistence-income fishery. The major source of protein and employment for male population (14+years). No evidence of commercial fishery. METHODS: Seine nets, box traps, fence traps, handlines longlines and spears.	PROBLEMS: Potential recruitment-overfishing as seagrass fishery targets juvenile fish. Increasing seasonal influx of itinerant fishermen from Nampula Province and southern Tanzania with a more commercial approach. SUSTAINABILITY: Expected to decline under current and projected pressures.
Shell Collection	SITES: within intertidal and shallow subtidal zones of all islands. SCALE: Commercial collection by itinerant fishermen for curio trade. Collection for food and curio trade by islanders (predominantly women and children) METHODS: Hand collection at low tides in the intertidal zone. Subtidal zone collection by snorkeling.	PROBLEMS: Overfishing of subtidal zone edible gastropods (personal observation). Anecdotal evidence of severe over-exploitation of curio shells (Gessner, personal communication) SUSTAINBILITY: Populations of targeted shell expected to decline under current and projected pressures.
Sea-cucumber collection	SITES: Intertidal and subtidal zones (to 50m depth) of all islands SCALE: Majority of collection by Tanzanian and Mozambican commercial diving operations. Opportunistic collection by islanders. METHODS: Commercial snorkeling/SCUBA collection. Incidental collection as by-catch from other intertidal zone exploitation.	PROBLEMS: Complete localized depletion of the more accessible areas (personal observation.) SUSTAINABILITY: Localized extinction of seven targeted species under current fishing pressure.
Crustacean collection: Crab	SITES: Within mangrove stands for the Mud Crab *Scylla serrata* and swimming crabs (*Portunus spp.*) SCALE: Low intensity artisanal collection. METHODS: Hand collection using metal crab hook and incidental by-catch of trap and net fishery.	PROBLEMS: None. SUSTAINBILITY: No decline in populations expected at current levels of exploitation.

Table 4.2 continued.

Crustacean collection: Lobster	SITES: Shallow subtidal areas of all islands. SCALE: Commercial collection by foreign operation. Artisanal collection by islanders. METHODS: Commercial snorkeling/SCUBA collection. Artisanal collection by spears and by-catch of the net fishery. PROBLEMS: Expected decline in populations with unregulated commercial exploitation. SUSTAINBILITY: Unknown.
Crustacean collection: Prawn	SITES: In river delta areas of adjacent coastline. Occasional collection from Ibo mangrove (Antonio, personal communication). SCALE: Seasonal commercial and artisanal collection. METHODS: Seine nets, push nets and by hand. PROBLEMS: Recent price rises dictated by foreign market forces has dramatically increased fishing intensity. SUSTAINBILITY: Sustainable with current gear technology and fishing practices.
Octopus collection	SITES: Intertidal zones of all islands. SCALE: Generally low intersity artisanal collection. METHODS: Hand collection using sticks (predominantly women and children). PROBLEMS: No perceived problems under current exploitation practices. SUSTAINBILITY: Unknown.
Tourism	SITES: None. SCALE: Occasional visiting yachts, sports fishermen and backpackers. Proposed tourism development on Quirimba and Matemo islands. ACTIVITIES: Snorkeling, diving, fishing and sightseeing. PROBLEMS: None. SUSTAINBILITY: Expansion of tourism development within the islands is highly likely. No assessment has been made of the potential impacts of these activities.

Fonseca (8) reported that the reefs were generally in a good condition although there was some evidence of coral extraction in the area. However, more recent reports from the area indicate that the scale of coral extraction has increased dramatically and there is now widespread damage to the reefs (Nogueira, personal communication).

Socio-Economic Importance. Mozambique Island has a long documented history (it was settled during the 14th and 15th centuries) and has already been declared as a Human Patrimony by UNESCO. It is still an important trade center for the entire coast of Nampula Province and products traded on the Island are exported as far as Malawi and Zambia. Fish, crops, art and crafts, jewelry and other merchandise are produced from the islands and play an important role in the economy of the local inhabitants and those from the adjacent coast. Mozambique Island still produces a substantial amount of fish, crustaceans and mollusks.

Unfortunately, the reef areas of Mozambique Island and the surrounding area of Nacala-Porto are also exploited for corals and shells for the curio trade which are collected by local people, marketed by entrepreneurs and middle men and exported to Portugal and other European countries. Scientists and government officials are attempting to stop this practice through the enforcement of proper legislation.

Due to its geographic location and historic architecture, Mozambique Island has the potential to be an important site for tourism development. Once the infrastructure has been rehabilitated from the effects of the war and several hurricanes, the number of cruise ships visiting the islands will most likely increase markedly.

Management and Research Developments. There is currently no management plan in place for Mozambique Island, although there are some movements towards the protection of the coral reefs in the area with the prevention of the exportation of corals. Scientific investigations are required to assess the damage from the collection of corals and shells as well as the effects of hurricanes in the region during the last few years.

Primeiras and Segundas Archipelago

Physical Description. The two strings of islands, the Primeiras and the Segundas, that form the archipelago are located between 8 and 20 km off the mainland coast of northern Mozambique (16°12'-17°17'S), between the coastal towns of Pebane (Zambezia Province) and Angoche (Nampula Province). The Primeiras to the south, comprise five islands and the Segundas, to the north, comprise a further five islands and two substantial reef complexes.

The islands lie on a shallow sandbar alongside the edge of the continental shelf of the Mozambique Channel. They are relatively small islands (less than 1 km²) and are in varying stages of vegetative development, from completely bare to dense climax thicket cover (30).

Reef Description and Status. Crescent-shaped fringing reefs have developed to the eastern sides of these islands, enclosing shallow lagoon areas and littoral zone coral platforms (30,35). Few studies have been made on the ecological condition of the reefs. Reefs of the islands to the north of the archipelago are strongly structured with regard to exposure to the southern monsoon winds and most are dominated by soft corals (35). Hard corals, mainly *Acropora* pp., were poorly developed, although within the pronounced "spur and groove" zones of the south-facing reefs they formed a dense, low-lying cover. This appears to differ from the previous assessment by Salm (27) that these were some of the finest reefs in Mozambique.

A major factor in the development of the reefs of the archipelago could be the occurrence of a seasonal up-welling of cold water from the Mozambique Channel which is thought to strongly influence the coastal fish populations of the islands (Kromer, personal communication). A marked thermocline at 16 to 24 m has been recorded in the Segundas islands with deeper water temperatures of approximately 17°C (35).

There are extensive seagrass beds between the islands and the mainland that support turtles and dugongs (33). The Primeiras Islands have been reported to have the most important Green turtle (*Chelonia mydas*) nesting beaches of Mozambique (10,14) with about 200 females nesting annually. Large specimens of Loggerhead turtle (*Caretta caretta gigas*) and Green turtle (*Chelonia mydas*) have also been recorded in the Segundas islands (35) although the presence of fishermen on most of the islands threatens the chances of breeding success. The region between the islands and mainland is the most important in the western Indian Ocean for Dugong (*Dugong dugon*) (33).

Socio-Economic Importance. Fishermen from the mainland regularly use the islands as a temporary base with the lack of freshwater preventing more permanent settlement (Kromer, personal communication). Due to low level of fishing technology, the exposed aspect of much of the fringing reef and the distance from the mainland, exploitation of the reefs has been at a relatively low intensity. Fishing activity is mainly centered on the seagrass beds where gill netting, seine netting and handlining are employed.

A large abundance of snappers (Lutjanidae), surgeonfish (Acanthuridae) and groupers (Serranidae) were reported (35) for the reefs of the northern Segundas islands.

Management and Research Developments. The islands have been designated a protected area several times (14,30,31). A number of initiatives are currently examining the setting up of a marine protective area within the islands, primarily focused on the protection of turtle nesting beaches. The Angoche delegation of the Institute for the Development of Small Scale Fisheries is making a study of the fishing activity around the Segundas islands. There is no reef-specific research currently taking place within the islands although a two year study is planned to commence in June 1998.

Bazaruto Archipelago

Physical Description. This archipelago has five islands: Magaruque, Bangué, Santa Carolina, Benguerua and Bazaruto and is located in Inhambane province, between the districts of Vilanculos and Inhassoro (Fig. 4.3). The islands are located between 21° 30'; 22° 10' S and 35° 22'; 35° 30'E.

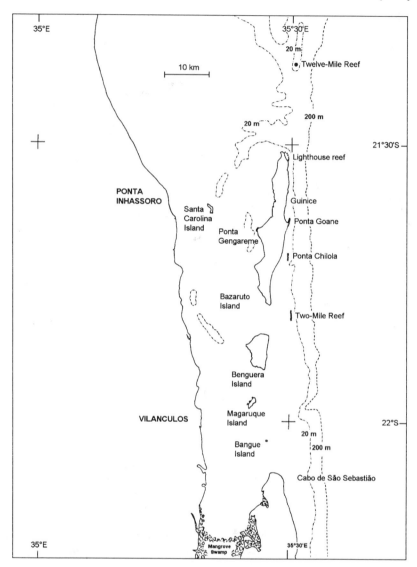

Figure 4.3. Map of Bazaruto Archipelago with location of major reefs.

Reef Description and Status. The eastern and southeastern offshore coral communities of Bazaruto can be classified as patch reefs on a submerged mid-Holocene coastline (5). Taxonomic studies, in which a hard coral species list for the archipelago is being compiled, are underway; to date, 33 coral genera comprising 26 scleractinian corals and seven soft corals have been found (Schleyer, M. personal observation).

The back-reef sand-flat environment is characterized by large *Porites* domes up to 2 m in diameter. Smaller domes of *Porites* and extensive thickets of large staghorn coral (*Acropora* spp.) dominate the back-reef coral fauna together with smaller colonies of *Pocillopora*, *Montipora* and *Pavona*. Coral cover in this area is high, up to 90%. The reef-flat environment is intertidal which results in a sparse coral fauna. Less abundant coral growth is evident on the fore-reef as this is subject to storm and turbulent conditions. *Acropora*, *Turbinaria* and *Pocillopora* are the conspicuous genera here. The fringing coral communities on the north-eastern shores of Bazaruto include the Coral Gardens area. These communities are dominated by the genera *Porites*, *Acropora*, *Pocillopora* but include faviids *Turbinaria*, *Tubastrea* and soft corals. There are sparse colonies of the ahermatypic corals *Dendrophyllia* and *Tubastrea*, to a depth of 12 m on the sheltered western shore of Bazaruto (Schleyer, M. personal observation).

True coral reef growth is restricted to depths of less than 3 m on the fore-reef; below this depth, scattered coral colonies occur. The depth constraint on reef growth is generally related to a reduction in light penetration and sedimentation. In the reef-front environment sandstone outcrops occur down to a depth of about 10 m.

Twenty seven species of Alcyonacea (soft corals) are reported from several reefs of the Bazaruto Archipelago (2), though hard corals cover the greater part of the habitable portions of the reefs (Schleyer, M. personal observation). Soft coral species are distributed among seven genera of the families Tubiporidae, Alcyoniidae and Xeniidae. The Alcyoniidae are the most common and are represented by 24 (89%) species dominated by the genera *Lobophytum*, *Sarcophyton*, *Sinularia* and *Cladiella*; two species (7%) belong to the Xeniidae, and *Tubipora musica* is also present.

There is a great abundance and diversity of marine mollusks. The principle ornamental shells (Gastropoda) from the Archipelago account for 155 species distributed among 39 genera. There are six endemic gastropods (5).

The coral reefs on the eastern coast of Bazaruto Island provide shelter for many resident fish species. Many migratory and pelagic species also pass through these waters, and approximately 300 species exist in the Bazaruto Archipelago (5). The best represented fish families observed on the reefs of northern Bazaruto Island are the: damselfishes (Pomacentridae), wrasses (Labridae), surgeonfishes (Acanthuridae), cardinalfishes (Apogonidae) and sweepers (Pempheridae) (Fiebig, S. personal communication).

Dugongs (*Dugong dugon*) have been reported and five species of turtles: Green turtle (*Chelonia mydas*), Hawksbill turtle (*Eretmochelys imbricata*), Leatherback turtle (*Dermochelys coriacea*), Loggerhead turtle (*Caretta caretta gigas*) and Ridley turtle (*Lepidochelys olivacea*) are known to exist in the archipelago (19). Loggerhead, and possibly Leatherback, Hawksbill and Green turtles, use the beaches on Bazaruto as nesting sites. The Loggerhead turtle nesting season in the archipelago is from November to March (5).

These reefs appear to be in good condition although further studies are necessary.

Socio-Economic Importance. Artisanal fishing is one of the main economic activities of the islanders. The most commonly practiced method is traditional hand-pulled beach seining; others include line fishing and the use of beach traps made of stone or wooden slats.

There are already well established tourism developments on the Islands of Magaruque, Benguerua and Bazaruto. These islands are international tourist destinations and the attractions available include 'big game' fishing, snorkeling and scuba diving. The facilities on Santa Carolina are in the process of being rehabilitated. There is also an airstrip on Bazaruto Island. Bazaruto is also a popular destination for cruise ships from South Africa, with an estimated 12 500 tourists arriving between June 1997 and June 1998.

Management and Research Developments. The Bazaruto Archipelago benefited from a Project funded by the European Union and implemented by the DNFFB (National Directorate of Forestry and Wildlife) and WWF (World-wide Fund for Nature). The aim of the Project was to improve the management and use of the natural resources with the involvement of local communities. At the end of the Project, the boundaries of the Marine Park would be enlarged and a Management Plan would be in place. During the implementation of this project, data on coral reefs has been collected.

Inhaca and Portugueses Islands

Physical Description. These southernmost islands (26°01'S, 32°56'E) of the country are located some 35 km due east of Maputo, the Capital. The coral reefs at Inhaca Island are not the most southerly on the east coast of Southern Africa, as it was believed until recently, but they are the most accessible from the shore (17).

Reef Description and Status. Three small, shallow-water, fringing reefs occur along the shores of Inhaca and Portugueses Islands with a combined length of about 3.5 km (Fig. 4.4). Patch reefs are also reported to occur offshore, in depths up to 15 m along the island's east coast (17). These are the best studied reefs in Mozambique, with records since 1935 (for example, 3,4,22,26). The Marine Biological Station was established on Inhaca Island in 1951, providing a focus for research in subsequent years.

The coral species composition of these reefs has recently been described in a comprehensive publication based on forty years of records. Boshoff (4) classified the corals found in Inhaca Island as belonging to 45 genera in 16 families of which most are hermatypic. A total of 160 species of reef-building corals have been described which represents approximately one third of the total number of species known in the Indian Ocean (17). An updated list of species is being completed for this area. The soft coral fauna is less well known (32). Fourteen species are known from the families Alcyoniidae and Xeniidae.

A number of reef-associated invertebrates have been reported as present. Two species of the giant clam occur on the reef, *Tridacna maxima* and *T. squamosa,* the former being more abundant. Several species of crustacea have been recorded, including the commercially important lobsters *Thenus orientalis, Panulirus ornatus, P. homarus* and *P. versicolor* (17). Brittlestars (Ophiuroidea) were the most abundant echinoderms recorded, comprising 18 different species. The Crown-of-thorns starfish *Acanthaster planci* has not been reported from these reefs (17).

About 25 families of fish are represented in Inhaca reefs. Benthic grazers (16 families) dominate the fish assemblage, particularly parrotfishes (Scaridae), surgeonfishes (Acanthuridae) and rabbitfishes (Siganidae). Turtles found at Inhaca and Portugueses Islands are: Hawksbill turtle (*Eretmochelys imbricata*),

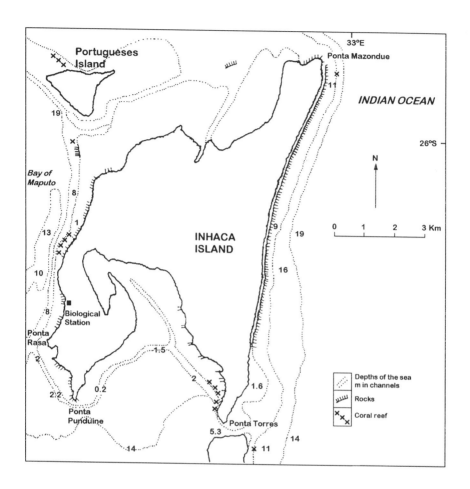

Figure 4.4. Map of Inhaca and Portugueses Islands showing location of major reefs.

Green turtle (*Chelonia mydas*), Loggerhead turtle (*Caretta caretta gigas*) and the Ridley turtle (*Lepidochelys olivacea*).

The reefs of Inhaca and Portugueses Islands are in a perpetual state of rejuvenation as a result of the short intervals between cyclones. In Maputo Bay, cyclones cause high levels of resuspension of the sand substratum, producing high turbidity and sedimentation that limit coral growth to a maximum depth of 10 m and cause physical damage to the reefs (17).

Socio-Economic Importance. As for Bazaruto, Inhaca Island is an attractive tourist destination, not only for Maputo inhabitants but also for tourists visiting the capital. Cruise ships from South Africa disembark tourists onto the tiny Portuguese Island, with an estimated 14 000 visitors per year. The clear, warm waters surrounding the small island and the pristine vegetation are the main attractions.

Inhaca inhabitants also utilize the natural resources, making their living from fishing, near-shore mollusks and other invertebrates. There is evidence that some of the fishery resources, such as holothurians, are already overexploited (11).

Management and Research Developments. An Integrated Development Plan was completed in 1990 but has not yet been officially approved by the Mozambican Government, and has not therefore, been implemented. The Plan takes into consideration the needs of the local population of the Island, estimated now at about 5000 inhabitants, the future development of tourism infrastructure, as well as the carrying capacity of the island for visitors.

Inhaca Island is also the site of the Eduardo Mondlane University Biological Station, a marine and terrestrial environment research facility. The Biological Station plays an important role in the training of students and post-graduates in coral reef research.

Ponta do Ouro to Cabo de Santa Maria

Physical Description. This coastal stretch extends from Ponta do Ouro (26°51'S;32°58'E) in the south to Cabo de Santa Maria (26°05'S;32°58'E) at the tip of the Machangulo Peninsula, in a distance of approximately 86 km. The coastline is linear, consisting primarily of extensive sandy beaches with well-vegetated sand dunes. The sandy beaches are interspersed with occasional rocky headlands from which subtidal rocky reefs extend seawards to depths of 5-15 m (23).

Reef Description and Status. A single study on the reefs of the area examined 11 coral reef localities (23). The study identified 19 genera of scleractinian and 10 genera of alcyonacean corals, together with the Black coral *Cirrhipathes* spp. Gorgonians (*Rumphella* spp.), sponges (9 genera) and tunicates (5 genera) were also reported as prominent in the sessile fauna of the reefs. Coral cover on the reefs varied from 33% to 93%, with soft coral generally dominant.

Robertson and colleagues (23) recorded some 150 species of fish in this area. In particular, the surgeonfishes (Acanthuridae), triggerfishes (Balistidae), butterflyfishes (Chaetodontidae), wrasses (Labridae), angelfishes (Pomacanthidae), damselfishes (Pomacentridae) and parrotfishes (Scaridae) were conspicuous.

Along the southern coast of Mozambique, four species of turtles are found but only the Loggerhead and Leatherback turtles are reported to nest along this coast. Turtle nesting activity is not evenly distributed along the beaches, but is concentrated in certain areas (23).

The reefs were reported to be generally in a good condition with the exception of some which were clearly surge-scoured and some which were seriously damaged by Crown-of-thorns starfish (*Acanthaster planci*) (23).

Socio-Economic Importance. Along this coastline, several species of invertebrates found on the rocky reefs (for example, rock lobsters, mussels, oysters, red bait and limpets), form an important part of the subsistence diet for local coastal communities. However, the sea is commonly rough in this area and consequently access in traditional boats to offshore resources is limited.

The National Tourism Policy for Mozambique (May 1995) identified this coastal stretch as an area of primary focus for tourism development. Currently, there are three large-scale dive operations in this area and on some of the reefs there are between 30 000 to 40 000 dives per year (23).

Management and Research Developments. The need to assess the effects of the tourism development has been highlighted for this area, however to date, no management plan exists.

Conservation Status

Parks and reserves were established under the Decree number 40 040, of 20 January 1955. There are four categories of protected areas: National Parks, Integral Natural Reserves, Partial Reserves and Special Reserves. Coutadas, which are areas set aside for hunting and photographic safaris, are also established in the same Decree.

Of the 2700 km of coastline in Mozambique, coral reefs are protected only within the Inhaca and Portugueses Islands Reserves and the Bazaruto National Park. The other coastal reserves and parks (Pomene and Maputo) only afford protected status to endangered species such as dugongs and turtles. The Ministry of Agriculture and Fisheries is responsible for protected area administration, with the exception of Inhaca and Portugueses Islands which are managed by Eduardo Mondlane University.

Considering the diversity of habitats along the length of the Mozambican coastline and the economic importance of the littoral waters, remarkably few coastal areas are under protected management.

Marine Protected Areas

Bazaruto National Park. Established in 1971, Bazaruto National Park was the first marine park in Mozambique (30). The park covers an area of 150 km², comprising 3 islands (Bangué, Magaruque and Benguera) and a 5 km buffer zone around them. Bazaruto and Santa Carolina islands are designated as special vigilance zones (19). An expansion of the park is currently being undertaken to include these two other islands and the contiguous marine environment. The marine environment of Bazaruto includes mangroves, coral reefs and seagrass beds. These marine habitats are reported to support a variety of marine mammals, including whales, dolphins and dugongs.

The National Directorate of Forestry and Wildlife is the government institution responsible for the management of the Bazaruto National Park. Currently, there is a resident Administrator, an officer responsible for law enforcement and nine guards. The Maritime Delegations of Vilanculos and Inhassoro are responsible for the control of territorial waters in the region (19).

In 1989, a Master Plan was elaborated for the sustainable development of the Bazaruto Archipelago based on conservation principles that would safeguard its ecological integrity, allowing at the same time, sustainable development of tourism that socially and financially benefits the islanders (5). Although corals were already protected in the Archipelago, the Master Plan focuses on the protection of selected coral reefs to prevent fishing and other destructive activities on them.

Inhaca and Portugueses Islands Reserve. Parts of the shore and dunes on Inhaca Island were declared nature reserves by Mozambique's government in 1965. It had become necessary to control excessive collecting of curio trade fauna by tourists in order to conserve typical habitats and to protect parts of the forest and mangroves from tree felling. The reserve areas include all the mangroves (except for a small area in the north to be used by the local population), two long strips of forest covering both the western and eastern dune ridges, some lagoon areas and all the coral reefs or scattered coral communities.

Since 1976, the management of these reserves has been the responsibility of Eduardo Mondlane University. There is a well-developed program for the protection and conservation of the reserves involving 12 guards employed by the University and headed by the resident biologist at the Marine Biological Station. These guards are posted at camps in the Reserves and they have considerable authority when dealing with violations of the rules (13).

An integrated Development Plan for Inhaca Island was devised under the aegis of the United Nations in 1990, with the participation of resident people in order to use the resources in a sustainable way (17). Three special sub-reserves were established for the coral reefs: Portugueses Island reserve (which protects the new coral reef situated in the lagoon), the Barreira Vermelha Marine Reserve (protects the coral reef area and an extra buffer zone of 200 to 300 m) and the Ponta Torres Marine Reserve (17). Diving is allowed on the reefs but fishing and any form of collection are strictly prohibited. Anchoring, navigation and water sports are not permitted close to the reefs.

The Inhaca and Portugueses islands marine reserves illustrate the degree of protection that reefs in Mozambique require in order to maintain their ecological integrity, support multiple resource use by the local communities, provide a site for scientific study and allow the growth of a sustainable tourism industry.

Proposed Marine Protected Areas

Several new marine protected areas have been proposed (7,14,27,28,29, 30,31,27). Some of the proposals refer only to the protection of endangered marine species such as dugongs and turtles, others to areas where important coastal and marine ecosystems are located - coral reefs, barrier coastal lakes, dune forests, deltas, mangroves, turtle nesting beaches and sea bird nesting sites (Table 4.3)

From the list mentioned above, only two of these areas are currently under consideration by the government: 1) the extension of Bazaruto National Park to include Bazaruto and Santa Carolina Islands as well as a larger marine area to include most of the coral reefs, and 2) the extension of Maputo Reserve to three miles off the coastline.

Table 4.4. Institutions involved in coastal zone research, planning and management. (a)= only for Inhaca Island (20).

Institution	Research	Planning	Management
Ministry of Coordination of Environment Affairs	X	X	X
University of Eduardo Mondlane			
Department of Biological Sciences	X		X (a)
Department of Geography	X		
Department of Forestry	X		
Department of Chemistry	X		
Ministry of Agriculture & Fisheries			
National Directorate of Forestry & Wildlife	X	X	X
National Agronomic Research Institute	X		
National Directorate of Geography & Cadastre	X		
Fisheries Research Institute	X		X
Small-Scale Fisheries Development Institute	X	X	
Ministry of Transport & Communications			
National Institute of Hydrography & Navigation	X	X	
National Marine Directorate			X
Maritime Administration	X		
National Meteorological Institute	X		
Ministry of Commerce & Tourism			
National Directorate of Tourism		X	X
Department of Commerce	X	X	
Ministry of Health			
Laboratory of Environmental Health & Water	X		
Ministry of State Administration			X
Ministry of Industry & Energy			X

Management and Research Priorities

Institutional and Legal Framework

A number of institutions have been given the task of coastal management but their mandates are either unclear, have many gaps, or are conflicting and overlapping. Table 4.4 shows the different institutions dealing with coastal zone and their current mandates over three main areas of action; research, management and planning (20).

Coastal Zone Management Programme (CZMP)

In June 1994, the Government approved the National Environmental Management Program (NEMP), which is the master plan for the environment in Mozambique. The Ministry for the Coordination of Environment Affairs (MICOA) has taken the lead in environmental management in Mozambique (21).

One of the priority areas of the NEMP is a number of activities related to integrated coastal zone management (ICZM). Coastal management is to be based on inter-institutional coordination between the relevant stakeholders in a program which will be elaborated and approved by them. The main issues in this program will be fisheries, coastal and marine ecosystems management, coastal and marine protection, marine parks and tourism. Within the framework of the NEMP, a National Coastal Zone Management Program (NCZMP) is now being prepared. It is further envisaged that one of the components of the NCZMP will address the critical ecosystems which comprise the coastal environment, including coral reefs, under the National Coral Reef Management Program.

The National Coral Reef Management Program (NCRMP). This aims to collect much needed information on Mozambique´s coral reefs, including; location, size, biological composition, and status. Work so far has highlighted three areas for attention: Quirimbas and Bazaruto Archipelagos and the reefs close to Xai-Xai. However, in terms of research capability and the quantity of existing information, Mozambique could be considered one of the poorest developed countries in the region. There still exists very little to no expertise within the country with the capacity to deal with the scientific issues related to coral reef conservation.

Conclusions

In the light of the above discussion, the authors propose four larger areas of activity that are vital for the sustainable management of coral reef resources in Mozambique:

• capacity building within the relevant fields required for effective sustainable management;
• collection and synthesis of relevant information and scientific data in support of sound management;
• development of an appropriate and effective network for the coordination of coral reef management related activities;
• identification, characterization and resolution of current and eventual problems with coral reefs and their management.

On a positive note, awareness of coral reef issues, scientific studies and training connected with the coral reef habitat are increasing markedly within the country. Government institutions and the private sector are now becoming more aware of the need to establish management plans for coral reefs and are helping to develop the capacity to do so. This culminated in February 1998 with the Ministry for the Coordination of Environmental Affairs producing a discussion paper which calls for the establishment of qualified working groups to directly address the country's weaknesses in coral-related issues.

References

1. Barnes, D.K.A., Corrie, A., Whittigton, M., Carvalho, M.A., Gell, F.R. in press. Coastal shellfish resource in the Quirimbas Archipelago, Mozambique. *Fisheries Management and Ecology*
2. Benayahu, Y., Schleyer, M.H. 1996. Corals of the South-west Indian Ocean III. Alcyonacea (Octocorallia) of Bazaruto Island, Mozambique, with a redescription of *Cladiella australis* spec. nov. *Investigational Report Oceanographic Research Institute* 69: 1-22
3. Boshoff, P.H. 1958. Development and Constitution on the Coral Reefs (at Inhaca Island). In *A Natural History of Inhaca Island, Mozambique*. eds. Macnae, W., Kalk, M. pp. 49-56. Johannesburg: Witwatersrand University Press
4. Boshoff. P.H. 1981. An annotated checklist of Southern African Scleractinia. *Investigational Report Oceanographic Research Institute* 49: 1-45
5. Dutton, P., Zolho, R. 1989. *Plano Director de Conservação para o Desenvolvimento do Arquipelago de Bazaruto*. Relatorio submetido ao Ministro da Agricultura. Maputo, Moçambique
6. Eichler, J.W. 1981. *Feasibility of Exporting Ornamental Fish from Mozambique and Particularly Reactivating their Export from Lake Nyasa*. Rome: FAO
7. Forjaz, J. 1985. *Conservation and Development Planning in the Coastal Zone of Mozambique*. Nairobi: UNEP
8. Fonseca, R. 1996. Perfil Ambiental da Ilha de Moçambique - Contribuição para um Plano de Desenvolvimento da zona Costeira. Paper presented at the *Integrated Coastal Zone Management Workshop*, 5-10 May, 1996. Inhaca, Maputo
9. Gell, F.R. 1997. *The Seagrass Fishery of the Quirimbas Island. Marine Biological and Resource Use Surveys of the Quirimbas Archipelago, Mozambique*. Technical Report 5, Society for Environmental Exploration, London and the Ministry for the Co-ordination of Environmental Affairs, Maputo
10. Groombridge, B. 1982. *The IUCN Amphibia-Reptilia Red Data Book, Part 1: Testudines, Crocodylia, Rhynchocephalia*. Gland : IUCN
11. Gujral, L. 1995. *Alguns Aspectos da Ecologia e Biologia da* Holothuria scabra *na Ilha da Inhaca*. Tese de Licenciatura, Universidade Eduardo Mondlane. Maputo, Mocambique
12. Hatton, J.C., Couto, M., Dutton, P., Lopes, L. 1994. *Avaliação da Situação Ambiental da Ilha de Moçambique e Zonas adjacentes*. Gabinete Técnico, Ministério da Cultura, Maputo
13. Hernroth, L., Gove, D.Z. 1995. Inhaca Island, Mozambique: A reborn base for biological research. *Ambio* 24: 513-514
14. Hughes, G.R. 1971. Preliminary report on the sea turtles and dugong of Mozambique. *Jornal de Veterinária de Mozambique* 4 : 45-62
15. IUCN/UNEP. 1982. *Conservation of the Coastal and Marine Ecosystems and Living Resources of the East African Region*. UNEP Regional Seas Reports and Studies. No. 11. Nairobi: UNEP

16. Kalk, M. 1959. A general survey of some shores of Northern Mozambique. *Revista de Biologia* Vol 2

17. Kalk, M. 1995. *A Natural History of Inhaca Island - Mozambique*. 3rd Edition. Johannesburg, Witwatersrand University Press

18. Lopes, L. 1996. Pressão populacional na zona costeira: mito ou facto. In *O Papel da Investigação na Gestão Costeira da Zona Costeira*. eds. Dias, D., Scarlet, P., Hatton, J., Macia, A. pp. 22-25. Maputo

19. Magane, S. 1996. *Perfil Ambiental do Archipelago de Bazaruto*. Relatorio apresentado no Workshop Nacional sobre Gestão Costeira em Moçambique, 5-10 de Maio 1996. Inhaca. Maputo

20. Massinga, A., Hatton, J. 1996. *Country Paper on the Status of the Coastal Zone, Mozambique*. Paper presented in the Integrated Coastal Zone Management Workshop, 5-10 May, 1996. Inhaca, Maputo

21. MICOA (Ministério para a Coordenação Ambiental) 1995. *Programa Nacional de Gestão Ambiental (National Environment Management Program)*. Maputo: MICOA

22. Nestler, A., Paech, H.J., Schmidt, W. 1984. Inhaca Island, Mozambique und die Entwicklung des Riffs vor Barreira Vermelha. *Petermanns Geographische Mitteilungen DDR* 1: 31-37

23. Robertson, W.D., Schleyer, M.H., Fielding, P.J., Tomalin, B.J., Beckley, L.E., Fennessy, S.T., van der Elst, R.P., Bandeira, S., Macia, A., Gove, D. 1996. *Inshore Marine Resources and Associated Opportunities for Development of the Coast of Southern Mozambique: Ponta do Ouro to Cabo de Santa Maria"*. ORI/UEM. Unpublished Report no. 130

24. Rodrigues, M.J. 1996. *Estudo da Estrutura da Comunidade de Corais da Zona do Farol da Ilha do Ibo*. Tese de Licenciatura. Universidade Eduardo Mondlane. Maputo

25. Saetre, R., da Silva, A.J. 1982. Water masses and circulation on the Mozambique Channel. *Revista de Investigação Pesqueira* 3: 1-78

26. Salm, R. 1976. The dynamic management of the Ponta Torres coral reef. *Memórias do Instituto de Investigação Cient'fica de Moçambique* 12 A: 1-23

27. Salm, R. 1983. Coral reefs of the Western Indian Ocean: A threatened heritage. *Ambio* 12: 349-353

28. Salm, R. 1983. Marine and coastal protected areas in the Western Indian Ocean. *Ambio* 12: 330-331

29. Tello, J. 1986. *Survey of Protected Areas and Wildlife Species in Mozambique with Recommendations for Strengthening Their Conservation*. Report to WWF, Gland, Switzerland

30. Tinley, K.L. 1971. Determinants of coastal conservation dynamic and diversity of the environment as exemplified by the Mozambican coast, pp. 125-153. Proceedings of the *Symposium on Nature Conservation as Form of Land Use*. Gorongosa National Park, Sarcus, Pretoria

31. Tinley, K.A., Rosinha, A.J., Lobao Tello, J.L.P., Dutton, T.P. 1974. Wildlife and wild places in Mozambique. *Oryx* 13: 344-349

32. Tixier-Durivalt, A., 1960. Les Octocoralliares de ile Inhaca. *Bulletin de la Musee Nationale d'Histoire Naturel* 32: 359-369

33. UNEP/IUCN. 1988. *Coral Reefs of the World Volume 2: Indian Ocean, Red Sea and Gulf*. Cambridge, The IUCN Conservation Monitoring Center

34. Whittington, M.W., Stanwell-Smith, D. in press. The status of marine habitats in northern Mozambique. *Biodiversity and Conservation*

35. Whittington, M.W., Heasman, M.S. 1997. *A Rapid Assessment of the Subtidal Habitats and Associated Commercial Fish Populations of the Segundas Islands: Santo Antonio and Mafamede Islands.* A Technical Report for the Institute for the Development of Small-Scale Fisheries (IDPPE), Mozambique. Society for Environmental Exploration, London and the Ministry for the Coordination of Environmental Affairs, Maputo

36. Whittington, M.W., Myers, M. eds. 1997. *Technical Report 1: Introduction and Methods. Marine Biological and Resource Use Surveys of the Quirimbas Archipelago, Mozambique.* Society for Environmental Exploration, London and the Ministry for the Coordination of Environmental Affairs, Maputo

37. Whittington, M.W., Carvalho, M., Corrie, A., Gell, F. 1997. *Technical Report 3: Central Islands Group - Ibo, Quirimbas, Sencar and Quilaluia Islands. Marine Biological and Resource Use Surveys of the Quirimbas Archipelago, Mozambique.* Society for Environmental Exploration, London and the Ministry for the Coordination of Environmental Affairs, Maputo

Chapter 5

Southern Tanzania

William R.T. Darwall & Martin Guard

The southern coast of Tanzania stretches for 690 km from Dar es Salaam to the Ruvuma River at the Mozambique border and supports one of the finest shallow-water coral reef and estuarine mangrove complexes in East Africa. Extending from Mafia Island to the Songo Songo Archipelago and bordered on the west by the Rufiji River Delta the shallow-water plateau is fringed on its eastern edge by a largely unspoiled outer reef which runs southwards from northern Mafia Island for an estimated 270 km to the Mozambique border (Fig. 5.1). The true extent of the reef, mangrove and seagrass systems and their supported diversities has only recently been revealed largely through the surveys of Frontier-Tanzania, a joint initiative between the University of Dar es Salaam and the Society for Environmental Exploration. These surveys have also highlighted a high degree of local dependence on the associated marine resources which are now suffering from the increasing demands of a rapidly rising coastal population. Overexploitation of these resources, coupled with the introduction of a number of highly destructive fishing techniques, makes the implementation of a management program for the sustainable use of resources a priority within the area.

Geographical Background

Hydrography and Seasonality

Climatic conditions along the Tanzanian coast are dictated by the northeast and southeast monsoons. Rainfall along the coast is highly variable with the highest yearly average for the country recorded at Mafia Island (900 to 1100 mm) and the lowest in the Mtwara District (<500 mm). The Tanzanian coast is outside the usual cyclone area. The most recent cyclones to hit the area were in 1872 at Zanzibar, and in 1952 at Lindi (52). Both cyclones were short-lived and caused little damage. Consequently, cyclones have not been a major influence on the physical or community structure of these reefs.

The East African Coastal Current travels in a northwards direction parallel to the coast with average current speeds of 1.1 to 2.1 m/s possibly

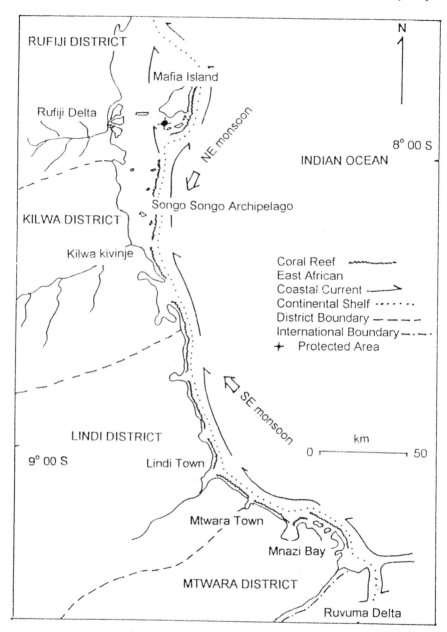

Figure 5.1. Coral reef distribution, coastal rivers and district boundaries from Mafia Island to the Mozambique border at the Ruvuma River.

accelerated up to 3 m/s by the prevailing winds during the southeast monsoon. Although primarily affecting offshore waters this current is responsible for major down-welling resulting in a predominance of low nutrient, warm and clear waters which encourage the extensive coral growth and benthic productivity associated with this stretch of coastline (40). Semi-diurnal tidal currents have an average range of 3.3 m which is one of the highest reported in the Tropical Indian Ocean (28). Peak outflow from rivers in April and May can markedly increase the amount of suspended sediments in the water column and the sediment plumes from the Rufiji and Ruvuma River deltas stretch for many kilometers up the coastline. These sediment inputs are the primary reason for the reduced coral growth north of Mafia Island and south of Ras Matunda, Mtwara. Water temperature averages 27° C but may drop to 25° C during June and July and rise to 29° C from January to March (42). The average surface salinity is 34.4 ppt (42).

Geology

One of the most notable features of the Tanzanian coastline is the extensive limestone coral cliffs (average 4 m high) and numerous coralline islets formed during the Pleistocene (130 000 years ago) and exposed by a subsequent drop in sea levels. These fossilized reefs which in some cases extend a kilometer inland represent past periods of extensive coral growth. With the exception of Mafia Island which arose from tectonic uplifting of the continental shelf (35), all islands in southern Tanzania were formed in this manner. Much of the coastal soils are highly alkaline and not suited to agriculture with small-scale farming primarily restricted to periods of high rainfall. In contrast, those soils overlying Mafia Island are more fertile and farming is more widespread. Similarly, in river basins such as the Rufiji and Ruvuma deltas fertile alluvial soils are prominent but agriculture is restricted to the drier months due to flooding throughout the rainy season. Consequently, the poor soil conditions in most areas ensure a high degree of local dependence on marine resources rather than farming.

Geography

Distribution of Coastal Zone Habitats. The width of the continental shelf averages 8 to 10 km, with the notable exception of the Mafia and Songo Songo archipelagos where it broadens significantly to a maximum of 35 km. Here it drops off rapidly to reach depths of greater than 200 m within 2 to 3 km of the islands. Coral reefs, seagrass and algal beds, and mangrove forests are found throughout the coastline. Coral reef development north of Mafia Island has been restricted to a few small offshore islands on account of the turbid waters from the Rufiji River which are carried north by coastal currents. South and east of the delta the shallow waters of the Mafia and Songo Songo archipelagos support a luxurious growth of coral patch reefs and seagrass beds. A fringing outer reef runs down the eastern side of both archipelagos to meet the mainland south of Kilwa Masoko from where it continues south to the Mozambique border. The reef is broken in places by a number of deep-water channels, river outlets and bays. The most developed bays in Mtwara also support a number of shallow patch reefs. Seagrass beds are widespread throughout the shallow waters of the Mafia and Songo Songo archipelagos and within the sheltered bays of the southern coastline from Kilwa Kivinje to Mtwara. Mangroves are found at most river outlets and on Mafia Island, but the highest concentration is within the Rufiji River Delta which supports the largest area of estuarine mangrove forest in East Africa at approximately 1000 km^2.

Location and Population Size of Main Urban Centers. The southern Tanzanian coastline is divided into five administrative districts; Mtwara, Lindi, Kilwa, Rufiji and Mafia (Fig. 5.1). Within these districts there are five main urban centers. Mtwara and Lindi towns are government administrative centers at both regional and district levels while Kilwa Masoko, Utete and Kilindoni act as administrative centers at only the district level. The total population for southern Tanzania is estimated at 2 million people and coastal communities represent 16% of the country's total population (Government Statistics 1988). The highest concentrations of people are found in the coastal towns of Mtwara, Lindi and Kilindoni on Mafia Island with the remaining population residing in villages scattered along the mainland and out-lying islands. The majority of coastal rural communities depend on a combination of fishing, subsistence farming, and small-scale trade in coconuts, lime, and fresh or dried fish. Small-scale tourism now provides an income to some, primarily on Mafia Island.

Location of Managed or Protected Areas. Eight marine reserves were designated in 1981 but were never implemented due to shortage of funds and personnel (8). Only two of these reserves were in southern Tanzania at Chole Bay and Tutia Reef and they are now included within the boundaries of Tanzania's only national government marine park at Mafia Island. Other proposed sites included the Songo Songo archipelago and Kilwa reefs, Ras Banura to Mchinga Bay in Lindi, and Ras Msamgamku to the Ruvuma River Delta in Mtwara (54). Management of these areas is, however, still limited to a few localized but valuable initiatives to be discussed below.

Ecological Surveys

The best studied areas within southern Tanzania are at Mafia Island, the Songo Songo Archipelago, and the Mtwara-Msimbati area (Fig. 5.2).

Mafia Island. The area which encompasses Mafia Island, the Mafia Channel and the Rufiji Delta forms one of the finest complexes of estuarine mangrove, coral reef and marine channel ecosystems; all lying within an area of some 1500 km^2. Mafia Island is centered at 7^0 40'S, 40^0 40'E, 120 km south of Dar es Salaam 21 km east of the Rufiji delta (Fig. 5.1). The population of the island is currently estimated at 40 000 people and the majority is dependent on the use of marine resources. The southern part of the island and it's associated islets (Fig. 5.2) was gazetted as Tanzania's first national marine park in 1995 (32) and has been the subject of a number of studies (3,11,14,17,19,31, 48,52,54). An estimated 15 000 people are resident within the marine park area. The development and implementation of the park are discussed later in this chapter.

The area enclosed within the park is approximately 300 km^2 and includes the southern part of Mafia Island and four small islands enclosing two interconnected bays. Water depth within the bays rarely exceeds 10 m except

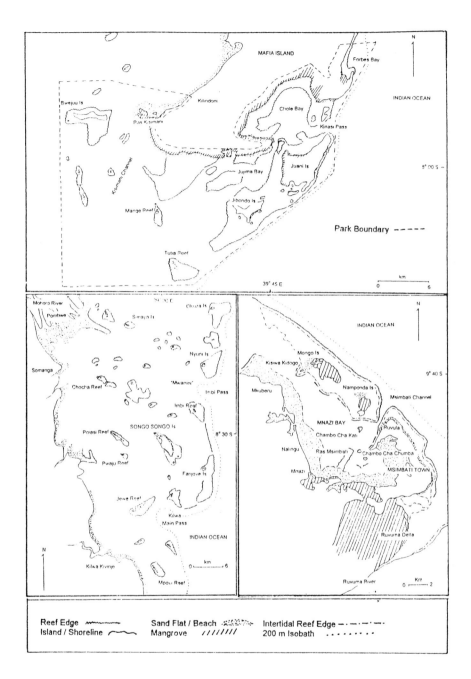

Figure 5.2. Coral reef distributions within the three main areas. focused on here. (top) South Mafia Island and associated islands showing the position of the marine park boundary. (bottom left) The Songo Songo Archipelago. (bottom right) Mnazi Bay and the Msimbati Peninsular.

in the tidal channels that bisect each bay where it drops to depths of 15 to 25 m. The deepest channel and the main point of tidal flushing is Kinasi Pass to the east where currents reach in excess of 2.1 m/s on spring tides. Outside the bays it drops off to depths greater than 200 m within 2 to 3 km of the islands.

A large variety of habitats are found within the park. These include both exposed and sheltered reef systems of hard and soft corals and algae, sandy and hard bottom intertidal flats, and extensive beds of seagrass, algae, and soft corals. On low spring tides the intertidal flats reach widths in excess of 2 km in places. Mangroves are present in a narrow fringe along much of the island coastline with two more extensive stands, one at Ras Kisimani on the western tip of the island, and another along the north side of Chole Bay. An outer fringing reef stretches for an estimated 33 km down the eastern side of the islands ending at Kitutia Reef on the northern the edge of the South Mafia Channel.

Hard coral (scleractinia) growth on the fringing reef is diverse with a mean surface cover of 40 to 50% to depths of 25 to 30 m but soft corals tend to dominate the lower slopes. Five to 10% of coral on the fringing reef was damaged, the damage was thought to be largely caused by waves. Rugosity is low, typical of an exposed reef. In contrast, within the sheltered bays of Chole and Jujima hard corals grow as highly rugose patch reefs and bommie fields (coral gardens). Coral damage was greater on the inner reefs (10 to 15%) and largely caused by fishing nets, explosives (for fishing) and boat anchors. Soft corals and algae grow together along the main tidal channels. Mixed beds of seagrass and algae cover an estimated 75% of the seabed within each bay. The Kisimani channel, which runs northwards along the western side of the park, separates a further group of patch reefs to the west. Coral growth on these reefs is less diverse than within the eastern bays and on the northern and western sides of Bwejuu Island coral growth is limited by periods of heavy sedimentation from the Rufiji River delta and octocorals tend to dominate. The mid-western coast of Mafia supports few reefs, the shoreline being predominantly sand and mud. There are, however, a number of small offshore islands and patch reefs supporting high levels of coral growth and an unsurveyed narrow fringing reef runs along the northwestern side of the island.

The Songo Songo Archipelago and Kilwa District.

The Songo Songo Archipelago, centered at 8⁰ 30' S, 39⁰ 30' E approximately 15 km northeast of Kilwa Kivinje on the mainland, supports one of the largest expanses of shallow coral reef in southern Tanzania (Fig. 5.2). The estimated surface area of living coral reef is 40 to 50 km^2 with 30 to 40 patch reefs, ranging in size from 10 km^2 to small clusters of reefs barely 200 m across, and five small coralline islands distributed over an area of approximately 400 km^2. The fringing reef, a continuation of that at Mafia, runs south from the South Mafia Channel for a further 30 km along the eastern side of the archipelago meeting the mainland just south of Kilwa Masoko. Three deep-water channels bisect the reef with dense seagrass beds at the channel mouths.

The largest island, at 7 km in length, is Songo Songo with a registered population of 5000 people. The four smaller islands are populated by semi-permanent camps of fisherfolk. Gas reserves were found below Songo Songo in the 1970s and the Tanzania Petroleum Development Corporation has had a presence on the island since that time. In 1995 funding was obtained to build a pipeline from Songo Songo Island to Dar es Salaam to allow use of these reserves and construction is underway. The implications of this development are discussed below.

The first detailed biological surveys of the area were conducted from 1995 to 1996 by Frontier-Tanzania (10,12,15,16,18,21,22,29) with financial support from the Norwegian Aid Agency (NORAD). The greatest cover of hard coral (50 to 60%) was found on reefs adjacent to deep water such as on the western slopes of Poiasi and Pwajuu reefs and along the length of the outer reef where coral growth extended to below 30 m. These reefs had suffered the least damage with less than 5% of coral dead or damaged below 6 m. Coral cover on the shallower reefs ranged from 10 to 40% with an average of 20% damaged or dead. Frequent sightings of large upturned table corals and occasional circular craters of coral rubble suggest that this damage is largely a result of dynamite fishing, a common practice throughout the area. The once productive reefs of Mpovi and Amani (30) near Kilwa Kivinje have suffered badly with only 5 to 10% coral cover remaining and with large areas of coral rubble and algae (29).

Mtwara and Msimbati. Mtwara and Lindi Districts combined have a 320 km coastline which includes the longest stretch of exposed coastal fringing reef in Tanzania and five major sheltered bay systems at Mnazi, Mtwara, Mikandani, Sudi and Lindi. Large settlements and towns have developed within the bays in the Mtwara and southern Lindi areas but the coastal communities north of Lindi Bay are restricted to a few small bays and inlets. Furthest south, Msimbati Town is the first landing site and immigration point for boats and passengers from Mozambique and represents a major route of small-scale trade between the adjacent coastal areas. North of Msimbati, Mnazi bay is the largest inshore area along the coast (Fig. 5.2). As on Songo Songo Island a gas reserve has been identified in the southern part of the bay to be developed following the completion of the Songo Songo to Dar es Salaam pipeline. Mtwara Bay is the south's only major industrial port although relatively small with a maximum capacity of 0.4 million tons of cargo per year.

Coral reefs are found outside the port, along the coast to Mikandani Bay, and adjacent to Mnazi Bay, Sudi, and Lindi Town, all of which are heavily exploited for their fisheries using seine nets and, more commonly now, explosives (26). Much of the reef within the Lindi District had not been surveyed and the following descriptions are for the Mtwara District (26). The most significant feature of the outer reef is the well-developed "spur and groove" zone with spurs extending seawards for 50 to 100 m and reaching heights up to 7 m with a diverse cover of corals. The surface cover of hard coral on the outer reef averaged 40% with less than 5% of coral damaged or dead.

Sheltered inside Mongo and Mana Hawanja islands Mnazi Bay supports a wide variety of habitats including large expanses of mangrove forest, intertidal reef flat, subtidal seagrass beds, and several large patch reefs. Coral cover on reefs within the bay was variable with some reefs, such as Chambo Cha Kati, having a mean surface cover of 60% hard coral, predominantly *Acropora formosa*, of which little was damaged or dead. In contrast, other reefs, such as Chambo Cha Chumba, were highly degraded with a mean coral cover of 10%, 30% of which was recorded dead or damaged. The observation of 37 craters within the coral along a 2 km stretch of reef near Ruvula suggests that much of the damage has been caused by dynamite fishing (26). The most unique area of

reef is adjacent to the narrow Msimbati Channel where tidal currents reach up
to 3 m/s and coral cover and fish diversity were high with a prevalence of
gorgonian seafans along the channel walls. Elsewhere along the coast patch
reefs have been observed in Lindi and Mikindani bays where, due to high
sediment inputs, the biological diversity is thought to be low and the reefs are in
a relatively poor condition.

Ecology

Diversity and Distribution Studies

Corals. General distribution studies have identified 51 scleractinian coral
genera in southern Tanzania (Table 5.1,22,26,31) which can be regarded as high
when compared to the 55 scleractinian genera recorded for the East African
Region (28,48,52). *Heterocyathus aequicostatus*, *Cynarina lacrymalis* and
Diploastrea heliopora were recorded for the first time in the southern Tanzania.
The main coral assemblages (Table 5.2) were similar to those described by
Hamilton and Brakel (28) for East Africa and are most diverse within the Songo
Songo Archipelago. *Acropora* is the dominant genus on most reefs exhibiting an
especially luxurious growth on the shallow sheltered inner reefs. *Galaxea* was a
characteristic feature of patch reefs along the western side of the Songo Songo
Archipelago.

Further down the coast exposed conditions restrict the growth of large stands
of *Galaxea* to a few isolated pockets, most notably in the Msimbati Channel,
Mtwara. *Pachyseris* was abundant on the lower reef slopes, especially in the
Mtwara District. Interestingly the fungiid *Halomitra pileus* completely
dominated sections of Poiasi and Pwajuu reefs (Songo Songo Archipelago) and
the entire outer reef adjacent to Msamgamku (Mtwara) where thousands of
individuals, many up to 75 cm across, were scattered over a large area of reef
slope (200 m). This phenomenon is rarely reported and it is not fully understood
why such large aggregations have occurred. Interestingly a reef solely
consisting of this species has been recently discovered in Fiji (38).

Coral genera were fairly uniformly distributed throughout the Songo Songo
Archipelago where an average of 33 were recorded on each reef, the maximum
number of 37 genera being recorded on Pioasi. The northwestern reefs near
Simaya Island, however, are influenced by high sediment outputs from the
Mohoro River and coral diversity is commonly reduced to large monospecific
coral stands of *Echinopora*, *Pachyseris* or *Montipora*. Further south in Mnazi
Bay the greatest number of genera was recorded on Ruvula Reef on the edge of
the Msimbati Channel where 42 genera were recorded. Elsewhere within the
bay the number of genera recorded ranged from 20 to 36. Coral distributions
were not recorded at Mafia Island.

The only detailed study of coral distributions within a reef system was for
Tutia Reef south of Mafia Island (52). The shallow algal zone at the top of the
outer reef was almost barren of coral with the exception of occasional heads of
Acropora corymbosa and a few small heads of *Porites* spp. The "spur and
groove" zone was, however, characterized by a great variety of corals
dominated by *Acropora*. On the lower reef slope *A. formosa* and *A. florida* were
still common but the dominant feature was of huge table form growths of *A.*

Table 5.1. Number of recorded taxa of flora and fauna at study sites.

	Mafia		Songo Songo		Mtwara		Combined Sites	
	Genera	Species	Genera	Species	Genera	Species	Genera	Species
Corals:								
Scleractinian	45	na	49	na	45	na	51	na
Non-scleractinian	na	na	12	na	11	na	na	na
Algae:	46	125	39	77	44	73	49	45
Chlorophyceae	18	50	15	30	15	33	16	57
Rhodophyceae	19	52	13	23	13	24	22	63
Phaeophyceae	9	23	11	24	16	16	11	29
Seagrasses	8	12	6	9	6	9	8	12
Gastropods	49	89	37	93	23	52	58	135
Mangroves	8	8	2	2	5	5	8	8
	Families	Species	Families	Species	Families	Species	Families	Species
Fish	59	396	52	270	68	330	na	na

Data taken from (9 to 12,14 to 19,21,22,26,31). Any discrepancies in species numbers given here with those at source are due to the inclusion of additional unpublished records from the Frontier-Tanzania research program. na = not available.

spicifera. On the sheltered inner reef areas *Acropora* species again dominated, but with *Montipora erythracea* and *Pocillopora verrucosa* fairly common. *Porites* was common in the more sheltered areas reaching huge sizes in some cases with colonies up to 3 m high. *Millepora* was common towards the reef base on the sheltered side. Interestingly, a comparison by Talbot in 1965 of the number of *Acropora* species found here with those recorded in Mozambique (5) found 17 species recorded at Inhaca following exhaustive collecting in comparison to 25 species recorded at Tutia with no attempt at exhaustive collecting.

Reef Fish. The most comprehensive survey of fish species to date has been for Mafia Island where almost 400 species have been recorded (Table 5.1) (31, Frontier, unpublished data). The species counts for all areas are given in Table 5.1 but the counts are not exhaustive with many species, especially the gobies, blennies, and damselfishes yet to be identified. New records include the first reports of *Pomacanthus asfur* (Pomacanthidae) south of Zanzibar in the Songo Songo Archipelago, and *Bolbometopon muricatum* (Scaridae) was recorded for the first time in southern Tanzania in the Msimbati channel (Frontier, unpublished data).

A comparative study of species distributions across reefs was made for a subset of 56 pre-selected species including representatives from each of the major trophic levels on the reef (19,22). The greatest numbers of species were recorded on the outer reef sites and along the edges of deep-water channels where an average of 90% of these species was observed. The site with the greatest number of recorded species was Rukyira Reef west of Kilwa Masoka, an outer reef site adjacent to deep water, where 92% of the censused species were observed. Fewer species were recorded on the more westerly reefs such as at Bwejuu Island, west of Mafia, and on Chocha Reef in the Songo Songo Archipelago where an average of 30% of the species were recorded. In the Mtwara area further south the greatest number of species was recorded on the outer reef sites near Namponda and Mongo islands where 86% were recorded. Within Mnazi Bay the proportion of species recorded was much reduced with only 12% recorded on the reefs in the southern part of the bay.

Table 5.2. A broad classification of coral reefs in southern Tanzania.

Reef Type	Distribution and biological characteristics
Outer fringing reef	North Mafia to Mtwara. Upper Levels: Algae dominated boulder rock, low-lying branching *Acropora*, *Pocillopora* and *Stylophora*, massive *Porites* and encrusting corals (such as *Cyphastrea*). 7 to 15 m: Branching and tabular *Acropora*, massive *Porites* and *Platygyra*. 15 to 20 m: *Porites* and *Pachyseris* and plate forms of *Montipora*
Leeward fringing and shallow patch reefs	Mafia / Songo Songo archipelago and southern bays. Upper levels: *Acropora*, *Millepora*, *Porites*, and *Goniastrea*. 4 to 10 m: Staghorn and tabular *Acropora*, thickets of *Millepora*, foliose *Montipora* and *Echinopora*, massive form *Diploastrea* and *Fungia*. 10 to 18 m: Staghorn *Acropora*, *Platygyra*, *Porites*, *Hydnophora*, *Fungia*, and alcyonarians.
Fringing or patch reefs associated with deep water channels	Kinasi Pass, South Mafia Channel; Imbi Pass; Kilwa Pass; Msimbati Channel. Upper levels: *Galaxea astreata*, branching *Acropora*, *Porites*. 8 to 16 m: Tabular *Acropora*, *Pavona*, *Porites*, *Platygyra*, *Diploastrea*, foliose *Montipora*, *Lobophyllia*, *Mycedium*, *Merulina* and *Pachyseris*. 16 to 30 m: *Pachyseris*, *Mycedium*, *Echinophyllia*, alcyonarians and seafans.
Fringing or patch reefs associated with turbid waters	Reefs near river outlets. Upper levels: Algae dominated, branching *Acropora* and *Stylophora*. 4 to 10 m: *Porites*, *Platygyra*, *Galaxea*. Monospecific stands of *Montipora* and *Echinopora*. Seagrass. 10 to 18 m: Monospecific stands of plate form *Echinopora*, seawhips, seafans and alcyonarians.

In a more detailed survey in 1965 Talbot censused the fish populations off Mafia Island using explosives and recorded 244 species of reef fish within the south Mafia area and 192 species from Tutia reef alone (52). On Tutia Reef 98 species were taken from the outer reef of which 4% were taken in the shallow seaward algal zone, 66% in the coral rich spur and groove zone, and 30% on the lower reef slope (>20 m depth). Talbot's species list was also considered incomplete with many of the benthic and cave-dwelling species being hard to recover following blasting. Fifty four percent of the species found were also recorded for Inhaca Island in Mozambique (25,51) and only 11% of species were considered endemic to Africa, the rest being common to the Indo-Pacific fauna. The greatest numbers of species were recorded in areas with a high density and diversity of coral as found on the inner reef where 66 species were taken in a single blast. In contrast, at the reef base, where coral cover was negligible, no small species were found and the fish fauna was reduced to occasional shoals of emperors (Lethrinidae) and large groupers (Serranidae).

Algae and Seagrass.

A total of 145 species of algae and 12 species of seagrass have been recorded at Mafia Island (31), Songo Songo Archipelago (12,21) and Mtwara District (26) combined (Table 5.1). Seagrass and algae beds were most prolific within the shallow sheltered bays of southern Mafia and throughout the Songo Songo Archipelago where the greatest abundance is found in an area known locally as "Mwanini" at the mouth of the deep water Imbi Pass (Fig. 5.2). Seagrass beds are also found within the sheltered bays to the south especially within Mnazi Bay. At Mafia Island the greatest floristic diversity was recorded within Chole Bay which contained virtually all algae and seagrass species recorded for the region and is suggested to be the center of marine floral diversity within the Mafia Island Marine Park (31). Within the Songo Songo Archipelago 66 of the algae species were also common to Mafia Island with 11 additional species recorded. In Mtwara District the highest diversity of algae was recorded on the intertidal area adjacent to the Msimbati outer reef and a further 9 species not previously recorded at either Mafia Island or Songo Songo have been identified.

Gastropod Mollusks.

Documented surveys of gastropod diversity are limited (6,9,34,43) with 135 species recorded to date (Table 5.1). The cryptic behavior and nocturnal habits of many species, however, suggest that this figure is considerably lower than the true total. Records for the rarer and more exotic species were mainly taken from the collections of local traders and fisherfolk.

Despite an increased collection pressure on these islands (Songo Songo and Fanjove Islands had six full-time resident collectors and traders in 1997) specimens of some of the larger and more exotic species such as *Cassis cornuta* and *Charonia tritonis* could still be found in 1997, although rarely on Mafia Island. Many of the lower value species such as *Lambis spp.* and *Cypraea tigris* were still common on the islands within the Songo Songo Archipelago in 1995. *Turbo marmoratus* is collected during September and October when it emerges from the coral to breed in open areas where ease of collection has led to heavy exploitation and it has become scarce throughout the region. The main species collected for food include the common murex (*Chicoreus ramosus*) and the tulip shell (*Pleuroploca trapezium*), which are collected on an opportunistic basis while hunting for octopii and sea cucumbers (holothuria). These two species are still fairly common although, again, less so around Mafia Island. Although a trade license is required for the collection and sale of gastropods this is poorly enforced and little information is held on the scale of collection and location of collection sites. Should future management of this resource require a reduction in current collection pressures alternative income sources will have to be provided for those involved as surveys on Mafia Island (9) found the income derived from shell collection forms up to 40% of the domestic income in some households.

Turtles.

All five species of marine turtles known to occur in the western Indian Ocean have been recorded in southern Tanzanian waters (24). The vast expanses of shallow seagrass beds and coral reefs of south Mafia Island, the Songo Songo Archipelago, and the sheltered southern bays near Mtwara provide ideal habitats for turtles. The green turtle (*Chelonia mydas*) and hawksbill turtle (*Eretmochelys imbricata*) are the most common species and are resident and breed in the area, the latter less commonly so. The olive ridley (*Lepidochelys olivacea*) and loggerhead turtles (*Caretta caretta*) are less common and in the latter's case are known to be seasonal migrants from Natal. Finally, the leatherback turtle (*Dermochelys coriacea*) is occasionally sighted coming in from deep water where it feeds on a diet of jelly fish.

The total number of green turtles nesting annually in southern Tanzania in 1975 was estimated at less than 170 with most nesting on the offshore islands (24). The lack of mainland nesting was mainly attributed to disturbance by local people and great emphasis was placed on the future protection of nesting sites on the more remote islands such as those within the Songo Songo

Table 5.3. Recorded sightings of live and dead turtles.

	No. recorded caught in nets	Estimated no. caught / year*	Underwater sightings	No. remains
Mafia Island (1994)	8	490	na	na
Songo Songo Archipelago (1995)	30	800	79 (1950 dives)	68
Mtwara (1996)	1/3 of all fishing trips	na	98 (720 dives)	na

* Based on an extrapolation from the proportion of fishing trips which caught turtles during the nine months of the year when the weather allows regular fishing with nets. na = information not available.

Archipelago. No such protection has been provided. With most of these beaches now occupied year round by visiting fisherfolk, few turtles are likely to nest successfully as nests are robbed of eggs and adults caught nesting are often slaughtered (13). More recently four active breeding sites have been identified at Mafia Island where both green and hawksbill turtles have been observed nesting and it is hoped that these beaches can now be protected within the boundaries of the Mafia Island Marine Park (31). In the Songo Songo Archipelago turtles are often sighted while diving and fisherfolk say that turtles do still nest there but that there are many fewer than before (13). On the smaller islands such as Simaya the cutting of vegetation was found to be increasing the rate of shoreline erosion and possible further loss of nesting beaches. To the far south turtles are reported to still nest on several beaches within Mnazi Bay and near Msimbati town but many of the nests are robbed.

Combined records of live sightings from dive surveys (1991 to 1997), turtle remains, and turtles captured in shark nets (Table 5.3) found 39% were greens, 39% hawksbills, 7% loggerheads, and 15% unidentified (Frontier, unpublished data). Fishers using shark nets report catch rates of up to 40 turtles in a week and up to 12 in a single day from around the Pombwe area at the mouth of the Rufiji River Delta. As these areas are fished heavily by the TAFICO prawn fishing fleet it is likely that large numbers of turtles are also taken in their nets although no information is currently available. The leatherback turtle has been reported off Kilwa Kivinje in November and recently a number have been seen in Mnazi Bay where on one occasion a specimen was observed being butchered on the beach for its meat. There are no recent confirmed sightings of the olive ridley.

In conclusion it appears that although turtles are still common throughout the region, populations are declining through a combination of loss of nesting sites and incidental capture in fishing nets. In response to one of the recommendations by Howell (33) the possibility of replacing shark nets with long-lines was investigated on Mafia and found to present a viable option to reduce the incidental capture of turtles by nets (14). Long-lines not only avoided the capture of turtles but also provided significant economic advantages over nets through greater catches, lower gear costs, and reduced maintenance costs. However, even if the incidental capture in nets is eliminated, some form of protective management of nesting beaches is essential if these populations are to persist.

Perceived Threats to Diversity

Potential threats to the shallow water marine ecosystems in southern Tanzania were assessed by UNEP (53,54) and the major causes for concern were identified as mangrove clearance for salt pans and agriculture, and the unsustainable use of marine resources.

Mangrove management in Tanzania has a history of falling under the ordinances of several different ministries, each with their own conflicting agendas. Management has largely failed as a result and, despite being declared as official "Mangrove Forest Reserves" large areas of mangrove have been cleared for salt production, agriculture and for use as building materials. Various agencies including NORAD have been working to sort out a more workable system of management and in 1991 the current management plan was completed. Implementation of the plan is, however, still in its early stages. The management conflicts became clear recently when permission was sought for large-scale mangrove clearance (19 000 ha) within the Rufiji Delta to make way for prawn farming. It now appears that, despite initial intervention by the government under pressure from donor agencies and the local population, permission has been granted for this project. The decision has not been received lightly, however, and at a recent workshop on mangroves and shrimp aquaculture in Kenya (February 1998) there was a call to reconsider the decision that has been made against the advice of NEMC, the environmental advisors to the Tanzanian Government. A growing local movement assisted by JET, an environmental NGO, is also against the project which they feel has been mishandled by the government.

The two largest rivers in the region, the Rufiji and Ruvuma, have already been subject to extensive mangrove clearance for agriculture and salt pans. During peak flow (April and May) the sediment plume from the Rufiji River now spreads across the Mafia Channel to within a few hundred meters of the most westerly reefs in the marine park. These reefs are already showing signs of stress from sedimentation with much of the shallow coral on the northern and western sides of Bwejuu Island dead and covered in a thick layer of silt. The reef fish population at Bwejuu Island, traditionally believed to be a fish breeding ground and nursery area, was the lowest recorded for all other sites surveyed within the marine park area.

The unsustainable use of marine resources is currently considered to pose the greatest threat to coral reef ecosystems in southern Tanzania.

Marine Resource Use

A rapidly rising coastal population has increased the demand on marine resources to a level where it has, in many areas, now outstripped the rate of supply by traditional means. In response fishers have developed and adopted more efficient extraction methods including the use of smaller mesh nets, explosives, and poisons. These new methods not only enable people to exploit the dwindling fish stocks beyond a sustainable level but they also destroy the very habitats upon which the fisheries depend. In addition, areas such as Mafia Island and the Songo Songo Archipelago, previously protected as natural "harvest refugia" on account of their remoteness, have now become accessible to visiting fisherfolk through an increase in the availability of outboard boat engines and ice for fish storage during transport.

Dynamite Fishing

The most destructive fishing method and possibly the greatest threat to the coral reefs themselves is thought to be the use of explosives (27). Dynamite easily purchased from road projects, quarry and mining sites, when detonated underwater sends out a powerful shock wave indiscriminately killing fish and non-target species many of which are never collected as they sink into the coral below (2). The coral itself is often damaged leading to a marked reduction in both fish abundance and diversity (23).

The immediate impacts of explosive fishing are difficult to quantify as the damage caused can range from a distinct crater in the coral to large areas of broken coral branches and upturned table corals (Fig. 5.3). The degree of damage caused depends on whether the dynamite was detonated in mid-water or directly above the coral. Dynamite fishing is, however, the only known destructive fishing technique in the region that can be employed directly above areas of dense coral, other gear suffering too much damage from the coral itself. The large areas of damage observed in the main coral stands are therefore unlikely to result from use of other fishing gears such as seine nets. The immediate advantages of dynamite fishing over traditional methods are seen as larger catches for a reduced fishing effort and elimination of the financial outlay to purchase traditional fishing gears such as nets and lines. These short-term gains are, however, soon likely to be outweighed by a rapid decline in the fishery through stock depletion and habitat degradation.

Although illegal in Tanzania, dynamite fishing is now very common and the shallow inshore coral reefs are reported as being degraded at an unprecedented rate (8,22,26). Recent reports indicate that up to 60% of all fish landed in the fish market at Mnazi Bay is caught using dynamite (Fisheries Officer, personal communication). At the time of writing, only at Mafia Island, where the gazettement of the marine park has resulted in regular dynamite patrols both within and adjacent to the park has this practice been reduced in southern Tanzania. Nevertheless, even here problems of dynamite use are evident with several fishers in 1996 held in possession of 29 kg of dynamite and over 3 m of fuse (G. Andrews, personal communication). Records compiled by Frontier-Tanzania (unpublished data) reveal a depressing picture throughout southern Tanzania as exemplified by 441 dynamite blasts recorded over a two month period (October to November 1996) at Mnazi Bay, Mtwara. The situation is similar in the Songo Songo Archipelago where a regular rate of 30 blasts were heard every three hours during calm conditions near Songo Songo Island. These records are all superseded by an incredible 100 blasts recorded at Mpovi reef (located adjacent to Kilwa Kivinje, the site of the District Fisheries Office) during one six-hour period in an area estimated at only five to six square kilometers.

Figure 5.3. Photo of an area of damaged reef, typical of dynamite fishing. Credit: Darwall.

In Mafia, Rufiji, and Kilwa Districts blast fishing is mainly practiced by "outsiders" who travel to the region from Dar es Salaam and Zanzibar aboard motorized sailing boats fitted with a central holding tank filled with ice. These men, usually sponsored by a single businessman or group, claim to be fish buyers using their ice to transport fish to the mainland markets. In reality few of these men buy all their fish from the local fishers and they obtain the large proportion of their fish using dynamite. The majority of these boats, known as "iceboats", have no visible registration and no traditional fishing gears. Based on small islands where villages have no police, each iceboat stays in the region for approximately ten days after which it returns to Dar es Salaam to sell the catch. Dynamited fish can often be identified by their broken bones and soft flesh, however, their detection at market is difficult as they are often mixed with fish bought from legitimate fishers using traditional gears.

The majority of local fishers express their disdain for fishing with explosives but many also claim to be dependent on the sale of fresh fish to these iceboats. Blast fishing in the southern districts of Lindi and Mtwara is mainly practiced by local youths using wooden canoes. With increased availability sometimes reducing the cost of dynamite to Tsh 1000 (US $1.60) a stick, dynamite use has markedly increased with local youth now finding little reason and motivation to save and purchase conventional fishing gear. Of even greater concern is the recent trend for fishers to make their own explosives from locally available materials such as sulfur flower, petrol and "*dawa ya ulaya*". The bombs made are now larger, obtain greater catches, and are more destructive than before. If this continues the very backbone of artisanal fishing may be threatened with local skills and knowledge being lost for future generations. With declining fish stocks necessitating increased fishing effort to maintain catches by traditional means the use of explosives becomes a more attractive option each day.

Local communities in all districts are aware of the negative impacts associated with this practice but are apathetic in dealing with the problem because of alleged corruption and leniency of sentences, perpetrators often being released with no charge. The widespread local belief that higher government officials and police are involved in the dynamite trade goes some way to explain the lack of community action and apathy. Action must be taken to include regular patrols, improved legislation, and increased fines and jail sentences for both users and those found in possession of explosives. More stringent regulations are also required for the use, movement, and accountability of explosives.

Programs such as the Marine Environment Protection Program (see this chapter) encompassing the Kilwa, Lindi and Mtwara Districts, and the Tanga Coastal Zone Conservation and Development Program (see Chapter 6), are working together with local government, local communities, and the police to prioritize local marine issues and their effect. As part of this process the use of explosives is being addressed and in Tanga has resulted in a degree of success with the cessation of dynamite use in some areas. If this success is to be replicated within other districts, and indeed throughout Tanzania, it needs to be recognized by all parties at local, district, regional and national levels that support for such a plan will require collaborative committed action.

The Finfish Fisheries

Ninety six percent of Tanzania's fisheries are reported to be small-scale artisanal fisheries (49) exploiting the inshore reef associated habitats. Ngoile and colleagues (44) concluded the optimum catch per fisher per year to be 4.6 metric tons and that fish stocks exploited by the artisanal fishers had already reached the optimum level by 1986. From 1990 to 1995 the average total catch per year was 48 400 metric tons (range 36 000 to 56 000) caught by 3232 registered fishing vessels (4) which, assuming an average crew of four in each boat, is only 3.7 metric tons per fisher per year.

Artisanal fishers employ traditional locally made wooden vessels. The largest vessels (3 to 10 m) are the *mashua* and *dhows* which are planked and sail powered, but more often now assisted by outboard engines. The smaller vessels include the *mtumbwi*, a small paddle or pole powered dugout canoe, and the *ngalawa*, a canoe with outriggers and in most cases a small sail. All these vessels are restricted to inshore waters. The fishing gears used include nets (seine, gill, and shark), lines (hand-line, troll-line, and long-line), traps (box and fence) and spears. All these fishing methods are employed on the inshore reef-associated habitats with coral habitats often damaged by boat anchors, seine nets, box traps and to a lesser extent shark nets.

The only known commercial fishery is for prawns off the Rufiji Delta. No recent figures for the fleet size have been obtained but in 1989 a Kenya-based company was fishing four boats an estimated 21 days a month with an average daily haul of one ton of prawns (54). No known stock assessment has been

Table 5.4. Number of people involved and estimated annual yields for the dominant finfish fisheries.

Gear Type	Mafia Island (1994)		Songo Songo Archipelago (1996)		Msimbati/Mnazi (1997)	
	No. People	Total yield (mt/y)	No. People	Total yield (mt/y)	No. People	Total yield (mt/y)
Seine Net	280	291	100	300	110 to 130	67[a]
Shark Net	175	32	55	170	35	na[b]
Long-line	35	12	0	0	0	0
Hand-line	260	200	140	200	>200	245
Box Trap	140	50 to 60	32	31	25	69
Fence Trap	10	19	4	na	12	86
Spear	Na	na	na	na	50 to 80	na

Data taken from: Mafia Island (14,17,31,37); Songo Songo (16); Mtwara; (26). "na" means the information is not available. "a": Women also fish with fine mesh mosquito nets ("kutanda") to catch "dagaa" (white bait). "b": Drifting shark net (jarife kulambaza); three catch records to date: lowest catch, 7.5 kg and highest catch, 183 kg

made. The by-catch is considerable and on occasions the sea has been coveredwith floating discarded fish. Damage is caused to the benthos during trawling and considerable quantities of sediments are re-suspended in close vicinity to the coral reefs. Local fishers consider the prawn trawlers to cause more damage than the dynamite fishers.

Government fishery catch statistics, collected since 1970, are extrapolated from a very small proportion of the catch and must be considered rough estimates at best. The most detailed surveys of the inshore reef fisheries are those conducted by Frontier-Tanzania at Mafia Island, Songo Songo Archipelago, and Mtwara (14,16,17,31). Of the three gear types most commonly used in these areas nets employed an estimated 775 fisherfolk, lines an estimated 635, and traps an estimated 215, with annual estimated catch yields of 850, 620, and 300 metric tons, respectively (Table 5.4). The main fish families targeted by the shark nets and long lines were Carcharhinidae, Dasyatidae and Myliobatidae (Table 5.5), whereas the seine nets and traps mainly targeted Lethrinidae, Acanthuridae, Scaridae, Siganidae and Carangidae (Table 5.6).

Shark and Ray Fisheries. An estimated 260 fishers fish full-time on the shark and ray fisheries of Mafia, Songo Songo and Mnazi Bay area near Mtwara (Table 5.4). Sharks are mainly valued for their fins which are exported to the Far-East. The flesh of both sharks and rays is salted and dried for local consumption and for sale on the mainland. The liver oil of the shark is used for weather proofing boats.

Shark nets, known locally as *jarife* target sharks, rays and larger pelagics. An average net is 240 m long and 5 m deep with a diagonal mesh of 12 to 30 cm. The nets are bottom set and fished from sailing boats on neap tides in water depths of between 10 and 30 m. Favored fishing sites include seagrass beds and area of coral rubble adjacent to deep-water channels. An average fishing team consists of four crew and a captain. A variation on this fishing method, known as *jarife kulambaza*, is employed by fishers from Msamgamku, Mtwara, where the nets are fished at night as drift nets with one end secured to the boat.

Table 5.5. Catch compositions for the shark net and long-line fisheries as % total catch by weight for dominant families. "Ma"= Mafia Island, "SS"= Songo Songo Archipelago, "Mt"= Mtwara (Mnazi & Mikandani Bays). "0"= less than 1% total catch and is grouped as "Other".

Family	SharkNets		Long-lines	
	Ma	SS	Ma	SS
Carcharhinidae	13	5	87	na
Dasyatidae	23	65	0	na
Mobulidae	0	3	0	na
Myliobatidae	19	21	2	na
Rhinobatidae	0	1	0	na
Rhyncobatidae	5	0	0	na
Other Fish	40	5	11	na

Data taken from: Mafia Island(14), Songo Songo(16).

Long-lines, locally known as *cocho* or *zulumati*, are currently used off Mafia and Mtwara having been first introduced to the fishery in 1991 by a Zanzibari fish trader to target sharks. A long-line typically consists of 80 to 100 m of rope with eight to 12 hooks mounted on 0.5 m lengths of chain. Moray eel is the most common bait although dolphin or turtle meat is preferred. Lines are fished near the seabed in similar habitats to the shark nets but can be fished in all tides and weathers unlike nets which are prone to tangling in strong tides and rough seas. The fishing team again consists of a four-man crew and the captain.

Catch compositions varied with fishing method and location (Table 5.5). Off Mafia Island net catches were dominated by rays and larger bony fish such as snappers (Lutjanidae), grunts (Haemulidae), and emperors (Lethrinidae) with sharks only forming 8 to 26% of the catch by weight. Catches of rays dropped significantly during the census period and many fishers have since moved further south to the Songo Songo Archipelago where catches of rays in 1995 were, on average, eight times greater at 82 kg/trip than at Mafia. Following this movement south local fishers in the Songo Songo Archipelago have reported a significant decline in their ray catches and say the fishery is in urgent need of management. In contrast to the nets the long-line catches were dominated by sharks (75 to 90% total catch by weight) with few rays caught. Only three catch records have been obtained for the drift nets off Mtwara but the target species are known to include large pelagics such as marlin, manta rays, sharks, and tuna.

Seine Net Fishery. An estimated 510 fisherfolk fish full-time on the seine fisheries of Mafia, Songo Songo and Mnazi Bay (Table 5.4) making it the most widely practiced fishery in these areas. The fish are sold both locally and to traders who transport catches on ice to mainland markets. Seine nets are usually fished from *mashua* and *dhows*, and occasionally from *ngalawa* and *mitumbwi*. The nets are made of 15 ply (or less) fiber with a stretched mesh ranging from 3 cm (*juya*) to 6 cm (*nyavu*). Although the use of *juya* nets is officially restricted to off-reef areas targeting small shoaling pelagics collectively known as *dagaa,* they are often fished illegally over shallow reef where they catch a high proportion of juvenile fish. The average net length for *nyavu* is 350 m and they are fished on spring tides as barrier nets over shallow coral, seagrass, and algal habitats. The fishers dive down to lift the nets over the coral heads but in many cases both nets and coral are badly damaged. The average crew size is eight to 10 for a *mashua* or *dhow* although 30 to 40 m lengths of net may be fished by crews of 2 to 3 from *ngalawa*. In the Mtwara

Table 5.6. Catch compositions as % total catch by weight for dominant families. "Ma" = Mafia Island, "SS" = Songo Songo Archipelago, "Mt" = Mtwara (Mnazi & Mikandani Bays). "0" = less than 1% total catch and is grouped as "Other".

Family	Shark nets			Long-lines			Seine nets			Hand-lines			Box Traps			Fence Traps		
	Ma	SS	Mt	Ma	SS	Mt	Ma	SS	Mt	Ma	SS	Mt	Ma	SS	Mt	Ma	SS	Mt
Carcharhinidae	13	5	na	87	-	-	0	0	0	0	na	na	0	0	0	0	na	0
Mobulidae	0	3	na	0	-	-	0	0	0	0	na	na	0	0	0	0	na	0
Rhinobatidae	0	1	na	0	-	-	0	0	0	0	na	na	0	0	0	0	na	0
Dasyatidae	23	65	na	0	-	-	0	0	0	0	na	na	0	0	0	5	na	0
Myliobatidae	19	21	na	2	-	-	0	0	0	0	na	na	0	0	0	0	na	0
Rhyncobatidae	5	0	na	0	-	-	0	0	0	0	na	na	0	0	0	0	na	0
BonyFish	40	5	na	11	-	-	0	0	0	0	na	na	0	0	0	0	na	0
Acanthuridae	0	0	na	0	-	-	17	4	0	0	na	na	22	17	0	0	na	0
Balistidae	0	0	na	0	-	-	6	0	9	0	na	na	0	8	0	0	na	0
Caesionidae	0	0	na	0	-	-	2	0	0	0	na	na	0	0	0	0	na	0
Carangidae	0	0	na	0	-	-	1	3	0	27	na	na	0	0	0	29	na	2
Chaetodontidae	0	0	na	0	-	-	0	0	0	0	na	na	13	3	0	0	na	0
Chanidae	0	0	na	0	-	-	0	0	0	0	na	na	0	0	0	1	na	0
Gerridae	0	0	na	0	-	-	3	0	0	0	na	na	0	0	0	17	na	0
Haemulidae	0	0	na	0	-	-	2	0	0	3	na	na	0	3	0	0	na	0
Hemiramphidae	0	0	na	0	-	-	0	0	0	0	na	na	0	0	0	5	na	1
Labridae	0	0	na	0	-	-	0	1	0	0	na	na	0	3	0	0	na	0
Lethrinidae	0	0	na	0	-	-	29	19	0	54	na	na	5	16	14	16	na	0
Lutjanidae	0	0	na	0	-	-	10	0	6	2	na	na	0	9	0	15	na	0
Mugilidae	0	0	na	0	-	-	0	0	0	0	na	na	0	0	0	4	na	4
Mullidae	0	0	na	0	-	-	4	19	0	0	na	na	0	6	5	0	na	0
Nemipteridae	0	0	na	0	-	-	2	16	0	0	na	na	0	0	0	0	na	0
Pomacentridae	0	0	na	0	-	-	0	0	11	0	na	na	0	0	0	0	na	0
Scaridae	0	0	na	0	-	-	11	19	9	0	na	na	22	25	0	0	na	0
Scombridae	0	0	na	0	-	-	0	0	0	0	na	na	0	0	0	0	na	90
Serranidae	0	0	na	0	-	-	0	0	0	5	na	na	0	0	0	0	na	0
Siganidae	0	0	na	0	-	-	9	17	43	4	na	na	8	9	63	0	na	0
Other	0	0	na	0	-	-	4	2	22	5	na	na	30	1	18	8	na	3

Data taken from Mafia Island (14,17,31,37), Songo Songo (16) and Mtwara (26)

area *kutanda* nets, basically 30 m lengths of mosquito netting, are used by women on foot to catch *dagaa* in shallow water. Seine nets may also be fished from the beach by a four to 10 man crew using a small canoe to take out the net.

Herbivores (30%) and generalist carnivores (29%) dominated the seine net fishery off Mafia with 218 species from 44 families recorded in the catches (Table 5.6). Lethrinidae (emperors) and Acanthuridae (surgeons and unicorns) formed the dominant part of the catch at 29% and 17% respectively. Further south in the Songo Songo Archipelago the trophic distribution of fish caught remained similar. Acanthuridae were, however, replaced by Scaridae and Siganidae as the dominant herbivores and Lethrinidae were replaced by Mullidae and Nemipteridae as the dominant carnivores. In Mtwara, where the fishery is predominantly over seagrass, catches were dominated by herbivores (Siganidae). The average size of fish caught was 20 cm with a minimum size of 9 cm.

Time-series data for the fishery is limited to a five-year period at Mafia Island ending in 1995 (Fig. 5.4). During this period the local fleet size had dropped by approximately 30% to 282 men fishing an estimated 6.2 km of net each day. The recorded drop in the local fleet size is thought to have been more than compensated for by an increase in the number of visiting fishers

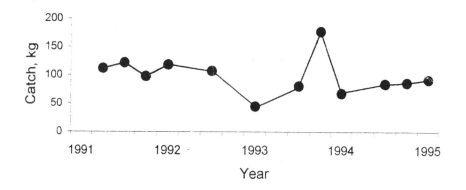

Figure 5.4. Catch per unit effort (CPUE) for the Mafia Island seine net fishery.

which was reported to rise ten fold in the period 1985 to 1990 (Mafia District fisheries statistics 1993). No significant changes in CPUE were detected over the time span of the census (Fig. 5.4) and the average catch rate (88 kg/trip) was similar to that obtained in the nearby Songo Songo fishery (84 kg/trip), and significantly higher than that at Mtwara (57 kg/trip). The catch composition remained fairly constant over the census period with no significant changes in size distributions within the dominant species.

The limited census period has made assessment of the sustainability of the fishery difficult. Comparisons with other fisheries in the western Indian Ocean (36), however, indicate that these catch rates were still relatively high at the time of census. Within the Mafia fishery catches from the three areas of Chole Bay, Jujima Bay, and the Western Reefs beyond the Kisimani channel, all partially separated by a combination of narrow and deep-water channels, were found to differ in species compositions suggesting that the fish stocks within each area may be distinct and should, if possible, be managed separately.

Madema Trap Fishery. Box traps, locally known as *madema*, are fished from small canoes and ngalawa in areas of shallow coral and seagrass. The traps are made locally from strips of tree bark and vines with a standard mesh size of 5 cm. Traps baited with seaweed, sea cucumbers, and starfish are placed in shallow water coral and seagrass areas and are retrieved on low spring tides using a long pole. The fishery is relatively small scale at Mafia and Songo Songo but is more significant in the Mtwara area.

Traps are often placed directly on the reef where they not only damage the coral but also capture a significant proportion of the smaller species of true coral reef fish such as butterflyfish. On Mafia Island, at the request of the local fisheries officer, a study was conducted to determine the value of these fish to the fisherfolk and whether they could be returned to the water as they are most often unharmed by the fishing process, unlike those caught using nets (37). The catch composition (Table 5.6), as a function of the number of individuals, was dominated by parrotfish (22%) and surgeonfish (22%) but with catches of butterflyfish up to 15% in coral habitats. The average size was 20 cm, the largest being a 51 cm parrotfish and the smallest a 6 cm surgeonfish. Six to

Table 5.7. The scale and estimated catch yields for the invertebrate fisheries.

	Mafia Island (1994)			Songo Songo (1995)			Mtwara (1997)		
	No. fishers	Catch / person	Est. yield (mt/y)	No. fishers	Catch / person	Est. yield (mt/y)	No. fishers	Catch / person	Est. yield (mt/y)
Octopus	>200	5.0 kg	150	>150	3.8 kg	62	>150	9	86
Sea cucumber	na	3.7 ind.	na	40 + many part-time	8.1 ind.	7	-	-	Fished out *
Spiny lobster**	na	na	na	5 to10	7 to10 kg	na	na	na	na

Data taken from Mafia Island (Frontier, unpublished data); Songo Songo (16); Mtwara (26). * An estimated 2 tons / week are imported from Mozambique. ** All small scale at present. "na" means the information is not available.

seven percent of the catch was discarded and mainly consisted of butterflyfish and surgeonfish all averaging 6 to 9 cm in length but a significant number of individuals under 10 cm in length were still retained and given to children.

Within the south east of Chole Bay the catches from an estimated 100 traps fished each day were extrapolated to give an estimated removal of 15 000 butterflyfish each year. The effect of removing this number of fish from such a restricted area is not known but it is worthwhile asking fisherfolk to return these fish which have little monitory value to themselves, an adult butterflyfish (12 to 14 cm) fetching 5 to 10 Tsh (<US $0.01) in 1995. Alternatively, the mesh size of traps could be increased to retain only those fish greater than 15 cm. Many fishers feel, however, that the smaller more colorful species such as the butterflyfish, once in the trap, attract other fish and hence their escape may result in lower catches of the targeted species. Fishers could also be encouraged to place traps in the seagrass areas where the capture of butterflyfish is replaced by rabbitfish, a more highly prized food fish.

Invertebrate Fisheries

Octopus are collected on the reef flat and shallow subtidal inner reef, occasionally for local consumption, but mainly for export to the Far East. The common octopus (*Octopus vulgaris*) and the white-spotted octopus (*Octopus macropus*) are taken, the former the more numerous of the two. As women, men, and children are involved in the fishery it forms an important source of income to the coastal-island populations. Octopus are caught either by wading in the shallow water or by diving on the shallow reef. They live in holes and crevices which can often be spotted by the piles of broken shell outside the entrance. A slender stick is inserted into the hole and, if occupied, the resident octopus will wrap itself around the stick and can be withdrawn.

The collection intensity can be very high on low spring tides with more than 25 collectors per km² observed on occasion. One concern is that such high rates of intertidal trampling have been recorded to have deleterious impact on other reefs (56). The current issue is, however, the "boom and bust" nature that seems to have overtaken this fishery. For example, the fishery on Mafia Island was severely depleted following two years of intensive collection in 1992 (31) and has still not recovered. This pattern looks likely to be repeated as traders systematically move their operations down the coast offering high prices to

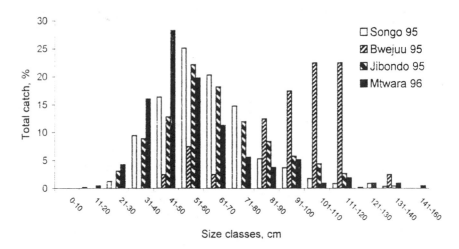

Figure 5.5. Octopus size distributions for catches landed at Jibondo Island (Mafia), Bwejuu Island (Mafia), Songo Songo Island, and Mnazi Bay.

stimulate rapid increases in fishing effort. In Mtwara catches have already declined from an average of 7.7 kg per person in 1996 to an average of 4 kg per person in 1997. To compound the problem the market has been further stimulated by the recent increase in availability of ice which now allows octopus to be sold fresh. An estimated 500 to 600 people collected over 280 metric tons/y of octopus in the combined Mafia Island, Songo Songo Archipelago and Mtwara areas (Table 5.7). The size distribution of octopus (average: 50 to 60 cm total length) was fairly consistent throughout with the exception of Bwejuu Island where the average total length in 1995 exceeded 100 cm (Fig. 5.5). As catches in Bwejuu are known to be on the decline it is thought that fishers may have been forced to collect in deeper water which may explain the larger-sized specimens.

Sea cucumbers are collected solely for export to the Far East; there is no known local consumption. They are collected from the intertidal flats (mainly at night) and by snorkel diving over sand and seagrass areas. At least 15 species are collected with prices varying considerably between species. Although sea cucumbers are collected by many people on an opportunistic basis, for example while octopus fishing, there are many organized groups of fishers who dive for them on a regular basis with a significant number of teams now using SCUBA to collect in deeper water. Catch yields were available only for the Songo Songo Archipelago where 40 full-time collectors and an unknown number of opportunistic fishers collected an estimated 7 mt/y in 1995 (Table 5.7). There is currently no enforced regulation on catch quotas or minimum sizes and the fishery has already been fished out at Mtwara and in some areas around Mafia. Sea cucumbers taken around Mafia were significantly smaller than those collected in the more recently developed fishery in the Songo Songo Archipelago (Fig. 5.6).

The lobster fishery in 1996 was small scale with the painted lobster (*Panulirus versicolor*), the ornate spiny lobster (*Panulirus ornatus*) and

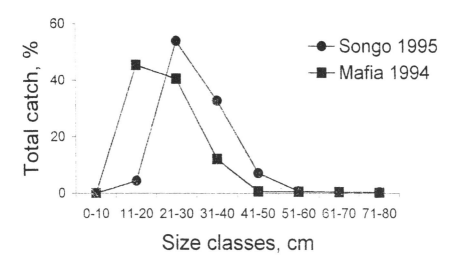

Figure 5.6. Sea cucumber size distributions for catches landed at Mafia and Songo Songo Islands.

occasional specimens of the flathead locust lobster (*Thennuorientalis*) taken by snorkel divers and nets. The fishery is mainly opportunistic with limited local demand. An increasing demand from tourism, especially on Mafia Island, combined with increased transport facilities, including regular air flights to Songo Songo from Dar es Salaam, is likely to lead to expansion of the fishery. An average catch by an experienced snorkel diver may be 7 to 10 kg taken over 3 to 4 hours with individuals taken ranging in size from juveniles at 100 to 200 g to large adults at 4 to 5 kg (Table 5.7). There is no regulation of the fishery and no effort is made to leave juveniles or egg-carrying females.

Coral Mining

Two forms of coral are mined, ancient limestone from fossil reefs and live coral. Fossil coral is mined from inland deposits and the raised coral rag along the shoreline for use either as building blocks or aggregate. Live coral is broken from shallow back reefs at low spring tides using iron bars. The denser coral forms such as *Porites* are preferred. Live coral is either used directly as a building aggregate or is burnt on open kilns to produce white lime for use as a cement alternative and as a white wash for houses. Live coral is preferred over ancient limestone as it has fewer impurities thus giving a higher quality "white" lime. Live coral is mined throughout southern Tanzania but the scale of mining is greatest around Mafia Island where an estimated 950 metric tons has been mined each year since 1985 (Table 5.8).

The negative effects of coral mining include the loss of natural breakwaters, indirect loss of sheltered marine habitats, direct loss of habitat for the many associated fish species (23), and loss of aesthetic value to reefs important for tourism (7). An enforced total cessation of mining is not practical as a good deal of local income is derived from the sale of lime and coral and there are often no economic alternatives for building materials. A variety of management

Table 5.8. Scale of collection and local involvement in coral mining.

Variable	Mafia District 1985-1994	Songo Songo Archipelago (1995)	Mtwara (1996)
No. People involved (secondary income)	475*	1 man full-time + many part-time	50 to 70
Est. tons / year	950**	100	480
Est. area (m^2) of reef mined to 0.5 m depth	48,000**	na	na

Data taken from (16, 20, 31) and * from (3). ** A proportion of this was mined from the Songo Songo and Kilwa reefs and brought back to Mafia for processing. na = information not available.

options have been tried in other parts of the world including mining of "sacrificial reefs" in the Maldives, and a partial ban on mining and provision of alternative materials in Sri Lanka. A more recent study on Mafia Island (20) demonstrated the potential use of sun-dried mud bricks as an alternative to coral (Box 5.1). Despite the obvious potential for the use of mud-bricks on Mafia Island many other sites such as Songo Songo Island have no suitable soils. Consequently, the building of higher quality, longer lasting buildings using imported and subsidized materials may be the only viable option.

Marine and Coastal Management

Discussions on the potential of marine parks and reserves in Tanzania have been undertaken since 1968 (46,54) with the first attempts to manage the marine and coastal environment areas initiated in 1975 through regulations under the Fisheries Act, 1970 (Table 5.9). Eight small areas of reef were declared Marine Reserves for total protection including two in southern Tanzania at Chole Bay and Tutia Reef off Mafia Island (Fig. 5.2). Lack of capacity led to these reserves being "paper reserves" with no active management established (8). Later pressure from various quarters urged the creation of larger, multiple use areas combining conservation and the concept of sustainable use and development (54). In April 1995 Mafia Island was gazetted as the first multiple use marine protected area in Tanzania (32).

Development of the Mafia Island Marine Park

Work towards developing the Mafia Island Marine Park (MIMP) was initiated in 1988 when the University of Dar es Salaam (through the Institute of Marine Science, IMS), with financial support from Shell Petroleum Development Tanzania Limited, and in collaboration with Frontier-Tanzania and a number of other agencies, sought to provide the baseline information upon which to develop the Park proposal. A marine park steering committee was formed in 1991 and the existing information including that provided by the IMS and Frontier-Tanzania collaboration (31) was presented and discussed by representatives in the local villages. Following a request from the Division of Fisheries (DOF) the Food and Agriculture Organization (FAO) agreed to sponsor the first of the Steering Committee activities and a consultant, in collaboration with the Attorney General's Chambers, began work in September 1991 to review the legislative base and propose recommendations. While forming a legislative structure specifically for the Mafia Park the team regarded

Table 5.9. A history of management recommendations and initiatives in southern Tanzania.

Year	Initiatives and recommendations
1968	First survey to assess the potential of Tanzania's coastal reefs for a national park (46). The Trustees of the Tanzania National Parks recommended the survey which was joint-funded by the New York Zoological Society, The Conservation Foundation and the African Wildlife Leadership Foundation. Recommendations for southern Tanzania included a biosphere reserve for the Mafia Island / Rufiji Delta complex and a reserve at Kilwa. Dynamite fishing and seine nets were identified as serious causes of reef destruction.
1970	Fisheries Act of 1970 outlawed dynamite fishing in Tanzania.
1975	Eight marine reserves were designated under the 1970 Fisheries Act. Two of these were in south Tanzania at Chole Bay and Kitutia Reef, Mafia Island. None were implemented.
1981	Review of the problems of marine conservation in Tanzania and call for government action (8).
1983	Only those reserves at Lathan Island and Mafia Island were still said to have intact reefs (50)
1984	UNEP identified resource use activities to have the greatest potential impact on marine environments in southern Tanzania (53).
1987	UNEP was invited to draw up a national action plan for the protection, management and development of Tanzania's marine and coastal environment.
1988	A workshop was held in Dar es Salaam on the "Ecology and Bioproductivity of the Marine Coastal Waters of Eastern Africa". A totally protected core area with a buffer zone of controlled use was recommended – no site was identified (39).
1989	(i) The Frankfurt Zoological Society suggested a study for a proposal to establish a marine park on Mafia Island. The initial study was implemented by the University of Dar es Salaam and Frontier-Tanzania with funding from Shell Petroleum Development Ltd. (45). (ii) UNEP published their recommendations for a national action plan for marine and coastal conservation and management (54). (iii) Frontier-Tanzania initiated a study to provide the information identified as necessary for the formulation of a marine park at Mafia island.
1991	WWF became facilitators for the proposed Mafia Island Marine Park (MIMP). NORAD provided funds for set up of infrastructure for the MIMP.
1993	Resolution passed at Arusha on Integrated Coastal Zone Management in East Africa.
1994	Marine Environmental Protection Program (MEPP) initiated for the Kilwa, Lindi and Mtwara Districts. Facilitated by the Rural Integrated Support Program (RIPS) funded by FINNIDA
1995	(i) Mafia Island Marine Park gazetted. (ii) Frontier-Tanzania initiated marine surveys of the Songo Songo Archipelago and Kilwa area.
1996	Frontier-Tanzania initiated marine surveys of the Mtwara area.

the Mafia plans as part of a longer-term program of developing a network of marine parks and reserves. The result was the drafting of a Marine Parks and Reserves Act and Regulations.

A workshop, funded by the World Wide Fund for Nature (WWF), was held on Mafia in October 1991 to present the proposals of the Steering Committee and to provide an opportunity for the island community and resource users to present their views. The workshop was well attended by a full range of potential and current stakeholders and included representatives from the local communities, commercial operators, and conservation bodies. The steering committee presented its proposals and following intensive discussion by all parties a proposal for the development of the MIMP was recommended. This workshop, which is often cited as being the centerpiece of community participation provided the basis for the development of the General Management Plan (GMP). The draft GMP developed post workshop (completed 1993) includes development proposals, zoning plans, and administrative arrangements.

Box 5.1. Mud Bricks, an Alternative to Coral?

Coral mining has been identified as an unsustainable use of resources and a significant source of habitat degradation in the Mafia District of Tanzania (3). Mined coral in this area has also been shown to be an important local building material and source of income to many people (1,2,4). If coral mining is to be prohibited in some areas then it is essential that alternative sources of building materials and income are first identified and accepted by the local people. A study was conducted on Mafia Island in 1994 by Frontier-Tanzania, with financial support from the Swedish International Development Agency (SIDA), to assess the feasibility of the production of pressed and sun dried mud bricks for use as an alternative building material and income source to mined live coral.

The technology for brick production is simple, inexpensive and readily available. Bricks are produced using a manually operated brick press (see photo) and are sun dried with no need for firing. The soil used needs to have an equal mix of sands and clays. Bricks can be made with little or no need for cement or lime stabilizer, although in these cases an outside coating is advised. Operation of the press and the full procedure for testing soil and brick quality are outlined clearly in a field operations manual available from the manufacturers of the brick press (see below).

Meetings were held in 21 villages and the people were found to be well aware of the problems associated with coral mining and open to the idea of using mud bricks as an alternative. Of the soil samples taken from 20 locations across Mafia and it's associated islets, the majority, with the notable exception of those from Jibondo Island, were found to be suitable and available in sufficient quantities for brick production and a demonstration house was built on one of the smaller islands.

Table. Summary of costs (1995) to build a small residential building for a range of alternative materials (excludes the costs for labor and transport of materials). Costs calculated at an exchange rate of 600 Tsh: US $ 1. A durability of 1 is most durable.

Building materials	Cost / US$	Durability
Unstabilized mud bricks	Nil	4
Mud bricks stabilized with lime	95	3
Wood poles and mud	163	6
Mud bricks stabilized with cement	422	2
Wood poles + mud + coral blocks	447	5
Cement + sand + cement blocks	650	1

An economic comparison of a range of traditional building technologies found mud bricks to provide a low cost and durable alternative (see Table). If constructed on a "self help" family basis, the main body of a house can be constructed using unstabilized mud bricks at no material cost thus providing a good building option for the poor. Commercial production of mud bricks was shown to be viable with a four man team able to produce 150 bricks per day which, if sold at 20 Tsh each, would provide an acceptable income alternative to that obtained through coral mining.

Finally, it was found that the benefits of building with mud bricks not only include a reduction in the need for coral but they also eliminate the need for mangrove poles in wall construction and firewood in the conversion of coral to lime. As firewood is in short supply on many of the smaller islands and mangrove cutting is illegal the option of using mud bricks is highly favorable. Since the completion

Photo. Operation of the CINVA-RAM brick press for the production of sun-dried mud-bricks.

of the project in 1995 two more houses have been built and, having been accepted by the local people, recommendations have been put forward to provide the villages with their own presses and to provide initial instruction in their use.

Note: The CINVA-RAM brick press can be obtained from the Crafts and Artisans Promotion Unit (CAPU), Morogoro, Tanzania, and the University of Dar es Salaam. A copy of the full report is available from: Frontier, P.O. Box 9473, Dar es Salaam or, Frontier, 77 Leonard St , London EC2A 4QS, UK

W.R.T. Darwall

References

1. Anderson, J.E.C., Ngazi, Z. 1995. Marine resource use and the establishment of a marine park: Mafia Island, Tanzania. *Ambio* 24: 475-481

2.   Darwall, W.R.T. 1996a. *Marine Biological and Resource Use Surveys of the Songo Songo Archipelago. Report No. 7: Marine Resource Use in the Songo Songo Archipelago.* A report submitted to the Royal Norwegian Embassy. The Society for Environmental Exploration and The University of Dar es Salaam. ISSN 1369-8788

3.   Dulvy, N.K., Stanwell-smith, D., Darwall, W.R.T., Horrill, C.J. 1995. Coral mining at Mafia Island, Tanzania: A management dilemma. *Ambio* 24: 358-365

4.   Horrill, J.C., Ngoile, M.A.K. 1991. *Mafia Island Report No. 2. Results of the Physical, Biological and Resource Use Surveys: Rationale for the Development of a Management Strategy.* The Society for Environmental Exploration, London. ISSN 1 873070 02 0

The new legislation was passed in November 1994 and the area was gazetted in April 1995 as the Mafia Island Marine Park. Many would, however, consider the park a misnomer and prefer to call it a coastal zone management project given the number of people who will continue to extract marine resources from within the area. Recent work by WWF and DOF has focused on rationalizing the GMP which was considered to be convoluted and overly ambitious with no clear vision for the future of the Park. It wasn't until 1996 that the management plan was translated into Swahili and by early 1997 the community had still not seen the full proposals for zoning or management. The Park remained without a full time warden until 1998 with no effective management in terms of the conservation objectives proposed within the GMP.

This loss of momentum was a product of the excessive time taken to establish the new institutional framework. The lack of active management was due to the time taken to appoint the Board of Trustees with its first meeting in November 1996, and to set up other institutional structures as outlined in the Act. Despite the general lack of active management WWF did manage to implement a successful anti-dynamite program within and around the MIMP through the district authorities and attempted to facilitate a more committed and rational community participation and development program. DOF with aid from NORAD also undertook a number of additional community projects aimed at creating alternatives to unsustainable resource use.

Both the Ministry and donors appear committed to establishing a working Marine Park. It was a combination of the establishment of a new institution and the struggle for control over the new enterprise that led to conflict between key participants. Hopefully this discord will be resolved and the process of implementation will be able to proceed in a more productive manner.

The Marine Environmental Protection Program

The other major initiative within southern Tanzania is the Marine Environmental Protection Program (MEPP) within which marine environmental management in the Kilwa, Mtwara, and Lindi Districts has developed over the past few years. Facilitated by the Rural Integrated Project Support Program (RIPS), funded by FINIDA, the MEPP was first initiated in 1994 following a participatory workshop in Sudi Town to discuss problems relating to the marine environment. By providing a platform for knowledge swapping, debate, and decision making on marine environmental issues the MEPP intends to foster community organization and empowerment (assisted by local government) to enable local people to manage and be responsible for their own local coastal and marine resources.

The first step towards this goal was the collaborative formulation and implementation of a number of initiatives including: (1) the formation of the Sudi Committee, (2) the introduction of seaweed farming, (3) a village credit revolving scheme to enable fishers to purchase much needed conventional fishing gears, (4) the construction of a fresh fish market in Kilwa Kivinje, (5) dynamite patrols, and (6) the production of media material such as community videos and radio programs through which local communities can express their views. With the notable exception of dynamite patrols, these initiatives have been successful, but more information is needed on the status of coastal and marine habitats and the levels and patterns of resource use in the region. The Frontier-Tanzania Marine Research Program in collaboration with the MEPP is collecting this information.

Further participatory workshops and group discussions are planned in order to formulate new management objectives and initiatives including the introduction of a voluntary fishery log-book scheme and the implementation of restricted fishing and gear use areas (zoning schemes) as advocated at previous meetings. Training will be given to fisheries officers and elected community representatives in simple marine survey techniques, basic data analysis and feedback techniques, to provide a core of local expertise able to train other villagers, and conduct future marine environmental monitoring in the area.

Local community representatives have recently written a constitution and are applying for registration of their own community environmental NGO (The Southern Zone Confederation for the Conservation of the Marine Environment) through which they can formally express their opinions and needs.

The Songo Songo Gas Development Project

The "Songas - Gas to Electricity Project" is one of the largest industrial developments along the coast of Tanzania. By late 1998 this project had planned to pipe natural gas from Songo Songo Island to Dar es Salaam. Approximately 25 kilometers of pipeline passes through the marine environment of which 0.5 km at either end will be entrenched to a depth of 2 m while the remainder will simply be laid on the surface of the seabed (55).

With a number of coral reef systems in close vicinity to the gas reserve, steps have already been recommended to mitigate against potential effects of sedimentation on reefs during pipe laying (55). With the only other foreseeable major impact arising from rupture of the pipeline by dynamite fishing Songas is to purchase a patrol boat to protect the pipeline. In recognition of the wider environmental impacts of dynamite fishing Songas has agreed to also provide the boat for marine police to patrol the entire Songo-Songo archipelago.

This action by Songas is seen to be an extremely positive gesture that should provide great benefit to the local environment and the dependent communities. The hope is that this will be an example of industry and conservation working together.

Conservation and Management Priorities

Southern Tanzania has been found to support a great diversity of marine habitats and a number of valuable fisheries upon which the coastal population are highly dependent. It is therefore of great concern that, at the time of writing, these resources still lack any effective management. Many of the fisheries show signs of overuse and the coral reefs are being degraded through activities such as fishing with explosives, seine netting, and coral mining. A management strategy is outlined below which suggests that habitats and fisheries should be managed separately and on different geographic scales.

The main priority is to halt the current destruction of coral reefs. A number of independent initiatives (MIMP, MEPP, and the Songas / Department of Fisheries collaboration) are currently addressing this issue but there is little coordination of activities between them and they are largely limited to operating within district boundaries. Habitats must be managed on a regional scale or the problems will simply be shifted from one area to another. The lack of coordination across district boundaries may have already put the reefs of the Songo Songo Archipelago at risk from increased dynamite fishing by fishers now barred from the MIMP. This problem has arisen following the initiation of regular dynamite patrols around southern Mafia. Although this action has undoubtedly benefited the reefs within the MIMP no prior provision was made to deal with the potential diversion of dynamite fishers to the neighboring reefs of the Songo Songo Archipelago. Furthermore with the intensity of reef destruction now more concentrated in localized areas, the overall impact may be more severe than if the effects had remained diluted over a larger area. Habitat management, which could be limited to policing against the use of destructive fishing techniques, must operate at a regional scale.

The lack of effective management of the fisheries is also of concern. Many of the fisheries currently have little if any management regulations and those that do exist are rarely enforced on account of insufficient personnel and finances to implement them. For example, the Songo Songo Archipelago which supports some of the most productive inshore fisheries in Tanzania has no resident fisheries officer (16). The nearest officer is based in Kilwa Kivinje and his visits to the area may be limited to two or three times each year. Fisheries officers must be adequately trained and equipped to both monitor fish catches and enforce regulations throughout the region. Wages may need to be increased as many fisheries officers claim to be so poorly paid that they are forced to take bribes instead of enforcing the regulations. In other cases they say they would simply rather take a bribe than arrest a fisher who will most often be released the next day, without charge, following a phone call from his sponsor in Dar es Salaam. Pressure from the powerful sponsors of illegal fishing activities must be stopped before progress can be made in trying to control such activities.

With limited reliable long-term catch data for any of the fisheries it is difficult to assess their current status and to provide specific management recommendations. The more intensive monitoring of fisheries catches must become a priority. Current catch monitoring is most often limited to those fish on sale at the markets and, with most fish being sold at sea, provides little information for the status of the local fishery. Ideally catches should be recorded at sea by the fishers themselves. Many fisherfolk have shown a keen competitive interest in comparing their catches so it may be possible to introduce a system of personal logging of catches if weighing scales are provided.

The provision of scales at a central point for the weighing of large fish such as sharks, rays and groupers may prove popular and also provide valuable information on catch compositions over time. Currently there is no information available on the size compositions of the larger fish which are most often cut into pieces, salted, and dried before reaching the markets. Despite the general lack of long-term catch data the ray fisheries (14,16) and the invertebrate fisheries were identified as being over-fished and are priorities for immediate management. Until more information is available a simple recommendation is to prohibit the use of SCUBA for the collection of invertebrates thus preserving the deeper water sites as harvest refugia.

In contrast to the management of habitats it has been shown in other areas that fisheries may be successfully managed on a local scale as small reserves while also providing benefits to the neighboring fisheries through an overflow of increased stocks from within the reserve (1,47, but see 41). It may therefore be practical for management of fisheries to be administered through the independent initiatives already operating within each district. The confinement of management within districts would greatly ease the difficulties of administration often associated with regional programs. Funding may be more readily obtained for a number of small-scale projects than for a single large-scale regional initiative. Such a management scenario does, however, still require a regional program for the management and policing of habitats to be in place before any reserves are implemented.

A final suggestion is that efforts should be made, as on Mafia, to include a number of turtle nesting beaches within the reserves. The turtle population has little chance for survival unless nesting beaches can be protected.

References

1. Alcala, A.C. 1988. The effects of marine reserves on coral fish abundances and yields of Philippine coral reefs. *Ambio* 17: 194-199
2. Alcala, A.C., Gomez, E.D. 1987. Dynamiting of coral reefs for fish. A resource destructive fishing method. In *Human Impacts on Coral Reefs: Facts and Recommendations*, eds. Salvat, B. pp. 51-60. French Polynesia: Antenne Museum. E.P.H.E.
3. Anderson, J.E.C., Ngazi, Z. 1995. Marine resource use and the establishment of a marine park: Mafia Island, Tanzania. *Ambio* 24: 475-481
4. Barnett, R. 1997. The shark trade in mainland Tanzania and Zanzibar. In *Shark Fisheries and Trade in the Western Indian and Southeast Atlantic Oceans*. TRAFFIC Report
5. Boshoff, P.H. 1958. Development and constitution of the reefs. In *A Natural History of Inhaca Island, Mocambique*. eds. Macnae, W., Kalk, M., pp. 49-56. Johannesburg: Witwatersrand University Press
6. Brown, A. 1996. *The Prosobranch Mollusks of Songo Songo, Tanzania: A Species list and an Investigation into the Commercial Shell Trade and the Methods Used by the Environmental Organisation Frontier to Assess It.*

Undergraduate Dissertation. Royal Holloway College, University of London

7.   Brown, B.E., Dunne, R.P. 1988. The environmental impact of coral mining on coral reefs in the Maldives. *Environmental Conservation* 15: 159-165

8.   Bryceson, I. 1981. A review of some of the problems of tropical marine conservation with particular reference to the Tanzanian coast. *Biological Conservation* 20: 163-171

9.   Choiseul, V.M. 1996. *The Status of the Marine Gastropod Fishery in the Mafia Island Marine Park, Tanzania.* The Society for Environmental Exploration and The University of Dar es Salaam. Unpublished Report

10. Choiseul, V.M., Darwall, W.R.T. 1995. *Marine Biological and Resource Use Surveys of the Songo Songo Archipelago. Report No.2: Fanjove Island.* A report submitted to the Royal Norwegian Embassy. The Society for Environmental Exploration and The University of Dar es Salaam

11. Choiseul, V.M., Darwall, W.R.T. 1996. *Mafia Island Report No.5. Results of Biological and Resource Use Surveys of the Western Reefs of the Mafia Island Marine Park.* The Society for Environmental Exploration and The University of Dar es Salaam. ISSN 1369-8788

12. Choiseul, V.M., Darwall, W.R.T. 1996. *Marine Biological and Resource Use Surveys of the Songo Songo Archipelago. Report No.3: Nyuni Island.* A report submitted to the Royal Norwegian Embassy. The Society for Environmental Exploration and The University of Dar es Salaam. ISSN 1369-8788

13. Cowper, D., Darwall, W.R.T. 1996. The current status of marine turtles of the Songo Songo archipelago, Tanzania. *Miombo* 15: 14-15

14. Darwall, W.R.T. 1995a. *Mafia Island Report No. 4. The Shark and Ray Fishery of the Mafia Island Marine Park: Current Status and Management Recommendations.* The Society for Environmental Exploration and The University of Dar es Salaam

15. Darwall, W.R.T. 1995b. *Marine Biological and Resource Use Surveys of the Songo Songo Archipelago. Report No. 1: Simaya Island.* A report submitted to the Royal Norwegian Embassy. The Society for Environmental Exploration and The University of Dar es Salaam. ISSN 1369-8788

16. Darwall, W.R.T. 1996a. *Marine Biological and Resource Use Surveys of the Songo Songo Archipelago. Report No. 7: Marine Resource Use in the Songo Songo Archipelago.* A report submitted to the Royal Norwegian Embassy. The Society for Environmental Exploration and The University of Dar es Salaam. ISSN 1369-8788

17. Darwall, W.R.T. 1996b. *Mafia Island Report No. 6. The Seine Net Fishery of the Mafia Island Marine Park: Current Status and Management Recommendations.* The Society for Environmental Exploration and The University of Dar es Salaam

18. Darwall, W.R.T. 1997. *Marine Biological and Resource Use Surveys of the Songo Songo Archipelago. Report No. 5: Songo Songo Island.* A report

submitted to the Royal Norwegian Embassy. The Society for Environmental Exploration and The University of Dar es Salaam. ISSN 1369-8788

19. Darwall, W.R.T., Dulvy, N.K., Choiseul, V.M. 1994. *Mafia Island Report No. 3: Results of Biological and Resource Use Surveys: Recommendations for Management.* The Society for Environmental Exploration and The University of Dar es Salaam

20. Darwall, W.R.T., Edward, J., Kabado, D. 1995. *Results of a Feasibility Study for the Production of Sun-dried Pressed Mud Bricks as an Alternative to the Use of Mined Live Coral on Mafia Island.* A report submitted to the Swedish Embassy, Dar es Salaam. The Society for Environmental Exploration and The University of Dar es Salaam

21. Darwall, W.R.T., Choiseul, V.M. 1996. *Marine Biological and Resource Use Surveys of the Songo Songo Archipelago. Report No.4: Okuza Island.* A report submitted to the Royal Norwegian Embassy. The Society for Environmental Exploration and The University of Dar es Salaam. ISSN 1369-8788

22. Darwall, W.R.T., Guard, M., Choiseul, V.M., Whittington M. 1996. *Marine Biological and Resource Use Surveys of the Songo Songo Archipelago. Report No. 6: Survey of Thirteen Patch Reefs (Vols.1-4).* A report submitted to the Royal Norwegian Embassy. The Society for Environmental Exploration and The University of Dar es Salaam. ISSN 1369-8788

23. Dulvy, N.K., Stanwell-smith, D., Darwall, W.R.T., Horrill, C.J. 1995. Coral mining at Mafia Island, Tanzania: A management dilemma. *Ambio* 24: 358-365

24. Frazier, J. 1976. Sea turtles in Tanzania. *Tanzania Notes and Records.* No.77 and 78: 11-14

25. Gabie, V. 1958. Fishes of Inhaca: supplementary list from records at the Department of Zoology, University of Witwatersrand. In *A Natural History of Inhaca Island, Mocambique.* eds. Macnae, W., Kalk, M., pp. 136-137. Johannesburg: Witwatersrand University Press

26. Guard, M., Muller, C., Evans, D. 1997. *Marine Biological and Marine Resource Use Surveys in the Mtwara District, Tanzania. Surveys of Fringing and Patch Reef within and adjacent to Mnazi Bay Report No. 1 Vols. 1,2.* The Society for Environmental Exploration and The University of Dar es Salaam

27. Guard, M., Msaiganah, M. 1998. Dynamite fishing in southern Tanzania: geographical variation, intensity of use and possible solutions *Marine Pollution Bulletin* 34: 758-762

28. Hamilton, H.G.H., Brakel W.H. 1984. Structure and coral fauna of East African reefs. *Bulletin of Marine Science* 34: 248-266

29. Hanaphy, F., Muller,C. 1997. *Report 8: Survey of Six Reefs: Amani; Mpovi; Mwanamkaya; Kiswani; Fungu Wango; and Rukyira, Kilwa District.*

Marine Biological and Resource Use Surveys in the Songo Songo Archipelago. Frontier-Tanzania Marine Research Programme. The Society for Environmental Exploration and the University of Dar es Salaam. ISSN 1369-8788

30. Hasset, D.V. 1983. *A Socioeconomic Report on the Fisheries in Kilwa District.* Report of the Mtwara/Lindi RIDEP project, London: U.K. Overseas Development Agency

31. Horrill, J.C., Ngoile, M.A.K. 1991. *Mafia Island Report No. 2. Results of the Physical, Biological and Resource Use Surveys: Rationale for the Development of a Management Strategy.* The Society for Environmental Exploration, London. pp. 46. ISSN 1 873070 02 0

32. Horrill, J.C., Darwall, W.R.T., Ngoile M.A.K. 1996. Development of a Marine Protected Area: Mafia Island, Tanzania. *Ambio* 25: 50-57

33. Howell, K.M. 1993. *A Review of the Conservation Status of Sea Turtles in Tanzania.* The Wildlife Conservation Society of Tanzania, Dar es Salaam

34. Kayombo, N.A. 1989. *Progress Report: Preliminary Study of the Ecology of the Intertidal Molluscs of Mafia Island, Tanzania.* National Museums of Tanzania

35. Kent, P.E., Hunt, M.A., Johnstone, M.A. 1971. *The Geology and Geophysics of Coastal Tanzania.* N.E.R.C. Geophysical paper No. 6

36. Laroche, J., Ramananarivo, N. 1995. A preliminary survey of the artisanal fishery on coral reefs of the Tulear Region (southwest Madagascar). *Coral Reefs 14*: 193-200

37. Lawley, S.L. 1996. *The Status of the Madema Fishery operating from Juani Island, and the Marine Impacts resulting as a consequence of the Mafia Island Marine Protected Area.* The Society for Environmental Exploration / The Department of Maritime Studies and International Transport, The University of Wales / The University of Dar es Salaam

38. Littler, M.M., Littler, B.M., Brooks, B.L., Kaven, J.M. 1997. A unique coral reef formation discovered at the Great Astrolobe Reef, Fiji. *Coral Reefs* 19: 51-54

39. Mainoya, J.R., Pratap, H.B. 1988. Marine conservation strategy for sustained bioproductivity in Tanzanian waters. In *Proceedings of the Workshop on Ecology and Bioproductivity of the Marine Waters of Eastern Africa*, ed. Mainoya, J.R. pp. 145-153. Dar es Salaam: University of Dar es Salaam

40. McClanahan, T.R. 1988. Seasonality in East Africa's coastal waters. *Marine Ecology Progress Series* 44: 191-199

41. McClanahan, T.R., Kaunda-Arara, B. 1996. Fishery recovery in a coral-reef marine park and its effect on the adjacent fishery. *Conservation Biology* 10: 1187-1199

42. Newell, B.S. 1959. The Hydrography of the British East African coastal waters. *Colonial Office Fishery Publication. London* 11: 1-18

43. Newton, L.C., Parkes, E.V.H., Thompson, R.C. 1993. The effects of shell collecting on the abundance of gastropods on Tanzanian shores. *Biological Conservation* 63: 241-245

44. Ngoile, M.A.K., Bwathondi P.O.J., Makwaia E.S. 1988. Trends in the exploitation of marine fisheries resources in Tanzania. In *Proceedings of the workshop on Ecology and Bioproductivity of the Marine Coastal*

Waters of East Africa. ed. Mainoya J.R. pp. 93-100. Dar es Salaam: University of Dar es Salaam

45. Ngoile, M.A.K. 1989. The Development of a Marine National Park, Mafia Island, Tanzania. University of Dar es Salaam, Institute of Marine Sciences, Zanzibar

46. Ray, G.C. 1968. *Marine Parks for Tanzania*. The Conservation Foundation: New York Zoological Society, Washington, D.C.

47. Roberts, C.M., Polunin, N.V.C. 1991. Are marine reserves effective in management of reef fisheries? *Reviews in Fish Biology and Fisheries* 1: 65-91

48. Rosen, B.R. 1975. The distribution of coral reefs. *Report of the Underwater Association.* 1: 1-16

49. Rumisha, C.H. 1995. *Fisheries Policy and Legislation. Technical Workshop on Legislation and Policy Review of Integrated Coastal Zone Management for Tanzania.* Dar es Salaam: Department of Fisheries

50. Salm, R.V. 1983. Coral reefs of the Western Indian Ocean: a threatened heritage. *Ambio* 12: 349-353

51. Smith, J.L.B. 1958. Fishes of Inhaca. In *A Natural History of Inhaca Island, Mocambique.* eds. Macnae, W., Kalk, M. pp.136-137. Johannesburg: Witwatersrand University Press

52. Talbot, F.H. 1965. A description of the coral structure of Tutia Reef (Tanganyika territory, East Africa), and its fish fauna. *Proceedings of the Zoological Society of London* 145: 431-474

53. UNEP.1984. *Socio-Economic Activities that May Have an Impact on the Marine and Coastal Environments of the East African Region: National Reports.* Nairobi: UNEP Regional Seas Reports and Studies No. 51

54. UNEP.1989. *Coastal and Marine Environmental Problems of the United Republic of Tanzania.* UNEP Regional Seas Reports and Studies No. 106

55. Wagner, G.M., Mgaya, Y.D., Benno,B.L. 1997. *Final Report of Environmental Assessment of the Songo-Songo Gas to Electricity Project: Impact on the Marine Environment.* Norplan A/S.

56. Woodland, R.V., Hooper, N.A. 1977. The effect of human trampling on coral reefs. *Biological Conservation* 11: 1-4

Chapter 6

Northern Tanzania and Zanzibar

J.C. Horrill, A.T. Kamukuru, Y.D. Mgaya & M. Risk

The northern section of the Tanzanian coast includes the mainland areas of Tanga, Bagamoyo and Dar es Salaam as well as the oceanic island of Pemba and the continental island of Unguja (often mistakenly called Zanzibar, Fig. 6.1). Zanzibar is, in fact, the name of the state which is comprised of the two islands of Unguja and Pemba. The 200 m depth contour, which indicates the approximate edge of the continental shelf, lies between six and 40 km from the mainland coast. Pemba being an oceanic island is separated from the continental shelf by a 400 m deep channel. The mainland coast and the islands are surrounded by coastal fringing reefs and patch reefs. The mainland fringing reef is broken by bays and river estuaries.

These reefs form an important source of subsistence and income for an estimated coastal population of 3.8 million people in 1988 representing 16% of the total population of Tanzania (49). Given an average annual growth rate of 4% (1988 census) this figure will be in the region of 4.6 million in 1997. The largest concentration of population is Dar es Salaam which has an estimated 2.5 million inhabitants with the population of Zanzibar town estimated at 300 000. Other large towns along the coast include Tanga and Bagamoyo. This chapter will describe the physical and biological aspects of the coral reefs of northern Tanzania, Zanzibar and Pemba, the social and economic characteristics, management issues, and a brief description of current management initiatives.

Geology

The present shape of the continental land forms (mainland coastline, Unguja Island) were developed during the Pleistocene when the sea level fluctuated by up to 100 m over the last 250 000 years depending on the amount of seawater locked up in the global ice sheets (14). Superimposed on this were land rises associated with geological faulting (51). During glacial times, sea level was low, and Unguja was part of the mainland. At that time, Unguja received input of siliciclastic sediments, brought in from areas further inland. During interglacial times, sea level rose, Unguja became an island, and carbonate platforms (coral reefs) developed. The present reefs are a relatively

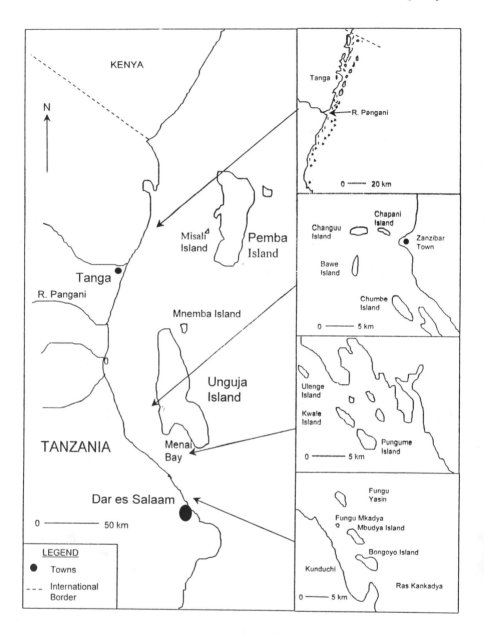

Figure 6.1. Map of the nearshore areas of northern Tanzania.

thin veneer developed on these pre-existing interglacial reefs. The oceanic island of Pemba is thought to have broken away from the mainland about 10 million years ago along a line known as the Pemba Rift (51).

Physical Oceanography

Climate

The climate is characterized by two main seasons dictated by the behavior of the Inter-Tropical Convergence Zone (ITCZ). The northeast monsoon (November to March) is characterized by higher air temperatures, lower wind speeds, calmer seas and a reduced velocity (1 to 2 knots) of the East African Coastal Current (EACC). The southeast monsoon (April to October), is typified by cooler air temperatures, higher winds, rougher seas with the velocity of the EACC increasing to a speed of 4 knots.

Hydrography

The waters off the Tanzanian coast are characterized by four water masses of different qualities occurring at increasing depths; tropical surface water, Arabian Sea water, Antarctic intermediate water and North Indian deep water which includes the outflow from the Red Sea. The tropical surface water has high salinity and oxygen content and is the most important for reef development. Reefs are protected from the deeper high salinity and low oxygen Arabian water by a thermocline. Although the depth of the thermocline varies seasonally from a maximum approaching 130 m at the end of the southeastern monsoon, to a minimum of some 60 m during the northeast monsoon (46), it does not allow significant upwelling or mixing of these two layers.

Due to high mixing the tropical surface water is essentially isothermal from the surface to the thermocline during the southeast monsoon. In the northeast monsoon surface water temperatures are, however, higher with a decrease in temperature with depth (46). The surface temperature reaches a minimum in September of just under 25 °C, and rises to a maximum of 29 °C in March and April. Oxygen concentration depends on temperature but approaches saturation throughout the year near the surface but there may be some reduction in oxygen tension before the thermocline is reached.

The tropical surface water also forms the northerly flowing East African Coastal Current (EACC) which dominates the general hydrography of the East African coast (46,47). The EACC has its origin as the South Equatorial Current which flows westwards across the Indian Ocean at a latitude of about 10°S striking the African coast at Cape Delgado in northern Mozambique, where it divides into the southerly Mozambique Current and the EACC. During the northeast monsoon the EACC meets the southerly flowing Somali Current with which it merges and then flow eastwards as the Equatorial Counter Current The point where this occurs is dependent on the monsoon winds. The winds of the northern monsoon impede the EACC, reducing its northward velocity to 0.5 knots. In the southeast monsoon the higher velocities of the EACC push this meeting point past the Kenya-Somalia border.

Tides

Although the EACC is important to reef development over larger geographical areas, tidal currents are very important locally. In Tanzania, tides are of the mixed semi-diurnal type, but the inequality of successive high and low waters, although more marked during neap tides, is never such as to obscure the rise and fall of the tides twice in every 24 hours. The mean spring range in both areas is high or macrotidal (63) for coral reef areas, being approximately 3.3 m. This high tidal range produces strong local currents which can reach speeds of up to three knots in restricted areas (45) and could be very important in determining local patterns of larvae dispersal.

Reefs of Northern Tanzania

Tanga

Tanga is the northern most region of Tanzania, extending 180 km south from the Kenyan border. The actual length of the coastline is about 407 km including bays and estuaries that account for 199 km of the total. Reef development along the coast is broken with 41 distinct sections of coastal fringing reef covering 97 km (47%) of the 208 km of coastline not taken up by bays and estuaries. There are also a total of 55 patch reefs along the length of the coast. Thirty of these patch reefs are adjacent to the continental shelf (outer patch reefs) with 25 patch reefs (inner patch reefs) located in shallow water (less than 25 m) between the coast and continental shelf. In total there are 96 reefs in Tanga with a total of 376 km of reef edge.

Studies of the condition of Tanga region's reefs have been sporadic. Early work tended to be descriptive (55,65) or sampled a small proportion of the reefs in a localized area (27,55,65). A wider survey of the reefs was undertaken in 1995 (22) with quantitative work on a small number of reefs conducted in 1996 (42). Nonetheless an impression of how some of these reefs have changed can be gained from Ray's (55) description of some of the reefs adjacent to Tanga town as being "among the best along Tanzania's coastline". By 1987 this situation had drastically changed. A study undertaken by IUCN concluded:

> "the reefs are extensively damaged throughout the Tanga Region. In most areas a percentage cover of live corals of less than 20% was recorded. In some areas live coral cover was less than 10%. On Niule reef '(leeward side) a live coral cover of less than 1% was estimated" (27).

These findings were supported by descriptive work on eight reefs adjacent Tanga town published two years later (65). This survey also found extensive damage to reefs especially in back reef areas and concluded that the locality no longer warranted gazettement as an area of special conservation value as recommended by Ray (55). Damage to these reefs was attributed to destructive fishing, especially the use of explosives such as dynamite.

A clearer impression of the overall status of reefs in Tanga was gained by the more extensive survey conducted in 1995. The purpose of that survey was to assess, the extent of reef degradation, reef biodiversity and levels of resource use. To accomplish this, management oriented rapid assessment procedures which involved resource users as well as local government officers were completed (23). The rapid appraisal procedure was based on other techniques

Table 6.1. Status of the reefs in Tanga region calculated using the percentage of original coral cover surviving. This was calculated as the percentage cover of live coral divided by the percentage cover of live plus dead coral. Percentages were estimated as the mid point of the percentage range of the ordinal values used in the survey. For example, the ordinal value 4 represented percentage covers of 50% to 75% the mid point of which is 67%.

Reef Status	% original coral cover surviving	Coastal Reefs	Inner Patch Reefs	Outer Patch Reefs	Total No.	Percentage of total
Destroyed	>75%	1	3	3	7	12
Poor	26%-75%	2	1	4	7	12
Moderate	11%-26%	8	4	18	30	52
Good	<10%	3	9	2	14	24
Totals		14	17	27	58	100

currently being used in the East African region or in other regions such as the manta board technique (13). The survey technique for reef condition assessed benthic cover (live coral, dead coral, macro-algae, soft coral, sand and reef rock) and densities of selected indicators (sea urchins, crayfish, giant clams, sea cucumbers and wing shells), for a sample of 58 (60%) reefs. This sample included 14 coastal reefs, 17 inner patch reefs and 27 outer patch reefs. Dead coral cover was estimated as the area covered by intact dead corals, dead areas within live colonies (for example killed by a bomb blast) and areas in which colonies had been totally fragmented by explosives or nets.

Reef condition was defined by using the percentage of original coral cover surviving which was calculated as the percentage of live coral divided by the sum of the percentages of live and dead coral multiplied by 100. Fish community structure was assessed for 85% of reefs using a rapid visual technique (61). The number of coral genera was used as an indicator of biological diversity as species diversity is often positively correlated with the number of genera. Moreover, high diversity of coral species is likely to indicate high diversity of other taxonomic groups associated with reefs. The number of coral genera was assessed for 83 reefs (37 coastal reefs, 19 inner patch reefs and 27 outer patch reefs).

From this broad sample of Tanga's reefs, it was estimated that 12% of reefs were completely destroyed, 24% were in good condition with the remaining 64% in poor or moderate condition (Table 6.1). Information from communities and monitoring systems that have been established since the assessment took place indicate that most of the damage to reefs north of the Pangani River was the result of dynamite fishing (24). Incidences of this type of fishing are an order of magnitude lower south of the river. It is also of interest that the majority of sampled reefs destroyed or in poor condition were adjacent to areas of high human population density, that is adjacent or to the north of Tanga town. Conversely, reefs in relatively good condition were adjacent to low human population density areas especially those south of the Pangani River.

A similar trend was noted for differences in fish community structure although not for benthic target species important for commerce, subsistence or conservation. Rankings of commercially important families (such as snappers, grunts and groupers) were low in 90% of the reefs sampled. Reefs with highest rankings for commercially important families were found adjacent to areas of low human population density south of the Pangani River. In contrast, reef type

Table 6.2   Abundance of benthic target species important for commerce (crayfish and sea cucumbers), conservation (giant clams) or subsistence (*Lambis spp.*) per 40 minute swim.

Reef Type	Crayfish /40mins Mean (sem)	Sea Cucumber /40mins Mean (sem)	Giant Clams /40mins Mean (sem)	*Lambis* spp. /40mins. Mean (sem)
Coastal Reefs (n=12)	1.17(0.73)	1.50 (0973)	0.33 (0.22)	0.00 (0.08)
Inner Patch Reef: Fore Reef (n=8)	1.00 (0.57)	0.00 (0.00)	0.00 (0.00)	0.00 (0.00)
Inner Patch Reef: Back Reef (n=10)	0.10 (0.10)	0.70 (0.70)	0.40 (0.22)	0.10 (0.10)
Outer Patch Reef: Back Reef (n=21)	0.33 (0.19)	3.29 (1.58)	1.24 (0.69)	0.38 (0.21)
Outer Patch Reef: Fore Reef (n=33)	2.55 (0.32)	2.33 (0.43)	1.39 (0.44)	0.39 (0.18)

seemed to be the biggest determining factor for the abundance of benthic target species important for commerce (crayfish and sea cucumbers), subsistence (wing shell species) or conservation (giant clams) with the outer patch reefs having the highest numbers (Table 6.2).

There is an increase in the median number of coral genera from coastal to outer patch reefs (Table 6.3). The maximum number of genera recorded was 39 for two outer patch reefs, Maziwe and Dambwe. The lowest value recorded was four for a coastal reef, Ras Nyama Kuu. Highly damaged reefs have very few genera. A total of 47 genera out of 63 for East Africa (19) were recorded in Tanga Region. This total is likely to increase with more intensive sampling techniques. Analysis of the coral community structure revealed two distinct community types with three outliers (Fig. 6.2). The first community type of 45 reefs was dominated by the patch reefs (80%) (eight coastal reefs, 15 inner patch reefs, 22 outer patch reefs). The second community type (35 reefs) was dominated by coastal reefs (77%, 27 coastal reefs, six inner patch reefs, two outer patch reefs). The three outliers were all highly damaged reefs and include the two reefs with the lowest genus number, Ras Nyama Kuu and Niule. The observed difference between coastal and patch reefs may be an effect of greater sedimentation on coastal reefs. The proximity of coastal reefs to the land makes it likely that they are more exposed to terrestrial run off. Differences in coral community species composition associated with sedimentation have also been found for some Kenyan reefs (39).

Dar es Salaam

Bongoyo Island, Fungu Yasin Sand Bank, Mbudya Island, and Pangavini Island are located to the north of the city of Dar es Salaam and along the seaward side there is a well-developed fringing reef. This series of reefs make up the Dar es Salaam Marine Reserves system which was gazetted in 1975. The shore of this area is mainly sandy beaches and dunes, but sometimes takes the form of coral cliffs and isolated estuaries with mangroves. The reserves are separated from the mainland by a 3 km lagoon and are continental in origin being just fragments of the nearby continent temporarily detached by rising sea level (59). The islands were formed from Pleistocene coral that is constantly being eroded by the sea to form rugged cliff shorelines, a characteristic of these islands.

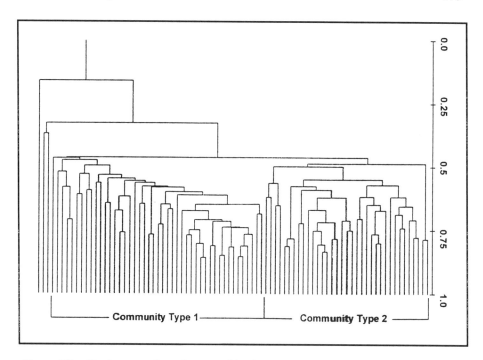

Figure 6.2. Dendrogram of coral communities in Tanga Region. Analysis used the Jaccard similarity coefficient and unweighted-pair groups method of clustering.

Table 6.3. Number of coral genera recorded per 20 minute swim for the coastal reefs, inner and outer patch reefs of Tanga Region.

	Coastal reefs	Inner Patches	Outer Patches
Median	20	24	28
Mode	16	26	34
Minimum	4	13	9
Maximum	31	32	39
No. of reefs sampled	37	19	27

South of the city there are three charted patch reefs and a broken coastal fringing reef mainly associated with headlands (Ras in Arabic and Swahili) such as Ras Kimbiji. There are also a number of other uncharted and unnamed patch reefs in this area (6). All the patch reefs have a spur and groove structure that is often extensively undercut. At the shallower points (5 m) benthic cover consists of hard and soft corals and sponges with deeper areas being mostly rock covered by macroalgae. Fore reefs slope steeply to a depth of 18 to 20 m with the back reefs being less than 5 m deep. High numbers of crayfish (lobsters), turtles, reef sharks, rays, jacks and barracuda were noted (6).

Hamilton's (18) descriptive work on the Dar es Salaam Reserves showed there was great variation in substrate with some areas having live coral cover of 80%, while other areas were being affected by dynamite fishing. His work indicated the presence of 88 coral species belonging to 34 genera. However, the collection was known to be incomplete and the addition of further genera and species especially from the family Acroporidae is anticipated. Other reports of the status of Dar es Salaam marine reserves are largely anecdotal, but described the reefs as extensively damaged by dynamite fishing and pollution (7,8,9,34,50,65).

Recent research conducted in the Dar es Salaam Reserves revealed an over fished condition (32,41) characterized by low fish abundance (200 kg/ha) with small-bodied fish contributing 70% of the total wet weight (Table 6.4). The low abundance of the commercially important families and the high abundance of small-bodied damselfish and wrasses is likely to be an indirect effect of fishing (28,36,58). Additionally, there was a significant negative relationship between sea urchin and the total wet weight of finfish (Fig. 6.3) indicating that sea urchins could be displacing some groups of finfish such as parrotfish and surgeonfish (40,41).

Only two reefs found evidence for the presence of triggerfish and densities of their sea urchin prey were found to be very high, up to 6000 kg/ha. This indicates that although the loss of the keystone predator, the red-lined triggerfish, may have been the initial cause of the sea urchin proliferation, it is not the currently limiting factor. This species has been shown to control sea urchin populations in protected Kenyan coral reef lagoons (35,38,66). The significant positive correlation between sea urchin abundance and turf algae (Fig. 6.3) indicates that food availability could be the present limiting factor on urchin populations. An alternative explanation for high sea urchin abundance is that sea urchins have proliferated because damage by dynamite and destructive fishing has opened up more substrate for them to colonize and feed on.

Gross substrate cover categories showed that hard corals and algal turf are the dominant groups. Coral cover varied considerably with depth and between reefs (Table 6.4). Coral cover was 70% on back-reef edges at 2 to 4 m of low-tide water depth but dropped to 30% on the shallower reef crests. Where coral cover was low there was a corresponding increase in sea urchins and algal turf (Fig. 6.3) which suggests that disturbance by sea urchins could be a factor in reducing hard coral cover or that urchins colonize dynamited and physically damaged reef sites.

Back-reef edges and reef crests are dominated by four coral genera which include *Acropora, Fungia, Galaxea* and *Montipora* (32,41). Species of two of these genera are reported to be well adapted to high turbidity, *Galaxea astreata* with long numerous polyps can remove fine sediment from its body while *Acropora formosa* by virtue of its finely upright branches impedes the settlement of sediments.

Damage from dynamite fishing reported on these (7,8,9,34,50,65) and other Tanzanian reefs (7,65) seems to be less evident on the visited leeward sides of Bongoyo, Mbudya and Pangavini islands' coral reefs. Nonetheless, dynamite damage was evident at Fungu Mkadya where circular craters of about 2 m radius can be seen and the explosives may be largely responsible for the poor condition of some reefs. During field work two underwater explosions per hour were heard. It is likely, given the distance that the sound caused by explosives travels underwater, that the dynamite fishing in this area is focused on schooling fishes in the vicinity of the seaward reefs which were not surveyed.

Table 6.4. Coral reef fish biomass, kg/ha (x ± sem), sea urchin biomass, kg/ha (x ± sem) and percentage substrate cover categories (x ± sem) in five sites of Dar es Salaam marine reserves system, 1997. Where NW=Northwest and SW=Southwest. Data from (42).

Fish Family kg/ha	Bongoyo NW Mean ± sem	Bongoyo SW Mean ± sem	Mbudya NW Mean ± sem	Mbudya SW Mean ± sem	Pangavini SW Mean ± sem
Surgeonfish	22.2 ± 6.3	21.1 ± 3.4	26.0 ± 5.7	45.0 ± 7.9	38.2 ± 8.2
Triggerfish	0.9 ± 0.9	0.0	0.0	0.0	0.5 ± 0.5
Butterflyfish	8.4 ± 2.2	7.6 ± 3.0	13.9 ± 2.9	24.4 ± 5.1	16.6 ± 7.4
Porcupinefishes	0.0	0.0	0.1 ± 0.0	0.0	0.0 ±
Grunts	1.6 ± 1.4	0.0	7.0 ± 3.4	15.8 ± 10.8	36.6 ± 14.5
Wrasses	21.1 ± 5.3	14.1 ± 3.1	26.7 ± 6.0	32.2 ± 10.6	15.4 ± 2.5
Snappers	4.2 ± 2.4	0.0	3.3 ± 1.2	19.8 ± 8.2	15.4 ± 3.8
Goatfishes	0.0	3.7 ± 2.4	2.6 ± 2.6	0.0	0.0
Angelfish	0.0	0.0	3.0 ± 1.8	0.0	4.3 ± 1.6
Damselfish	50.0 ± 7.8	49.0 ± 11.6	29.7 ± 5.3	102.3 ± 9.6	41.2 ± 7.5
Parrotfish	8.8 ± 1.8	16.3 ± 4.8	21.9 ± 6.0	22.9 ± 7.7	13.2 ± 1.8
Rabbitfish	0.4 ± 0.4	0.0	1.7 ± 1.7	5.3 ± 3.4	18.6 ± 4.6
Others	57.0 ± 18.8	60.1 ± 13.2	94.2 ± 30.2	40.9 ± 11.0	74.7 ± 20.0
Total	174.6 ± 29.2	171.9 ± 20.5	230.1 ± 29.3	308.7 ± 41.0	274.6 ± 27.2
Urchin species kg/ha					
D. savignyi	5444.3 ± 702.6	2107.4 ± 221.6	799.7 ± 286.0	784.6 ± 351.3	135.3 ± 103.4
D. setosum	367.5 ± 78.5	1597.0 ± 268.3	159.0 ± 89.6	60.1 ± 26.0	10.6 ± 6.8
E. mathaei	0.0	0.0	0.0	0.0	13.5 ± 13.5
E. molaris	0.0	0.0	0.4 ± 0.1	0.0	0.0
Echinothrix spp	567.6 ± 82.7	595.3 ± 202.7	3045.8 ± 894.0	650.7 ± 370.5	415.3 ± 142.5
T. gratilla	301.9 ± 222.6	0.0	462.1 ± 163.0	67.8 ± 32.4	18.5 ± 18.5
Others	0.0	0.0	0.0	0.0	0.0
Total	6681.3 ± 628.4	4299.7 ± 411.3	4467.0 ± 842.9	1563.2 ± 247.7	593.2 ± 227.4
Substrate cover (%)					
Algal turf	38.3 ± 4.0	45.0 ± 4.3	40.0 ± 5.9	6.5 ± 1.1	12.9 ± 2.6
Calcareous algae	0.0	0.0	0.3 ± 0.2	0.2 ± 0.2	0.0
Clam	0.3 ± 0.2	0.1 ± 0.1	0.2 ± 0.1	0.1 ± 0.1	0.1 ± 0.1
Coralline algae	6.4 ± 1.8	5.6 ± 1.9	17.4 ± 5.1	11.2 ± 2.1	7.3 ± 3.2
Fleshy algae	0.5 ± 0.2	1.8 ± 1.6	1.6 ± 1.2	0.0	0.3 ± 0.3
Hard coral	48.9 ± 2.1	34.7 ± 3.4	37.1 ± 4.4	81.2 ± 1.8	77.9 ± 3.1
Sand	2.5 ± 1.9	6.2 ± 5.9	0.0	0.3 ± 0.3	0.0
Sea ± anemone	1.3 ± 0.6	0.6 ± 0.4	0.5 ± 0.5	0.3 ± 0.2	0.3 ± 0.3
Seagrass	0.0	0.3 ± 0.3	0.0	0.2 ± 0.2	1.2 ± 1.0
Soft coral	1.9 ± 1.3	4.5 ± 1.6	3.0 ± 1.9	0.0	0.0
Sponge	0.0	1.2 ± 0.9	0.0	0.0	0.0

Unguja Island

There is scattered coral development all around the island of Unguja. On the eastern coast and northern and southern extremities there is a fringing reef which is broken by Chwaka Bay. There is also a well developed reef formation associated with Mnemba Island in the northeast and two deeper reef formations to the north at Leven Bank and south of the island at Bedford Bank. On the west there are a number of patch reefs and islands extending from Menai Bay up to Ras Nungwi.

Quantitative studies have been conducted on a number of the patch reefs as well as Mnemba Island (20,26,48,56,65). An unpublished semi-quantitative

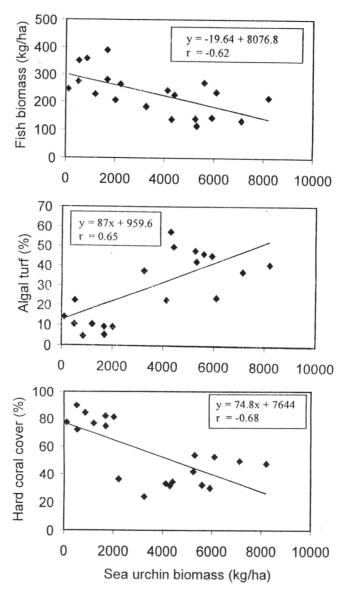

Figure 6.3. Scatterplot and correlation statistics between (top) fish and sea urchin wet weights, (middle) turf algae cover and sea urchin wet weights, and (bottom) hard coral cover and sea urchin wet weights observed in the Dar es Salaam marine reserves system in 1997. Data from (42).

study using the management oriented rapid appraisal procedure mentioned in the Tanga section (23) also assessed benthic cover of the eastern fringing reef. These studies were conducted to 1) describe the benthic composition and fish communities of the different reefs surveyed, 2) investigate the effect of reduced fishing pressure on fish communities at Mnemba Island, and 3) compare the benthic and fish communities of Chapani and Chumbe Island.

Benthic Composition and Fish Communities. The highest levels of live hard coral cover have been found on the islands and patch reefs adjacent to Zanzibar town with the exception of Chapani Island (Table 6.5). The highest cover was found on the seaward reef of Pungume Island, which had 88% coral cover, but most of the reefs to the south west (group 3) have live coral cover values of between 12% and 29% with the eastern reefs of Mnemba Island and the fringing reef having 11% or less. The eastern side of Unguja is subject to much more vigorous wave action than the western side. Therefore the eastern reefs are subjected to greater physical disturbance through wave action than those on the west. This may explain the observed higher coral cover for reefs on the western side of the island. A similar observation has been recorded for reefs at Dar es Salaam (42). Data on the number of coral genera is limited. Of the reefs that have been assessed highest numbers were found at Pange, Murogo, Chumbe and the fore reef of Mnemba Island.

Highest levels of dead coral have been found on the reefs of Menai Bay to the southeast of Zanzibar Town, such as Kwale, Pungume and Ukombe Islands. The high levels of dead corals on these reefs were attributed to the impact of destructive fishing techniques (26). The *kigumi* technique (21) was responsible for the majority of damage on Kwale and Ukombe Islands. The *kigumi* technique is a version of *muro-ami* fishing used in the Philippines where fish are driven into a seine net by swimmers beating the benthos with poles. This technique pounds the more fragile coral into rubble. Fishing with dynamite had caused most damage on Pungume Island. Local fishers report that dynamite fishing at the island is undertaken by fishers from Dar es Salaam and Makunduchi, a village on the southern tip of Unguja Island.

Fish population densities, excluding damselfishes, were nearly an order of magnitude higher on the back and fore reefs of Mnemba Island and Chumbe Island (Table 6.5). Lowest fish population densities were found on the islands adjacent to Zanzibar town including Chapani, Changuu and Bawe Islands. The number of fish species was also highest on Mnemba and Chumbe Islands and lowest on Chapani, Changuu and Bawe.

Effect of Reduced Fishing Pressure. In 1989 the Institute of Marine Sciences, Zanzibar was commissioned to collect baseline data on the benthic and fish communities of Chapani, Changuu, Bawe and Mnemba Islands because of a proposal to lease these islands to tourist operators. Development on the former three islands did not take place, but on Mnemba Island the investor was given the sole rights including a 200 m exclusion zone around the island. This exclusion zone was strictly enforced while there were no such measures taken on the other three sites. Permanent transect lines were established at Chapani Island, Changuu Island, Bawe Island, and on the fore and back reefs of Mnemba Island (48). A follow-up survey was conducted two years later in 1991 (20). It was conducted at the same permanent transect sites, during the same season, and using the same methods but, unfortunately, the benthic data from the 1989 survey is not available. The method, choice of fish families and number of species used for the fish counts was similar to that used for a survey of Kenyan reef fishes (60), which in turn, was based on the method developed by the Great Barrier Reef Marine Park Authority (16).

Table 6.5. Percentage of live and dead coral cover, number of coral genera per 100m transect (* per 20 minute count) and the density and species numbers of the fish populations per 1000 m² on 10 reefs of Zanzibar. n/a = data not available (Sources: 15,20,26,56,65)

Reef	Live Coral (%)	Dead Coral (%)	Number of coral genera/100m transect	Mean fish density including damsel fish/1000m²	Mean fish density excluding damsel fish/1000m²	Mean no. of fish species/1000m²	Commercial fish density /1000m²
Chapani Island	55.3	12.4	28	1293	81	29	7
Changuu Island	69	3	18	1805	58	43	14
Bawe Island	57	2	15	1602	32	38	2
Pange Reef	~80	n/a	39*	n/a	n/a	n/a	n/a
Murongo Reef	~80	n/a	48*	n/a	n/a	n/a	n/a
Chumbe Island	76.1	12.6	n/a	587	492	70	30
Kwale Island West	25.6	15.8	n/a	1726	221	54	76
Kwale Island East	12	5.5	n/a	290	181	42	87
Pungume Island East	14.4	34.2	n/a	1742	196	53	53
Pungume Island West	88.4	2.6	n/a	1196	95	35	20
Ukombe Island	26.5	31.3	n/a	2342	324	42	13
Mnemba Island	11	1.8	35	4538	1225	74	580
Fore Reef							
Mnemba Island	8	0.1	28	2059	511	73	446
Back reef							

The most significant finding was the decrease in the population densities and species numbers of the majority of families at the unprotected sites, at Chapani, Changuu and Bawe Islands, whereas at Mnemba densities and species numbers mostly increased (Table 6.6). The largest differences were found in those families targeted by fishers. These fish species included the parrotfish, emperors, snappers, goatfish, rabbitfish, groupers and grunts. With the exception of the numbers of damselfish, the overall trend was for fewer fish and fish species at Chapani, Changuu and Bawe, with greater numbers and species at Mnemba. At all sites there were large increases in the numbers of damselfishes. At Mnemba this was largely due to an increase of the fusilier damsel (*Lepidozygus tapienosoma*). This is an interesting result given the explanation for high abundances of small-bodied fishes given in the Dar es Salaam section above. The likely explanation for the changes in Zanzibar may be good recruitment of the juvenile schooling species.

Very few large fish-eating species were recorded. In comparable work in the Philippines, White (68) found increased densities of piscivores after a similar period of closure to fishing. This difference between sites may be have been the consequence of the low population densities of these species in other parts of Mnemba. Thus, there were no individuals to immigrate into the areas closed to fishing. An alternative explanation is that enforcement of the closed areas was not efficient and poaching removed the piscivores.

Benthic and Fish Communities of Chapani and Chumbe Islands

Differences in reef communities between the two islands were studied by comparing benthic cover, the number of coral species, population densities of sea urchins, coral associates, and the reef fish of Chapani (polluted and heavily fished) and Chumbe Islands (a control for site for fishing and pollution). This study lacked good replication of reefs and may have been confounded by different levels of fishing between sites but some patterns are indicative of the effects of human influences.

Historically, fishing was not supposed to be allowed on the western side of Chumbe Island as it was within a military zone but anecdotal evidence suggests that this regulation was not effectively enforced until after this study when the island was gazetted as a marine protected area in 1994 (see Chapter 16). Consequently, fishing was taking place at Chumbe during this study although probably at much lower levels than at Chapani Island because of its remoteness from Zanzibar town. Chumbe Island is located 10 km south of Zanzibar town adjacent to the shipping channel between the towns of Dar es Salaam and Zanzibar. As the reef nearest to Zanzibar town, Chapani Island is closest to the discharge points of raw sewage. Measurements of nutrients associated with sewage (nitrate, ammonia and phosphate) taken at Chapani and two adjacent reefs showed fluctuations with tidal currents, with highest values at Chapani. At Chumbe Island, nutrients never rose above detection levels (Table 6.7, 5).

Coral diversity at Chapani was significantly lower than at Chumbe: the average number of coral species encountered on a 20 m transect at Chapani was 6.1, while at Chumbe the figure was 14.8. The live coral cover was higher ($p<0.001$), and the ratio of live to dead coral also higher on Chumbe (Table 6.7). There was, however, no difference in the cover of dead coral and hardground between the islands. A summary of coral growth rate data shows the

Table 6.6. Comparison of the density of fish and number of species per 1000m² summarized for protection and year. Where unprotected reefs were Chapani, Changuu and Bawe and protected reefs were the fore and back reefs of Mnemba Island.

	Unprotected					Protected					
	1990		1992			1990		1992			
Species/1000m²	Mean	sem	Mean	sem	%Difference	Mean	sem	Mean	sem	%Difference	
Surgeonfish	1.7	1.2	2.0	1.0	20.0	9.5	2.1	11.0	1.4	13.6	
Triggerfish	0.0	0.0	0.0	0.0	0.0	2.5	2.1	1.5	0.7	-66.7	
Butterflyfish	6.7	3.1	6.7	4.6	0.0	10.0	5.7	9.0	1.4	-11.1	
Grunts	1.3	1.5	0.3	0.6	-75.0	0.0	0.0	0.5	0.7	100.0	
Wrasses	12.0	1.0	7.7	3.5	-36.1	14.0	0.0	11.5	2.1	-21.7	
Emperors	0.0	0.0	0.7	0.6	0.0	0.0	0.0	3.0	0.0	100.0	
Snappers	0.3	0.6	0.3	0.6	0.0	2.0	0.0	4.5	0.7	55.6	
Goatfish	1.0	1.0	0.3	0.6	-66.7	3.0	0.0	5.0	0.0	40.0	
Angelfish	1.7	1.5	1.0	0.0	-40.0	2.0	0.0	2.0	0.0	0.0	
Damselfish	17.7	2.3	15.0	3.5	-15.1	13.5	1.4	14.5	3.5	6.9	
Parrotfish	3.7	1.5	1.3	0.6	-63.6	4.5	2.1	6.5	0.7	30.8	
Groupers	2.0	0.0	0.7	0.6	-66.7	2.0	0.7	2.0	1.4	0.0	
Rabbitfish	0.3	0.6	0.3	0.6	0.0	0.0	0.0	1.0	0.0	100.0	
Total	49.3	3.5	36.7	7.1	-25.7	64.5	6.4	73.5	0.7	12.2	
Total less Damselfish	31.7	2.1	21.7	4.9	-31.6	51.0	8.5	59.0	4.2	13.6	
Density/1000m²											
Surgeonfish	2.0	1.7	2.7	2.1	33.3	182.0	172.5	206.5	9.2	11.9	
Triggerfish	0.0	0.0	0.0	0.0	0.0	4.0	1.4	6.5	0.7	38.5	
Butterflyfish	23.0	13.5	12.0	3.0	-47.8	34.0	26.9	50.5	27.6	32.7	
Grunts	2.0	2.0	0.3	0.6	-83.3	0.0	0.0	0.5	0.7	100.0	
Wrasses	36.7	7.6	15.3	7.5	-58.2	73.5	31.8	60.0	26.9	-22.5	
Emperors	0.0	0.0	0.7	0.6	0.0	0.0	0.0	107.0	49.5	100.0	
Snappers	0.3	0.6	0.7	1.2	100.0	43.5	44.5	171.0	5.7	74.6	
Goatfish	1.3	1.2	0.3	0.6	-75.0	16.0	8.5	104.0	1.4	84.6	
Angelfish	1.7	1.5	1.0	0.0	-40.0	2.5	2.1	26.0	29.7	90.4	
Damselfish	983.3	251.5	1762.7	200.0	79.3	1244.5	644.2	2430.5	1248.0	48.8	
Parrotfish	7.3	6.1	2.7	1.5	-63.6	98.5	106.8	118.5	103.9	16.9	
Groupers	2.7	0.6	2.7	3.8	0.0	3.5	0.7	4.5	2.1	22.2	
Rabbitfish	0.7	1.2	0.3	0.6	-50.0	0.0	0.0	5.0	5.7	100.0	
Total	1082.7	218.9	1801.7	197.0	66.4	1847.0	603.9	3498.5	1470.1	47.2	
Total less Damselfish	99.3	36.2	39.0	16.6	-60.7	602.5	40.3	1068.0	222.0	43.6	

Table 6.7. Summary table of nutrient concentrations (micro moles, μM), coral cover (%) and fish densities (per 1000m^2) and quadrat studies for both urchins and associates. UD = undetectable, N.S = not significant, * = p < 0.05, ** = p < 0.001, *** = p < 0.001.

	Chapani Mean ± sem	Chumbe Mean ± sem	Significance
Phosphate (μM)	1.93 ± 2.67	UD	
Nitrate (μM)	7.45 ± 7.05	UD	
Ammonia (μM)	4.16 ± 3.90	UD	
Live coral (%)	55.3	76.1	***
Dead coral and hardground (%)	12.4	12.6	N.S
Live:Dead ratio	4.5	6	
Associate density per m^2	87	38	***
Urchin density per m^2	6.4	1.2	***
Fish densities per 1000 m^2			
Surgeonfish	0.03 ± 0.00	8.77 ± 0.07	***
Triggerfish	0.00 ± 0.00	0.37 ± 0.22	
Butterflyfish	2.16 ± 0.01	3.88 ± 0.01	N.S
Wrasses	1.51 ± 0.01	6.50 ± 0.02	**
Angelfish	0.00 ± 0.00	0.65 ± 0.00	**
Commercial family group[1]	1.92 ± 0.03	7.45 ± 0.04	**
Damselfish[2]	603.20 ± 1.16	547.10 ± 1.36	N.S
Total density less the African Demoiselle	74.50 ± 0.17	492.84 ± 1.44	**
Total density	612.5 ± 1.21	587.09 ± 1.21	N.S
Density of specific urchin predators /1000m^2			
Red lined triggerfish (Balistapus undulatus)	0.00 ± 0.00	0.12 ± 0.00	
Maori wrasses (Cheilinus spp.)	1.25 ± 0.31	0.62 ± 0.24	N.S
Coris wrasses (Coris spp.)	0.37 ± 0.27	0.00 ± 0.00	
Total	1.56 ± 0.45	0.75 ± 0.23	N.S

1. includes: Goatfish, parrotfish, grunts, groupers, rabbitfish, snappers and emperors.
2. includes both shoaling and solitary damselfish

average growth rate at Chumbe was 0.70 ± 0.13 cm/y which was significantly lower (p<0.001) than Chapani at 1.0 ± 0.43 cm/y. The difference in mean growth rate between the two sites is probably the result of enhanced growth as a response to eutrophication at Chapani (64). The response of reefs to enhanced nutrient input has been termed the "Janus Effect" (12), after the two-faced Roman god of entrances and exits. The immediate response of corals to increased nutrients is increased growth rate, but as nutrient inputs continue to build, the corals are beset with borers, associates, and smothered by algae. At some point, Janus shows his other face, and the corals deteriorate.

In addition to the differences in the coral communities, there were significant differences in fish, sea urchin and coral-associated communities. At Chapani, sea urchin density was significantly higher at 6.4 per m^2 compared to Chumbe at 1.2 per m^2. At Chapani the density of coral associates on *Porites lobata* was higher (87.5 per m^2) than at Chumbe (32.3 per m^2, p<0.001). There was no significant difference in the total numbers of fish at the two islands (Table 6.7) with planktivorous damselfish making the largest overall contribution to fish population density. At Chapani, the yellowtail demoiselle (*Neopomacentrus azyron*) was extremely abundant, making up 85% of the observed fish population. Without damselfish, however, all the visually obvious (including the ecologically important triggerfish) and the commercially important families (emperors, snappers, parrotfish and groupers) were more abundant at Chumbe.

These data suggest that fishing and pollution have combined to produce more coral-associates, more reef pests, such as sea urchins, and reduced diversity of corals, despite higher coral growth rates. It is difficult to know whether or not these differences were attributable to increased recruitment success and growth or reduced predation on these species. In the case of sea urchins, McClanahan (37,38,42) has found that the red-lined triggerfish is an important predator that can often control sea urchin populations and that fishing quickly reduces the abundance of this predator. Muthiga (43) found, however, that the abundance of chlorophyll in the water, a measure of nutrient enrichment, is positively associated with sea urchin larvae and their rate of settlement can increase with increasing chlorophyll or algal concentrations. There is evidence that some species of sea urchins can obtain up to 75% of their food requirements by direct absorption of dissolved organic matter (2,33,53), although no studies have been undertaken on East African species. In a detailed study of one important sea urchin, *Echinometra mathaei*, Muthiga (43) found that adult populations were not controlled by the abundance of larvae or their rates of settlement but rather by the post-recruitment mortality of both juvenile and adults, largely attributable to predation. Thus, when predators are removed by overfishing there could be greater recruitment of sea urchin populations in sites of higher nutrient availability such as Chapani. Both factors of increased larval success and reduced predation could, therefore, be the causes for the high level of sea urchins and coral-associates at Chapani compared to Chumbe.

Social and Economic Characteristics

There is growing and justified recognition of the importance of social and economic factors in conservation. Management can be focused on habitats, ecosystems, species or people but, since people cause most of the manageable impacts, it is ultimately people who are being managed. Thus, it is not only important to gain an understanding of the resources involved, but also of the people who are affecting the resources. In northern Tanzania these people include coastal communities and commercial interests.

Types and Patterns of Resource Use

Coral reefs in northern Tanzania are used by local communities and commercial interests in a number of ways. These are fishing, collection of octopus, sea cucumbers, crayfish (lobsters), shells (both for food and curios), corals (for building, lime production and curios) and more recently mariculture, especially of the red seaweed *Euchema* spp. (17, Box 6.2). Fishing is undertaken with a variety of gears including handlines, longlines, trolling (for pelagics), traps, entanglement nets, seine nets, purse seine nets, gill nets, scoop nets, stake nets, fence traps, spears, spear guns, poisons and explosives. The major demersal fish catch includes: carnivores, scavengers, piscivores (emperors, wrasses, goatfish, snappers, grunts and groupers) and herbivores (rabbitfish and parrotfish).

Octopuses are collected from the reef flat by walkers using spears or from shallow water by divers with face masks. Sea cucumbers are collected by

Box 6.1. Reefs of Pemba Island

Pemba Island is 62 km long, and 22 km at its broadest point. The eastern shore and northern and southern extremities of the island are rocky and exposed to heavier wave action than the western side. The western shoreline has a number of large bays lined with mangroves as well as peninsulas and islands with their associated coral reefs. It is estimated that there are 1100 km of reef in Pemba, representing 45% of the coral reefs of Tanzania. Corals have been recorded as deep as 64 m (1).

Despite its obvious importance, there have been few studies of Pemba's reefs. The western fringing reef has a narrow reef flat which is extensively damaged in places (3). In contrast, the fore slope has coral cover between 21 and 60% and few dead corals (Table). The eastern fringing reef is more exposed and has variable coral cover which does not exceed 15%. The northern and eastern reefs of Misali Island have the highest recorded coral cover, 75% and 53% respectively. Dead coral accounted for approximately 10% of cover for both these reefs. The eastern reef was dominated (in order of importance) by branching, massive, encrusting and sub-massive colonies, the northern reef by encrusting, massive, branching and tabulate forms with the western reef by encrusting colonies (2). Coral genera and fish species richness at Misali Island is high with 40 coral genera and 350 fish species recorded and with the diversity highest on the northern and western reefs.

Table. Summary of the percentage benthic cover of the eastern, northern and western reefs of Misali Island, Pemba. Data is presented as means and standard errors (sem).

Cover Type	Eastern Mean	sem	Northern Mean	sem	Western Mean	sem
Live coral	53.0	6.6	75.5	2.4	21.3	7.8
Dead coral	10.4	3.1	9.8	2.1	1.4	0.8
Damaged coral	0.9	0.3	4.3	0.7	6.8	3.5
Soft coral	8.6	3.2	0.7	0.3	1.3	1.0
Sponge	1.6	0.7	1.3	1.0	11.3	2.0
Calcareous algae	1.1	0.5	0.1	0.1	3.5	2.1
Macro algae	2.4	0.9	0.9	0.5	13.5	4.6
Others	4.2	0.9	0.2	0.1	0.3	0.2
Rock	8.0	3.3	4.7	1.5	13.7	11.8
Sand	5.7	3.4	1.2	0.8	23.3	6.5
Water	4.2	1.9	1.4	0.3	3.6	3.3

The island is used extensively by local communities for fishing, octopus and sea cucumber collection and there are several temporary fishers' camps on the island. Important fishing techniques are handlines, traps and nets. Drag nets and dynamite fishing have damaged some of the reefs in the area. At present, the damage is not great but will increase if these fishing techniques are not restrained.

Misali Island was chosen as the pilot marine conservation area for Pemba because of the high diversity of reef-building coral, its role as a source area for the reefs to the north and as a breeding ground for commercial fish species, its importance for threatened species, the established research interest, its small and manageable size, and the unusual coastal forest and terrestrial species present on the island. Following the recommendations that Misali Island be given protected area status (1,2,3), the Environment and Development Group

(EDG), an English consultancy firm, began working with the Government of Zanzibar in October 1996. The two objectives of this project are 1) to help the Zanzibar government establish a self-sustaining national system of nature conservation areas, both marine and terrestrial and second, and 2) to develop a pilot conservation area on and around Misali Island.

A participatory approach has been adopted by EDG, whereby all the resource users are involved in the management, including the design of the park management regime. The local fishing communities have been involved throughout the planning process, and it was unanimously declared at a workshop in March 1997 that Misali should receive protected area status. Following this decision, an initiative was taken to incorporate the commercial resource users offering marine activities, namely SCUBA diving and deep sea fishing operations, into the management process.

J.C. Horrill & J. Church

References

1.   Horrill, J.C. 1992. *Status of the Coral Reefs of Misali Island.* Environmental Study Series 13. Commission for Lands and Environment, Zanzibar
2.   Horrill, J.C., Machano, H., Omar, S.H. 1994. *Misali Island: Rationale for a Marine Protected Area.* Environmental Study Series 17. Commission for Lands and Environment, Zanzibar
3.   UNEP. 1989. *Coastal and Marine Environmental Problems of the United Republic of Tanzania.* UNEP Regional Seas Reports and Studies No. 106. Nairobi: UNEP

walkers, divers with face masks and increasingly, because of their scarcity, by divers with SCUBA. Crayfish are collected by divers using spears, spear guns or traditionally with a dead octopus to scare them from their shelter. Shells are collected in a similar manner to octopus but without the use of spears. There are few larger scale collectors using baited nets or traps. Corals are mined from the reef edge and flats using crowbars. An increasing use of the reef is tourism (fishing and diving) which is now rapidly expanding in Zanzibar (Unguja and Pemba Islands) and to a lesser extent Dar es Salaam.

Resource use is dependent on the sex of the user, the area, and the market. Traditionally, women were gleaners of the reef flat and sold already caught fish while men built boats and fished offshore. The types of markets in the area determined what is collected, be it shells, sea cucumbers or octopus. The recent rise in seaweed farming has attracted many women (54, Box 6.2). The primary income earner for most men is fishing for finfish. Those that free dive or with SCUBA often target abundant or marketable species. The finfish fishery is the most important source of food (17,25), and is estimated to supply95% of the protein requirements of Zanzibar (29). This high degree of dependence is also probably true for most rural areas of northern Tanzania.

In Tanga, the boat and gear ownership of male fishers is private (17). Fishers mostly own their boat alone or occasionally own more than one boat. Where a boat is owned by more than one person, they invariably belong to one family. This is also the case in Mafia Island (25). The case of seaweed farming differs in that the farmers are often given equipment by the buyer on condition that they sell to that buyer for a fixed price. Sale of other produce such as finfish, octopus, are on an auction basis or to a specific buyer as in the case of seaweed farming. When fishers do not have their own gears they use those of others in return for a proportion of the catch. The proportion varies with area, in Tanga, it is about 50% (17), but 70 to 80% in Mafia (25). Fishers can also receive a wage from the gear owner for operating that gear. This is often the case for boats operating with large seine nets and dynamite (Horrill, C. personal observation) where the young divers are paid on a daily basis. The money received depends on the value of the catch.

An interesting challenge for conservation management is the rapid development of recreational use of Pemba's marine resources. Since 1992, when the Zanzibar government permitted commercial use of the marine environment around Pemba, SCUBA diving and deep sea fishing operations have increased. Both activities are considered "world class" with the diving being comparable to that of the Red Sea and the Maldives. Of the eleven SCUBA diving and fishing operators, nine are based in Kenya, one in mainland Tanzania, and one on the northwestern shore of Pemba Island itself. Kenya, being closer to Pemba than Zanzibar, has provided better support, infrastructure and services required for private investors in marine tourism. Management of tour operators based in Kenya will provide a unique challenge for conservation and management in Tanzania.

Indigenous Management and Knowledge

There is increasing recognition in conservation of the importance of indigenous management and knowledge. In northern Tanzania, there is an interesting difference between the islands of Pemba and Unguja and the mainland in terms of indigenous management systems. In Tanga (mainland), a number of studies found no evidence of existing or previous traditional indigenous management (17,22,62). This was despite the fact that the studies had investigated every type of indigenous management mechanism (such as closed areas and restricted access) reported in the literature. A likely reason for this is that coastal society is now mobile and homogeneous, the many different tribes and cultures which originally made up this society having gradually blended over time (62). The mixing of mainly African and Arab cultures, and to a smaller extent Indian, has resulted in a coastal and almost tribeless culture. People see themselves as coastal and not as Swahilis which is the name given to them by inland peoples. The lack of tribalism has reduced potential spheres of cultural influence typical of tribal areas. This, coupled with a previous history of low human population density, has encouraged a view of open access to marine resources (4).

In contrast to the mainland, there are vestiges of indigenous management in Zanzibar (21). Recent examples of this include the closure of fishing areas by the village of Ras Kisimkasi and camping restrictions on the island of Kwale by the joint efforts of four villages on the Fumba peninsula. Indigenous management has, however, probably weakened after independence as a result of a directive and socialist government. Since independence, the centralized and socialist governments increasingly took control over resource management and local community control decreased.

Box 6.2. Seaweed Farming in Tanzania

The history of seaweeds in Tanzania dates back to the 1930's when people traditionally harvested wild seaweeds from the Zanzibar Islands. The seaweeds were sold to businessmen who exported them to Europe. In the early 1950's, about 400 tons (dry weight) of the red seaweed *Eucheuma* were harvested (1). Continuous harvesting without replacement led to a decrease of the wild resource. The trade collapsed between 1973 and 1975 mainly due to the failure of the Zanzibar crop to compete with the cleaner farmed seaweeds from the Philippines. This collapse was probably attributable to harvesters mixing a variety of wild seaweeds and this led to the need for seaweed farms that have greater control over seaweed quality.

At nearly the same time of the wild *Eucheuma* collapse, a University of Dar es Salaam botanist Professor K. Mshigeni was studying in the Philippines and documented the potential for seaweed farming in Tanzania. Mshigeni completed the first successful experiments on seaweed farming in 1985 which led to the first Tanzanian seaweed farms (2). Commercial production did not start until 1989, however, because of lack of funds. Two private entrepreneurs, a Tanzania national and a foreigner, started experimental farms at Paje and Jambiani villages on the east coast of Unguja. By 1992, seaweed farming was established in Pemba and Mafia Islands (4). The industry has since quickly expanded and in 1997 covered nearly 25 villages or about two thirds of the coastal area of Unguja Island. On mainland Tanzania, commercial seaweed farming started in 1995 and, in 1996, the first seaweed farms were sold to private entrepreneurs (5). The Institute of Marine Sciences (IMS) of the University of Dar Es Salaam conducted the first environmental impact of seaweed farming between 1992 and 1995 (5).

When seaweed farming started in Unguja in 1989, both men and women joined the industry but now more than 90% of the farmers are women. Men started leaving the industry to women and returned to fishing and activities triggered by tourism, including road construction, making lime for white wash, construction of houses and working in guest houses. Men say that they need money every day and that women are more patient to complete the cycle of planting, weeding, harvesting and selling.

Seaweed farming may reduce the fishing pressure on the reefs but it can depend on the amount of men who previously fished that change occupations. Seaweed farming is mostly done by women on Unguja Island but, on Pemba Island, seaweed is mainly farmed by men. The reason is that the topography of the two islands determine the farming technique as well as the danger of farming and economic alternatives. Unguja has shallow bays and intertidal areas that allow farming at low tides by fixing seaweeds onto nylon ropes held by wooden pegs driven into the sediments. In contrast, Pemba Island has more steep cliffs and less tourism and the Pemba technique uses a floating method in deeper waters that requires the use of boats. This danger reduces women's participation. On mainland Tanzania, however, both sexes are equally involved and this may be because of the greater geological diversity of the coastline and lower concentration of tourists relative to Unguja. In addition, many people realized that destructive fishing methods have destroyed their marine environments and they, therefore, concentrate on seaweed farming and promote nondestructive fishing methods (7,10).

Why Farm Seaweed?

Seaweeds are important because they contain polysaccharides such as agar, alginate and carrageenan which are used in food, pharmaceutical, cosmetic and agricultural industries. The seaweed *Eucheuma* contains a high fraction of the extractable polysaccharide carrageenan. Over harvesting and factors of quality would make it difficult to satisfy the seaweed industries with wild seaweeds. Seaweed farming, if successful, is a good source of cash income especially for people in developing countries who have had little or no income generating activity. For example, if fish catches are reduced fishers frequently lack alternative incomes and this sometimes encourages destructive fishing methods. Seaweed farming generally produces higher incomes than alternative activities such as handicraft, collecting octopus, fishing, petty trade and agriculture. In mainland Tanzania a seaweed farmer with an ordinary plot of 50 ropes receives 13 000 Tanzanian shillings (US $22.7) per harvest and harvesting is done every two to three weeks, most farmers have more than one plot and other sources of income (the minimum wage in Tanzania is US $600 per year, 5). An ordinary fisher receives an annual income of about US $565 compared to US $1000 for a seaweed farmer. Farmers have managed to purchase radios, kitchenware, clothes and furniture, old homes have been improved and new houses built, and the number of children suffering from malnutrition has decreased in the villages where seaweed is farmed (7). Some fish species also use the shelter of the seaweed for nursery grounds or, like the rabbitfish, graze on the farmed seaweed. Seaweed farmers usually bring back home some fish catch from their farms.

Some Negative Effects of Seaweed Farming

Negative effects include direct and indirect impacts on the abundance and diversity of intertidal organisms including macrophytes, macrobenthos and meiobenthos (6,9). In some areas, there has been an overgrowth of the *Eucheuma* by other algae, particularly in areas with high nutrients. Farmers also kill sea urchins on their farms and throw them away because they are afraid of their poisonous spines. Seaweed farms often kill seagrasses and algae growing underneath them and expose bare substrates which increases sediment erosion. Opportunistic organisms, such as tubeworms, use the roots of the dead seagrasses for shelters (6). Further, *Eucheuma*, when under stress, produces chemicals including hydrogen peroxide that are toxic to other intertidal organisms (8).

Social relationships of Zanzibari households have been affected by seaweed farming. Zanzibari women traditionally did not have the means for earning money and this new income often brings domestic conflicts. Some husbands say that their wives have become less obedient and some women say they give their husbands money to "cool them down" and allow them to continue seaweed farming (3). Some men claim that their wives no longer join them in the terrestrial farms because of seaweed farming. People have also faced problems of caring for their young children. For example, younger children were left at home to be looked after by older brothers and sisters, many of whom were not old enough to care for themselves. In one instance, a child, who had followed the mother to their seaweed farm, died from drowning. As a result, villagers contributed to build a day-care center to care for the children of seaweed-farming mothers. Seaweed farming has also increased the drop-out rate for primary school children. Even pupils without plots retrieve and sell the broken and floating seaweed that accumulates along the beach. The Ministry of Education has, however, tried to reduce this problem. Seaweed farmers have also complained that sun exposure hurts their eyes and that they often get stung by fishes and rays and the sores take many months to heal.

Flower E. Msuya

References

1. Mshigeni, K.E. 1973. Exploitation of seaweeds in Tanzania. The Genus *Eucheuma* and other algae. *Tanzania Notes and Records* No. 72, pp 19-36

2. Mshigeni K.E. 1985. *Pilot Seaweed Farming in Tanzania: Progress Report and Future Trends.* Dar es Salaam: University of Dar es Salaam

3. Msuya F.E. 1997. Women seaweed farmers in the Zanzibar Islands, Tanzania. *Intercoast Network*, No. 29

4. Msuya, F.E., Mmochi, A.J. 1995. The seaweed farming industry in Zanzibar: Marketing frustrations and conflicts. *Swedmar Review* November 1995, pp 17-21

5. Msuya, F.E. 1996 *Seaweed Farming in Lindi and Mtwara regions, Phase-Two, Implementation and Expansion.* Consultancy report for RIPS Programme, Mtwara Tanzania

6. Msuya F.E., Ngoile, M.A.K., Shunula, J.P. *1996. The Impact of Seaweed Farming on the Macrophytes and Macrobenthos of the East Coast of Unguja Island, Zanzibar, Tanzania.* Report submitted to the Canadian International Development Agency (CIDA), Zanzibar, Tanzania

7. Msuya F.E., Dickinson T., Whittick, A. 1994. *Community in Transition: The Impact of Seaweed Farming on the Women of Paje, Zanzibar, Tanzania.* Video production, Zanzibar: Institute of Marine Sciences

8. Mtolera M.S.P., Collen, J., Pedersen M., Semesi, A.K. 1995. Destructive hydrogen peroxide production in *Eucheuma denticulatum* (Rhodophyta) during stress caused by elevated pH, high light intensities and competition with other species. *European Journal of Phycology* 30:289-297

9. Olafsson, E., Johnstone, R.W., Ndaro, S.G.M. 1995. Effects of intensive seaweed farming on the meiobenthos in a tropical lagoon. *Journal of Experimental Marine Biology and Ecology* 191: 101-117

10. Rural Integrated Project Support 1995. Marine Environment Protection, Complete Project Document, January 1995, Mtwara Tanzania

Recognition of the economic importance of coral reefs among local fishers in most of northern Tanzania is high (21,22,26,62). For example, fishers are aware that increased fishing pressure and the use of destructive methods are putting the fishery under increasing pressure. They often have specific names for sites at sea and also have firm views on which areas are important to the fishery in terms of different gears, the species of fish caught, and breeding sites (21,22,26). The vast majority of communities know that explosive and seine net fishing is destroying the reefs and attribute declining fish stocks and catches to the prevalence of these techniques. This is contrary to the beliefs and activities of many government agencies and projects which often advocate the use of awareness programs to educate fishers about the adverse effects of destructive fishing. Ironically, villagers often accuse the government of not being aware of the impact of dynamite fishing and use the number of fishers arrested and released without trial or punishment as an indication of the government's lack of awareness of this problem.

Threats

The most widespread threat to the reefs in northern Tanzania is the use of destructive fishing techniques. These include; the use of explosives, the *kigumi* or "*juya la kojani*" technique (21), seine nets (*juya*) and poisons. With the exception of *kigumi*, all of these techniques have now been used for many years. It is estimated that dynamite has now been used for over 30 years (7), seine nets were used in Zanzibar since the 1960s and the use of poisons was recorded as far back as 1900 (1). Alexander (1) stated that the use of poison was in decline even in 1961 as before that date whole villages were involved in fishing with poisons.

The most common naturally-occurring poison used is an extract from the *Euphorbia* plant. The sap is soaked in sisal wads and four or five of these wads are released into the water. Fish are killed or stunned instantaneously and are collected from the water or trapped by a fence trap (*uzio*) placed across the estuary or creek. Although, the use of poisons is less than the days of Alexander (1), users of this technique now use a greater variety of poisons in a greater number of habitats.

The prevalence of destructive techniques depends greatly on the location. For instance, dynamite is the biggest threat to reefs on the mainland, followed by the use of seine nets and poisons. In Zanzibar, *kigumi* is most prevalent with poisons and dynamite being less prevalent. The *kigumi* method has caused the greatest damage to the reefs of Pemba (Evans, personal communication). The use of dynamite in Pemba is more prevalent than in Zanzibar, probably because of its nearness to Tanga.

Simple overfishing is another major problem. Beyond the evidence given above, there is an additional comparative study of Kisite and Chumbe Parks, Tanga-Pangani reefs and the Dar es Salaam marine reserves (42). This study found a highly significant 67% decrease in the estimates of fish wet weights in fished compared to unfished reefs (Table 6.8). The most abundant groups in the protected reefs are predators and herbivores. A more detailed Discrete-Group Sampling technique for calculating numbers of individuals and species showed, however, that there was 275% more damselfish and 31% more wrasses in the unprotected reefs.

Further evidence for overfishing comes from the relationship between the number of fishers versus the catch of selected resident coral reef fish from 1971 to 1992 in Dar es Salaam which indicates that the optimum level of production had already been surpassed (Fig. 6.4). The optimum level of production was 700 metric tons from 1150 fishers (Fig. 6.4). The same trend in catch of coral reef fishes was found in Tanga and Zanzibar where total production was kept constant only through a combination of increasing effort and higher catches of sardines and Indian Mackerel respectively (29,52).

The types of overfishing reported in Tanzania include Malthusian, growth, recruitment and economic. In Tanga, local fishers state that there are too many fishers for too few fish (22) which has been described by Russ (57) as Malthusian overfishing. A study of seine catches at Dar es Salaam found that 51% of the catch was immature, 38% had developing gonads and only 8% were in a spawning state. Thus, almost 90% of the beach seine catch had had no chance to spawn in their lifetime (3). This study concluded that there was evidence for both growth and recruitment overfishing since most of the beach seines used had mesh sizes not exceeding 1.2 cm.

A cost benefit analysis conducted in Dar es Salaam region by Kamukuru (31) indicated poor economic performance of motorized boats. The motorized handline fishery could only cover daily operating expenses and had both negative return on investment and pay back period, an indication of economic overfishing. Motorized basket trappers could, on average, make profits compared to motorized handliners by combining both engines and sails. It was realized that fuel and lubricants cut deeply into the daily net revenues leaving only a small portion to be shared among owners and crew. Given human population trends, economic growth, which is slower than population increase, and the perception that "there is always fishing" as a source of income, the expected trend is for an increase in the numbers of fishers and a decrease in catch. This will further exacerbate the fisheries profit unless fishers move to other economic activities or find additional fish resources, such as seasonal pelagics.

Walking on the reef for collecting or mariculture has a widespread and significant impact. Reefs are harvested at low tide for food and commercial purposes (octopus, mollusks and shells for the curio trade). The impact of reef trampling has been well documented (44,67), but the effect of mariculture especially seaweed farming may also be significant (Box 6.2). Research in Unguja on this topic found that seaweed farming lowers bacterial production and abundance of smaller animals such as nematodes (30). The cause of the observed differences is unclear but may be the result of increased disturbance, differences in fish feeding behavior and bacterial production or nutrient dynamics. Additionally, differences may be caused by the release of toxins, mainly strong oxidants such as hydrogen peroxide as well as volatile halogenated compounds, from the farmed algae (10).

Rapid urbanization and the lack of waste-water treatment has resulted in high levels of pollution near towns and cities. In Zanzibar, there is no sewage treatment on the island, and sewage treatment has broken down in Dar es

Table 6.8. Wet weight estimantes (kg/ha) of the studied fish families at each of the sites. At the bottom of the table the ANOVA comparison of differences between protected and unprotected reefs based on the site averages is given. F values are given and level of statistical significance. NS = not significant. Data from (42).

Sites		Surgeons	Trigger-fish	Butterfly-fish	Wrasses	Snappers	Goatfish	Angelfish	Damsel-fish	Parrotfish	Rabbitfish	Others	Total
Protected Reefs													
Kisite 1	mean	142.2	23.8	15.1	42.7	176.6	0.9	17.1	48.4	156.7	0.5	59.2	683.3
	S.D.	17.0	19.3	8.8	3.1	44.0	0.3	6.8	4.3	20.7	0.4	12.1	7.4
Kisite 2	mean	170.6	15.8	21.4	29.6	386.5	11.7	9.2	101.1	100.3	3.2	152.3	1001.6
	S.D.	25.6	2.6	0.0	20.0	82.5	16.4	9.0	17.2	62.1	4.5	47.2	243.7
Kisite 3	mean	88.5	19.5	11.0	29.8	4.7	1.1	11.5	59.3	109.2	0.3	27.4	362.4
	S.D.	31.7	4.1	5.2	2.8	4.0	0.4	10.7	28.8	38.9	0.4	5.1	121.6
Unprotected reefs													
Ufunguni	mean	60.2	0.0	11.6	74.5	19.2	8.5	5.5	47.2	51.3	1.5	28.5	307.9
	S.E.	1.4	0.0	3.8	32.7	5.4	10.6	5.5	9.2	35.1	0.8	27.3	61.8
Makome	mean	35.2	0.0	6.5	25.7	3.7	0.9	5.0	75.6	16.8	0.1	17.0	186.5
	S.D.	4.8	0.0	0.9	0.0	3.9	0.2	6.2	3.9	5.0	0.2	1.5	3.9
Taa	mean	74.1	0.9	6.5	37.7	31.0	0.2	4.5	74.1	22.4	4.8	73.8	329.9
	S.D.	3.7	1.3	6.6	4.1	15.1	0.3	1.6	0.2	6.5	2.3	48.9	40.4
Changale	mean	49.5	0.0	9.8	18.0	24.3	7.1	6.0	76.8	12.5	3.7	9.4	217.1
	S.D.	28.8	0.0	3.8	10.7	7.7	9.9	8.5	6.8	8.2	3.7	12.1	49.6
Mbudya 1	mean	43.3	0.0	9.2	30.2	7.9	0.0	0.0	59.3	17.3	1.1	25.6	193.9
	S.D.	33.4	0.0	3.0	8.1	8.3	0.0	0.0	22.0	13.3	1.0	2.3	25.5
Mbudya 2	mean	16.7	0.0	25.9	35.7	0.5	0.0	0.0	133.4	13.8	0.6	7.5	234.1
	S.D.	10.6	0.0	15.9	5.0	0.7	0.1	0.0	11.4	4.8	0.8	6.5	23.1
Bongoyo 1	mean	27.7	0.0	6.2	31.0	15.5	0.3	2.4	57.4	6.7	0.0	19.7	167.0
	S.D.	12.9	0.0	6.3	2.5	2.7	0.1	0.0	10.2	4.6	0.0	13.1	8.5
Bongoyo 2	mean	9.2	0.0	7.3	35.6	0.0	0.3	0.0	93.8	16.5	0.0	19.7	182.3
	S.D.	10.4	0.0	5.4	17.8	0.0	0.3	0.0	24.0	6.1	0.0	10.7	32.4
Protected	mean	133.8	19.7	15.8	34.1	189.3	4.6	12.6	69.6	122.0	1.3	79.6	682.4
	S.D.	41.7	4.0	5.2	7.5	191.2	6.2	4.1	27.8	30.3	1.6	64.9	319.6
Unprotected	mean	39.5	0.1	10.4	36.0	12.8	2.2	2.9	77.2	19.7	1.5	25.1	227.3
	S.D.	21.8	0.3	6.6	16.8	11.6	3.5	2.6	26.9	13.5	1.8	20.9	60.5
Difference (%)		-70.5	-99.4	-34.5	5.8	-93.3	-52.5	-76.7	10.9	-83.9	10.0	-68.4	-66.7
F-value		25.63	225.70	1.64	0.03	8.26	0.69	22.35	0.17	65.82	0.01	5.08	17.69
Significance		0.001	0.001	NS	NS	0.018	NS	0.001	NS	0.000	NS	0.051	0.002

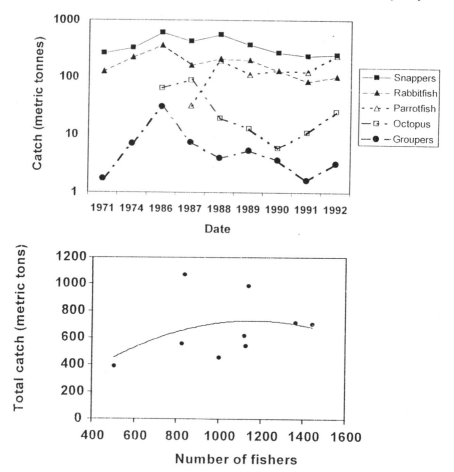

Figure 6.4. (top) Trend in fish production of selected resident coral reef finfish and shellfish landed at Kunduchi and Msasani landing sites and (bottom) the relationship between number of fishers and total catch of selected resident coral reef finfish and shellfish within the Dar es Salaam marine reserves system between 1971 and 1992.

Salaam and Tanga. Diffuse village-size populations do not pose a major threat, but urban centers such as Dar es Salaam, Tanga and Zanzibar do, as does future hotel construction. Other sources of pollution are industries and agriculture. Litter is also an increasing problem especially plastic and latex products.

Upland deforestation and increased land clearance are liable to increase problems of sedimentation. The descriptions of the coral communities given above show that although Northern Tanzanian reefs have developed under conditions of sediment stress, it is not presently possible to predict the outcome of this further stress. Unusual weather patterns, such as those caused by the El Niño can bring increased rainfall variation, exacerbating this problem.

The burning of coral for lime is less of a problem in northern Tanzania compared to the south (11, Chapter 5). Although traditional lime kilns dot the coastal landscape it is usually Pleistocene reef rock being processed, not mined coral.

Management Initiatives

There are six conservation initiatives being implemented including projects at Tanga, the Dar es Salaam Reserves and Kunduchi on the mainland as well as Chumbe Island, Menai Bay and Misali Island in Zanzibar. These projects represent a diverse range of management strategies including a locally based collaborative management program in Tanga, a collaboration between central government and local communities in Menai Bay, Kunduchi and Misali Island, a solely central government initiative for the Dar es Salaam Marine Reserves and private initiative at Chumbe Island. This broad range of initiatives should produce important lessons and guidelines for reef conservation and management in this region.

Tanga

The Tanga Coastal Zone Conservation and Development Programme is being implemented by the Office of the Tanga Regional Administrative Secretary with technical assistance from the World Conservation Union (IUCN) and funding from Irish Aid. The program addresses two critical issues facing the Tanga coast which include 1) unsustainable use of the coastal resources, as evidenced by declining yields of fish, and 2) the deteriorating condition of the coral reefs, mangroves and coastal forest habitats. Coupled to these resource problems is that previous government and community management programs have been inadequate to stop these problems.

The program developed a collaborative approach between government agencies and local resource users where participatory resource assessments identified the issues and possible actions. The resource assessment was followed by a participatory process involving issue analysis, action planning, implementation, monitoring and evaluation. This was initiated at village level, but with support and facilitation of government staff. Village initiatives included the formulation and enforcement of bylaws, undertaking of patrols to prevent destructive fishing, management agreements for reef zoning with three reef closed to replenish fish stocks, and the testing of mariculture options. Preliminary analysis of fish catch statistics in one of these villages has shown an increase in the number of fish per fisher (also see Chapter 16).

Dar es Salaam Marine Reserve

The original regulations for the Dar es Salaam Reserve allowed for no use other than nonextractive tourism. Management was top down, only the Division of Fisheries had decision making powers and enforcement was to be undertaken by armed guards and patrol units. Many decisions were merely political, and due to a lack of funds no practical protective management was implemented and a combination of these factors made the management process a total failure.

This failure resulted in a complete review of marine protected area management in Tanzania culminating in the Marine Parks and Reserves Act of 1994. The Act was followed by the formation of an institutional framework for the management and development of marine protected areas. This framework allows for collaboration at all levels from central government to resource users. Using the powers of this new Act, a collaborative management agreement between the central government and a private tour company has been signed. This has resulted in more effective policing of the area in 1998 which has reportedly reduced dynamite fishing. Mbudya Island will provide a site for another collaborative agreement involving central government, the Wildlife Conservation Society of Tanzania and the management of a nearby hotel. Clean-up campaigns, mapping, the establishment of dive centers and guarding against dynamite fishing have started. Fungu Yasin Sand Bank and Pangavini Island have, however, yet to benefit from the powers of the new Act.

The Dar es Salaam marine reserves system are also likely to benefit from the proposed Kunduchi Integrated Coastal Area Management Programme (KICAMP). The program will work in the area to the north of Dar es Salaam. Some of the objectives of the program will be training and overall public awareness for conservation of all the resources within the area.

Zanzibar

There are two marine conservation initiatives currently being implemented on Unguja Island. The Chumbe Island Coral Park and Environmental Education Center is managed by a private company, Chumbe Island Coral Park Ltd formed in 1992 (see Chapter 16). The company has an advisory committee whose membership includes representatives from the Ministry of Agriculture and Natural Resources, the Department of Environment, the Institute of Marine Sciences of the University of Dar es Salaam, and neighboring villages. The island was gazetted as a marine protected area by the Government of Zanzibar in 1994. The protected area does not allow any extractive use and includes a reef and forest sanctuary (see Chapter 16 for more details).

The Menai Bay Conservation Area is supported by the World Wide Fund for Nature (WWF), and is working with local communities and the Government of Zanzibar to develop sustainable resource use practices and conserve biodiversity. The main management issues are reduction of destructive fishing techniques such as *kigumi*, dynamite fishing and poisons, and overfishing.

References

1.   Alexander, C.S. 1964. Fish poisoning along the northeast coast of Tanganyika. *Tanganyika Notes and Records* 62: 56-71
2.   Bamford, D. 1982. Epithelial absorption. In *Echinoderm Nutrition*, eds. Jangoux, M., Lawrence, J.M. pp. 317-330. Rotterdam: A.A. Balkema
3.   Benno, B.L. 1992. *Some Features of the Beach Seine Fishery along the Dar es Salaam Coast, Tanzania.* MSc Thesis, University of Kuopio, Finland
4.   Berkes, F. 1995. Community-based management of common property resources. *Encyclopedia of Environmental Biology* 1:371-373
5.   Björk, M., Mohammed S. M., Björklund M., Semesi, A. 1995. Coralline algae, important coral reef builders threatened by pollution. *Ambio* 24: 501-505
6.   Brown, K. 1994. *Ras Kutani Beach Resort: A Survey of Nearby Submarine Resources.* Unpublished Report
7.   Bryceson, I. 1978. Tanzanian coral reefs at risk. *New Scientist* 80: 115

8. Bryceson I. 1983. Pollution of Dar es Salaam coastal environments by industrial and domestic effluents. In *Status and Problems of Marine Resource Development in Tanzania*, ed. Mainoya, J.R. pp. 32-41. Dar es Salaam: University of Dar es Salaam

9. Bryceson, I., DeSouza, F., Jehangeer, I., Ngoile, M.A.K., Wynter, P. 1990. *State of the Marine Environment in the Eastern African Region*. UNEP Regional Seas Reports and Studies No. 113. Nairobi: UNEP

10. Collen, J., Mtolera, M., Abrahamson, K, Semesi, A., Pederson, M. 1995. Farming and physiology of the red algae *Euchema*: Growing commercial importance in East Africa. *Ambio* 24: 497-501

11. Dulvey, N.K., Stanwell-Smith D., Darwall, W.R.T., Horrill, C.J. 1995. Coral mining at Mafia Island, Tanzania. *Ambio* 24: 358-365

12. Edinger, E. 1993. *Mass Extinction of Caribbean Corals at the Oligocene-Miocene Boundary: Paleoecology, Paleoceanography, Paleobiography.* MSc Thesis, Geology, McMaster University, Hamilton

13. English, S, Wilkinson, C, Baker, V. 1994. *Survey Manual for Tropical Marine Resources*. Townsville: Australian Institute of Marine Sciences

14. Gallup, C.D., Edwards, R.L., Johnson, R.G. 1994. The timing of high sea levels over the past 200,000 years. *Science* 263: 796-800

15. Gaudian G. 1992. Scleractinian coral survey. In *Ecological Baseline Surveys of Coral Reefs and Intertidal Zones around Mnemba Island and Zanzibar Town*. ed. Ngoile, M.A.K. pp. 20-29. Environmental Study Series 9. Zanzibar: Commission of Lands and Environment

16. GBRMPA. 1978. *Great Barrier Reef Marine Park Authority on Reef Fish Assessment and Monitoring*. GBRMPA Workshop Series. ISSN 0156-5842 No.2

17. Gorman, M. 1995. *Report on Socio-Economic Study/ Participatory Rural Appraisal. Tanga Coastal Zone Conservation and Development Programme*, P.O. Box 5036, Tanga, Tanzania

18. Hamilton, H.G.H. 1975. *A Description of the Coral Fauna of the East African Coast*. MSc Thesis. Volume 1, Dar es Salaam: University of Dar-es-Salaam

19. Hamilton, H.G.H., Brakel, W.H. 1984. Structure and Coral Fauna of East African reefs. *Bulletin of Marine Science* 34:248-266

20. Horrill, J.C. 1992a. *Ecological Monitoring of the Coral Reefs Associated with Mnemba, Chapwani, Changuu and Bawe Islands*. Environmental Study Series 11. Zanzibar: Commission of Lands and Environment

21. Horrill, J.C. 1992b. *Status and Issues of the Marine Resources of the Fumba Peninsula*. Environmental Study Series 12. Zanzibar: Commission of Lands and Environment

22. Horrill, J.C. 1996. *Coral Reef Survey: Summary Report.* Tanga Coastal Zone Conservation and Development Programme, P.O. Box 5036, Tanga, Tanzania

23. Horrill, J.C. 1996. *Management Oriented Rapid Assessment Procedures.* Tanga Coastal Zone Conservation and Development Programme, P.O. Box 5036, Tanga, Tanzania

24. Horrill, J.C. 1997. *An Evaluation of the Enforcement Trials.* Tanga Coastal Zone Conservation and Development Programme, P.O. Box 5036, Tanga, Tanzania.

25. Horrill, J.C., Mayers, C.J. 1992. *Marine Resource Users in the Proposed Mafia Island Marine Park, Tanzania: A Preliminary Survey.* A Report for the Mafia Island Marine Park Technical Committee. WWF Country Office Tanzania, P.O. Box 63117, Dar es Salaam

26. Horrill, J.C., Seif, I., Ameir, O.A., Omar, S.H., Machano, H., Khatib, A.A., Omar, M., Kibwana I. 1994. *Baseline Monitoring Survey of the Coral Reefs and Fisheries of the Fumba Peninsula, Zanzibar.* Environmental Study Series 16. Zanzibar: Commission of Lands and Environment

27. IUCN. 1987. *The Coastal Resources of Tanga Region, Tanzania: Report of a Preliminary Study of the Status and Utilization of Tanga's Natural Resources with Management Recommendations.* Nairobi: IUCN East Africa Regional Office

28. Jennings, S., Polunin, N.V.C. 1996. Impacts of fishing on tropical reef ecosystems. *Ambio* 25: 44-49

29. Jiddawi, N.S., Issa, S., Shariff, M. 1991. Review of the marine fisheries sub-sector for Zanzibar. In *Proceedings of the Workshop on the Priorities for Fisheries Management and Development in the South West Indian Ocean.* eds. Ardil, J.P., Sanders, M.J., Albion: FAO Fisheries Report No. 457 FIPP/R45791

30. Johnstone R.W., Olafson, E. 1995. Some environmental aspects of open water algal cultivation: Zanzibar, Tanzania. *Ambio* 24: 465-469

31. Kamukuru, A.T. 1992. *Costs and Earnings of Basket Trap and Handline Fishery in the Dar-es-Salaam region of Tanzanian Coast.* MSc Thesis, University of Kuopio, Finland

32. Kamukuru, A.T. 1996. *Assessment of the Biological Status of the Dar es Salaam Designated Marine Reserves of Tanzanian Coast.* Unpublished report submitted to International Oceanographic Commission (IOC)

33. Kholodov, V.I. 1975. Assimilation of different forms of food by *Strongylocentrotus droebachiensis. Hydrobiology Journal* 11: 41-46

34. Mainoya, J.R., Pratap, H.B. 1988. Marine conservation strategy for sustained bioproductivity of the Tanzanian coastal waters. In *Proceedings of the Workshop on Ecology and Bioproductivity of the Marine Coastal Waters of Eastern Africa,* ed. Mainoya, J.R. pp. 145-153. Dar es Salaam: University of Dar es Salaam

35. McClanahan, T.R. 1992. Triggerfish: coral reef keystone predators. *Swara* 15:15-16

36. McClanahan, T.R. 1994. Kenyan coral reef lagoon fish: effects of fishing, substrate complexity, and sea urchins. *Coral Reefs* 13:231-241

37. McClanahan, T.R. 1995. Fish predators and scavengers of the sea urchin *Echinometra mathaei* in Kenyan coral-reef marine parks. *Environmental Biology of Fishes* 43: 187-193

38. McClanahan, T.R., Shafir, S.H. 1990. Causes and consequences of sea urchin abundance and diversity in Kenyan coral reef lagoons. *Oecologia* 83:362-370

39. McClanahan, T.R., Obura, D. 1997. Sedimentation effects on shallow water coral communities in Kenya. *Journal of Experimental Biology and Ecology* 209:103-122

40. McClanahan, T.R., Nugues, M., Mwachireya, S. 1994. Fish and sea urchin herbivory and competition in Kenyan coral reef lagoons: the role of reef management. *Journal of Experimental Marine Biology and Ecology* 184:237-254

41. McClanahan, T.R., Kamukuru, A.T., Muthiga, N.A., Yebio, M.G., Obura, D. 1996. Effect of sea urchin reductions on algae, coral and fish populations. *Conservation Biology* 10: 136-154

42. McClanahan, T.R., Muthiga, N.A., Kamukuru, A.T., Machano, H., Kiambo, R.W. 1999. The effects of marine parks and fishing on the coral reefs of northern Tanzania. *Biological Conservation* 89: 161-182

43. Muthiga, N.A. 1996. *The Role of Early Life History Strategies on the Population Dynamics of the Sea Urchin* Echinometra mathaei *(de Blaiville) on Reefs in Kenya.* PhD Dissertation, Nairobi: University of Nairobi

44. Muthiga, N.A., McClanahan, T.R. 1997. The effect of visitor use on the hard coral communities of the Kisite Marine Park, Kenya. *Proceedings of the 8th International Coral Reef Symposium* 2: 1879-1882

45. Mwaipopo, O.U. 1989. Hydrography. In *The Development of a Marine National Park, Mafia Island, Tanzania. The Current State of the Environment of the South Mafia Island Channel.* ed. Ngoile, M.A.K. pp. 10-11. Zanibar: University of Dar es Salaam, Institute of Marine Sciences

46. Newell, B.S. 1957. A preliminary survey of the hydrography of the British East African coastal waters. *Fishery Publication,* London 9:1-21

47. Newell, B.S. 1959. The hydrography of British East African coastal waters. II. *Fishery Publication,* London 12:1-18

48. Ngoile, M.A.K. 1990. *Ecological Baseline Surveys of Coral Reefs and Intertidal Zones around Mnemba Island and Zanzibar Town.* Environmental Study Series 9. Zanzibar: Commission of Lands and Environment

49. Ngoile, M.A.K., Horrill, J.C. 1993. Coastal ecosystems, productivity and ecosystem protection: coastal ecosystem management. *Ambio* 22: 461-467

50. Ngoile, M.A.K., Bwathondi, P.O.J., Makwaia, E.S. 1988. Trends in the exploitation of marine fisheries resources in Tanzania. In *Proceedings of the Workshop on Ecology and Bioproductivity of the Marine Coastal Waters of Eastern Africa,* ed. Mainoya, J.R. pp. 93-100. Dar es Salaam: University of Dar es Salaam

51. Ngusaru, A. 1997. Geological history. In *A Guide to the Seashores of Eastern Africa and the Western Indian Ocean Islands.* ed. Richmond, M.D. pp. 7-8. Sida, Department for Research Cooperation, SAREC

52. NRI. 1993. *Report on Integrated Coastal Zone Management Study, Tanga, United Republic of Tanzania.* Natural Resources Institute, London: Overseas Development Administration

53. Pequignat, E. 1966. "Skin digestion" and epithelial absorption in irregular and regular sea urchins and their probable relation to the outflow of spherule-coelomocytes. *Nature* 210: 397-399

54. Pettersson-Lofquist, P. 1995 The development of open water algae farming in Zanzibar: Reflections on the socioeconomic impact. *Ambio* 24: 487-491

55. Ray, G.C. 1968. *Marine Parks of Tanzania.* Washington D.C.: Conservation Foundation

56. Risk, M.J., Dunn J.J., Horrill, C. 1993. Reef monitoring in Maldives and Zanzibar: Low-tech and high-tech science. In *Global Aspects of Coral Reefs: Health, Hazards, and History.* ed. Ginsburg, R.N. pp. M36-M42. Miami: University of Miami

57. Russ, G.R. 1991. Coral reef fisheries: effects and yields. In *The Ecology of Fishes on Coral Reefs.* ed. Sale, P.F. pp. 601-635. San Diego: Academic Press

58. Russ, G.R., Alcala, A.C. 1989. Effects of intense fishing pressure on an assemblage of coral reef fishes. *Marine Ecology Progress Series* 56:13-27

59. Salm, R.V., Clark, J.R. 1984. *Marine and Coastal Areas: A Guide for Planners and Managers.* Gland: IUCN

60. Samoilys, M.A. 1988. Abundance and species richness of coral reef fish on the Kenyan Coast: The effects of protective management and fishing. *Proceedings of the 6th International Coral Reef Symposium* 2:261-266

61. Sanderson, S.L., Solonsky, A.C. 1986. Comparison of a rapid visual and a strip transect technique for censusing reef fish assemblages. *Bulletin of Marine Science* 39:119-129

62. Scheinman, D., Mabrook, A. 1996. *The Traditional Management of Coastal Resources.* A Consultancy Report for Tanga Coastal Zone Conservation and Development Programme, P.O. Box 5036, Tanga, Tanzania

63. Stoddart, D.R. 1971. Environment and history in Indian Ocean reef morphology. *Symposium of Zoological Society*, London 28: 3-38

64. Tomascik, T., Sander, F. 1985. Effects of eutrophication on reef building corals. *Marine Biology* 87:143-155

65. UNEP. 1989. *Coastal and Marine Environmental Problems of the United Republic of Tanzania.* UNEP Regional Seas Reports and Studies No. 106. Nairobi: UNEP

66. Watson, M., Ormond, R.F.G. 1994. Effect of an artisanal fishery on the fish and urchin populations of a Kenyan coral reef. *Marine Ecology Progress Series* 109:115-129

67. Woodland, R.V., Hooper, N.A. 1977. The effect of human trampling on coral reefs. *Biological Conservation* 11:1-14

68. White, A.T. 1988. The effect of community managed marine reserves in the Philippines on their associated coral reef fish populations. *Asian Fisheries Science* 2: 27-41

Chapter 7

Kenya

David O. Obura, Nyawira A. Muthiga & Maggie Watson

In 1989 Kenya's coastal population was recorded as 1.83 million people, with an annual growth rate of 3.7% (25), of which a large proportion is due to migration of people from other parts of Kenya. Increasing economic activity, due to shipping, freight handling and tourism, provides a strong draw for migrant workers, as well as creating conditions for environmental degradation. Marine resource use is largely unregulated but the establishment, in 1968, of East Africa's first marine protected areas has provided for the protection and conservation of several reef areas. This has also provided an opportunity for research on the effects of resource use, and the effectiveness of levels of protective management, outlined in the first part of this chapter. In the second part of the chapter, the principal conservation and environmental issues affecting Kenya's reefs are described on a case study basis, using each of the five main protected areas to highlight the principal human population and resource pressures, and the findings of research in each of the areas.

Coastal Geography and Climate

The Kenya coast is approximately 500 km long, between latitudes 1 and 5° S (Fig. 7.1). Geologically the coast is differentiated into two regions; the southern half, from the Tanzania border north to Malindi, consists of tiers of Pleistocene reefs above and below sea level, the most prominent one being the intertidal platform that forms the current fringing reef. North of Malindi, the coast is formed by broad sedimentary plains of Quaternary and Tertiary origin, drained by Kenya's two largest rivers the Tana and Athi-Sabaki Rivers. These geological differences have had a profound influence on the coastal terrestrial and marine environments, with coastal hills and coral reefs in the south and broad plains and soft substrate environments in the north. Together, the geological and habitat differences have affected patterns of human settlement and its effects on coral reef ecosystems, with greater settlement on the rocky shores of the south coast.

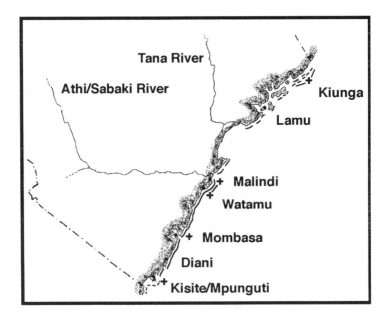

Figure 7.1. Map of Kenya coast showing the extent of continuous (solid lines) and intermittent (broken lines) fringing reefs, and marine parks and reserves (crosses). Scale bar = 20 km.

Monsoon winds are the dominant climatic influence on the Kenya coast, blowing from the northeast (December to March) and southeast (May to October) with a 1 to 2 month transition period in between characterized by variable and lower winds. Secondary in influence to the monsoon winds, the northern Kenya coast is seasonally bathed by the Somali Current system, receiving cold upwelling waters pushed southwards during the northeast monsoon (NEM). Offshore, this influence can reach as far south as Malindi (27), though the presence of cold upwelled waters on coral reefs in Malindi has not yet been recorded.

The influence of river discharge on coral reefs is controlled by local geological history. In the south, coastal hills prevent the penetration of major rivers from the hinterland, resulting in low influence of freshwater runoff and river discharge. In the north, however, the low sedimentary plains allow the Tana and Sabaki rivers to drain much of the south and central portions of Kenya. The coastline north of Malindi is dominated by river influence with long stretches of sandy beaches and dunes, and predominantly sandy bottoms. Riverdischarge plumes are transported north or south by prevailing coastal currents and winds - southwards during the NEM, and northwards during the SEM (7).

Physical and Chemical Oceanography

As with other parts of the East African coast, Kenya is bathed by waters of the East African Coastal Current (EACC), formed by the northward deflection of the Southern Equatorial Current when it hits the African mainland in

Table 7.1. Physical oceanographic conditions on the Kenya coast, monthly means (mean, standard error), and East African Coastal Current (EACC) speed and direction. Northeast monsoon (NEM): December - April; Southeast monsoon (SEM): May - November. Sources: 3,9,33,61,62, 65,67, unpublished data (Coral Reef Conservation Project). Notes - (a) salinity in Malindi during rainy season discharge of Sabaki River.

		NEM		SEM	
		mean	sem	mean	sem
Temperature (°C)	EACC	28.4	0.2	26.4	0.2
	Reefs	29.8	0.1	27.7	0.2
Salinity (ppt)	EACC	34.2	0.5	34.9	0.1
	Reefs	34.4	0.1	34.6	0.1
Transparency (m)	EACC	11.2	0.8	16.7	1.7
	Reefs	16.3	0.5	15.2	0.9
	Malindi[a]	7.4	0.6	9.3	0.5

East African Coastal Current:	*December*	*March*	*May*
Speed (m/s)	0.23-0.52	0.13-0.26	0.58-0.74
Direction (degrees)	020-040	300-350	340-346

Tanzania. The EACC flows northwards throughout the year. Its speed is faster during the southeast monsoon (SEM) when reinforced by the prevailing winds, and slower during the NEM when the monsoon winds blow counter to the current (Table 7.1). Water movement within reef lagoons and over the shallow reef front is strongly influenced by tidal flushing patterns, and tends to flow with prevailing winds rather than the offshore EACC. As mentioned earlier, the influence of the EACC on the northern part of the Kenya coast is moderated by the Somali Current during the NEM.

Coral reef waters show consistent seasonal temperature variations, driven by monsoon wind reversals (Fig. 7.2a). In normal years, temperatures vary between approximately 25 and 31°C, with a minimum during the SEM when cloud cover is high, and cold, deeper waters are brought to the surface by strong monsoon winds. There are two temperature maxima, corresponding to transition periods between the monsoon seasons, when winds are light and variable and insolation is high. The first maximum occurs at the end of the SEM in October/November when reef water temperatures can rise to 3°C. The second maximum occurs at the end of the NEM in March/April when insolation is highest, and reef water temperatures can rise to 31 to 32°C, with localized midday peaks of 36°C in shallow, still areas. Compared to offshore values (Table 7.1), temperatures experienced by coral reefs are more variable, with higher extremes. In "warm" years, such as 1994 and 1998, the latter associated with El-Niño seawater warming trends, peak temperatures in March and April exceeded "normal" levels by over 1°C.

Salinity variation is low and controlled by rainfall during the monsoon seasons. Minimum salinity values in reef waters of 32 to 33 ppt are associated with localized heavy rainfall, or with heavy river discharge following heavy rains in upcountry watersheds, for example in Malindi during heavy flow of the Sabaki River (Fig. 7.2b).

Chemical parameters of offshore waters in East Africa show strong seasonal patterns under the influence of the monsoons (33). Figure 7.3 summarizes

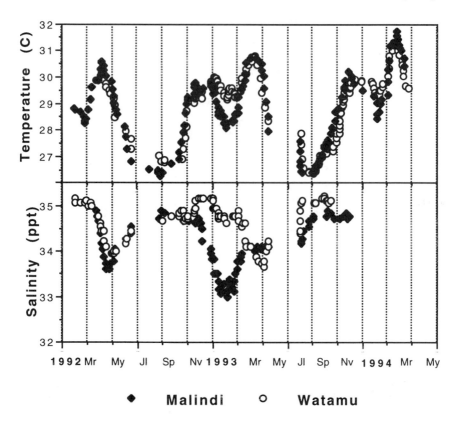

Figure 7.2. Seasonal variation of a) temperature and b) salinity in Malindi and Watamu coral reef waters, 1992-94 (moving average of low tide measurements).

phosphate (9,62), nitrate (9) and chlorophyll (9) measurements for offshore waters in East Africa, with ammonia, nitrate and nitrite, phosphate and chlorophyll sampled in reef and mangrove creek waters around Mombasa in 1996 to 1997 (60). Ammonia shows peak values in reef and creek waters during both monsoon seasons, with highest values in creek waters at the onset of the SEM. Nitrate/nitrite concentrations in creek waters are highest in April to May, and are continually low in reef waters. Offshore concentrations of nitrate are highest during the NEM. Principal nitrogen sources include nitrogen fixation, terrestrial runoff and upwelling. Nitrogen fixation is thought to cause the offshore peak concentrations during the NEM (9,33), while the peaks in creek waters in May and potentially November, which occur during the rainy seasons, may be due to runoff and terrestrial sources.

Phosphate concentrations in offshore waters peak in June during the SEM, with minima in November and April during the calm inter-monsoon transition periods. In reef and creek waters, phosphate shows strong cycling with maxima during the SEM and minima during the NEM (January to April). Principal sources of phosphate include water column mixing, upwelling and runoff (33). Water column mixing may contribute to the offshore peak of phosphate in the

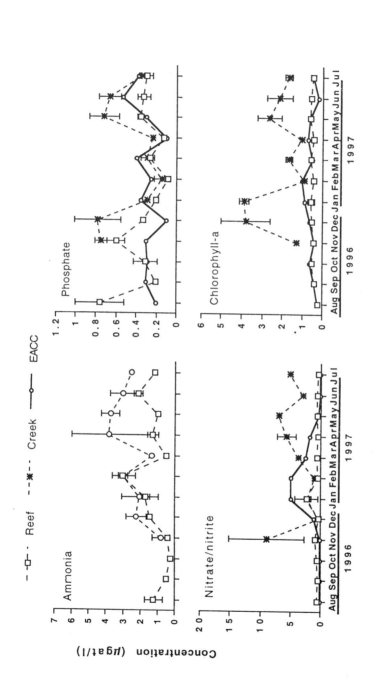

Figure 7.3. Concentrations of ammonia, nitrate/nitrite, phosphate and chlorophyll-a in Mombasa Marine Park (n=4 sites) and Mtwapa Creek (n=2 sites), August 1996-July 1997, and in open sea (East Africa Coastal Current). Sources: (9,60,62)

SEM, while creek waters, and the adjacent reefs may also receive phosphate from runoff, especially following the rains in November and December. Chlorophyll-a concentrations in reef and offshore waters show little seasonal variability. By contrast, chlorophyll concentrations in creek waters show a very high maximum in November and December, and a lower one in May. These coincide with the onset of both NEM and SEM when rainfall and water column mixing are initiated. All parameters presented here were found at higher concentrations in creek water compared to reef and offshore waters (Fig. 7.3), indicating significant inputs of nutrients from fresh water runoff.

Climate Change

Recent studies (15) of the quantities of trace metals and isotopes of oxygen and carbon incorporated in the skeletons of large *Porites* coral heads growing on the Kenya coast give some insight into recent climate variability of Eastern Africa, and provide independent climatological assessments for comparison with glacial records from Mt. Kenya (22,23). The ^{18}O trace of a single coral core dating back to 1801 suggests water temperatures in Malindi have risen by 1.5°C, with half of that rise occurring in the last 30 years (15). Fluctuations in the concentration of barium and uranium in the core reflect seasonal input of freshwater and terrigenous sediment to Malindi, and may prove useful in determining historic changes in river influence. However, ecological evidence of recent increases in sediment discharge to Malindi reefs (3,28,65,86 and "Sediment Effects" section) are not reflected in the barium/uranium signature of the initial core, requiring further work.

Coral Reef Geography

Ancient and Modern Reefs

Coral reefs have fringed the Kenya coast throughout the Holocene and Pleistocene periods. The position of these ancient reefs advanced up and down the shore following fluctuations in sea level caused by glacial cycles. These remnant reefs form the major geological and topographical features along the southern Kenya coast - the present-day intertidal reef platform, the beach cliffs and rocky platforms that form most of the coastline, and deeper platforms at 8 to 15 and 25 to 30 m depth. There are ongoing efforts to find traces of deeper remnant reef platforms in the Indian Ocean, down to 150 m depth, about the limit of lowest sea level during glacial maxima. The influence of the Tana and Athi-Sabaki Rivers on the northern Kenya coast has persisted at least for the duration of the Pleistocene, resulting in poor and patchy development of ancient and modern reefs in the area.

The historical distribution of coral reefs appears to have been similar to present distributions (12), suggesting stable marine environmental conditions over recent geological time in East Africa. During the Last Interglacial period (around 125 000 years ago), the rocky platforms that are now exposed on land were shallow subtidal reef habitats. The vertical stratification of corals on this platform suggests similar ecological conditions as on present-day reefs (11), with successional transitions from early-colonizing species, through *Acropora-*

dominance in intermediate successional stages, to an assortment of massive species (*Porites*, faviids) as the final stage. At the higher sea level stand the shallow subtidal and intertidal reef area was considerably larger than today's, providing a larger area of suitable habitat for coral growth. Sedimentation rates may also have been higher, resulting in greater habitat heterogeneity. A feature common on Pleistocene reefs not found today were large banks of the calcareous alga *Halimeda*, in some areas covering 50 km² with thicknesses over 5 m (12). Such *Halimeda* banks are found in other extant coral reef areas, for example the Great Barrier Reef (32).

Biogeography

Pleistocene versus Present Distributions. Comparisons of Pleistocene and modern reef gastropod assemblages suggest that species diversity on modern reef flats has decreased since the Pleistocene. Estimates of the decline range from 2 (based on species presence/absence, 12) to 35 species lost (based on sampling effort and abundance, 36) out of about 170 extant species, that is, from 1 to 21% species loss. Crame's studies (11,12) on coral succession and ecological zonation of Pleistocene corals indicate similar species and assemblages to today's reefs, with two primary assemblages - *Acropora*-dominated assemblages in high-energy locations, and *Porites*-faviid assemblages in calmer water.

Present Distributions. The cover, size and diversity of coral reef ecosystems decreases northwards along the Kenya coast, due to increasingly poor conditions for reef development. Patterns of species abundance and diversity are not always clear, however, reflecting multiple factors and levels of influence, from the regional influence of the Somali current, through the sub-regional influence of river discharge to the local influence of species interactions, habitat and human intervention. For example, gastropod diversity in Kenya is lower than in Tanzania, suggesting there is a decrease in diversity northwards, away from a center of diversity where the South Equatorial Current meets the African continent in Tanzania (36,83,96,97). Within Kenya, gastropods show a slight decrease in diversity northwards, however the decline in species diversity is small compared to the decrease in density (see Distribution Studies). Coral and fish diversity have not been studied to specifically address the question of diversity clines from south to north, however indications are that they are lower on reefs north of Lamu than along the southern Kenya coast (78,94).

Ecological, Resource Use And Conservation Studies

Taxonomic Studies

Reef Building Corals. Much of the work on the hard coral fauna of the Kenyan coast has been concentrated within the Malindi-Watamu reef complex. This area consists of a well-developed fringing reef extending from Watamu to Vasco da Gama point south of Malindi town, with several patch reefs including North reef in the Malindi Marine park. The most comprehensive

species list of scleractinian corals from this area is derived from studies carried out by Hamilton (20) at North Reef and similar sites in Tanzania (20,21). Hamilton recorded 55 genera and 140 species of scleractinian corals on reefs in Kenya and Tanzania. From reefs in Malindi and Watamu, an additional four genera and 43 species were added (31).

Most work on scleractinian corals has been restricted to shallow reef habitats including reef flats, reef lagoons, back reef and reef edge sites. The most speciose genera include *Acropora, Montipora* and *Porites* while the most abundant genera include *Porites, Pocillopora, Acropora, Platygyra, Galaxea, Echinopora, Montipora*, and *Astreopora* (18,21). The Kenyan coral fauna is similar in composition to other parts of East Africa and the western and central Indian Ocean (21,31,75,80), supporting the suggestion (see Chapter 1) that there is a high degree of homogeneity of corals at the species level throughout the Indian Ocean (81,87).

There may have been a higher species diversity of hard corals on Kenyan reefs during the Pleistocene era (11) but the dominant genera remain the same including *Porites, Acropora, Montipora Cyphastrea* and *Platygyra*. There is a gap in knowledge of the coral fauna especially of Northern Kenyan reefs and deeper reef habitats. Knowledge of the soft coral fauna of Kenyan reefs is also lacking. Currently a hard coral reference collection is housed at the KWS Malindi resource training center. Additional materials from Kenyan reefs are housed at the British Museum of Natural History and the National Natuurhistorisch Museum, Leiden, The Netherlands.

Algae and Seagrasses.
The Kenyan coast has a rich and diverse fauna of marine algae including 90 species of Chlorophyceae, 10 species of Cyanophyceae 45 species of Phaeophyceae and 132 species of Rhodophyceae. Additionally, 12 species of marine angiosperms have been recorded in Kenya (10,26,54,55,56). The high diversity of marine algae along the Kenyan coast has been attributed to the heterogeneous nature of the habitat and the wide tidal range (54). Despite the spatial variability in the algal composition along the Kenyan coast, the overall faunal composition is similar to other coastlines in East Africa and the western Indian Ocean (1,30). Currently a reference collection of marine plants is housed at the National Museums of Kenya herbarium. No taxonomic information exists on the coralline algae of the Kenyan coast.

Mollusks.
The earliest records of the molluskan fauna of the Kenyan coast (12) lists 173 species of gastropods from 32 families and 103 bivalves from 40 localities along the coast, including coral reef habitats. Additional information includes a survey of gastropod populations in Diani (96) and a checklist of cowries of East Africa (68). More recently a survey of prosobranch gastropods in thirteen localities from Zinyika in the north to Kisite in the south recorded 135 species from 25 families in reef lagoon, reef flat and reef edge habitats (36).

These surveys indicate that the Kenyan coast has a rich and diverse reef-associated gastropod fauna that is similar in composition to assemblages in other areas within the Western Indian ocean (84). There is little evidence of endemism in the gastropod fauna except for *Vasum rhinoceros*, a species found on reef flats only in Kenya and Zanzibar (36). Comparison of present day species with the Pleistocene molluskan fauna indicates a 45% reduction in species, including the bivalves *Tridacna gigas* and *T. crocea*, and the gastropods *Strombus bulla* and *Cerithrium salebrosum* (12).

Finfish Fauna. Information on finfish on Kenyan reefs is derived from several sources, as no comprehensive taxonomic species list is available. One study recorded 188 species from 15 families from reef slope sites in 19 localities along the Kenya coast from Shimoni in the north to Kiunga in the south (78) Bock (4) compiled checklists of 350 species of lagoon fish of Diani and Kilifi reefs. Additional information is available in Bock (5) and FAO species identification guides for the Western Indian Ocean (16). Although more taxonomic studies need to be carried out, the information available so far indicates a faunal composition similar to other reefs in the Western Indian ocean, with low levels of endemism.

The finfish fauna of shallow Kenyan reefs is severely effected by fishing. In a survey of eight reef lagoons with differing protection levels from fishing, of 110 species from eight target families on protected reefs, only 58 species were found on unprotected reefs (38). The families surveyed did not include some of the major commercial families, such as the Serranidae and Lethrinidae, thus the effect of fishing on finfish community structure is likely greater than indicated in that study. Some species of fish, such as *Pomacentrus baenschi*, are now largely seen in protected areas (2,37). Nevertheless, as in other highly disturbed habitats, some fish species appear to thrive better on unprotected reefs, such as the regional endemic *Amphiprion allardi* (37,38).

Distribution Studies

Coral assemblages on Kenyan reefs are characterized by pocilloporid, poritid, acroporid and faviid species, with localized dominance of genera such as *Echinopora*, *Goniastrea* and *Galaxea* depending on local environmental factors (21). The upper zones of seaward reef slopes that experience strong wave action are dominated by branching acroporids and poritids such as *P. nigrescens*. Below this zone in deeper waters lies a mixed zone of massive poritids and faviids, including *Platygyra* and *Montastrea*. Sheltered reef slopes are dominated by extensive stands of *Galaxea astreata* and *Lobophyllia* spp., with branching forms of *Acropora* and massive poritids and faviids in deeper water. Lagoon patch reefs are dominated by *Porites*, with locally high abundance of *Pocillopora*, *Pavona*, and *Stylophora*. Broad scale surveys of 12 reefs along the Kenyan coast indicate that reef edge sites have a higher diversity of coral species than reef lagoon sites (Muthiga, N. unpublished data, Fig. 7.4).

Management has had a major effect on the diversity of coral reefs in Kenya. Coral cover and diversity are higher in protected reefs than in unprotected reefs of similar structure (43). Additionally coral cover increased in the Mombasa Marine National Park following several years of protection (41,46) showing the positive effects of protection on the coral community. High diversity and cover of corals usually results in high topographic complexity, and thus high diversity, abundance and biomass of other reef-associated taxa such as fish (35,92). Management actions restricting destructive human effects to coral communities therefore help prevent reductions in diversity and abundance of the associated

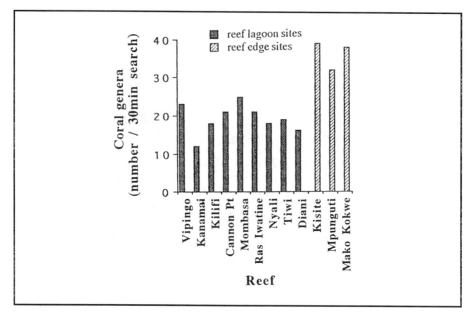

Figure 7.4. Coral diversity on reef edge and reef lagoon sites.

taxa. Of eight fish families surveyed in reef lagoons under a range of management types (protected versus unprotected) seven families had reduced numbers of species and densities on unprotected compared to protected reefs. In some cases indirect human effects may supersede direct effects from fishing: on protected fore reef slopes exposed to sedimentation in Malindi, species diversity of commercially important fish was lower than on unsedimented, unprotected reefs (78). Dynamite fishing on the Kenya-Tanzania border was also noted to reduce commercially important fish especially on Mbijira reef (78).

Management also has an effect on the distribution and species diversity and abundance of reef-associated invertebrates. For both sea urchins and gastropods, protected reefs have lower diversity and abundances than unprotected reefs (Table 7.2). Sea urchin diversity is higher and density lower in protected areas than in unprotected areas, the causes of which are discussed in the section "Indirect Effects of Fishing" (46). Superimposed on the south-north decline in gastropod diversity and density (36), is the effect of predation release of gastropods on unprotected reefs (35). For all but the two favored commercially harvested species (*Lambis truncata* and *L. chiragra*) the removal of gastropod-eating finfish on unprotected reefs has resulted in a net increase in the diversity and density of gastropods on these reefs, in spite of the removal of shells by fishers for sale (35,46).

Modern Fisheries Development and Management

The coral reef resources of Kenya are managed by the Fisheries Department under the Fisheries Act (Ministry of Environment and Natural Resources and the Kenya Wildlife Service (KWS) under the Wildlife Conservation and

Box 7.1 Patterns of Reproduction of an Important Grazer on Kenyan Reefs

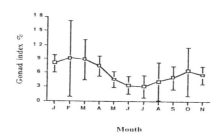

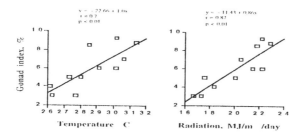

Figure 2. The relationship between mean monthly gonad indices of *Echinometra mathaei* and (left) mean monthly temperature and (right) mean monthly light on Kenyan reefs

Many temperate marine invertebrates reproduce during restricted periods usually linked to times of the year (spring and summer) when environmental conditions are suitable for growth of the young. The mechanisms that control reproduction in tropical marine invertebrates have received less attention.

Studies of the reproduction of *Echinometra mathaei* (de Blainville) at several locations on the Kenyan coast over a three-year period revealed that reproduction is seasonal with gonad growth peaking in February during the northeast monsoon (NEM) and spawning occurring in March through April at the end of the NEM (Fig. 1). Gonad growth was significantly correlated with monthly sea water temperatures and monthly light levels suggesting that these two factors play a role in cueing reproduction in *E. mathaei* (Fig. 2).

Echinometra mathaei is widely distributed throughout the Western Indian Ocean but only exhibits seasonal reproduction in locations where minimum sea water temperatures fall below 18°C (2). This suggests that temperature may not have a key role in controlling spawning in *E. mathaei* in Kenyan waters. Temperatures and light however may have an indirect effect by controlling growth of phytoplankton. Phytoplankton concentrations in Kenyan waters also show a seasonal pattern peaking at around the same time that light and temperatures peak. Spawning in sea urchins has been shown to be induced by phytoplankton (1,3) however this was not tested in this study.

E. mathaei spawns at the time when temperatures are highest and light levels are highest and when availability of food for the young is greatest. These factors acting together would form a strong cue in controlling spawning even in tropical environments where the magnitude of change in temperature, light and chlorophyll is not as great as in temperate environments.

Nyawira Muthiga

References

1.   Himmelman, J.H. 1980. Synchronization of spawning in marine invertebrates by phytoplankton. *Advances in Invertebrates Reproduction* 3-19
2.   Pearse, J.S., Phillips, B.F. 1968. Continuous reproduction in the Indo-Pacific Sea urchin *Echinometra mathaei* at Rottnest Island, Western Australia. *Australian Journal for Marine Freshwater Resources* 19:161-172
3.   Starr, M., Himmelman, J.H., Therriault, J. 1992. Isolation and properties of a substance from the diatom *Phaeodactylum tricornutum* which induces spawning in the sea urchin *Strongylocentrotus droebachiensis*. *Marine Ecology Progress Series* 79:275-287

Management Act). Other institutions with local jurisdiction include the Forestry Department that manage mangroves and the Coast Development Authority. Most reef fisheries are artisanal in origin, using handlines, basket traps, spearguns and small pull- and gill-nets. Offshore fishing from sail-powered dhows includes handlining, trolling and gill-netting. New fisheries that are growing in importance include beach seining and netting for aquarium fish within coral reef areas, and sport-fishing in offshore waters. The Fisheries Act prohibits destructive forms of fishing such as dynamite fishing. The Fisheries Department is in charge of collecting fisheries catch data at fish landing sites, organizing fishermen into cooperatives, enforcing fisheries regulations and developing fisheries policy in Kenya. It is, unfortunately, understaffed and underskilled with few enforcement capabilities. The KWS has a mandate to manage marine resources within marine parks and reserves. In the latter, only "traditional" fishing methods are allowed, using handlines and traps. The KWS has trained rangers and Wardens that manage marine parks and enforce conservation regulations.

Fish and Fisheries Studies

Research on reef fish has focused on the effects of different management strategies on fish abundance and diversity, and concomitant effects on coral reef community structure and function. Results have differed primarily as a result of the reef zone under study. Surveys of outer reef slopes in 1987 found little difference in the abundance of reef fish between protected and fished reefs (78) with most of the variation attributed to other factors such as sedimentation and the use of destructive fishing methods (such as dynamite). By contrast, studies of lagoon patch reef fish communities from 1988 to the present have found large differences as a result of protection status (38,39). In lagoons, fish population densities and sizes are much smaller, and the number of species is up to 50% lower, in unprotected compared to protected reef lagoons (38). Acanthurids (surgeonfish), balistids (triggerfish), chaetodontids (butterflyfish), pomacanthids (angelfish), and scarids (parrotfish) have all suffered population and diversity reductions, in addition to families targeted by fisheries (see below). Labrids (wrasses), pomacentrids (damselfish) and diodontids (puffers) were apparently less affected by fishing pressure, and in some cases increased in numbers. Increased numbers of wrasses on unprotected reefs is due to larger numbers of small and juvenile individuals, but with a decrease in overall biomass. Damselfish and puffers appear to do well in disturbed reefs, the former capturing newly available substrate for algal lawns. The comprehensive reduction in fish populations, and simplification of food webs and functional groups has multiple direct and indirect effects on reef community structure, outlined in the section below (and see Chapter 2).

Annual fisheries yields reported for Kenya are highly variable, though consistent with levels reported for other parts of the western Indian Ocean. Yields of 2.6 to 13.3 tons/km²/y have been reported from Kisite (89,90), 5.1 to 12.9 tons/km²/y from unprotected reefs in Kilifi (63), 10.5 to 13.1 tons/km²/y for Diani (50) and approximately 13 tons/km²/y adjacent to the Mombasa Marine Park (41). These levels are comparable to 0.8 to 5.0 tons/km²/y reported for Tanzania, and approximately 12 tons/km²/y for a reef fishery dominated by emperors and rabbitfish in Madagascar (29). A large difference in estimated maximum sustainable yield (MSY) for coral reef fisheries exists, ranging from 5 tons/km²/y estimated by FAO in 1979 for coral reefs and associated continental shelves, to 10 to 20 tons/km²/y by Munro and Williams in 1985, for coral reefs only (in 41). With most regional fisheries far above the FAO estimate, it is likely that an MSY of 10 to 20 tons/km²/y is more reasonable (McClanahan, T. personal communication), and therefore most fisheries in the region are at or near their MSY. The small size of fish characteristic of the low-yield fisheries in Kenya (41,50) suggest that unprotected reefs are exploited well beyond their MSY, leading to resource depletion. With fisher populations approaching 20 per km² (50), the most depleted reefs in Kenya are utilized well above a threshold level of 7 fishers/km² suggested by McClanahan in modeling studies (see Chapter 2).

Catch per unit effort (CPUE) varies among gear types, with typical artisanal gear including handlines, basket traps, spearguns, gill nets, and seine nets. Measurements of CPUE cover most of these categories, including 0.6 kg/hook/hr (89,90) and 4.7 kg/man/d (50) for handlines, 6.5 kg/man/d for gill nets, 4.1 kg/man/day for seine nets, 4.1 kg/man/d for basket traps, and 3.6 kg/man/day for spearguns (50). The value for handlines is at the low end of the "normal" range of 0.5 to 2.0 kg/line/h reported by Dalzell (13).

The reef fishery at Kisite demonstrates some of the difficulties in determining the "health" of a coral reef fishery. Surveys in the Kisite MNP and Mpunguti MNR in 1992 (92) found the biomass of commercially important lethrinids, lutjanids and serranids up to ten times greater in the unfished park compared to the adjacent exploited reserve. While biomass within the protected park had increased dramatically from levels recorded in 1987 (78), Mpunguti showed no such recovery, and there are even tentative indications of

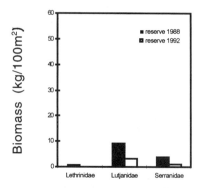 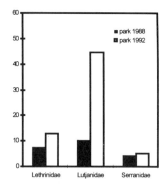

Figure 7.5. Differences in biomass of fish families in unprotected and protected reefs. A) Biomass of commercially important lethrinidae, lutjanidae and serranidae on fore reef slopes in the unprotected Mpunguti MNR and unfished Kisite MNP in 1988 and 1992 (92). Note that the lutjanid biomass of the protected park in 1992 exceeds average total fish biomass levels, likely caused by patchy distribution of large schools of lutjanids. B) Biomass of selected fish families on lagoon patch reefs in unprotected and protected reefs between 1988 and 1994 (41).

a further decline (Fig. 7.5a). Similarly, the biomass of several fish families, including non-commercial ones, is several times lower on unprotected lagoon reefs than protected ones (fig. 7.5b). The order of magnitude differences in fish densities between protected parks and unprotected reserves suggests very high levels of fishing, and potentially overfishing, on unprotected reefs. However, in spite of the high density differences, there are variable differences in the diversity and species richness of fish, with both no difference (92) and significant decreases in species richness (38) being recorded

Marine protected areas can have significant effects on fish populations and fisheries yields. Follow-up studies of the Kisite/Mpunguti park and reserve in 1994 and 1995 (89,93) showed small increases in fish abundances over 1992 levels at Kisite MNP but more substantial gains across the commercially important guild at Mpunguti. Several factors may have contributed to these increased fish populations in the park and secondarily in the reserve, including: a) larval replenishment, b) adult migration from park to reserve (but see below, and recent reviews in 14,73,76), and c) improved management of fisheries in the reserve.

From 1980 to 1985 the total demersal catch of the Mpunguti fishery (Fig. 7.6, 93) remained relatively stable although the proportion of herbivorous rabbitfish increased while piscivore and invertebrate-eating lethrinids (emperors) decreased. Following this switch, a major slump in the landings of almost all families occurred from 1985 culminating in a trough in 1988 when catches were approximately 35% of 1980 to 1985 levels. Following improved management of the park and reserve in 1989, total catch recovered substantially, due to recovery in the catch of rabbitfish and emperors. The recovery in both herbivorous and predatory fish landings since 1989, and the co-dominance of herbivorous and predatory fish in the catch (Fig. 7.7) suggest the fishery at Kisite is not overfished. Although the largest fish, such as groupers, are probably depleted at Mpunguti, the piscivorous and invertebrate-eating emperors show no sign of ecosystem overfishing as defined by Pauly (69).

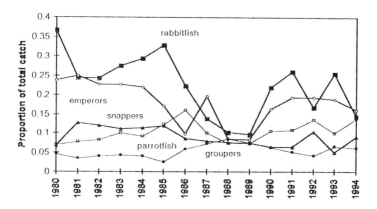

Figure 7.6. The proportion of five commercially important families in the demersal catch associated with Mpunguti MNR between 1980 and 1994.

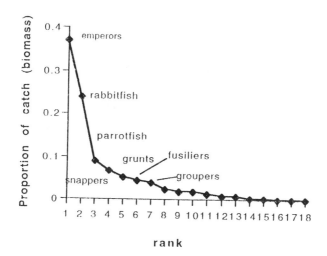

Figure 7.7. Ranked proportional biomass of demersal fish grouped by family in the commercial catch associated with Mpunguti MNR. After groupers, proportion of catch due to (in descending order): goatfish, wrasses, spadefish, crocodile fish, mojarras, bream, damselfish, squirrelfish, monos, lizardfish, surgeonfish.

Ecosystem overfishing as defined by significant indirect effects (section below), does, however, probably occur.

Added to the above difficulties in determining whether a fishery is overexploited or not, are a complex of social and cultural factors (see Chapter 2). Fisher behavior and social factors not covered by traditional fisheries science may have important consequences on fisheries. Gear type has important effects on fisheries catch and composition. Selection of a gear type by a fisher can have both historical (training and preference), as well as income and resource competition components (50, Obura unpublished data, Chapter 2). Fishers tend to define themselves by the gear they use, only switching under strong economic pressure. This may be caused by dwindling catch and income causing individuals to group together to pool resources, and switching to more competitive gear, principally beach seines, which catch smaller fish and discriminate less among species (50). Individual fishers also may have very different skill levels: although more than 180 fishers were recorded landing their catch at Mkwiro fishing cooperative in Kisite over 12 months between November 1993 and January 1995, 13 and 28 fishers caught 50% and 75% of the fish biomass respectively (89,90).

Indirect Effects of Fishing on Coral Reef Ecology

Artisanal and small-scale commercial reef fisheries have had a dramatic effect on the ecology of Kenyan reefs. Most artisanal fisheries in Kenya are concentrated within reef lagoons, and during the calm northeast monsoon, on the shallow fore reef. Removal of the predatory fish, the preferred fisheries catch (see Fish and Fisheries Studies section), and of non-preferred but keystone predators such as triggerfish (39,49), has led to predation release within the shallow reef grazing sea urchin assemblage (44,45,59), which is comprised principally of *Diadema setosum, D. savignyi, Echinometra mathaei* and *Echinothrix calamaris*. The result has been large increases in sea urchin populations on heavily fished reefs, where predation on sea urchins has decreased to very low levels (Fig. 7.8). Sea urchins compete with many herbivorous fish, such as the acanthurids and scarids, and sea urchin increases appear to be reducing the abundance and feeding rates of scarids (52).

Sea urchins are keystone grazers in coral reef communities, prompting a number of studies on their biology and ecological interactions (Box 7.1, 34,39,42,43,45,49,51,52,58,59). Within the sea urchin guild, the lack of predation has led to strong resource competition (34). The small rock-boring urchin, *E. mathaei*, is the competitive dominant under these conditions (49), where intense grazing of algae reduces resources to levels below those sustainable for the larger-bodied diadematids (42). Heavily fished shallow reefs are clearly dominated by *E. mathaei*, which can reach population densities of > 30 per m². Where water depth increases (> 1 m) and there is access to the fore reef through reef breaks enabling both incursion of predators from the fore reef and higher water energy from waves, *Echinothrix diadema* tends to dominate. In both cases, incidental abrasion and direct grazing on sessile benthic invertebrates (hard and soft corals and sponge) and erect algae results in reduced diversity and cover of these organisms (Fig. 7.9). Algal turf is the only cover form resilient to the intense disturbance from grazing urchins, and becomes dominant on hard substrates under these conditions (59). It is also suggested that increased production of sand from urchin bioerosion may enhance invasion of seagrass, converting hard to soft substrates (42,59).

Recent large-scale sea urchin removal experiments, in which sea urchins were removed from areas of 50 x 50 m, and then 100 x 100 m (51), and observations following the creation of a new park in Mombasa that was previously intensively fished (see Mombasa Marine Park section), have provided some answers on the reversibility of the indirect effects of fishing (and see Chapter 2). Following sea urchin removals there was a dramatic increase in fleshy algal cover due to the reduction in herbivory, and increases in fish

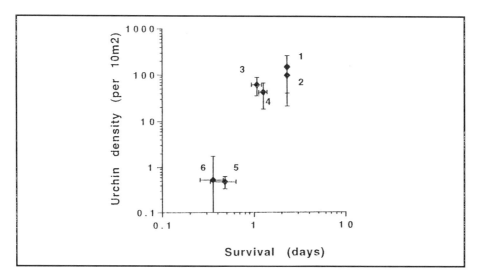

Figure 7.8. Sea urchin density versus survival from predation (as an indicator of fishing intensity on coral reefs). See text for explanation. 1-Diani, 2-Kanamai, 3-Bamburi, 4-Vipingo, 5-Watamu (park), 6-Malindi (park). Source (49).

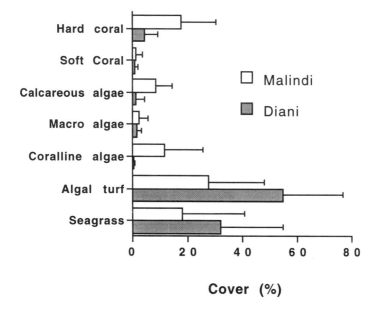

Figure 7.9. Percent cover (mean ± s.d.) of benthic cover categories under conditions of low (Malindi) and high (Diani) sea urchin density. Source (49).

populations attracted to the algae and associated epifauna. The increase in fish abundance was, however, dependent on the level of fishing: on fished reefs there was a smaller increase of fish populations in urchin removal plots than on

Table 7.3. a) Environmental conditions (visibility and sedimentation rate (mean, standard error of the mean)) in Malindi and Watamu (control). Percent hard cover, number of colonies and genus richness of b) hard corals and c) soft corals in 90 m.transects.

	Malindi		Watamu	
	mean	*sem*	*mean*	*sem*
a) Environmental conditions				
Visibility (m)	8.1	3.8	15.7	4.3
Sedimentation rate $(mg/cm^2/day)$	13.8	18.02	5.6	6.3
b) Hard corals				
Cover (%)	34.9	3.8	32.2	7.8
No. colonies	115.3	17.04	112.5	22.7
No. genera	18.0	1.6	21.5	4.1
c) Soft corals				
Cover (%)	10.9	3.1	18.5	10.4
No. colonies	37.6	9.4	85.0	44.1
No. genera	4.9	0.7	3.7	1.8

protected reefs. This resulted in lower herbivory rates on macroalgae on the unfished reefs from the combined repression of fish and urchin populations. The initial increases in fleshy algal cover caused decreases in hard coral cover, but in the park, over the course of the 1.5 to 2 year experiment, coral cover increased due to reduced disturbance from sea urchins (51, unpublished data).

Sediment Effects

River discharge is one of the dominant physical factors influencing coral reefs along the northern coast of Kenya. The phenomenon has been studied by a number of groups over a period of two decades in the Malindi area (18,47,65,86). Excessive sediment in coral reef waters is known to be detrimental to coral reefs, due to high absorption of light by suspended particulate matter in the water column, and increased settlement rates of sediment causing smothering of benthic organisms. Additionally, nutrient enrichment associated with sediments can cause eutrophication of reef waters, reducing suitability for coral and associated communities. However, the levels at which sediment influence becomes harmful varies considerably between different sites, and it is now accepted that many continental-margin coral reefs thrive in sediment conditions previously thought unsuitable.

Sedimentation rates measured at Malindi are greater than the threshold of 10 mg/cm²/y suggested for normal reef development (74), and water clarity is reduced compared to control reefs in Watamu (Table 7.3, 65). The proportion of fine silt and terrigenous components is also higher in Malindi (28,65,86). This has resulted in increased incidence of "coral stress" indicators (18,65,86), such as bleaching, the presence of excess mucus and sediment on coral tissue, recently dead colonies, and a high sediment load in algal turf mats growing on rocky surfaces. In spite of these effects, long-term population studies have not found greater mortality of corals in shallow water (65) nor decreased coral cover and diversity of Malindi reefs (Table 7.3). Nevertheless, there is some indication of a change in coral species composition of sediment-influenced reefs to dominance by resistant coral genera (47,65).

Coral Bleaching and Resilience of Reefs

Bleaching of reef corals and other sessile invertebrates harboring photosynthetic symbionts (zooxanthellae) occurs in response to a variety of external or environmental stressors that perturb the symbiosis (Box 2.3, 8,17). Bleaching sporadically occurs on Kenyan reefs during maximum temperature and insolation periods in March and April, when the sea is calmest and the sun is directly overhead (Obura, D. personal observation), and at times bleaching is also a response to high sediment influence (65). Large-scale bleaching was observed in 1987, 1994 and 1998 (McClanahan, T. personal communication). Bleaching and mortality rates recorded from March to June 1998 were at unprecedented levels for the Kenya coast, corresponding to a 2°C temperature anomaly, the highest so far recorded for the Kenyan coast. This severe bleaching and subsequent mortality of corals is consistent with other bleaching reports from around the world during development of the El-Niño Southern Oscillation (ENSO) from mid-1997 to 1998, and to ENSO related bleaching reported in previous years, where over 90%, and sometimes 100% mortality of corals has been reported for some locations (Box 2.3, 8,17,95).

Marine Parks And Reserves - Their History And Importance To Marine Conservation Studies

All of Kenya's marine parks are embedded in larger reserves (Table 7.4), where limited extraction of resources is permitted. The intention of reserves is to form buffer zones between the uncontrolled exploitation of marine resources outside of parks from protected reefs within parks. In practice, marine reserves generally experience similar levels of resource use as unprotected areas. Previous sections of this chapter have compared resource use levels, and the ecological effects of exploitation, between park and reserve or unprotected areas. This section presents the management implications of resource use and human impacts, using each of the Marine Protected Areas (MPAs) to illustrate the dominant threats affecting reefs in Kenya.

Kisite Marine National Park

Kisite MNP and Mpunguti MNR are unlike other park-reserve complexes in Kenya, as the park area is adjacent to, not contained by, the reserve. At the far southern extent of the Kenya coast, the two protected areas did not have high levels of use from either fishing or tourism, until the 1980s. Initially, one of the principal threats to the park was the practice of dynamite fishing by fishers from neighboring Tanzania, the lack of patrol boats and enforcement, making it impossible for the park authorities to pursue and arrest poachers. Since the 1980s, however, poaching in the park has been stopped, increasing numbers of tourists are visiting the unique island reefs, and fishing intensity for both food and aquarium export is rapidly increasing. Recent studies of fish community structure and fisheries at Kisite and Mpunguti suggest some benefits of zoned

Table 7.4. Kenyan marine parks and reserves, principal users and conflicts.

Reserve/Park Name	Year gazetted	Size (km^2)	Principle Users/ Human Influences	Issues/conflicts
Mpunguti Reserve	1978	11	Fishing, Tourism (day-trips, diving, snorkelling)	Fisher identity-local versus Tanzanian, prevention of dynamite fishing.
Kisite Park		28		
Mombasa (both)	1986	Res: 200 Prk: 10	Tourism, Urban, Fishing	Loss of fishing area (gazetted in 1989), prevention of beach seining, reduction of commercial/development effects.
Malindi-Watamu (both)	1979 (Biosphere 1979)	Res: 177 Mal: 6.3 Wat: 12.5	Fishing, Tourism (diving snorkelling)	Tourism/land development, effects to intertidal and reef habitats, beach mobility.
Kiunga (reserve only)	1979 (Biosphere 1980)	250	Fishing	Fear of loss of fishing grounds, external supervision of communities.
Diani (reserve only)	1995	75	Fishing, Tourism, Commercial development	Fear of loss of fishing grounds, loss of local empowerment, tourism revenue sharing.

fisheries management, using the core protected area as a source of fish for the adjacent fished area.

In 1992 the abundances of commercial species, six species of butterflyfish, and two species of triggerfish were up to 10 times higher in the Kisite MNP than in the reserve (Fig. 7.5, 92), and findings presented in the "Fish and Fisheries Studies" section (above) suggest some export of fish from the park to the reserve. However, direct evidence of "spillover" of adults or larval replenishment, the two major mechanisms of fisheries enhancement by protected areas (70) is still largely lacking. Most adult fish are unlikely to move the 1.7 km distance from Kisite to the reefs at Mpunguti, particularly since much of the intervening substrate is sandy habitat. Other studies have found that significant adult spillover may be restricted to a several hundred meters (73), and that export of fish from protected to fished areas may be slow to develop (77). The hydgrography of the Kisite area and its influence on larval retention is not known. However, local retention of larvae around islands has been commonly found (79), and larvae can influence their own dispersal through behavioral adaptations (6). Even if local retention does not occur it is probable that Kisite helps seed more northerly Kenyan reefs with pelagic reef fish larvae.

Equally importantly, Kisite and Mpunguti may depend on "up current" Tanzanian reefs for recruits. If this is so, local fisheries controls might not protect the reefs from stock collapse caused by increasing exploitation elsewhere, and an international approach is required for effective management. Providing a secure source of pelagic larvae to neighboring fisheries is likely to be the most important and widespread benefit of MPAs (73) and an international network of MPAs linking sources and sinks could insure against stock collapse (72). MPAs are an insurance against over-exploitation (14) and embody a rare application of the precautionary principle in resource management. Moreover, the leakiness that has caused management difficulties in terrestrial conservation may be seen as a positive advantage in MPAs. Combining the designation of chains of MPAs among countries to enhance larval exchange, with size and area considerations to ensure sustainability of populations and community structure in each MPA (see Chapter 2) should be a regional priority for the western Indian Ocean.

Mombasa Marine National Park

The Mombasa Marine Park is the most recently gazetted marine park on the Kenya coast, formally established in 1989. Situated on the heavily populated and urbanized north coast of Mombasa, the park and surrounding reserve were created to manage the various user groups, and to derive revenue from tourism to snorkelling sites. Since effective control of the park in 1991 the diversity and abundances of both finfish and the benthic community have increased dramatically (see also Chapter 2). Exclusion of fishers from the park (65% of the reef area) resulted in a similar proportion of fishers leaving the area, hence fishing effort did not change greatly (41). Catch per unit effort did increase (by 10%), with fishers concentrating their effort along the boundary of the park (Fig. 2.7) presumably to catch adult fish "leaking" out of the protected zone. This build up of fishing effort on the edge of the park may prevent the hoped-for increase in fish populations and overall catch in the reserve. Maximization of fisheries seeding by the park may require redesigning park boundaries such that the edge-to-area ratio is higher (41) but this could also reduce the abundance of fish in the park. Park managers reduced the park's size in 1995, resulting in a short-term increase in fish catches (Fig. 2.7) though this was followed by a decline as the adult fish in the deregulated area were rapidly extracted.

Creation of the Mombasa Marine Park has led to increased diversity and abundance of fish, coral cover and diversity of benthic communities. Fish populations increased by a factor of almost 10 from 1991 to 1994, then decreased after 1995 following the reduction in park area mentioned above. Coral cover in the park increased from 8% to 45%, and the cover of fleshy algae, coralline algae, and soft corals also increased after park creation, resulting in a more diverse and robust coral reef community (40). Sea urchin populations have steadily decreased in the park, while predation rates on experimentally tethered sea urchins have increased, though the large-bodied urchin *Echinothrix diadema* appears very tolerant to predation and still occurs at high population densities in some areas (40).

Watamu Marine National Park

The Watamu Marine Park illustrates some of the interacting and synergistic factors affecting all of Kenya's marine parks. The principal user groups of the park and it's surrounding reserve include local fishers, a growing tourism industry, and local residents living along the park boundary. There have been no major events affecting either the management structure or reef communities of the park, however long-term trends suggest slow reef degradation (40). From 1988 to 1997 there has been a slow but persistent decrease in fish biomass from 2000 to 900 kg/ha, and an increase in fleshy algal cover from 4% to 14%, in some patches covering over 70% of the substrate. The decrease in fish abundance may suggest persistent poaching by fishers or a response to increased algal cover. Whether reduced herbivory or pollution from sewage and shore-based activities, or both, is responsible for the increased algal cover is uncertain, though these two influences are likely to reinforce one another. In

Table 7.5. Unprotected and protected reefs exposed to sediment influence from the Sabaki River, Malindi. Algal "canopy" heights were recorded as "short" or "tall" for each category, giving a ratio of tall/short for the prevalence of low-herbivory (tall canopy) to high-herbivory (short canopy) forms. Source: (65).

| | Fished | | | Protected | | | t-test |
	mean	*sem*	*N*	*mean*	*sem*	*N*	*sign.*
Hard corals							
Cover (%)	34	4.8	5	36	2.5	5	ns
No. colonies	118	20.5	5	113	12.6	5	ns
No. genera	16	1.5	5	20	1.8	5	<0.05
Soft corals							
Cover (%)	12	3.9	5	10	2.0	5	ns
No. colonies	36	10.2	5	39	8.6	4	ns
No. genera	5	1.0	5	5	0.3	4	ns
Algal cover							
Turf	22	4.1	5	31	4.6	5	<0.05
Halimeda	10	2.3	5	7	2.4	5	ns
Macroalgae	10	3.2	5	2	1.2	5	<0.001
Coralline	9	4.0	5	4	1.4	5	ns
Algal canopy ratios							
(tall/short)							
Turf	1.8	1.8	5	0.3	0.2	4	ns
Macroalgae	1.8	0.9	5	0.7	0.3	4	<0.10

the long run, they will be of increasing importance to the long term integrity of reefs in Watamu and the other marine parks, and will need research and some interventions to prevent long term decline. A study which reduced algal cover in one area of the park found an increase in the abundance of fish occupying these plots (Chapter 2, McClanahan, T. unpublished data).

Malindi Marine National Park

The Malindi Marine Park has offered a "natural experiment" for investigation of the interaction of sediment influence and fishing (47,65,86). Surveys of reefs within the Malindi Marine Park indicate healthy coral communities showing minor indications of sediment stress (47,65), though not with the high rates of mortality predicted in the past (86). Comparisons of reefs within the Malindi Park, and of fished reefs closer to the Sabaki River, found that coral cover and number of colonies were similar between the sites but that at the fished sites coral genus diversity and cover of turf algae decreased, while the abundance of fleshy algae increased (Table 7.5). As a further indication of reduced fish populations from fishing, the height (and therefore biomass) of fleshy algae was higher on the unprotected reefs (65), suggesting lower herbivory. If fished reefs in Malindi are exposed to the same intensities of fishing as on other parts of the Kenya coast, the simplified coral communities may have lesser resilience to withstand stresses from river sediment. This would result in even greater reductions in reef productivity than has been found for other parts of Kenya (see section Fish and Fisheries Studies). Conversely, protection from fisheries in the Malindi Park may confer added resilience to coral reefs in the area to withstand terrigenous sediment influence, and provide an important seed or source area for adjacent reefs exposed to sediment and fishing.

Coral community composition of reefs in the Malindi Marine Park may have altered in response to increasing sediment influence in the last 30 years (47). Coral cover in the park is among the highest observed on Kenyan reefs, at 35 to 40%, indicating sediment stress is not causing community deterioration. Surveys showed that certain genera occurred at higher abundances in Malindi than in sediment-free control reefs (*Echinopora*, *Galaxea*, *Hydnophora*, *Millepora* and *Platygyra*) while other genera were less abundant (*Favia*, *Montipora* and *Pocillopora*), suggesting a gradual shift in coral community structure towards corals more tolerant of high-sediment conditions (47).

Marine Reserves - Resource Management by Whom and for Whom?

The regulation of marine resource exploitation is a contentious issue due to the fact that fish and other reef resources are frequently viewed as common property, and the widely held view that their supply is limitless. Conflicts in resource management within reserves therefore focus on authority and the setting and enforcement of extraction limits (Chapter 2). Reserves permit "traditional fishing", thus the principal conflicts in reserve management involve the identity of fishers and local communities, the type of fishing gear used, physical access to the resource, involvement and cooperation of communities with management, and enforcement of regulations. Additionally, fishers and communities adjacent to marine parks – which tourists are allowed to use but fishers are not – fear that government management of reef resources by the Kenya Wildlife Service (KWS) is only a step towards total control by the government and prohibition of fishing to service the wealthy tourist and "conservation" industries. Broad scale ecological surveys of outer reef and lagoon sites in both Diani (24), and Kiunga Marine Reserves (66) show that both areas experience high and moderate levels of fishing respectively, with evidence of similar ecological repercussions to other utilized reefs (see sections above, 45).

The Kiunga and Diani marine reserves differ from the other marine reserves in that they do not include central park areas (Table 7.4). They illustrate differing potential outcomes of attempts to engender co-management between KWS and local resource users. Kiunga is a remote region, in the far north of the Kenya coast (Fig. 7.1), with resource use limited to subsistence and small-scale commercial extraction, and only the beginnings of small-scale, exclusive SCUBA and nature tourism. A joint KWS/WWF Participatory Rural Appraisal project has been working with fishers since 1996 to build a co-management process involving fishing villages and KWS (19). While the remoteness of the region hinders effective implementation of management mechanisms devised centrally, it enables the slow growth of the participatory mechanisms that build the trust and shared responsibilities necessary for community and government co-management. Implementation of a sustainable resource management plan for Kiunga is still far away, but steps are being taken to identify and design one.

In contrast, Diani, on the south coast, is Kenya's oldest, and one of the most developed, tourism resort-hotel areas, in addition to supporting fishing communities that extend back more than 200 years (82, see Chapter 2). It is also the most degraded shallow reef on the Kenya coast, due to extraction of fish and other organisms. Efforts to implement a marine reserve in Diani in

Table 7.6. Principal impacts to Kenyan reefs and possible options for mitigation.

Impact	Level	Areas affected	Interventions
Fishing / extraction	High - critical	Malindi southwards, all major settlements, Lamu islands.	Extraction limits, co-management of government and users.
	Moderate	Rest of coast	Co-management of government and users, anticipation of over-use.
Sediment and eutrophication	High - critical	Malindi (Sabaki R.) to Ras Tenewi (Lamu) (Tana R.)	Soil conservation and watershed management upcountry. Protection of important reef species and guilds.
	Moderate	Fringing reefs adjacent to creek mouths	Local interventions - mangrove preservation, etc.
Population growth	High - critical	Mombasa, tourism centers (Diani, Malindi-Watamu)	Urban planning, sewage and solid waste disposal, pollution regulation.
	Moderate	Rest of coast	Sewage and solid waste disposal, agriculture & chemical controls
Commercial & tourism growth	High - critical	Mombasa, tourism centers (Diani, Malindi-Watamu)	Land, zoning and environmental impact legislation.
	Moderate	Minor tourism centers	Land, zoning and environmental impact legislation. Small-scale, eco-tourism incentives

1994 were largely supported from the tourism industry due to the potential offered for greater revenue generation and restoration of the highly degraded coral reef. While revenue-sharing and reef restoration would also assist local communities, distrust of the government, the poor history of revenue-sharing in other Kenyan parks and reserves, and political manipulation resulted in rejection of the reserve management plan by fishing communities, effectively blocking implementation of reserve management. While easy access to the Diani area may have favored effective implementation of co-management, the number of interest groups involved, the high economic (and hence political) stakes, and the extreme differences between traditional and modern methods of fishery regulation (Chapter 2, 50) prevented the dialogue and compromises necessary for implementation of reserve management.

Principal Threats and Conservation Initiatives

The principal threats to reefs in Kenya are similar to those in many other parts of the region, and with other parts of the world (for example see 85). Table 7.6 summarizes the main threats discussed previously in this chapter, and suggests interventions that will be needed to alleviate the increasing degradation of coral reef environments throughout Kenya. To be effective, all interventions require the coordination of management and implementation agencies, dedication of resources to applied research, community involvement and participation, and appropriate legislation.

Table 7.7. Principal initiatives and institutions involved in coral reef conservation and research in Kenya.

Activity	Scope	Institutions	Sponsors
Integrated Coastal Area Management (ICAM)	Pilot project, Mombasa north coast	Coast Development Agency (CDA) Kenya Wildlife Service (KWS) Kenya Marine and Fisheries Research Institute (KMFRI) Fisheries Department(FD)	University of Rhode Island USAID.
Management and Research	Memorandum of Understanding	Kenya Wildlife Service (KWS) Kenya Marine and Fisheries Research Institute (KMFRI)	Netherlands government Wetlands Project.
Research and monitoring		Coral Reef Conservation Project (CRCP) Kenya Wildlife Service (KWS) Kenya Marine and Fisheries Research Institute (KMFRI)	various.
Education and Training		Kenya Marine and Fisheries Research Institute (KMFRI) Moi University School for Environmental Studies University of Nairobi Coral Reef Conservation Project (CRCP) Kenya Wildlife Service (KWS) Kenya-Belgium Project	various.
Public awareness and action		Kenya Turtle Conservation Committee, Wildlife Clubs of Kenya	various.
International collaborations	Local to international.	United Nations Environment Program (UNEP), The World Conservation Union (IUCN), World Wide Fund for Nature (WWF)	various.

The principal initiatives focusing on coral reef conservation and research, and the principal institutions involved are outlined in Table 7.7. Interest and involvement of individuals, groups, private companies, and government agencies in coral reef conservation in Kenya is rapidly growing. While this is partly a reflection of the global increase in concern about the plight of coral reefs, it also shows the increasing awareness of the dependency of the coastal economy on healthy and clean reefs. All of the initiatives incorporate cooperation and collaboration among different groups for addressing the multi-sectoral issues facing Kenya's marine environment.

The Future

Kenya's coral reefs have benefited from early protection in marine parks and reserves, with the added benefit of local awareness of the importance of conservation to the economy, principally in terms of tourism. Recent ecological research has demonstrated the benefits of protected areas directly to resource exploitation, by the maintenance of healthy and productive source populations within parks, and the spill-over effect of adult fish and potentially recruits to fishing zones outside the park boundaries. Continuing increases in human populations in Kenya, as in other countries, has focused research and management attention on the vulnerability of reef ecosystems to interacting threats, such as fishing and eutrophication, on the potential for reef restoration, and on ways of incorporating and developing indigenous cultural attitudes into conservation interventions. With the growing threat of global scale perturbations in the earth's climate, such as portended by the 1997-1998 El-Niño phenomenon and widespread bleaching in the Indian Ocean, conservation planning will have to focus on national and regional scale coordination, over and above individual protected area sites and management systems.

With a relatively short coastline compared to other countries in the region, Kenya's coral reefs will perhaps be some of the first to face a severe threat of nation-wide degradation. The diversity of initiatives and institutions involved in coral reef research and conservation (Table 7.6 and 7.7) offer some hope for successful interventions. However, fundamental changes in resource use practices, economic valuation, legislative protection and regional cooperation will be necessary to halt the current persistent erosion of coral reef health and vitality.

References

1.   Aleem, A.A. 1984. Distribution and ecology of seagrass communities in the Western Indian Ocean. *Deep Sea Research* 31: 919-933
2.   Allen, G.R. 1991. *Damselfishes of the World*. Hans A. Baensch, Melle
3.   Blom, J., van der Hagen, H, van Hove, E, van Katwijk, M, van Loon, R, Meier, R. 1985. *Decline of the Malindi-Watamu Reef Complex: Quantitative and Qualitative Survey of the Coral Growth*. Laboratory of Aquatic Ecology, Catholic University, Nijmegen, The Netherlands.
4.   Bock, K.R. 1972. Preliminary checklist of lagoonal fishes of Diani, Kenya. *Journal of East African Natural History Society and National Museum* 137: 1-6
5.   Bock, K.R. 1978. *A Guide to Common Reef Fishes of the Western Indian Ocean*. Macmillan Education Limited, London
6.   Botsford, L., Moloney, C., Hastings, A., Largier, J., Powell, T., Higgins, K. and Quinn, J. 1994. The influence of spatially and temporally varying oceanographic conditions on meroplanktonic metapopulations. *Deep Sea Research* 41: 107-145
7.   Brakel, W. 1984. Seasonal dynamics of suspended sediment plumes from the Tana and Sabaki rivers, Kenya: analysis of Landsat imagery. *Remote Sensing of the Environment* 16: 165-173
8.   Brown, B. ed. 1990. Coral bleaching: special issue. *Coral Reefs* 8: 153-232
9.   Bryceson, I. 1982. Seasonality of oceanographic conditions and phytoplankton in Dar es Salaam waters. *University Science Journal (Dar University)* 8: 66-76
10.   Coppejan, E. 1989. *Caulerpa* section (Chlorophyta, Caulerpales) from the Kenyan coast. *Nova Hedwigia* 49: 381-393
11.   Crame, J.A. 1981. Ecological stratification in the Pleistocene coral reefs of the Kenya Coast. *Palaeontology* 24: 609-646
12.   Crame, J.A. 1986. Late Pleistocene molluscan assemblages from the coral reefs of the Kenya coast. *Coral Reefs* 4: 183-196
13.   Dalzell, P. 1996. Catch rates, selectivity and yields of reef fishing. In *Reef Fisheries*. eds. Polunin N.V.C., Roberts, C.M. pp. 161-192. Chapman and Hall London

14. Dugan, J., Davis, D. 1993. Applications of marine refugia to coastal fisheries managment. *Canadian Journal of Fisheries and Aquatic Sciences* 50: 2029-2042

15. Dunbar, R., Cole, J. 1996. Field Report of Preliminary Coral Coring in Malindi, Kenya. Report to Kenya Wildlife Service

16. Fischer, W., Bianchi, G. 1984. FAO Species Indentification Sheets for Fishery Purposes. Rome: FAO.

17. Glynn, P. 1993. Coral reef bleaching: ecological perspectives. *Coral Reefs* 12: 1-17

18. Green, F. 1983. The Leopard and Watamu reef expeditions to Kenya. Report

19. Gubelman, E., Kavu, B. 1996. *Traditional Utilization of Natural Resources within and around Kiunga Marine and Dodori National Reserves, Kenya: Results of Participatory Rural Appraisal and Recommendations for Integration of Local Communities into Management Planning for KM&DNRs*. Nairobi: World Wildlife Fund-East Africa Regional Programme Office

20. Hamilton, H.G.H. 1975. A description of the coral fauna of the East African Coast. Msc Thesis, University of Dar-es-Salaam

21. Hamilton, H.G.H., Brakel, W.H. 1984. Structure and coral fauna of East African reefs. *Bulletin of Marine Science* 34: 248-266

22. Hastenrath, S., Kruss, P.D. 1992. The dramatic retreat of Mt. Kenya's glaciers between 1963 and 1987: greenhouse forcing. *Annals of Glaciology* 16: 127-133

23. Hastenrath, S. 1993. Towards the satellite monitoring of glacier changes on Mount Kenya. *Annals of Glaciology*. 17: 245-249

24. Holliday, L. 1994. *Kenya Diani Marine Reserve Expedition, 1993: Report on the Distribution of Habitats and Species of the Diani Coast*. University of York and Hull, U.K.

25. ICAM. 1996. *Towards Integrated Management and Sustainable Development of Kenya's Coast. Findings and recommendations for an action strategy in the Nyali-Bamburi-Shanzu area.* Report of the ICAM committee. p. 1 - 77. Coast Development Authority, Kenya

26. Isaac, F.M. 1968. Marine Botany of the Kenya Coast: Angiosperms. *Journal of the East African Natural History Society and Museum* 116: 29-47

27. Johnson, D., Mutua Nguli, M., Kimani, E. 1982. Response to annually reversing monsoon winds at the southern boundary of the Somali Current. *Deep Sea Research* 29: 1217-1227

28. Keech, R. 1980. Grainsize and mineralogical analysis of recent sea bed sediments in the Malindi National Marine Park, Kenya. Msc Thesis, University of Durham, UK

29. Laroche, J., Ramananarivo, N. 1995. A preliminary survey of the artisanal fishery on coral reefs of the Tulear Region (southwest Madagascar). *Coral Reefs* 14: 193-200

30. Lawson, G. W. 1969. Some observations on the littoral ecology of rocky shores in East Africa (Kenya and Tanzania). *Transaction of the Royal Research Society in South Africa* 38: 329-340

31. Lemmens, J.W.T.J. 1993. Reef-building corals (Cnidaria: Scleractinia) from the Watamu marine national reserve, Kenya; an annotated species list. *Zoologische Mededelingen* 67: 453-465

32. Marshall, J., Davies, P. 1988. *Halimeda* bioherms of the northern Great Barrier Reef. *Coral Reefs* 6: 139-148
33. McClanahan, T.R. 1988a. Seasonality in East Africa's coastal waters. *Marine Ecology Progress Series* 44: 191-199
34. McClanahan, T.R. 1988b. Coexistence in a sea urchin guild and its implications to coral reef diversity and degradation. *Oecologia* 77: 210-218
35. McClanahan, T.R. 1989. Kenyan coral reef-associated gastropod fauna: a comparison between protected and unprotected reefs. *Marine Ecology Progress Series* 53: 11-20
36. McClanahan, T.R. 1990. Kenyan coral reef-associated gastropod assemblages: distribution and diversity patterns. *Coral Reefs* 9: 63-74
37. McClanahan, T.R. 1994a. Endemic survives adversity. *Coral Reefs* 13: 104
38. McClanahan, T.R. 1994b. Kenyan coral reef lagoon fish: effects of fishing, substrate complexity, and sea urchins. *Coral Reefs* 13: 231-241
39. McClanahan, T.R. 1995. Fish predators and scavengers of the sea urchin *Echinometra mathaei* in Kenyan coral-reef marine parks. *Environmental Biology of Fishes* 43: 187-193
40. McClanahan, T.R. 1997. Effects of fishing and reef structure on East Africa coral reefs. *8th International Coral Reef Symposium* 2: 1533-1538
41. McClanahan, T.R., Kaunda-Arara, B. 1996. Fishery recovery in a coral-reef marine park and its effect on the adjacent fishery. *Conservation Biology* 10: 1187-1199
42. McClanahan, T.R., Kurtis, J.D. 1991. Population regulation of the rock-boring sea urchin *Echinometra mathaei* (de Blainville). *Journal of Experimental Marine Biology and Ecology* 147: 121-146
43. McClanahan, T.R., Mutere, J.C. 1994. Coral and sea urchin assemblage structure and interrelationships in Kenyan reef lagoons. *Hydrobiologia* 286: 109-124
44. McClanahan, T.R., Muthiga, N.A. 1988. Changes in Kenyan coral reef community structure due to exploitation. *Hydrobiologia* 166: 269-276
45. McClanahan, T.R., Muthiga, N.A. 1989. Patterns of predation on a sea urchin, *Echinometra mathaei* (de Blainville), on Kenyan coral reefs. *Journal of Experimental Marine Biology and Ecology* 126: 77-94
46. McClanahan, T.R., Obura, D. 1995. Status of Kenyan coral reefs. *Coastal Management* 23: 57-76
47. McClanahan, T.R., Obura, D. 1997. Sediment effects on shallow coral communities in Kenya. *Journal of Experimental Marine Biology and Ecology* 209: 103-122
48. McClanahan, T.R., Obura, D. 1998. Marine Ecological Monitoring of Coral Reefs in the Masoala Peninsula. CARE/Wildlife Conservation Society, Madagascar
49. McClanahan, T.R., Shafir, S.H. 1990. Causes and consequences of sea urchin abundance and diversity in Kenyan coral reef lagoons. *Oecologia* 83: 362-370

50. McClanahan, T.R., Glaesel, H., Rubens, J. Kiambo, R. 1997. The effects of traditional fisheries management on fisheries yields and the coral-reef ecosystems of southern Kenya. *Environmental Conservation* 24: 1-16

51. McClanahan, T. R., Kamukuru, A. T., Muthiga, N. A., Gilagabher Yebio, M., Obura, D. 1995. Effect of sea urchin reductions on algae, coral and fish populations. *Conservation Biology* 10: 136-154

52. McClanahan, T.R., Nugues, M., Mwachireya, S. 1994. Fish and sea urchin herbivory and competition in Kenyan coral reef lagoons: the role of reef management. *Journal of Experimental Marine Biology and Ecology* 184: 237-254

53. McClanahan, T.R., Done, T., Polunin N.V.C. in press. Resiliency in coral reef ecosystems. In *Resiliency and Sustainability in Large-Scale Ecosystems*. eds Gunderson, L., Hollings, C.S., Jansson, B.-O., Folke, C. SCOPE, John Wiley & Sons

54. Moorjani, S.A. 1978. The Ecology of Marine Algae of the Kenyan Coast. University of Nairobi, Kenya. PhD Dissertation, University of Nairobi

55. Moorjani, S.A. 1982. Rocky shore zonation in Kenya: horizontal and vertical distribution patterns in the marine flora. *Symposium on the Coastal Marine Environment of the Red Sea, Gulf of Aden and Tropical Western Indian Ocean*, Khartoum 2: 1-17

56. Moorjani, S., Simpson, B. 1988. *Seaweeds of the Kenya Coast*. Nairobi: Oxford University Press

57. Munro J.L, Williams D.McB 1985. Assessment and management of coral reef fisheries: biological, environmental and socio-economic aspects. *Proceedings of the 5th International Coral Reef Congress* 4: 544-578

58. Muthiga, N.A. 1996. The role of early life history strategies on the population dynamics of the sea urchin *Echinometra mathaei* (de Blainville) on reefs in Kenya. PhD Dissertation, University of Nairobi

59. Muthiga, N.A., McClanahan, T.R. 1987. Population changes in the sea urchin (*Echinometra mathaei*) on an exploited fringing reef. *African Journal of Ecology* 25: 1-8

60. Mwangi, S. 1997. *An Assessment of Marine Pollution in the Mombasa Marine Park and Reserve*. Interim report submitted to the KWS Wetlands programme

61. Newell, B.S. 1957. A preliminary survey of the hydrography of the British East African coastal waters. *Fisheries Publications* 9: 1-11

62. Newell, B.S. 1959. The hydrography of the British East African coastal waters. *Fisheries Publications* 12: 1-17

63. Nzioka, R.M. 1979. Observations on the spawning seasons of East African reef fishes. *Journal of Fish Biology* 14: 329-342

64. Nzioka, R. M. 1990. Fish yield of Kilifi coral reef in Kenya. *Hydrobiologia* 208:

65. Obura, D. 1995. *Environmental Stress and Life History Strategies, a Case Study of Corals and River Sediment from Malindi, Kenya*. PhD Dissertation, University of Miami

66. Obura, D., Mwadzaya. H, Wekesa, E., Church, J, Muthiga, N. 1998. *Rapid Assessment of Coral Reef Bio-physical and Socio-economic Conditions in the Kiunga Marine Reserve, Kenya: Methods Development and Evaluation.* Nairobi: FAO/UNEP Water Branch

67. Okera, W. 1974. The zooplankton of the inshore waters of Dar es Salaam (Tanzania, S.E. Africa) with observation on reactions to artificial light. *Marine Biology* 26: 13-25

68. Osborne, J.F. 1977. Further notes on cowries of the coasts of Kenya and Tanzania. *Journal of the East African Natural History Society and Museum* 32: 1 - 12

69. Pauly, D. 1988. Some definitions of overfishing relevant to coastal zone management in Southeast Asia. *Tropical Coastal Area Management* 3: 14-15

70. Plan Development Team. 1990. *The Potential of Marine Fisheries Reserves for Reef Management in the U.S. Southern Atlantic.* (ed) Bohnsack, J.A., NOAA NMFS Technical Memo. NMFS-SEFC-261

71. Polunin, N.V.C., Roberts, C.M. 1993. Greater biomass and value of target coral-reef fishes in two small caribbean marine reserves. *Marine Ecology Progress Series* 100: 167-176

72. Roberts, C. 1994. Marine reserves: a brief guide for decision makers and users. Barbados:

73. Roberts, C. M., Polunin, N. V. C. 1991. Are marine reserves effective in management of reef fisheries? *Review in Fish Biology and Fisheries* 1: 65-91

74. Rogers, C. 1990. Responses of coral reefs and reef organisms to sedimentation. *Marine Ecology Progress Series* 62: 185-202

75. Rosen, R. 1971. The distribution of reef coral genera in the Indian Ocean. *Symposium of the Zoological Society of London* 28: 263 - 299

76. Rowley, R.J. 1994. Marine reserves in fisheries management. *Aquatic Conservation - Marine and Freshwater Ecosystems* 4: 233 - 254.

77. Russ, G., Alcala, A. 1996. Do marine reserves export adult fish biomass? Evidence from Apo Island, Central Philippines. *Marine Ecology Progress Series* 132: 1-9

78. Samoilys, M.A. 1988. Abundance and species richness of coral reef fish on the Kenyan Coast: The effects of protective management and fishing. *Proceedings of the 6th International Coral Reef Symposium* 2: 261-266

79. Schultz, E., Cowen, R. 1994. Recruitment of coral reef fishes to Bermuda: local retention or long distance transport? *Marine Ecology Progress Series* 109: 15-28

80. Sheppard, C. 1987. Coral species of the Indian Ocean and adjacent seas: a synonymized compilation and some regional distributional patterns. *Atoll Research Bulletin* 307: 1-32

81. Sheppard, C.R.C., Sheppard, A.L.S. 1991. *Corals and Coral Communities of Arabia.* Fauna of Saudi Arabia, Saudi Arabia

82. Spear, T. T. 1978. *The Kaya Complex: A History of the Mijikenda Peoples of the Kenya Coast to 1900.* Nairobi: Kenya Literature Bureau

83. Spry, J.F. 1961. *The Sea Shells of Dar es Salaam: Gastropods.* Dar es Salaam: Tanzania Society

84. Taylor, J.D. 1971. Reef associated molluscan assemblages in the Western Indian Ocean. *Symposium of the Zoological Society of London* 28: 501 - 534

85. UNEP/IUCN. 1988. *Coral Reefs of the World*. Gland: IUCN/UNEP

86. van Katwijk, M., Meier, N., van Loon, R., van Hove, E., Giesen, W., van der Velde, G., den Hartog, D. 1993. Sabaki River sediment load and coral stress: correlation between sediments and condition of the Malindi-Watamu reefs in Kenya (Indian Ocean). *Marine Biology* 117: 675-683

87. Veron, J.E.N. 1985. Aspects of the biogeography of hermatypic corals. *Proceedings of the 5th International Coral Reef Congress* 4: 83 - 88

88. Veron, J.E.N. 1995. *Corals in Space and Time: The Biogeography & Evolution of the Scleractinia*. Sydney: UNSW Press

89. Watson, M. in prep. Catch composition and effort in an artisanal reef fishery in southern Kenya.

90. Watson, M. 1996. *The Role of Protected Areas in the Management of Kenyan Reef Fish Stocks*. D.Phil. Thesis, University of York, York, UK

91. Watson, M.R., D.A. Austin, T.J., Ormond R.F.G. 1996. The effects of fishing on coral reef fish abundance and diversity. *Journal of the Marine Biological Assciation of the United Kingdom* 76: 229-233

92. Watson, M., Ormond, R.F.G. 1994. Effect of an artisanal fishery on the fish and urchin populations of a Kenyan coral reef. *Marine Ecology Progress Series* 109: 115-129

93. Watson, M., Ormond, R.F.G., Holliday, L. 1997. The role of Kenya's marine protected areas in artisanal fisheries management. *Proceedings of the 8th International Coral Reef Symposium, Panama* 2: 1955-1960

94. Weru, S. 1991. *An Appraisal on the Kiunga Marine National Reserve*. Nairobi: Kenya Wildlife Service

95. Williams, E., Bunckley-Williams, L. 1990. The world-wide coral reef bleaching cycle and related sources of coral mortality. *Atoll Research Bulletin* 335: 1-63

96. Yaninek, J. 1976. Survey of gastropod populations at Diani and at Malindi Marine National Park, Kenya. *Journal of the East African Natural History Society and Museum* 31: 1-10

97. Yaninek, J. S. 1978. A comparative survey of reef-associated gastropods at Maziwa Island, Tanzania. *Journal of the East African Natural History Society and Museum* 31: 1-16

Chapter 8

The Red Sea

D. Medio, C.R.C. Sheppard & J. Gascoigne

In the Red Sea, scientific work increased substantially in the 1970s and 1980s. Considerable work on both ecological and physiological aspects has come from one or two laboratories in the region, though most still comes from visiting scientists. Some of the latter have conducted several wide-scale surveys along large expanses of coastline, especially on the Arabian shore. Two substantial and fairly recent compilations both review this material and add details of some new work, on a wide range of aspects (7,41). In the last few years, emphasis has been placed on conservation aspects and on application of previous work. This has been a valuable process and has led to some useful conservation developments and increase in more effective protection in some areas. The balance of this article follows this work, with greater emphasis placed on human effects and conservation, and less on repeating conclusions of the well-reviewed survey work.

It remains true that substantial swathes of the Red Sea are very little explored. On the eastern side of the Red Sea proper, pockets of well studied areas exist around the towns of Yanbu and Jeddah, while a program of very useful broad-scale surveys was conducted at intervals of a few kilometers along the entire coast (27,28,29,30). The Sinai is fairly well researched, particularly in its southern tip and at the northern end of the Gulf of Aqaba. The African coast is less well studied, outside pockets around Sudanese ports, though fisheries work is expanding the knowledge of areas such as Eritrea which previously offered very limited access. Islands of the Red Sea are not well known from a biological point of view, especially those of the southern archipelagos which promise to contain much that is of interest.

The Red Sea extends over a wide latitudinal range (Fig. 8.1) and the intense insolation of the region results in correspondingly large gradients of temperature and salinity along its length. While many popular accounts continue to assume that this sea is fringed with coral reefs throughout its length, in fact the southern third is relatively poor in reefs, having a sedimentary character which favors higher abundance of macro-algae, seagrasses and mangroves. The sea as a whole also appears to be a catchment for larvae of the Indian Ocean in that diversity for several groups is relatively high, partly because of annual pumping of water into the Red Sea from the Gulf of Aden (37). This incoming water is rich in nutrients from the Arabian upwelling system, causing a Red Sea gradient of nutrients where the south is enriched while the north is oligotrophic. The Red Sea, technically an ocean rather than a sea because of its spreading center (5), very unusually has no marked thermocline, resulting in a more extensive vertical tropical zone than is commonly the case in low latitude seas. The following account summarizes what is known about reefs and biological communities of the Red Sea, adding new information where possible.

Physical Characteristics

Bathymetry

The Red Sea is a long and, relative to its size, deep trough with an average depth of 491 m (25). It is a part of the great rift system which extends from eastern Africa to the Dead Sea. Its bathymetry is well known following several cruises up to the middle of this century (for example, the Mabahiss, 1934 to 1935, 4,25), including exploration of its deeper regions, in which abyssal hot spots are found. Three main bathymetric regions are recognized in the Red Sea. The coastal shelves, including the coral reef zone, descend from the shore to the main trough at 300 to 600 m. This then gradually deepens to about 1000 m near the central axis. This deep trough is about 1500 m deep along much of its entire length, and between 22°N and 19°N it contains a continuous isobath in excess of 1500 m and in places more than 2000 m deep and 20 km wide. The southern third of the Red Sea is shallower, containing broad sedimentary plains, until at the entrance to the Red Sea at Bab el Mandeb there is a sill only about 160 m deep. From this shallow plain arise some of the southern islands and archipelagos.

The topography of the Red Sea is irregular as is well exemplified by a series of submarine pinnacles rising from the ocean floor to the surface. The most conspicuous of these are at the El-Akhawein islets (Brothers) and the Abu el Kizan reefs (Daedalus). Within the central deep axis lie the hot brine pools of the Red Sea which are among the most extreme habitats on this planet (19).

The Gulf of Aqaba at the northern end is a similarly very deep basin which is in excess of 1000 m deep. It is separated from the Red Sea by a relatively shallow sill (Strait of Tiranof only 340 m which may constrain water exchange between the two bodies (41). Two depressions have been identified; one to the north of the sill about 1100 m deep and, separated by a submarine sill, one to the south with depths of 1420 m. The maximum depth recorded is 1829 m (25).

The Gulf of Suez, in striking contrast, is a shallow, flat bottomed gulf which for the most part is only 50 to 73 m deep and probably nowhere greater than 90 m. At the mouth of the gulf the bottom drops abruptly to depths in excess of 300 m. It is at this steep shelf where, to a large degree, the water circulation of the whole of the Red Sea is controlled. The Gulf of Suez contains the most northerly reefs of the Indian Ocean.

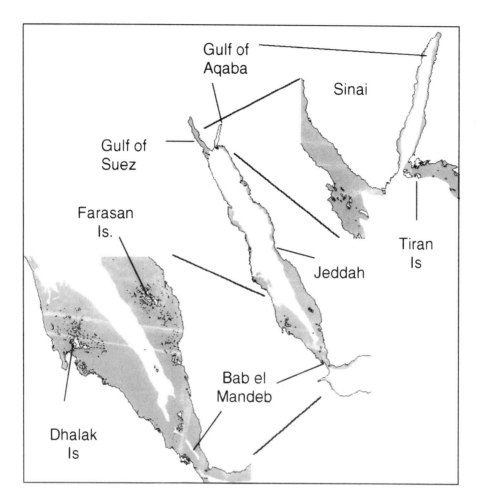

Figure 8.1. Details of Red Sea. Shaded area within the sea is the 200 m bathymetric contour. Insets are enlargements of the extreme northern and southern ends.

Geomorphology

The Red Sea is considered to be a young ocean which has witnessed major environmental upheavals in a relatively short span of time (5). Until approximately 200 mya, most of the Red Sea region was land. It was not until the Oligocene, around 40 mya, that it became established as a trough, and during this period the area was periodically covered by sea. Major environmental changes began in the late Miocene, from between 25 to 5 mya, and the Red Sea basin has been connected at different times to the proto-Mediterranean as well as to the Indian Ocean through the Straits of Bab el Mandeb.

About 5 mya, the rifting processes, which had ceased during the Miocene period, recommenced creating the deep axial trough present today. The link with the Mediterranean was closed and a connection with the Indian Ocean was established, once again allowing colonization by Indo-Pacific fauna. In particular, coral reefs began to grow in shallow areas. During the Pleistocene Ice Ages there were extensive sea level fluctuations, so the shallow areas where this Pleistocene reef growth took place were variously spread over a vertical range of at least 100 m, resulting in development of several substantial limestone ridges which, in today's higher sea level, are now located offshore. In a final glaciation when sea level dropped about 140 m, the Red Sea was isolated or nearly isolated from the Indian Ocean, allowing hypersaline conditions to develop (3,5), decimating the tropical fauna. During the following Holocene transgression, normal Indian Ocean fauna reappeared, and about 5000 years ago the sea reached its present-day level. The present coral reefs are therefore very young, founded upon, and in many cases, veneering, much older reef systems formed during earlier interglacial periods. During this period, substantial alluvial fan systems formed from outwashed terrestrial material. Reefs grew on these also, and repeated episodes of outwash and reef growth formed thick layers of alternating reef and alluvial material in many locations (41).

Raised fossil reefs are found on the shores here providing clear testimony to the tectonic uplift and sea level changes which have taken place. Fossil reefs occur in series of different heights in relationship to sea level, in which height is related to age (Fig. 8.2). The well visited Ras Mohammed peninsula contains some good examples of fringing reefs developed at different times in the past 120 000 years (see Fig. 8.3 for an example from the central Red Sea).

Volcanic material, which is important in the adjacent Gulf of Aden (see Chapter 9), is exposed much less frequently in the Red Sea (3) so that the surface materials of the present Red Sea are mainly carbonates of Pleistocene age or later.

Climate and Oceanography

The climate of the Red Sea is among the hottest and driest in the world. Despite its latitudinal span it is uniformly dry throughout the year, and winds cause strong year-round evaporation. Both African and Arabian coasts of the Red Sea are bounded by mountain ranges which ensure that the wind systems blow predominantly along its length. Winds are controlled to a great extent by the movement of the Inter-Tropical Convergence Zone (see Box 1.1 and Fig. 9.6), so that the main winds flow along the sea's axis, although thermally generated winds blow obliquely or perpendicular to the shore. In the northern Red Sea above 20°N the prevailing wind is from the north-west all year round with southerly winds blowing only occasionally in winter months. In the southern Red Sea below 20°N, winds are the same as the northern Red Sea during the summer period (May to September) but flow north, up the Red Sea in the winter (October to April).

Air temperature changes seasonally. In winter, mean temperature averages about 15°C in the north, the Gulf of Suez being slightly cooler, though

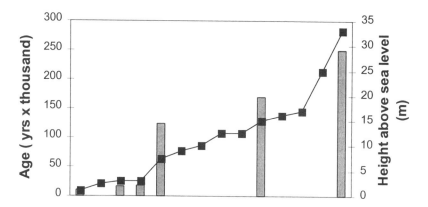

Figure 8.2. Elevations of Red Sea fringing reefs and their ages. Line (right axis) shows elevations of 14 fringing reefs in central Red Sea and Gulf of Aqaba, arranged in order of height. Histogram bars (left axis) shows ages of those which have been dated in thousands of years. Data from various sources summarized in (41).

air temperature may fall considerably, to 4°C on occasion. In the south the average temperature is 25°C. In July-August temperatures average 30°C in the north and 36°C in the south, at about latitude 16°N. The average temperature range is therefore smaller in the south, and cold extremes in the south are never below about 12°C in Sudan. South of latitude 16°N the Red Sea is one of the most consistently hot areas in the world, though other regions may have higher temperature peaks. In addition some parts of the southern Red Sea are very humid with over 150 days a year of extreme human discomfort (8).

Throughout the Red Sea, high temperatures coupled with effects of coastal mountain ranges lead to localized onshore and offshore winds caused by differential heating and cooling of the mountains and the sea. The strength of these can temporarily overwhelm the prevailing wind effect, causing marked and important localized rises and falls of sea level, exposing shallow biota to strong desiccation.

Rainfall throughout the Red Sea is minimal and sporadic, mostly occurring in winter with origins in the Mediterranean air mass, but affected greatly by local mountains. Average precipitation is less than 5 mm at Hurghada in the north, while it is 63 mm at Jeddah in the central part, and up to 200 mm at Massawa (Eritrea). Water input comes mainly from flash flooding which moves vast quantities of desert material into shallow water, developing extensive and important alluvial fan systems with very important consequences to local reef survival and formation (41).

The water balance in the Red Sea is negative. Annual precipitation is rarely over 10 mm while evaporation is about 2 m/y. In addition, the Red Sea has a higher tidal height than the Mediterranean, so there has been a further small net loss of water northwards since the opening of the Suez Canal. The balance is made up by an inward flow through the Bab el Mandeb, and it is estimated that water renewal time in the upper 200 m (the water above the thermocline) is in the order of six years, while the time for turnover of water for the whole Red Sea is about 200 years (41).

Figure 8.3. A classical Red Sea fringing reef, only about 50 m wide. The 100 m contour typically lies no more than 100 m to seaward of the reef crest. The shore is a fossil reef tectonically uplifted about 3 m.

Sea surface mean temperature is also one of increasing values from north to south, with the exception of the extreme southern part influenced by the Indian Ocean. Mean surface values range from 17.5°C at Suez and 27°C at 18°N (February) to >32°C at Hodeidah (Yemen) and Massawa (Eritrea) in August and September. Temperature extremes occur mostly in inshore waters. Low extremes may drop to less than 10°C in the Gulf of Suez, while high values of 36 to 38°C have been recorded in the southern Red Sea. Temperatures of at least 45°C are common in shallow lagoons behind fringing reefs.

Surface salinity increases through evaporation as water flows northwards throughout the length of the Red Sea. Typically it increases from 36.5 parts per thousand (ppt) in the extreme south, to about 40.5 ppt at the extreme northern part of the Red Sea. In the shallow Gulf of Suez, surface salinity increases to about 42.5 ppt, mainly through evaporation but also possibly by addition from ancient sub-surface salt deposits. At the northern end, the increasingly dense water turns under, returning south beneath the northward flowing surface layer. This returning flow has a constant salinity of 40.5 to 40.6 ppt and a constant temperature of 21.5°C. This major circulation is persistent, and other currents tend to be weak and greatly variable. A clear and detailed description of Red Sea currents has proved to be difficult, partly because currents are weak and variable. Basically the fundamental movements follow the winds, so that the northerly wind in summer drives surface water south for about four months while in winter the flow is reserved, pushing water into the Red Sea from the Gulf of Aden (8).

Tides in the Red Sea are simple, and are not closely linked to those of the Indian Ocean with which it communicates. There is an oscillating tide of small amplitude and semi-diurnal period causing high water at one end when it is low at the opposite end, with a period of about 12 hours. Average spring range is about 0.6 m in the northern and 0.9 m in the southern ends, with maxima in the Gulfs of Aqaba and Suez of 1.2 and 1.5 m respectively. This decreases to no appreciable semi-diurnal tide in the central area near Port Sudan and Jeddah. Because of the wind regime and water forcing through the Bab el Mandeb, there is a marked annual "tide", in which water levels are up to 50 cm higher in winter than in summer. This is the only tide in the central region, and has important consequences for the shallow biota.

Water masses of the central and northern Red Sea have low nutrient concentrations with a fairly clear latitudinal pattern (Table 8.1). During the summer when the Arabian upwelling is at its greatest, Gulf of Aden water entering the Red Sea is enriched with nutrients and particulate organic matter (POM), raising nutrient and organic levels in the south (45). Nutrient levels decrease from south to north in a manner inversely related to oxygen content, which increases throughout the water column towards the north. In the shallow Gulf of Suez, wind-induced mixing ensures that there is an almost uniform vertical distribution of oxygen and nutrients, while in the Gulf of Aqaba, distribution of nutrients can be influenced by local coastal upwelling and, in the extreme northern part, even by wind blown phosphate fertilizer (11,12,13,25). Considerable plankton enters the Red Sea via the Bab el Mandeb and consequently, the introduced particles lead to increased turbidity in the southern Red Sea reducing the euphotic zone layer to a depth of only about 30 m. This also has a considerable effect on the distribution of coral reefs in this part of the Red Sea.

Primary production in the Red Sea is low because the thermocline and halocline prevents nutrients from recycling between deeper water and the photic zone, and because there is little terrestrial runoff (45). The enriching influence of the Gulf of Aden on the southern Red Sea is shown in Table 8.1, and these high values of water-column productivity in the south may be added to bathymetric and water quality factors which inhibit reef growth.

Character and Distribution of Reefs

The clear, warm waters of the northern and central Red Sea support some of the most attractive and most studied coral reefs anywhere in the world. Studies date back to the early work of Forsskal, Haeckel, Klunzinger and Crossland. Modern quantitative investigations of the reefs started with in the 1970s (21) and comprehensive outlines of coral reef distribution, development and taxonomy followed (36,38).

Coral Reef Types

A number of different reef types have been described, arising in part because the Red Sea, more than most parts of the world, is tectonically active (3) and because in many places the reefs are only thin veneers overlying much older substrate (Fig. 8.4). Typically fringing reefs are by far the most abundant reef type, lying close to shore and varying greatly in size. Contour reefs develop on sites where the magmatic mountains submerge into the sea and continue to

Table 8.1. Comparison of some water conditions of the north, central and south parts of the Red Sea which affect coral growth and reef development. Data from (41,45).

Characteristics	North	Central	South
Salinity range	40.5-42	36-40	36.5
Surface temperature	17.5	24-28	>32
Plankton cells /m^3 (winter)	14 000	58 000	21 000
Plankton cells /m^3 (summer)	180	300	3000
Production gC/m^2/d	0.21(greater near banks)	0.39	1.60
Bathymetry	Steep, close to shore	Steep, close to shore	Broad sedimented slope
Commonest island types	Reefal (Tiran)	Low cays	Volcanic or low uplifted fossil reefs (Farasans, Dhalaks)
Main reef types	Contour, Fringing	Fringing, Barrier	Broad fringing
Volcanic substrates	No	Uncommon	Common

descend almost along a straight line. Such a structure does not provide sufficient support for colonization and development of large biogenic communities. Contour reefs are typically only 3 to 4 m wide, but may extend outward to as much as 1 km in embayments and old *wadi* systems (13, 41). This is not considered to be a result of poor conditions for reef growth since crests of fringing reefs which extend over 1 km from shore may be seen immediately adjacent, where bathymetry allows. On the largest fringing reefs, substantial lagoons may develop between shore and reef crest, penetrated by narrow channels, called *marsas* or *sharms*. These fringe drowned river valleys and are generally still connected to *wadis* or seasonal rivers.

Barrier reefs are formed where reef grows on older, offshore limestone platforms, the latter probably being old Pleistocene fringing reefs. These now lie some distance from land, along depth contours of between 50 to 200 m deep, in other words, along the line of old Pleistocene shorelines. One linear structure running for 200 km off Saudi Arabia is a large barrier reef, known as the Little Barrier Reef (38). Patch reefs typically occur where factors such as temperature and salinity and, most importantly, high sedimentation, constrain greater coral reef development. Most patch reefs lie on calcareous sandy and silty substrate from 1 to 5 m deep. Ridge reefs were first described as longitudinal ridges lying along the axis of the Red Sea (14), their substrate being the result of normal faulting and underlying salt deposits moving upwards along these faults. As far as atoll formations are concerned, Sanganeb (Sudan) has been described as the only atoll in The Red Sea. However, many structures on the barrier reef are similarly dish-shaped, and in the Red Sea as much as anywhere, a semantic preoccupation with classification of reef types tends to overlook the fact that reef construction will occur wherever substrate and environmental conditions have allowed. In the tectonically active and young Red Sea, variation in substrate is considerable, leading to a corresponding variety of reef type.

Distribution of Reefs

Until the early 1980s the distribution of coral reefs in the Red Sea was largely based on observations made in the northern part. Consequently it was widely

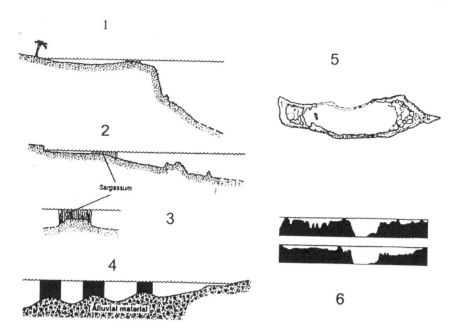

Figure 8.4. Typical Red Sea reef types. 1. A classical Red Sea fringing reef, only about 50 m wide. 2. A broad central and southern fringing reef. 3. Patch reefs in the central and southern region. Like 2, these commonly support broad stands of *Sargassum*. 4. Series of patch reefs prograding to seaward, based commonly on alluvial fans, though sometimes (more commonly in the north) also on limestone platforms. 5. Sanganeb atoll, central Red Sea. 6. Two cross section through the north-central barrier reef region, from shore to barrier reef. Shore is to the right. Barrier reef sections are up to 5 km wide, separation of barrier reef from shore is likewise 5 km wide and over 100 m deep.

believed that the whole of the Red Sea, on both coasts, was lined with continuous fringing reefs (20) even though, much earlier, naturalists had reported that reefs were much less numerous in the southern part (26). In the past two decades, analysis of coral data from the full length of the Red Sea has shown strong north-south gradients, with the best developed reefs in the northern and central regions (27,38).

The most northerly reefs in the shallow and sedimented gulf of Suez are patch reefs on the eastern shore, 1 to 3 m in height. The main limiting factor here appears to be high sedimentation rather than cool temperature and high salinity. The dominant corals are branching forms of the genera *Acropora* and *Stylophora*, the former genus often accounting for more than 60% of total coral cover (38). On the western shores of the Gulf of Suez, a long stretch of fringing reefs are found within 50 km of Suez town. These lead into the Red Sea proper, where extensive, illuminated and shallow substrate allows the growth of some of the largest reefs found in the northern Red Sea.

The Gulf of Aqaba is like a small scale Red Sea. The 200 m deep sill at its entrance supports luxuriant reefs including some of the most recreationally dived reefs anywhere in the world (24). Most of the Gulf of Aqaba has only narrow fringing reefs, or contour reefs, though in embayments and on alluvial fan systems, such as at Nabq and Wadi Kid, they broaden to almost 1 km. The narrowest examples reveal interesting geological features. In many places the reef has split, revealing the underlying basements and thus showing the way in which these reefs conform to their basement contours (41). The classical fringing reefs of the Red Sea extend southward along both coasts to 18° or 20° N (Fig. 8.4). Mostly these extend only 10 to 50 m from the shore. Thus, because the Red Sea slopes steeply, only very limited substrate is shallow enough to be illuminated. Exceptions occur where alluvial fans have extended shallow substrate to seaward, and around island groups such as the Wedj bank with its rich complexes of seagrass, reefs and mangroves (27,28).

Important reef areas are also found offshore in the northern and central Red Sea where the barrier reef complex off Saudi Arabia, probably mirrored by a similar structure off southern Egypt and Sudan, has the most diverse reef communities known in the Red Sea (38). Narrow fringing reefs extend as far as the central Red Sea, where the mix of offshore banks and both broad and narrow fringing reefs is similar to that in the north. In the central region there is a general broadening overall, with wider and more frequent lagoons. The African coast has been explored enough to suggest that it is similar to the Arabian coast. The Egyptian peninsula of Gebel Elba juts outwards 70 km into the Red Sea, and its marine environment remains mostly unexplored. Further south, the 750 km long Sudanese coastline is home to some of the best reefs in the Red Sea (17), including the well studied Sanganeb atoll. On this coast south of about 20°N, fringing reefs are considerably reduced in size while increasingly, muddy substrates and mangroves along the coast cause reef development to take place further from shore.

The southern Red Sea region is generally poor in reefs. This is attributed to a combination of increasing sedimentary conditions, shallowing bathymetry, and higher nutrient levels originating in the Gulf of Aden, favoring algal growth over coral development. South of 20°N the continental shelf becomes broader and fringing reefs become intermittent, being replaced in many places by sand or mud substrates and mangroves. Where fringing reefs do occur, the gradual sub-surface slope has allowed them to extend considerable distances to seaward (Fig. 8.5). Further south, sandy shores and sub-littoral habitats near shore support almost no coral, and mangroves become increasingly dominant. In Yemen this is the case for most of the coast. Where coral development does occur, such as on the offshore reefs and the coast between Al Mokha and Bab el Mandeb, reefs have low coral cover and diversity. Similarly, in Eritrea only rudimentary reefs can be found. Reasons for inhibition of reef development are the same as for the Arabian shore, but with possibly greater influence also from a high energy environment in which strong wind and wave action results in high scouring as well. One remote area in Eritrea, Zula Bay, has well developed reefs but these are in a small bay which protects the reef from the major winds, currents, and sediments.

In the southern part of the Red Sea, at least along the Arabian side, a different reef type dominated by algae can be found in sheltered locations. These algal reefs are calcareous red algal constructions analogous to oceanic coral reef crests. They arise from sandy substrates where water is 2 to 4 m deep, support few corals and are typically covered in *Sargassum*, whose fronds form thick mats on the water surface. These provide extensive hard substrate in otherwise sandy areas.

Figure 8.5. A broad southern Red Sea fringing reef, looking toward land from the seaward edge. Corals are sparse, and *Sargassum* lies on the reef flat. A lagoon of about 5 m lies between reef and beach, and the latter supports mangroves.

The two large archipelagos found in the southern Red Sea, the Farasan and Dhalak, rise from shallow sedimented and uplifted platforms. Inner parts of both are poorly colonized with corals, though the islands and more deeply submerged areas present fairly luxuriant coral (38). The reefs of the Dhalak archipelago, a relict and uppermost layer of a larger carbonate platform (1,2), are thin and in the form of fragmentary fringing or patch reefs. Partial coral cover on rocky substrates is more common than true reefs in Eritrea and the Dhalak Archipelago. Such areas do not have the density and diversity of corals and other reef fauna seen further north. South of Massawa, Eritrean reefs support dense seasonal growth of *Sargassum* and other brown and green macroalgae, which appear around November, reach a maximum in January and die back in April or May. This coincides with the south wind period which brings nutrient rich water into the southern Red Sea from the Gulf of Aden.

Biological Patterns

Major environmental gradients that correlate with latitude are salinity and low winter temperatures, both of which become more severe further north. By contrast, temperature fluctuations and nutrients increase southwards. There is also a major shallowing in the south, affecting the degree of sedimentation and suitability of substrate. Using a mixture of dominant coral species, fish communities and overall appearance or quality, four main zones distributed north-south within the Red Sea have been determined (27,28,29,30). These are:

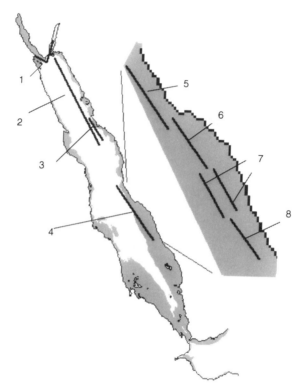

Figure 8.6. Principal coral communities along the Arabian side of the Red Sea. Inset is a section of the central-southern region where there is a marked change in the nature of the reefs and of the coral communities. The intent is to illustrate the degree of geographical separation; for details of various combinations within each block of dominance, character and diversity see (91).

a) the Gulf of Aqaba;
b) northern Red Sea southward to near Jeddah;
c) the mainland coast around Jeddah together with some islands in the southern Red Sea; and
d) the southern mainland coast and southern Farasan Islands.

Not included in the analysis was the African side of the Red Sea, though the few localities known suggest that the same pattern would also be expected there. There are lesser patterns across the width of the Red Sea, from shore to offshore reefs, with the African and Arabian coasts appearing to mirror each other closely. Patterns with longitude have been much discussed, and little additional work has been done since this subject has been reviewed (41). The following summarizes the major patterns.

Corals. Analysis of coral data from nearly 200 sites from both of the northern Gulfs and the Arabian mainland coast to 16.5°N on the Yemen border (38,40) showed 13 principal coral communities (Fig. 8.6). Several sections themselves can be subdivided further along latitudinal lines. Most of the defined coral communities are limited to either the northern, central, or southern

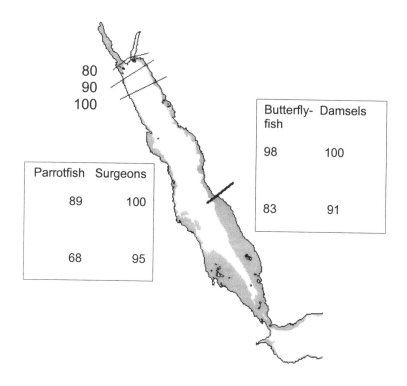

Figure 8.7. Principal division of reef fish assemblages. Thick line in central region marks 20°N. Values in boxes are results of cluster analyses on species presence/absence data for the four families shown, of percentage number of sites correctly classified on the basis of location north or south of 20°N. In boxes, top line = north, bottom line = south. Marks in northern end of Red Sea show clines in average number of species per site for the same fish families plus wrasses and groupers, all families combined.

areas of the Red Sea, only a few communities span two of these areas, and only one type of community is spread throughout. This distribution of community pattern was attributed largely to offshore depth, exposure and sedimentation. In the central-southern region where the change in these factors occurs, the latitudinal changes in coral communities present is particularly striking. Coral reproduction in the Red Sea shows differences from Indo-Pacific locations (Box 8.1), affected by the particular seasonality and environment of the Red Sea.

Reef Fishes. Reef fish assemblages of the Red Sea are equally varied from north to south, showing marked differences among regions in species richness, assemblage composition and species abundance. Detailed studies made along the Saudi Arabian coast (27,28,33,34) show that major differences occur in faunal composition and relative abundance of species in all families investigated. Two main regions exist in the Red Sea proper, a north and central region, and a region south of a fairly abrupt transition around 20°N, over a distance of only about 60 km of coast (33). The results of these analyses (Fig. 8.7) show that, in terms of species composition or on the basis of the

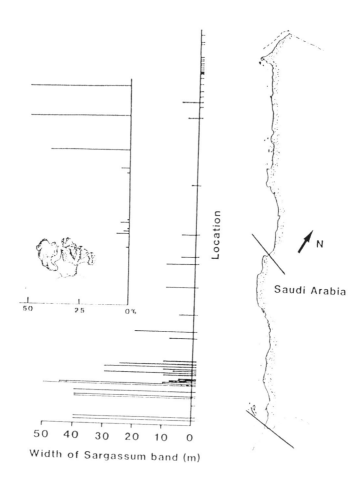

Figure 8.8. Latitudinal pattern of *Sargassum* (main graph), showing occurrence of *Sargassum* and the width of the *Sargassum* band on the reef crest. Inset shows percent cover by soft corals on the fringing reefs; lines drawn on coastline of Arabia show northern and southern limits of the soft coral graph.

abundance of the species present, these two areas are very different. As with the corals, more detailed examination of smaller areas (Fig. 8.7 inset) reveals finer distribution patterns as well. The differences are clear in the field with major shifts in species dominance between regions.

Soft Corals and Macroalgae. The distribution of two other groups, soft corals and macro-algae, mainly *Sargassum* illustrates well the latitudinal gradient in the Red Sea (Fig. 8.8). For both groups, a similar area in

Box 8.1. Patterns of Coral Recruitment and Mortality

An accurate understanding of all aspects of recruitment is essential to understanding the distribution and maintenance of coral communities, and consequently to effective management of reefs. Early studies on the recruitment and reproduction of Red Sea corals indicated settlement rates of between 1 and 5 new colonies per m^2 /y or up to 60 small recruits per m^2 (1,3). The coral *Stylophora pistillata* released larvae for up to eight months a year (6), though spawning periods of all species occurred in different seasons, different months or different lunar phases within the same month (7).

More recently, coral recruitment in the Egyptian Red Sea was investigated by examining distribution of coral spat on settlement plates and by censusing juveniles (2). Settlement averaged 18.6 recruits/m^2 (around 37.1 /m^2/y), lower than that recorded elsewhere in the Red Sea and considerably lower than the Great Barrier Reef (GBR, between 131 and 879 /m^2/ y). It is possible that lower rates of settlement in the Red Sea are associated with geographical trends rather than seasonal factors.

Reproductive patterns from the Red Sea are in marked contrast to those in a number of other Indo-Pacific coral reefs. Unlike the annual synchronized spawning event in the GBR (5), in the Red Sea spawning occurs over a longer period of time, with most brooders appearing to be iteroparous, releasing larvae over a large part of the year. The extended breeding seasons in the Red Sea have been linked to both physical and biological factors. Ranges and amplitudes of variables such as tides and temperature are limited, thereby providing adequate conditions for larval dispersal and settlement over longer periods of time. It may be that physical and biological controls on post-spawning success are quantitatively different in the Red Sea, with post-settlement mortality being greater on Pacific and Caribbean reefs due to either higher biological disturbance or to more extreme physical disturbances such as hurricanes.

About 4.5 to 4.8 coral colonies /m^2 showed partial mortality, that is, around 11% of total coral cover and over 50% of coral colonies (2). This frequency of damage to corals typically occurs over a period of a few months to a year. Extrapolating from age classes of coral juveniles based on size frequency distributions and rates of juvenile mortality and growth gives a mean recruitment rate of about 4.7 juveniles /m^2/y. Size frequency distributions which indicate similar numbers of one and two year old juveniles also suggest a decline in recruitment in the last few years. This could be attributed to increased larval, spat and juvenile mortality, or alternatively a decline in larval output linked to natural fluctuations or perhaps anthropogenic disturbance.

The northern end of the Red Sea and particularly the Gulf of Aqaba, may be considered a small sub-region of the Red Sea (4). Its morphology, oceanography, hydrodynamics, coastal development, and coral community may all influence the patterns of damage to corals, larval supply, post settlement mortality and ultimately coral recruitment.

D. Medio

References

1. Loya, Y. 1976. Settlement, mortality and recruitment of a Red Sea coral population. In *Coelenterate Ecology and Behaviour.* ed. Mackie, G.O. pp 89-100. New York: Plenum Press
2. Medio, D. 1996. *An Investigation into the Significance and Control of Damage by Visitors to Coral Reefs in the Ras Mohammed National Park, Egyptian Red Sea.* DPhil, University of York, UK
3. Mergner, H. 1971. Structure, Ecology and Zonation of Red Sea Reefs (in Comparison with South Indian and Jamaican reefs). In *Regional Variation in Indian Ocean Coral Reefs.* eds. Stoddart, D.R., Yonge, C.M. London: Academic Press
4. Ormond, R.F.G., Dawson-Shepherd, A., Price, A., Pitts, R.G. 1984. *Report on the Distribution of Habitats and Species in the Saudi Arabian Red Sea.* IUCN/MEPA
5. Richmond, R.H., Hunter, C.L. 1990. Reproduction and recruitment of corals: comparisons among the Caribbean, thr tropical Pacific and the Red Sea. *Marine Ecology Progress Series* 60:185-203
6. Rinkevich, B., Loya, Y. 1979. The reproduction of the Red Sea coral Stylophora Pistillata. II. Synchronisation in breeding and seasonality in planulae shedding. *Marine Ecology Progress Series* 1:145-152
7. Shlesinger, Y, Loya, Y 1985. Coral community reproductive patterns: Red Sea versus the Great Barrier Reef. *Science* 228:1333-1335

the southern third of the Red Sea is a major pivotal location. There, soft corals decline, alongside the marked change in hard coral communities noted above, and *Sargassum* begins to occur not only occasionally and in sheltered patches such as in *sharms*, but in dense and broad stands along the seaward edges of reef flats. In the southernmost sites studied in Saudi Arabia, *Sargassum* also densely colonized small patch reefs and the algal reefs remarked upon earlier. The location of the major shift lies south of Jeddah, and is near the point where the depth contours sweep away from land. At this point, near-shore reefs change from clear, low nutrient conditions to increasing nutrients and warmer summer temperatures.

In all of the above groups, differences occur between the two northern Gulfs of Suez and Aqaba. The Gulf of Suez is shallow and sedimented, perhaps resembling the northern part of the Arabian Gulf more than other parts of the Red Sea in terms of reef development and coral community type (41), while the Gulf of Aqaba may best be viewed as a continuation of the Red Sea. There is evidence, however, of some increased speciation of corals in the far north of the Red Sea and Gulf of Aqaba, but whether this is an artifact of the increased sampling that has been done there compared with that of the central Red Sea requires investigation. While considerable amounts of ecological work have now been carried out in the Red Sea, the sampling and locations of sites has not been equitable along its length, which may give rise to biased conclusions in terms of species distributions.

Human Effects

Most tropical intertidal and nearshore marine environments have come under increasing pressure from several types of human effect and the Red Sea is no different (7). Human effects to coral reefs are divided here in three main groups: industrial and domestic pollution, effects of coastal construction and effects of subsistence and recreational activities including fishing and collecting.

Sewage and Oil Pollution

The effects of pollution in the Red Sea are increased significantly by its enclosed nature and limited water exchange with the Indian Ocean, which means that the potential for dispersion of pollutants is limited, exacerbated in the central region by a lack of tides. Lack of widespread sewage treatment facilities in most Red Sea countries has resulted in extensive damage to coral reefs as well as serious human health problems. Considerable outputs occur around large cities such as Suez, Jeddah, Yanbu and Port Sudan, and increasingly in recently built-up areas including those developed for tourism. Well researched examples of damage to coral reefs by sewage have been reported in several countries of the Red Sea (12,23,44). Sewage and similar forms of pollution such as phosphate contamination have been linked to increased death rate in corals, inhibition of calcification and an overall increased sediment and nutrient load, leading to increased algal growth.

Considerable amounts of rubbish enter the sea at urban and recreational areas as well as from ship traffic. Twenty years ago one report noted that the entire coast of Saudi Arabia is seriously polluted by plastic deposits, and occasionally covered in oil (46). The situation is similar in Egypt, Yemen, Sudan and Eritrea. Although the extent of biological damage to coral reefs has not been investigated the aesthetic damage is considerable. Where fishing gear is among the items discarded on and near reefs, the damage to corals is considerable.

Oil pollution can have severe consequences to Red Sea coral reefs particularly in view of the enclosed nature of this body of water. Most of the worst oil pollution is reported near and around oil fields and refineries in the Gulf of Suez, though terminals and refineries at Yanbu and Jeddah (Saudi Arabia), at Hodeidah and Mokha (Yemen), and Port Sudan also cause contamination. Operational discharges as well as discharges from ships are significant (6). The degree of oil pollution on Red Sea coasts is such that a major report completed in 1979 concluded that "coastal pollution by oil was found to be a very serious problem along major sections of the Gulf of Suez and Egyptian Red Sea coast... The degree of pollution is not uniform for the long coastline involved... However, a number of areas (in the Red Sea) must rank with some of the worst polluted coastlines of the world" (47). In the last decade, much has been achieved in some areas, at least in terms of visible oil contamination. Several countries have introduced more stringent regulations and trained oil spill response teams that work closely with international companies. Examples include the oil spill response facilities at Zeit Bay and

Hurghada in the north-western Red Sea. Another such facility is being deployed within the Ras Mohammed National Park in Egypt. In some cases these are, however, paper operations only and practice has not lived up to regulation, but they at least form a basis on which to develop.

Coastal Development and Tourism

Disturbance may also arise from construction and operation of both large and small coastal industries. Dredging and land fill especially cause effects which can extend several kilometers along a coast from the site of operations. Effects of these have been rarely studied in the Red Sea, though information is available from the geographically close Arabian Gulf coastline. The largest and most prolonged development is probably in Jeddah, where demand for sea-frontage is such that development has extended for over a hundred kilometers. Construction of roads and recreational facilities on the reef flat itself has been an engineering marvel, much admired and pictured even on the Jeddah telephone directory (Fig. 8.9). The ecological consequences include, however, many kilometers of destroyed reefs and stagnant bodies of shallow water. Covering water fronts with concrete or vast quantities of sand also causes unwelcome environmental costs such as destruction of productive seagrass beds and some changes to coastal equilibria resulting in shoreline erosion. On the reef slopes near the center of Jeddah severely affected sites showed recolonization, but mainly of the opportunistic coral *Pocillopora*. Further efforts are underway to construct houses near some coastal areas suggested for protective management (43).

Highly saline discharges from desalination plants are commonly cited as causing environmental problems. Observations around large plants indicate that in the steep and deep Red Sea, discharge effects are limited to distances of less than two or three hundred meters from the release, a relatively small radius in view of the immense importance of the product. More important than salinity may be the additives such as biocides. Biocides have been known to kill important grazing littorinid gastropods (41) which keep intertidal algae in check. Death of these gastropods causes green algae to colonize and reduce the diversity of mud flats and mangrove areas.

Coastal construction and the resulting sedimentation may be the greatest manageable coral reef problem in this region (39). Certainly much of the damage is localized, at least at scales of the whole Red Sea but it is often exactly these areas that have the potential for tourism that requires a clean marine environment (24). In the Sinai a 4000 m² beach was created from land fill and in Hurghada over 90% of all hotel development has taken place on landfilled back reef (18,23). These projects result in heavy sedimentation and reef deterioration. A number of laws aimed at protecting natural coastal habitats have been passed, and it is hoped that further development of the country's coastline south of Hurghada will comply with the current legislation. Legislation includes a ban on construction within 200 m of the reef and a ban on effluent discharge (9,29).

Divers and snorkellers in high densities can cause significant damage to back reef and fore-reef slopes (15,16,32). Studies on heavily visited sites have found significantly more broken corals, lower coral cover and smaller

Figure 8.9. A reef flat in central Jeddah (the corniche), much built upon and admired locally for its design and engineering. The reef flat is almost totally destroyed, with stagnant pools and high algal growth soon after the development. Reef slopes were severely impacted, though some parts are recovering.

coral colonies at heavily used sites and visitor damage appears to be the major cause of coral mortality (Box 8.2, 24,29).

In Israel, the Eilat infrastructure includes a phosphate factory, oil refinery, military harbor, commercial port, hotel development, artificial lagoons and marine reserve, as well as a visible untreated sewage outlet on the northern outskirts of the city. Arguably, this is one of the most heavily developed 10 km of coastline in the world.

Countries bordering the southern Red Sea are less developed as they have been torn by serious political and military turmoil over the past two decades, but are still affected by some of the same environmental problems. In Yemen, pollution due to sewage and industrial development is as acute in localized areas as some of the central and northern sections of the Red Sea, and has already lead to visible degradation of the coastline. This is particularly relevant in the light of the rapidly expanding coastal population and the country's tourism aspirations. Oil pollution is a particularly serious problem in Yemen, as is coastal erosion. Unfortunately, there is no information specifically connected with reef condition.

The coast of Eritrea, on the other hand, is sparsely populated, partly due to the extreme heat and aridity of the coastal plain and party due to the effects of the prolonged war with Ethiopia. Port and coastal areas were the focus of battles which largely depopulated coastal areas. Apart from the main coastal town of Massawa in the center and Assab in the far south, other towns are few and have small populations. A total absence of sanitation facilities causes localized pollution around settlements but the high energy marine environment usually restricts this problem to a short distance from shore. Settlements tend to become established in the more sheltered embayments, which also harbor the best coral areas.

Fishing

In much of the Red Sea, past fishing effort was sustainable, mostly as a result of limited efficiency and a lack of a proper market structure and refrigeration. These natural controls have been overcome through improved fishing technology and infrastructure to supply the ever-increasing populations in Red Sea countries. This has led to uncontrolled fishing or very selective fishing, decreasing the populations of exploited species. This may lead to deterioration of the community structure of coral reef fishes, with direct and indirect effects on the coral reef ecosystem (10).

Heavily fished areas include the Gulf of Suez where trawling is heavy, and most areas adjacent to heavily populated coasts (such as Suez, Jeddah, Port Sudan and Hodeidah). In addition several countries, such as Egypt and Yemen, have made great efforts to increase catches (42). In Yemen, very cheap subsidized fuel has made fishing from small outboard driven boats profitable, despite the high fuel consumption. Large numbers of Yemeni fishers make trips throughout the southern Red Sea, frequently fishing in Eritrean and Somali waters. It is thought that most fishing effort on Eritrean reefs comes from Yemen, where high value reef-associated species such as snapper, grouper and grunt are sought. This was probably the case throughout the War of Independence when few Eritreans lived near the coast. Some foreign trawlers from Saudi Arabia are also licensed to fish in Eritrean territorial waters (inside 12 miles) and others fish without licenses.

Trawling is widespread on all shallow banks in the Red Sea for shrimp and commercially important large pelagics including jacks and cuttlefish. Trawlers operate out of Egypt, Saudi Arabia and Yemen, and there is concern about shrimp and cuttlefish resources, especially since these are often trawled close inshore while they are spawning. These fisheries supply the more affluent parts of the region with luxury foods rather than sustaining local populations.

Lack of ice in Eritrea means that fishing effort by Eritreans themselves is largely confined to shark, which can be dried. Eritreans eat very little fish and, therefore, most fish is exported and currently sold in Yemen and some to Saudi Arabia, where Eritreans also purchase all fishing gear and fuel. A dependence on Yemen undermines the ability of Eritrea to manage its reefs, since attempts to prevent or control fishing leads to reprisals. The conflict over the Hanish Islands between Yemen and Eritrea has also led to severe hardship in Eritrean coastal communities.

Box 8.2. Ras Mohammed National Park

In 1983 the land and surrounding coral reef on the peninsula of Ras Mohammed at the southern tip of Sinai was recognized by the Egyptian Government as a National Park (Law 102). Both the land and the surrounding coral reefs, including the island of Tiran, are multiple-use areas in which traditional grazing and fishing by Bedouins is permitted but development is strictly controlled. Recently, the National Park complex was extended to include the remaining coastal waters of the Gulf of Aqaba as far as the border with Israel (5). The coral reefs of this area are some of the most popular and spectacular areas for SCUBA diving, and have seen a remarkable growth in coastal and reef-related tourism, such that by 1995 there were 40 international hotels (with more under construction), 32 dive centers and 240 dive boats using the geographically constrained fringing reef plus a small number of offshore reefs, inevitably resulting in reef damage (1,2).

By one measure, the establishment of the Park must be viewed as a major achievement, and is a response to environmental concerns and recognition that the reef environment forms almost the sole basis for local revenue. Laws include a set-back of usually 30 to 60 meters between extreme high tide and construction work including sewage treatment facilities (3,4,5). Reef recreational activities are, however, now the major cause of damage to the Park's coral reefs (6). At some sites physical damage to corals on the back reef and reef crest affected up to 10% of total coral cover and between 30 and 60% of the more damage-prone branching corals. At some of the most heavily used sites, coral cover has decreased considerably and high physical damage to branching corals may have affected community composition. Damage to corals by SCUBA divers is now being mitigated by education programs. Damage due to divers, snorkellers, and coastal modification and construction are slowly being controlled. Consequently, it is being suggested that coastal development can be made compatible with reef protection provided that appropriate measures are insisted upon (3).

D. Medio

References

1. Hawkins, J. and Roberts, C. 1992. Effects of recreational SCUBA diving on fore-reef slope communities of coral reefs. *Biological Conservation* 62: 171-178
2. Hawkins, J., Roberts, C. 1993. The growth of coastal tourism in the red sea: present and possible future effects on coral reefs. In *Global Aspects of Coral Reefs: Health, Hazards and History*, ed. Ginsburg, R.N. pp. 385-391. Miami: Rosensteil School of Marine and Atmospheric Sciences
3. Medio, D. 1995. *Conservation and Tourism Development in the Ras Mohammed National Park, Egypt. Case Study for the Survey of Wildlife Management Regimes for Sustainable Utilisation.* A Darwin Initiative Project, UK Department of the Environment. World Conservation Monitoring Centre (WCMC), Cambridge, UK

4.   Medio, D. 1996. *An Investigation into the Significance and Control of Damage to Coral Reefs by Tourists in the Ras Mohammed National Park, Egypt.* DPhil Thesis, University of York, UK

5.   Medio, D., Ormond, R.F.G., Pearson, M.P. 1996. Assessment and management of diving related tourism in the Ras Mohammed National Park, Red Sea, Egypt. In *Proceedings of the International Conference on Coastal Change* 1: 840-848

6.   Ormond, R.F.G., Hassan, O., Medio, D., Pearson, M. P., Selem, M. 1997. Effectiveness of coral protection programmes in the Ras Mohammed National Park, Egyptian Red Sea. In *Proceedings of the 8th International Coral Reef Symposium* 2: 1931-1936

7.   Pearson, M.P. 1995. Sustainable financing of protected areas in southern Sinai. In *Proceedings of a Workshop on Sustainable Financing Mechanisms for Coral Reef Conservation*, pp 72-77. Environmentally Sustainable Development Proceedings Series No.9, The World Bank: Washington D.C.

The high levels of traditional and informal interchange across the southern Red Sea means that reef fisheries in this area are very difficult to monitor and manage. There is also some concern in Eritrea and Yemen that trawlers which fish coastal waters do so closer inshore than regulations permit. Catch statistics from trawlers operating in Eritrean waters in 1996 show a proportion of reef-associated species such as parrotfish, butterflyfish and slipper lobster, as well as emperor, grunt, snapper and grouper in the catch, indicating that trawling strays on to reef areas. There is also concern that trawls might be catching a large number of turtles, although little data has been collected (22).

Collection of reef invertebrates such as shells, corals and sea-stars, for food or as souvenirs has been carried out by beach-combers and divers alike. The increase in coastal populations and tourist activities in the last two decades or so has in some cases denuded large areas of reef organisms such as shells, sea cucumbers, corals, sea stars and black coral. Other natural resources affected include mother of pearl shell (*Trochus*) which is very intensively collected in Sudan, and the few turtle colonies on the Saudi Arabian coast typically used for food. Some Red Sea countries such as Jordan, Egypt and Israel have recently introduced legislation to control collection of reef organisms such as hard corals, shells and fish (23).

The potentially high-earning aquarium industry has until recently faced practical limitations such as the lack of efficient airport infrastructure throughout the Red Sea with the exception of Jeddah in Saudi Arabia. Recent improvements in communication and airport infrastructure have led to an increase in aquarium trade and there is presently a concern that the aquarium fish business may contribute to the deterioration of reef communities.

References

1.   Angelucci, A., Matteucci, R, Praturlon, A. 1981. Outline of geology and sedimentary environments of the Dahlak Islands, (Southern Red Sea). *Bollettino della Societa Geologica Italiana* 99: 405-419

2. Angelucci, A., Carbone F., Matteucci R. 1982. La scogliera corallina di Ilisi nelle Isole dei Bagiuni (Somalia meridionaleonale) Somalia. *Bollettino della Societa Paleontologica Italiana* 21:201-210

3. Behairy, A.K.A., Sheppard, C.R.C., El Sayed, M.K. 1992. *A Review of the Geology of Coral Reefs of the Red Sea.* UNEP Regional Reports and Studies. No 152

4. Berman, D. 1981. *Assault on the Largest Unknown. The International Indian Ocean Expedition.* Paris: Unesco Press

5. Braithwaite, C.J.R. 1987. Geology and palaeogeography of the Red Sea region. In *Red Sea,* eds. Edwards, A.J., Head, S.M. pp. 22-44. Oxford: Pergamon Press

6. Dicks, B. 1987. Pollution. In *Red Sea.* eds. Edwards, A. & Head S.M. pp.383-404, Oxford: Pergamon Press

7. Edwards, A .J., Head S.M. eds. 1987. *Red Sea.* Oxford: Pergamon Press

8. Edwards, F. J. 1987. Climate and oceanography. In *Red Sea.* eds. Edwards, A.J., Head, S.M. pp. 45-69. Oxford: Pergamon Press

9. Fawzi, M.A. 1995. *Economic Assessment of the Ras Mohammed National Park.* Egyptian Environmental Affairs Agency (EEAA), National Biodiversity Unit, Natural Protectorates Department, Cairo, Egypt

10. Ferry, R. E., Kohler, C. C. 1987. Effects of trap fishing on fish populations inhabiting a fringing coral reef. *North American Journal of Fisheries Management* 7: 580-588

11. Fishelson, L. 1973. Ecology of coral reefs in the Gulf of Aqaba (Red Sea) influenced by pollution. *Oecologia* 12:55-67

12. Fishelson, L. 1973. Ecological and biological phenomena influencing coral-species composition on the reef tables at Eilat (Gulf of Aqaba, Red Sea). *Marine Biology* 19:183-196

13. Fishelson, L. 1980. Marine reserves along the Sinai peninsula (northern Red Sea). *Helgolander wissenschaftliche Meeresuntersuchungen* 33: 624-640

14. Guilcher, A. 1988. A heretofore neglected type of coral reef: the ridge reef. Morphology and origin. *Proceedings of 6th International Coral Reef Symposium*, Townsville, Australia, 3:399-402

15. Hawkins, J., Roberts, C. 1992. Effects of recreational SCUBA diving on fore-reef slope communities of coral reefs. *Biological Conservation* 62:171-178

16. Hawkins, J., Roberts, C. 1993. The growth of coastal tourism in the Red Sea: present and possible future effects on coral reefs. In *Global Aspects of Coral Reefs: Health, Hazards and History*, ed. Ginsburg, R.N. pp. 385-391. Miami: Rosensteil School of Marine and Atmospheric Sciences

17. Head, S.M. 1987. Corals and coral reefs of the Red Sea. In *Red Sea*, eds. Edwards, A.J., Head S.M. pp.128-151. Oxford: Pergamon Press

18. Jones, A. P. 1995. *Report to Hurghada Environmental Protection and Conservation Agency* (HEPCA) Hurghada, Egypt

19. Karbe, L. 1987. Hot brines and the deep sea environment. In *Red Sea*, eds. Edwards, A.J., Head, S.M. pp. 70-89. Oxford: Pergamon Press

20. Longhurst, A.R., Pauly, D. 1987. *Ecology of Tropical Oceans.* London: Academic Press

21. Loya, Y. 1972. Community structure and species diversity of hermatypic corals at Eilat, Red Sea. *Marine Biology* 13:100-123

22. Lundin, C. Undated. World Bank Working Paper on Eritrea. The World Bank: Washington, DC
23. Medio, D. 1995. *Conservation and Tourism Development in the Ras Mohammed National Park, Egypt. Case Study for the Survey of Wildlife Management Regimes for Sustainable Utilisation.* A Darwin Initiative Project, UK Department of the Environment. World Conservation Monitoring Centre (WCMC), Cambridge, UK
24. Medio, D. 1996. An investigation into the significance and control of damage to coral reefs by tourists in the Ras Mohammed National Park, Egypt. D. Phil Thesis, University of York, UK
25. Morcos, S.E. 1970. Physical and chemical oceanography of the Red Sea. *Oceanographic and Marine Biology Annual Reviews* 8: 73-202
26. Neibuhr, C. 1972. *Travels through Arabia, and Other countries in the Far East, Performed by M. Neibuhr, Now a Captain of Engineers in the Service of the King of Denmark.* Reprint of the Libraire du Liban, Beirut, Vil 1 424 pp, Vol 2: pp. 437
27. Ormond, R.F.G., Dawson Shepherd, A.R., Price, A.R.G., Pitts, J.R. 1984. *Report on the Distribution of Habitats and Species in the Saudi Arabian Red Sea.* No. 1, Kingdom of Saudi Arabia: IUCN/MEPA
28. Ormond, R.F.G., Dawson Shepherd, A.R., Price, A.R.G., Pitts, J.R. 1984. *Report on the Distribution of Habitats and Species in the Saudi Arabian Red Sea.* No. 2, Kingdom of Saudi Arabia: IUCN/MEPA
29. Ormond, R.F.G., Dawson Shepherd, A.R., Price, A.R.G., Pitts, J.R. 1984. *Management of Red Sea Coastal Resources: Recommendations for Protected Areas.* Kingdom of Saudi Arabia: IUCN/MEPA
30. Ormond, R.F.G., Dawson Shepherd, A.R., Price, A.R.J, Pitts, R.J. 1986. *Distribution of Habitats and Species Along the Southern Red Sea Coast of Saudi Arabia.* Report No. 11, Kingdom of Saudi Arabia: IUCN/MEPA
31. Ormond, R. F. G., Hassan, O., Medio, D., Pearson, M. P., Selem, M. 1997. Effectiveness of coral protection programmes in the Ras Mohammed National Park, Egyptian Red Sea. In *Proceedings of the 8th International Coral Reef Symposium*, Panama 2: 1931-1936
32. Riegl, B., Velimirov, B. 1991. How many damaged corals in the Red Sea reef systems. *Hydrobiologia*, 216: 249-256
33. Roberts, C.M. 1986. *Aspects of Coral Reef Fish Community Structure in the Saudi Arabian Red Sea and on the Great Barrier Reef.* D.Phil. Thesis, University of York, UK
34. Roberts, C.M., Ormond, R.F.G. 1987. Habitat complexity and coral reef fish diversity and abundance on Red Sea fringing reefs. *Marine Ecology Progress Series* 41: 1-8
35. Roberts, C.M., Ormond, R.F.G, Dawson Shepherd, A.R. 1988. The usefulness of butterflyfishes as environmental indicators on coral reefs. *Proceedings of the 6th International Coral Reef Symposium*, Townsville, Australia 2:331-36
36. Scheer, G., Pillai, C.S.G. 1983. Report on the stony corals from the Red Sea. *Zoologica, Stuttgart* 133: 1-198
37. Sheppard, C.R.C. in press. Biodiversity patterns in Indian Ocean corals, and effects of taxonomic error in data. *Biodiversity and Conservation*
38. Sheppard, C.R.C., Sheppard, A.L.S. 1991. Corals and coral communities of Arabia. *Fauna of Saudi Arabia* 12: 3-171

39. Sheppard, C.R.C., Wells, S. 1988. *Directory of Coral Reefs of International Importance: Indian Ocean Region.* Gland: IUCN

40. Sheppard, C.R.C. 1988. Similar trends, different causes: Responses of corals to stressed environments in Arabian seas. *Procedings of 6th International Coral Reef Symposium,* Townsville, Australia 3:297-302

41. Sheppard, C.R.C., Price, A.R.G., Roberts, C.J. 1992. *Marine Ecology of the Arabian Area: Patterns and Processes in Extreme Environments.* London: Academic Press

42. UNDP-GEF 1992. *Yemen: Protection of Marine Ecosystems of the Red Sea Coast.* Project Document. United Nations Development Programme, Global Environment Facility, New York, US

43. UNEP, 1987. *State of the Marine Environment in the Red Sea Region.* (Draft). Nairobi: UNEP Regional Seas Reports & Studies

44. Walker, D.I., Ormond, R.F.G. 1982. Coral death from sewage and phosphate pollution at Aqaba, Red Sea. *Marine Pollution Bulletin* 13: 21-25

45. Weikert, H. 1987. Plankton and the pelagic environment. In *Red Sea,* eds. Edwards, A.J., Head, S.M. pp 90-111. Oxford: Pergamon Press

46. Wennink, C.J., Nelson Smith, A. 1977. *Coastal Oil Pollution Study for the Kingdom of Saudi Arabia.* Vol. 1 Red Sea coast, Vol. 2 Gulf coast. London: International Maritime Organisation

47. Wennink, C.J., Nelson Smith, A. 1979. *Coastal Oil Pollution Study for the Gulf of Suez and Red Sea Coast of the Republic of Egypt.* London: International Maritime Organisation

Chapter 9

Reefs and Coral Communities of the Arabian Gulf and Arabian Sea

C.R.C. Sheppard, S.C. Wilson, R.V. Salm & D. Dixon

The seas included in this chapter are the Arabian or Persian Gulf (simply "the Gulf" in local usage), several of its components which experience extreme environmental characteristics, as well as the Gulf of Oman, Arabian Sea and Gulf of Aden (Fig. 9.1). These are all marginal seas of the Indian Ocean, partly because of latitude, but also because of extreme environmental stresses other than temperature. All these bodies of water are linked by the circulatory patterns of the Arabian Sea, and by the great weather and current systems of the Indian Ocean.

These seas exhibit marked seasonal variability, resulting in some of the most remarkable effects seen in tropical waters. Extremes of cold are as important as the heat generally associated with this region. In embayments, especially in the Arabian Gulf, very high evaporation coupled with low winter temperatures create saline density gradients that drive water circulation, but also reduce biological diversity. In the Arabian Sea, seasonally reversing winds drive the important Arabian upwelling, which results in a substantial fishery and an enclave of southern temperate biota within this tropical area.

Much of the coast of this region is difficult to access. Most has never been visited in a scientific sense. Reefs of Iran, especially Baluchistan in the northern Arabian Sea, and much of the Yemen coast have received, at best, only cursory survey. Recent surveys of parts of the Gulf of Aden have discovered patches of unexpectedly rich coral and reef development. This region is better known geologically, because of its oil, and has a well-studied upwelling, because of the important fishery. The following account reflects this bias, but provides a background for future reef research in the region.

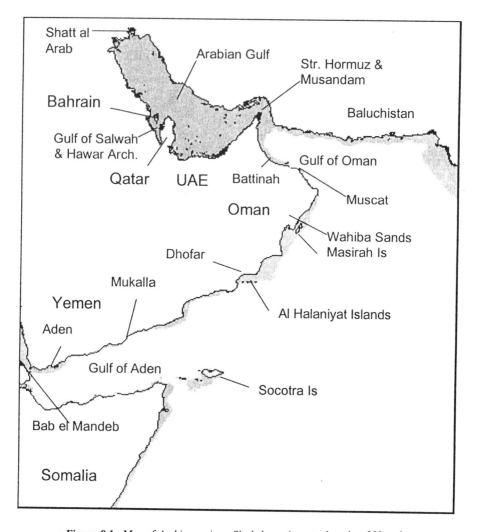

Figure 9.1. Map of Arabian region. Shaded area is water less than 200 m deep.

Geological, Geographical and Physical Background

Structure and Form

The Arabian Gulf. The Arabian Gulf is a large Miocene, carbonate basin, whose deepest depression runs along the northern, Iranian side. It is about 1000 km long by 200 to 300 km wide, with an average depth of about 35 m, dipping to about 60 m near Iran and to about 100 m deep at its entrance in the Straits of Hormuz. Its Arabian shoreline is geologically stable, while its Asian shoreline is unstable (52). Carbonate sediments dominate, derived mainly from microfauna, though the hot, arid climate of the area stimulates formation of evaporitic minerals including dolomite. Rivers have only localized effects on hydrology and sediments, terrigenous inputs coming mainly from flash floods (51,52).

Throughout the Gulf are vast areas of limestone substrate, thinly covered by carbonate sand. These platforms are commonly flat, featureless expanses with remarkably little relief, but in many cases they exactly resemble patch reefs. Possibly the largest is a chain of patch reefs in the Gulf of Salwah running north-south, east of Bahrain. The summits of these are near low-water level, but they have no corals at present due to the severe environmental conditions, and instead support large brown algae. These are formed in part from upward forcing of surface limestone by underlying salt domes (66) in a manner similar to that which led to the creation of archipelagoes in the southern Red Sea (see Chapter 8). Similar structures appear to exist in the eastern Gulf.

The Arabian shore supports terraces of reefs. These terraces are found in the highest parts of the island of Bahrain and small island groups such as the 10 to 15 m high reefs of the Hawar Archipelago between Bahrain and Qatar. The small Saudi Arabian islands probably also have uplifted limestone at their core, though these are now coral cays, ringed by modern coral and coralline algal construction which provide the most diverse hard substrate habitats known in the Gulf.

The United Arab Emirates (UAE) coast in the southern Arabian Gulf is a large, shallow embayment supporting a complex mixture of limestone patches and sedimented areas colonized by seagrasses and algae. Sediments, dominated by foraminifera, are produced in great excess to form banks and shoals, driven towards the mainland by northerly winds and waves. Cementation of limestone sediment proceeds rapidly, causing extensive Holocene limestone crusts in shallow and intertidal water, while the extremely hot and arid climate also leads to the formation of dolomite and other evaporite deposits. This environment supports little or no coral, but is biologically productive due to dense plant cover.

Straits of Hormuz. The entire Arabian peninsula has rotated about 7° anti-clockwise since the opening of the Red Sea, which has pushed northeastern Arabia into the Asian plate. This has led to the remarkable, fjord-like and mountainous structures of Musandam in the Straits of Hormuz. Musandam is a 90 km spur of limestone mountains, valleys and cliffs, of Permian through to Cretaceous origin, long recognized as unusual geologic structures in Arabia (Fig. 9.2). They are reefal, built by algae, rugose and scleractinian corals. They are folded and tilted approximately 10° from horizontal, added to which there is also at least 60 m of localized subsidence. While it is contiguous with Arabia, Musandam is part of the Iranian mountain system (26).

The coastline of this steep and convoluted area is mostly accessible only by sea. Although only 90 km long, its linear coastline is probably over 600 km. This is of considerable biological importance because Musandam provides a substantial rocky substrate and stepping stone for reefal species whereas for hundreds of km on either side the shore is formed by uncolonizable soft substrate. While the Iranian shoreline on the opposite shore is rocky too, the available evidence suggests that its sublittoral is mainly exposed, coarse-grained soft substrate. The area is extremely spectacular, beautiful and, on land at least, inhospitable. The phrase "going round the bend" originated here; the

Figure 9.2. Section of the Musandam peninsula showing steep cliffs and sheltered sections.

steep sided *khawrs* shut off breeze, so that officials posted to a telegraph relay station in Khawr ash Shamm in the 1860s were driven to distraction by boredom and heat. Missing the marvelous opportunities for studying nature, they instead gave this area the reputation of being the most oppressive place in the world.

Figure 9.3. Wahiba sands. Dunes and mobile sand continue seaward for hundreds of meters, such that all rock surfaces are heavily scoured. The upwelling provides the basis for a rich artisanal fishery.

Gulf of Oman. The Gulf of Oman is sedimentary, and its water has a near-normal salinity. Its Al Battinah coast is a gently sloping sandy bay over 300 km long. Groups of islands including the Daymaniyat Islands some 40 km offshore provide the only significant coral substrates, until the Muscat Area of Oman is reached. The reefs of the Daymaniyats are among the best examples of reef formation in the Sultanate.

The 250 km stretch from the Muscat area to Ras al Hadd, the easternmost tip of Arabia, is ecologically the best-known region in the Arabian Sea (56). It is mainly composed of various sandstone and dolomite outcrops, along with some limestones and metamorphosed basalt interspersed with small pocket beaches. At elevations of 2 to 10 m along this section of coast, fossil scleractinian corals exist which were deposited in the early Pleistocene (26). Some of these are "stacked bioherms" rather than true fossil reefs (25), in which layered coral communities alternate with coarse *wadi* deposits and storm debris. The coral layers are not fully consolidated reef, a condition which continues today in this region. Semi-fossilized drowned reefs have also been discovered along the 20 m depth contour along this stretch of coast.

Arabian Sea. The Arabian Sea shoreline is poorly known for much of its length. From Ras al Hadd southward, sweeping sandy bays backed by low-lying dunes or salt pans dominate, with the notable exception of Masirah Island. The extensive dunes of the Wahiba Sands continue to the sea (Fig. 9.3).

Figure 9.4. Dhofar Cliffs. Steep cliffs facing the Arabian sea generally terminate near low water level, either at sand substrate or a short "bench" colonized mainly by algae.

Further south, rocky cliffs alternate with long stretches of littoral sand dunes, but cliffs generally terminate near low water level and are heavily scoured (Fig. 9.4). As a result, the sublittoral of this coastline is predominantly soft substrate environment below the first few meters of water. This coast is mostly a high-

Figure 9.5. Socotra southern-facing bay. This island faces extreme wave scour in the summer monsoon. Rocky patches deeper than about 15 m support fairly dense algae but corals are restricted to sheltered coves or to deeper water.

energy environment, though some sheltered flats support enormous seabird populations. The coastal rock here is a complex mix of tertiary calcareous shales, limestone and gypsum, with chert and marly bands interbedded with limestone, and some igneous rock.

The Socotra Archipelago lies on the Carlsberg Ridge. The southern rocky shores of the four main islands are very steep and are exposed to the full force of the summer monsoon, but sheltered northern shores support significant coral communities between rocky outcrops dominated by macroalgae (Fig. 9.5). The islands themselves lie on a broad, shallow sedimented platform, from which originates much of the sediment that controls the marine communities. This piles up into immense beaches in some areas.

Gulf of Aden. The Gulf of Aden extends from the straits of Bab el Mandeb to a line drawn between Baghashwa in Yemen and Ras Asir on the Somali peninsula. Almost half of the northern coast is composed of sweeping, high-energy beaches between magnificent limestone headlands such as Ras Fartak. Where ancient lava flows reach the sea, coral communities provide 10 to 60% cover. Further west, where the fetch of the Gulf of Aden is reduced by the landmass of Africa, there are less exposed sites where low reef frameworks have developed. The towering calderas that guard the entrance to Aden harbor provide suitable substrate for relatively mature coral communities. In

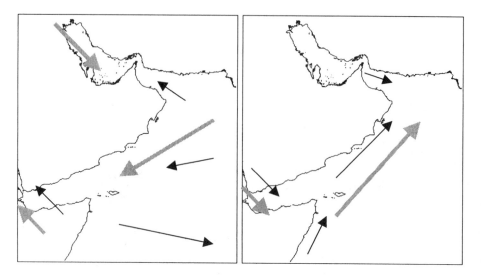

Figure 9.6. Map of winds and surface currents in winter (left) and summer (right). Winds are thick, gray arrows, currents are thin, black arrows.

more sheltered waters still, nearer Bab el Mandeb, patches of mixed coral and seagrass habitat are found in the sheltered *khawrs*.

Climate and Oceanography

Regional Climate Pattern

The Indian Ocean monsoon pattern, and the seasonal migration of the Inter-Tropical Convergence Zone (ITCZ), dominate the marine climate (Box 1.1). In low latitudes of the western Indian Ocean, trade winds north of the equator blow essentially from the northeast, while south of the equator they blow from the southeast. The winds meet at the ITCZ where air rises to over 12 km high, creating clouds and rain (21).

In the first quarter of each year the northeast monsoon is fully developed and the ITCZ lies far south of Arabia (Fig. 9.6). Winds cross the Arabian Sea from the east or northeast and usually remain below 5 m/s, but along the eastern edge of Arabia they are deflected by mountains and flow down that coast. In the Gulf of Aden, winds are similarly deflected, flowing towards the central Red Sea because of the low pressure there.

In the second quarter the southwest monsoon develops. The ITCZ migrates northwards, passing along the southeast coastline of Arabia, through the Gulf of Aden almost into the Red Sea. Rising air temperature drives strong winds in the Arabian Sea, which now lies south of the ITCZ. Winds flowing down the Red Sea enter the Gulf of Aden, and then are deflected to the northeast, parallel to the coast of Arabia. The clockwise airflow over the Arabian Sea reinforces this, causing sustained southwesterly winds of over 15 m/s along this coast for about four months in the summer, before the ITCZ migrates southward again.

This summer monsoon blows warm surface water offshore, and is replaced by deep upwelling water, which is cold and nutrient rich. The wind during the Arabian summer, the *khareef*, is both strong and persistent, forming waves typically 3 m high. On land, living conditions are extremely harsh in much of the area, in part due to the sustained, wind-driven sand, though along part of the Arabian coast, mountain escarpments cause persistent fine rain to fall.

Local Wind Systems

Large temperature differentials in this desert region drive strong local winds which are as important as the monsoon system to shallow marine ecosystems. In summer, thermal winds build up strongly to strike the coast obliquely. In the Arabian Gulf they may be the strongest winds experienced, temporarily raising sea level by up to 0.3 m. Intense thermal winds may blow from land at night too, lowering water level and exposing shallow reefs by over 0.5 m. The resulting desiccation effects have marked influences on distribution and alignments of coral reefs and mangroves.

Cold *Shamal* wind flow down from the Iranian mountains in winter for several days at a time, reducing air temperatures to near freezing, and sea temperatures to 4°C nearshore and 14°C offshore (20,69). Waves in the southern Gulf can reach 5 m high, and this combination causes extensive marine mortality, limiting the range of many important biotic groups. Mangrove distribution in particular is limited by these cold episodes more than by high salinity of the area. In the Gulf of Oman and northern Arabian Sea, local winds can produce waves of 3 m (43).

Evaporation

Evaporation by dry winds is as intense in winter as in the hot summer. Over the whole Arabian Gulf, evaporation averages 144 to 500 cm/y (53), most occurring in the shallow embayments in the south where evaporation locally exceeds 2000 cm/y. Evaporation substantially exceeds fresh water input, despite the substantial Tigris, Euphrates and several smaller Iranian rivers, whose 110 km^3 per year of freshwater is equivalent to 46 cm/y of depth (53). Net water loss is replaced by surface inflow from the Gulf of Oman.

Under the influence of the coriolis force, dense water formed from evaporation sinks and drives a geostrophic current. The dense water flows out of the Gulf below the inflowing fresher surface water (29,53). Several mathematical models have been developed for the Gulf flows (36). It is likely that the turnover time of water in the Gulf due to the circulation, defined as the time needed for all Gulf water to come within the influence of the open sea boundary, is estimated to be about 2.4 years (29). Flushing time is estimated to be about 3 to 5.5 years because of the effects of vertical mixing and other turbulent processes.

In the shallow bays of the southern Arabian Gulf where most evaporation occurs, salinity exceeds 50 ppt over hundreds of square km, exceeding 70 ppt in large expanses. Although largely devoid of corals, the area remains highly productive and important in terms of carbon and nitrogen fixation.

Arabian Sea Upwelling and Productivity

During the southwest monsoon in July and August, upwelling water is approximately 16 to 17°C (60,70), and affects almost all the Arabian Sea shoreline. Cooling is greatest, and biota most affected, off many rocky promontories where the continental shelf is narrow, and temperatures remain less depressed where the continental shelf is broad. The upwelling is separated into two main parts, that of the Arabian Sea proper, and that off the Somalia coast, known as the Somali upwelling, separated by warm water flowing out of the Gulf of Aden into the central Arabian Sea (70). These upwellings are most important to reef development because both nutrient enrichment and cold water are major inhibitors of corals and reefs.

Cold water pulses extend north into the Gulf of Oman in most years. In winter, gyres of cold water generated on the Iranian shores, spin intermittently across the Gulf of Oman to Omani shores. These are sufficient to force the biota towards a more temperate character (66). Locally driven currents also create episodic upwelling events, but of a more minor nature than that from the main, sustained upwelling typical of the main part of the Arabian Sea (56). Typical daily temperature fluctuations of 6°C and extreme fluctuations of up 8°C have been reported for the waters off Muscat in summer months (12).

The upwelling and induced high fertility is substantial. In the Indian Ocean, high fertility may generally be defined as surface water chlorophyll concentrations of >0.5 mg/m^3 (34). Only the Arabian Sea and east coast of southern Africa during summer show such high values (55,60). In Arabia, the pelagic productivity increase in upwelling months may be two orders of magnitude greater than in winter (see Fig. 1.10, which is a Coastal Zone Color Scanner enhancement showing averaged production, contrasting winter with summer upwelling).

Dissolved oxygen saturation in most surface waters is about 4.8 to 6.5 ml/l depending on temperature and salinity. The saturated layer generally extends to about 100 m deep, so in the Arabian Gulf it extends to the bottom, since this water body is less than 60 m deep. The Arabian Gulf is one of the most productive bodies of water on Earth, partly because of high benthic production in the vast shallows (see Landsat enhancement in Fig. 1.7). In the Arabian Sea, oxygen levels drop when beneath 100 m due to high salinity intrusions from the Arabian Gulf and Red Sea (70) and a rain of organic matter from above. This produces low O_2 values of 0.2 to 1 ml/l between 200 to 1200 m deep and this oxygen minimum extends south to 3°N.

Other Currents and Tides

Other important currents exist (17,21,29,53). The Indian northeast monsoon current flows towards Arabia and diverges in the Arabian Sea. One branch curves southward along the Arabian Peninsula coast, passing the entrance to the Gulf of Aden, returning eastwards with the Equatorial Counter Current. The other branch turns northwards towards the Gulf of Oman but dips down to return southward as deeper water. Important in a biogeographical sense is the South Equatorial Current. This flows westwards throughout the year, exceeding 2 km/h. Because it crosses the major atoll groups of the Maldives, Chagos and

Seychelles before reaching Arabia, it is important to regional biodiversity, being a possible source of species for an Arabian sink (66).

Below the oxygen minimum layer noted earlier, oxygen rich water appears again (54). Its origin is the southern Indian Ocean and Antarctica, and it is focused onto this coast by the high salinity wedges exiting the Gulf and Red Sea. It is the source of much of the nutrients, and may also be the source of some of the unusual biota of the Arabian region, such as the enclave of southern hemisphere, temperate water kelp (*Ecklonia*) found along the south eastern coast of Arabia (4,5).

The high salinity wedges exiting the Red Sea and Arabian Gulf are important regionally as well. Water of salinity >40 ppt flows into the Arabian Sea at 800 m deep from the Red Sea and 300 m deep from the Gulf (70). Because of the higher density of this water, these plumes help drive a circulation pattern in the Indian Ocean, especially in winter (19,62).

Tides in the Arabian Gulf are in co-oscillation with those in the Gulf of Oman and Arabian Sea. There is a mixture of semi-diurnal tidal movement which is superimposed on to a diurnal constituent (29), resulting in mixed diurnal and semi diurnal tides. Gulf spring tide amplitudes exceed 1 m, reaching 3 m at the Shatt al Arab (32) driving tidal currents of over 0.5 m/s. Tides in the Gulf of Oman and the Arabian Sea are oceanic in type where frictional effects are minimal. Tide heights range from 1.5 m, in the Arabian Sea, to 2.5 m in the Gulf of Oman, being predominantly semi diurnal (44) and correlating closely with that of the Indian Ocean. Generally, tidal flow in unconstrained coastal areas is less than 1 knot. However, tidal streams passing through constrictions caused by reefs and low islands commonly exceed 1 to 2 m/s. Consequences of the enhanced water exchange to shallow biota of the Gulf are immense (66) and allow many enclosed embayments to support considerably richer biota than could otherwise be expected given the temperatures and salinities encountered.

Historical Sea Level

At the start of the Holocene, sea level was probably somewhere between 120 to 150 m below present level, for perhaps 1000 to 2000 years (see Box 1.2). This probably had greater consequences to the Arabian region than many parts of the Indian Ocean. The Arabian Gulf, for example, simply dried out, apart from the courses of the Tigris and Euphrates rivers which exited along the present Iranian coast. During this time, the marine ecosystems of the Gulf were effectively reset, and in the biogeographical context, recruitment of marine life into the Gulf commenced anew.

Large changes in monsoon and upwelling strength occurred over this time (46,47), and even the present aridity of the region is relatively recent (33). Pollen and foraminifera in sediment cores show that stronger monsoons occurred in interglacial periods and weaker monsoons in glacials, over the past 140 000 years (Fig. 9.7). During the early part of the Holocene transgression, both monsoon and upwelling were considerably reduced for a period, then became considerably stronger, finally declining to its present state. Thus recruitment of Indian Ocean fauna into the region in the early Holocene took place when upwelling was reduced (64). Although the barrier increased later, possibly

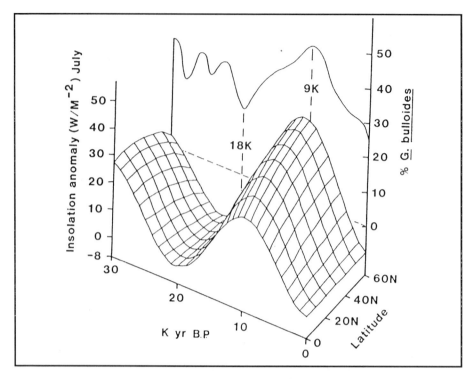

Figure 9.7. Strength of the Arabian Sea upwelling over the past 30 000 y (46,47). The percentage abundance of the diatom *Globigerina bulloides* is termed the "upwelling index".

substantially, this pattern permitted the redevelopment of the relatively rich and diverse biota seen in Arabian Seas today (66). During Pleistocene times, several marine groups had a wider distribution than at present. Raised beach gravel deposits along the northern Oman coast contain corals no longer found alive there, but which are now common only in southern Oman. Likewise, several mollusks are found in the deposits which are no longer found living anywhere in Oman (56). It is likely that the time since the transgression has not been long enough for complete recolonization (66).

Reef Development in the Arabian Sea and Gulfs

Regional Distribution of Reefs and Coral Communities

Arabian Gulf. Many of the islands and banks of hard substrate forced upwards by underlying salt domes are now colonized by corals. The banks now provide much of the limited vertical relief. On the Arabian side, there is a very gradual slope and a gradual blending of marine conditions with terrestrial, sometimes extending across a band of several km, especially in the UAE. This contrasts with the Iranian side where the Zagros Mountains exceed 1000 m elevation close to the shoreline.

Reefs of the Saudi Arabian islands are the best known in this region, and were studied in detail for over 20 years. Several were included in recent work connected with the creation of a Marine Wildlife Sanctuary following the Gulf War (35). The offshore Saudi Arabian islands are coral cays (8,9), have the greatest diversity of corals and a variety of dominant species in different zones (68). These islands contain the most developed reefs in the Gulf. In Jana and Karan Islands, massive *Porites* dominate the upper reef slopes, from about 2 m to about 5 m deep, providing very high coral cover. Below this, are several more small zones: a community of encrusting and foliose *Montipora*, then an intermittent zone of bushy *Acropora* or *Pocillopora*, and finally a zone of encrusting and massive faviids with conspicuous *Turbinaria*. At about 18 m, this last zone forms the deepest coral community known for the Gulf, though free living forms such as *Psammoseris* may be common deeper still. Most of the reef communities have not been analyzed quantitatively, but are well illustrated (8). Patch reefs closer to the mainland are much less diverse (40,41) and are usually dominated by *Porites compressa*. The most northerly reefs in the Gulf lie around islands off Kuwait (20) where around 26 species are present, and like most known reefs in the Gulf, they support insignificant coral growth below 15 meters. Corals also occur in isolated colonies on rocky outcrops on the southern mainland of Kuwait, but further north, the influence of the Shatt al Arab estuary precludes corals.

Reefs of Qeshim Island in the Straits are reported to have high coral cover (27,39). The only other reported coral reefs from the entire Asian coast of the Gulf are at Shotur Island. This probably reflects only the lack of data from Iran, as this northern part of the Gulf is the steepest and deepest of all, and will probably eventually be shown to have the most developed fringing reefs in the Gulf.

The low-lying southern Gulf coast along the UAE is generally muddy and unsuitable for most corals. There are numerous patch reefs dominated by *Acropora* offshore. Fringing reefs grow around some low islands, as well as along the east and north coasts of Qatar. These areas tend to have a high coral cover, but a low diversity of perhaps less than 20 species. Their lack of diversity is probably because of high sedimentation and periodic decimation in near freezing winter air temperatures (69). Coral reefs off Bahrain and west of Qatar develop the typical reef profile of a reef flat at or near low water level, and a reef slope that descends relatively steeply (66), but many banks off the UAE are bare limestone with few corals, kept scoured by mobile sediments.

Only reefs well removed from land develop the typical reef profile of a reef flat at or near low water level, and a reef slope which descends relatively steeply. Reefs near land are domes, with gentle slopes that may or may not reach the low tide mark. Domes are more common and extensive than true fringing reefs but the two conditions intergrade. Dome profiles with poor coral cover are not actively growing (63). However, many limestone mounds with extremely gentle slope and sparse coral cover may have been actively growing in the Pleistocene.

Where water is too saline for corals, such as the Gulf of Salwah between Qatar and Saudi Arabia, macro-algae replace corals on the limestone. Where corals do grow, they form a veneer on older limestone structures. The limestone platforms are friable, erosion is evident and attachment of corals to the substrate is weak.

Straits of Hormuz. Almost the entire 600 km of this mountainous and scenic coast offers extensive, steeply sloping hard substrate appropriate for coral settlement and growth to great depths. Clear water provides good conditions for corals and other coelenterates (16). Corals are diverse, with several growth forms not found elsewhere in Arabian seas. Although some reefs in Musandam form true reef frameworks, most corals do not form reefs. Coral in this area is not quite as varied as in the Gulf of Oman but is more abundant. From year to year, Crown-of-Thorns starfishes, *Acanthaster planci*, are abundant, causing considerable damage to corals and influencing coral communities on the east and north coasts (23).

Reefs in this area are made from, and are heavily dominated by, *Porites lutea*, with various *Acropora* abundant too. Coral diversity is highest around the mouths of fjords, and the mixed communities contain both abundant *Acropora* and faviid zones, and sometimes dense *Pocillopora damicornis*. As tidal flushing becomes less efficient deeper within the *khawrs*, some of which are 25 km long, coral assemblages become more depauperate.

Gulf of Oman. Reefs are common in this area and grow on different substrate types including Semail Ophiolite which is uplifted, dark green non-limestone oceanic crustal material (26) and on ancient limestones known as Oman Exotics (10). The reef studded section of coast is limited to the north by the sandy Al Batinah coast which sweeps for 200 km towards the Straits of Hormuz. The Iranian coast of the Gulf of Oman consists mainly of sand dunes and sandy beaches, but there appear to be cliffs and some bays containing corals only in eastern Baluchistan.

Porites is the dominant builder of framework reefs throughout Oman. Colonies fuse in the shallows to form reef-flats up to tens of meters wide that may be settled by other coral species. These fused colonies probably form the oldest continuously living reefs in the Sultanate, with some individual colonies estimated to be several hundred years old. Good examples can be found at the Daymaniyat Islands and in the bays near the old city of Muscat itself. The Daymaniyat Islands contain good examples of the principal coral reef types that are common throughout the Gulf of Oman. On rocky leeward shores are fringing frameworks of fused colonies of *Porites lutea* extending from the low water mark to 3 m depth. Generally, this leads to a zone of mixed corals dominated by *Acropora clathrata* with an understory of massive faviids and smaller *Porites* colonies. In some places, however, large undulating monospecific stands of *Pocillopora damicornis* form reef frameworks 2 to 3 m thick. In sheltered, leeward coasts of headlands and islands, conditions favor mixed communities dominated by *Acropora*.

Arabian Sea. Upwelling increases southward, causing the marine biota to gradually assume an increasingly temperate character. South of the tip of Somalia more typical tropical conditions return (17). An important consequence of the upwelling-induced increase in marine productivity is the large fishery off Yemen, Oman and Somalia.

South of Ras al Hadd (see Fig. 9.1) the Arabian shoreline borders the great Wahiba Sands desert. Sand dunes continue into the sea, providing a sandy, very high energy sublittoral substrate which is unsuitable for corals. South of the Wahiba Sands lie the flat salt pans of Barr al Hikman off which an extensive and spectacular reef solely composed of *Montipora foliosa* is located. Other areas off Masirah and Barr al Hikman have well developed coral reefs dominated by *Platygyra* and *M. foliosa*. Low ridges of limestone have allowed the extensive reef development in this area. The diversity of corals here is not high, reaching only 27 genera, but some reefs are the largest true coral reefs in the Sultanate. A broad dune system formed of coralline sand extends several hundred meters inland, behind a wide beach, and indicates that the reefs are at least several thousand years old. The ecology of the area is unusual and requires research. For example, there are many rare and little known species of fishes, including a recently discovered butterflyfish *Chaetodon dialeucos* (59).

From Masriah Island to Dhofar the coast is predominately sandy and so again is unsuitable for coral growth. In the few rocky areas, upwelling also inhibits reef development. Nonetheless, in the northern sheltered bays of the Al Halaniyat Islands, a group of five rocky islands approximately 30 km offshore, support coral communities with over 75% coral cover, though these grow on non-reef substrate. Framework reefs of up to 3 m thick do occasionally occur but the corals grow in association with dense algae during the summer monsoon.

The southern region of Oman, Dhofar, has been studied fairly extensively (3,4,5,6,45), mostly from the viewpoint of its algae but scattered corals grow beneath the algal canopy. Where sea cliffs exist, seasonal wave energy and scouring is intense and corals are all but absent. Even in the most sheltered coves, large coral growths are few. There seems to be no true reef growth, although *Acropora* forms occasional exceptions, and *Porites lutea* develops some enormous solitary growths which support high seasonal breeding concentrations of the spiny lobster *Panulirus homarus*. More extensive coral communities have, however, been recently discovered in deeper water (15 to 25m depth) with live coral cover reaching 30% in places. Reef development does not occur anywhere on the Yemen coast of the Arabian Sea, but a low diversity of corals occurs among macroalgae as described for southern Oman.

Gulf of Aden. On the north coast of the Gulf of Aden, information is sparse. Reef formation is severely limited by the combined effects of unsuitable substrate and upwelling. Significant coral communities are found only to the west of Mukalla at a few sites where igneous rock outcrops and larva flows meet the sea. At these sites, the contrast between the white coralline sand, black igneous rock and turquoise sea can be spectacular.

Bir Ali, over a hundred kilometers west of Mukalla, is the most westerly site in the Gulf of Aden with significant coral cover. With its excellent anchorage, formed by surrounding islands and headlands of igneous rock, Bir Ali was an important trading port in medieval times. Patches of coral are well developed on the sheltered sides of the islands surrounding the main bay, but while live coral cover may be as high as 60% in some places, there is no sign of reef framework. At nearby Belhaf, massive *Porites* colonies have, however, formed a more substantial reef structure a few meters thick on ancient lava flow, and live coral cover is greater than 50%. A further 250 km west, the area is dominated by lava fields which fan out to the sea over a 20 km stretch of coast. Here a rudimentary fringing reef has formed with a classic reef profile. The reef flat extends 100 to 150 m followed by a reef slope which steps down 2 to 5 m across the reef face. Coral cover on the flat is very low at 5%, but reaches 20 to 40% cover on the slope. Though the framework is only a few meters thick it is probably the most extensive reef framework on the southern coast of Yemen.

Nearer Aden, the coast is dominated by fine sandy beaches until the calderas of Aden where the modern port has been built around this natural harbor. Here again, volcanic boulder fields extend into the sea and are colonized by a veneer of massive and encrusting corals. The steep sides of the volcanoes themselves plunge into the Gulf and coral cover may reach 80%. West of Aden, 70 km from the mouth of the Red Sea is the most important area of mixed seagrass and coral habitat anywhere on this coast. It was proposed as a center for farming green turtles, *Chelonia mydas* (28). Here, patches of branching corals are most abundant where tidal flushing generates strong currents.

Coral growth on the Socotran Archipelago was first though to be poor (61), attributable to the upwelling and associated temperature and turbidity extremes in the southwest monsoon. Recent investigations have, however, revealed that hermatypic corals are widespread, although no biogenic reef structures have been recorded. Differences in coral communities between northeast and the western coast of Socotra arise due to the nature of the substrate, the degree of exposure, or localized temperature differences round the island caused by the upwelling system trapping warmer water against the shore in some places and dispersing it others (Box 9.1).

Djibouti on the African coast has few fully developed reefs. It was the site of some notable earlier taxonomic work by Gravier (24) but, unfortunately, little has been done since his studies in the 1910s. In Somalia, a shallow rock shelf fringes much of the Gulf of Aden coast and coral communities dominate the western half (42). Few framework reefs exist, but in places corals are dense and diverse, with a mix of coral and fish species typically found in western Indian Ocean, Red Sea and Arabian Sea reefs. The eastern half of the Gulf of Aden is dominated by algae, and it is likely that most of this coast has few reefs and only scattered corals. The paucity of corals here is probably due to influence of the upwelling water, a condition which continues down the Indian Ocean coast of Somalia for at least 500 km. The dominant algae are large browns, while seagrasses are abundant on soft substrates. There is apparently no further significant coral growth until the southern part of Somalia but few studies have been completed to confirm this assertion (Box 9.1).

Coral and Reef Growth Under Extreme Conditions

Severe temperature, salinity and upwelling conditions mean that numerous areas of exposed, hard substrate are not dominated or even colonized by corals. Instead, soft corals and macroalgae generally dominate. The algae may grow alone or coexist with corals and may even form canopies growing over corals (Fig. 9.8). Reef growth over geologic time is interrupted by episodic coral

Box 9.1. Reefs of the Gulf of Aden and Socotra Archipelago

The Gulf of Aden and the northern Somali coast have traditionally been considered unsuitable for development of coral reefs, due to seasonal upwelling of cold and nutrient-rich waters to the north (Oman) and south (Somalia) of the mouth of the Gulf (13). The first reports of coral reefs in the area were by Gravier in the 1910s (2,3,4,5), followed by unpublished reports of fringing reefs supporting well developed reef fish communities in Djibouti, (1), and sparse algal-dominated reefs in Socotra (11,12).

With the end of political instability in the region, surveys for biological diversity and resource hot spots have been conducted to anticipate economic development and environmental degradation. Three areas have been studied: the Socotra Archipelago at the mouth of the Gulf of Aden (15), the Saad ed Din Islands off Zeila town at the western edge of northern Somaliland (6), and the coast of Djibouti (7). All three locations have well-developed and complex coral reef communities, and it is possible these communities will also exist along the Indian Ocean coast of Somalia, and along the Yemen coast, in areas sheltered from the direct effects of the cold upwelling.

Two basic benthic communities were recorded in these studies: 1) coral-dominated communities forming carbonate-accreting reef structures in some areas, and 2) algal-dominated communities with a predominance of fleshy algae at Socotra, (8,9) and coralline algae at the Sept Freres Islands in Djibouti (7). Segregation of these two communities was very marked between northern and southern sites at Socotra (figure), and in a similar cluster analysis between the Sept Freres islands compared to coastal reefs of Djibouti (7). These differences are due to exposure to cold upwelling waters on the southern coast of Socotra, and at the Sept Freres Islands. Scheer (11,12) described similar low coral and high algal cover benthic communities on the south coast of Abd-al-Kuri.

The five main groupings in the dendrogram illustrate the types of reef communities found in the region. These are: 1) a highly distinctive shallow water *Acropora* community, consisting of large arborescent *Acropora*, very low soft coral cover, few other macro-invertebrates and no macroalgae, 2) sites with >30% soft coral cover and moderate hard coral cover of between 16% and 22%, 3) sites with high cover of hard corals, principally tabulate *Acropora*, and low cover of soft corals, 4) low coral cover sites, frequently dominated by non-scleractinian macroinvertebrates, an algal mat or turf, and small macroalgae, and 5) extremely low coral cover sites of <1%, frequently with extensive areas of encrusted rock and macroalgae

The northern coast of Socotra, the continental coast of Djibouti and the Saad ed Din islands .harbor extensive hard and soft coral communities that resemble those of southern Oman (9). Common Indo-Pacific coral species predominated with the addition in the Gulf of Aden of species (*Acropora hemprichii, Porites nodifera*) and colony morphologies (for example *Stylophora pistillata, Echinopora* cf. *fructiculosa*) characteristic of the Red Sea (14). Provisional totals, at different levels of sampling, of 99 species of corals in 43 genera were recorded at Saad ed Din (6), 170 species in 51 genera in Djibouti (7), and 33 genera in Socotra (9).

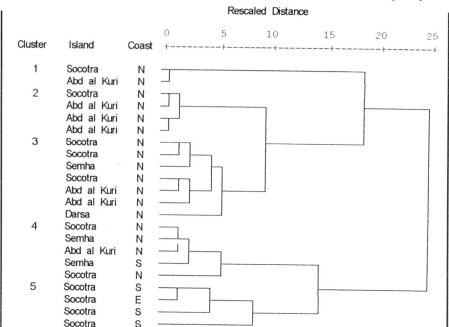

Figure. Dendrogram based on cluster analysis of 15 life-form categories at Socotra Archipelago sites (March 1996). This analysis demonstrates divergence between sublittoral communities of northern (N) and southern (S) coasts. The single eastern site (E) is at the highly exposed extreme eastern end of Socotra.

The coral reefs in the area support abundant and diverse communities of coral reef fish. The fish community of Socotra is basically south Arabian, but with a strong east African influence which gives rise to previously unrecorded sympatry between a number of Arabian endemic species and their Indian Ocean sister species (9). There were few Red Sea species recorded at Socotra (10). The fish communities at Saad ed Din and Djibouti included species from the Indian Ocean, Red Sea and Arabian Sea. One hundred and thirty two species of reef-associated fish were found in 3.5 hours of sampling at Saad ed Din, and 80 species from a restricted set of 10 families in Djibouti. The number of planktivorous fish (*Chromis*, triggerfish and pelagics) and pelagic predators on exposed reefs was very high (6,7), suggesting high water-column productivity from the nutrient rich waters upwelling at the mouth of the Gulf of Aden. In addition, the size of the top predators and scavengers (Serranidae - groupers, and Lethrinidae - emperors) at Saad ed Din was exceptional, some reaching up to 1 m in length and probably close to or over 100 kg in weight (6).

Exploitation of reef resources throughout Somalia and the Socotra Archipelago is minimal, with government programs to increase fishing effort in Djibouti. As a whole, therefore, shallow marine communities are in exceptionally good condition. This situation is likely to change rapidly with development and political stability, with increasing demand for fish and potentially also for coral-based construction materials on the north coast of

Socotra. This surge in exploitation is already evident in the shark-fishing industry presently dominated by non-Somalis, highlighting the need for timely research and protection of the unique reef communities of this region.

J. Kemp & D.O. Obura

References

1. Barratt L, Medley, P. 1990. Managing multi-species ornamental reef fisheries. *Progress in Underwater Science* 15: 55-72
2. Gravier, C. 1910a. Sur les recifs coralliens de la Baie de Tadjourah et leurs Madreporaires: Gulf of Aden. *Compte Rendu Hebdomadaire des Seances de L'Academie des Sciences, Paris* 151: 650-652
3. Gravier, C. 1910b. Sur quelques formes nouvelles de Madreporaires de la Baie de Tadjourah: Gulf of Aden. *Bulletin du Museum d'Histoire Naturelle* 16: 273-276
4. Gravier, C. 1910c. Sur quelques particularites biologique des recifs madreporiques de la Baie de Tadjourah: Gulf of Adean. *Compte-rendu de L'Association Francais pour l'Avancement des Sciences, Paris.* 39: 167-169
5. Gravier, C. 1911. Les recifs de coraux et les madreporaires de la Baie de Tadjourah: Gulf of Aden. *Annales de L'Institute Oceanographique, Paris* 2: 99
6. IUCN. 1997. *Preliminary Ecological Assessment of the Saardin Islands, Awdal Region.* Nairobi: IUCN
7. IUCN. 1999. *Marine and Coastal Assessment, Djibouti.* Nairobi: IUCN
8. Kemp, J.M. 1997. Extensive coral communities of the Socotra Archipelago, Gulf of Aden. *Coral Reefs* (Reef Sites) 16: 214
9   Kemp, J.M. 1998. The Occurrence of *Nizamuddinia zanardinii* (Schiffner) P.C.Silva (Phaeophyta: Fucales) at the Socotra Archipelago. *Botanica Marina* 41: 345-348
10. Kemp, J.M. in press. Zoogeography of the coral reef fishes of the Socotra Archipelago. *Journal of Biogeography*
11. Scheer, G. 1964. Korallen von Abd-el-Kuri. *Zoologische Jarhbucher, Abteilung fur Systematik, Okologie und Geographie der Tiere* 91:451-456
12. Scheer, G. 1971. Coral reefs and coral genera in the Red Sea and Indian Ocean. *Symposium of the Zoological Society of London* 28: 329-367
13. Sheppard, C., A. Price, Roberts, C. 1992. *Marine Ecology of the Arabian Region: Patterns and Processes in Extreme Tropical Environments.* Academic Press, London
14. Sheppard, C., Sheppard, A. 1991. *Corals and Coral Communities of Arabia.* Fauna of Saudi Arabia, 12
15. United Nations Development Programme/Global Environment Facility Report. 1996. *Mission Report (Marine Team) for the Conservation and Sustainable Use of the Biodiversity of Socotra.* 19th February - 20th March 1996. MacAlister Elliott and Partners Ltd, Lymington, UK

Table 9.1. Coral species which survive high salinity (lasting 1-3 months at least in the Gulf of Salwah and Bahrain region. (Data from 63).

Salinity (parts per thousand)	46	48	50	>50
Cyphastrea serailia	------------>			
Porites compressa	------------>----?--->			
Platygyra daedalea	-------------------------->			
Favia pallida	-------------------------->			
Favites chinensis	-------------------------->		*Sargassum* only	
Leptastrea purpurea	-------------------------->			
Porites nodifera	---------------------------------->			
Cyphastrea microphthalma ------------------------------------>				
Siderastrea savignyana	-------------------------------------->			

mortality. In Oman this appears to be confined to more exposed locations, but elsewhere restrictions on coral and reef development may occur from many different combinations of temperature, exposure and salinity extremes.

Coral and Reef Growth under Extreme Conditions

Work done mainly in this Arabian region has shown that as environmental conditions become more severe, the processes of coral growth and reef growth become uncoupled (66). The processes required for coral reef accretion fail well before corals cease to exist along environmental gradients of salinity, temperature or nutrients (see Chapter 1), after which algae increase and then dominate.

The decline of coral abundance along these gradients is often not accompanied by a fall in coral diversity. A considerable number of corals are known to withstand salinities between open ocean (33 ppt) and 42 ppt (66). Only above 45 ppt and up to 50 ppt in the Arabian Gulf is there then a significant negative association between salinity with species number. Some corals survive as much as 50 ppt (Table 9.1) but in this higher range, least squares regression suggests a drop of 1.1 coral species for each 1 ppt increase in salinity (63). Although this study only considered salinity, it was recognized that a combination of salinity and temperature was probably most important in influencing coral survival. Low temperatures and their duration were recognized as being important (14). Water temperature fluctuations for several Arabian sites are greater than most tropical areas (Table 9.2). Where the duration of cold weather affects corals, mortality is most pronounced near the surface. Water depth provides some protection from cold-air chilling but not for cold upwelling water. A decline in coral diversity can be matched with temperature fluctuations (Table 9.3), and some of the species that disappear relatively early are those commonly viewed as important reef builders.

Upwelling water is cool, but rarely falls below about 17°C. In the past, cold upwelling waters was frequently cited as lethal to corals, as indeed they are, for example, in many oceanic areas. In the Arabian region, however, many species have adapted to these cool temperatures, so again, a combination of factors, including range of temperature fluctuation, are more important than the absolute low values. Another important factor is increased nutrients, which both inhibit corals directly and give a competitive advantage to algae. High nutrients

Table 9.2. Temperature extremes recorded in reef areas in embayments in the Arabian region (66) and numbers of coral species.

Location	Latitude	Min (°C)	Max (°C)	Range	Coral diversity
Saudi Gulf	27°N	11.4	36.2	24.8	60
Qatar Gulf	24°N	14.1	36.0	21.9	40-60
Abu Dhabi Gulf	25°N	16.0	36.0	20.0	40-60
Kuwait	29°N	13.2	31.5	18.3	40
Gulf of Suez	29.5°N	17.5	30.0	12.5	100
Gulf of Aqaba	29°N	20.0	28.0	8.0	150+

Table 9.3. Coral species which survive temperature extremes of the range indicated. Data from (14,63,68).

Temperature fluctuation (oC)	8-15	15-20	20-28	30
Acropora horrida	------------------>			
Stylophora pistillata	------------------------------------>			
Porites nodifera	-->		*Sargassum* only	
Cyphastrea microphthalma	--->			
Siderastrea savignyana	--->			
Porites compressa	--->			
Platygyra daedalea	--->			
Porites lutea	--->			
Psammocora contigua	--->			
Pavona varians	--->			
Coscinaraea monile	--->			
Leptastrea purpure	--->			
Favia pallida	--->			
Favia speciosa	--->			
Favia favus	--->			
Favites pentagona	--->			
Turbinaria crater	--->			

is a factor consistently associated with poor coral abundance and failing reef construction (see Table 1.5 in Chapter 1). Widespread bleaching during the summer months of 1990 was reported in Musandam and in the Muscat Area (56), possibly as a response to greater than usual temperatures and so even high temperatures may, at times, be a cause for poor coral reef development in this region.

In the Arabian Seas a combination of moderately low temperatures (about 16 to 20°C), raised salinities (about 38 to 42 ppt or more) and ambient nutrient levels (about 0.1 to 1 mg C/m²) allows corals to survive but reduces the chances for proper reef development. Curiously, coral communities on non-accreting substrata are indistinguishable from those on accreting reefs. At the extreme end of this range algae, which are present throughout the range, assume increasing dominance. With increasing salinity in the Arabian Gulf, coral diversity eventually collapses, but under increasing upwelling in the Arabian Sea, diversity is maintained even though corals become sparse and reefs do not develop. In the latter case, the gradation may continue through a condition of scattered colonies co-existing among green algae or under a canopy of brown algae, to an ecological community where only algae exist (Fig 9.8).

Figure 9.8. Mixed assemblage of macroalgae and corals in the Arabian Sea. Most of the algae are of the *Sargassum* family. This scene is unusual in that it also shows *Ecklonia*. The corals grow on mixed substrate and are not accreting reefs. (Photo L. Barratt).

Biological Factors Affecting Community Structure

In addition to physical factors, biological factors such as *Acanthaster planci* and coral diseases determine the distribution and diversity of Arabian Sea and Gulf of Oman coral communities (22,23). *Acanthaster planci* favors acroporid (*Acropora* and *Montipora*) over *Porites* species and this prey preference influences the species composition of coral assemblages. In the past 20 years, *A. planci* outbreaks have been reported in northern Oman which have devastated stands of *Acropora* but left *Porites* reefs untouched. An outbreak of Crown-of-Thorns starfish during the 1980s reduced the number of sites supporting rich *Acropora* communities, but *Acropora clathrata* which escaped starfish predation have now attained large sizes and dominate several sites. While major outbreaks have marked effects, low level *A. planci* infestations following disturbances, such as a storm, may also be important. *A. planci* may continue to selectively prey on recruiting corals and low level predation can reduce recovery rates as was found for the reefs in northern Sharkiyah following a severe storm in 1991.

The incidence of coral disease in Arabian waters may reflect the degree of physiological stress resulting from harsh oceanographic conditions. A new disease, Yellow-Band Disease, has recently been reported for the southern Arabian Gulf, alongside the more common Black Band and White Band diseases (Box 9.2). An outbreak of disease in the Gulf of Oman affected 20% of

Box 9.2. Coral Diseases in the Western Indian Ocean

Anthropogenic factors such as coastal development, agricultural runoff and other forms of pollution, reef mining, dynamite fishing, careless anchoring and careless divers, are well known human influences associated with coral reefs. More insidious and much less well known is the destruction of living corals by disease. Coral diseases were first described in the Caribbean in the early 1970s (1), and it is from this region that coral diseases have been most widely documented. In the middle 1980s, diseases were also found in the Indo-Pacific (3). Diseases specific to the western Indian Ocean were discovered shortly thereafter (see 5,6,8,11).

Disease has been rigorously defined as "any impairment (interruption, cessation, proliferation, or other disorder) of vital body functions, systems or organs usually characterized either by 1) an identifiable group of signs (observed anomalies indicative of disease), and/or 2) a recognized etiologic or causal agent, and/or 3) consistent structural alterations (such as developmental disorders, changes in cellular composition or morphology, and tumors)" (13).

Best known of the coral diseases are the "Band Diseases" (2). Band diseases kill living coral tissue by forming an active band on or around the coral, eventually decaying and then sloughing off, leaving only the denuded coral skeleton. Band Diseases have a characteristic color which is used to identify or distinguish them. Four band diseases are currently recognized - Black, White, Red, and Yellow Band Disease.

The Band Diseases

Black Band Disease (BBD) has received the most attention and was the first coral disease where a pathogen was identified. Studies indicate that the primary pathogen is the cyanophyte *Phormidium corallyticum* (16). BBD is contagious as it is possible to transplant BBD to other, previously uninfected colonies using scrapings of infected colonies (4). The distribution of BBD infected colonies are, however, not always clumped, so although contagious, BBD is not highly infectious (9). While BBD is prevalent in the western Atlantic and present in the Indo-Pacific region, it is apparently rare in the western Indian Ocean. It has been reported from the Red Sea (5), Mauritius (6), and from the southern (11) and northern parts of the Arabian Gulf (Fadlalla, Y. personal communication).

White Band Disease (WBD) was the second of the band diseases to be described and first referred to as "White Death" or "Plague". Unlike BBD, little is known about WBD etiology and a pathogen has yet to be ascribed to this disease (18). This may be due, in part, to the fact that WBD can be confused with two other syndromes of corals that also exhibit whitening - coral bleaching and Shut Down Reaction (SDR, see 7). Corals infected with WBD are recognized as having a characteristic bright white band or patches of freshly denuded white skeleton, with a sharp and well-defined border between healthy tissue and the newly exposed skeleton. Coral bleaching differs in that the coral skeleton is still covered by tissue - although the coral appears white, it is because the coral tissue is translucent due to the loss of zooxanthellae.

Making the distinction between WBD and SDR is slightly more difficult. While denuded skeleton is also evidence for SDR, SDR attacks very fast and tissue loss is usually over the entire individual, unlike WBD which is patchy. WBD is not contagious (4) but is considered common and widespread. In the western Indian Ocean, WBD was first reported from the Red Sea (5) and is still prevalent at places along the central Saudi coast (J.M. Kemp, personal communication). WBD has also been reported from Mauritius (6), Gulf of Oman (8) and from the southern (11) and northern parts of the Arabian Gulf (Y. Fadlallah, personal communication).

Red Band Disease (RBD) is a newly discovered coral disease in which the identity of the primary pathogen is unclear. The term RBD was first used to describe a brick-red cyanobacterial infection on scleractinian corals in the Bahamas (15). There is, however, prior record of a brown variant of what was thought to be a BBD infection of gorgonians (17). The BBD pathogen, *P. corallyticum* was, however, not present in the gorgonian infection; instead, two species of *Schizothrix* were the dominant cyanobacteria. The Bahama samples yielded two species of yet another cyanobacteria, *Oscillatoria*. So it is presently unknown if there is now more than one disease with a reddish coloration. It is also unknown if RBD is contagious. To date, there have been no reports of RBD from the western Indian Ocean.

Yellow Band Disease (YBD) is a very recently reported disease (11), and as yet, the pathogen is unknown. Instead of exposing white coral skeleton, as usually the case in a band disease, skeleton denuded by YBD retains the characteristic yellow coloration, occasionally turning greenish. YBD is contagious - transplanting a YBD infected piece of coral to a non-infected colony results in the transmission of YBD to the healthy colony (Korrubel, J., Riegl, B. unpublished observations). Another "yellow syndrome" - termed Yellow-blotch Disease - was recently reported from the Lower Florida Keys, and has subsequently been reported from other sites in the Caribbean (see 18). From the descriptions released, it appears doubtful that YBD and Yellow-blotch are the same condition. To date, there has been only a single report of YBD worldwide - from the southern Arabian Gulf (11). Aside from Florida and Caribbean (18), there have been no other reports of Yellow-blotch.

Quantifying Coral Disease

Techniques for obtaining and analyzing data on coral reef diseases are similar to other coral-reef methods (see 10). Probably the fastest method is the Manta Tow, in which an observer is surface-towed behind a small boat. A subsequent swim survey of the area (usually using SCUBA) can then be used to make observations on several variables simultaneously - such as the percentage cover of diseased, live, and dead coral - over a fairly wide area. Combined observations from a number of tows and swims may be used to obtain quite accurate estimates of spatial distribution of the infestation. In addition, underwater videography is fast becoming a method favored in the study of corals allowing, for example, the collection of a permanent visual record of diseases in a particular area. More quantitative methods are generally intensive and very time consuming, but may be used to investigate finer scales. For example, line

Photo. Examples of yellow band diseases.

transect methods are the most frequently used and can include estimates of the cover or frequency of disease in corals.

Cause and Consequences of Diseases

Current thinking proposes that the spread of coral disease is facilitated by environmental and anthropogenic stress. Tissue damage by coral-eating fishes (such as chaetodonts, scarids and pomacentrids), snails (such as *Coralliophila* or *Drupella*), polychaete worms (such as *Hermodice*), and starfish (*Acanthaster planci*) are considered vectors of infection. In addition, animals that live in a parasitic or commensal relationship with corals (such as the coral crabs, family Xanthidae) may also injure coral tissues. Such tissue damage may degenerate to form open wounds, which are a potential site for pathogenic invasion (see 12). Anthropogenic factors, pollution in particular but perhaps global warming as well, may influence the onset and development of coral diseases (14). While it appears that infection by coral disease is patchy (where infection is found, the level of infection is usually low, only affecting a small percentage of the total coral population), it is thought that under certain conditions, and in combination with stressful factors, coral disease(s) could reach epidemic proportions.

Chronic infestations of disease would substantially increase bare substratum. The denuded coral skeleton creates free space for colonization by other marine organisms. Overgrowth by algae may inhibit coral tissue regrowth, and settlement by bioerosive organisms (such as sponges) severely weakens the remaining coral skeletons, making them greatly susceptible to breakage and ultimately leading to a collapse of the reef's topography. Furthermore, the loss of live coral tissue results in a reduction in the potential for producing new recruits, and a reduction in the availability of food for corallivorous fish. Coral diseases are therefore considered to be an important factor in modifying the structure and function of entire coral reef communities over time.

Coral diseases are poorly known despite some 25 years of research. Further research is needed to 1) identify the pathogens and mechanisms of spread, 2) quantify the distribution and abundance of coral diseases, 3) assess environmental and biotic conditions which may result in the onset of diseases, and perhaps most importantly, 4) identify and evaluate methods to prevent and treat coral diseases. A number of new coral diseases have recently made their appearance, and in some cases, pathogens have already been implicated. Thorough description and quantifying their occurrence and association with stress factors remains a high priority.

J.L. Korrubel

References

1. Antonius A. 1973. New observations on coral destruction in reefs. *Tenth Meeting of the Association of Island Marine Laboratories of the Caribbean*: 3 (Abstract)
2. Antonius A. 1981. The 'band' diseases in coral reefs. *Proceedings of the 4th International Coral Reef Symposium* Miami 2: 7-14
3. Antonius A. 1985. Coral diseases in the Indo-Pacific: a first record. PSZNI: *Marine Ecology* 6: 197-218
4. Antonius A. 1985. Black band disease infection experiments on hexacorals and octocorals. *Proceedings of the 5th International Coral Reef Congress* 6: 155-60
5. Antonius A. 1988. Distribution and dynamics of coral diseases in the eastern Red Sea. *Proceedings of the 6th International Coral Reef Symposium* 2: 293-98
6. Antonius A. 1993. Coral reef health in Mauritius. *Proceedings of the 1st European Regional Meeting of the ISRS* 2. (Abstract)
7. Antonius A. 1995. Pathologic syndromes on reef corals: a review. In *Coral Reefs in the Past, Present and Future*, ed. Lathuillere, B., Geister, J., pp. 161-169. Publications du Service Geologique du Luxembourg
8. Coles S.L. 1994. Extensive coral disease outbreak at Fahl Island, Gulf of Oman, Indian Ocean. *Coral Reefs* 13: 242
9. Edmunds F.J. 1991. Extent and effect of black-band disease on a Caribbean reef. *Coral Reefs* 10: 161-65
10. English S., Wilkinson C., Baker V. 1997. *Survey Manual for Tropical Marine Resources*. 2nd Edition. Townsville: Australian Institute for Marine Science
11. Korrubel, J.L., Riegl B. 1997. A new coral disease from the southern Arabian Gulf. *Coral Reefs* 17: 22
12. Peters E.C. 1984. A survey of cellular reactions to environmental stress and disease in Caribbean scleractinian corals. *Helgolander Meeresuntersuchungen* 37: 113-37
13. Peters E.C. 1997. Diseases of coral reef organisms. In *Life and Death of Coral Reefs*, ed. Birkeland, C. pp. 114-139. New York: Chapman and Hall
14. Peters E.C., Gassman N.J., Firman J.C., Richmond R.H., Power E.A. 1997. Ecotoxicology of tropical marine ecosystems. *Environmental Toxicology and Chemistry* 16: 12-40

15. Richardson L.L. 1993. Red Band Disease: a new cyanobacterial infestation of corals. *American Acadamy of Underwater Scientists 10th Annual Scientific Diving Symposium*: 153-60
16. Rutzler K., Santavy D.L. 1983. The Black Band Disease of Atlantic Reef Corals. I. Description of the cyanophyte pathogen. PSZNI: *Marine Ecology* 4: 301-19
17. Rutzler K, Santavy DL, Antonius A. 1983. The Black Band Disease of Atlantic Reef Corals. III. Distribution, ecology, and development. PSZNI: *Marine Ecology* 4: 329-58
18. Santavy D.L., Peters E.C. 1997. Microbial pests: coral disease in the western Atlantic. *Proceedings of the 8th International Coral Reef Symposium* Panama 1: 607-12

sites in 1996 (11), *Platygyra* being the most commonly infected genus. Also a white patch disease, where necrotic coral tissue sloughs rapidly off colonies of *Platygyra* exposing the white skeleton beneath, is prevalent in parts of Musandam, and appears to be a significant cause of mortality for the genus. No invasion of coral tissue by pathogens is visible *in situ*, and tissue specimens were not collected for further study.

Coral bleaching also affects many communities throughout Oman. Although recorded seawater temperatures in the Muscat area reach higher levels (39°C) than those in other parts of Oman and cause extensive bleaching, they are not sustained for long and the corals largely recover. Coral bleaching can be severe to a depth of 3 m in the fjord-like bays of Musandam, where it can cause widespread mortality of the affected corals (56).

Bioerosion of damaged or dead corals has a serious effect on development of reef framework. The principal agents of bioerosion include boring algae, sponges, the mussel *Lithophaga*, and the echinoids *Diadema setosum*, *Echinothrix diadema*, and *Echinometra mathaei*. *Diadema* forms the densest accumulations, massing on talus areas around the bases of live coral colonies.

The Simplest Reefs

Some of the simplest true reefs of all occur in this region. Bays protected from extremes of upwelling contain numerous aggregations of enormous coral colonies, mainly *Porites*. Adjacent colonies tend to fuse together forming a structure whose cross-sectional profile is identical to that of a small reef, referred to as "incipient reefs" (22). No matrix of bound sediment need be involved for their formation. Large aggregations of *Pocillopora* form patch reefs, and both these and the large *Montipora* reefs have been mentioned (Box 9.3). Even though carbonate sediments are trapped in *Pocillopora* reefs they may not be durable because secondary calcification and binding in the reef fabric, largely by algae and sponges, is limited.

Rudimentary fringing reefs are generally dominated by tabular and ramose *Acropora* species or by *Porites*. Talus banks exist, formed from the fragments of dead branching corals. Colonization of these banks by corals is, however, variable. Expanses of alcyonarians covering rock or dead coral colonies are common in the Arabian region.

Sparse coral communities and weak or non-existent reefs are not restricted to one clearly defined locality but occur throughout the region, sometimes over hundreds of kilometers of coast. Coral diversity is low compared to other Indian Ocean locations but, monospecific reefs aside, total coral diversity on even the most simple reefs exceeds 100 or 150 species and, therefore, remains higher than that found in many entire Pacific Archipelagoes and indeed higher than the whole of the Caribbean.

In the Arabian region there is relatively little hard substrate deeper than 12 to 18 m and, therefore, coral communities tend to be shallow. In all areas, the percentage cover of live corals drops abruptly below 10 m, even where it exceeds 75% cover in shallow water. Deeper than this, the region seems particularly rich in non-zooxanthellate corals (56). The maximum depth of zooxanthellate corals is determined by the general progression from rock to soft substrate and by the common presence of a thermocline at 10 to 15 m (but occasionally less) below which the water is both turbid and cold (56). Underwater visibility is unpredictable in much of the region, changes daily, and generally is less than 10 to 12 m (66). Interestingly, one of Omans' most striking endemic, zooxanthellate corals, *Acanthastrea maxima*, appears to favor the conditions found at depths greater than 10 m and is most common on rock surfaces with less than 10% live coral cover (67).

Slightly more complex reefs in the central part of the Arabian Gulf show several different zones or communities, even where the total number of coral species was less than 30 (63). Recorded salinity was high, often 43 to 45 ppt. Despite this, coral cover was high, and did not depend on, or even correlate with, coral diversity. Staghorn *Acropora* dominate in the least saline and least turbid conditions, while a deeper community dominated by *Porites compressa* occurred below this in lower salinity sites, while *Porites nodifera* dominated where salinities reached 43 to 45 ppt. In higher salinities still, diversity and coral cover fell drastically, and then disappeared. This pattern occurred on both actively accreting and sometimes large reefs, as well as on some limestone domes which do not reach the surface and which probably are not accreting.

Human Influences

Dredging and Landfill

Coastal land fill (euphemistically called "reclamation" by engineers) and dredging cause substantial effects on several reef systems in the Arabian Gulf (37). Coasts which include intertidal flats, mangroves, shallow embayments and patch reefs are favored areas for residential and industrial construction and destruction activities ("development" by those same engineers), despite the large quantity of empty land slightly further from the sea. Approximately 40% of the Saudi Arabian Gulf coast is now artificial (65), and a similar situation occurs in other Gulf states (38). Throughout this region, construction of ports and other facilities without due care has disrupted sediment flow and land-sea equilibrium, resulting in severe erosion along long stretches of coast. Once underway, this erosion can only be prevented from causing further loss of property by the use of "hard engineering", or the construction of concrete

Box 9.3. Monospecific Reef Formations

In several parts of the world, large monospecific stands of corals occur. They are nowhere more striking than in parts of the Arabian Sea. Pure stands of *Pocillopora damicornis* up to several hundred meters across are common, and examples of monospecific communities can be found of *Pavona cactus*, *Goniopora djiboutiensis*, *Acropora clathrata*, *Porites lutea*, *Stylophora pistillata*, *Lobophyllia* sp., and *Galaxea fasicularis*.

The most extensive monospecific stands are formed of *Montipora foliosa* south of Barr al Hikman in Oman, where tens of square kilometers are composed of this species alone. At its most shoreward extreme, the reef here has a narrow zone dominated by faviids, principally *Platygyra daedalea*, which runs parallel to shore. Further offshore, the substrate becomes increasingly dominated by *Montipora foliosa* whose colonies become larger in size until 100% of the seabed is exclusively composed of green whorls of this species 2 to 3 m in diameter in less than 5 m of water. This extends several kilometers out to sea in two lobes, each with an area of over 15 square kilometers, the largest monospecific stand of coral yet reported.

The restriction of such communities to one species only is not fully understood, though in some cases a high level of interspecific aggression has been suggested (3,4). In the case of *Pocillopora damicornis*, branches of adjacent colonies may interlock and fuse (2) to form a coherent structure capable of resisting greater wave energy than could individual colonies alone. In other cases, a combination of broadcast spawning and brooding larvae (5) causes a positive feedback which enables this species to reduce susceptibility to storm damage and limit larval dispersal in an environment characterized by mobile sediments. The Crown-of-Thorns Starfish is known to influence coral community structure in Arabian Seas (1), and may be a factor enabling *Acropora clathrata*, a non-preferred prey species, to dominate to the exclusion of other corals in sheltered areas.

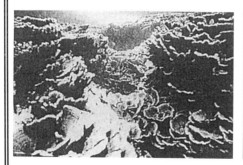

Photos. Single species reefs: *Montipora foliosa* (left), *Pocillopora damicornis* (right)

Simon Wilson

References

1. Glynn, P.W. 1992. Monsoonal upwelling and episodic *Acanthaster* predation as probable controls for coral reef distribution and community structure in Oman, Indian Ocean. *Atoll Research Bulletin* 379:1- 66
2. Hidaka, M., Yurugi, K., Sunagawa, S., Kinzie, R.A. III. 1997. Contact reactions between young colonies of the coral *Pocillopora damicornis*. *Coral Reefs* 16:13-20
3. Sheppard, C.R.C. 1979. Interspecific aggression between reef corals with reference to their distribution. *Marine Ecology Progress Series* 1:237-247
4. Sheppard, C.R.C. 1981. Roles of interspecific and intraspecific competition in coral zonation. *Progress in Underwater Science* 6:57-60
5. Ward, S. 1992. Evidence for broadcast spawning as well as brooding in the scleractinian coral <u>Pocillopora damicornis</u>. <u>Marine Biology</u> 112:641-646

barriers. These barriers, temporarily and at great cost, achieve a maintenance of the required disequilibrium between the forces of sea and land.

Land fill usually increases sedimentation which may directly smother habitat or limit photosynthesis of coral reefs and other communities (30,31). Large developments in Saudi Arabia dredged an estimated 47 km² of coastal habitats, removing more than 200 million m³ of sediments adjacent to the development site (30). In Bahrain, 15 to 20 km² of shallow coastal waters and habitats have been dredged during recent decades (37). The ecological effects of dredging are similar to those described above for coastal landfill, and include both direct habit loss and various secondary effects such as smothering by sediment and loss of illumination (30,31,37,38). In parts of the Gulf, sedimentation from dredging has created new sandy bottom areas which support the feeding of some wading birds (30), but generally, ecological effects are undoubtedly more adverse than beneficial, especially to coral reefs.

In Oman, the recent increase of major industrial development has been and will continue to be concentrated in the four main coastal cities of Sohar, Muscat, Sur and Salalah. Petrochemical installations, fertilizer plants, an aluminum smelter, desalination plants, ports, harbors, and large hotels are among the planned infrastructure which require offshore dredging, some of which will inevitably impact coral reefs whether or not mitigation measures are planned or undertaken. The principal problem is smothering by fine sediments during construction, later compounded by associated discharges of cooling water and concentrated brine from desalination processes.

Oil Pollution

This region is the world's largest oil production area (18) and most oil produced is exported by sea. The Arabian seas are therefore among the busiest tanker routes with, for example, 20 000 to 35 000 individual tanker passages annually through the Strait of Hormuz (37).

For these reasons, reports of widespread pollution in the Arabian Gulf and Arabian Sea Gulf region, are not surprising. Apart from accidents, well blow-outs and the notorious deliberate Gulf oil spill of 1991, tanker and ship traffic results in the deliberate discharge of dirty ballast and bilge water, estimates of which range from 400 000 to 750 000 tons in 1986 in the Gulf (37). The Gulf of Aden is one area deliberately selected for discharge because detection in this area is unlikely. Along the coast of North Yemen, oil was recorded at 58% of 131 coastal sites (7), and along the southern Yemen coast it was recorded at 57% of 91 coastal sites. Numerous reports also exist documenting the tar balls and oil fouling on shores throughout the region. One survey of the western Arabian Gulf encountered tar balls at 77% of visited sites (50) and tar concentrations in some localities have been estimated at 1 to 10 kg per linear meter of the Gulf shoreline (15), or up to 100 times greater than other regions of the world. Beach tar concentrations in the Muscat area from 1993 to 1995 are among the highest in the world, greater than those reported anywhere on the Oman coast in the past decade (13).

Ecological effects of oil on reefs may not be as great as they are on habitats such as seagrasses, mangroves and rocky intertidal shores. Spawning and nursery areas undoubtedly occur in many shallow coastal areas, especially for penaeid shrimp such as *Penaeus semisulcatus* (8,48). It is often these shallow coastal waters that are exposed to oil pollution and other coastal pressures. On the coast of Oman oil has threatened breeding seabirds on the Al Halaniyat islands and contaminated recreational beaches (56).

Effects of Fishing

Human influences attributable to fishing were found at 69% of the 85 sites surveyed, the most severe impacts being on Omani reefs (1). Of a total of 87 gillnets or fragments of gillnets found on reefs, over 20% had been lost less than one year previously. This reflects an increase in artisanal fishing activity stimulated by fishing gear subsidies.

Fisheries activities, including the effects of gill nets, ropes, anchors, fishing line, fish traps and litter, was the most commonly recorded cause of damage by humans, and the one with the most severe effects. Damage to coral colonies is caused as fishing gear strikes and drags across the substrate, smothering and breaking corals. Damage is mostly caused by discarded gear, which may remain on a reef for decades, causing acute and chronic degradation. Fishing gear is discarded by fisherfolk who are unable to retrieve ropes, and it subsequently becomes entangled on the seabed. Nets, in particular, become entangled on coral reefs after being lost in storms or heavy seas. Other fishing gear, judged by fishers to be beyond repair, is simply dumped, where some of it is carried by currents and wave action onto coral reefs. Gillnets remain effective even when dumped, lost or abandoned. Nets abandoned for six years have been observed with freshly caught fish. Such "ghost fishing" is damaging to fish but also lobster which become entangled while scavenging on fish carcasses caught in the nets.

Damage to coral reefs by abandoned gill nets varies from tissue loss affecting a few coral colonies to mortality of entire reefs. Attempts by fishers to retrieve entangled nets by force often causes significant damage, tearing up and breaking coral colonies. Nets lying passively provide substrate for algae, which subsequently reduces the light available to underlying corals, and reduces water exchange. Algae then begin to colonize and overgrow adjacent coral colonies.

The action of waves, currents and tidal ebb and flow moves nets, resulting in tissue loss through abrasion and breakage. Natural stresses, such as pathogens and boring organisms, are more likely to invade damaged reefs (Box 9.2).

Of the 239 coral communities described for Musandam, Muscat and Dhofar, at least 162 (68%) were damaged by fishery activities, litter and *A. planci* predation (56). Musandam has the highest incidence of damage, followed by the Muscat area with 48 sites. Patches of *P. damicornis* and *Acropora* spp. were found to be particularly vulnerable to damage from abandoned fishing nets, with up to 80% of *Pocillopora* reefs destroyed in this way.

Conservation

Arabian Gulf Conservation. The most notable conservation effort in the Gulf has involved the Jubail Marine Wildlife Sanctuary which covers about 2500 km^2 of shore and sea, including some islands (35). This project arose following the deliberate oil spill in the 1991 Gulf War. The original objectives were to assess damage caused by the oil spill on coastal and marine habitats and biota, develop methods for rehabilitation of habitats and species, assess and document biological diversity, and address, on a manageable spatial scale, the major conservation and management needs for improving the environmental quality of the Gulf region. Within this, some 35 research and development projects were conducted over more than three years, producing a very substantial body of over 100 publications, several in a volume which serves as the best entry to this detailed literature (35). Apart from the scientific investigations, a major achievement was the investigation of what methods, if any, were best applied to different habitats for removal of spilled oil.

Gulf of Oman and Arabian Sea. A cross-sectoral, coastal zone management plan in Oman has been particularly successful. The coastal and marine protected areas within this plan were selected from hundreds of sites throughout the Musandam to the Dhofar region (2,56,57,58). Detailed coastal zone management plans were then developed for specific sites and a number of protected areas established (49). Of special interest are the voluntary conservation measures including those taken by fisherfolk in the Bar Hikman region, by which fishing is deliberately carried out offshore and away from the reefs, where fish abundance is lower, leaving the productive inshore sites as "cold storage areas" (56) for use during bad weather.

To date the Daymaniyat Islands Nature Reserve, declared in 1997, is the only coastal protected area in the Gulf of Oman and Arabian Sea which includes coral reefs. It encloses 203 km^2 of sea and seabed and includes the nine islands, rocks, reefs and offshore shoals which lie approximately 20 km off the Al Batinah coast. As well as being an important site for coral reefs, a variety of seabirds and turtle species use the beaches for nesting since they have remained free from mammalian predators. Strict regulations controlling activities in the reserve are in force, preventing over-night camping and interference with wildlife. Mooring buoys have been installed at dive sites, and anchoring is prohibited throughout the reserve as a means of protecting corals, including some good examples of monospecific *Pocillopora* stands.

References

1. Al Jufaili, S., Al-Jabri, M., Al-Baluchi, A., Baldwin, R.M., Wilson, S.C., West, F., Matthews, A.D. in press. Human impacts on coral reefs in the Sultanate of Oman. *Estuarine, Coastal and Shelf Science*
2. Anderlini, V.C. 1985. *Protected Areas System Plan for the Sultanate of Oman*. WWF/IUCN Project 9069. Gland: IUCN, Gland
3. Anonymous. 1988. *Ecological Studies of Southern Oman Kelp Communities*. Summary Report. Kuwait: Regional Organisation for Protection of the Marine Environment
4. Barratt, L., Ormond, R.F.G., Wrathall, T. 1986. Community structure and persistence. In *Ecology and Productivity of the Sublittoral Algae* Ecklonia radiata *and* Sargassopsis zanardini. *Part 1. Ecological Studies of Southern Oman Kelp Communities*. Council for the Conservation of the Environment and Water Resources, Muscat, Oman, and Regional Organisation for the Protection of the Marine Environment, Kuwait, pp. 1.1-1.22.
5. Barratt, L., Ormond, R.F.G., Wrathall, T. 1986. Growth and Production. In *Ecology and Productivity of the Sublittoral Algae* Ecklonia radiata *and* Sargassopsis zanardini. *Part 1. Ecological Studies of Southern Oman Kelp Communities*. Council for the Conservation of the Environment and Water Resources, Muscat, Oman, and Regional Organisation for the Protection of the Marine Environment, Kuwait, pp. 2.1-2.20.
6. Barratt, L. 1984. *Ecological Study of Rocky Shores on the South Coast of Oman*. Report to IUCN and UNEP Regional Seas Programme. Geneva: IUCN
7. Barratt, L., Dawson Shepherd, A.R., Ormond, R.F.G., McDowall, R. 1987. *Yemen Arab Republic Marine Conservation Survey. Vol. I. Distribution of Habitats and Species along the YAR coastline*. IUCN Red Sea and Gulf of Aden Environment Programme/TMRU York, UK.
8. Basson, P.W., Burchard, J.E., Hardy, J.T., Price, A.R.G. 1977. *Biotopes of the Western Arabian Gulf*. Dhahran: Aramco Ltd
9. Burchard, J.E. 1979. *Coral Fauna of the Arabian Gulf*. Dhahran: Aramco, Ltd
10. Clarke, J.E., al-Lumki F., Anderlini, V.C., Sheppard, C.R.C. 1986. *Sultanate of Oman. Proposals for a System of Nature Conservation Areas*. Gland: IUCN
11. Coles, S.L. 1994. Extensive coral disease outbreak at Fahl Island, Gulf of Oman, Indian Ocean. *Coral Reefs* 13:202.
12. Coles, S. L. 1997. Reef corals occurring in a highly fluctuating temperature environment at Fahal Island, Gulf of Oman (Indian Ocean). *Coral Reefs* 16: 269-272
13. Coles, S.L., Al-Riyami, K.A. 1996. Beach tar concentrations on the Muscat coastline, Gulf of Oman, Indian Ocean, 1993-1995. *Marine Pollution Bulletin* 32: 609-614
14. Coles, S.L., Fadlallah, Y.H. 1991. Reef coral survival and mortality at low temperatures in the Arabian Gulf: new species-specific lower temperature limits. *Coral Reefs* 9:231-237
15. Coles, S.L., Gunay, N. 1989. Tar pollution on Saudi Arabian Gulf beaches. *Marine Pollution Bulletin* 18: 214-218

16. Cornelius, P.F.S., Falcon, N.L., South, D., Vita-Finzi, C. 1973. The Musandam expedition 1971-2. Scientific results: Part 1, biological aspects. *Geographical Journal* 139: 400-403

17. Currie, R.I., Fisher, A.E., Hargreaves, P.M. 1973. Arabian Sea upwelling. In *The Biology of the Indian Ocean*. ed. Zeitschel, B. pp 37-52. New York: Springer Verlag

18. Dicks, B. 1987. Pollution. In *The Red Sea*. eds. Edwards, A., Head S.M. pp. 383-404. Oxford: Pergamon Press

19. Dietrich, G. 1973. The unique situation in the environment of the Indian Ocean. In *The Biology of the Indian Ocean*. ed. Zeitschel, B. pp 1-6, New York: Springer Verlag

20. Downing, N. 1985. Coral Reef communities in an extreme environment: The northwest Arabian Gulf. *Proceedings of the 5th International Coral Reef Congress*, Tahiti. 6: 343-348

21. Edwards, F.J. 1987. Climate and oceanography. In *The Red Sea*. eds. Edwards, A.J., Head, S.M. pp 45-69, Oxford: Pergamon Press

22. Glynn, P.W. 1983. *Final Report on the Effects of the Sea Star* Acanthaster *on Omani Coral Reefs, with some Recommendations for Further Study*. Report to Ministry of Agriculture and Fisheries and the Omani-American Joint Commission for Economic and Technical Cooperation, Muscat, Oman

23. Glynn, P.W. 1992. Monsoonal upwelling and episodic *Acanthaster* predation as probable controls for coral reef distribution and community structure in Oman, Indian Ocean. *Atoll Research Bulletin* 379: 1-66

24. Gravier, C. 1911. Les recifs de coraux et les madreporaires de la Baie de Tadjourah: Gulf of Aden. *Annales de l'Institut Oceanographique, Paris* 2: 99

25. Green, F.W. 1983 Comparison of present-day coral communities off the Oman coast with mid-tertiary corals from the Mam reef, near Seeb, Oman. Paper read to International Society for Reef Studies, 8-9 December 1983, Nice

26. Green, F., Keech, R. 1986. *The Coral Seas of Muscat*. London: Middle East Economic Digest

27. Harrington, F.A. 1976. Iran: surveys of the southern Iranian coastline with recommendations for additional marine reserves. In *Promotion of the Establishment of Marine Parks and Reserves in the Northern Indian Ocean Including the Red Sea and Persian Gulf*. Gland: IUCN Publication New Series No 35

28. Hirth, H.F., Kilkoff, L.G., Harper, K.T. 1973. Seagrasses at Khor Umeirah, People's Democratic Republic of Yemen with reference to their role in the diet of the green turtle, *Chelonia mydas*. *Fishery Bulletin* 71: 1093-1097

29. Hunter, J.R. 1986. The physical oceanography of the Arabian Gulf: a review and theoretical interpretation of previous observations. In *First Gulf Conference on Environment and Pollution* eds. Halwagy, R., Clayton, D., Behbehani, M. pp 1-23. Kuwait: Kuwait University Publication

30. IUCN. 1987. *Arabian Gulf. Saudi Arabia: An Assessment of Biotopes and Coastal Zone Management Requirements for the Arabian Gulf*. MEPA Coastal and Marine Management Series, Report No. 5. Gland: IUCN

31. IUCN/UNEP. 1985. *The Management and Conservation of Renewable Marine Resources in the Indian Ocean Region in the Kuwait Action Plan Region.* Nairobi: UNEP Regional Seas Reports and Studies. No. 63.
32. Jones D.A. 1986. *A Field Guide to the Sea shores of Kuwait and the Arabian Gulf.* Poole: University of Kuwait and Blandford Press
33. Klein, R., Loya, Y., Gvirtzman, G., Isdale, P.J., Susic, M. 1990. Seasonal rainfall in the Sinai desert during the late Quaterny inferred from flourescent bands in fossil corals. *Nature*, London, 345: 145-147
34. Krey, J. 1973. Primary production in the Indian Ocean. In *The Biology of the Indian Ocean.* ed. Zeitschel, B. pp. 115-126. New York: Springer Verlag
35. Krupp, F., Abuzinada A.H., Nader, I,A. 1996. *A Marine Wildlife Sanctuary for the Arabian Gulf.* Brussels: European Commission
36. Lardner,R.W., Al-Rabeh, A.H., Gunay, N., Hossain, M., Reynolds, R.M., Lehr W.J. 1993. Computation of the residual flow in the Gulf using the Mt. Mitchell Data and the KFUPM/RI Hydrodynamical Models. *Marine Pollution Bulletin* 27:61-70
37. Linden, 0., Abdulraheem, M.Y., Gerges, M.A., Alam, I., Behari, M.A., Borhan, M.A., Al-Kassab, L.F. 1990. *State of the Marine Environment in the ROPME Sea Area.* Kuwait: UNEP Regional Seas Reports and Studies. No. 112
38. Madany, I.M., Ali, S.M., Akhter, M.S. 1987. The impact of dredging and reclamation in Bahrain. *Journal of Shoreline Management* 3:255-268
39. Marini, L. 1985. Study of a locality in Iran suitable for a marine biological station. In *I Parchi Costieri Mediterranei.* ed. Dhorn, P. pp 685-706. Proceedings of International Conference, Castellabate, June 1973. Regione Campania Assesorato per il Turismo
40. McCain, J.C. 1984. Marine ecology of Saudi Arabia. The nearshore, soft-bottom benthic communities of the Northern Area, Arabian Gulf, Saudi Arabia. *Fauna of Saudi Arabia* 6: 79-97.
41. McCain, J.C., Tarr, A.B., Carpenter, K.E., Coles, S.L. 1984 Marine Ecology of Saudi Arabia. A Survey of Coral Reefs and Reef fishes in the Northern Area, Arabian Gulf, Saudi Arabia. *Fauna of Saudi Arabia* 6: 102-120.
42. McClanahan, T.R., Obura, D. 1997. *Preliminary Ecological Assessment of the Saad ed Din, Awdal Region.* Somali Natural Resources Management Programme. Nairobi: IUCN Eastern Africa Programme
43. Murty, T.S.,. El Sabh, M.I. 1984. Storm tracks, storm surges and sea state in the Arabian Gulf, Strait of Hormuz and the Gulf of Oman. In *Oceanographic Modelling of the Kuwait Action Plan Region.* Paris: UNESCO
44. National Hydrographic Office. 1997. *Sultanate of Oman Tide Tables 1998.* Royal Navy of Oman, Muscat
45. Nizamuddin, M., Hiscock, S., Barratt, L., Ormond, R.F.G. 1986. The occurrence and morphology of Sargassopsis gennov. (Phaeophyta, Fucales). In *Ecology and Productivity of the Sublittoral Algae Ecklonia radiata and Sargassopsis zanardini. Part 1. Ecological Studies of Southern Oman Kelp Communities.* ed. pp 7.1-7.13. Kuwait: Council for the Conservation of the Environment and Water Resources, Muscat, Oman, and Regional Organisation for the Protection of the Marine Environment

46. Prell, W.L. 1984. Variation of monsoonal upwelling: A response to changing solar radiation in climate processes and climate sensitivity. *Geophysical Monograph* 29: 48-57

47. Prell, W.L., Kutzbach, J. 1987. Monsoon variability over the past 150,000 Years. *Journal of Geophysical Research* 92: 8411-8425

48. Price, A.R.G. 1982. Distribution of penaeid shrimp larvae along the Arabian Gulf coast of Saudi Arabia. *Journal of Natural History* 16:745-757

49. Price, A.R.G., Salm, R.V., Dobbin J.A. 1993. Coastal protected areas of the Arabian Peninsula. In *Application of the Biosphere Reserve Concept to Coastal Marine Areas.* eds. Price A.R.G., Humphrey S., pp. 107-109. Gland: IUCN

50. Price, A.R.G., Wrathall, T.J., Bernard, S.M. 1987. Occurrence of tar and other pollution along the Saudi Arabian shores of the Gulf. *Marine Pollution Bulletin* 18:650-651

51. Purser, B.H. 1973. *The Persian Gulf.* New York: Springer Verlag

52. Purser, B.H., Seibold, E. 1973. The principal environmental factors influencing Holocene sedimentation and diagenesis in the Persian Gulf. In *The Persian Gulf.* ed. Purser, B.H. pp. 1-9. New York: Springer Verlag

53. Reynolds, R.M. 1993. Physical Oceanography of the Gulf, Strait of Hormuz and the Gulf of Oman-Results from the Mt. Mitchell Expedition. *Marine Pollution Bulletin* 27: 35-59

54. Rochford, D.J. 1966. Source regions of oxygen maxima in intermediate depths of the Arabian Sea. *Australian Journal of Marine and Freshwater Research* 17:1-30

55. Ryther, J.H., Hall, J.R., Pease, A.K., Bakum, A., Sones, M.M. 1966. Primary organic production in relation to the chemistry and hydrology of the western Indian Ocean. *Limnology and Oceanography* 11:371-380

56. Salm, R.V. 1993. Coral reefs of the Sultanate of Oman. *Atoll Research Bulletin* 380:1-84.

57. Salm, R.V., Dobbin J.A. 1987. A coastal zone management strategy for the Sultanate of Oman. In *Coastal Zone 87, Proceedings of the Fifth Symposium on Coastal Zone Management.* eds. Magoon, O.T., Converse, H. Miner, D., Tobin, L.T., Clark, D., Domurat, G., pp. 97-106. New York: American Society Civil Engineering

58. Salm, R.V., Dobbin J.A. 1989. Coastal zone management planning and implementation in the Sultanate of Oman. In *Coastal Zone 87, Proceedings of the Fifth Symposium on Coastal Zone Management.* pp. 72-78. New York: American Society Civil Engineering

59. Salm, R.V., Mee, J. 1989. *Chaetodon dialeucos*, sp. nov. A new species of shallow water butterflyfish from the northwest Indian Ocean. *F.A.M.A.,* 12: 8-11, 131.

60. Savidge, G., Lennon, H.J., A.D. Matthews. 1988. A shore based survey of oceanographic variables in the Dhofar region of southern Oman, August-October 1985. In *Ecology and Productivity of the Sublittoral Algae* Ecklonia radiata *and* Sargassopsis zanardini. *Part 1. Ecological Studies of Southern Oman Kelp Communities.* pp 4-21. Kuwait: Council for the Conservation of the Environment and Water Resources, Muscat, Oman, and Regional Organisation for the Protection of the Marine Environment

61. Scheer, G. 1971. Coral reefs and coral genera in the Red Sea and Indian Ocean. *Symposium of the Zoological Society*, London, eds Stoddart, D.R., Yonge, C.M. pp. 329-367. London: Academic Press
62. Shapiro, G.I., Meschanov, S.L. 1991. Distribution and spreading of Red Sea Water and salt lens formation in the northwest Indian Ocean. *Deep-Sea Research* 38: 21-34
63. Sheppard, C.R.C. 1988. Similar trends, different causes: Responses of corals to stressed environments in Arabian seas *Proceedings of the 6th International Coral Reef Symposium*, Townsville 3: 297-302
64. Sheppard, C.R.C., Dixon, D.J. 1998. Seas of the Arabian Region. In *The Seas*. eds Robinson, A.R., Brink, K.H. pp. 915-931. San Diego: Wiley
65. Sheppard, C.R.C., Price, A.R.G. 1991. Will marine life survive in the Gulf? *New Scientist* 1759:6-40
66. Sheppard, C.R.C., Price, A.R.G., Roberts, C.J. 1992. *Marine Ecology of the Arabian Area. Patterns and Processes in Extreme Environments.* London: Academic Press
67. Sheppard, C.R.C., Salm, R.V. 1988. Reef and coral communities of Oman, with a description of a new coral species (Order Scleractinia, genus *Acanthastrea*). *Journal of Natural History* 22: 263-279
68. Sheppard, C.R.C., Sheppard, A.L.S. 1991. Corals and coral communities of Arabia. *Fauna of Saudi Arabia* 12:1-191
69. Shinn, E.A. 1976. Coral reef recovery in Florida and the Persian Gulf. *Environmental Geology* 1:241-254
70. Wyrtki, K. 1973. Physical oceanography of the Indian Ocean. In *The Biology of the Indian Ocean.* ed. Zeitschel, B. pp. 18-36. New York: Springer Verlag

Chapter 10

India and Sri Lanka

Gerald Bakus, Rohan Arthur, Suki Ekaratne, & S.S. Jinendradasa

The subcontinent of India occupies a large area of the tropical Indian Ocean, but it has a scant growth of coral reefs along its coasts. Several factors limit reef development here, chief among them being turbid waters stirred by monsoonal systems, fresh water runoff from rivers, and a heavy human population and development pressure along the entire coastline (136). The island complexes around India, in contrast, show healthy reef growth and support high species diversities (Fig. 10.1). The biological affinities of the reefs include species assemblages typical of the western Indian Ocean and the southeast Asian and central Pacific fauna, and a large variety of habitats and environmental conditions (Chapter 1).

The reefs of India and Sri Lanka include some of the most used and degraded, as well as some of the most untouched in the region. Although marine protected areas in this region originate from the 1980s, environmental managers rely on an incomplete knowledge of the status and ecology of the reefs. With increasing resource-extraction pressure on these reefs, due to increasing human population and tourism, there is a danger of losing these ecosystems through ignorance and unplanned management. In this chapter we will give a broad overview of the physical and biogeographic influences that shape the reefs of the subcontinent and its islands, and present the major threats to their conservation. The conservation of these reefs may be more limited by their shared cultural and economic institutions so we will also attempt to synthesize the social, economic, and political environment within which rational management will take place, and to identify priority areas for future research and management.

History of Coral Reef Studies

Despite several decades of coral reef research in India and Sri Lanka, the state of our present knowledge of these systems is patchy at best (see 7 for a review). There are fundamental gaps in basic distribution and status information for most reef areas in the region (136). The earliest coral reef study in the Indian region

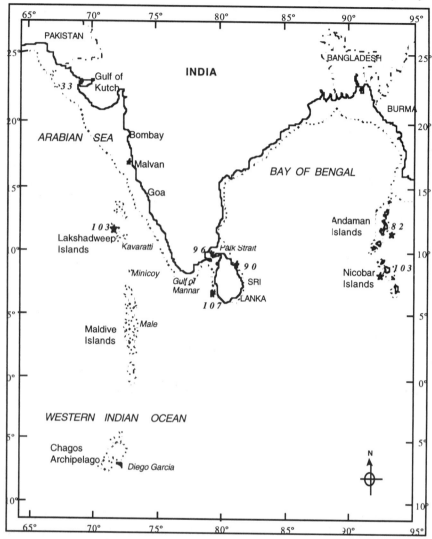

Figure 10.1 India, Sri Lanka and surrounding islands. Major reef locations discussed are marked, with figures for the number of hard coral species found at each site, where known. Few surveys have attempted a complete coral listing for the patchy reef formations off Malvan.

was a brief account of the Nicobar Islands by Rink in 1847 (108) and later, major contributors to knowledge about Indian and Sri Lankan coral reefs are Sewell, Gardiner, Mergner, Scheer and Pillai (7). Dr. Pillai has contributed a series of papers on the scleractinian corals and coral reefs of India (76-86) which describe the taxonomic diversity of these reefs, and the Central Marine Fisheries Research Institute has published a collection of papers on the exploitation potential of the Andaman-Nicobar Islands (117).

Although the taxonomy, natural history, and productivity of coral reefs in India have been studied, there is virtually no modern experimental ecological research.

There are several institutions in Sri Lanka and India whose primary mandate includes marine research but their focus has historically been on oceanography, taxonomy, and fisheries. The extensive literature cited in Bakus and colleagues (7) is dominated by species lists and taxonomic records, followed by studies on fishery exploitation potential, short survey reports, and lastly by a variety of other ecological studies which largely include studies of productivity, species distributions, and behavior. While such documentary research is essential for building a knowledge base, it is vital to take such basic research further to try and understand reef community organization, species behavior, and the ecological influence of human activities.

Meteorology and Oceanography

The Indian Ocean north of the equator comes under the influence of a monsoonal current gyre (Fig. 10.2). India and its islands experience semiannual reversals of atmospheric as well as oceanic surface water circulation in April and October, associated with the northeast and southwest monsoons (92,113,114,142). In January, when the northeast monsoon is at its peak, winds flow from the northeast, and ocean currents follow the coastline with a northerly component off the east coast and a southerly component off the west coast of India. During the southwest monsoon, which is intense in both the Arabian Sea and the Bay of Bengal, the overall direction of the winds over the northern Indian Ocean is from the southwest. In June and July, as the southwest monsoon reaches its peak, the flow is generally in the opposite direction (132). Considerable departure from this direction occurs from place to place on small scales. Tides are mainly semidiurnal with spring tides ranging from 0.3 to 2.0 m. Selected oceanographic data for the Lakshadweep and Andaman Seas, emphasizing coral reefs, are summarized in Table 10.1.

Diversity, Biogeography, and Endemicity

Indian reefs are subject to different biogeographic influences, with predominantly Indo-Pacific affinities and low levels of endemicity. There is a pronounced latitudinal gradient in the number of coral species (Fig. 10.1, Table 10.2). The lowest values are reported from the Gulf of Kutch and vary between 33 (Pillai, C. personal communication) and 44 reported species (74) which increases to about 96 species for southeast India (77). The Lakshadweep Islands are contiguous biogeographically with the Maldivian reefs and the southernmost atoll, Minicoy, has close faunal affinities with the Maldives (116). The Lakshadweep and Maldive Islands play an important role in the biogeography of the western Indian Ocean because they serve as a bridge between the Southeast Asian and East African fauna (Chapter 1, Box 1.1). The reefs of southeast India are faunistically closer to those of Sri Lanka and even the Gulf of Kutch (116). At the other longitudinal extreme, the Andaman and Nicobar reefs contain a high diversity of corals characteristic of the southeast Asian region. The marine biota here is strikingly Indo-Malaysian with some Burmese and Polynesian influences (84). The reefs here have been unreliably surveyed and between 135 (81) and 179 species (125) of hard corals have been reported for the Andaman Islands and about 116 species for the Nicobars (112).

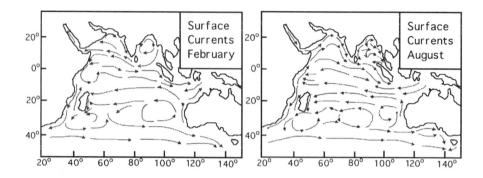

Figure 10.2. Indian Ocean surface currents, February and August (modified from 142).

Table 10.1. Oceanographic characteristics of the Laccadive and Andaman Seas, Indian Ocean. Mean values of surface waters, unless otherwise indicated. *=0-250 m, or deeper; **=0-50m; ***=0-100 m. Sources: 7,64,65. Much of the NIO data are from 30 stations in the Laccadive Sea between March 20 and April 6, 1978 and 50 stations in the Andaman Sea during January 29 to February 27, 1979, plus additional information from Drs. Wajih Naqvi and Joaquim Goes.

Characteristic	Laccadive Sea	Andaman Sea
Temperature (°C)	29-30	27-32 (near islands)
Salinity (ppt)	35-36	24.8-34
Euphotic zone (m)	69-81	75-90
		(30-50 near islands)
Secchi disk (m)	23-27	-
Total suspended matter (g dry wt/m^2)	105*	112
Total detritus (g dry wt/ m^2)	10.4*	-
Chl a (total) (mg/m^3)	0.08	0.033
(mg/ m^2)	4.9*	3.64
Phytoplankton cells/l	1900-8200	>5000
	(2000-4000 near islands)	(1100-4000 near islands)
Primary production		
(mg C/ m^3/day)	6.2 (1.4-30.2)	5.3 (1.3-9.7)
(mg C/ m^2/day)	372 (254-830)	273 (134-615)
Phytoplankton C (mg/ m^2)	115*	181
Zooplankton dry weight	50*	285
(mg/ m^2)	(sea 588, lagoon 835; high values due to ostracod swarms)	
Zooplankton C (mg/ m^2)	-	97
PO$_4$-P (μM or μg-at/l)	0.2-1.0**	0.17-0.54**
	(low day-high night; 0.34 open sea, 0.23 lagoon)	
NO$_2$ (μM)	0-0.1 (0.35 high)	-
NO$_3$-N (μM)	0.-1.0**	0**; 0-20.2***
	(high day-low night; 0.46 open sea, 0.53 lagoon)	
NH$_4$-N (μM)	<0.35-1.74 (open sea) 0.77 (lagoon)	0.39-3.82
Dissolved organic N (μM)	9.4-22.4	-

Table 10.2. Species richness of hermatypic corals from South Asian reefs. The numbers of species of stony corals is low in some regions, such as the Andamans and Nicobar Islands, because surveys did not include extensive collections by scuba diving. Sources: 83, C.S.G. Pillai, B. Mukherjee and M.V.M. Wafar, personal communications.

Locality	No. of Species and Subgenera	No. Genera	Sources
India and Sri Lanka			
Gulf of Kutch	~ 33	21	73,74; Pillai (personal communication)
Lakshadweep Islands	103	37	85
Palk Bay and Gulf of Mannar	96	36	Pillai (personal communication)
Tuticorin	21	19	80
Sri Lanka	183	68	100, 101
Andaman Islands	82	>31	55,81,125
Nicobar Islands	103	43	112
Adjacent localities			
Mergui Archipelago, (Myanmar)	77	36	19,31
Phuket, Thailand	173	66	17
Maldive Islands	197	64	87,139

The diversity of other faunal groups known from Indian includes 640 species of crabs and 3271 species of mollusks (4,13,122), 200 species of sea cucumber (37), 624 species of algae (130), 451 species of sponges (Patanayak, J.G. personal communication), and more than 450 species of polychaetes (27). The echinoderms are represented by 75 species from the Lakshadweep Islands, 96 species from southeast India, and 256 species from the Andaman-Nicobar Islands (36). The Lakshadweep Islands have about 603 species of fishes (40) and the Andaman-Nicobar Islands at least 600 species (125,126).

Geography of Coral Reefs

Modern reef growth related to the present sea level began about 5000 years ago (119) but many continental coastal areas are devoid of corals and coral reefs because of freshwater runoff and siltation. Coral reefs in India occur principally in the Lakshadweep, Andaman and Nicobar Islands (Fig. 10.1). Remote sensing has unveiled the existence of the following coastal reef flat areas: Gujarat 148 km^2, Tamil Nadu 65 km^2, Lakshadweep Islands 140 km^2, Andaman-Nicobar Islands 813 km^2, and other lagoon knolls and reefs 50 km^2 (51). Reefs in these areas have a dominance of *Acropora* on exposed seaward reefs and *Porites* communities on protected reefs, as originally described by Sewell (115). Below we will describe the basic environmental conditions and reef structure in each of the major reef areas of India and some of the environmental problems associated with each region.

Coastal Reefs

Gulf of Kutch. This is the northernmost extent of reef growth in the Indian Ocean by about 1000 km, between latitudes 22°15'N and 23°15'N, and longitudes

69°00'E and 70°40'E (140). Along the southern lip of the Gulf of Kutch, and around several of the 42 islands in the gulf, the reefs are mostly patch coral formations with a few fringing reefs that are restricted to a vast intertidal region. The coasts of the Kutch are subject to the highest tidal regime in the country (4 to 7 m amplitude) and up to 5 kilometers of coast is exposed during extreme low tides. The Gulf of Kutch has a very high rate of sedimentation, resulting in a relatively poor coral fauna today (84).

The entire Gulf of Kutch (Fig. 10.1) has between 33 and 44 species of Scleractinian corals and 12 species of alcyonarian corals (73,74, Pillai, C.S.G. personal communication). No branching forms of coral have been found alive in these reefs, although there is plenty of evidence that branching *Acropora* grew in the past because semi-fossilized fragments are found among the coral rubble and sand bars (140, Arthur, R. personal observation) The Poshetra Point area has intertidal rock reefs and pools with a 10% coverage of the non-branching corals *Favia*, *Favites*, and *Montipora* (73,86). The intertidal fringing reef has nine genera of stony corals and 45% coverage.

The reefs of the Gulf of Kutch face several anthropogenic forces, including heavy oil-tanker traffic (with pipelines running through the reefs), large-scale trawling and other commercial fisheries, mostly for export, and industries which discharge waste into the Gulf. Coastal people have traditionally depended on fishing, and although much of this fishery is for pelagics, the reef is still used considerably for small-scale and bait fishing, as a harboring site, and for harvesting conchs, ornamental shells, and windowpane oyster (74; Krishnan, S. personal communication). Several reefs, including those of Pirotan Island (Sastry, D.R.K. personal communication), have been severely damaged by the extraction of limestone for cement, and the associated siltation. This activity was stopped in 1986 when the area was declared India's first Marine National Park, but the mining effects are still evident (74). Sedimentation levels are high due to coastal development and mangrove degradation with water visibility typically less than 1 m (84). Coral reefs in the Gulf of Kutch are under constant pressure of economic development because of the importance of the Gulf for the industry of this region.

West Coast. It was previously believed that the west coast of India was too turbid for corals to thrive, but there have been several recent reports of reef-building corals, and scattered reefs along the coast from Bombay south to Goa (Fig. 10.1). Research is restricted to brief status surveys and location reports, but they indicate that intertidal corals are present at Ratnagiri, Malvan and Redi located between Bombay and Goa (Fig. 10.1,97,121). The reefs of Malvan are reported to have the richest faunal diversity (208 species of macroscopic invertebrates), and the area has been proposed for a park (72, Pillai, C.S.G. personal communication).

Intense siltation and heavy wave action along this coast presumably makes it difficult for branching corals to survive. There are nine recorded species of stony coral with *Porites* being the dominant genus (72, C.S.G. Pillai, pers comm.). Two species of corals (*Pseudosiderastrea tayamai* and *Porites lichen*) were reported from the intertidal rocks of Bombay (136). Angria Bank, about 150 km southwest of Ratnagiri, has some coral development but the reef community is undescribed. Gaveshani bank, located about 100 km west of Malpe, has five species of stony corals at depths of 32 to 40 m (61). Patch reefs were also reported from Vizhinjam (M.V.M. Wafar, manuscript) and stony corals have been recorded off

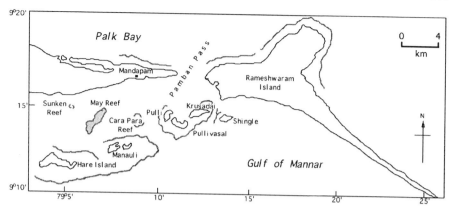

Figure 10.3. Islands in the Gulf of Mannar, southeast India. Source: (80).

Mormugao Head in Goa (Untawale, A.G. personal communication). The coast of Quilon to Enayam has 29 species of Scleractinia, 13 of these from shallow waters (84) This area has not attracted conservation-oriented research and, therefore, little is known about the threats to corals and other marine habitats.

Southeast India. A series of fringing reefs occur on continental edges between southeast India and Sri Lanka as well as some patch reefs off the coastal islands (Fig. 10.3). The region between Mandapam and Tuticorin is a 140 km stretch of coastline which is fringed by 20 small islands each measuring about 5 km^2 (7). These islands were formed by a 1.5 m uplift that occurred 5000 years ago, resulting in the emergence of contemporary reefs and islands (80). The islands are typically bordered by patch reefs. Radiocarbon dating places the age of an uplifted reef at Mandapam at 4020 ± 160 years (120). This region has 96 species (36 genera) of scleractinian corals, seven species of which are ahermatypic (78).

Unlike the west coast of India, most of the rainfall in this region occurs during the winter rains of the northeast monsoon and ranges between 76 and 127 cm/y. This causes salinity to drop to between 25 and 27.5 ppt in January but it returns to near normal seawater salinities between 33 and 36 ppt during the rest of the year (77). Islands in the Gulf of Mannar are low-lying and have no permanent freshwater streams. Air temperatures range between 25° C and 31° C and water temperature between 25° and 30° C in January and May, respectively. The conditions for coral growth are poor as the northeast winter monsoon stirs the water column reducing water visibility to < 0.5 m for more than six months of the year (53).

The corals of the Gulf of Mannar are both more diverse and more abundant than those of Palk Bay (77). The fringing reefs near Mandapam display an indistinct zonation (77). Coral zonation becomes more evident along the southeast coast of Sri Lanka (52). Palk Bay has lagoons of 1.0 to 2.0 m depth but they are generally devoid of corals except for a single reef that is interrupted at Pamban Pass on the seaward side of the reef. Dominant stony corals on the seaward side of the reef include the families Acroporidae, Poritidae, and Faviidae, the genera *Montipora* and *Acropora* representing 40% of the species (76,78).

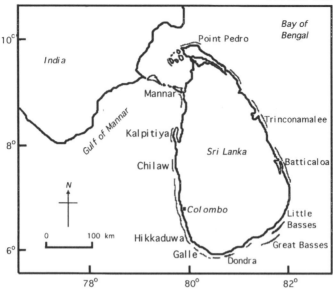

Figure 10.4. Sri Lankan coral reefs. Source: Ekaratne.

Research on these islands dates back to 1895 when Thurston described the marine fauna of Rameswaram Island (124) and the first underwater observations and distribution of coral reefs were made in the early 1970s (104). Manauli and Krusadai Islands, located near Mandapam, and Hikkaduwa of Sri Lanka are the best-known locations with coral reefs (53,60). The islands of the northern part of the bay are rich with 30 to 60 species of stony corals, especially *Acropora*, *Pocillopora*, and species in the Poritidae and Faviidae families. Calcium carbonate accretion in *Acropora* at Karichalli Island, near Tuticorin, is discussed by Ramanujam and colleagues (105).

The Manuali reef once contained 30 species of stony corals and seven species of mangroves but the reef has since been partially destroyed due to extraction for cement factories (Kumaraguru, A.K. personal communication). Dominant reef corals included *Acropora*, *Porites*, *Goniastrea*, *Favia*, *Pocillopora*, and *Montipora*. Krusadai Island has a lagoon with boulders and corals and a well-developed fringing reef. Foraminiferans comprise 15% of the sediments, representing mostly benthic-associated genera (29).

Local fishermen harvest marine products from the reefs, and are depleting the populations of ornamental mollusks (140). Spear fishermen break corals to extract hidden fish and, therefore, much of the reef is composed of broken and dead corals. These reefs are also a favorite site for college excursions and reef walking has resulted in considerable coral breakage. Additionally, the indiscriminate collection of college laboratory specimens reached such alarming proportions that a ban was imposed (140). Carbide factories and white cement plants have led to the considerable removal of corals from the Gulf of Mannar and Palk Bay (93). The Gulf of Mannar suffers especially from siltation, sewage effluents, and mining (45). Chandrika and Pillai (14) found considerable traces of *Escherichia coli* from reef sediments and in collections of *Acropora formosa* from the Manauli reefs, presumably because of improper waste and sewage management.

Sri Lanka. Sri Lanka is a tear-drop shaped island of 65 610 km², located off the southern coast of India, with a human population of 17 million. Nearshore reefs, mainly of the fringing type, are found along 2% of its 1585 km coastline (60, Fig. 10.4). Patch reefs on rocky bottoms, reefs growing on beach-rock and sandstone as well as three barrier reefs and two ridge-colonized reef formations comprise the reef ecosystems of Sri Lanka (20,23,103).

The reefs of Sri Lanka have not been comprehensively mapped but the major reef formations are found within a 30 m depth contour. The major reefs are off of the Jaffna Peninsula in the north of the island and from Trincomalee to Kalmunai in the east. Reefs extend from the south, near Tangalle, to the southwest, near Ambalangoda. Along the west coast, they extend from Mannar in the northwest to Kalpitiya. The three barrier reefs are located along the west coast at Vankalai, Silavathurai and off Kalpitiya, the latter known as Bar Reef. The two ridge-covered reefs are off the southeast coast of the island, known as the Great and Little Basses (20, 103).

The knowledge base on Sri Lankan reefs is sparse and there are less than a handful of people engaged in reef research. Some of the reefs have been surveyed qualitatively for fish and scleractinian coral cover, but not for other organisms The extensive reef formations in the north and east have not been surveyed because the area is defended by secessionist rebels. Surveys have revealed the existence of 183 species of stony corals in 68 genera, and over 300 species of fishes in 62 families, including 35 species of butterflyfish, and also the occurrence of spiny lobsters, dolphins, whale sharks, and five species of sea turtles. The common reef-building corals belong to the families Acroporidae, Agariciidae, Faviidae, Caryophyliidae, Merulinidae, Mussidae, Oculinidae, Pocilloporidae and Poritidae. Common octocorals include *Sarcophyton*, *Sinularia* and dendronephthids (24,53,100,101). The marine fishes of Sri Lanka are described in part by Munro (56) and De Bruin and colleagues (16), marine mammals by Leatherwood and Reeves (48), and the marine birds by De Silva (18).

Studies on coral have been limited to growth and recruitment. At Hikkaduwa Sanctuary, coral recruitment extended almost throughout the year, and was maximal from May to August. In southwest reefs *Acropora formosa* grew linearly from 5.0 to 18.7 mm/month, with maximum growth between February and March, and a lesser peak in September and October. *Acropora formosa* weight increments were high from March to July, peaking in June and July in phase with the recruitment period.

Southwest reefs experienced high loads of particulate matter, including sandy material, from May to November, in concert with the rough seas of the southwest monsoon rainy period, with maximum sediment loads of up to 3.2 kg/m²/ day. Experiments with *Acropora* coral transplants are viewed as promising for reef rehabilitation. Among the reef-associated habitats that have high biodiversity, *Halimeda* mats harbor a rich diversity of organisms that include polychaetes, amphipods, shrimps, crabs, mollusks, bryozoans, ascidians, foraminiferans, echinoderms, nemerteans, pycnogonids, and platyhelminths. During periods of strong wave action, *Halimeda* clumps also serve as a protective nursery habitat for a number of reef-associated organisms, including pipefish, gobies, ophiuroids, holothuroids, echinoids, crabs, olive snails, and other mollusks (24).

Most of the known reefs, particularly readily accessible nearshore reefs, are degraded due to human-induced damage (23). Reefs with over 50% of live hermatypic cover are present at Bar Reef, at the Great and Little Basses and at a few reefs on the southern coast, including Hikkaduwa in the southwest. Hikkaduwa and Bar Reef constitute the only two legally protected Marine Sanctuaries in Sri Lanka, the former having been accorded sanctuary status in 1979, and the latter in 1992 (75). Marine sanctuaries were established under the Fauna and Flora Protection Ordinance (99). Although legal enactments for reef and reef-related protection are in place, implementation and monitoring are inadequate, effectively permitting the continuation of reef degradation practices (23). The relevant laws which protect coral reefs and related habitats include the Coast Conservation Act No. 57 of 1981, National Environmental Act No. 47 of 1980, Fisheries Ordinance No. 24 of 1940, Fauna and Flora Protection Ordinance No. 2 of 1937, with their subsequent amendments (62,141). The Sri Lankan Coast Conservation Act of 1981 protects development on land within 300 m of the coast and 2 km seaward of the coast (41). There are 3 marine protected areas and 12 coastal sites.

Among the foremost destructive practices adversely impacting the physical structure of the reef are the removal of coral for conversion into lime, reef organism removal for the export aquarium industry (valued at US $ 2 million in 1985 and estimated at about US $ 10 million per year in the 1990s), and fishing practices that employ explosives and the indiscriminate use of fishing nets. Sediment loads arising from unsound land-use practices, agro-chemicals derived from agricultural overuse, other polluting wastes draining into reefs, including those from sewage and industry, are the major agents destabilizing reef ecosystem processes leading to reef degradation and loss of reef biodiversity (22,23,33,66,141). Populations of coral-eating crown-of-thorns starfish, *Acanthaster planci*, have been reported to periodically increase and form large population aggregations in reefs on the northwest and the east (Box 2.2, 15,102). In the wake of anthropogenic disturbances, location-specific invasions of Sri Lankan coral reefs have taken place by other organisms such as sea urchins, corallivorous gastropods, sponges, and algal genera such as *Halimeda* and *Ulva* (24).

Oceanic Coral Reefs

Lakshadweep Islands. The Lakshadweep (previously Laccadive) Archipelago consists of 12 atolls, three reefs, and five submerged banks (Fig. 10.5). Of its 36 islands covering a total area of 32 km², the largest island is Androth (4.8 km²) and the smallest Bitra (0.1 km²) and only 10 (all atolls) are inhabited. The Lakshadweep, Maldives and Chagos Archipelagoes are aligned along the ninety-degree ridge, a 3000 km ridge of coral limestone capping massive sunken volcanoes (Chapter 1, 119). All inhabited Lakshadweep Islands are protected by an outer reef which encloses a shallow lagoon with the exception of Androth Island, which is exposed on all sides (40). The islands receive heavy southwest monsoonal rain ranging between 156 and 225 cm/year with most of it falling between June and September (79) with air temperatures ranging between 20.1° to 32.9° C. The lagoons have surface seawater temperatures of 22° to 28° C, salinities of 36 to 39.4 ppt, and oxygen levels between 1 and 15 ml/l (28).

The best surveyed island in the island chain is Minicoy. The island height is 1.8 m above MSL, and has a 10 km² lagoon. The windward outer reef has spur and groove formations. The infauna of the sand flat consists principally of

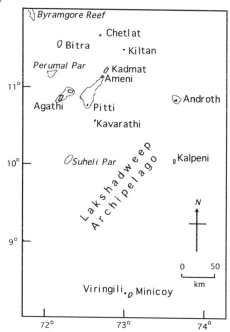

Figure 10.5. Lakshadweep Archipelago showing the extent of coral reefs (modified from 36).

polychaetes, sea anemones, sipunculid worms, the enteropneust *Ptychodera*, and a cephalochordate (Pillai, C.S.G. personal communication). Many corals in the lagoon have been affected by siltation (82), but at least 103 species (26 genera) of hermatypic corals have been recorded (85). The seagrasses *Thalassia hemprichii, Cymodocea* spp. and *Syringodium isoetifolium* are abundant from the low intertidal to 100 m offshore but are occasionally also found further offshore (63). *Acanthaster planci* has occasionally been observed in the intertidal, the lagoon, and deeper regions (35,118).

The Lakshadweep are the most densely populated islands in India with more than 54 000 people living on 32 km² of land (25). The Lakshadweep Islands consist of the northern inhabited Amindivi (or South Kanara) Islands, including Ameni, Kadamat, Chetlat, Kiltan, Bitra and Agathi (Fig. 10.5). The southern or Malabar Islands include Minicoy, Kavaratti (the government center), Kalpeni, and Androth. The Lakshadweep Islands have about 3000 artisanal fishermen (7). The annual fish catch in the Laccadive Sea is 2000 to 5000 tons (mostly tuna, 70% of the catch, and shark, 39). Smoking and sun-drying of fish are common. Fishing is the chief occupation of the Lakshadweep islanders and the locals are highly dependent on bait fish (such as sprats, pomacentrids, and apogonids) which they use for pole and line tuna fishery. Species like *Spratelloides delicatus* and *S. japonicus* are much sought after for live bait (46). The reef also serves as a food source (rays, perches, carangids, belonids, halfbeaks) when tuna fish catches are low, and there is a shell-craft industry (140). Fisherfolk use the lagoon very seasonally and some Lakshadweepans practice transhumance, fishing off the Suheli Par Island between November and April, and moving back to their homes on the main islands for the remaining months (Koya, S.I. personal communication). Tourism is highly restricted and only Bangaram Island has a tourist resort open to foreign tourists. Indian tourists are allowed limited access to the other islands.

Lakshadweep is a heavily subsidized economy as are the Andaman and Nicobar islands. They are dependent on the mainland for all essential supplies including fuel, vegetables and packaged foods, and infrastructure. In the absence of sufficient subsidies on conventional construction materials, the islanders find it a simpler option to harvest the lagoons for coral which they use for houses, roads, and other construction (140, Koya, S.I. personal communication). Though the collection of coral from lagoons has been largely regulated, the collection of coral shingle from the shore continues unabated, resulting in an ever-weakening beach front (84). Dredging activities in lagoons around many inhabited islands have created severe disturbances in the past, the removal of the reef front in some areas to allow the passage of large boats has permanently affected current flows in and out of the lagoon (82,84). This activity has killed off large areas where healthy reefs once thrived.

Andaman and Nicobar Islands. The Andaman and Nicobar Islands include more than 550 islands, islets, and rocky outcrops, of which 38 are inhabited (Fig. 10.6). These islands border the Andaman Sea on the east, which is adjacent to Burma, Thailand and Sumatra, and the Indian Ocean on the west. The Andaman-Nicobar Islands are elevated mountain ranges (submarine extensions of the Ara rocks), basically sedimentary in nature, with fringing reefs on the eastern side, and barrier reefs, with a lagoon up to 40 m deep, on the western side. The Andaman Islands occupy a land area of 6475 km^2 and the Nicobar Islands 1645 km^2, much of it heavily forested. The Andaman-Nicobar Island chains are separated by a deep oceanic ridge located at 10° N. latitude. The islands are high islands and receive abundant precipitation (318 cm/y) with a dry season between December and April.

Remote sensing of coral reefs and mangroves of the southern Andaman Islands has been undertaken (43) Reef platforms extend about 500 m from shore in the Andaman Islands and up to 1000 m from shore in the Nicobar Islands, the latter having small surge channels (107). The reef flats of coastal reefs are fringed with mangroves and are typically 50 to 100 m wide on the flat and descend steeply. Most of the fringing reefs occur at depths of 5 to 7 m, with luxuriant coral growth near Port Blair (60). Coral growth is richer on the west than east coast. The Andaman and Nicobar Islands have more than 135 species (59 genera) of stony corals, of which 110 species and 45 genera are hermatypic. Thirty two genera are known from Great Nicobar (81). The soft corals *Sarcophyton* and *Lobophytum* are common throughout the islands, as well as in the Lakshadweep (35).

Coral cover and diversity are generally high. The Nicobar Islands are richer in coral growth than are the Andaman Islands (81). Reddiah (107) reported that the dominant reef flat stony corals included *Porites, Favia, Pocillopora, Acropora, Heliopora,* and *Tubipora* with no clear pattern of zonation. The Nancowry Island area of the Nicobar Islands is dominated by *Porites, Acropora,* and *Pocillopora* (49, 107). Tillachong Island, Nicobar Islands, has a fringing reef with 30 genera of stony corals. *Acropora palifera* occupies 26% of the total stony coral cover and *Porites* sp. 23% (111, 112). The Long Island of the North Andaman Islands has a 75% stony coral cover (107).

The reefs of the Andamans and Nicobars are the most pristine reefs remaining in India. The population of the Andaman and Nicobar Islands in 1991 was 203 968

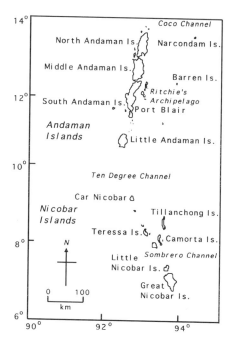

Figure 10.6. The Andaman and Nicobar Islands, India (13).

which includes a number of small tribes, namely the Andamanis, Onges, Nicobaris, Jarawas and the Sentinels, which number less than a 1000 individuals (69, Box 10.1). There are 516 villages in the Andaman-Nicobar Islands and the principal crops are rice, coconut and betel nut. The islands are still rather remote and inaccessible for full-scale commercial exploitation, and until recently, tourists had a daunting time getting to the Andamans. The Nicobars are still closed to tourists. With a new international airport under construction in Port Blair, this situation will change. The Andamans are fast becoming a popular holiday destination and the few islands that have been opened to tourism have a heavy visitation rate of about 100 tourists/day.

The average reported finfish landings in the Andaman-Nicobar Islands was between 1500 to 4000 tons/y in 1983. Other commercially important species in the Andaman Sea include 12 species of prawns, six species of lobsters, eight species of edible crabs, four species of edible oysters, seven species of holothurians, the snails *Trochus* and *Turbo*, and the giant clam *Tridacna* and *Hippopus* (various authors in 7,51). Some 22 species of gorgonians are exported from India, particularly for biomedically important chemicals (123).

The Andaman-Nicobar Islands are rich in finfish resources but underutilized by local Indian settlers who prefer to eat freshwater fish (117). These settlers have, however, developed a well-established underground network to transport protected marine species or to bypass harvesting regulations. Their focus is often on sea cucumbers, shark fin, *Trochus* shells, and other reef products popular in the markets of southeast Asia (109). The reefs are also used by fisherfolk from Burma and Thailand who also collect these species as well as live crocodiles. The Andaman government considers these fisherfolk poachers and

Box 10.1. The Aboriginal People of the Andamans: Cultural Conflict Threatens Coral Reefs

Among the earliest records from the Andamans, the Chinese traveler I'Tsing in 671 AD tells of a demonic and cannibalistic people inhabiting these islands (4). These people are the aboriginal tribe that live today in ever-dwindling numbers, struggling to ward off extinction but also preserving some of the least disturbed reefs in the Indian Ocean. The Andaman tribes belong to the Negrito ethnographic group, with small populations scattered among islands in the Malacca Peninsula (the Semangs), the Philippines (the Aetas) and extinct tribes of Tasmania. The Andaman tribes include four extant ethnic groups, the Andamanese, the Onges, the Jarawas and the Sentinels (3). All of these populations have had different historical influences but are now all facing extinction.

The Andamanese, the most numerous of the tribes, fought fiercely against colonization, but soon submitted to the superior weapons of the British (3). They made peace with the British, but several villages succumbed to skin infections, sexually transmitted diseases, and occasional skirmishes. By 1901 their population was as few as 625 individuals and are now further reduced to less than fifty. These last individuals live on small Strait Island, confined by the Indian government (4). The Onges, more accessible and friendly than the Andamanese, have followed a similar path towards extinction, fueled by disease and loss of traditional lands. They are also supported by the Indian Government in tiny tribal reserves.

The Sentinels and the Jarawas on the other hand have remained fiercely hostile to attempts to befriend them. The Jarawas occupy a large portion of the western shores of South and Middle Andaman islands, afforded protection in officially declared tribal reserves. Jarawas have two distinct clans, the Eremtaga or forest dwellers, and the Arioto or coast dwellers, who fish actively during the dry season and move inland during the rainy months (3,3). The Sentinelese are confined to the relatively secluded island of North Sentinel, and very little is known about their culture or their population status. Hostility with the British served to decimate the populations of the aboriginal tribes of the Andamans through war and disease, but the present migration of settlers from India and Bangladesh is perhaps more insidious in the decline of these tribal populations. These settlers were first encouraged to populate the Andamans by the Indian government in the 1960s, and the influx of people has not stopped (7). Settlers have put a heavy demand on the land resources of the Andaman Islands, and the aboriginal tribes are hemmed in on all sides by their settlements. While the Sentinels, the Onges and the Andamanese are restricted to fairly secluded parts of the Andamans chain, the Jarawas face the brunt of this cultural conflict.

The Andaman Trunk Road, a highway built on traditional Jarawa hunting grounds, heightens antagonism. Skirmishes are frequent along this road, and vehicles travel with armed escorts passing through Jarawa territory. Though the Jarawa waters are off-limits for fishing and passage, fishermen from settler villages nearby are constantly enticed back to these rich fishing grounds. This leads to further conflict, and many of these incidents result in serious injury and death. The Jarawas organize raiding missions stealing metal utensils which they use to fashion arrowheads. In equal share, the settlers encourage their cattle to graze in Jarawa lands. These cattle are known to sully the Jarawa's traditional watering holes, making the water unfit for consumption (7). There are also several reports of contractors logging timber in Jarawa land.

Aboriginal Andaman people play an important role in the ecology of the Andamans as their antagonism is unwittingly responsible for the conservation of these unique islands. The Jarawa region possesses the largest remnant stands of the Giant Tropical Evergreen Forest left on these islands. The reefs, which have never been quantitatively surveyed, do not share the same pressures of fishing and development as reefs outside the region. All aboriginal Andamans are keen fisherfolk and hunt fish, turtle, and dugong with arrows and spears. They maintain a low level sustenance fishery unlikely to significantly threaten the reefs they exploit (1). Their traditions are becoming increasingly threatened as is their effectiveness in deterring settlers who will use the land and sea more intensively. The loss of Jarawa tradition will open the gates to development and ecological degradation.

Rohan Arthur

References

1. Bhaskar, S., Whitaker, R. 1983. Sea turtle resources in the Andamans. In *Mariculture Potential of Andaman and Nicobar Islands - an Indicative Survey,* eds. Silas, E.G., Alagarswami, K. pp. 94-97. CMFRI.: Cochin
2. Lidio, C. 1966. *The Andaman Islanders.* London: Weidenfield and Nicholson
3. Portman, M.V. 1899. *A History of our Relations with the Andamanese.* Calcutta: Office of the Superintendent of Government Printing
4. Singh, N.I. 1978. *The Andaman Story.* New Delhi: Vikas Publishing House
5. Saldhana, C.J. ed. 1989. *Andaman, Nicobar and Lakshadweep: an Environmental Impact Assessment.* Oxford and IBH: New Delhi

will, therefore, arrest them if caught (109). The area is, however, poorly patrolled and well-organized poachers using fast-powered dugouts (called *'doongies'*) are effective at removing most of the reefs' resources. Andaman tribes have hunted fish, turtle, and dugong using traditional methods (such as bow and arrow and spear) for centuries (Box 10.1), and likewise Burmese and Thai fisherfolk have been fishing in these reefs for hundreds of years. However, the commercialization and present illegality of the fishing has resulted in more opportunistic and less sustainable practices than in the past, for example, in the gaining popularity of blast and cyanide fishing.

Land requirements of settlers in the Andaman Islands have reduced the tropical forests and converted the acreage to rice fields. This has resulted in a loss of topsoil and resultant sedimentation on coral reefs. Large-scale logging activities and illegal timber trade have exacerbated the problem.

The Coral Reef Ecosystem

The coral reefs of the subcontinent differ functionally from each other based on their biogeographic location, reef structure, and local oceanographic and geographical factors. Both coasts of the continental mainland of India are turbid

coastlines, controlled by monsoonal systems. As a consequence, reefs do not
proliferate on mainland India, and the continental fringing and patch reefs found
here are poorly developed. In general they support low reef-associated diversity
but high net production. The Andaman and Nicobar reef complexes are
characterized by mountainous islands which supply a high influx of terrigenous
sediment into the reef waters, and by high current flows between the islands. The
reefs here are high-diversity fringing reefs that have a faunal composition
influenced by their proximity to the reefs of south-east Asia. The Lakshadweep
chain of islands on the other hand are flat coral atolls with large lagoonal reefs.
They are high productivity reefs that also support high faunal diversities.

Productivity

The coral reef productivity of selected islands indicates coral-reef production
values between 2.4 and 9.5 g $C/m^2/d$ (Table 10.3) which are typical for coral reefs
throughout the world (42). Reported gross production in the Lakshadweep and
Gulf of Mannar were generally about twice as high as estimates for the Andamans.
P/R ratios for Lakshadweep and Gulf of Mannar were high (6.1 and 3.2
respectively), and generally higher than the world average of 1.0 (42). Ten
species of hard corals from Palk Bay and the Gulf of Mannar had gross P/R ratios
of 1.97 to 3.58 (60). While these data suggest differences in auto versus.
heterotrophy between Lakshadweep and Gulf of Mannar reefs, further studies are
needed to corroborate their results

Water-Column Biota

Plankton and Microbes. *Trichodesmium* blooms are common and occur
almost every year during the pre-monsoon season in the Laccadive Sea (90,91),
and also occur in coastal regions such as Tuticorin (110). During these blooms
the density of cells and chlorophyll can increase by two orders of magnitude
(110). Primary production of the plankton in the Laccadive Sea was between 254
and 830 $mgC/m^2/day$ (mean = 372), chlorophyll a 1.4 to 15.4 mg/m^2 (mean = 4.9),
and phaeopigments 1.16 - 17.2 mg/m^3 (mean = 4.6) (11). Phytoplankton
production in surface waters of the Gulf of Mannar was 89 to 91 g $C/m^3/year$ (88).
Surface chlorophyll a averaged 0.041 mg/m^3 or 1400 to 4900 cells/l (54).
Nanoplankton (<64 μm) represent 65 to 75% of the total phytoplankton production
(135).
    Zooplankton biomass in the Lakshadweep Islands generally increases from the
north to south and decreases 23 to 61% from the ocean to the atoll lagoon.
Copepods represent 74 to 88% of total plankton counts (127). In shallow waters
the mean zooplankton biomass is 289 mg C/m^2 (50) and is a mixture of oceanic
and neritic species. The dominant organisms are copepods, particularly calanoids.
    There are few data on benthic bacterial counts near coral reefs. The microbial
density at or near the ocean surface in the Lakshadweep Islands averages 18
bacteria/ml (59). The density of nitrifying bacteria in living corals varies from 4
to 260 x 10^3 cells/mg coral tissue (138). The average nitrate production was 9.4 ±
6.0 nmol/mg coral tissue/hr. Nitrification by reef corals appears to be an important
pathway of nitrogen cycling (137). Very little is known about detritus but
particulate organic aggregates, comprising mucus and entrapped organic matter,

Table 10.3. Productivity of some coral reefs in India.

Locality	Benthic Gross Production (g C/m²/day)	Respiration (g C/m²/day)	P/R Ratio	Source
Gulf of Mannar				
Manauli Reef	7.3	0.3	–	60
Krusadai Reef	2.4	2.0*	1.2	9
Palk Bay Reef	4.9-9.5	2.3-3.3	2.2-3.4	9
Andaman Islands				
Andaman Reef	3.9	17.1	4.4	60
Chiratapu Reef	2.8	3.5	0.8-1.4	55
Lakshadweep Islands				
Minicoy Reef	9.1	0.1	91.0	60
Kavaratti Reef	6.2**	2.4	2.6	96
Kavaratti seagrass bed	12.0	6.2	1.9	95

* low productivity probably due to the destruction of corals (see text); ** not corrected for diffusion

may account for as much as 20% of the gross primary production of these coral reefs (94).

Benthic-Associated Biota

Plants and Algae. Some 159 species of Chlorophyta, 141 species of Phaeophyta, 307 species of Rhodophyta, and 17 species of Cyanophyta have been recorded from coastal India (130). At least 180 species of benthic algae have been reported from the Gulf of Mannar and Palk Bay (128), where green algae predominate. Standing crops of algae ranged from 0.08 to 1.16 kg/m². Minicoy Island (Lakshadweep) has 37 known species of benthic algae. Sixty four species of benthic algae are known from the Andaman-Nicobar Islands (34). Very few studies have been conducted on the ecology of benthic marine algae. The annual yield of seaweed ranges from 900 mt in Palk Bay to 100 000 mt in the Gulf of Kutch (130).

Extensive seagrass beds (12 species) occur in Palk Bay, the Gulf of Mannar near Mandapam, and around the islands in the Gulf of Mannar (Jagtap, in press). The standing crop of seagrasses in 3.58 km² of Palk Bay was about 2000 tons and the maximum biomass occurred at a depth of 1.5 to 2.0 m (129, Jagtap, in press). Five species of seagrasses occur in the Lakshadweep Islands (35). In comparison, the Andaman and Nicobar Islands are relatively poor in seagrass growth (34).

There may be as many as 60 species of mangrove plants in India (12). Mangroves (mangals) are well developed in southeast India. They are also abundant in the Andaman-Nicobar Islands because of an abundance of freshwater runoff (47). There they commonly occur within 2 to 5 m of well-developed fringing reefs (2). The Lakshadweep Islands lack mangroves except for Minicoy Island (131). Approximately 60% of India's coastal marine fish species are dependent on the mangrove estuarine complex as a feeding, breeding and nursery grounds (30). Mangroves are being rapidly destroyed throughout the country, especially for land reclamation and wood.

Macrofauna and Meiofauna of Soft Bottoms. The benthic macrofauna and meiofauna of soft bottoms of India are poorly known. The mean biomass of the benthos is 0.93 g/m² in the Lakshadweep Islands and 7.62 g/m² in the Andaman-Nicobar Islands (72). The standing crop of meiofauna from the

Andaman-Nicobar Islands is 21 mg wet wt/10 cm^2; for macrofauna it is 5 to 21 g/m^2 (71). Some 195 species of interstitial fauna are known from the Andaman-Nicobar Islands, dominated by copepods, isopods and polychaetes (106).

Marine Vertebrates. More than 1340 species of marine fishes have been reported from India, with over 600 species each from the Lakshadweep and Andaman-Nicobar Islands (32, 40, 125, 133). Few of the fishes have been studied except for commercial species. Marine ornamental fishes of the Lakshadweep Islands are discussed by Emmanuel and colleagues (26) and those of some Andaman Islands by Mustafa and colleagues (58).

Coastal waters of southern India have 20 species of seasnakes. Seasnakes are especially common in the Andaman-Nicobar Islands (1). There are five species of marine turtles in India including the olive, green, hawksbill, leatherback and loggerhead (98). The commonest turtle is the green turtle. Crocodiles (*Crocodilus porosus*), once nearly extinct, are now protected in the Andaman Islands.

Twenty-three species of birds commonly occur in the Lakshadweep Islands and some 50 species of breeding birds in the Andaman-Nicobar Islands. The seabirds are poorly known in the latter region (126). Shorebirds in the Gulf of Mannar are discussed by Balachandran (8).

Twenty-two species of marine mammals are reported from India (10,38,134). Dolphins are relatively common in Palk Bay, Gulf of Mannar, and the Andaman Islands (Kumaraguru, A.K. personal communication). Marine mammals of the Lakshadweep, Andaman and Nicobar Islands are virtually unstudied. Dugongs are an endangered species, occasionally sighted (in the Gulf of Mannar and Gulf of Kutch), yet considered nearly extinct by some observers.

Reef Use

Fisheries and Shellfisheries

The coastal lands of India and Sri Lanka are densely populated. Coral reefs represent a vital part of the social and economic environment of local communities that live near them, with daily sustenance and commerce focused around the exploitation potential of the reefs. South Asian coastal communities employ a large diversity of fishing practices in reefs, and each reef area has its own characteristic fishery ranging from low-end sustenance fishery to large scale commercial trawling which has very little dependence on the reef. Some 24 stocks of fisheries (20 groups of fishes) and shell-fisheries are being exploited in coastal waters of India. Approximately 150 species of crustaceans are of commercial importance in India, including 117 species of prawns (landings for 1989 were 292 365 tons), 17 species of lobsters, 12 species of crabs, and 4 species of stomatopods (122). The collection of other marine products for ornamental purposes and for the exotic food market has also become an increasingly popular money earner for local communities and, without adequate laws to control this trade, pressure on the reef fauna is high. Pearl harvesting was once a major reef industry here, among the three best pearl fisheries in the world, but the species has been overexploited to commercial extinction (140). A summary of fisheries and management techniques in India is presented by Bakus (6) and Murty and Rao (51).

Destruction of Coral Reefs

Coral reefs of India have been exploited since before recorded history but it is only in the past century that the rate of exploitation has increased dramatically, due in large part to the increase in the human population. Except for some of the Andaman-Nicobar Islands, no pristine coral reefs exist today (84).

Coral remains a cheap and easily available raw material for constructing houses, roads, and walls. Coral mining has been banned in national parks since their creation in the 1980s, but large-scale mining is still prevalent in parts of the Lakshadweep and Nicobar Islands, Gulf of Mannar, and Sri Lanka despite recent legal protection (45,103,140). Legal harvesting, in the Lakshadweep Islands where there are no parks, is presently restricted to dead coral shingle. Coral mining has, however, left scars that will take decades to repair.

Conservation

Marine Protected Areas

There are 10 Marine Protected Areas (MPA's) in India as well as six parks that include coastal sites (Table 10.4, 41). The India Wildlife (Protection) Act of 1972 provides for the establishment of national parks and sanctuaries by state governments which are administered by the Ministry of Environment and Forests (Table 10.4, 41). The Gulf of Kutch Marine Sanctuary and Marine National Park, the Gulf of Mannar National Park, and Wandoor Marine National Park (Andaman Islands) have been established primarily to protect marine habitats. The Andaman and Nicobar chain of islands has 99 sanctuaries and national parks (69), but many are uninhabited islands without management or staff. A biosphere reserve, The Great Nicobar Biosphere Reserve, has no legal status but includes a number of marine habitats. No legal protection exists for the Lakshadweep Islands. There is a need to declare the reefs near Tamil Nadu a Biosphere Reserve (45, 89).

Tourism. Reef-related tourism is not yet a large industry, but with tourist infrastructure increasing in Sri Lanka, the Andaman Islands, and the Lakshadweep Islands, more tourists are being attracted. It is only in the last decade or so that the tourist industry has paid attention to the reefs as a potential tourist destination. There are, however, several official restrictions that prevent uncontrolled tourism in the best reefs areas of the country. The Lakshadweep atolls, with their palm-fronted beaches and docile lagoons, are a natural tourist destination, yet only restricted tourism is permitted on these islands, ostensibly to guard the sensibilities of the conservative Muslim population. Foreign nationals are permitted to visit only the tiny uninhabited island of Bangaram which has an international tourist facility, while Indian visitors have to choose one of the limited government or government-affiliated tourist packages (140, Kakkad, P.

Table 10.4. South Asian Marine Protected Areas affording protection to coral reefs and related habitats (41). The Andaman and Nicobar Islands have 99 protected areas, most of them tiny uninhabited islands (69). The Great Nicobar Biosphere Reserve does not yet have legal status. The islands and reefs of the Lakshadweep have no protected areas.

Protected Area	Important Habitats/Species
INDIA	
Gulf of Kutch Marine National Park and Sanctuary, Gujarat,west coast	Mangroves, coral reefs, turtles, dugong, water birds
Malvan Sanctuary, south of Bombay	Coral reefs, turtles, mangroves
Gulf of Mannar National Park, south-east coast	Mangroves, segrass beds, coral reefs, dugong, dolphins, turtles
Sundarbans National Park, northern Bay of Bengal	Extensive mangrove forests
Bhitar Kanika Wildlife Sanctuary, east coast	Mass nesting site for Olive Ridley turtles
Mahatma Gandhi (Wandur) Marine National Park, Andaman Islands	Coral reefs, turtle, dugong, mangroves, estuarine crocodile
Great Nicobar Biosphere Reserve, Nicobar Islands	Coral reefs, mangroves, estuarine crocodile
SRI LANKA	
Hikkaduwa Marine Sanctuary	Coral reefs
Bar Reef Marine Sanctuary	Coral reefs
Kokkilai Lagoon Sanctuary	Sea-grass beds, mangroves, water birds

personal communication). Overnight visits on the islands are strictly regulated, and the average tourist is allowed only a whistle-stop tour of the Lakshadweeps.

The Andaman Islands have been chosen as a site for large-scale tourism development, and they are presently witnessing a large investment in tourism infrastructure. Until recently, however, most reefs were off limits for tourism and very little was done to encourage reef recreational activity. With many of these controls being eased, and with the construction of an international airport for the Andamans, the reefs are poised for a large tourist influx (Acharya, S. personal communication). This development will increase disturbances on the fragile landscape of these islands, and could be a conservation problem if not adequately controlled (109). The Nicobar Islands on the other hand, are still closed to all tourism, and the reefs here are probably less in danger from uncontrolled tourism development.

Conclusions

Science

Bakus and colleagues (7) summarized the information gaps and deficiencies in methodology in coral reef studies in India. Among the most important points were the lack of planned, long-term, and comprehensive research programs, the lack of experimental research and statistical analysis of the collected data, the lack of data on the effects of humans on coral reef ecosystems, and the lack of an infrastructure to educate young children about the beauty and scientific value of coral reef ecosystems. Additionally, the training of reef researchers in ecological concepts, research design, and methods is crucial if research is to be given meaningful direction. There seems to have been little change in the status of reef research in the past several years.

The number of papers published on coral reefs of India since 1992 has been remarkably small, only a few dozen short papers and only a handful in major scientific or conservation journals. The lack of sustained and experimental studies that are designed to answer problems of reef status, degradation and responses to anthropogenic stresses severely limits the ability of managers to make well-informed decisions. The training of reef researchers in ecological concepts, research design and methods is crucial if this hurdle is to be overcome and to give research a meaningful direction. One potential source of support is The Ministry of Environment and Forests in New Delhi which maintains a national committee (Coral Reef Committee operating from 1980) that funds research on coral reef and mangroves species and ecosystems (Pillai, C.S.G. personal communication). Although the present infrastructure and finances are inadequate for elaborate research programs, the most immediate hurdle is a lack of interest in undertaking extensive coral reef field studies. This situation appears to be changing with several institutions contemplating long-term research in several Indian reefs, but it is clear that a vast amount remains to be done before research here can catch up with the needs of conservation.

Conservation

The multitude of current reef exploitative and degradatory practices, together with the paucity of knowledge on reef ecology, dictates that a precautionary approach incorporating an integrated course of action be speedily adopted for the sustainable management of Indian and Sri Lankan coral reefs (20-24). Kumaraguru (44,45) suggests the following conservation strategies for coral reefs: 1) establish marine parks, sanctuaries and bio-reserves but also initiate alternative employment opportunities for the fishermen, 2) enforce the protection of these preserves with a sea-worthy police force, 3) educate the illiterate fishermen concerning the value of preserving coral reefs, and 4) locate alternate raw materials for construction. A single and separate government authority, with expertise in coral reef ecology and management, is also badly needed to manage Indian coral reefs (84).

As in many developing countries, both education and law enforcement are greatly needed to preserve coral reefs (5). Perhaps one of the most effective methods is to educate young children on national television. Another is to stimulate environmental groups and individuals to monitor human activities or ecologically important reef species, and to make this information available to the general public and marine scientists. Finally, enforcement of laws is essential for the maintenance of all natural areas. Although regions such as the Andaman-Nicobar Islands are protected by national park or other sanctuary status, the laws need to be enforced and even strengthened. Government management can often emphasize terrestrial rather than marine habitats or can develop policies for the terrestrial resources that jeopardize marine habitats. For example, government-sponsored timber extraction in the Andamans results in forest destruction and consequent siltation of reefs which can easily undermine management of the marine environment (57). Consequently, greater effort to coordinate, as well as enforce, laws is required.

References

1. Ahmed, S. 1975. Seasnakes of the Indian Ocean in the collections of the Zoological Survey of India together with remarks on the geographical distribution of all Indian Ocean species. *Journal of the Marine Biological Association of India* 17: 73-81.

2. Anand, P.E.V. 1995. Proximity of coral reefs and mangroves in the Andaman Islands. *Coral Reefs* 14: 108

3. Anand, P.E.V., Pillai, N.G.K. 1995. Studies on some aspects of biology and ecology of coral reef fishes of Lakshadweep with observations on other coral reef ecosystems of India. *Marine Research Under the Postgraduate Programme in Mariculture. Part 6*, ed. Rengarajan K. No. 61:99-111. Cochin: Central Marine Fisheries Research Institute

4. Appukuttan, K.K. 1996. Marine molluscs and their conservation. In *Marine Biodiversity Conservation and Management*. eds. Menon, N.G., Pillai, C.S.G., pp 66-79. Cochin: Central Marine Fisheries Research Institute.

5. Bakus, G.J. 1983. The selection and management of coral reef preserves. *Ocean Management*. 8: 305-316.

6. Bakus, G.J. 1985. Multidisciplinary marine fisheries resource management program for developing countires: with comments on the Indian Ocean. In: *Proceedings of the International Conference on Biology of Benthic Marine Organisms*, eds. Thompson, M.-F., Saroyini, R., Nagabhushnam, R. pp. 425-450. Aurangabad, India

7. Bakus, G.J., Wright, M., Schulte, B., Mofidi, F., Yazdandoust, M., Gulko, D. Naqvi, W., Jagtap,T., Goes, J., Naik, C. 1994. *Coral Reef Ecosystems*. New Delhi: Oxford & IBH Publishing Co. Distributed by A. Balkema, Rotterdam

8. Balachandran, S. 1995. Shore birds of the Marine National Park in the Gulf of Mannar, Tamil Nadu. *Journal of the Bombay Natural History Society* 92:303-313

9. Balasubramanian, T., Wafar, M.V.M.. 1974. Primary productivity of some fringing reefs of the southeast India. *Mahasagar*. 7: 157-164.

10. Bensam, P., Menon, N.G. 1996. Conservation of marine mammals. In: *Marine Biodiversity Conservation and Management*, eds. Menon, N.G., Pillai, C.S.G. pp 133-142. Cochin: Central Marine Fisheries Research Institute

11. Bhattathiri, P.M.A., Devassy ,V.P. 1979. Biological characteristics of the Laccadive Sea. In *The Laccadive Sea (Lakshadweep)*. pp. 80-92. National Institute of Oceanography Technical Report

12. Bhosale, L.J. 1987. The mangrove ecosystems in India. In *Mangrove Ecosystems of Asia and the Pacific*, eds. Field, C.D., Dartnall ,A.J. pp. 24-30. Townsville: Australian Institute of Marine Science.

13. Central Marine Fisheries Research Institute. 1983. *Mariculture Potential of Andaman and Nicobar Islands - An Indicative Survey*. Cochin: Central Marine Fisheries Research Institute, Bulletin 34:108

14. Chandrika, V., Pillai, C.S.G. 1992. Bacterial flora on corals, sponges and reef sediments of Manauli Island in Gulf of Mannar. In *Association of Microbiologists of India 32nd Annual Conference*, Madurai. Abstract

15. De Bruin, G.H.P. 1972. The Crown of Thorns starfish *Acanthaster planci* (Linne) Ceylon. *Bulletin of Fisheries Research Sri Lanka* 23:37-41

16. De Bruin, G.H.P., Russell, B.C., Bogusch, A. 1955. *The Marine Fisheries Resources of Sri lanka.* Rome: FAO

17. Ditlev, H. 1976. Stony corals (coelenterata: Scleractinia) from the west coast of Thailand. *Phuket marine Biological Center, Research Bulletin* 13: 1-14

18. De Silva, R.I. 1990. The seabirds of Sri Lanka (an annotated checklist). *Ceylon Journal of Science, Biological Sciences.* 21:28-33

19. Duncan, P.M. 1989. On the Madreporaria of the Mergui Archihpelago collected for the Trustees of the Indian Museum by Dr. John Anderson, F.R.S., Superintendent of the Museum. Journal of the Linnean Society (Zoology) 21: 1-25

20. Ekaratne, S.U.K. 1989. *Status of Sri Lankan coral reefs.* Country Report for workshop to establish funding priorities for management of biologically diverse ecosystems, Department of Zoology, University of Colombo, Sri Lanka

21. Ekaratne, S.U.K. 1989. Research priorities into effective management of coral reef resources of Sri Lanka: country report. In: *United States National Science Foundation - United States Agency for International Development Regional Workshop,* pp. 160-170. Bangkok

22. Ekaratne, S.U.K. 1990. Development of alternatives for the effective management of coral Reef resources of Sri Lanka. *International Interdisciplinary Symposium on Ecology and Landscape Management in Sri Lanka*

23. Ekaratne, S.U.K. 1990. Man-induceed degradation of coral reefs in Sri Lanka. *Fifth MICE Symposium for Asia and the Pacific,* Nanjing University Press, China, pp. 22–27

24. Ekaratne, S.U.K. 1997. *Final report on Coral Reef Ecology at Hikkaduwa Marine Sanctuary.* Coastal Resources Management Project, USAID

25. Elliot, H.F.I. 1976. Island ecosystems and conservation with particular reference to the biological significance of islands of the Indian Ocean and consequential research and conservation needs. *Journal of the Marine Biological Association of India* 14: 578-608

26. Emmanuel, P, Anand, P.E.V., Varghese, T.J. 1990. Notes on marine ornamental fishes of Lakshadweep. *Seafood Export Journal (India).* 22:13-18.

27. Fauvel, P. 1953. *Fauna of India. Annelida Polychaeta.* Allahabad: Indian Press Ltd

28. Girijavallabhan, K.G., Davidraj, I.., Alavandi, S.V. 1989. Hydrobiology of the lagoons. In: *Marine Living Resources of the Union Territory of Lakshadweep,* eds. James, P.S.B.R., Susselan, C., pp. 200-211. Central Marine Fisheries Institute Bulletin No. 43

29. Gnanamuthu, C.P. 1943. The foraminifera of Krusadai island (in the Gulf of Manaar). *Bulletin of the Madras Government Museum of Natural Science, Natural History Section.* 1: 1-21.

30. Gopinathan, C.P., Selvaraj, G.S.D. 1996. The mangroves - importance, conservation and management. In: *Marine Biodiversity Conservation and Management.* eds. Menon, N.G., Pillai, C.S.G., pp 4-15. Cochin: Central Marine Fisheries Research Institute

31. Harrison, R.M., Poole, M. 1909. Marine fauna of the Mergui Archipelago, Lower Burma, collected by Drs. D. Simpson, M.A., B.Sc. and R.N.

Rudmore-Brown, B.Sc. University of Aberdeen: Madreporaria. *Proceedings of the Zoological Society of London* 1909: 897-912

32. Heere, A.W.C.T. 1941. A list of fishes known from the Andaman Islands. *Memoirs Indian Museum.* 15: 331-403

33. Herath, J.W. 1990. *The coral and shell industry of Sri Lanka.* Sri Lanka German Technical Cooperation and Coast Conservation Department, Colombo

34. Jagtap, T.G. 1985. Studies on the littoral flora of Andaman Islands. In *Marine Plants: Their Biology, Chemistry and Utilization*, ed. Krishnamurthy, V., pp. 43-50. Goa: Proceedings of the All India Symposium in Marine Plants

35. Jagtap, T.G. 1987. Distribution of algae, seagrasses and coral communities from Lakshadweep Islands, eastern Arabian Sea. *Indian Journal of Marine Science* 16: 256–260

36. James, D.B. 1986. Zoogeography of shallow-water echinoderms of Indian Seas. In *Recent Advances in Marine Biology.* ed., James, P.S.B.R. pp. 569-591. New Delhi: Today and Tomorrow Printers and Publishers

37. James, D.B, 1996. Conservation of sea cucumbers. In *Marine Biodiversity Conservation and Management*, eds. Menon, N.G., Pillai, C.S.G., pp 80-88. Cochin: Central Marine Fisheries Research Institute

38. James, P.S.B.R., Mohan, R.S.L. 1987. The marine mammals of India. *Marine Fisheries Information Service Technical External Series* No. 87:1-13

39. Jones, S. 1986. Lakshadweep - general features and some considerations. *Central Marine Fisheries Research Institute Marine Fisheries Information Service* Bulletin No. 68: 3-6

40. Jones, S., Kumaran, M. 1980. *Fishes of the Laccadive Archipelago.* Kerala: The Nature Conservation and Aquatic Sciences Service

41. Kelleher, G., Bleakley, C., Wells, S. 1995. A global representative system of marine protected areas. Vol. III. Great Barrier Reef Marine Park Authority, World Bank, World Conservation Union

42. Kinsey, D. W. 1983. Standards of performance in coral reef primary production and carbon turnover. In *Perspectives on Coral Reefs.* ed. Barnes, D.J. pp. 209-220. Manuka: Brian Clouston Publisher

43. Krishnamoorthy, R., Bhattacharya, A., Natarajan, T. 1993. Mangroves and coral reef mapping of South Andaman Islands through remote sensing. In *Sustainable Management of Coastal Ecosystems.* eds. Swaminathan, M.S., Ramesh, R. pp. 143-151. Madras: Swaminathan Research Foundation

44. Kumaraguru, A.K. 1991. Indian coral reefs and the need for conservation. *Environmental Pollution and Resources of Land and Water.* (1991):73-81

45. Kumaraguru, A.K. 1997. *Coral Reefs in the Gulf of Mannar and the Conservation Strategies Required.* Unpublished Manuscript

46. Kumaran, M., Pillai, P.P., Lal Mohan, R.S., Murty, V.S., Gopakumar, G. 1989. Live-bait resources and development. *Central Marine Fisheries Research Institute Bulletin* No. 43: 39-45

47. Lal Mohan, R.S. 1983. Cultivable finfish resources. In *Mariculture Potential of Andaman and Nicobar Islands - An Indicative Survey.* pp. 52-53. Central Marine Fisheries Research Institute Bulletin No. 34

48. Leatherwood, S., Reeves, R.R.. 1989. *Marine Mammal Research and Conservation in Sri Lanka 1985-1986.* UNEP Marine Mammal Technical Report No. 1, Nairobi, Kenya

49. Mahadevan, S., Easterson, D.C.V. 1983. Topographical features of areas surveyed. In *Mariculture Potential of Andaman and Nicobar Islands - An Indicative Survey.* pp. 10-25. Central Marine Fisheries Research Institute Bulletin No. 34

50. Marichamy, R. 1983. Zooplankton production in coastal waters. In *Mariculture Potential of Andaman and Nicobar Islands - An Indicative Survey.* pp. 33-35. Central Marine Fisheries Research Institute Bulletin No. 34

51. Menon, N.G., C.S.G. Pillai eds. 1996. *Marine Biodiversity, Conservation and Management.* Cochin: Central Marine Fisheries Institute

52. Mergner, H. 1971. Structure, ecology and zonation of Red Sea reefs (in comparison with South India and Jamaican reefs). *Symposium of the Zoological Society of London* 28:141-161

53. Mergner, H., Scheer, G. 1974. The physiographic zonation and the ecological conditions of some South Indian and Ceylon coral reefs. *Proceedings of the Second International Coral Reef Symposium,* Brisbane 2: 3-30

54. Movachan, O.A. 1973. *Soviet Fisheries Investigations in the Indian Ocean.* ed. A.S. Bogdanov, Translated from the Russian. Israel Program for Scientific Translations, Jerusalem

55. Mukherjee, B. 1985. An integrated system analysis of the coral reef environment and ecology at Chiriatapu in South Andamans. PhD Thesis. Ranchi: Ranchi University

56. Munro, I.S.R. 1955. *The Marine and Freshwater Fishes of Ceylon.* Canberra: Department of External Affairs

57. Mustafa, A.M. 1990. Increasing environmental stress on the coral reef ecosystem around South Andaman. *Journal of the Andaman Science Association.* 6:63-65

58. Mustafa, A.M., Dwivedi, S.N., Warwadekar, Y.M., Abidi, S.A.H.. 1987. Endangered coral reefs of Bay Islands and their ornamental fishes. Symposium on the Management of Coastal Ecosystems and Oceanic Resources of the Andamans, Port Blair. In *Proceedings of the Symposium on Management of Coastal Ecosystems and Oceanic Resources of the Andamans,* eds. Singh, N.T., Gangwar, B., Rao, G.C., Soundararajan, pp. 60-65

59. Nair, S. 1979. Microbial characteristics of the Laccadive Sea (Lakshadweep). In *The Laccadive Sea (Lakshadweep).* pp. 108-120. National Institute of Oceanography Technical Report

60. Nair, P.V.R., Pillai, C.S.G.. 1972. Primary productivity of some coral reefs in the Indian seas. In *Proceedings of the Symposium on Corals and Coral Reefs, 1969,* eds. Mukundan, C., Pillai, C.S.G. pp. 33-42. Cochin: Marine Biological Association of India

61. Nair, R.R., Qasim, S.Z. 1978. Occurrence of a bank with living corals off the south-west coast of India. *Indian Journal of Marine Science* 7: 55-58

62. Nakatani, K., Rajasuriya, A., Premaratne, A., White, A.T. eds. 1994. *The Coastal Environmental Profile of Hikkaduwa, Sri Lanka.* Colombo: Coastal Resources Management Project

63. Namboodiri, P.N., Sivadas, P. 1979. Zonation of molluscan assemblage at Kavarati Atoll Laccadives). *Mahasagar.* 12: 239-246

64. National Institute of Oceanography. 1979. The Laccadive Sea (Lakshadweep). *NIO Technical Report.* 1/79
65. National Institute of Oceanography. 1980. The Andaman Sea. *NIO Technical Report.* 2/80
66. Ohman, M., Rajasuriya ,A., Linden, O. 1993. Human disturbances on coral reefs in Sri Lanka: A case study. *Ambio.* 22:474-480
67. Ohman, M.C., Rajasuriya, A., Olafsson, E. 1997. Reef fish assemblages in north-western Sri Lanka: distributional patterns and influences of fish practices. *Environmental Biology of Fish* 49:45-61
68. Olsen, S., Sadacharan, D., Samarakoon, J.I., White, A.T., Wickremeratne, H.J.M., Wijeratne, M.S. 1992. *Coastal 2000: A Resource Management Strategy for Sri Lanka's Coastal Region.* Sri Lanka: Coastal Resources Management Project and CCD. Two Volumes
69. Pande, P., Kothari, A., Singh, S. eds. 1991. *Directory of National Parks and Sanctuaries in Andaman and Nicobar Islands: Management Status and Profiles.* New Delhi: IIPA
70. Parulekar, A.H. 1981. Marine fauna of Malvan, central west coast of India. *Mahasagar* 14: 33-44
71. Parulekar, A.H., Ansari, Z.A.. 1981. Benthic macrofauna of the Andaman Sea. *Indian Journal of Marine Science* 10: 280-284
72. Parulekar, A.H., Hankantra, S.N., Ansari, Z.A.. 1982. Benthic production and assessment of demersal fishery resources of the Indian seas. *Indian Journal of Marine Science* 11: 107-114
73. Patel, M.I. 1978. Generic diversity of scleractinians around Poshetra Point, Gulf of Kutch. *Indian Journal of Marine Science* 7: 30-32
74. Patel, M.I. 1988. Patchy corals of the Gulf of Kutch. In *Proceedings of the Symposium on Endangered Marine Animals and Marine Parks*, ed. Silas, E.G. pp. 411-413. Cochin: Marine Biological Association of India
75. Pernetta, J.C. 1993. *Marine Protected Area Needs in the South Asian Seas Region, Volume 5: Sri Lanka,* IUCN, Switzerland
76. Pillai, C.S.G. 1969. Corals and coral reefs. *Symposium on Corals and Coral Reefs.* Marine Biological Association of India. Souvenir Issue pp. 9-17
77. Pillai, C.S.G. 1971a. Composition of the coral fauna of the southeastern coast of India and the Laccadives. *Symposium of the Zoological Society of London* 28: 301-327
78. Pillai, C.S.G. 1971b. The distribution of corals on a reef at Mandapam, Palk Bay. *Journal of the Marine Biological Association of India* 11: 62-72
79. Pillai, C.S.G. 1971c. The distribution of shallow water stony corals at Minicoy Atoll in the Indian Ocean with a checklist of species. *Atoll Research Bulletin* 141: 1-12
80. Pillai, C.S.G. 1977. The structure, formation and species diversity of South Indian reefs. *Proceedings of the Third Internationa Coral Reef Symposium,* Miami 1: 47-53
81. Pillai, C.S.G. 1983a. Coral reefs and their environs. In *Mariculture Potential of Andaman and Nicobar Islands - An Indicative Survey.* pp. 36-43. Central Marine Fisheries Research Institute Bulletin No. 34
82. Pillai, C.S.G. 1983b. The endangered marine and terrestrial habitats of Minicoy Island in Lakshadweep - A matter of concern for naturalists. *Seminar on World Conservation,* pp. 24-28. Bombay Natural History Society, December 1983

83. Pillai, C.S.G. 1983. Structure and genetic diversity of recent Scleractinians of India. *Journal of the Marine Biological Association of India* 25: 78-90
84. Pillai, C.S.G. 1996. Coral reefs of India, their conservation and management. In *Marine Biodiversity Conservation and Management*, eds. Menon, N.G., Pillai, C.S.G., pp. 16-31. Cochin: Central Marine Fisheries Research Institute
85. Pillai, C.S.G., Jasmine, S. 1989. The coral fauna. *Central Marine Fisheries Research Institute Bulletin* 43: 179-194
86. Pillai, C.S.G., Rajagopalan, M.S., Varghese M.A. 1979. Preliminary report on a reconnaissance survey of the major coastal and marine ecosystems in the Gulf of Kutch.. *Marine Fisheries Information Service T & E Series.* 14: 16-20
87. Pillai, C.S.G., Scheer, G. 1976. Report on the stony corals from the Maldive Archipelago. *Zoologica* 126: 1-81
88. Prasad, R.R., Nair, P.V.R.. 1960. A preliminary production and its relation to fisheries of the inshore waters of the Gulf of Mannar. *Indian Journal of Fisheries* 7: 165-168
89. Purjava, G.R., Ramesh, R. 1993. Ecology, conservation and restoration of coral reef ecosystems. In *Sustainable Management of Coastal Ecosystems.* eds. Swaminathan, M.S., Ramesh, R. pp. 103-113. Madras: Swaminathan Research Foundation
90. Qasim, S.Z. 1970. Some characteristics of a *Trichodesmium* bloom in the Laccadives. *Deep-Sea Research* 17: 655-660
91. Qasim, S.Z. 1973. Productivity of specialized environments. *Mahasagar* 6: 95-100
92. Qasim, S.Z. 1982. Oceanography of the northern Arabian Sea. *Deep-Sea Research* 29: 1041-1068
93. Qasim S.Z. 1995a. Indian Ocean and coral reefs. *Journal of Indian Ocean Studies* 3:7-20
94. Qasim, S.Z. 1995b. Specialized marine ecosystems - Corals and coral reefs. In: *Felicitation volume in honour of Professor C. Suriyakumaran at the 50th Anniversary of the United Nations*, Colombo: K.V.G. de Silva & Sons
95. Qasim, S.Z., Bhattathiri, P.M.A. 1971. Primary production of a seagrass bed on Kavaratti Atoll (Laccadives). Hydrobiologia 38:29-38
96. Qasim, S.Z., Bhattathiri, P.M.A., Reddy, C.V.G. 1972. Primary production of an atoll in the Laccadives. Int. Revue. ges. Hydrobiol. 57: 207-225
97. Qasim, S.Z., Wafar, M.V.M. 1979. Occurrence of living corals at several places along the west coast of India. *Mahasagar.* 12: 53-58
98. Rajagopalan, M. 1996. The marine turtles and their conservation. In *Marine Biodiversity Conservation and Management*, eds. Menon, N.G., Pillai, C.S.G. pp 126-132. Cochin: Central Marine Fisheries Research Institute
99. Rajasuriya, A. 1994a. Marine sanctuaries and conservation of fishery resources. In *Report and Proceedings of the Sri Lanka FAO National Workshop on Development of Community-Based Fishery Management, Colombo.* eds. Morris, M.J., M.-Hotta, Atapattu, A.R. pp. 175-182
100. Rajasuriya, A. 1994b. Three genera and twelve species of stony corals new to Sri Lanka (abstract). Paper presented at the *2nd Annual Scientific Sessions of the National Aquatic Resources Agency*, Colombo
101. Rajasuriya, A., de Silva, M.W.R.N. 1988. Stony Corals of Fringing Reefs of the Western, South-western and Southern Coasts of Sri Lanka.

Proceedings of the 6th International Coral Reef Symposium, Australia, Vol. 3: 287-296

102. Rajasuriya, A., Rathnapriya, K. 1994. The abundance of the Crown-of-thorns starfish *Acanthaster planci* (Linne, 1758) in the Bar Reef and Kandakuliya areas and implications for management. Colombo: *Second Annual Scientific Sessions of the National Aquatic Resources Agency.* Abstract

103. Rajasuriya, A., White, A.T. 1995. Coral Reefs of Sri Lanka: Review of their extent, condition, and management status. *Coastal Management* 23: 77-90

104. Rajendran, A.D.I., David, K. 1972. A preliminary underwater survey of the extent of the coral reefs in and around some of the islands in Gulf of Mannar. In *Proceedings of the Symposium on Corals and Coral Reefs*, eds. Mukundan, C., Pillai, C.S.G., pp. 231-238. Cochin: Marine Biological Association of India

105. Ramanujam, N., Mukesh, M.V., Preeja, N.B. 1992. Calcium carbonate accretion, mechanical properties and adaptive sugnificance of the coral *Acropora cervicornis* (sic) in the windward side of Karichalli Island, Gulf of Mannar. *Journal of the Indian Association of Sedimentology* 11:89-94

106. Rao, G.C. 1975. The interstitial fauna in the intertidal sands of Andaman and Nicobar group of islands. *Journal of the Marine Biological Association of India* 17: 116-128

107. Reddiah, K. 1977. The coral reefs of Andaman and Nicobar Islands. *Records of the Zoological Survey of India* 72: 315-324

108. Rink., H. 1847. Om Koralrevene ved Nikobarerne. *Forhandlinger ved de Skandinaviske Naturforskers.* Möte 5: 556-568

109. Saldhana, C.J. ed.. 1989. *Andaman, Nicobar and Lakshadweep: An Environmental Impact Assessment.* New Delhi: Oxford and IBH

110. Santhanam, R., Srinivasan, A., Ramadhas, V., Devaraj, M. 1994. Impact of *Trichodesmium* bloom on the plankton and productivity in the Tuticorin Bay, southeast coast of India. *Indian Journal of Marine Sciences* 23:27-30

111. Scheer, G. 1971. Coral reefs and coral genera in the Red Sea and Indian Ocean. *Symposium of the Zoological Society of London* 28:329-367

112. Scheer, G., Pillai, C.S.G.. 1974. Report on the Scleractinia from the Nicobar Islands. *Zoologica* 127: 1-75

113. Sen Gupta, R., Naqvi, S.W.A.. 1984. Chemical oceanography of the Indian Ocean, north of the equator. *Deep-Sea Research.* 31A: 671-706

114. Sen Gupta, R., Qasim, S.Z. 1985. The Indian Ocean - an environmental overview. In *The Oceans - Realities and Prospect.* ed. Sharma, R. C. pp. 7-40. New Delhi: Rajesh Publications

115. Sewell, R.B.S. 1922. A survey season in the Nicobar Islands on the R.I.M.S. "Investigator", October 1921 to March 1922. *Journal of the Bombay Natural History Society* 28: 970-989

116. Sheppard, C.R.C. 1987. Coral species of the Indian Ocean and adjacent seas: a synonymized compilation and some regional distributional patterns. *Atoll Research Bulletin* 307: 1-32

117. Silas, E.G., Alagarswami. K. eds. 1983. Mariculture potential of Andaman and Nicobar Islands - an indicative survey. *Central Marine Fisheries Research Institute Bulletin.* No. 34

118. Sivadas, P. 1977. Report on the occurrence of *Acanthaster* sp. in Lakshadweep waters. *Mahasagar.* 10: 179-180

119. Stoddart, D.R. 1971. Environment and history in Indian Ocean reef morphology. *Symposium of the Zoological Society of London.* 28: 3-38

120. Stoddart, D.R., Pillai, C.S.G.. 1972. Raised reefs of Ramanathapuram, South India. *Transactions Institute of British Geographers* 56: 111-125

121. Sukhtankar, R.K., Pandit, S.J., Shirke, A.J. 1993. Occurrence of the coral reefs on the Bhandarpule Coast, District Ratnagiri, Maharashtra. *Journal of the Geological Society of India* 42:405-409

122. Suseelan, C. 1996. Crustacean biodiversity, conservation and mangement. In *Marine Biodiversity Conservation and Management*, eds. Menon, N.G., Pillai, C.S.G. pp 41-65. Cochin: Central Marine Fisheries Research Institute

123. Thomas, P. A. 1996. The gorgonid resources and their conservation in India. In *Marine Biodiversity Conservation and Management*, eds. Menon, N.G., Pillai, C.S.G. pp 32-40. Cochin: Central Marine Fisheries Research Institute

124. Thurston, E. 1895. Ramesvaram Island and fauna of the Gulf of Manaar. 2nd edition. Madras: *Madras Government Museum Bulletin* No.3

125. Tikader, B.K., Daniel, A., Subbarao, N.V. 1986. *Sea Shore Animals of Andaman and Nicobar Islands.* Calcutta: Zoological Survey of India

126. Tikader, B.K. Das, A.K. 1985. *Glimpses of Animal Life of Andaman and Nicobar Islands.* Calcutta: Zooloigcal Survey of India

127. Tranter, D.J., George, J. 1972. Zooplankton abundance at Kavaratti and Kalpeni Atolls in the Laccadive Sea. In *Proceedings of the Symposium on Corals and Coral Reefs*, eds. Mukundan, C., Pillai, C.S.G. pp. 239-256. Cochin: Marine Biological Association of India

128. Umamaheswara Rao, M. 1972. Coral reef flora of the Gulf of Mannar and Palk Bay. In *Proceedings of the Symposium on Corals and Coral Reefs*, 1969, eds. Mukundan, C., Pillai, C.S.G. pp. 217-230. Cochin: Marine Biological Association of India

129. Umamaheswara Rao, M. 1973. The seaweed potential of the seas around India. In: *Proceedings of the Symposium on Living Resources.* Cochin: Central Marine Fisheries Research Institute

130. Untawale, A.G., Dhargalkar, V.K., Agadi, V.V. 1983. *List of Marine Algae from India.* National Institute of Oceanography, Goa

131. Untawale, A.G., Jagtap, T.G.. 1984. Marine macrophytes of Minicoy (Lakshadweep) coral atoll of the Arabian Sea. *Aquatic Botany* 19: 97-103

132. Varadachari, V.V.R., Sharma, G.S. 1967. Circulation of the surface waters in the North Indian Ocean. *Journal of the Indian Geophysical Union* 4: 61-73

133. Venkateswarlu, T. 1984. Scientific, common and vernacular names of fishes of India. *Records of the Zoological Survey of India* 56: 1-96

134. Venkateswarlu, T. 1990. Marine mammals of Indian seas. *Environmental Ecology.* 8:1050-1052

135. Wafar, M.V.M. 1977. Phytoplankton production of two atolls of Indian Ocean. *Mahasagar.* 10: 117-122

136. Wafar, M.V.M. 1986. Corals and coral reefs of India. *Proceedings of the Indian Academy of Sciences.* (Animal Science/Plant Science) Supplement. November, pp. 19-43

137. Wafar, M., Wafar, S., David , J.J.. 1990. Nitrification in reef corals. *Limnology and Oceanography* 35: 725-730

138. Wafar, M.V.M., Wafar, S., Rajkumar, R. 1993. Nitrogen uptake kinetics of freshly isolated zooxanthellae. *Indian Journal of Marine Science* 22:83-88

139. Wells, J.W., Davies, S.P. 1966. Preliminary list of stony corals from Addu Atoll. *Atoll Research Bulletin* 116: 43-55

140. Wells, S.M., Sheppard, C. eds. 1988. *Coral Reefs of the World. Volume 2: Indian Ocean.* UNEP Regional Seas Directories and Bibliographies. Gland and Cambridge

141. White, A.T., Ekaratne, S.U.K. 1995. Coastal Tourism in Sri Lanka: Guidelines for Environmental Protection. In: *Eco-tourism: Concept, Design and Strategy*, eds. Hiranburana, S, Stithyudhakarn, V., Dhambutra P. pp 115-134. Bangkok: Srinakharinwirot University Press

142. Wyrtki, K. 1973. Physical Oceanography of the Indian Ocean. In *The Biology of the Indian Ocean*, ed. Zeitschel, B. pp. 18-36. New York: Springer-Verlag

Chapter 11

The Maldives: A Nation of Atolls

Michael J. Risk & Robert Sluka

The Maldives are a double chain of islands in the Indian Ocean stretching for almost 1000 km south of Sri Lanka (74,75). There are more than 1200 islands (only 202 are inhabited), grouped into 19 atolls. The word atoll itself comes from Dhivehi, a Sinhalese dialect which is the language of the Maldives, and means an administrative district (4). The name Maldives is believed to have originated from the Sanskrit word *malodheep*, meaning garland, presumably from the appearance of the chain of islands from the deck of a ship. Marco Polo called the Maldives 'the flower of the Indies'.

The Maldives has been a trading crossroads for the Indian Ocean for more than four thousand years. It is said that an ancient group of sun-worshipping people called the Redin came to Maldives from Sri Lanka, or from the northwest in general, 4000 years ago, bringing with them their beliefs in spirits (*djinni*). Some legends describe the Redin as white people, tall, with brown hair, big hooked noses, and blue eyes (27). The Redin's first landfall was at the northwest tip of the Maldives, from there, they spread to the south and east. They were later replaced or displaced by waves of other Buddhist and Hindu settlers, largely from the Indian subcontinent, but the early beliefs in spirits, and reliance on the sea, had a strong cultural influence.

Maldive people converted to Islam in 1153, a watershed in the history of the archipelago. According to legend, a sea-*djinni* named Rannamaari held sway on Malé Atoll, and threatened to destroy the town of Malé unless a virgin girl was sacrificed every month. A visiting North African learned of this sad state of affairs, and offered to take the place of the virgin. He made his way to the temple reserved for sacrifices, disguised as a girl, and sat by a window piously reciting verses from the Koran. When the spirit appeared, he began reciting the verses even more loudly, causing the spirit to squeal with pain and disappear forever. The local people converted to Islam immediately thereafter.

The post-conversion history of Maldives involves a series of Sultans, invasion by the Portuguese, rebellions, competing influences from the nearby mainland, and, near the end of the 19th Century, an agreement between Sultan Muhammad Muenuddin and the British government on Ceylon (later Sri Lanka), turning Maldives into a British Protectorate.

Maldives was declared a republic in 1953, although the British maintained an air force base on Gan, in the south. This arrangement broke down in 1976.

Maldives was granted full independence from Britain on July 26, 1965. The current President, Maumoon Abdul Gayoom, has served since 1978, being reelected four times.

Culture and Economy

As befitting a group of islands lying astride some of the world's oldest maritime trading routes, the (approximately) 250 000 inhabitants of the Maldives are an ethnic mix, primarily of Sinhalese, Dravidian and Arab stocks, with influence also from Africa. The state religion is Sunni Muslim, and no other religions are permitted, although *djinni* are still blamed for unexplained occurrences.

The area of the country is 67 000 km^2, but most of this is ocean: less than 4% of the total area, about 300 km^2, is in fact dry land, the maximum elevation being 3 m. As little of this land is arable, most food has to be imported. The population growth rate is about 3.5%.

The capital city, Malé, is located on an island of the same name, at the south edge of North Malé Atoll. The population of Malé is hard to estimate, because much of it is transient: the official figure is 65 000, but at some times there may easily be as many as 100 000 people in town. The land area of Malé is 2 km^2, giving a population density of about 50 000 per km^2. The island has been enlarged several times via 'reclamation' (a word suggesting that people are taking back from the sea what rightly belongs to them). In the south, on Addu Atoll, the influence of the British base on Gan is clearly seen. Causeways were built linking several of the islands, and it is possible that these have altered the local pattern of water movement. Causeways were also built by a prominent Maldivian connecting three islands in Laamu Atoll

From very early times, the islands were known for two export products: the money cowry, *Cypraea moneta*, and Maldive fish. Fish was exported especially to Sri Lanka and was produced by boiling, smoking, curing and drying skipjack tuna, a process which results in a black fillet with many of the attributes of wood, and astonishing keeping qualities. It was an ideal source of protein, and quickly became a staple in the cuisine of the Indian subcontinent. Maldive fish is still produced throughout the country, but generally only for local consumption. Recently, several tuna canning factories have been built.

The major earner of foreign exchange is tourism. In recent years, 200 000 people have visited the Maldives annually, largely to enjoy diving on pristine reefs in crystal-clear water. It is estimated that more than 60% of visitors to the Maldives dive at least once during their visit. Over 70 of the uninhabited islands have been reserved for tourism developments, with many of them catering to the desires of specific nationalities.

Climate

Generally, the Maldivian climate is monsoonal, especially in the northern islands. Addu, to the south, is out of the monsoon belt (69). The northeast monsoon, the *iruvai*, lasts from December to March. These are the dryer months, and the time most favored by tourists. The southwest monsoon, the *hulhangu*, lasts from April to November. During this time, rain can sometimes be torrential, winds very strong, and storms severe. Transitions between these two seasons are not abrupt, however, and rains can occur during the dry season. There is little variation in wind direction through the year. The daytime air temperature year-round is about 28°C, and nights are not much cooler. Humidity is high, and the air is salty. Tides are mainly semidiurnal, with a microtidal range of 0.7 m in the north to about 1 m in the south.

Geologic History

Plate Tectonics and Pleistocene Sea Level Changes

The Maldives Islands are a series of coral atolls, cays and faroes developed on the Laccadives-Chagos Ridge, which in turn was generated by the northern drift of the Indian Plate over the Réunion hotspot (6, see Chapter 12). The Maldives shallow carbonate system was initiated during the early Eocene, with carbonate deposition on previously erupted marine lava. Subsequent geologic history of the island chain is a complicated picture of sea level changes, reef and carbonate platform development and erosional events. Large sea-level changes in the Pleistocene resulted in periodic exposure and flooding of the atolls, with corresponding erosional and solution events. Seismic records (6) show that exposure during Pleistocene glacial low sea level times resulted in dissolution and karstification of the shallow reef bank tops, which were exposed to rainfall. During the past 10 000 years, sea levels have been rising and this recent Holocene physiography is formed of shallow reefal accumulation above the older karsted solution horizons formed during the Pleistocene.

Holocene Reef Development

Holocene reef development in the Maldives has resulted in a number of large atolls up to several 10s of km in diameter. The lagoon depth in these large atolls is on the order of 50 to 100 m and depths are greater in the south than in the north. This distribution of lagoon floor depths probably represents Holocene reef growth on a surface previously eroded almost flat by the sea-level drop. Developed on the floor of these lagoons in the northern atolls are an immense number of ring reefs, or faroes, that are basically miniature atolls. These range in diameter from 10s to 100s of meters; if central lagoons are present, they range in depth from a few meters to a few 10s of meters. Faroes are absent in the southernmost atoll of Addu (68,69).

There is considerable north-south variation in the structure and development of the islands and atolls of the Maldives chain (75). In the north, atolls are broad banks, discontinuously fringed by reefs, with small peripheral islands and many faroes. To the south, atoll lagoons are deeper, faroes are rare or absent, and the atoll rim becomes stronger and more cemented. The reasons for the north-south change in lagoon depths are far from obvious. Darwin (18) suggested that this was caused by greater subsidence. Daly (17) thought it was caused by inhibition of reef growth. On the other hand, it may simply reflect the history of submarine ridge activity. The hotspot that drove the Indian subcontinent up into Asia created a magma bulge in the upper mantle, which could very well have tilted the Maldives-Laccadive Ridge upwards and towards the north.

Together with the neighbor group of islands, the Lakshadweeps, the Maldivian chain of atolls and faroes is the largest and most extensive on the planet. The reasons for this unique reef development pattern must lie in the unique aspects of the geological history. The location of the main atolls was almost certainly controlled by the location and geometry of the underwater volcanic peaks originating on the ridge as spreading initiated. Atolls are known from many locations, but the existence of the faroes seems unique to Maldives.

There has as yet been no drilling program designed to elucidate the origin and development of these reefs within reefs, but the explanation may very well lie in the interplay of steady state and catastrophic climates, combined with the relatively symmetrical wind roses. The steep sides of the atolls themselves represent the seaward accretion expected of reefs growing under moderate energy conditions. Maldives can, however, experience severe wind and wave conditions. For example, a series of large waves submerged all of the reclaimed land at the edge of Malé several years ago. When storms of this severity hit, pieces of reef will be torn from the reef front and hurled into the lagoon. This is the process of reefs growing landward under high-energy conditions, first described by Davies (19), on the Great Barrier Reef. Most of these transported blocks of reef will die, of course. Some will survive, and begin to grow up, accreting and shedding sediment and debris, much as miniature reefs. Upward accretion during the Holocene Transgression under conditions of ever shifting wind directions, will result in ring reefs, at least in the northern islands. To the south, where monsoonal climates do not occur and major storms are rare, faroes are less common. In what is believed to be a similar process, reefs from the Karimunjawa Islands, Java Sea, show little or no windward-leeward differentiation, possibly due to varying wind patterns associated with monsoonal climates (22).

The Holocene section on Maldives is generally about 15 to 20 m thick. A drilling program on the northern rim of Malé, part of an investigation into a possible harbor extension, penetrated a bit less than 18 m into the Holocene (75). Much of the core was sand or rubble; in the entire core, two samples of massive faviid corals, large enough to date, were encountered. The extent of these massive corals was 30 cm, or somewhat less than 2% of the total core. This is not surprising, even for an atoll rim location, as the low frequency of storms favors the accumulation of sand. Maldivian islands are mostly sand (69,70,75), and exposed boulders are rare.

Dating of the Malé core, and a series of observations on other islands, the following Holocene history of Maldivian atoll reefs. Reef growth began about 6000 years BP, and the reefs grew upwards in a catch-up mode at 3 to 10 mm/y for the next 3000 years. In the last 3000 years reefs have grown up to the surface. Because the reefs are now in the surf zone sediments have been shed into the lagoons and channels at increased rates which, combined with sand thrown up from occasional storms, forms islands.

Biogeography, Zonation, Reef Structure

Coral reefs are certainly the most-studied ecosystem in the Maldives and fish have also been the subject of several recent works (see later sections on reef fisheries). There are nearly 200 species of hermatypic corals in nearly 60 genera (see Chapter 1). Generic diversity also increases from north to south (56). There is very little attenuation of coral diversity across the Indian Ocean (Chapter 1, 73). The broad north-south gradients that do exist in the Indian Ocean are thought to be imposed by river drainage from Asia in the north, and lack of suitable substrate to the south. In the Indian Ocean, Maldives lies in the zone of maximum coral diversity. The reasons for this probably involve the existence of suitable substratum, such as erupted lava, and the environmental conditions of warm and clear water. Sea water temperature in the Maldives is the highest among reefal areas in the Indian Ocean (52).

Generally, the lushest growth and highest diversity of corals is found at a depth of about 10 m, on what we have termed the upper fore-reef slope. Coral cover ranges from essentially 100%, on actively-growing atoll fore-reefs, to a typical value of about 35 to 40%. A typical 20 m coral survey transect encounters about 40 genera of corals, indicating a very diverse coral fauna. This, and the variety and abundance of fish, are what attract tourists. Maldivian reefs, however, do seem to be qualitatively different from other shallow-water reefs in the Indian Ocean, in that they display high abundance and diversity of branching *Acropora*. This in turn leads to relatively loose, open reef frameworks (69). The tops of faroes are usually covered with loose coral rubble, mostly *Acropora* debris, and sand. Live, massive corals occur at the rims of these structures.

Considerable work has been done on the modern reefs of Maldives. Matteuci and Russo (37) describe facies sequences and coral communities on some Maldivian reefs. Risk and colleagues (49) provide an overview of a large Canadian-Maldivian program on reef monitoring. Studies on the impacts of coral mining (9) and on reef rehabilitation efforts and the importance of coral reproduction (11,12,13) have taken place and will be discussed later in this chapter.

In a recent paper, Bianchi and colleagues (7) describe reef structure, sediments and geomorphology of a Maldivian reef in relatively pristine condition, the fringing reef around Alimathaa Island, Felidu Atoll. As this setting is typical of most Maldivian reefs, the description is summarized here. The island itself is sand, grading to coral rubble as the reef edge is approached. Outer slopes are very steep and the area down to about 15 m is covered with lush corals, yet the width of this zone is usually less than 30 m. The outer reef slope, here as elsewhere in the Maldives, is characterized by a series of reef terraces representing past sea level still stands. Typically, there are terraces at depths of 3 to 6 m, 15 to 30 m, and a deeper one at 50 m. On steep slopes, there may be caves incised into terrace faces. The modern coral growth is a veneer over older reef rock, but the existing community is constructional down to a depth of at least 50 m.   In the upper levels, reef building is by zooxanthellate corals, but in deeper zones this role is sometimes taken over by the azooxanthellate branching coral, *Tubastrea micranthus*, which may reach heights of 2 m.   The dividing line between these two coral types is seemingly controlled by water movement, usually at depths of about 45 m.

Interestingly, a significant proportion of the sediment on the lagoon floors and the passes of Felidu is detrital dolomite, which implies erosion and reworking of poorly-consolidated Pleistocene sands.   Maldivian reef sediments are, in general, characterized by an abundance of coral fragments, especially in the coarse size fractions (gravel and coarse sand).   *Halimeda* is abundant in the sand fraction, as are large foraminifera.

The suite of boring organisms found in Maldivian corals is typical of most of the Indo-Pacific: several species of *Lithophaga,* various polychaete worms, and several species of boring sponges.   The bright purple or blue boring sponge, *Cliona schmidtii*, is especially common.

The relatively pristine nature of the Maldivian marine environment was emphasized by a series of geochemical analyses performed as part of the Canadian-Maldivian project.   Coral skeletons were analyzed for most of the common heavy metals, using advanced geochemical equipment.   In all cases, values were below detection limits.   Coral tissues were analyzed for organic fractions, and again values of extraneous organics were typically very low, except for hydrocarbon residues found in corals near the island that serves as a fuel store for the airport.

Relationship Between Reefs and Fish Communities

The relative abundance of coral reef fish has been shown to vary based on specific features of a particular reef such as geomorphology, current regime, and location on the continental shelf (54,55).   Several studies have also shown that the absolute abundance of some species of coral reef fish can be predicted from particular habitat measures such as complexity or live coral cover (30,50). However, there seems to be little trend in these habitat-abundance relationships; there are species and location specific relationships between habitat parameters and fish abundance.

The fish fauna of the Maldives has been relatively little studied, but Randall and Anderson (47) provide a checklist of epipelagic and shore fishes and the Marine Research Section of the Ministry of Fisheries and Agriculture has finished a more complete checklist.   Studies of the ecology of coral reef fishes include exploratory reef fish surveys, studies of coral mining and its influence on fish assemblages, and studies on grouper-habitat relationships.

An exploratory survey of reef fish resources was conducted in North Malé Atoll (70,71) using longlining and hook and line fishing.   This survey was later expanded to include Shaviyani, Alifu, and Laamu atolls (4,5).   There were distinct trends in reef fish abundance among habitats and from north to south within a habitat type.   The southern-most atoll studied (Laamu) differed from the more northern atolls by a lower catch rate and different species composition, specifically, more snappers.   The grouper *Epinephelus sonnerati* was caught in more northern atolls, but not in the most southern atoll while Jacks (family Carangidae) showed the opposite trend.   There is no readily apparent reason for these differences. Based on qualitative data, the shallow-water reef fauna does not vary markedly along the length of the Maldives islands (4). There was, however, a trend towards increasing catches per hook in the central atolls. This may be related to the volume of reefs inside the atolls (but not around the atoll ring) (5). Alifu and N. Malé have abundant internal reefs, Laamu relatively few, and Shaviyani few, but relatively large reefs. These internal reefs could influence the abundance of fish susceptible to long lining by providing shelter for juveniles as well as sources of prey items (5).

Effects of coral mining on reef flat and reef-slope fish assemblages where coral mining occurred on reef flats indicated clear differences in fish assemblage structure between mined and unmined reefs (21). Eighty percent of the indicator fish species were more abundant on unmined than mined flats. There was also a significant relationship between habitat complexity and fish numbers on faro reef flats (10). Planktivores were more abundant on reef slopes than flats, while herbivores showed the opposite pattern. Most species were more abundant on reef slopes than flats. Species that were more abundant on mined than unmined reef flats preferred sand and low rugosity rubble habitat.

The alteration of habitat had significant effects on reef fishes which may be due to the reduction in coral cover associated with mining (9) or to the decrease in structure due to coral removal. The loss of structure resulted in a decrease in the abundance of many species of fish which presumably relied on the intact reef flats for protection and prey. Coral mining is now regulated and coral cannot be mined on tourist resort's 'house' reefs, atoll rim reefs, and common bait-fishing reefs. More restrictive legislation has been written for two of the atolls where most of the damage has occurred (15). Experimentation with artificial reef structures in mined reef flats has shown that the fish community that develops is initially quite different from that on unmined reef flats. Species such as *Myripristis vittata*, *Pempheris vanicolensis*, *Chromis viridis*, and *Apogon apogonoides* are abundant on artificial structures, but not in unmined reef flats (14).

Groupers and Maldivian Reefs

Groupers are ecologically and economically important top-level predators found on coral reefs (25,43). The relative abundance of groupers has been shown to vary among coral reefs at several spatial scales. At the largest spatial scale, there are biogeographic differences in grouper relative abundance. For example, several species of grouper are found on coral reefs along the continental shelf regions of the northern Indian Ocean that are not found in the atolls of the Maldives (26). Within a biogeographic province, the relative abundance of groupers has been shown to differ among different types or zones of coral reefs (3,60,63,65). These differences may be consistent among biogeographic provinces. For example, *Cephalopholis argus* is most abundant on reef crests in both the Gulf of Aqaba and the Republic of Maldives (60,63).

Among several types of habitats in Gaagandu, North Malé Atoll and Olhugiri, Thaa Atoll, smaller groupers were found more often in the shallow lagoons while larger individuals where found on the reef crests and slopes (63). Superficially this observation may suggest recruitment to shallow areas and subsequent movement offshore with increasing size, as observed in many

Caribbean grouper species (53), but the species composition of grouper in lagoons was quite different from crests and slopes. Small individuals of abundant slope or crest species are rare in lagoons but occasionally observed in reef crests and slopes and, therefore, it is likely that most grouper species are recruiting directly to adult habitats (Sluka, R. personal observation).

At Thaa Atoll, *Cephalopholus. argus* was common on both the outer and inner reef crest while *C. urodeta* was more abundant on the outer reef crest (63). In Laamu Atoll, *C. urodeta* are also more abundant on outer than inner reef slopes (Sluka, R. personal observation). Some species of grouper are known to be site attached and several species of grouper, such as *Plectropomus* spp., *Variola louti*, and *Gracila albomarginata*, were found loosely attached to structural features of coral reefs. *Aethaloperca rogaa* appeared intermediate between free-roaming species and the more site-attached species such as *Cephalopholis* and *Epinephelus* pp. *C. argus* was found more often in sites with a higher vertical relief, greater massive coral cover, and lower sand cover. This is similar to many grouper species that prefer areas with high vertical relief (40,62). These observations and those of grouper species in the Caribbean (61,62,65), indicate that grouper movement patterns and behavior are significantly affected by specific and quantifiable features of coral reefs.

Threats to the Reefs

The Republic of Maldives is in a unique position, in that the islands are relatively free from the anthropogenic effects from which reefs are suffering in other parts of the world, while at the same time being threatened, perhaps more than any other nation on the globe, by the possible effects of sea level rise. At an international meeting in Miami, in 1993, there was general agreement among reef scientists that reefs, worldwide, suffered from three major threats. These are:

1. Sediment stress, largely from deforestation and agriculture,
2. Sewage stress, and
3. Inappropriate fishing methods: overfishing, bombing, cyanide fishing, muro-ami and others.

Maldives are no more than 3 m above sea level. There are no rivers anywhere in the country. Anthropogenic sediment stress, therefore, comes only from dredging activities, and these influences are relatively short-lived. Dredging has deepened the harbor at Malé, and dredging occurs around the airport on Hululé, but sediment stress is not nearly as intense as in other parts of the world. Sewage stress has affected Maldivian reefs (Fig. 11.1), and will become increasingly important as the population grows, and the flight to the capital continues. The Maldivian government is trying to alleviate some of the stresses by developing one island near the capitol (Vilingilli) and creating a new island near the airport (Hululé) by reclamation. Interestingly, sewage stress from the resort islands is relatively insignificant. Every resort is required to install a system for dealing with its sewage. Some resorts, on large islands, have

Figure 11.1. Effect of sewage on Maldivian reefs: Top, healthy reef from an area of low human population density; Bottom, reef on Malé, same depth and orientation, but impacted by large discharge of untreated sewage.

septic systems, while others, on smaller islands, sometimes have large holding tanks, that are periodically pumped out, with the waste discharged in deep channels far at sea. If these regulations are adhered to, then sewage stress on the Maldivian reefs will increasingly come from the local populations, and not from tourists.

Sea Level Rise and Global Change

Recent projections of the rate of sea level rise due to melting of the polar ice caps suggest a rise of around 0.5 m in the next 50 years (28). There is also evidence that major shifts in the Earth's climate may be far more rapid than previously estimated (66). A rapid increase in sea level obviously poses a serious threat to the reefs of the Maldives, as it will to other low-lying small-island states, such as Fiji, Solomons and Samoa. In addition to sea level rise will be the added danger of the increased frequency of tropical storms, and increased storm run off (67,39). As sea level rises, those islands that still retain freshwater lenses will experience an illusory increase in the availability of fresh water. This will be illusory because the fresh water will rise as it floats on the rising sea water. As it rises, the fresh water will be subject to increased evaporation and will, therefore, be exhausted more quickly (42). From work on microatolls from Maldives, Woodroffe (75) found no significant changes in sea level over the last few decades, but this is no guarantee change will not occur in the future.

In response to the perceived threat from sea level rise, the Government of Maldives has begun construction of a 3-m high gabion seawall around Malé, with the help of a $30 million grant from Japan. Although this reaction is understandable, it may be questioned. Projections of rates of sea level rise in the next century, although undoubtedly subject to errors, suggest that healthy reefs will be able to keep pace (41). After all, the reefs that created Maldives survived and flourished through one of the greatest sea level changes the globe has experienced, the Holocene Transgression, during which sea level rose approximately 75 meters. The best breakwater for an atoll is a healthy reef. Sewage input causes reef bioerosion rates to increase dramatically (22,23,29,51) and, therefore, constructed seawalls will be undermined by the sewage.

Even if Maldivian reefs are able to keep pace with rising sea levels there may, however, be a greater threat from rising seawater temperatures. Earlier, it was pointed out that the high coral biodiversity in Maldives may be due to the fact that average sea water temperatures are relatively high, with minimum values of about 28°C (52). There have been reports in Maldives of coral bleaching associated with elevated temperatures (8, Sluka, R. personal observation). The upper lethal temperature for many reef corals is about 30 to 31°C, so corals in Maldives are potentially in danger. As the oceans begin to warm, corals will be killed, not by the average temperature values, but by the periodic and often unpredictable upward excursions.

It is probably true that human intervention in the Earth's climate systems will bring about changes that we cannot yet imagine. The effects of these changes will fall disproportionally on some countries and areas. On the other hand, we should not allow our focus on global change to divert us from local impacts and responsibilities. In most reef areas, the effects of global change are not as immediate a threat as are land-based pollution and human intervention.

Structural Stability

Residential and industrial development on Malé has accelerated, and major construction projects are common. These projects usually involve use of heavy equipment, pile drivers, and sometimes blasting. Most of the buildings on Malé are constructed from live coral, which is 'harvested' from nearby reefs (9). Population increase on Malé has resulted in greater demand on the groundwater supply. The groundwater lens in the center of Malé has shrunk greatly over the past 20 years. In 1983, it was estimated that groundwater supplies would last only about 10 years. In 1993, there was only one public tap supplying water to the populace, and many of the wells had suffered severe saltwater intrusion. For this reason, the Maldivian government, through development aid loans, has now invested heavily in desalination plants for Malé. The intake pipes for these plants were placed in channels blasted in the reef surface.

All of the sewage from Malé is discharged untreated over the reef, with predictable results: the coral communities around Malé are seriously degraded relative to other islands (49). The atoll which supports the city of Malé has passed from a constructive, aggradational stage typical of reefs growing at stable sea level, to a destructive phase during which physical and biological destructive processes will begin to accelerate.

There is growing concern over the observation of cracks in the Malé "House Reef" (the Maldivian term for the reef surrounding a village or habitation). Some of these cracks are simply normal growth sutures that can now be observed in shallow water on Malé, because the corals are all dead (48), but eventually an atoll that has ceased to grow will suffer mass wasting. This is a serious concern on an island so densely inhabited.

To provide information on location and extent of fresh water supplies and to investigate the problem of the alleged 'reef cracking' we performed resistivity and shallow seismic investigations of Maldivian reef structures. We used offset seismic reflection techniques with 50 m long geophone arrays and a sledgehammer as the sound source (49). Records were taken on Tari, a resort island in North Malé Atoll, and on Malé itself. These measurements were designed to demonstrate the utility of shallow seismic techniques as tools for investigating reef growth and sea level change (49). These are among the first results of shallow seismic studies on reefs at any location, and are the first for the Central Indian Ocean (49). This study found no detectable freshwater lens on Malé, except for a thin veneer (only a few cm) in the vicinity of the Palace. These results are very worrisome because previous reports, from 20 years earlier, described a 3 m freshwater lens. The seismic results show excellent geologic facies detail down to depths of about 100 m. Reef facies can be clearly seen, including details of debris interfingering at the backreef-lagoon transition, seaward dipping reef front deposits, and recent land reclamation infilling. Stacking of successive reef sequences is especially evident. The thickness of the Holocene section in most areas, on both islands, is about 15 m.

Two short closely-spaced sections at the south end of Tari both show a strong reflector at about 20m, which we interpret as the Holocene-Pleistocene disconformity. Above that is a relatively homogeneous section that represents Holocene sands. Below the Holocene-Pleistocene contact are a series of horizons with irregular topography, that are earlier karstified reef surfaces. Other sections taken on Tari show four stacked reef sequences, with the first strong reflector, the base of the Holocene, at 20 m. All the Tari sections correlate, and suggest the following history: at least four successive periods of reef growth and cementation, each one followed by a sea level drop and subsequent karstification, resulting in complex subsurface topography.

The sections on Malé show that the island is developed on an atoll rim reef. Facies present include fore reef shallow slope, reef flat, lagoon infill, backreef rim, debris shoals and backreef debris beds dipping into the main lagoon. The seismic record taken at the headquarters of the Marine Research Section was located at the historic edge of the atoll. This section shows a shallow Holocene reef at 10 m, partly buried under reclamation fill. Again, at 20 m, is an irregular, strong reflector we interpret as the top of the Pleistocene. The uppermost Pleistocene sequence shows some progradation over the lower reefal units. Beneath that are two more buried reef horizons, each strongly karstified, with steep seaward dips. A reverse fault with about 5 m of vertical displacement occurs in the lower part of these seaward beds, but does not cut through the top of the Pleistocene. On the other hand, to landward are three normal faults, with several meters' displacement, all of which penetrate the Holocene sequence.

Other sections, taken on a traverse through the island, show lagoon infill, the transition between sediments of the internal rim-reef lagoon and backreef debris, then atoll rim sequences, complete with backward-driven debris sheets: as the reef grows to sea level, it begins to shed sediments and debris back into the lagoon. The depth of the lagoon, throughout the Holocene development of the reef at Malé, was about 10 m. The Malé records show, again, stacking of reef sequences, each one successively karstified during lowstands.

At National Security Service headquarters, the seismic section clearly shows the transition between sediments of the internal rim-reef lagoon and the backreef complex. A strong reflector at 10 m represents the modern backreef, now buried under reclamation. Under that, a strong reflector representing the top of the Pleistocene rises from the old lagoon surface at 25 m, with shallow dip, to the backreef complex at 15 m. The depth of the Pleistocene lagoon in the center of Malé was therefore about 10 m. This same pattern is repeated three more times with depth, with each deeper reflector showing progressively more extensive karstification. A reverse fault cuts the Pleistocene-Holocene disconformity, and extends upwards into the Recent section.

The sections from Malé show how these atoll-rim reefs develop. These results will be of interest to earth scientists. Of much greater interest to the Maldivians, however, is the pattern of faulting we observed in the upper part of the section. We saw no evidence of any faulting in the records from Tari, which is also on the outer rim of the main atoll. The Malé sections show some deep-seated faulting that resembles the pattern described by Aubert and Droxler (6). These same sections also show several faults, some with several meters displacement, that are restricted to the upper part of the Holocene section. It is very unlikely that these shallow faults have been caused by compaction, as sufficient loading was never present and Tari does not show them.

The shallow faulting on Malé may be a direct result of the main difference between the two study areas: Malé is densely inhabited, and under the sort of development pressures that generate shallow stresses on the underlying reef. The normal biological repair processes are inoperable here. With all appropriate scientific caution, we are compelled to point out that, should movement on one of these faults result in collapse of part of the atoll rim, the result would be loss of life numbering in the tens of thousands. Such mass wasting could be caused by a nearby earthquake, or by human activities such as pile driving or blasting. Relative sea level rise, for some of the inhabitants of Malé, could be very rapid indeed.

Coral Mining

Coral has been mined for building material on Maldives for generations. Traditionally, coral rock has been the material of choice for construction of houses and mosques. This is now the main building material used in Malé, Addu, and on tourist islands. Massive species such as *Porites, Goniastrea* and faviids are preferred, but bases of large *Acropora* are also used. Mining is usually concentrated on the rims of shallow faroes: a *dhoni* will anchor in shallow water, and several men armed with crowbars and hammers will fill it with coral. No diving equipment is used, so mining is restricted to depths of a few meters. The coral, much of it still alive, is then stacked somewhere out of the way to dry, to let the rains leach the salt out, and to let the smell drop to acceptable levels. Pieces are then broken up into suitable sizes, and mortared into walls. It is estimated that about 93 000 m^3 have been mined from Maldivian reefs from the early 1970's to the mid-1980's (9). The growth of the tourist industry, the need for larger buildings on Malé and adjacent islands, building of an international and regional airports, and the increase in the population all put a great strain on the coral resources of Maldives.

Before investigating possible solutions, the size of the problem should be estimated. Our reef survey work on Maldives showed that the typical coral cover on the rims of atolls and faroes was approximately 30%. Adding up the reef-building species such as *Porites*, faviids, *Goniastrea, Pavona*, and even throwing in genera such as *Montipora*, gives a figure of only about 10% of total coral cover, at most. In other words, even in areas of healthy coral growth, much of what is available is unsuitable. The total coastline of Maldives is 644 km. Let us assume that this length represents the length of reefs in the area (there will be unmapped faroes not included here, but their addition of reef length will be partly compensated for by parts of the 644 km, above, not having healthy reef development). Assume further that the area of reef available to be mined by non-divers is a strip 10 m wide (an overestimate). Applying the estimate, above, of 30% coral cover, with 10% of that cover being suitable for building, yields a mineable resource with an area of (about) 200 000 m^2. This is for the entire country. The corals in this resource base will accrete upwards about 1 cm/y, giving an increase in volume, each year, of 2000 m^3.

A typical (large) Maldivian house is perhaps 5 x 7 m, with one interior partition. Assume walls 2 m high, no (or little) coral used in the roof framing, no coral used in the mortar. Such a house will require a little more than 10 m^3 of coral - the walls will be somewhat porous, and in fact are made that way for air circulation. If the coral resources of Maldives are to be extracted on a steady-state basis, and if houses are built only of coral, then the entire country can sustainably build 200 houses, and no mosques or government buildings, per year. The present population growth on Maldives adds 10 000 to 12 000 people every year. Consequently, there will be a housing problem if coral is the main source of building material.

Of course, this exercise is highly oversimplified. There is no allowance for transportation problems within the atolls, no consideration of re-occupation or recycling of older houses, losses of corals to bioerosion, storms and other factors. Perhaps more important, it does not take into account the destabilizing of reef tops by the mining activity itself, which seems to feed back into further reef destruction. Nonetheless, these simple calculations help place in focus the size of the problem facing the islanders if they continue to build houses from coral.

There is not only a supply problem. The tops of faroes are usually moated by live coral, and topped by a mobile sheet of coral rubble and sand. Surveys of mined faroes taken 20 years after mining (supposedly) stopped have shown few signs of coral recovery (13). If the corals on the rim of a faro are mined, the interior unconsolidated material begins to shift with the prevailing winds. The outer rampart may be breached, and sediment delivered to deeper water. This erodes and destabilizes the live corals at the edges of the gap, and they in turn will fall into deeper water (accelerating the natural process described earlier). In fact, coral mining generates a positive feedback loop, destabilizing the atoll top and eventually leading to its demise.

Stabilizing these faro tops and repairing the damage done by coral mining is not trivial. Corals, of course, transplant wonderfully well, anywhere the water is clear (16). On the Maldivian faroes, the problem is providing stable substrate. Coral planulae can settle on rubble, but if the rubble shifts, the corals will be killed. So neither natural settlement nor coral transplanting will work until the substrate has been stabilized. Clark and Edwards (13) report the results of British Council work on rehabilitation of Maldivian reef tops, in which large concrete 'mats' are set down on the substrate. Corals do settle on these mats, and coral transplants have reasonable success rates. On the other hand, the expense of providing these concrete structures for every mined Maldivian faro puts this remediation method out of the reach of Maldives, or even of the wealthiest of countries.

It has been evident for years that coral mining cannot be sustained at the present rate. A radical solution to the problem was proposed: select a "sacrificial" faro, and mine out the whole reef to a depth of 10 m, thereby producing enough coral rock to satisfy demand for the next decade (9). In the long run, as the authors point out, Maldivians will have to learn to use other materials, such as blocks made from the ubiquitous coral sand. At the present, however, there is cultural reluctance to accept the use of blocks, coupled with some past disasters that occurred when blocks made from unleached sand failed in use.

The faro-mining solution needs careful examination, however, before large sums of money are spent on implementation. Only the atoll rims will preserve any massive corals, and, as we have seen earlier, this sort of preservation is extremely rare. The atoll rim core described by Woodroffe (75) is only about 2% massive corals, and only a fraction of a faro is in fact reef core. Most of the framework is loose *Acropora* debris, unsuitable for building. The seismic work showed no head corals anywhere in the Holocene, within the limits of resolution (about 1 m). What is more, data from a core taken on the rim of a ring reef should not be used to generalize the internal subsurface contents of an entire faro: most of this will be sand.

Maldives is not the only country in which coral is used as building material. In Indonesia, for example, some of the migratory 'sea gypsy' tribes, such as the Bugis and the Bajo build houses, piers and breakwaters from coral.

Figure 11.2. Building construction in Laamu Atoll mixed traditional (coral) and modern styles.

Indonesia has achieved moderate success in changing the habits of these coral-users, via education programs. Maldivians will be better off, in the long run, the faster they are able to wean themselves from the use of live coral.

In order to abate the destruction of coral reefs due to mining for construction material, the government has encouraged and in some cases required the use of concrete blocks. Recent legislation has recognized the environmental and economic damage of coral mining and seeks to limit spatially and numerically the extent of coral removal. Coral mining is now regulated and specifically coral cannot be mined on tourist resort's 'house' reefs, atoll rim reefs, and common bait fishing reefs. More restrictive legislation has been written for two of the atolls where most of the damage has occurred (15). Villagers may apply to local island offices to remove coral from distant faros, but may be turned down and urged to build with locally made concrete blocks. Many village homes show a mixture of the old and new building materials (Fig. 11.2). Concrete can be obtained in Malé' and is transported by *dhoni* to the outer island villages. Sand is taken from the beach and mixed with water and concrete and then poured into a mold. Care has to be taken to wash the sand, as salt makes the blocks weak. Many villagers consider buildings made from coral stronger, but the environmental, economic and time (the speed of construction) advantages of using concrete blocks are also recognized (38).

Crown-of-Thorns Starfish

Research on crown-of-thorns (COT) distribution in Maldives was made available by the Marine Research Section (MRS) of the Ministry of Fisheries and Agriculture. Two previous outbreaks have been recorded in recent history. One occurred in the 1970s in Ari Atoll and the other in mid 1980s in Kaafu Atoll (1). The MRS visited 80 sites in 1987 to 1988 and found COT on only five sites among eight different atolls (33). In 1990, MRS visited 111 sites along the entire stretch of the Maldivian archipelago (32). COTs were mainly observed in the central atolls (Alifu and Kaafu) and in the south in Gaaf Alif and Gaaf Dhaal. In 86 of 111 sites no COT were observed and at only one site over 99 COT were observed. Four sites in Laamu Atoll were visited, with no COTs observed. In Kaafu Atoll, however, four tourist resorts reported collecting a total of 30 500 COTs from their dive sites! Another survey in early 1991 indicated that 8 of 31 resort dive sites had COTS, with densities ranging from 0 to 48 COT per hour (34). An outbreak on one patch reef was reported from sourthern Ari Atoll in May 1991 (35). Recent data suggest that there is no outbreak occurring among resort island dive sites (Nadeehu, I. personal communication).

Based on the available data, it appears that there are no crown-of-thorns outbreaks occurring in the Maldives. Given the dispersed nature of this island country and thus the difficulty in monitoring all coral reefs, outbreaks could occur in more remote areas not generally visited by people able to recognize and record these occurrences.

Overfishing

In some maritime regions with abundant reefs and associated marine resources, there are traditional systems of resource utilization: perhaps the best-known of these is *sasi*, employed in the Molukus, Indonesia. Under this system, all marine resources to the farthest breaking wave seen from shore is under the management and control of the village. There is, in Maldivian society, the concept of the 'house reef'. Any inhabited reef is the property of those living there, who also are responsible for maintaining the resources of that reef. One should not, for example, come ashore on a house reef without asking permission. As has been pointed out earlier, however, most Maldivian islands are not inhabited, and hence there is open access to most marine resources. And, in fact, there is no legal basis for the 'house reef' concept as the State does not recognize any proprietorship rights to reefs or reef resources.

Traditionally, Maldivians have focused fishery efforts on catching skipjack tuna. Recently, however, several coral reef fisheries have started due to lucrative external markets and the internal tourist demand. This has led to some spectacular crashes in recent times, and management of some of the marine resources bears examination.

The Livebait Fishery. For centuries, Maldives has been the site of a thriving tuna fishery, largely targeting skipjack tuna. As this is an open water, pole-and-line fishery, the only direct stress on the reefs is the taking of live bait, which are generally small reef-associated pelagic species (2). The live bait fishery is ancient, having been reported from at least the 14th Century.

While the tuna grounds are far offshore in deep, oceanic waters, baitfish can be collected within the atoll lagoon near coral reef structures. There are over twenty fish species regularly used as livebait, but these fall into three main categories: 1) fusiliers, family Caesionidae, 2) cardinalfishes, family Apogonidae, and 3) the silver sprat, *Spratelloides gracilis* or shorthead anchovy

Encrasicholina heteroloba (36). Traditionally, baitfish were collected in small sailing vessels using nets. The amount taken was low but any fish could be taken from any reef (Shakeel, H. personal communication). This was sustainable, because humans were intercepting only a part of the food chain in which natural mortality rates were very high. Baitfish schools also move significantly throughout the atoll lagoon and any form of limited access to reefs would have likely proven detrimental to tuna fishing (Anderson, C. personal communication).

Recent improvements in technology, such as nylon nets and better aeration of baitwells, have allowed dramatic increases in the baitfish catch. Currently, mechanized fishing boats with 5 to 10 fishers collect baitfish with nets. These nets may be left on the reef for several days before collection (for example if a storm prevented retrieval). This procedure kills much of the coral underneath the net. Baitfish not needed on a particular day are stored in net cages which float near reefs in the atoll lagoon. There is significant mortality of these fish when held overnight. In addition, some fishers use lights to collect fish at night. There is no quota on baitfish collection, but fisherfolk may not collect from tourist resort house reefs. As yet, there is no documented stock decrease as a consequence of increased catches, although there are complaints from fishers of local shortages. It is likely that the baitfish stock itself is subject to large annual fluctuations due to climate changes, and hence patterns due to exploitation will emerge only with difficulty.

Money Cowries. Small cowries (*Cypraea moneta*) were probably one of the earliest forms of money. Their use in China dates at least from the Shang Dynasty (1700 to 1100 BC). The Maldives were one of the major sources of the shells, which were pierced and hung on long strings. Later Chinese money was even cast to resemble cowry shells. Export routes at first were through the Indian subcontinent, but later on there was direct shipments to Africa, SE Asia, and Europe. Cowries were one of the main forms of exchange used in the slave trade, and their use was widespread in Asia and Africa. In fact, in the mid-1800's there was a 500-fold decrease in the value of money in Uganda following wholesale importation of cowries from Maldives (20).

Traditionally, the Sultan had control over cowry collecting. Palm fronds were placed in shallow reef flat or seagrass environments, where thin films of algae would grow on them (2). Cowries would crawl up onto the leaves in search of food and the palm leaves were periodically taken up onto the beach and the cowries shaken off. The shells were buried in the sand to deflesh them and were then ready for export. In the 1720's, at the height of the slave trade, about 500 000 000 cowries were exported into West Africa alone. Developments in international banking, and the decline of the slave trade, put an effective end to the trade in money cowries, although there is still some export to India and Asia for use in ornamentation. The trade was, however, sustainable for almost 4000 years. Reasons for this sustainability include control by a central authority, the Sultan, collection was near villagers homes and, therefore, exploitation was spatially limited, and fecundity and turnover of the resource was high.

Sea Cucumbers. This fishery is aimed at the Chinese market and started in 1985 (2). Sea cucumbers were mostly collected by hand from shallow lagoons, either by snorkeling or SCUBA. Sea cucumbers were grossly overfished and stocks crashed in less than a decade. Bans, controls and limits are, however, not enforced. Prices remain high for quality sea cucumbers at approximately US $30 per kilogram dry weight and, therefore, the incentive is high to collect any available sea cucumbers.

Giant Clams. A fishery aimed at the Taiwanese market began in 1990: in 1990 to 1991, 20 tons of frozen adductor muscle were exported to Taiwan, equivalent to 125 000 clams. The prime target species, *Tridacna squamosa*, was absent from reefs that had been fished, and had to attain an age of at least eight years before it was of harvestable size. It was clear that this fishery was not sustainable, and the issuing of licenses ceased in 1991.

Grouper. Maldivians have traditionally relied on pelagic resources for food and their economic livelihood. However, subsistence level fishing of reef fish has always occurred, especially in atolls far from good tuna fishing spots. During bad weather or special times of the year (such as the fasting month) reef fish constitute the main source of protein for the islanders. In recent years, the demand for reef fish resources by the tourist industry (such as lobster and predatory reef fish) and lucrative foreign markets (for Napoleon wrasse, giant clams, sea cucumbers and groupers) has resulted in the commercialization of reef fish fisheries (31). Prices for tourist and foreign markets are considerably higher than the low prices paid for tuna, the current beach-side price for tuna is US $0.30 per kilogram. This provides a large incentive to switch to these non-traditional fishery resources. The two main threats of these fisheries are overexploitation and conflicts with other user groups (59). Presently, the main conflict is with diving tourism which requires large predatory fish to attract customers.

The most recent of these non-traditional reef fish fisheries is the live grouper trade. The fishery for grouper started about January 1993 (57). Grouper export rose from 200 tons in 1994 to 1000 tons in 1995 (59). Exports for 1996 were expected to show about a 10-fold increase above the 1995 level (Adam, M.S. personal communication). Groupers are bought from local Maldivian fishers by a Maldivian collector who is a middleman for foreign importers who are usually from Hong Kong.

There are at least 40 species of grouper known from Maldivian waters (47), but only a few of these are commercially targeted. The price paid for live grouper depends upon demand, species, and size. In Laamu Atoll, for example, the highest prices are paid for the *Plectropomus* species, *Epinephelus fuscoguttatus* and *E. polyphekadion* (Sluka, R. personal observation). *Cephalopholis* spp, *Anyperodon luecogrammicus*, and *Aethaloperca rogaa* may fetch one fifth to one tenth of the price of the former species. In fact, the *Cephalopholis* species have been used to feed the more expensive species rather than using space for these less expensive species. The hold of one vessel with a 14 ton capacity was filled with only *E. fuscoguttatus* and species of *Plectropomus* (Sluka, R. personal observation).

Grouper are caught by handlining with live bait, by fisherfolk snorkeling in the water. A variety of boats are used depending on the number of fishers, from small .i.rowboats; (1 to 2 people) and sailing vessels (3 to 4 people), to large mechanized boats (7 to 8 people, 57,58). Sailing vessels may catch 50 to 80 fish per day, while mechanized boats, 100 to 170 (57). The preferred bait is the goldband fusilier (*Pterocaesio chrysozona*) which is caught in nets much like in the live-bait fishery: minced tuna fish is used to attract the fusiliers above a net placed on the seafloor. Fishers hold each of the nets' four corners and lift it out of the water once the baitfish have been attracted over the net. The live golden fusilier are then hooked near the tail and dangled in front of the grouper. The fishers enter the water using mask, fins, and snorkel to spot individual groupers they would like to catch, and handline with the live bait while in the water. Once hooked, grouper are rapidly brought to the surface and transferred to the boat hold.

The daily catch of fisherfolk are either placed in their own small cages or directly brought to the collectors' larger cage facility. Shakeel (57) estimates a 5 to 20% mortality rate in boat holds due to poor water quality, overcrowding, and damage to the fish during catching and processing. Many fish die from internal bleeding after swallowing the hook and ruptured swimbladders are common from pulling the fish to the surface too rapidly. The fishers release the air from the bladder with a sharp tool, but many times pierce too deeply resulting in internal bleeding.

The fishery is already showing signs of overfishing (see Box 11.1). Collectors have shifted away from the atolls close to Malé' and now have collection sites in all atolls (Haleem, M. personal communication). In Thaa Atoll, the main collector has noticed that the fish he is receiving from fishers are distinctly smaller than at the beginning of the trade (Afeef, M. personal communication). Shakeel (57,58) estimated the maximum sustainable yield of groupers from the different atolls and, for example, estimated a yield of 27 tons per year from shallow coral reefs of Laamu Atoll. The foreign collection vessels have capacities of approximately 14 to 16 tons and may collect from more than one atoll, depending on where the Maldivian intermediary has collection bases. Recently, one vessel collected approximately 7 to 8 tons of grouper on one trip to Laamu Atoll (Sluka, R. personal observation) and one or two vessels are expected at least every 6 to 8 weeks. These figures suggest that 40 to 140 tons were collected per year which is almost two to five times the maximum sustained yield estimate. In 1994, fisherfolk were already reporting that their catches were declining, especially in Alifu and Vaavu Atolls (57). Based on export figures of 1000 tons and the mortality rate in fisherfolk's and exporter's holding facilities, that the maximum sustainable yield for grouper was probably surpassed in 1995 (59).

The Aquarium Fish Trade. Exports of fish for the aquarium fish trade began about 1980, and were limited to a few companies employing less than 25 people (24). The trade has not been economically important to the overall Maldivian economy. The economic value of this trade never constituted more than 1% of the total value of marine exports.

The collection of aquarium fishes is centered around the capitol Malé due to the proximity of international flights. Most fish are flown to Sri Lanka where they are subsequently re-exported, but some fish are flown directly to overseas markets. Consequently, reefs in the central atolls are heavily fished while the more southern and northern atolls are not fished at all.

Box 11.1. Groupers: Group-Spawning Predators in Need of Conservation

Groupers (Pisces: Serranidae, subfamily Epinephelinae) are top-level predatory fish found in warm waters throughout the world (4). Of the 15 genera and 159 species known to date, eight genera and 66 species are found in the western Indian Ocean, Red Sea or Persian Gulf (4). The most abundant genus in this region is *Epinephelus*, constituting 68% of known species. The reproductive ecology of groupers is influenced greatly by the biology and behavior of these species. Biologically, the most important feature of grouper reproduction is protogyny, or changing sex from female to male at some stage in their lives, and most species of grouper are considered to be protogynous. There are few species, however, for which this life-history characteristic has be unequivocally confirmed and a few species for which it appears that some males may directly develop from juveniles (13,15). Transition from female to male appears to be socially rather than biologically mediated, as there is a wide range of ages and sizes at which transitional individuals have been recorded (15).

Indo-Pacific groupers exhibit a wide variety of spawning patterns including non-migratory pair spawning, such as found for *Cephalopholis spiloparaea*, *C. urodeta*, non-migratory haremic spawning, such as for *C. argus* and *C. miniata*, and migratory pair and group spawning, such as for *Epinephelus fuscoguttatus*, *Plectropomus areolata* and *P. leopardus* (2,3,6,7,14,16). The migration of large numbers of groupers to specific sites during a few months of the year has been termed a spawning aggregation. Indo-Pacific groupers begin to gather in aggregations several days before the new moon, with spawning behavior noted throughout the day culminating in pelagic fertilization. Spawning usually commences 10 to 20 minutes prior to sunset and ends 10 to 20 minutes after sunset.

Grouper spawning aggregations are the focus of commercial, recreational, and artisanal fisheries throughout subtropical and tropical regions of the world (7,8). Groupers appear to be especially susceptible to overfishing at this time due to a) behavioral changes rendering them less wary of fishers, b) fishing of spawners prior to gamete release, c) selective removal of larger males, potentially resulting in sperm limitation (1), d) aggregations returning to same place at same time each year, and e) concentration of populations, thus effectively fishing a very large area as groupers may travel many kilometers to the aggregation. Intense fishing of grouper spawning aggregations has lead to decreases in abundance and mean size of individuals as well as strongly female-biased sex ratios (11,12). In some cases, aggregations which were successfully fished artisanally have disappeared due to the increased pressure brought about by gear improvements or outside markets. The high-priced market for live grouper in Southeast Asia has resulted in intense fishing with spawning aggregations being an easy target for quick economic gain, regardless of biological and ecological consequences.

Johannes (5) suggested that spawning aggregations of coral reef fish be protected from fishing due to the destructive nature of this practice. The reoccurrence of these aggregations at specific sites during several months of the year allows for relatively simple management of catch and effort. Once spawning sites and seasons are delimited, restrictions can be imposed, potentially for only a few days around the new moon (5), so that groupers can reproduce and replenish depleted populations. The high price currently paid for live grouper (up to a days wage per kg to fisherfolk in Laamu Atoll, Republic of Maldives) will make enforcement a challenge. Size and/or bag limits on fishing aggregations are unlikely to be effective due to hook induced mortality (18, Sluka, R. personal observation) and the practice of continued fishing to obtain the largest individuals possible within the bag limit (previously caught, dead grouper are thrown back when a larger individual is caught). Ideally, grouper aggregations sites should be preserved within a system of marine protected areas (MPAs). MPAs have been shown to effectively protect grouper populations such that abundance and mean size are greater inside than outside the MPA. MPAs also result in the export of grouper biomass through adult movements (17) and larval export (9). A series of permanently protected MPAs which contain grouper spawning aggregations would be a big step towards the conservation of grouper populations throughout the Indo-Pacific.

Robert D. Sluka

References

1. Bannerot, S., Fox, W.W. Jr., Powers, J.E. 1987. Reproductive strategies and the management of snappers and groupers. In *Tropical Snappers and Groupers: Biology and Fisheries Management*. eds. Polovina, J.J., Ralston, S. pp. 561-603. Boulder: Westview Press

2. Donaldson, T.J. 1995. Courtship and spawning behavior of the pygmy grouper, *Cephalopholis spiloparaea* (Serranidae: Epinephelinae), with notes on *C. argus* and *C. urodeta. Environmental Biology of Fishes* 43:363-370

3. Goeden, G.B. 1982. Intensive fishing and a 'keystone' predator species: Ingredients for community instability. *Biological Conservation* 22:273-281

4. Heemstra, P.C., Randall, J.E. 1993. *Groupers of the World (Family Serranidae, subfamily Epinephelinae). An Annotated and Illustrated Catalogue of the Grouper, Rockcod, Hind, Coral grouper, and Lyretail Species Known to Date*. FAO Fisheries Synopsis No. 125. Vol. 16. Rome: FAO

5. Johannes, R.E. 1980. Using knowledge of the reproductive behavior of reef and lagoon fishes to improve fishing yields. In *Fish Behavior and its Use in the Capture and Culture of Fishes*. eds. Bardach, J.E., Magnuson, J.J., May, R.C., Reinhart, J.M. pp. 247-270. ICLARM Conference Proceedings 5. Mainila: International Center for Living Aquatic Resources Management

6. Johannes, R.E. 1981. *Words of the Lagoon : Fishing and Marine Lore in the Palau District of Micronesia*. Berkely: University of California Press

7. Johannes, R.E. 1988. Spawning aggregation of the grouper, *Plectropomus areolatus* (Ruppel) in the Solomon Islands. *Proceedings of the 6th International Coral Reef Symposium* 2: 751-755

8.   Olsen, D.A., LaPlace, J.A. 1978. A study of a Virgin Island grouper fishery based on a breeding aggregation. *Proceedings of the Gulf and Caribbean Fisheries Institution* 31:130-144

9.   Plan Development Team. 1990. *The Potential of Marine Fishery Reserves for Reef Fish Management in the U.S. Southern Atlantic.* NOAA Technical Memo NMFS-SEFC-261

10. Parrish, J.D. 1987. The trophic biology of snappers and groupers. In *Tropical Snappers and Groupers: Biology and Fisheries Management.* eds. Polovina, J.J., Ralston, S., pp. 405-463. Boulder: Westview Press

11. Sadovy, Y. 1994. Grouper stocks of the Western Central Atlantic: The need for management and management needs. *Proceedings of the Gulf and Caribbean Fisheries Institutions* 43:43-64

12. Sadovy, Y. in press. The case of the disappearing grouper: *Epinephelus striatus* the Nassau grouper, in the Caribbean and western Atlantic. *Proceedings of the Gulf and Caribbean Fisheries Institutions* 45

13. Sadovy, Y., Colin, P.L. 1995. Sexual development and sexuality in the Nassau grouper. *Journal of Fish Biology* 46:961-976

14. Samoilys, M.A., Squire, L.C. 1994. Preliminary observations on the spawning behavior of coral trout, *Plectropomus leopardus* (Pisces: Serranidae), on the Great Barrier Reef. *Bulletin of Marine Science* 54:332-342

15. Shapiro, D.Y. 1987. Reproduction in groupers. In *Tropical Snappers and Groupers: Biology and Fisheries Management.* eds. Polovina, J.J., Ralston, S. pp. 295-327. Boulder: Westview Press

16. Shpigel, M., Fishelson, L. 1991. Territoriality and associated behaviour in three species of the genus *Cephalopholis* (Pisces: Serranidae) in the Gulf of Aqaba, Red Sea. *Journal of Fish Biology* 38:887-896

17. R. Sluka., Chiappone, M., Sullivan, K.M., Wright, R. 1997. The benefits of marine fishery reserve status for Nassau grouper *Epinephelus striatus* in the central Bahamas. *Proceedings of the 8th International Coral Reef Symposium* 2:1961-1964

18. Wilson, R.R. Jr., Burns, K.M. 1996. Potential survival of released groupers caught deeper than 40 m based on shipboard and in-situ observations, and tag-recapture data. *Bulletin of Marine Science* 58:234-247

Collection of ornamental fish in the Maldives is generally by handnet. This avoids the environmental damage caused by using poisons like cyanide (46). Some damage may occur, however, if fish are chased into crevices in the coral reef and corals removed to trap the fish. No collection can occur on tourist resort house reefs and total and species quotas are in effect.

Conclusions

The islands of the Maldives chain are unique among reef systems. Although the geological reasons for its particular formation remain unclear, they are the largest chain of atolls and ring reefs anywhere in the world. At the present, the combination of low human population density and a broad expanse of reefs has allowed Maldives to escape many of the environmental problems associated with reefs elsewhere. Coral cover is high, and reef fish are abundant. Nonetheless, there are problems. Maldivian reefs are threatened by predicted increases in sea level. The practice of mining coral to build houses must be curtailed because the present harvest is not sustainable. Sewage discharge has damaged some of the reefs near densely-populated areas. In addition, the trade in live fish, especially groupers, is presently unsustainable. In summary, although the present status of Maldivian reefs is excellent, the future may be influenced by some ominous trends.

References

1. Adam, M.S. 1989. *Status Report and Survey Results.* COT Busters Program, Marine Research Section, Ministry of Fisheries and Agriculture, Malé, Republic of Maldives
2. Adam, M.S., Anderson, R.C., Shakeel, H. 1997. Commercial exploitation of reef resources: examples of sustainable and non-sustainable utilisation from the Maldives. *Proceedings of the 8th International Coral Reef Symposium*, Panama 2: 2015-2020
3. Alevizon, W., Richardson, R., Pitts, P., Serviss, G. 1985. Coral zonation and patterns of community structure in Bahamian reef fishes. *Bulletin of Marine Science* 36:304-317
4. Anderson, R.C. 1992. North-south variation in the distribution of fishes in the Maldives. *Rasain* 12:210-226
5. Anderson, R.C., Waheed, Z., Arif, A., Rasheed, M. 1992. *Reef fish resources survey in the Maldives.* Phase II. Bay of Bengal Program/WP/80
6. Aubert, O., Droxler, A.W. 1992. General Cenozoic evolution of the Maldives carbonate system (Equatorial Indian Ocean). *Bulletin Central de Recherche* 16: 113-136
7. Bianchi, C.N., Colantoni, P., Geister, J., Morri, C. 1996. Reef geomorphology, sediments and ecological zonation at Felidu Atoll, Maldive Islands (Indian Ocean). *Proceedings of the 8th International Coral Reef Symposium*, Panama 1: 431-436
8. Brown, B.E. 1987. Worldwide death of corals-natural cyclical events or man-made pollution. *Marine Pollution Bulletin* 18: 9-13
9. Brown, B.E., Dunne, R.P. 1988. The impact of coral mining on coral reefs in the Maldives. *Environmental Conservation* 15:159-165
10. Brown, B.E., Dawson-Shepherd, A., Weir, E., Edwards, A. 1989. Effects of degradation of the environment on local reef fisheries in the Maldives. *Rasain* 2:1-12
11. Clark, S. and A.J. Edwards. 1993. Coral transplantation: an application to rehabilitate reef-flat areas degraded by coral mining in the Maldives. *Proceedings of the 7th International Coral Reef Symposium*, Guam 1:636
12. Clark, S., Edwards, A.J. 1994. The use of artificial reef structures to rehabilitate reef flats degraded by coral mining in the Maldives. *Bulletin of Marine Science* 55: 726-746
13. Clark, S., Edwards, A.J. 1995. Coral transplantation as an aid to reef rehabilitation: evaluation of a case study in the Maldive Islands. *Coral Reefs* 14: 201-213

14. Clark, S. 1994. Artificial reef structures as tools for marine habitat restoration in the Maldives. *Rasain* 14:197-202

15. Cooke, A., Anuradha, R.V. 1996. A review of legal instruments and law relevent to the management of coastal ecosystems in the South Asia region. In *Proceedings of the International Coral Reef Initiative South Asia Workshop.* ed. Bennett, A.J. pp. 80-163

16. Cortes, J., Risk, M.J. 1985. A reef under siltation stress: Cahuita, Costa Rica. *Bulletin of Marine Science* 36: 339-356

17. Daly, R.A. 1915. The glacial-control theory of coral reefs. *Proceedings of the American Academy of Arts and Science* 51: 155-251

18. Darwin, C.R. 1842. *The Structure and Distribution of Coral Reefs.* London: Smith, Elder and Co

19. Davies, P.J. 1977. Modern reef growth-Great Barrier Reef. *Proceedings of the 3rd. International Coral Reef Symposium*, Miami 2: 325-330

20. Davies, P.J. 1983. Reef growth. In *Perspectives on Coral Reefs.* ed. Barnes, D.J. pp. 69-101. Canberra: Brian Clouston Publisher

21. Dawson-Shepherd, A.R., Warwick, R.M., Clarke, K.R., Brown, B.E. 1992. An analysis of fish community response to coral mining in the Maldives. *Environmental Biology of Fishes* 33:367-380

22. Edinger, E.N. 1998. *Effects of Land-based Pollution on Indonesian Coral Reefs: Biodiversity, Growth Rates, Bioerosion, and Applications to the Fossil Record.* PhD. Dissertation, McMaster University, Hamilton Canada

23. Edinger, E.N., Risk, M.J. 1992. Bioerosion of modern and fossil reefs: causes, consequences and corroboration. *Proceedings of the 7th International Coral Reef Symposium*, Guam 2: 437-438

24. Edwards, E.J., Dawson-Shepherd, A. 1992. Environmental implications of aquarium-fish collection in the Maldives, with proposals for regulation. *Environmental Conservation* 19:61-72

25. Goeden, G.B. 1982. Intensive fishing and a 'keystone' predator species: Ingredients for community instability. *Biological Conservation* 22:273-281

26. Heemstra, P.C., Randall, J.E. 1993. Groupers of the world (Family Serranidae, subfamily Epinephelinae). *An annotated and illustrated catalogue of the grouper, rockcod, hind, coral grouper, and lyretail species known to date.* FAO Fisheries Synopsis No. 125

27. Heyerdahl, T. 1986. *The Maldive Mystery.* London: George Allen and Unwin

28. Hoffman, J.E. 1984. Estimates of future sea level rise. In *Greenhouse Effect and Sea Level Rise: A Challenge for This Century.* eds. Barth, M.C., Titus, J.G., pp. 79-104. New York: Nostrand Reinhold Co

29. Holmes, K.E. 1997. Eutrophication and its effects on bioeroding sponge communities. *Proceedings of the 8th International Coral Reef Symposium,* Panama 2: 1411-1416

30. Luckhurst, B.E., Luckhurst, K. 1978. Analysis of the influence of substrate variables on coral reef fish communities. *Marine Biology* 49:317-323

31. Maniku, M.H. 1994. The status of coral reef resource systems and current research needs in the Maldives. In *The Management of Coral Reef Resource Systems. Conference Proceedings* 44. eds. Munro, J.L., Munro, P.E. pp. 25-27. Manila: International Center for Living and Aquatic Resource Management

32. Marine Research Section. 1990a. COT Newsletter. No. 11

33. Marine Research Section. 1990b. COT Newsletter. No. 6

34. Marine Research Section. 1991a. COT Newsletter. No. 12

35. Marine Research Section. 1991b. COT Newsletter. No. 13

36. Marine Research Section. 1995. Tuna baitfish research. *Maldives Marine Research Bulletin* No. 1

37. Matteuci, R., Russo, A. 1985. Principali facies a coralli nell'atollo di North Malé (Isole Maldive). *Bolletino Della Società Geologica Italiana* 104: 311-326

38. Sluka, R., Miller, M.W. 1998. Coral mining in the Maldives. *Coral Reefs* 17:288

39. Miller, D.L.R., MacKenzie, F.T. 1988. Implications of climate change and associated sea-level rise for atolls. *Proceedings of the 6th International Coral Reef Symposium*, Townsville 3: 519-522

40. Nagelkerken, W.P. 1979. Biology of the graysby, *Epinephelus cruentatus*, of the coral reef of Curacao. *Studies on the Fauna of Curacao and other Caribbean Islands* 60:1-118

41. Neumann, A.C., Macintyre, I. 1985. Reef response to sea level rise: Keep-up, catch-up or give-up. *Proceedings of the 5th International Coral Reef Symposium,* Tahiti 3: 105-110

42. Oberdorfer, J.A., Buddemeier, R.W. 1988. Climate change: effects on reef island resources. *Proceedings of the 6th International Coral Reef Symposium*, Guam 3: 523-527

43. Parrish, J.D. 1987. The trophic biology of snappers and groupers. In *Tropical Snappers and Groupers: Biology and Fisheries Management.* eds. Polovina, J.J., Ralston, S. pp. 405-463. Boulder: Westview Press

44. Pillai, C.S.G., Scheer, G. 1976. Report on the stony corals from the Maldives Archipelago. *Zoologica* 126: 1-83

45. Price, A., Firaq, I. 1996. The environmental status of reefs on Maldivian resort islands: a preliminary assessment for tourism planning. *Aquatic Conservation* 6: 93-106

46. Randall, J.E. 1987. Collecting reef fishes for aquaria. In *Human Impacts on Coral Reefs: Facts and Recommendations.* ed. Salvat, B. pp. 29-39. French Polynesia: Antenne Museum E.P.H.E.

47. Randall, J.E., Anderson, R.C. 1993. Annotated checklist of the epipelagic and shore fishes of the Maldive Islands. *Ichthyological Bulletin of the J.L.B. Smith Institute of Ichthyology* No. 59

48. Risk, M.J., Scott, P.J.B. 1991. Final Report to International Centre for Ocean Development, Maldives Project.

49. Risk, M.J., Dunn, J.J., Allison, W.R., Horrill, C. 1993. Reef monitoring in Maldives and Zanzibar: Low-tech and high-tech science. In *Global*

Aspects of Coral Reefs. ed. Ginsburg, R.N. pp. 66-72. Miami: Rosenstiel School of Marine and Atmospheric Science

50. Roberts, C.M., Ormond, R.F.G. 1987. Habitat complexity and coral reef fish diversity and abundance on Red Sea fringing reefs. *Marine Ecology Progress Series* 41:1-8

51. Rose, C. S., Risk, M.J. 1985. Increase in *Cliona delitrix* infestation of *Montastrea cavernosa* on an organically polluted portion of the Grand Cayman fringing reef. *Marine Ecology* 6: 345-363

52. Rosen, B.R. 1971. Principal features of reef coral ecology in shallow water environments of Mahe, Seychelles. *Symposium of the Zoological Society of London* 28: 163-183

53. Ross, S.W., Moser, M.L. 1995. Life history of juvenile gag, *Mycteroperca microlepis*, in North Carolina Estuaries. *Bulletin of Marine Science* 56:222-237

54. Russ, G.R. 1984a. Distribution and abundance of herbivorous grazing fishes in the central Great Barrier Reef. I. Levels of variability across the entire continental shelf. *Marine Ecology Progress Series* 20:23-34

55. Russ, G.R. 1984b. Distribution and abundance of herbivorous grazing fishes in the central Great Barrier Reef. II. Patterns of zonation of mid-shelf and outershelf reefs. *Marine Ecology Progress Series* 20:35-44

56. Sheppard, C.R.C. 1981. The reef and soft substrate coral fauna of Chagos, Indian Ocean. *Journal of Natural History* 15: 607-621

57. Shakeel, H. 1994a. Grouper fishery: benefits, threats and challenges. *Rasain* 14:183-196

58. Shakeel, H. 1994b. Study of grouper fishery and live grouper holding operations in the Maldives. Unpublished report. Marine Research Section, Ministry of Fisheries and Agriculture, Malé, Maldives

59. Shakeel, H., Ahmed, H. 1996. Exploitation of reef resources: grouper and other food fishes. Workshop on Integrated Reef Resources Management, Ministry of Fisheries and Agriculture, Malé, Republic of Maldives

60. Shpigel, M., Fishelson, L. 1989. Habitat partitioning between species of the genus *Cephalopholis* (Pisces: Serranidae) across the fringing reef of the Gulf of Aquaba (Red Sea). *Marine Ecology Progress Series* 58:17-22

61. Sluka, R.D. 1995. *The Influence of Habitat on Density, Diversity, and Size Distribution of Groupers in the Upper Florida Keys and Central Bahamas*. Ph.D. Disseration. University of Miami, Coral Gables

62. Sluka, R.D., M. Chiappone, Sullivan, K.M. 1996. Habitat preferences of groupers in the Exuma Cays. *Bahamas Journal of Science* 4:8-14

63. Sluka. R.D., Reichenbach, N. 1996. Grouper density and diversity at two sites in the Republic of Maldives. *Atoll Research Bulletin* 438:1-16.

64. Sluka., R.D., Sullivan, K.M. 1996. The influence of habitat on the size distribution of groupers in the upper Florida Keys. *Environmental Biology of Fishes* 47:17-189.

65. Sluka, R.D., Chiappone, M., Sullivan, K.M., deGarine-Whichatitsky, M. in press. Habitat characterization and space utilization of juvenile groupers in the Exuma Cays Land and Sea Park, Central Bahamas. *Proceedings of the 45th Gulf and Caribbean Fisheries*

66. Smith, J. E., Risk, M.J., Schwarcz, H.P., McConnaughey, T.A. 1997. Rapid climate change in the North Atlantic during the Younger Dryas recorded by deep-sea corals. *Nature* 386: 818-820
67. Smith, S.V., Kinsey, D.W. 1976. Calcium carbonate production, coral reef growth and sea level change. *Science* 194: 937-939
68. Spencer Davies, P., Stoddart, D.R., Sigee, D.C. 1971. Reef forms of Addu Atoll, Maldive Islands. *Symposium of the Zoological Society of London* 28: 217-259
69. Stoddart, D.R. 1973. Coral reefs of the Indian Ocean. In *Biology and Geology of Coral Reefs.* eds. Jones, O.A., Endean, R. pp. 51-92. New York: Academic Press
70. Van der Knaap, M., Waheed, Z., Shareef, H., Rasheed, M. 1989a. *Reef fish resources survey in the Maldives.* Bay of Bengal Programme/WP/64
71. Van der Knaap, M., Z. Waheed, H. Shareef and M. Rasheed. 1989b. Reef fish research and resources survey: major findings. *Rasain* 2:22-29.
72. Van der Knapp, M. 1989. *Monitoring Program.* COT Busters Program, Marine Research Section, Ministry of Fisheries and Agriculture, Malé, Republic of Maldives
73. Veron, J.E.N. 1995. *Corals in Space and Time.* Sydney: University of New South Wales
74. Wells, S.M. 1988. *Coral Reefs of the World: Indian Ocean, Red Sea and Gulf.* Gland: UNEP/IUCN
75. Woodroffe, C.D. 1992. Morphology and evolution of reef islands in the Maldives. *Procedings of the 7th International Coral Reef Symposium,* Guam 2: 1217-1226

Chapter 12

The Mascarene Islands

Odile Naim, Pascale Cuet & Vijay Mangar

The Mascarenes consist, from west to east, of Reunion, Mauritius and Rodrigues. The archipelago lies 800 km east of Madagascar between 21°07' and 19°40' south and 55°13' and 63°30' east (Fig. 12.1). The three islands of the archipelago consist of geologically and topographically distinct units with a narrow island shelf. Surface areas and highest points are 2512 km^2 and 3069 m in Reunion, 1865 km^2 and 905 m in Mauritius, and 110 km^2 and 400 m in Rodrigues, respectively. The birth of the Mascarene islands through volcanic action (Box 12.1), and their separation from the African and Asian continents, as well as the distance between them, has led to a separate evolution and a high degree of endemism. The archipelago was first visited by Europeans in the 16th century but remained uninhabited until the 17th century. By the 18th century most of the terrestrial endemic animals had been decimated.

The Mascarene marine environment has a comparatively high biological diversity and coral reefs have developed significant structures. Coastal fishing activities and tourism on reefs have a considerable economic importance in Mauritius and Reunion. Economic development has, however, led to deforestation and urbanization. In the last decade, agriculture has become increasingly demanding, using more and more chemical products and water from rivers. Surface waters transport residues of fertilizers and various pesticides to the marine environment, and during the cyclone season, discarded rubbish. Sources of disturbance also include waste waters discharged from urban developments, effluents from sewage works and from industries, as well as the erosion of soils due to deforestation and urbanization. Thus there have been drastic modifications in the structure of the reef communities, shown by a decrease in the abundance and diversity of the reef fauna. In Reunion, coastal erosion has resulted from coral reef degradation. Throughout the archipelago, increasing human populations and economic pressure make management and conservation difficult. Further research is needed to determine the ecological status of reefs in the Mascarenes, especially since some reef flats at present appear to be undergoing natural recovery from previous impacts.

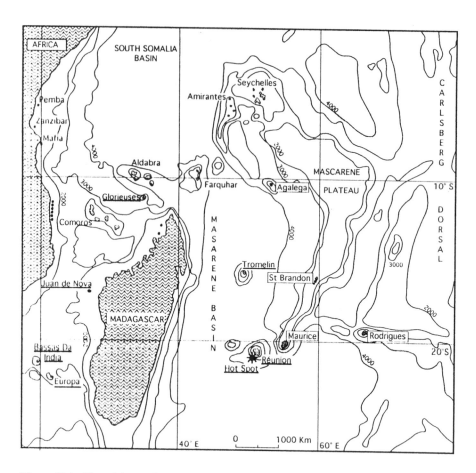

Figure 12.1. Map of the south-west Indian Ocean, including Mauritius and Reunion dependencies.

Further, experiments in Reunion of algae removal and coral and fish transplantation suggest the possibility of restoring reef flats, and these methods could help accelerate the recovery of Mascarene coral reefs.

Political Context and Population

The principal islands of the Mascarene Archipelago belong to two different states, Mauritius and France. The present Creole population results from a mixture of the first Europeans, slaves from Africa, and free workers originating from India, China and Madagascar.

Table 12.1. A selection of reef banks. Their distance from the island of Mauritius and surface area above -35m (from 74).

Name	Distance from Mauritius (km)	Surface (km^2)
Soudan	208	823
Hawkins	400	240
Saint-Brandon	421	3087
Nazareth	672	10 633
Saya de Malha	1024	11 000

The Republic of Mauritius includes the islands of Mauritius and Rodrigues, but also the Saint-Brandon islets or Cargados Carajos shoals (a complex of 22 islets, cays and shoals on a submarine reef platform situated 16°23'S and 59°27'E), and the Agalega islands (2 cays at 10°24'S and 56°38'E, 16,91), and six submerged banks, including the bank of Saint-Brandon (75, Fig. 12.1, Table 12.1). The population is around 1.3 million inhabitants.

The French Republic in the Mascarene Archipelago includes Reunion as an administrative division of France. "Les îles éparses", under Reunion jurisdiction, consists of îles Glorieuses (and the submerged bank of Geyzer and Zélée), Tromelin, Juan de Nova, Bassas da India and Europa (75, Fig. 12.1; Table 12.2). Most of these islands were established as nature reserves in 1971 and formally gazetted in 1975. The human population of Reunion will reach 700 000 inhabitants in the year 2000.

In 1984, Madagascar, Mauritius and the Republic of Seychelles created the COI (Commission de l'Océan Indien) that Reunion and Comoros joined two years later. The cooperation between the islands includes joint protection of the rich fishing areas, observation and warnings of cyclones, and industrial development. The COI includes 13 million inhabitants, 594 000 km^2 of emergent lands and 3 millions km^2 of Exclusive Economic Zone.

Coral Reefs

Reefs are highly developed in Rodrigues and Mauritius (Fig. 12.2), mostly due to the extension of the island shelf (72). The entire coast of Rodrigues is bordered by a fringing reef that covers 200 km^2 with a maximum width of 8 km. This island has the most substantial and best developed reef in the Mascarenes. In Mauritius, barrier and fringing reefs are interrupted by major river mouths and cover 300 km^2, with a maximum width of 4 km. In Reunion, reefs are fringing, discontinuous and narrow (only 550 m wide in the largest part, Fig. 12.2), and cover 7.3 km^2. Reef platforms are abundant in Reunion, present in Rodrigues and absent in Mauritius. In the archipelago, only one reef cay is recognized: "l'île Flamand" in Mauritius. Reefs have an emergent reef flat at low tide. Muddy accumulations, and thus mangroves, are best-developed, though still poor, in Mauritius, rare in Rodrigues, and absent in Reunion. The main scientific studies of this region are listed in Table 12.3.

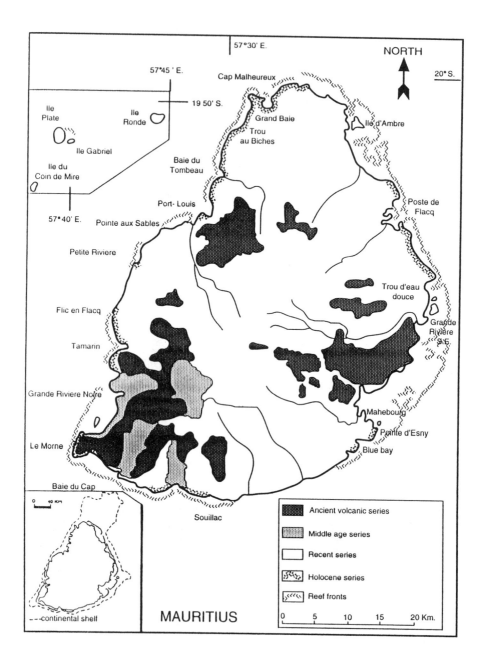

Figure 12.2. Maps of Mauritius (above), Rodrigues (facing page, above), and Reunion (facing page, below). Adapted from (71).

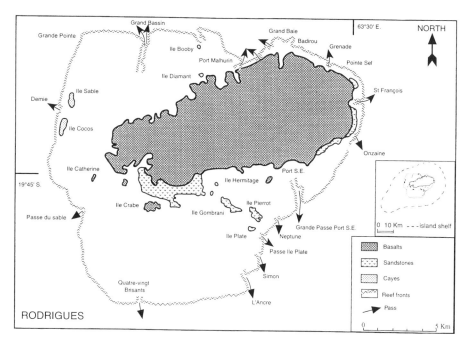

RODRIGUES

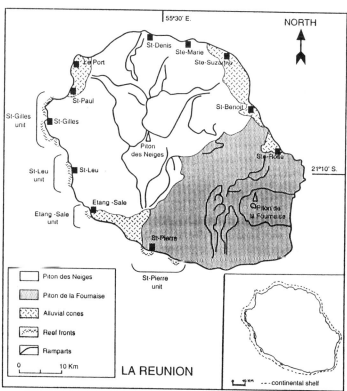

LA REUNION

Table 12.2. Iles éparses natural reserves, except Juan de Nova and the bank of Geyser and Zélée ; see (99) for more information.

Iles éparses	Latitude Longitude	Distance from other islands	Length/width (height or minimum depth)	Fauna and economic value
Iles Glorieuses	(two islands lying on a large coral platform)			
	11°35'S 47°18'E	220 km from Madagascar	Grande Glorieuse: 2.3 km / 1.7 km (12 m)	green turtles nesting, sea birds, coconut crabs
Geyser and Zélée	(two submerged banks depending on the Glorieuses. 11 km between the banks)			
	12°S 46°E	about 100 km N-E of Mayotte	Banc de Geyser ≈ 20 km/20 km (some parts emerging at low tides). Banc de la Zélée ≈ 22 km/14 km (minimum depth ≈ 10 m)	fishing area from Mayotte
Tromelin	(emerged cay)			
	15°53'S 54°31'E	560 km N-NW of Reunion	1.6 km / 0.7 km (6 m)	green turtles nesting (declared reserve IUCN 1984), sea birds
Juan de Nova	(raised fossil reefs ?)			
	17°03'S 42°43'E	175 km from Madagascar	6 km / 1.6 km (12 m)	phosphorite
Bassas da India	(atoll with a closed lagoon)			
	21°28'S 39°42'E	350 km from Madagascar	diam. 12 km (barely emergent at low tide)	
Europa	(atoll in filling phase. Shallow lagoon <1m deep, fringed with mangroves. Rim = karst structure)			
	22°21'S 40°21'E	330 km from Madagascar	6.5 km / 6.5 km (6 m)	green turtles nesting, sea birds

Hydrology and Seasonal Patterns

Ocean swells are casued by the southeast trade winds. During the cool season (from June to October), winds (7 to 11 km/h) produce swells of one to 2 m amplitude. During the hot season (from November to May) weak winds (less than 6 km/h) generate swells with a maximum amplitude of 0.5 m. During the southern summer, the archipelago is subjected to cyclones, which generate whirlwinds of between 180 to 250 km/h, high swells (five to 6 m in height) generally in a N-NE direction, and high rainfall (up to 0.8 to 1.4 m of rain in 24 hours). The coasts are also affected by swells of long wavelength (occasionally up to 600 m) known as austral swells that originate more than 3000 km south of the Mascarene Archipelago, and which rarely last more than 24 hours. In the same way as swells generated by cyclones, these swells play an important role in the morphological evolution of the coastal regions (71). Tides are semi-diurnal with low amplitude. For example, the tidal amplitude in Reunion is a maximum of 0.9 m and seems to be the lowest in the western Indian Ocean (30), but tides are somewhat higher in Rodrigues at 1.2 m.

Reef Structure

Studies by Pichon (81,82) and Faure and Montaggioni (34,35) have defined the common reef characteristics of the Archipelago. Comparative studies of the

Table 12.3. List of some geological, biological and physico-chemical studies in the Mascarenes.

Region	Subject	Authors
Mascarene archipelago	Reefs	Gardiner (1936)
	Reef geomorphology	Montaggioni (1978)
	Species of corals and ecology	Faure (1982)
Mauritius	Geomorphology and sedimentology	Mondon (1976)
	Leeward outer slopes	Faure and Montaggioni (1971b)
	Windward outer slopes	Faure and Montaggioni (1976)
	Benthic communities	de Baissac et al (1962), Pichon (1967)
	Algae	Borgesen (1940-57)
	Alcyonarians and Gorgonians	Stiasny (1940)
	Mollusks	Lienard (1877)
	Crustaceans (Decapods, Stomatopods)	Bouvier (1915)
	Some Echinoderms	Michelin (1845)
	Fish	Vinson (1937-39), de Baissac (1949-71), Cornic (1987)
	Flora and fauna of the rocky shores	Hodgkin and Michel (1960)
Rodrigues	Reefs	Faure and Montaggioni (1971a)
Reunion	Algae	Payri (1985)
	Coral ecology	Bouchon (1981)
	Coral growth	Guillaume (1988)
	Fauna associated with *Pocillopora*	Ribes (1978)
	Benthic communities	Naim (1993)
	Fish	Letourneur (1992)
	Interrelations fish and corals	Chabanet (1994)
	Holothurians	Conand (1996)
	Biogeochemistry	Lison de Loma (1996)
	Bioerosion and calcification	Conand et al. (1997)
	Bierosion and sedimentology	Chazottes (1994)
	Groundwater discharge	Cuet (1989)
	Physico-chemistry of the open ocean	Leroy and Barbaroux (1980), Gamberoni et al (1984)
Mauritius and Reunion	Geology and geomorphology	Montaggioni and Nativel (1988)
	Algae	Jadin (1936)
	Shells	Drivas and Jay (1988)
	Benthic communities	Pichon (1971)

outer slopes suggest a similar ecology between the three islands. Differences that do appear are linked mainly to the geological history (70) such as the extent and continuity of the island shelf.

Considering their narrowness, the reef flats of Reunion, Mauritius and the sector north-east of Rodrigues have a marked similarity although the reef flat is far more diversified in Reunion. Sectors west and south of the reef flat of Rodrigues present an affinity with the reefs of Tulear and that of Mayotte (42) in that the reef flats have a width of 2 km, a succession of compact reef flats, coral strips and scattered coral heads. Additionally, one notes the presence, within the reef structure, of depressions varying between 15 and 45 m diameter for a depth of 6 to 10 m (region of Pointe de l'Ancre, south Rodrigues). Common to many coral reefs in the Indian Ocean is the absence of a true algal crest on the reef front (93). In Reunion, the back reef areas are characterized by low levels of sediment accumulation. In contrast, in Mauritius and Rodrigues, these areas have large sandy accumulations that favor the establishment of seagrasses.

Box 12.1. Origin of the Islands

Dating of volcanic materials indicate that the cone of Mauritius grew some 8 million years ago (=mya, 5), while the oldest dated rocks of Reunion give ages around 2.1 mya (4). Dating from Rodrigues indicate ages between 1.6 and 1.3 mya (6). Mauritius and Reunion originated from a single stationary hotspot which earlier produced a volcanic ridge underlying a large part of the carbonate upper layers of the Mascarene Plateau, the Chagos Bank, the Maldives and Laccadive Islands, and the huge flood basalt volcanism of the Deccan Traps in western India (2). According to this model, the relative motion of the surface expression of the hotspot is SW, with the following ages of the primitive basaltic series: Reunion 0 to 2 Ma, Mauritius 7 to 8 Ma, Mascarene Plateau (Nazareth Bank) 36 Ma, Chagos Bank 48 Ma, Maldive Islands 55 to 60 Ma, and the Deccan Traps (west India) 66 to 68 Ma (3). The proposed ages should be considered as relevant to the end of the volcanic activity rather than the date of the main building period.

The present location of the asthenospheric heat source is supposed to be at about 300 km SW of Reunion (1). Rodrigues is not situated on the track of this hot spot. The island forms the eastern culmination of an EW trending ridge and lies roughly halfway between the Mid-Indian Ocean Ridge and Mauritius. The origin of the Rodrigues Ridge remains uncertain. A connection with the evolution of the Rodrigues triple junction has been proposed (7). Alternatively, Morgan (8) suggests a channeled asthenospheric flow from the Reunion hot spot track towards the Mid-Indian Oceanic Ridge to explain the Rodrigues volcanism. Bonneville and colleagues (1) proposed that Rodrigues island was created near the Mid-Indian Ocean Ridge and that the Rodrigues Ridge constitutes a "trail effect" as the Mid-Indian Ocean Ridge moved away from Reunion. Very few geologic studies have been made on Rodrigues island where only the upper structure of the volcanic edifice is accessible to investigations.

P. Bachelery

References

1.   Bonneville, A., Barriot, J.P., Bayer, R. 1988. Evidence from geoid data of a Hot Spot origin for the southern Mascarene Plateau and Mascarene islands (Indian Ocean). *Journal of Geophysical Research* 93 (B5): 4199 - 4212

2.   Duncan, R.A. 1981. Hotspots in the southern oceans - an absolute frame of reference for motion of the Gondwana continents. *Tectonophysics* 74: 29 - 42

3.   Duncan, R.A., Backman, J., Peterson, L. 1989. Reunion hotspot activity through tertiary time: initial results from the Ocean Drilling Program LEG 115. *Journal of Volcanology and Geothermal Research* 36: 193-198

4.   McDougall, I. 1971. The geochronology and evolution of the young oceanic island of Reunion, Indian Ocean. *Geochimica and Cosmochimica Acta* 35: 261 - 270

5. McDougall, I., Chamalaun, F.G. 1969. Isotopic dating and geomagnetic polarity studies on volcanic rocks from Mauritius, Indian Ocean. *Geological Society American Bulletin* 80: 1419 - 1431
6. McDougall, I., Upton, B.G.J., Wadsworth, W.J. 1965. A geological reconnaissance of Rodriguesz island, Indian Ocean. *Nature* 206: 26 - 27
7. McKenzie, D.P., Sclater, J.P. 1971. The evolution of the Indian Ocean since the late Cretaceous. *Geophysical Journal of the Royal Astronomical Society* 25: 437 - 528
8. Morgan, W.J. 1978. Rodriguesz, Darwin, Amsterdam., a second type of hot spot island. *Journal of Geophysic Research* 83: 5355 - 5360

Biological Diversity

Since the colonization of islands by Europeans, the terrestrial biodiversity has decreased. Eliminated endemic animals were largely birds belonging to parrot, pigeon, dove, flamingo and hawk families (15), the most well-known extinctions including the Dodo (family Raphidae, 17) in Mauritius, and the Solitaire (family Pezophapidae) in Rodrigues (and perhaps in Reunion as well). There were also more than twelve species of tortoise (*Testudo* spp.) occurring in herds of 2000 to 3000 individuals living near the marshes on the three islands that were completely destroyed (83). In the marine environment there are fewer known extinctions. However, the last mention of dugongs (*Dugong dugon*) was in the late 1700s when they disappeared from Mauritius, killed for their meat (52). Moreover, some ancient collections of the National Museum of Natural History of Paris show species of fish from the island Bourbon (the ancient name for Reunion) which have never since been observed there (Durville, P. personal communication).

Algae and Marine Plants. Around 40 species of dinoflagellates have been recorded in Reunion (Quod J. and Turquet, J. unpublished data). Concerning macroalgae, Payri (80) recorded 156 species of algae in Reunion, of which 146 are located on the reefs. Banks of seagrasses (Phanerogames) are abundant in Mauritius (six species: *Thalassodendron ciliatum, Syringodium isoetifolium, Halophila ovalis, H. stipulacea, Halodule universis* and *Halodule sp.*), less abundant in Rodrigues (two species: *Halophila ovalis* and *H. balfouri*), and monospecific and rare in Reunion *(Syringodium isoetifolium, 32)*, although *Halophila stipulacea* has been recorded out of the reefs (La Possession, -15 m, Bigot, L. unpublished data.

Hydroids. Around 90 species of hydroids have been recorded in Reunion (Gravier-Bonnet, N. unpublished data).

Corals. In the Mascarene Archipelago, Faure (31,32) identified more than 50 genera and 186 species of corals (ahermatypic and hermatypic Scleractinians, and Hydrocorallines, Milleporina and Stylasterina, of which the majority are reef builders) compared to 70 genera from the Mollucas-Philippines region which is considered to be the maximum for coral diversity (85,97).

Table 12.4. Principal economic features of Mauritius and Reunion.

	Mauritius	Reunion
GNP per capita	8800 F	36 000 F
agriculture (exports of sugar cane)	14% (600-700 000 t/y.)	10% (250 000 t/y.)
production/industry	26%	27%
services/education	60%	63%
number of professional fishermen	2500	382
number of tourists/y	>300 000	200 000

Investigations by Faure (32) have shown that among the recorded coral genera, 70% are common to the three islands, 76% to Reunion and Mauritius, 75% to Mauritius and Rodrigues, 70% to Reunion and Rodrigues. This degree of affinity is similar to that of Tulear (Madagascar) and Reunion (74%).

Mollusks. Detailed surveys have produced more than 2500 species of mollusks in Reunion and more than 3500 in Mauritius (28). Several hundreds are micro-mollusks with body sizes of less than 1 cm. The number of endemic species, like *Harpa costata, Clanculus mauritianus, Cypraea cribellum* and *Bursa bergeri* comprise approximately 10% of the recognized species.

Fish. More than 650 species of fish have been recorded in Reunion (61). By comparison, on the Geyser and Zélée bank (îles Glorieuses), 297 species have been recorded (Chabanet, P. and colleagues unpublished report). In Reunion, the diversity of fish is generally higher on the outer slope (Shannon index H' = 4.18) than on the reef flats (H' = 2.39) (9). Endemic species are the surgeonfish *Acanthurus polyzona* (rare in Mauritius but can be locally abundant in Reunion at Cap la Houssaye, St. Philippe, Grande anse); the angelfish *Centropyge debelius*, occurring from -46 to -90 m in Mauritius and Reunion (rare) and *Apolemichthys guezei*, -60 to -80 m in Reunion, and the boxfish *Oxtracion trachys*, from -15 to 130 m in Mauritius (rare).

Marine Turtles. Green (*Chelonia mydas)* and Hawksbill turtles (*Eretmochelys imbricata)* occur in the Mascarenes, the green turtle still using beaches to lay eggs, but now very rarely.

Economic Importance of Reefs

The economy of the archipelago is largely based on the sugar cane industry, tourism and fishing (Table 12.4). On both islands, reefs constitute a center for tourist development and in Mauritius the luxuriance of the coral reefs and large beaches acts as a major tourist asset attracting more than 300 000 tourists per year. Tourist pressure is greatest in the north-west of the island (Grand Baie, Trou-aux-Biches), with subsidiary centers in the east at Trou d'Eau Douce and Blue Bay, and in the south-west at Le Morne. In contrast, reef-based tourism in Reunion is much less developed and tourism in Rodrigues is low but developing.

In Mauritius, fishing is done in the lagoons with basket traps. Mesh size, by law, must not be less than 4 cm in diameter. Outside the lagoon, fishing is done by handlines and basket traps. There are about 2500 fishermen on the main island and some 2000 tons of fish are landed from the lagoon (99). An

Table 12.5. The four reef units of Reunion and their proportion of the total reef area of the island.

Reef Unit	Reef areas, from north to south	Area %
Saint-Gilles	- platforms of Cap Champagne, Cap Homard and Grand Fond.	61
	- reef complex of Saint-Gilles/La Saline.	
	- platform of La Souris Chaude.	
Saint-Leu	- platforms of Pointe des Chateaux, La Chaloupe, and La Fontaine.	18.5
	- fringing reef of Saint-Leu.	
	- platform of La Pointe au Sel.	
Etang-Salé	- fringing reef of Etang-Salé.	6
Saint-Pierre	- fringing reefs of Saint-Pierre and Terre-Sainte.	14.5
	- platform of Grands-Bois.	

important supply to the economy is fishing on the outer banks by a fleet of 17 vessels. To avoid over-exploitation, a licensing system for bank fishing vessels has been in effect since 1992 which, from 1994, has been consolidated by a fish catch quota. Fish Aggregating Devices (FADs), made of floating material anchored at sea to attract pelagic fishes such as tuna and marlin, have been developed, with 26 deployed off Mauritius. Tuna fisheries account for 60% of the total fish catch and canned tuna represents almost 90% of the export in fish and fish products, though a proportion of this catch is from wide ragnging vesels that fish distant banks in the Indian Ocean. Marine fish farming is also developed (74). Moreover, the exploitation of fish for the aquarium trade has been developed but has not been well studied.

In Reunion, coastal fishing is poorly developed and fishers strictly use handlines although some gill-nets can be observed at Etang-Salé. Among the 1500 ton yield from coastal fishing, only 100 to 150 tons per year are considered to be coral reef fish (Tessier 1997, unpublished report). There are 36 FADs off Reunion. Due to the shallowness of the reef flats, the reefs are largely frequented by non-professional fishermen who catch octopus and small fish occurring within corals. These activities have never been evaluated in terms of the yield but these fishers walk on the reef flat, and probably contribute to reef degradation.

Disturbances

Heavy sedimentation, eutrophication, the collection of shells, walking on coral, over-fishing and boat anchors are responsible for the severe degradation of the islands' coral reefs. On remote islands (islets in Rodrigues, îles éparses), past extraction of guano or phosphates, collection of eggs from breeding colonies of sea birds, and the introduction of animals like rats and goats may have had unknown impacts. The reefs of Reunion (Table 12.5) have been the subject of scientific study since 1975, which has enabled an historical evaluation of some reef species and populations such as hard corals.

Disturbances in Reunion

Most studies have focused on the Saint-Gilles/La Saline reef complex, which is the most important reef area in Reunion (48% of the total surface of reef flats). Major changes in the structure of its ecological communities was attributed to a

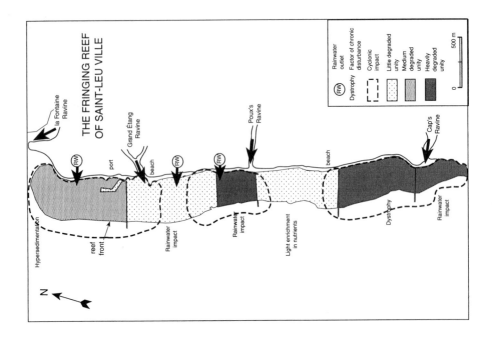

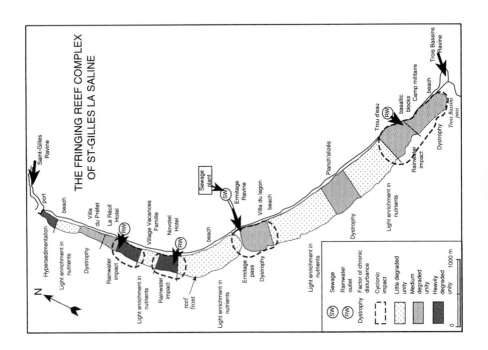

Figure 12.3. Maps of (a) Saint-Gilles/La Saline reef complex, (b) Saint-Leu fringing reef.

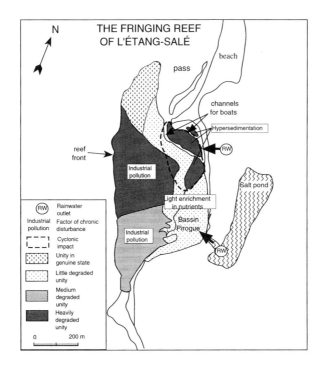

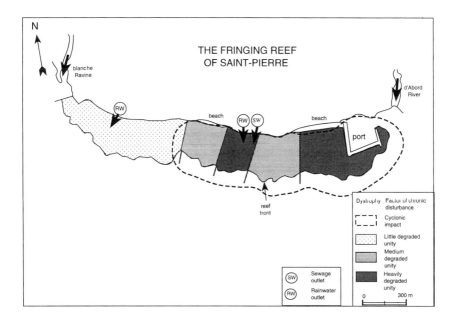

Figure 12.3. *(continued)* (c) Etang-Salé fringing reef, and (d) Saint-Pierre fringing reef.

combination of natural factors, such as cyclones or very low tides, and anthropogenic factors such as polluted groundwater discharge (45). On the other reefs, other well-identified sources of disturbance include run-off, farming, industrial wastes and sewage.

Groundwater Discharge. Excessive runoff is often responsible for transitions from coral-dominated to algae-dominated benthic communities. Sources may include groundwater discharge (26,53,62), which constitutes the main source of freshwater affecting the Saint-Gilles/La Saline reef (49), although some dry ravines flow into the reef in periods of heavy rains (Fig. 12.3). As shown by the low salinity and the high silicate values found near the shoreline (Table 12.6), groundwater discharge occurs in the back-reef zone. High silicate values are due to a high content in groundwater (up to 1.3 mM in the coastal area, 41).

From 1971 to the present, coastal urbanization has increased, and many tourist accomodations have been built. This development may have contributed to an increase in the nutrient content of groundwater, whose mean concentrations were 314 ± 81 μM for nitrates ($\pm$ 95% confidence interval) and 3.9 ± 0.4 μM for phosphates in 1985-1986 (22). At this time sewage was treated in cesspools and septic tanks, and may have contaminated the shallow groundwater. Groundwater enriched in nitrates occurred during the rainy season (Fig. 12.4a), probably through leaching of the soil by rainwater. Sources of nitrates may have included ammonium derived from nitrogen fixation of terrestrial plants and the decomposition of plant litter, domestic sewage, fertilizers and rain (26), although rainfall is low in nitrates in Reunion (41).

The groundwater flow rate was estimated to be about 1.2 l/s per 100 m of coastline in the north of the reef during the 1986 low-water period (49) but significant spatial variations occurred (25) probably due to the hydrogeology of the reefs. Coastal sedimentary formations lie over a highly permeable volcanic aquifer. Where these permeable sedimentary formations do not exceed a few meters in thickness, groundwater discharges between the shoreline and the reef front. Where sediments are thicker, the volcanic aquifer discharges mainly beyond the reef front (49,50). Seasonal variations in reefal water salinity (Fig. 12.4b) may be explained by variations in both the groundwater flow rate (see 62) and the water residence time on the reef, often affected by trade-wind conditions. Tidal variation is also responsible for short-term variability (Fig. 12.4c).

Groundwater discharges significant amounts of nitrogen to the reef (Table 12.6), though enrichment of phosphates was limited (Table 12.7). Biological uptake and release may obscure the physical processes of advection and mixing (89), and a weak, although significant, linear relationship was found between phosphates and silicates (23). This was not the case with nitrates, which had a more conservative behavior with respect to both salinity and silicates, reflecting dominant control by hydrographic supply (22).

Nutrient-enriched zones (called dystrophic zones, Fig. 12.3a), have: 1) a high coverage of macro-algae (76) with a biomass comparable to values found in the worst affected areas of the polluted Kaneohe Bay in Hawaii (88,90), 2) corals subjected to competition with cyanophytes, macro-algae and epilithic algal communities which tended to penetrate or entirely cover coral colonies (76,77), and 3) fewer branching corals, like the normally dominant *Acropora*

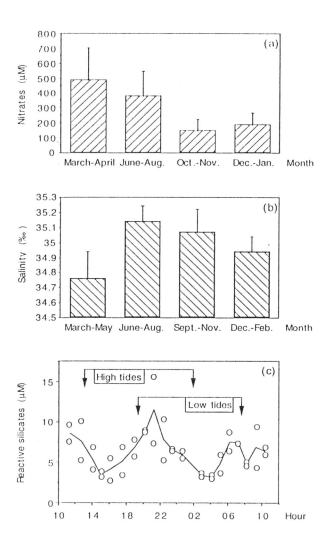

Figure 12.4. (a) Mean nitrate concentrations (± 95% confidence interval) in eight wells located in the vicinity of the reef complex of Saint-Gilles/La Saline from March 1985 to January 1986. (b) Mean salinity (± 95% confidence interval) on eight sites of the reef complex of Saint-Gilles/La Saline (four on the shoreline, four on the inner reef flat) from January 1985 to April 1986. (c) Reactive silicate concentrations over 24 hours on the shoreline of the reef complex of Saint-Gilles/La Saline (February 1985). Data from (22).

formosa. Some species like *Montipora circumvallata,* and *Porites (Synaraea) rus,* dominated the coral community (25,12, Naim and Cuet in preparation). In contrast, oligotrophic reef flats were composed of branching corals dominated by the genus *Acropora,* and had a high cover and diversity of corals on one of the locations monitored (12, Naim and Cuet in preparation). On non degraded reefs, macroalgae and cyanophytes were inconspicuous (88).

Table 12.6. Mean (± 95% confidence interval) salinity, inorganic nutrient concentrations, and particulate organic carbon content (POC) from samples collected from January 1985 to April 1986 on the reef complex of Saint-Gilles/La Saline (four stations on the shoreline, four stations on the inner reef flat). Number of samples in brackets. Ammonium concentrations were measured from September 1985 to April 1986 only. Data from (22). Superficial oceanic water data from (1, 39, 55). * : significant difference between shoreline and inner reef flat (Mann-Whitney, p = 0.0001). ** : nitrates + nitrites.

	Shoreline	Inner reef flat	Superficial oceanic waters
Salinity *	34.8 ± 0.2 (64)	35.12 ± 0.06 (64)	35.1 - 35.2 (all year)
Reactive silicates * (μM)	10 ± 3 (64)	3.7 ± 0.5 (63)	3 (winter)
Nitrates * (μM)	2.4 ± 0.7 (63)	0.8 ± 0.3 (63)	0 - 0.2 (winter)** / 0 (summer)**
Nitrites (μM)	0.16 ± 0.03 (64)	0.12 ± 0.02 (63)	
Ammonium (μM)	0.37 ± 0.08 (35)	0.30 ± 0.06 (36)	0.1 (winter)
Phosphates (μM)	0.31 ± 0.07 (62)	0.32 ± 0.06 (60)	0.15 - 0..3 (winter) / 0.1 (summer)
POC (μg C)	185 ± 19 (66)	174 ± 20 (64)	–

Table 12.7. Mean estimated groundwater-linked nutrient enrichment on the reefs of Saint-Gilles/La Saline (data from 22), Saint-Leu (data from 79), and Etang-Salé (data from 24). Nutrient enrichment was calculated from the mean salinity measured on the reefs, using the theoretical dilution line drawn from oceanic values (Table 12.6) and nutrient content of groundwater (Saint-Gilles/La Saline: measured. Saint-Leu and Etang-Salé: roughly estimated as the ordinal intercept value obtained from regression lines drawn from samples taken on the shoreline). * : nitrates + nitrites. LT - measurements made at low tide only.

		Saint-Gilles/ La Saline (1985-86)	Saint-Leu (1992-93)	Etang-Salé (1986)
Mean groundwater	Nitrates	314	148*	82*
nutrient content (μM)	Phosphates	3.9	?	2.6
Mean salinity	Shoreline	34.79	32.74 (LT)	32.78
	Inner reef flat	35.12	35.01	34.69
Potential groundwater-	Shoreline	3.2	10.1*	5.5*
linked nitrate enrichment (μM)	Inner reef flat	0.3	0.6*	1.1*
Potential groundwater-	Shoreline	0.04	?	0.16
linked phosphate enrichment (μM)	Inner reef flat	?	?	0.03

According to a PCA analysis of the benthic community structure (Naim and Cuet in preparation), one of the back reef locations monitored was characteristic of non-degraded areas, while another was characteristic of degraded ones. The two back reef areas clearly differed with respect to salinity, silicates and nitrates, indicating higher groundwater discharge into the degraded reef compared to the non-degraded one (22). On the reef flats, mean yearly values of groundwater tracers did not differ between the degraded and non-degraded areas. Groundwater, however, occasionally reached the degraded reef (25), especially during the warm season when algal growth is enhanced and eutrophication has the most critical effect (76). This suggests that the algae takes advantage of increases in nutrient levels occurring in short pulses (see 27). Large numbers of herbivorous fish were observed in the degraded areas (11,57), whereas omnivores dominated in non-degraded ones (9). On the contrary, grazing sea-urchins (*Echinometra mathaei* and Diadematidae) were rare in degraded areas, and numerous in non degraded ones (20,88). This suggests that the algal development observed on the degraded areas of the reef flat may have resulted from an imbalance between nutrient availability and herbivory pressure (64).

Nutrient availability on the degraded area of the reef flat was possibly enhanced both by acceleration of nutrient recycling and an input of exogenous organic matter. The degraded reef had higher nutrient concentrations and epilithic algae and digestive content had a higher proportion of organic matter than the oligotrophic reef (65). The recycling of nutrients by the herbivorous damselfish *Stegastes nigricans* appeared to be enhanced, both through a rapid dissolving of nutrients from fecal matter, and probably through the action of microorganisms. These results indicate that eutrophication may accelerate nitrogen and carbon cycles when *S. nigricans* is a key herbivorous species (76). On the other hand, the gross production to respiration ratio of the degraded reef flat in the summer was about 0.8, suggesting that exogenous organic matter may supplement this reef. Perhaps detrital algae originating in the back reef may settle on the reef flat, and enhance the heterotrophic part of the food web. Heterotrophs might, in turn, release nutrients into the water column further contributing to the build-up of algae (68).

River Run-off. At the end of the 1980s, dystrophic zones similar to those of the Saint-Gilles/La Saline reef were common on all the Reunion reefs (Cuet, P. and Naim, O. unpublished). Reefs were observed to be more or less nutrient-enriched through groundwater seepage, nitrate concentrations reaching the record value of 180 μM on the Saint-Pierre shoreline (unpublished). Corals can, however, support relatively high nutrient concentrations (2), and in Reunion, some coral communities were found to tolerate groundwater-linked nutrient enrichments (Table 12.7), notably on the inner reef flat of Saint-Leu (79).

Before 1989, Saint-Leu and Saint-Pierre were among the richest reefs of Reunion in terms of coral abundance, species richness and diversity of the associated fauna (34). Severe disturbances were recorded on both reefs during the January cyclone period of 1989, where superficial waters flowed onto the reef, as recorded in Kenya (66). Heavy sedimentation generated by cyclone Firinga was responsible for a coral mortality of 99% on most of the reef flats of Saint-Leu (60,79) and Saint-Pierre. At Saint-Leu, corals were buried by sediments and most died with the exception of massive *Porites lutea* and colonies of *Pavona divaricata*. These two species dominated two years after the impact. The slopes of the d'Abord river adjacent to Saint-Pierre had been used as a dumping ground for many years and after the hurricane the waters became so unhealthy that swimming was forbidden for two months. Scleractinians were buried by mud and rubbish. Only some *Galaxea* survived (unpublished) and most fish died or left the reef (56).

The mass coral mortality observed at Saint-Leu was followed by colonization of algae on the dead coral skeletons (79), as observed on other reefs struck by hurricanes (46). Large shifts in benthic community structure also occurred following other stochastic events such as very low tides (45).

Sewage from Turtle Farming. Raw effluent from a sea turtle farm (*Chelonia mydas*) developed in 1979 was being discharged onto the Pointe des Chateaux reef platform. Sea-water dumped by the turtle farm was analyzed in

1984 (54). While the annual production of turtles averaged 60 tons per year, the farm discharged 135 kg of suspended matter daily, or the equivalent of 1500 human inhabitants. Dumped sea-water (nearly 20 000 m^3 per day) was loaded with dissolved inorganic nitrogen (about 18 μM on average, mainly in the form of ammonium) and phosphorus (about 5 μM). The outfall was near the pass to the reef platform, so hydrodynamic and hydrological features allowed fast dilution (54). Regardless, the benthic communities were heavily affected within 200 m of the outfall (Naim O. unpublished report). Large filamentous algae were observed in the back reef and hard corals were replaced by soft corals (Alcyonarians) on the reef flat and outer slope, as is often observed in turbid waters enriched with organic matter (33). Under pressure from CITES, removal of wild young turtles from Tromelin, for growth in turtle farms, ended in 1994. Nevertheless, the farm will maintain the already existing adult stock for an additional 10 years (Derand, D. unpublished report).

Industrial Sewage. Prior to the building of the Etang-Salé sewage treatment plant in 1986, coral mortality of up to 90 to 100% occurred on the reef flat (24) and dead coral substrates were covered by up to 80% by the boring sponge *Cliona inconstans*. The main factor causuing degradation might be sea-borne industrial wastes, mainly from a sugar cane refinery located south of the reef (equivalent to 275 000 to 425 000 inhabitants 100 days a year) (DDASS, 1986). Coral mortality was lower in the inner zone of scattered colonies, although most of the micro-atolls of *Porites lutea* were covered with algal turfs and corallimorphs. Presumably due to eutrophication of the reef flat, oceanic waters were enriched with inorganic phosphorus (about 0.5 μM in January-February) and this, along with nitrogen-enriched groundwater discharge (Table 12.7), may have favored the development of algal turfs. It is interesting to note, however, that the highest growth rate of *Porites lutea* in the world (2.21 ± 1.49 cm/y; maximum of 3.5 cm/y) was recorded in this area (44).

Coastal Erosion. Coral reefs play a major role in the protection of the coast by reducing the energy of the waves and currents and by enriching beaches with sand. Beach erosion has been reported in Reunion (Mespoulhé and Troadec 1994, unpublished report) due to the disappearance of branching corals and a reduction in reef topographic complexity. This might have a disastrous influence on the durability of the coastal area in an island where swells and impact of cyclones are high.

Carbonate budget studies were carried out in 1994 at Trou d'Eau, an oligotrophic area of the Saint-Gilles/La Saline reef complex (19). Gross $CaCO_3$ deposited on the Trou d'Eau reef flat was estimated at around 8 $kg/m^2/y$ or twice the estimated world average (51), suggesting good vitality for this reef. Calcium carbonate dissolution prevails in the back reef. In total, combining the reef flat and back reef, 2.9 tons of $CaCO_3$ are deposited every year on the Trou d'Eau study transect. The calculation of bioerosion was based on estimates of the feeding activity of sea urchins (*Echinometra mathaei*) and parrotfish (*Scarus sordidus*) which are responsible for the major part of the observed bioerosion on experimental substrates (14). Parrotfish had a negligible effect on bioerosion (< 0.2 $kg/m^2/y$) due to their limited abundance and average small body sizes, the high population densities of sea urchins giving them the major role. In total, 2.3

tons of $CaCO_3$ were transformed into sediment every year on the study transect. Although all the processes involved in the carbonate budget have not been analyzed, a simple comparison suggests an equal rate of growth and decay, and a significant supply of sediments to the beach.

Examination of the same parameters in degraded areas should improve our understanding of beach erosion in Reunion. Bioerosion by *E. mathaei* was found to be negligible in the studied dystrophic zone (20), but the calcification rate was also low (3.5 kg/m²/y) when measured in summer (68).

Status of Reunion Reefs

Coral Degradation. Disturbances in Reunion come from 1) natural, high impact factors, and 2) chronic, anthropogenically altered factors such as freshwater run-off, turbidity and siltation due to harbor construction or modification, nutrient-enrichment through groundwater inputs, and discharges from industrial activities and livestock. Hurricanes were also important such that the same area may be affected by short but severe impacts as well as being chronically degraded (Table 12.8).

The degree of alteration of communities by each factor was assessed (see Fig. 12.3, Table 12.8) by analyzing the health and the percentage of mortality of corals, but also the relative abundance of coral competitors like cyanophytes, algae, sponges, other cnidarians or ascidians, and by analyzing the abundance of some herbivores like the damselfish *Stegastes nigricans*, sea-urchins and some detritivores like holothurians (78).

The degree of alteration of the different coral formations varies greatly according to which anthropogenic pressures and environmental factors were resonsible. Only 1% of the reef flats were condsidered to be in an original 'pristine state', 54% were lightly degraded, 32% moderately degraded, and 13% heavily degraded by chronic factors. Hurricane impacts degraded 18% of the reef flats. In total, 28% of the reef flats were heavily degraded by chronic impacts and hurricanes. Considering chronic perturbations, nutrients affect 26% of the reef flats, harbor activities 8%, heavy sedimentation due to surface waters 7%, and industrial wastes 5%. Additionally, bleaching of corals occurs each summer and can kill 30 to 100% of the coral community (25, unpublished).

Communities of the outer slopes are also degraded, mainly by heavy sedimentation in areas close to ravine outlets, but also by heavy spearfishing, collection of lobsters and shells by scuba-diving, high use by divers and anchoring, but possibly also by nutrient-enriched groundwater seepage (11). The current state of knowledge does not, however, make it possible to quantify the disturbances to the outer reef slopes.

Natural Recovery of Coral Reefs. After the impact of cyclone Firinga in 1989, on Saint-Leu and Saint-Pierre, the reefs are undergoing regeneration. Macroalgae have been slowly decreasing on the Saint-Leu inner reef flat (79) which is being colonized by a pioneer coral community (Naim, O. unpublished), corals being most abundant and diverse where chronic disturbance does not occur. At Etang-Salé and in La Saline, facies of dystrophy have decreased or disappeared (24, Dutrieux, E. and colleagues, unpublished).

Table 12.8. Degreee of degradation, given by the percent of coral reef area affected by disturbances, on the reef flats of Reunion.

Index of reef degradation	St-Gilles/ La Saline	Saint-Leu	Etang-Salé	Saint-Pierre	All reef flats
CHRONIC DISTURBANCES					
Not degraded	0%	0%	11%	0%	1%
Little degraded	62%	44%	22%	36%	53%
Medium degraded	32%	41%	21%	36%	34%
Heavily degraded	6%	14%	47%	12%	11%
Total	100%	100%	100%	100%	100%
IMPACT OF CYCLONES (example of Firinga, January 1989)					
Heavily degraded	12%	76%	11%	64%	27%

Two factors might be involved. First, the building of sewage treatment plants on the west coast began in 1986, including the treatment of the sugar cane refinery effluent south of Etang-Salé. Only the town of Saint-Pierre, whose sewage treatment plants are obsolete, was not involved. The treatment of domestic sewage should have decreased groundwater contamination, but the connection of users to the sewerage system is not yet complete, and often treatment is inefficient due to poor management and a low rate of water collection. Second, Reunion has not experienced heavy rains since hurricane Clotilda in 1987, and groundwater and run-off may be reduced.

Potential for Localized Marine Extinctions. Degradation of coral appears to have led to a spectacular decrease in biological diversity. In Reunion, some species seem to have disappeared. This is the case for some mollusks opisthobranchs, a few starfish, like *Culcita*, and some holothuroids that were common ten years ago (Naim, O. personal observations).

Benthic communities in the dystrophic zones of the reef flat and outer slope of the Saint-Gilles/La Saline reef complex have suffered a loss of biodiversty and the replacement of fragile species by more opportunistic ones (9). Recently a decrease in abundance and diversity of fish on all the reef flats of Reunion has occurred (58,59). Reef flats constitute nurseries for fish (38), but in dystrophic zones, the abundance of juvenile fish greatly decreased (8,10), suggesting that the effect of coral degradation may influence the continued subsistence of local human populations on reef fishes.

Mauritius and Rodrigues

In Mauritius, over the past 200 years, natural forest cover has been reduced to less than 1% of its original cover (95). The fringing reefs around Mauritius are badly affected by nutrients and both those from Mauritius and Rodrigues by siltation (29,86,96,99). Rodrigues was formerly reported to be a biologically luxuriant island, but because of deforestation, people now have water resource problems.

Reefs on the west coast of Mauritius are considered to be the most accessible and vulnerable to tourist activities while reefs on the east and south, subject to heavy swells for much of year, are naturally protected. The extensive sandy beaches and the reefs which often shelter them are increasingly being used by a vigorous tourist industry. Consequently, a large trade in corals and

Table 12.9. Survey of coral degradation in Mauritius: percentage of living coral cover and dominant species of corals on seven transects from the beach to the deep reef, located around Mauritius (data collected between September 1991 and May 1992).

Station	Shore reef	Back reef	Fore reef	Dominant species of corals
Ile aux Bénitiers	49.0%	44.3%	16.7%	*Acropora grandis, Pavona cactus, Acropora formosa, A. hyacynthus*
BalaClava	60.4%	-	9.0%	*Montipora tuberculosa, Acropora formosa, Favites abdita*
Trou aux Biches	47.5%	60.2%	27.4%	*Acropora grandis, A. formosa, A. hyacynthus*
Anse la Raie	-	65.3%	26.6%	*Montipora tuberculosa, Acropora formosa*
Trou d'Eau Douce	44.8%	1.2%	0.0%	*Pavona cactus, Cyphastrea microphthalma*
Bambous Virieux	26.7%	34.1%	-	*Pavona cactus, Fungia spp.*
Bel Ombre	37.7%	48.1%	-	*Pocillopora damicornis, Acropora hyacynthus*

shells, taken from the local reefs, has developed (99). The Government of Mauritius is concerned about the over-exploitation of shells and corals, and black coral, which is globally threatened, is now very rare around the island.

Over-fishing is becoming a problem throughout much of the island (99). Total catches have declined from 2500 tons in 1976 to 1375 tons in 1984. Use of dynamite and small mesh nets in the lagoon have contributed to the deterioration of the reefs. Outbreaks of *Acanthaster planci* have been recorded (Box 2.2). Habitats like mangroves and seagrass beds are also being degraded and destroyed.

A survey was made on seven reef sites around Mauritius using line transects (Table 12.9). Ile aux Bénitiers was considered as the control site for human influences. The Trou aux Biches region is considered to be one of the spots experiencing the greatest tourist development in Mauritius and, thus, the dominant human influences were attributed to activities like boating and boat anchoring. In Bambou Virieux, high sedimentation was observed due to terrigenous run-off from nearby agricultural areas and some signs of eutrophication were obvious. A striking feature in the area was the presence of whip corals attaining three meters in height along the channel slope. In Belombre, the coral community has been degraded by effluent from a sugar factory. At Anse la Raie, signs of eutrophication and colonization by macro-algae was observed. At Pointe aux Sables, no biological observations were made. Nevertheless, numerous sources of disturbance were obvious including industrial effluents, sewage, shipping and power plant influences. This study suggests that Mauritian reefs display degradation similar to that recorded for Reunion. Before an overall picture of the status of Mascarene reefs is developed, further surveys and inventories in Mauritius and Rodrigues are required.

Management and Conservation

In the Mascarene Archipelago, economic pressures and human population increase make management difficult. In Mauritius, the Fisheries Act of 1980 and Fisheries Regulations of 1983 prohibit taking undersized and female

Table 12.10 Marine reserves in Mauritius and Reunion.

	Mauritius	Reunion
Fishing reserves	Black River	All reef flats
	Blue Bay/Le Chaland	Outer slope of Saint-Gilles/La
	Grand Port/Mahébourg	Saline to 20 m depth
	Port-Louis	Reefs of Cap La Houssaye
	Rivière du Rempart-Poudre d'Or	
Nature reserves	Cargados Carajos shoals	Iles Glorieuses
	Ile aux Aigrettes and Ile Marianne	Tromelin
	Ile Plate and Ilot Gabriel	Bassas da India
	Ile aux Cocos and Ile aux Sables	Europa
	(Rodrigues)	

lobsters bearing eggs, the use of poisons and explosives, the import or export of live fish, corals and shells without a permit, and the collection of turtles and marine mammals. Spear-fishing is prohibited and the government has banned all spearguns and harpoons. In Reunion, many similar decrees control fishing and prohibit collection of corals and shells but, on this island, many of these decrees are poorly enforced.

Abiotic disturbances like chemicals or soil erosion, despite their high occurrence, have not degraded the Mauritian barrier reefs due to the large distance of these reefs from the coastal outlets and the existence of strong tidal currents that discharge polluted coastal waters through reef passes. Rodrigues is less well known and needs further ecological investigations. Fringing reefs in the three islands are closer to the coast, and their conservation, therefore, requires a major limitation on pollution sources. Sewage treatment plants should eventually reduce the industrial and domestic pollution on the reefs. Some other sources of pollution cannot, however, be controlled without difficulty. The urbanization of the supra-littoral zone and the construction of roads increase the volume of freshwater run-off and modifies its natural course. The expansion of agriculture increases non-point sources of chemicals and sedimentation. Management should focus on controlling and limiting these sources of disturbance.

Management should also promote the rehabilitation of the degraded reefs. In Reunion, an experiment to restore the reef flat of Saint-Leu after the cyclone Firinga suggested that the removal of fleshy algae induced the settlement of a new algal community controlled by herbivorous organisms, especially sea urchins (79). This initial experiment opens the possibility for restoring reef flats that are in decline after accidental impacts. Research is in progress on transplanting corals and associated fishes (13).

Major efforts are needed to promote environmental awareness and to integrate conservation with sustainable resource use. Marine reserves are numerous in Mauritius, while rare in Reunion (Table 12.10). Nevertheless, a nature reserve project, including all Reunion reefs, is under development. The creation of marine protected areas would make it easier to solve the multiple problems linked to the management of coral reefs in this region. A program elaborated in the COI context (1996-2000) has the goal of enhancing the overall implementation of Integrated Coastal Area Management (ICAM) in the COI region. Recommendations for projects included a survey of coastal and marine resources, improvement in pollution control and a marine education program.

References

1. Anonymous 1986. *Etude du Milieu Marin en Baie de la Possession et Baie de St-Paul. Campagne 1985.* Centre d'Océanologie de Marseille - Université de la Réunion Unpublished Report
2. Atkinson, M.J., Carlson, B., Crow, G.L. 1995. Coral growth in high-nutrient, low-pH sea-water : a case study of corals cultured at the Waikiki Aquarium, Honolulu, Hawaii. *Coral Reefs* 14: 215-223
3. Baissac (de), J. 1949-1971. Contributions à l'étude des poissons de l'île Maurice. *Proceedings of the Royal Society of Arts and Science,* Mauritius
4. Baissac (de), J., Lubet, P.E.K., Michel, C.M. 1962. Les biocœnoses benthiques littorales de l'île Maurice. *Recueil des Travaux de la Station Marine d'Endoume, Marseille* 25: 253-291
5. Borgesen, F. 1940-1957. Some marine algae from Mauritius. *Biologiske Meddelelser,* Royal Danish Academy of Sciences and Letters, Kubenhavn, Munksgaard
6. Bouchon, C. 1981. Quantitative study of the scleractinian coral communities of a fringing reef of Reunion Island (Indian Ocean). *Marine Ecology Progress Series* 4: 273-288
7. Bouvier, E.L. 1915. Décapodes marcheurs et Stomatopodes recueillis à l'île Maurice par M. Paul Carié. *Bulletin Scientifique de la France et de la Belgique* 48: 1-141
8. Chabanet, P. 1992. Comparison of coral reef fishes between two sectors (non-disturbed and disturbed) in Saint-Gilles la Saline fringing reef (Reunion Island). *Proceedings of the 7th International Coral Reef Symposium* 1: 344
9. Chabanet, P. 1994. *Etude des Relations entre les Peuplements Coralliens et les Peuplements Ichtyologiques sur le Complexe Récifal de Saint-Gilles la Saline.* Doctorat en Environnement Marin, Université d'Aix-Marseille III, Marseille
10. Chabanet, P., Letourneur, Y. 1995. Spatial pattern of size distribution of four fish species on Reunion coral reef flats. *Hydrobiologia* 300-301: 299-308
11. Chabanet, P., Join, J.-L., Cuet, P., Naim, O. 1995. Spatial variability in submarine groundwater discharge (SGD) occurrence and benthic and fish communities patterns on Saint-Gilles la Saline reef : a tentative interpretation through an hydrogeological model (Reunion Island). *European Meeting of the International Society for Reef Studies,* Newcastle. Abstract
12. Chabanet, P., Ralambondrainy, H., Amanieu, M., Faure, G., Galzin, R. 1997. Relationships between coral reef substrata and fish. *Coral Reefs* 16: 93-102
13. Chabanet, P., Naim, O., Gapper, C., Kay, T., Choussy, D. 1998. Restoration of a damaged coral reef flat on Reunion Island by the removal of buddings of corals and their associated fish fauna : preliminary results. *American Zoologist* 37(5): 40A
14. Chazottes, V. 1994. *Étude de la bioérosion et de la sédimentogenèse en milieu récifal : effets de l'eutrophisation (île de la Réunion, Océan Indien*

occidental). Doctorat en Sédimentologie, Université d'Aix-Marseille II, Marseille

15. Cheke, A.S., Elliot, H.F.I. 1987. *Studies of Mascarene Island Birds.* Cambridge: British Ornithological Union

16. Cheke, A.S., Lawley, J.C. 1983. Biological history of Agalega, with special reference to birds and other land vertebrates. *Atoll Research Bulletin* 273: 65-108

17. Clark, G. 1866. Note sur la découverte récente des débris de Dodo à l'île Maurice. *Annales des Sciences Naturelles: Zoologie et Paléontologie.* Paris: Masson

18. Conand, C. 1996. Asexual reproduction by fission in *Holothuria atra* : variability of some parameters in populations from the tropical Indo-Pacific. *Oceanologica Acta* 19: 209-216

19. Conand, C., Chabanet, P., Cuet, P., Letourneur, Y. 1997. The carbonate budget of a fringing reef in la Reunion Island (Indian Ocean) : external bioerosion and benthic flux of $CaCO_3$. *Proceedings of the 8th International Coral Reef Symposium* 1: 953-958

20. Conand, C., Heeb, M., Peyrot-Clausade, M., Fontaine, M.F. 1998. Evaluations of bioerosion by two types of the sea-urchin *Echinometra mathaei* on several sites of a fringing reef in La Reunion Island (Indian Ocean) and comparison with other sites. In *Echinoderms.* eds. Mooi, R., Telford, M. pp. 609-615. Rotterdam: A.A. Balkema

21. Cornic, A. 1987. *Poissons de l'île Maurice.* Rosehill, Mauritius: Éditions de l'Océan Indien

22. Cuet, P. 1989. *Influence des Résurgences d'eau Douce sur les Caractéristiques Physico-chimiques et Métaboliques de L'écosystème Récifal à La Réunion.* Doctorat en Chimie de l'Environnement, Université d'Aix-Marseille III, Marseille

23. Cuet, P. 1994. Sources de l'enrichissement en sels nutritifs de l'écosystème récifal à la Réunion : impact des eaux souterraines. In *Environnement en Milieu Tropical.* Coudray, J., Bouguerra, M.L. eds. pp. 105-110. Paris: ESTEM

24. Cuet, P., Naim, O. 1992. Analysis of a blatant degradation in la Reunion Island (l'Étang-Salé fringing reef). *Proceedings of the 7th International Coral Reef Symposium* 1: 313-322

25. Cuet, P., Naim, O., Faure, G., Conan, J.Y. 1988. Nutrient-rich groundwater impact on benthic communities of la Saline fringing reef (Reunion Island, Indian Ocean): preliminary results. *Proceedings of the 6th International Coral Reef Symposium,* Townsville 2: 207-212

26. D'Elia, C.F., Webb, K.L., Porter, J.W. 1981. Nitrate-rich groundwater inputs to Discovery Bay, Jamaica: a significant source of N to local coral reefs? *Bulletin of Marine Science* 31: 903-910

27. Done, T.J. 1992. Phase shifts in coral reef communities and their ecological significance. *Hydrobiologia* 247: 121-132

28. Drivas, J., Jay, M. 1988. Coquillages de la Réunion et de l'île Maurice. Papeete : Les Éditions du Pacifique

29. Fagoonee, I. 1988. Un profil de l'état des récifs coralliens de l'île Maurice. *Le Journal de la Nature, Université de la Réunion, Laboratoire de Chimie Organique* 1: 47-55

30. Farrow, G.E, Brander, K.M. 1971. Tidal studies of Aldabra. *Philosophical Transactions of the Royal Society of London* B260: 93-121

31. Faure, G. 1977. Annotated check list of corals in the Mascarene archipelago, Indian Ocean. *Atoll Research Bulletin* 1203: 1-26

32. Faure, G. 1982. *Recherche sur les Peuplements de Scléractiniaires des récifs Coralliens de l'Archipel des Mascareignes (Océan Indien Occidental)*. Doctorat ès Sciences, Université d'Aix-Marseille II, Marseille

33. Faure, G. 1994. Principales dégradations de l'écosystème récifal. In *Environnement en Milieu Tropical*. eds. Coudray, J., Bouguerra, M.L. pp. 86-97. Paris: ESTEM

34. Faure, G., Montaggioni, L.F. 1970. Le récif corallien de Saint-Pierre de la Réunion (Océan Indien): géomorphologie et répartition des peuplements. *Recueil des Travaux de la Station Marine d'Endoume, Marseille. Fascicule hors-série* 10: 271-284

35. Faure, G., Montaggioni, L.F. 1971a. Le récif corallien de l'Ile Rodrigues (Archipel des Mascareignes, Océan Indien): géomorphologie et répartition des peuplements. *Symposium on Indian Ocean and Adjacent Seas, Cochin*, p. 30

36. Faure, G., Montaggioni, L.F. 1971b. Les récifs coralliens sous le vent de l'Ile Maurice (Archipel des Mascareignes, Océan Indien) : morphologie et bionomie de la pente externe. *Comptes-Rendus de l'Académie des Sciences, Paris* D 273: 1914-1916

37. Faure, G., Montaggioni, L.F. 1976. Les récifs coralliens au vent de l'Ile Maurice (Archipel des Mascareignes, Océan Indien) : morphologie et bionomie de la pente externe. *Marine Geology* 21: M9-M16

38. Galzin, R. 1987. Structure of fish communities of French Polynesian coral reefs. II. Temporal scales. *Marine Ecology Progress Series* 41: 137-145

39. Gamberoni, L., Geronimi, J., Murail, J.F. 1984. Structure hydrologique aux abords immédiats de l'île de la Réunion en période hivernale (août-sept. 1982). Résultats de campagnes océanographiques du M.S. Marion-Dufresne et de prospections littorales de la Vedette 'Japonaise', *CNFRA* 55: 41-47

40. Gardiner, J.S. 1936. The reefs of the western Indian Ocean. II. The Mascarene region. *Transactions of the Linnaean Society of London* 19: 426-436

41. Grunberger, O. 1989. *Etude Géochimique et Isotopique de l'infiltration sous Climat Tropical Contrasté - Massif du Piton des Neiges - Ile de la Réunion*. Doctorat en Hydrogéologie, Université de Paris XI, Paris

42. Guilcher, A., Berthois, L., Le Calvez, Y., Battistini, R., Crosnier, A. 1965. Les récifs coralliens et le lagon de l'île de Mayotte (archipel des Comores). ORSTOM Report 11

43. Guillaume, M. 1988. *La Croissance du Squelette de* Porites lutea,

Scléractiniaire Hermatypique, sur le Récif Frangeant de la Saline, Ile de la Réunion, Océan Indien. Doctorat en Océanographie Biologique, Université d'Aix-Marseille II, Marseille

44. Guillaume, M. 1993. *La Croissance Exceptionnelle de Porites lutea, Scléractiniaire Hermatypique, sur le Récif de l'Étang-Salé à l'île de la Réunion.* Réunion de la Société Géologique de France, Carbonates Intertropicaux, Paris

45. Guillaume, M., Payri, C.E., Faure, G. 1983. Blatant degradation of coral reefs at la Reunion island (West Indian Ocean). *European Meeting of the International Society for Reef Studies, Nice*

46. Harmelin-Vivien, M. 1994. The effects of storms and cyclones on coral reefs: a review. *Journal of Coastal Research* 12: 211-231

47. Hodgkin, E.P., Michel, C. 1960. Zonation of plants and animals on rocky-shores of Mauritius. *Proceedings of the Royal Society of Arts and Science, Mauritius* 2: 121-145

48. Jadin, M.F. 1936. Liste des algues récoltées en 1890 aux îles de la Réunion et de Maurice. *Bulletin de l' Académie de la Réunion* 13: 87-120

49. Join, J.-L. 1991. *Caractérisation hydrologique du milieu volcanique insulaire, le Piton des Neiges, île de la Réunion.* Doctorat en Hydrogéologie, Université de Montpellier II, Montpellier

50. Join, J.-L., Pommé, J.B., Coudray, J., Daesslé, M. 1988. Caractérisation des aquifères basaltiques en domaine littoral. Impact d'un récif corallien. *Hydrogéologie* 2: 107-115

51. Kinsey, D.W. 1985. Metabolism, calcification and carbon production. I - Systems-level studies. *Proceedings of the 5th International Coral Reef Congress* 4: 505-526

52. La Housse de Lalouvière, P. 1994. Dugongs, extinct mammals of Mauritius. Diodon, Bulletin d'information du MMCS No. 3

53. Lapointe, B.E. 1997. Nutrient thresholds for bottom-up control of macroalgal blooms on coral reefs in Jamaica and southeast Florida. *Limnology and Oceanography* 42: 1119-1131

54. Le Gall, J.Y., Fesquet, J.M. 1985. Le lagon comme environnement aquacole de la ferme d'élevage de la tortue verte marine *Chelonia mydas* à l'île de la Réunion (Océan Indien). *Proceedings of the 5th International Coral Reef Symposium*, Tahiti 5: 481-486

55. Leroy, C., Barbaroux, O. 1980. *Observations physiques et chimiques effectuées sur le milieu marin autour de l'île de la Réunion.* ISTPM Nantes Unpublished Report

56. Letourneur, Y. 1991. Modifications du peuplement de poissons du platier récifal de Saint-Pierre (île de la Réunion, Océan Indien) consécutives au passage du cyclone Firinga. *Cybium* 15: 159-170

57. Letourneur, Y. 1992. *Dynamique des Peuplements Ichtyologiques des Platiers Récifaux de l'île de la Réunion.* Doctorat en Océanographie Biologique, Université d'Aix-Marseille II, Marseille

58. Letourneur, Y. 1996a. Dynamics of fish communities on Reunion fringing reefs, Indian Ocean. I. Patterns of spatial distribution. *Journal of Experimental Marine Biology and Ecology* 195: 1-30

59. Letourneur, Y. 1996b. Dynamics of fish communities on Reunion fringing reefs, Indian Ocean. II. Patterns of temporal fluctuations. *Journal of Experimental Marine Biology and Ecology* 195: 31-52
60. Letourneur, Y., Harmelin-Vivien, M., Galzin, R. 1993. Impact of hurricane Firinga on fish community structure on fringing reefs of Reunion Island, S.W. Indian Ocean. *Environmental Biology of Fishes* 37: 109-120
61. Letourneur, Y., Taquet, M., Chabanet, P., Tessier, E., Parmentier, M. 1999. Preliminary check-list of marine fishes of Reunion Island, south-western Indian Ocean. *Atoll Research Bulletin*, in press
62. Lewis, J.B. 1987. Measurements of groundwater seepage flux onto a coral reef : spatial and temporal variations. *Limnology and Oceanography* 32: 1165-1169
63. Lienard, E. 1877. *Catalogue de la Faune Malacologique de l'île Maurice et de ses Dépendances.* Paris
64. Littler, M.M., Littler, D.S. 1984. Models of tropical reef biogenesis: the contribution of algae. *Progress in Phycological Research* 3: 323-364
65. Lison de Loma, T. 1996. *Transformation de la Production Primaire Algale par* Stegastes nigricans *(Pisces, Pomacentridae) sur les Récifs Coralliens de la Réunion: Influence de L'eutrophisation.* D.E.A. en Sciences de l'Environnement Marin, Université de la Méditerranée, Marseille
66. McClanahan, T.R., Obura, D. 1997. Sedimentation effects on shallow coral communities in Kenya. *Journal of Experimental Marine Biology and Ecology* 209: 103-122
67. Michelin, M. 1845. *Zoophytes, Echinodermes et Stelleridae.* Essai d'une faune de l'île Maurice. Mag. Zool. 2: 3-6
68. Mioche, D., Cuet, P. 1999. *Metabolisme du Carbone et des sels Nutritifs en Saison Chaude, sur un Récif Frangeant Soumis à une Pression Anthropique (Ile de la Réunion, Océan Indien).* Comptes-Rendus de l'Académie des Sciences, Paris, in press
69. Mondon, J.M. 1976. *Contribution à la Géomorphologie et à la Sédimentologie des Récifs Coralliens de l'île Maurice (Archipel des Mascareignes, Océan Indien).* Doctorat en Sédimentologie, Université de Provence, Marseille
70. Montaggioni, L.F. 1974. Coral reefs and quaternary shorelines in the Mascarene archipelago (Indian Ocean). *Proceedings of the 2nd International Coral Reef Congress,* Brisbane 2: 579-593
71. Montaggioni, L.F. 1978. *Recherches géologiques sur les complexes récifaux de l'Archipel des Mascareignes (Océan Indien occidental).* Doctorat ès Sciences, Université d'Aix-Marseille II, Marseille
72. Montaggioni, L.F., Faure, G. 1980. Les récifs coralliens des Mascareignes (Océan Indien). Collections des Travaux du Centre Universitaire, Université de la Réunion
73. Montaggioni, L.F., Nativel, P. 1988. *La Réunion. L'île Maurice. Géologie et Aperçus Biologiques.* Guides Géologiques Régionaux. Paris: Masson
74. Munbodh, M., Ramyead, T.S., Kallee, P. 1988. L'importance économique des récifs coralliens et tentatives d'aquaculture à Maurice. *Le Journal de la Nature,* Université de la Réunion, Laboratoire de Chimie Organique 1: 56-68

75. Naim, O. 1988. Les récifs coralliens des îles du sud-ouest de l'Océan Indien. Géomorphologie, dégradations, ressources et protection : premier bilan. *Le Journal de la Nature*, Université de la Réunion, Laboratoire de Chimie Organique 1: 105-120

76. Naim, O. 1993. Seasonal responses of a fringing reef community to eutrophication (Reunion Island, Western Indian Ocean). *Marine Ecology Progress Series* 99: 307-315

77. Naim, O. 1994. Structure des communautés benthiques et eutrophisation en milieu corallien. In *Environnement en Milieu Tropical*. eds. Coudray, J., Bouguerra, M.L. pp. 99-104. Paris: ESTEM

78. Naim, O. submitted. Les récifs coralliens de la Réunion. Bionomie des peuplements et dégradation. *Ecologie*

79. Naim, O., Cuet, P., Letourneur, Y. 1997. Experimental shift in benthic community structure. *Proceedings of the 8th International Coral Reef Symposium, Panama.* 2: 1873-1878

80. Payri, C.E. 1985. Contribution to the knowledge of the marine benthic flora of Reunion island (Mascarene archipelago, Indian Ocean). *Proceedings of the 5th International Coral Reef Congress*, Tahiti 6: 635-640

81. Pichon, M. 1967. Caractères généraux des peuplements benthiques des récifs et lagons de l'île Maurice (Océan Indien). *Cahiers de l'ORSTOM (série Océanographie).* 5: 31-45

82. Pichon, M. 1971. Comparative study of the main feature of some coral reefs of Madagascar, la Réunion and Mauritius. *Symposium of the Zoological Society of London* 28: 185-216

83. Pritchard, P. 1979. *Encyclopaedia of Turtles.* THF Publications

84. Ribes, S. 1978. La macrofaune vagile associée à la partie vivante des Scléractiniaires sur un récif frangeant de l'île de la Réunion (Océan Indien). Doctorat en Océanographie Biologique, Université d'Aix-Marseille II, Marseille

85. Rosen, B.R. 1971. The distribution of reef coral genera in the Indian Ocean. *Symposium of the Zoological Society of London* 28: 263-300

86. Salm, R.V. 1983. Coral reefs of the Western Indian Ocean: a threatened heritage. *Ambio* 12: 349-353

87. Scheer, G. 1971. Coral reefs and coral genera in the Red Sea and Indian Ocean. *Symposium of the Zoological Society of London* 28: 329-367

88. Semple, S. 1997. The use of temporal variations in algal cover and biomass as a tool for the quantification of the degree of eutrophication of a fringing coral reef in Réunion Island, S.W. Indian Ocean. *Oceanologica Acta* 20: 851-861

89. Smith, S.V. 1984. Phosphorus versus nitrogen limitation in the marine environment. *Limnology and Oceanography* 29: 1149-1160

90. Smith, S.V., Kimmerer, W.J., Laws, E.A., Brock, R.E., Walsh, T.W. 1981. Kaneohe bay sewage diversion experiment: perspectives on ecosystem responses to nutritional perturbation. *Pacific Science* 35: 279-395

91. Staub, F., Gueho, J. 1968. The Cargados Carajos shoals on Saint-Brandon. Resources, avifauna and vegetation. *Proceedings of the Royal Society of Arts and Science, Mauritius.* 3: 7-46

92. Stiasny, G. 1940. Alcyonaria und Gorgonaria von Mauritius. *Archives Néerlandaises de Zoologie,* Amsterdam 4: 334-351

93. Stoddart, D.R. 1973. Coral Reefs of the Indian Ocean. In *Biology and Geology of Coral Reefs*, Volume 1: Geology. eds. Jones, O.A., Endean, R. pp 51-92. London:Academic Press

94. Taylor, J.D. 1971. Reef associated Molluscan assemblages in the Western Indian Ocean. *Symposium of the Zoological Society of London* 28: 501-534

95. UNEP 1982. *Environmental Problems of the East African Region.* UNEP Regional Seas Reports and Studies 6

96. UNEP 1984. Unpublished Country Report on Mauritius. UNEP: Nairobi

97. Veron, J.E.N. 1986. *Corals of Australia and the Indo-Pacific.* London: Angus and Robertson Publishers

98. Vinson, L. 1937-1939. Les Poissons de Maurice. *Proceedings of the Royal Society of Arts and Science, Mauritius* 5 (8)

99. Wells, S. 1988. *Indian Ocean, Red Sea and Gulf.* In Coral Reefs of the World, Volume 2. Cambridge: UNEP/IUCN

Chapter 13

The Seychelles

S. Jennings, S. S. Marshall, P. Cuet & O. Naim

The reefs of the Seychelles are among the most extensive in the western Indian Ocean. They range from heavily exploited and intermittently polluted fringing reefs on the coasts of the large granitic islands of Mahé, Praslin, and La Digue to isolated atolls such as Aldabra where fishing pressure and pollution levels are low. Reefs may sustain important artisanal fisheries, provide coastal protection and are an important resource for the dive tourism industry. Reefs have been studied in most detail on the granitic islands and Aldabra. Reclamation, sedimentation and eutrophication threaten reefs around the large granitic islands and military development once threatened Aldabra. Approximately 15% of the islands' reefs now have protected status but it has proved difficult to advance from protection by law to protection in practice (Box 13.1). Nevertheless, the extensive reefs of Seychelles, coupled with a small population have allowed the country to address marine conservation issues which appear insurmountable elsewhere.

Geography and Geology

The Seychelles is an archipelagic nation of 42 granitic and 74 coralline islands with a total land area of 455 km² contained within an Exclusive Economic Zone (EEZ) of 1 374 000 km². For government administrative purposes the archipelago is divided into four groups, the Inner Seychelles, where 97% of the 75 000 human population now reside, and the southern groups of Amirantes, Farquhar and Aldabra (Fig. 13.1). The Seychelles are characterized by two types of island, the granitic inner Seychelles to the north and the outer coralline islands and atolls of the Amirantes, Farquhar and Aldabra groups to the south and west (Fig. 13.2). The granitic islands have a land area of 277 km² and are remnants of Gondwanaland, the ancient continent which split to form Africa, Madagascar, the Seychelles, India, Antarctica and Australia. Today the granitics rise from the Seychelles Bank, an area of 31 000 km² with mean water depths between 44 to 65 m (10,48).

The coralline islands are usually classified as high or low-lying islands. Low-lying islands are found on the Seychelles and Amirantes Banks. Three

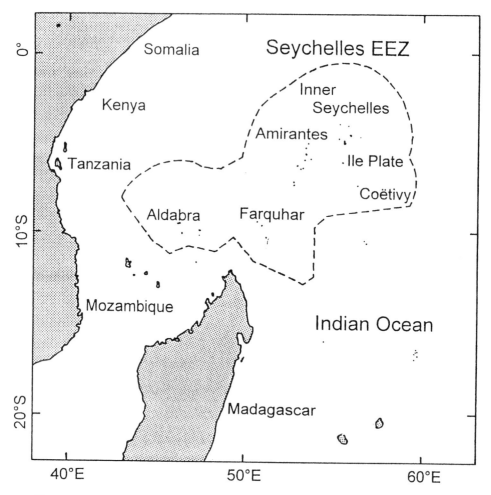

Figure 13.1. The four island groups of the Seychelles Exclusive Economic Zone (EEZ). Of the 42 granitic and 74 coralline islands in the Seychelles, Ile Plate and Coëtivy are the only islands which are not assigned to these groups.

low-lying islands rise from the Seychelles Bank, Denis and Bird Island from depths of around 55 m on the northern rim and Coëtivy from 36 m on the southern rim. Other low-lying islands rise from the Amirantes Bank to the west. The Amirantes Bank is approximately 6300 km² in area, with a rim at depths of 11 to 27 m and a deeper central zone. In contrast with the Seychelles Bank, no volcanic rocks are exposed, but they lie close to the surface. The low lying coralline islands of the Amirantes Bank are rarely more than 2 to 3 m above sea level and are formed of sands that has been deposited onto coral platforms by waves and currents.

The westernmost atolls of Aldabra, Assumption, Astove, Cosmoledo and St. Pierre (Fig. 13.2) are often referred to as the high limestone islands because they may reach heights of 8 m above sea level. These atolls have formed on

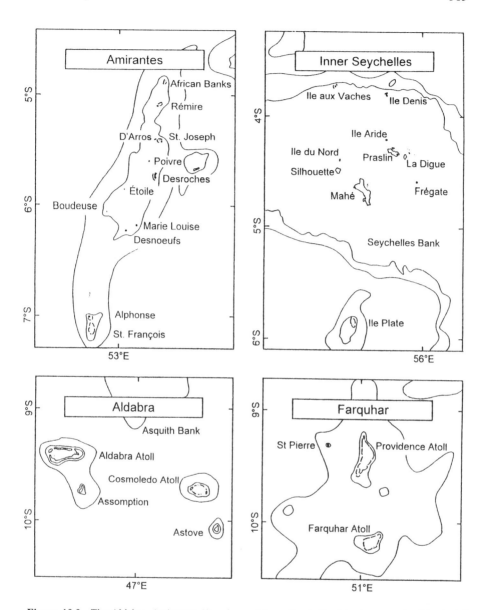

Figure 13.2 The Aldabra, Amirantes, Farquhar and Inner Seychelles island groups. Land is shaded and the 2000 m and 200 m depth contours are shown. All the larger islands in the Inner Seychelles are granitic, but there are no granitic islands in the other groups.

top of volcanic structures and rise from water depths of over 2000 m. As a result, the outer reefs slope rapidly to depths of several hundred meters. The high limestone islands are much older than the low-lying coralline islands, and they are characterized by terraces which reflect changes in sea levels during the last glacial cycle (10,49).

Climate and Oceanography

The climate of Seychelles has a significant influence on the distribution and development of reefs and there are marked seasonal changes in climate due to monsoonal wind shifts. Annual climate changes are induced by seasonal air pressure changes over the Indian subcontinent, changes in the position and intensity of the southern Indian Ocean subtropical anticyclone, the seasonal passage of intertropical troughs and ocean currents, and the sea surface temperature in the equatorial Indian Ocean. From May to October the trade winds blow from the southeast (southeast monsoon) and from December to March they tend to blow from the northeast (northeast monsoon). In the transition months of April and November, intertropical troughs lie over Seychelles and winds tend to be light and variable. Rainfall is lower on low than high islands and varies from around 2500 mm/y on the granitic islands to 1000 mm/y on Aldabra. Air temperatures over the Seychelles range from 19 to 36°C, and mean temperatures are 25 to 28°C. Tropical cyclones do not affect the northern granitic islands, but there are occasional records of cyclones in the southern groups of Aldabra and Assumption (53).

The Seychelles lie in the south equatorial current and sea-surface temperatures range from 26 to 31°C and salinities from 34.5 to 35.5 ppt. Tidal ranges on the open ocean reefs are only 0.3 to 1 m, but they increase to 1 or 2 m around the granitic islands and 2 to 3 m in the Aldabra group. The oceanic water surrounding the Seychelles is characterized by low and variable rates of production. Atolls may, however, induce upwelling and this adds to downstream oceanic productivity. An example of this effect was provided by the study of gross primary production around Astove Atoll (Fig. 13.3); while production is low in the adjacent ocean and on the windward side of the island, the island has induced upwelling which leads to increased production around the reef and in the wake of the island (16).

Colonization and Government

The history of human colonization has largely determined the rate and intensity at which the natural resources in the Seychelles were exploited and the effects of pollution, reclamation, and tourism on the marine environment. France claimed possession of the Seychelles in 1756, and the first settlers arrived in Seychelles from Réunion and Mauritius. Settlers established a settlement close to the current capital of Victoria on Mahé but disregarded their orders to develop plantations and spice gardens and proceeded to amass wealth from trade in timber and the native fauna. Trees were felled for ship building, and giant tortoises, turtles and birds were slaughtered for subsistence and sale.

In 1794, the British took control of the islands but continued disputes between the British and French meant that the islands were rarely a true possession of either country until the islands became a British dependency in 1815. Both Britain and France promoted the slave trade and by 1803, the population of Seychelles was 2101, of which 1820 were slaves. The slaves were forced to work on plantations where introduced crops such as cinnamon, cloves, coffee, bamboo, chili, lemon, tea, mango, avocado, paw-paw, castor oil, cotton,

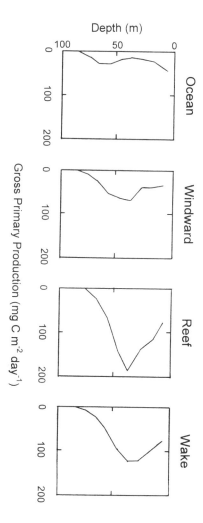

Figure 13.3. Estimates of gross primary production at four sites around Astove Atoll (see Fig. 13.2). The oceanic and wake stations were 7.4 km and 1.8 km from the island respectively. Redrawn from (16).

vanilla and nutmeg were grown. When slavery was abolished in 1835, the population of Seychelles was approximately 10 000 people.

Throughout the nineteenth century the Seychelles continued to be administered with Mauritius but, in 1903, the Aldabra group and Seychelles were merged to form a separate Crown Colony. The population continued to rise steadily, exceeding 25 000 by 1930. In 1965, the Aldabra, Farquhar and Desroche groups were annexed to form part of the British Indian Ocean Territory. This was a precursor to the proposal that Aldabra should be developed as a military base, but the proposal was not adopted and the islands were returned to Seychelles when the country attained independence in 1976.

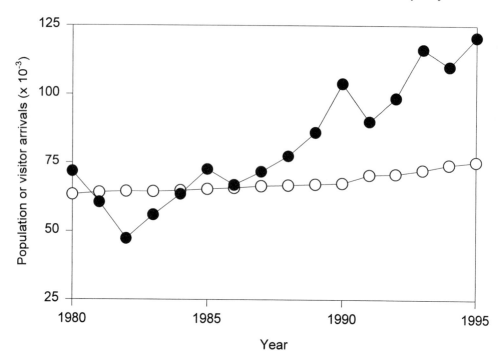

Figure 13.4. The resident population (open circles) and number of tourist visitors (filled circles) to Seychelles from 1979 to 1995.

An international airport opened in 1972, and tourism became an increasingly important source of foreign revenue. By the late 1970's both the resident population and the number of tourist visitors exceeded 60 000, and since 1993 over 100 000 tourists have arrived each year (Fig. 13.4).

Reef Ecology

A History of Reef Studies

The first descriptions of the natural history of Seychelles come from the visit of the 'Ascension' in 1609. Investigative rather than descriptive studies began with the Fairfax Moresby Hydrographic studies in 1822, and many other expeditions made taxonomic collections of reef fauna and flora in the late nineteenth and early twentieth centuries (Table 13.1). The most comprehensive studies of Seychelles reefs followed the Percy Sladen Memorial Trust Expedition in 1905 (20), and the International Indian Ocean Expedition in 1964. In addition, studies of the Aldabra reef were conducted by scientists based permanently on Aldabra following the establishment of a Royal Society research station.

In recent years, resident scientists on Aride and Cousin Islands have worked on reefs, as have staff of the Government Conservation and National Parks Service (now the Marine Parks Authority) and the Seychelles Fishing Authority. In addition, the Soviet-American Expedition of 1989 and the Netherlands Indian

Ocean Program (Tyro Expedition) of 1992 to 1993, surveyed reefs and made coral, fish and invertebrate collections throughout the Inner Seychelles and Amirantes (30,51).

Recent expeditions have added much to our knowledge of the western Indian Ocean reef fauna. Indeed, 91 new fish records were recorded during the Tyro Expedition (40). Detailed knowledge of reefs and corals mostly come from research conducted during the International Indian Ocean Expedition (9,10,11,31,32,41,49) and the more recent Soviet-American and Netherlands Oceanic Reefs Expeditions (30,51). There are few long term and detailed studies of Seychelles reefs and they have not received the same scientific attention as the terrestrial fauna (48). The Marine Parks Authority has, however, recently implemented a reef survey program in collaboration with the Swedish Development Agency (SIDA) and the Great Barrier Reef Marine Parks Authority (GBRMPA) and it is hoped that this program will provide a basis for more extensive research on Seychelles reefs.

Reef Types and Distribution

The reefs of Seychelles can be classified into three major groups: fringing reefs, platform reefs, and atolls. Fringing reefs have developed around the coasts of the granitic islands Water depth and exposure govern the development of these reefs and they are most extensive around Mahé and Praslin where they occupy areas of 20 and 27 km² respectively (Fig. 13.5). Fringing reefs on the other islands total 10 km². The vertical extent of fringing reefs is typically limited to 15 to 20 m by the shallow depths on the Seychelles Bank and their morphology is largely determined by their aspect.

There are marked differences between reefs exposed to the southeasterly trades and those in sheltered locations. Thus reefs on the southeast coast of Mahé are exposed to the trade winds and tend to be continuous and unbroken with a width of 500 to 750 m whereas in northwest Mahé the reefs are sheltered and tend to be highly irregular, with many gullies and channels (49). On the west coast of Mahé, the granite cliffs between bays plunge steeply into the sea and true fringing reefs have only developed in the sheltered bays such as Baie Ternay and Port Launay. In the exposed areas, corals grow directly on the granitic substrate. Fringing reefs around Praslin are extensive and may extend 3 km from the shore (Fig. 13.5), but much of the coral is currently dead.

Platform reefs have developed in the Amirantes and Farquhar groups. These total over 200 km² in area. Stoddart recognized two types of platform reef, those which have a considerable area of dry land following the accumulation of detrital deposits and those with shallow lagoons and reef and a very small land area as found at African Banks, Ile Plate and Providence. Assumption and St. Pierre are raised platform reefs reaching heights of 8 m above sea level. These raised reefs were used as nesting sites by seabird colonies and have been extensively mined for guano.

Farquhar, St. Joseph, St. Francois and Alphonse in the Amirantes are atolls. The combined area of peripheral reef in these Atolls is around 120 km² and they are virtually unstudied. The remaining reefs in Seychelles are found around the raised atolls of Aldabra, Cosmoledo and Astove in the Aldabra group. The total area of peripheral reef in the raised atolls is approximately 200 km² and the lagoons are largely devoid of coral growth.

Table 13.1. A condensed history of *Research, Development*, conservation, *Management* and related laws and treaties in Seychelles.

Date	Activity
1820-	*Research*: Fairfax Moresby Expedition (Hydrographic survey)
1839	*Development*: Whaling Station opens on Ste. Anne
1860-	*Management*: Darwin and Huxley voice concern over conservation in Aldabra to Governor
1879	of Mauritius
1880-	*Research*: Deutschen Tiefsee Expedition (Geology)
1899	'Alert' Expedition (Biological Collection)
1900-	*Research*: 'Sealark' (Percy Sladen Trust) Expedition (Biological Collection)
1909	*Development*: Turtle hunters establish permanent bases on Aldabra and Assumption; Sea cucumber export begins
	Management: First attempts to control turtle exploitation
1910-	*Development*: Turtle shell export peaks; End to export of turtle bones for fertilizer
1919	
1920-	*Research*: 'Dana' Expedition (Oceanography)
1929	*Management*: Turtle egg collection banned; Turtle size limits introduced
1930-	*Research*: 'Mabahiss' Expedition (Oceanography)
1939	
1940-	*Research*: 'Albatross' Expedition (Oceanography)
1949	
1950-	*Research*: JLB and MM Smith Reef fish collection; 'Galathea' Expedition
1959	(Oceanography); 'Calypso' (Cousteau) Expedition (Filming)
	Development: Tuna long lining begins; Salt fish and green snail exports peak
	Management: Green turtle capture restricted on Aldabra
1960-	*Research*: JE Bohkle, JC Tyler, RH Rosenblatt, WA Starck II (Fish collection); 'Te
1969	Vega' Expedition (Oceanography and collection); Royal Society (UK) begin work on Aldabra; 'Anton Bruun' (International Indian Ocean) Expedition (Coral *Research*)
	Development: Proposal to develop Aldabra as military base
	Management: Green turtle capture banned; International Council for Bird Preservation (ICBP) purchase Cousin Island
	Laws & Treaties: Act to create Seychelles National Parks and Nature Conservancy Commission (NPNCC) passed; Aldabra leased by Royal Society (UK)
1970-	*Research*: Randall and Woodland (Fish collection); 'Manihine' Expedition (Collection)
1979	*Development*: Reefs reclaimed to create Mahe airport; Purse seining for tuna begins
	Management: Exclusive Economic Zone declared; Seychelles Islands Foundation (SIF, corporate body to manage Aldabra) established; Marine National Parks (MNP) established at Ste Anne, Curieuse, and Baie Ternay; Cousin Island gazetted as a special reserve
	Laws & Treaties: Publication of white paper on conservation strategy; Seychelles signs International Convention for Regulation of Whaling, International Convention on Civil Liability for Oil Pollution Damage; Convention on the Prevention of Marine Pollution by Dumping of Wastes and Other Matter; Convention on International Trade in Endangered Species (CITES)
1980-	*Research*: International Union for the Conservation of Nature (IUCN) turtle study; CMPI
1989	study of coastal erosion; Study of dredging and land reclamation of reefs on Ste Anne MNP in Victoria; Soviet- American Expedition
	Development: European Vessels gain access to EEZ; Tuna processing plant opens in Victoria; Shell button and jewelry factory opens; Construction of sewage works
	Management: Aldabra designated as World Heritage Site; Aldabra handed to SIF for *Management*; African Banks declared as protected areas; Silhouette MNP established
	Laws & Treaties: Seychelles signs UN convention on Law of the Sea; Signs convention for Protection, Management and Development of the Marine and Coastal Environment of the East African Region; Signs convention for Protection of World Cultural and Natural Heritage; Fisheries Acts limit catches and mesh sizes; Department of Environment (DoE) created
1990-	*Research*: 'Tyro' Expedition (Biological Collection and Reef Description)
	Laws & Treaties: Biodiversity Agency replaces Conservation and National Parks Service (CNP) at DoE; Seychelles signs Rio Biodiversity Convention

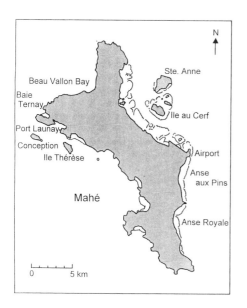

Figure 13.5. Distribution of fringing reefs around the largest granitic islands of Mahé and Praslin.

There are marked differences in the nutrient regime around the granitic and coralline islands and these are likely to affect reef development and the species which dominate the reef community. Nutrient input to the coralline islands is mainly from oceanic water, localized upwelling (Fig. 13.3) and nitrogen fixation. Moreover, the carbonate sediments surrounding the low-lying islands may further reduce phosphorus levels as a result of their geochemical scrubbing.

The granitic islands in the inner Seychelles receive more rainfall and are often forested, so high nutrient concentrations are expected to be present in runoff (33). Analyses of water samples collected in February and March 1989 supported these theories and, in general, mean nutrient levels around the granitic islands were higher than those around the coralline islands. The high nutrient levels around the granitic islands appear to lead to crustose coralline algal and frondose macroalgal dominance whereas the nutrient poor regimes around the coralline islands tend to lead to hermatypic coral dominance (33).

Detailed studies of the corals on Seychelles reefs have largely been limited to the granitic islands and Aldabra, although there have been some recent collections and surveys conducted in the Amirantes (30). On the fringing reefs of Mahé, Rosen (41) described reef development in relation to water movement and exposure. In the surf zone, the coral community is dominated by *Pocillopora* spp. Where there was considerable water movement, but no direct surf action, *Acropora* spp. tended to dominate and in sheltered areas *Porites* spp. are found. Most coral growth occurs at depths to 6 m, and corals are increasingly scarce at depths in excess of 10 to 15 m.

The outer reef slope is characterized by *Acropora pharaonis, A. divaricata, A. irregularis, A. palifera, A. humilis, Seriatopora caliendrum* and *Fungia fungites*. At greater depths and in more sheltered areas there are species of *Porites*, *Favia* and *Leptoria*. The reef edge habitat is typically 20 to 40 m wide and exposed to wave action. It is dominated by corals such as *Millepora dichotoma*, *Pocillopora danae*, *P. meandrina*, *Acropora digitifera* and *Goniastrea pectinata*, and by calcareous algae. The algal ridge is 10 to 20 m wide, and parts of this area dry during low water spring tides. Coral colonies are scarce and small, but may be diverse.

Shoreward of the algal ridge, there are a series of cobble ridges and sand-filled troughs which run parallel to the reef front. Algal species such as *Sargassum* and *Turbinaria* may be abundant and some coral colonies develop in the troughs (41,49). The algal flora of Seychelles remains poorly known and approximately 350 species of chlorophyta, phaeophyta, and rhodophyta have been recorded to date (15,29).

Seagrass beds are often found between the cobble ridges and the shore. In south Praslin such seagrass beds are very extensive and occupy several km^2. Eight seagrass species are found in Seychelles: *Cymodocea serrulata*, *Cymodocea rotundata*, *Halodule uninervis*, *Halophila decipiens*, *Halophila ovalis*, *Halophila stipulacea*, *Syringodium isoetifolium*, *Thalassia hemprichii* and *Thalassodendron ciliatum* (29).

The zonation of corals around the atolls is very different from that on the fringing reefs of the granitic islands. Gorgonians, *Porites* spp. and *Dendrophyllia* spp. dominate at depths below 38 m. From 28 to 38 m encrusting corals, especially *Agariciella* spp. and *Plesiastrea* spp. are dominant. At 14 to 28 m, the coral community is dominated by faviids, *Echinophyllia* spp., *Herpolitha* spp., *Pachyseris* spp., *Symphyllia* spp., *Podabacia* spp. and *Porites lichen*. In areas shallower than 6 m, there is a highly diverse region of soft corals and faviids. The reef edge is dominated by *Acropora glochiclados* and *Stylophora mordax*, with *Acropora*, *Astreopora*, *Porites* and *Millepora* species just below (6,42). The differences between reefs on the atolls and granitic islands are largely due to the shallow Seychelles Plateau which surrounds the granitic islands and supports the development of a wide fringing reef (49).

Prior to the Netherlands Oceanic Reefs Expedition in 1992 and 1993, 51 genera of corals, 45 of which were hermatypic, had been recorded from the granitic Seychelles and 47, of which 44 were hermatypic, from Aldabra (42,49). Collections during the Netherlands Oceanic Reefs Expedition produced 40 new records of stony reef corals (scleractinia, hydrocorals and octocorals) and a total species list of 161 species (excluding *Acropora* spp.). Reef surveys during the same expedition suggested that the area specific species richness of corals was higher in the Amirantes than around the granitic islands (23,24).

Invertebrate Fauna. The coral reefs of Seychelles provide habitats for many invertebrate species but they are mostly poorly collected and studied. Studies of invertebrates have largely focused on taxonomy and basic distribution and a minimal amount of small scale ecological work has been conducted. Some 129 species of marine caridean shrimps are known from the region, but 200 are expected to occur. The first major invertebrate collections were made at the turn of the century on the 'Alert' and 'Sealark' expeditions (Table 13.1), but the majority of work followed the 'Anton Bruun' cruise during the International Indian Ocean Expedition of 1964 (13). This collection included 64 species of palaemonid shrimps, and another 29 were collected during the

Netherlands Oceanic Reefs Expedition in 1992 and 1993 (17). Of the 89 species recorded in both collections, 17 are endemic to the western Indian Ocean. Forty nine species of Brachyuran decapod crustaceans (coral crabs) were described on the basis of those removed from corals collected during the Netherlands Oceanic Reefs Expedition (21).

Approximately 150 species of echinoderms have been described from the islands, including 33 species of sea-urchin, 32 starfishes, 35 holothurians, 44 ophiuroids and 9 crinoids. The sea urchin community is dominated by *Diadema savignyi* and the coral eating starfish *Acanthaster planci* is becoming increasingly common. It is not known whether this increase is due to natural or human (direct or indirect) effects. Over 70% of the echinoderms which have been recorded have widespread Indo-Pacific distributions, and six are possible endemics to the East African region (14).

The molluscan fauna of Aldabra was studied in the late 1960s (50) and that of reefs around Mahé, Desroches and Cosmoledo was surveyed between 1987 and 1989 in order to identify resources which could be exploited by the artisanal shell trade. At depths of 0 to 20 m, 450 species of mollusc in 79 families were recorded. Three species of Trochidae and two species of Turbinidae were favored for exploitation, but 63 potentially valuable species were identified (19). Collections of sponges and sea anemones were also been made during the Soviet- American and Netherlands Oceanic Reefs Expeditions, and species lists for sites in the granitic islands and Amirantes are available (22,43,52).

Fishes and Turtles. Almost one thousand species of fish have now been recorded from the Seychelles plateau. The majority of reef associated species have widespread Indo-Pacific distribution. Two hundred and eleven species were recorded from the islands before 1900 (Playfair 1867) and around 300 species had been recorded when J.L.B and M.M. Smith visited the islands in 1954. Their collections were by far the most extensive at that time and when their book *The Fishes of Seychelles* was published in 1968 (45), they included approximately 800 species from the northern islands and listed others which were likely to occur. This list included pelagic and deep water fishes in addition to those collected from the reefs.

Between 1970 and 1997 several other fish collections were made (38-40). These collections added over 100 species to those which had already been recorded. Their collections also indicated that a number of species recorded by Smith and Smith were initial or terminal phases of wrasses and parrotfish which were already known by other names. The reef-associated fauna probably currently consists of around 400 species, and most of these species have a widespread Indo-Pacific distribution. There are few, if any, endemics. The distribution and abundance of fishes around the granitic islands is determined by the habitat type and fishing effort (25,26). The true fringing reefs, patch reefs, and corals growing directly on a granitic substrate all have distinctive fish faunas and coral-associated species such as corallivorous chaetodontids. These are most abundant on fringing reefs.

Four species of sea turtle have been recorded in Seychelles which include the leatherback turtle *Dermochelys coriacea*, the loggerhead *Caretta caretta*, the hawksbill *Eretmochelys imbricata* and the green *Chelonia mydas*. The hawksbill and green are the most abundant and widely distributed species in Seychelles. Hawksbill turtles feed on sponges and soft corals and sleep in crevices in the reefs. Hawksbills nest on at least 20 islands in the Seychelles. A large nesting population is observed in the Cousin Island reserve, where 30 to 40 nest annually, predominantly from October to January. Green turtles feed on algae and seagrasses. They nest throughout the archipelago and throughout the year, although they are most abundant in the Aldabra group (18).

Human Impacts

A History of Exploitation

The biological resources of Seychelles, in common with many isolated oceanic islands, have been intensively exploited. Even before the arrival of the first colonists, seafarers frequently took turtles, tortoises and fishes from the islands to provision their vessels during long sea voyages. By the late eighteenth century, trade in marine animals and their products was the mainstay of the economy, and few islands remained unexploited. By 1832, a whaling station had opened on Ste. Anne Island and fisheries for bony fishes, sea-cucumbers (trepang or bêche de mer), green snail *Turbo marmoratus*, and black-lip pearl oyster *Pinctada margaritifera* were thriving. The nacreous (mother-of-pearl) shells of the green snail and the black-lip pearl oyster were highly prized for lacquer ware, jewelry and button manufacture. The whaling station closed in 1915 and the focus of sea-cucumber, snail and oyster fisheries largely moved on to South Pacific reefs. Fishing, however, remains the most significant human exploitative activity on the reefs of Seychelles and a variety of gastropods are still collected for button manufacture and the tourist trade (27).

Historically, turtles were the most intensively exploited marine species in Seychelles. Some 28 000 green turtles were taken from Aldabra between 1906 and the outbreak of World War I. Green turtle meat was eaten fresh and meat and flippers were salted and preserved. In early years, little of the turtle was wasted, turtle oil and turtle bone meal were produced and the carapace was used as a container. Subsequently, calipee, a gelatinous cartilage used in soup, formed the basis of a flourishing export market and the availability of increasing quantities of turtle by-products caused prices to collapse and much meat to be discarded. So many turtle bones had accumulated on Aldabra in the 1930's that a small windmill was constructed in order to crush them for fertilizer. Hawksbill turtle were killed for their carapace, and the epidermal scutes were used to produce 'tortoise' shell. Prior to 1967, up to 4 tons of tortoiseshell was exported from the Seychelles annually. In later years, annual catches of hawksbill were around 500. The general turtle industry prospered until the late 1960's, but the production and sale of turtle-shell ornaments continued until the early 1990's.

Fisheries and their Impacts

Since the bans on the capture and sale of turtles were implemented, fishing has had the most significant impact on reefs and their biota. The reefs around the granitic islands of Mahé, Praslin and La Digue are fished by the artisanal fishery. Fishers operate on foot or by boat. Fishers on foot usually target octopus and catch 0.5% of the total estimated yield in the artisanal fishery. Four types of boat are used by artisanal fishers: pirogues, small open boats which are powered by oars or outboard engines of up to 15 HP (4 to 6 m in length); outboards, which have larger outboard engines and are usually a fiberglass design, the 'Mini-Mahé', which was introduced in 1971 (5 to 6 m); whalers, undecked wooden boats powered by inboard diesel engines (6.5 to 8 m); and schooners, which are large fully decked fishing boats with inboard engines (10 to 25 m) (3,4).

Pirogues, outboard and whaler-based fishers usually set fish traps over reefs and on seagrass beds or fish with lines and setnets. All spear fishing is banned in Seychelles. These smaller boats operate almost exclusively around the granitic islands. Pirogues account for 35% of the total catch by weight, but they often target low-value species such as rabbitfishes (Siganidae). Whalers and schooners account for 50% of the total catch, fishing both inshore reefs and the more accessible offshore banks. In 1992, the Seychelles fishery was composed of 87 pirogues, 198 outboards, 95 whalers, and 60 schooners (4).

Schooners are the largest vessels used in the artisanal fishery and fishing usually relies on hand-lines and electric fishing reels. The schoonerfleet accounts for approximately 15% (1987 to 1989) of the artisanal catch but the fish that they target tend to be the most valuable of those landed locally. Catch rates are typically 35 to 50 kg/person/d and the catch consisted of 52% Lutjanidae, 18% Serranidae and 13% Lethrinidae in 1987 to 1989 when a detailed study of the fishery was completed by the Seychelles Fishing Authority (37). The schooners can travel considerable distances and are the only boats in the artisanal fleet which routinely fish on the Mahé and Amirantes plateaus. Fishing effort and catches are higher in the calmer inter-monsoonal periods. The number of schooners fishing in recent years has declined as their fishing activities have not been profitable. Many fishers have loans to repay on their schooners over five-year periods and few skippers and crew receive an income commensurate with the hardships of a life at sea.

In the late 1980s, 475 to 640 Seychellois were considered to be full-time fishers and another 500 fished on a casual or seasonal basis. The full-time fishers in the artisanal fishery averaged 2.5% of the working population. Fishers tended to be relatively old and highly experienced. Average ages of skippers and crew are 43.7 and 39.2 years, and average experience was 21.3 and 16.1 years respectively. In the late 1980s there were less people entering the fishery than in previous years, it is considered very difficult to make an adequate living in many larger boats. The average number of people reliant on a fisher's income was 5 for skippers and 4.3 for crew. The fisher was the sole contributor to income in 50% of households (36).

In 1992, total fishing effort was dominated by handlining and trapping with 70 600 person days of handlining and 178 900 trap sets estimated in that year. Handlines accounted for 78.3% of the 5718 tons landed by the artisanal fishery. The inshore fishery is considered to be optimally exploited and there are clear changes in fish communities in intensively fished areas. These changes involve marked decreases in the abundance of larger species and those from higher trophic levels (26). As a result, the offshore banks and the Mahé and Amirantes plateau are increasingly targeted in order to maintain yields. Over 50% of the artisanal catch is landed in Victoria on Mahé. Many of the more valuable species are exported fresh to other countries; predominantly Réunion, Mauritius, Germany, and England. Fresh fish and frozen fish exports were 200 and 839 tons respectively in 1992.

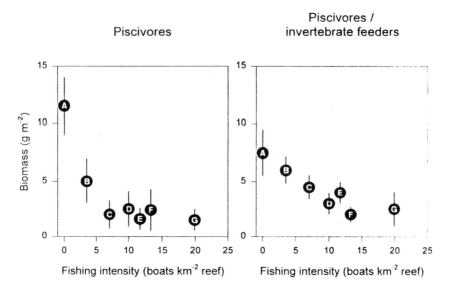

Figure 13.6. Relationship between fishing intensity and the biomass (mean ± 95% CL) of piscivorous fishes and piscivorous/ invertebrate feeding fishes on Seychelles reefs. A. Cousin Island, B. Ste. Anne Marine National Park, C. north-east Praslin, D. east Mahé, E. west Mahé, F. south-west Praslin, G. north-west Mahé. Data from reference (26).

The significance of the artisanal fishery is currently being eclipsed by a burgeoning tuna industry. Following the establishment of the Exclusive Economic Zone (EEZ) the Seychelles licensed tuna vessels to fish in its EEZ and Victoria, the capital on Mahé, is now the largest tuna trans-shipping port in Indian Ocean and the site of a successful tuna cannery.

The assessments of the Seychelles Fishing Authority suggest that inshore fish stocks are now optimally or over-exploited, and they are trying to develop offshore fisheries on the Mahé plateau. The effects of fishing on the structure of fish communities on the fringing reefs and associated habitats within 2500 m of the coasts of the granitic islands have been investigated using fishery independent underwater visual census techniques (26). These reefs are predominantly fished by pirogues and outboards using traps (casiers), although declines in the abundance of target species have encouraged many fishers to set traps further offshore in recent years. The intensity of fishing around the islands of Mahé and Praslin varies considerably, from the very intensively fished areas off northwest Mahé to the unfished Marine Reserve at Cousin.

A census of 134 reef-associated fish species on three types of reef habitat (fringing reef with a carbonate framework, coral growth on granitic substrate in exposed locations and small patch reefs on a predominantly sandy substrate) in each of seven areas subject to different levels of fishing intensity demonstrated that there was a clear relationship between the biomass of target fishes in the reef at higher trophic levels recorded by underwater visual censuses and fishing intensity (Fig. 13.6). Similarly, the diversity (measured as species richness) of fishes in the snapper (Lutjanidae) and emperor (Lethrinidae) families, which are among the most valuable targets of the reef fishery, was significantly lower in more intensively fished areas. For the species which showed the strongest responses to fishing, differences in the responses on the three different types of reef habitat were rare and inconsistent. Despite significant decreases in the biomass of piscivorous fishes at higher fishing intensities, the biomass of small (< 20 cm) corallivores, detritivores, omnivores and invertebrate feeders which were not targeted by the fishery did not increase. This suggested that predator-prey relationships between the target species were not tightly coupled and that the implementation of a fishing strategy which deliberately removes piscivores in order to increase the biomass of their prey would not be successful (26).

Fish yields from heavily fished reefs around Seychelles appear to be sustainable, but it is important to recognize that the yields from these reefs may only be maintained because larvae can recruit from adjacent and less heavily fished areas. The effects of fishing on the closely spaced reefs on the Seychelles Bank must be treated as collective, and the existence of marine reserves and less intensively fished areas may ensure that young fishes continue to recruit to the fishery. There has been no study of the relationships between fish communities on these reefs and it is important to adopt a precautionary approach to management until more is known.

Reclamation, Sedimentation, and Pollution

Population growth, increasing urbanization, demands for land, deforestation and a growing tourist industry have, directly or indirectly, been responsible for many adverse human influences on Seychelles reefs. The most extensive direct losses of reefs have resulted from development and reclamation in the vicinity of Victoria in northeast Mahé. There has been incremental reclamation of the reef and mangrove areas around the port of Victoria and 5 to 6 km^2 of fringing reef to the south of Victoria was reclaimed in order to build the international airport. The steep and rugged granitic environment of Mahé means that coastal reclamation will continue to be viewed as a potentially important source of flat ground for development. Direct, but localized, damage to coral has been caused in a number of areas when visiting boats have anchored on reefs at Ste. Anne, Curieuse, and Baie Ternay Marine National Parks. Ile Coco was closed to visitors in 1987 following such damage (34).

The proposed development of Aldabra posed one of the greatest threats to the reefs of Seychelles. Jacques Cousteau visited the reefs of Aldabra in 1954, and the popular media coverage which followed brought much publicity and affirmed their biological importance. However, with the cold-war at its height following the Cuban missile crisis and Aldabra then forming part of the British Indian Ocean Territory, the British and US governments signed a 1965 treaty to state that the islands of the territory would be available for defense purposes. The British Labour Government was clearly unappreciative of the ecological importance of Aldabra. The minister responsible had responded to a question in the House of Commons by stating that "the island of Aldabra is inhabited- like Her Majesty's Opposition Front Bench- by giant turtles (*sic*), frigate birds and boobies; nevertheless, it may well provide useful facilities for aircraft".

The Royal Society, Smithsonian Institution, National Academy of Sciences, and other bodies vigorously opposed development. The protests of these bodies culminated with the Royal Society expedition to Aldabra. This commenced in 1967 with the aim of obtaining all possible information on the islands before any development started. Devaluation of the British pound rendered the military scheme too expensive and subsequent changes in international relations and

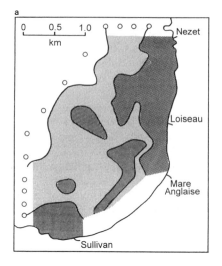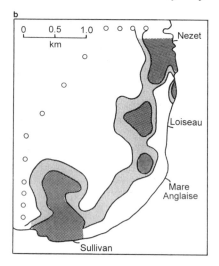

Figure 13.7. Spatial distribution of dissolved inorganic nutrients in Beau Vallon Bay during October 1989. The four rivers which flow into the Bay are marked. a. Nitrogen: dark shading >0.5 mM, light shading 0.2 to 0.5 mM and unshaded < 0.2 mM. b. Phosphorus: dark shading > 0.25 mM, light shading 0.23 to 0.25 mM and unshaded <0.23 mM. The seaward extent of the survey grid is denoted with circles.

defense strategy meant that development never occurred, but partly as a result of the threat, the reefs of Aldabra are among the most thoroughly studied in Seychelles Islands (7,46,47).

The input of terrigenous sediment has profound effects on the growth and development of corals (12). Sedimentation results primarily from the clearance of land for building, but also from poor agricultural practice and deforestation. Much of Mahé is susceptible to erosion even though regulations stipulate that cultivated land should be terraced (44). Sedimentation has also resulted from sand extraction, the clearing of river mouths, and the construction of sea walls, groins, breakwaters and piers. Sedimentation has had adverse impacts on the corals of the Ste. Anne Marine National Park

Polluting inputs of nutrients have been recorded at a number of developed coastal sites. At Beau Vallon Bay in northwest Mahé, the turn-over of water is very poor, leading to decreases in salinity when runoff is high, and the retention of nutrients and polluting substances. The release of polluted water from houses, hotels, and farms may be acutely toxic to hard coral species and lead to a community dominated by soft corals.

Nutrient rich effluents from pig farms have also been identified as a threat to reefs in Baie Ste. Anne. There are concerns that coral recruitment and the re-colonization of corals and seagrass following storms would be affected by land-derived pollution (Kelly, G. personal communication).

A key study of the effects of nutrient enriched discharges on the inshore reef environment was conducted in Beau Vallon Bay on Mahé in 1989. The study examined the links between nutrient enrichment and the degradation of corals and provided insights into the potential impacts of these processes at other sites. Beau Vallon is one of the most intensively used tourist sites on Mahé, and in 1990 there were 458 tourist rooms available in hotels adjacent to the bay and some 3700 people living in the Beau Vallon district. Many of the local people

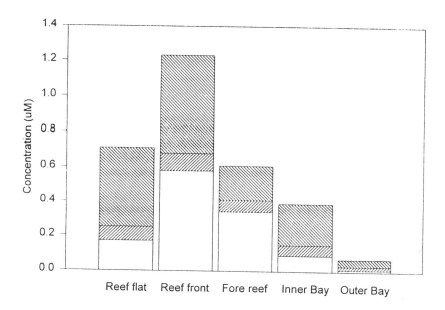

Figure 13.8. Concentration of dissolved inorganic nitrogen in different regions of Beau Vallon Bay during October 1989. Upper bar, ammonium; middle bar, nitrites; lower bar, nitrates.

are involved in farming and much of their waste water flows into the bay via the Sullivan River (Fig. 13.6). Concentrations of dissolved inorganic nitrogen (Fig. 13.7a) and dissolved inorganic phosphorus (Fig. 13.7b) are highest in inshore reef flats adjacent to the river mouths. Nutrient levels in these areas and on the reef front were above potential eutrophication thresholds (Fig. 13.8) (8) and, in conjunction with heavy sedimentation, may account for the absence of coral on parts of this reef. Nutrient levels around the reef in Beau Vallon Bay were comparable with those which have been recorded around Cerf Island (east of Mahé); an area which is affected by nutrient inputs from Victoria Harbor (33).

Tourism

The biological resources which first attracted colonists to Seychelles now attract tourists. Coral reefs and their fauna are one of the principal attractions. The number of tourists arriving in Seychelles has risen since the international airport opened (Fig. 13.4) and approximately 25% of all visitors pay to enter the Marine National Park (MNP) at Ste. Anne, Mahé, and a further 10% visit the MNP at Curieuse. Although Seychelles is currently diversifying the economy into offshore services, trans-shipment and export processing, tourism is likely to remain the most important source of foreign revenue. Seventeen percent of the workforce is engaged in tourist related activities and tourism is so consequential that a discussion of Seychelles macro-economic development continues to be substantially a discussion of the tourist sector (1,2). Seychelles' reliance on tourism means that the economy is vulnerable to the vagaries of the tourist market. Although activities such as cruise, conference, and thematic "eco-tourism" are now being promoted, the majority of tourists arrive in search of a safe, sunny, sandy seaside refuge from cold European winters. As such, pollution of the coastal and marine environment could have dramatic effects on the future of the tourist industry and the Seychelles economy.

Brochures proclaim that the Seychelles are 'unique by a thousand miles'. For the tourist seeking the opportunity to see Seychelles' fauna and flora in their natural surroundings, the slogan advertises the islands' main advantage. However, such isolation also increases trading costs, and with a current trade deficit exceeding $150 million, the economy is increasingly reliant on tourism. At present, Seychelles is an ideal location for the ecotourist, but visitors may threaten the viability of the species which they come to observe, and the ecotourism industry must be developed sustainably if it is to provide long-term benefits in an increasingly competitive global market. It is possible to balance the desires of tourists and conservationists: BirdLife International, for example, have demonstrated that the income from carefully managed tourist visits to Cousin Island Special Reserve (Box 13.1) can fund many of their conservation activities.

More than one quarter of all tourists arriving in Seychelles visit the Ste. Anne MNPeach year. Here, the difficulties of balancing tourist access with reef conservation are increasingly apparent. Increased development in the park has meant that the management of waste water, solid waste, discharges from boats and the direct physical impacts of snorkellers and divers on the reefs has become an increasing concern. Fortunately, in this relatively successful park, there was sufficient Government and International support to establish a visitor center where the aims of management and conservation can be disseminated to a wider audience. Moreover, a number of international organizations are providing assistance with zoning the park for different activities, providing mooring buoys and monitoring the effects of tourist visits.

Conservation and Management

A History of Conservation

While there has been a long standing tradition of exploitation in Seychelles there has also been a long standing tradition of conservation (Table 13.1). In 1788, only eighteen years after the first permanent settlement was established, governor Jean Baptiste Philogene de Malavois enacted strict conservation laws. de Malavois was alarmed by the rate of deforestation and by his own calculations which suggested that two thirds of the giant tortoise population had already been shipped from the islands. He banned the felling of trees for firewood and the slaughter of hawksbill turtles and tortoises. His laws were ineffective, but provoked an interest in conservation which has persisted. Throughout the late nineteenth and early twentieth centuries, government officials and visiting scientists continued to press for effective conservation laws. A number of extinctions such as those of giant tortoises, dugongs, crocodiles, and the green parakeet on Mahé had been widely publicized and there were increasing concerns for the remaining fauna. In 1874 the first terrestrial nature reserves were established on the recommendation of botanist John Horne and today, 43% of the land area has protected status.

While the desire for conservation was epitomized by dramatic events in the terrestrial environment, the protection of marine and reef biota has been central to Seychelles' conservation policy. In the course of this century, the emphasis of conservationists has moved from species to habitat-based concerns. The basis for contemporary management of reefs is a network of Marine National Parks, although there are specific and more detailed regulations for fisheries and the control of activities which lead to marine pollution. Turtles received the first attention from conservationists in the 1920s and legal controls on green turtle hunting on Aldabra were instituted in 1955, followed by the declaration that the capture of green turtles was illegal in 1968. In 1969, the National Parks and Nature Conservancy Ordinance was passed and this act led to the creation of the Seychelles' National Parks and Nature Conservancy Commission (NPNCC). It was at this time that the emphasis of conservation strategy shifted from species to area protection, and in the period 1973 to 1991, the NPNCC and their successors, Conservation and National Parks (CNP) worked with a number of international organizations to oversee the development of the Marine National Parks, two special reserves which provide protection for reefs and a UNESCO World Heritage Site at Aldabra Atoll.

Protected Area Management

Six sites in the Inner Seychelles Group have been designated as Marine National Parks and two as Special Reserves which included protection for marine habitat (Table 13.2, Fig. 13.9, (34)). Two protected areas operate with the blessing of the current government but are run and administered from outside Seychelles. Thus Cousin Island is owned and managed by BirdLife International (Box 13.1) and Aride Island was purchased by Christopher Cadbury and is managed by the Royal Society for Nature Conservation (RSNC). The reefs around both these islands, which are primarily managed as bird reserves, are protected from fishing and the beaches provide protected nesting sites for turtles. Aldabra was leased by the Royal Society until 1980 when it was handed over to the Seychelles Islands Foundation (SIF), a corporate body governed by an international board of trustees. In 1981, Aldabra also received 'special reserve' status from the Seychelles government, prior to being designated a World Heritage Site by UNESCO in 1982.

The regulations which govern activities in MNP's differ in detail, but all state that reef habitats must not be damaged and that fishes must not be captured. There are a number of practical constraints which prevent the effective implementation of the regulations (1,5). The lack of wardens and patrol boats, disregard for park regulations and a lack of visitor facilities have been identified (1). Only Curieuse and Sainte Anne have sufficient staff to ensure that park regulations are largely enforced and the independently managed Cousin Island Special Reserve is also effectively patrolled (Box 13.1).

Seychelles is largely reliant on fish exports and tourism for foreign revenue and it is important that conflicts between conservation and exploitation can be resolved if sustainable development and the protection of natural resources are to be assured (27). Marine National Parks are viewed as a central component of the strategy to resolve these conflicts and to ensure the successful co-existence of activities which rely upon a shared resource base. The extent to which MNP's in the Inner Seychelles provide protection for reef fish

Table 13.2. Marine protected areas of the Seychelles.

Marine Protected Area	Year	Area (Sea) km²	Management Responsibility	Management Action
Cousin	1968	1.2 [1]	BirdLife International	Managed & Policed[2]
Aride	1973	to 200m	Royal Society for Nature Conservation[3]	Managed & Policed
Ste Anne	1973	10	Marine Parks Authority	Managed & Policed
Curieuse	1979	10.8	Marine Parks Authority	Managed & Policed
Baie Ternay	1979	0.8	Marine Parks Authority	Basic Management[4]
Port Launay	1979	1.6	Marine Parks Authority	Basic Management
Silhouette	1979	to 1 km	Marine Parks Authority	No Management
Shell reserves in E. Mahe, N. La Digue and N Praslin	1981	to 400	None	No Management
Aldabra	1981	350	Seychelles Islands Foundation[5]	Basic Management
Ile Cocos, Ilot Platte & Ile la Fouche	1997	0.7	Marine Parks Authority	Basic Management
African Banks	1987	0.3	Ministry of Defence[6]	No Management

Notes:

1. The reef is protected to 500 m from the low water mark.
2. A reserve which is managed and policed, is delineated by boundary markers and has regular anti -
poaching patrols. See text for details of activities in specific MPAs
3. Aride Island was also recognised as a Special Reserve in 1979 government legislation
4. Basic management implies that the boundary of the reserve is marked and the function of the
reserve is advertised.
5. Aldabra was recognised as a Special Reserve in 1981 government legislation and as a UNESCO
World Heritage Site in 1982
6. African Banks is used as a naval firing range

communities was investigated in 1994. Fish communities were censused at coralline and granitic sites in Cousin Island Special Reserve, Sainte Anne MNP, Baie Ternay MNP and Curieuse MNP, four of the seven MPA's in the Inner Seychelles. All these parks have been designated for at least 15 years (Table 13.2), but the park regulations are difficult to enforce and they receive different degrees of protection.

Cousin Island was purchased as a bird and turtle reserve by the International Council for Bird Preservation (ICBP), but near total protection is provided for the fringing reef up to 500 m from the island. Poachers have been virtually eliminated from Cousin in recent years and the island is thought to be one of the most important turtle breeding sites in the Inner Seychelles. Sainte Anne MNP is one of the most popular tourist sites in Seychelles and 21 645 tourists, more than 25% of all those arriving in Seychelles, paid to snorkel, dive or view the reef from glass-bottom boats in 1993 (5). The reserve is actively patrolled, but its close proximity to Victoria means that poaching remains a problem and over 100 illegally placed casiers (fish traps) are removed from the park annually. There are also fishing concessions for the residents of Ste. Anne MNP and approximately 10 casiers and some hand-lines are used annually. In 1994, when the reef fish communities in Seychelles MNP's were studied (28), Baie Ternay MNP was regarded as a 'paper park': a protected area in name only. Little attempt was made to enforce park legislation and the reefs were fished until the Marine Parks Authority began to manage this MNP in 1996. Curieuse

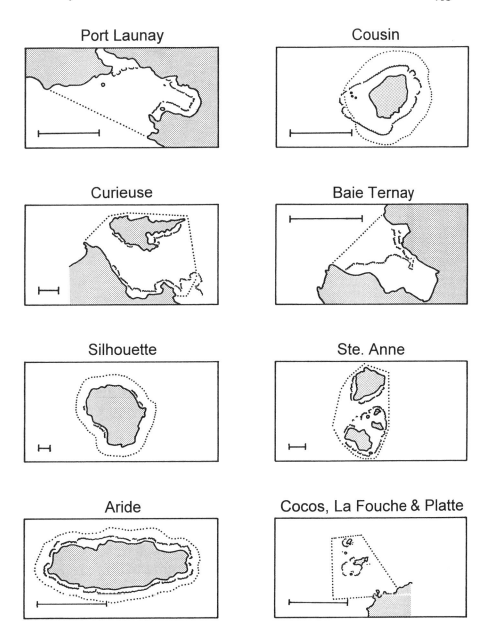

Figure 13.9. The marine reserves of the Inner Seychelles. Broken lines indicate reserve boundaries, land is shaded and fringing reefs are shown. The scale bar is 1 km and the general location of the reserves is shown in Fig. 13.2 and 13.5. The Cocos, La Fouche and Platte reserve is to the north of Félicité (north-east of La Digue Fig. 13.2 and 13.5).

MNP was visited by 8964 tourists in 1993 but it was not managed or patrolled on a full-time basis.

Comparison of the fish communities in the four MPA's indicated that the species richness and biomass of the total fish community, and species richness

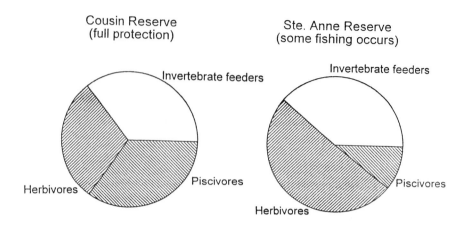

Figure 13.10. Biomass composition of the non-cryptic diurnally active reef-associated fish community on coralline sites at the Cousin Island Reserve and Ste. Anne Marine National Park. Data from (28).

and biomass of many families were higher on both coralline and granitic reefs in Cousin Island Special Reserve and Ste. Anne MNP than in Baie Ternay MNP and Curieuse MNP. The biomass of three families of fishes targeted by the fishery (Lethrinidae, Lutjanidae, Serranidae) was, however, significantly lower in Ste. Anne MNP than in Cousin Island Special Reserve. This was attributed to illegal fishing and the fishing concessions offered to local people in Ste. Anne MNP. The study concluded that poaching and minor fishing concessions did not affect the biomass and overall species richness of reef fishes: those attributes of the fish community which were likely to be most important to tourist visitors. A very small level of fishing effort did, however, lead to dramatic changes in the trophic structure of the fish community (Fig. 13.10). It is notable that many of these very small MPA's (Table 13.2) must be stocked by larval fishes which are the progeny of adults living many kilometers away. As such, the protected area cannot operate in isolation to maintain biomass and diversity and requires that other reefs in the region are subject to low fishing intensities and harbor stocks of adult reef fishes.

Making Management Work. Approximately 15% of reefs in Seychelles now have 'protected' status but there are continuing concerns about the sustainability of tourism, development and exploitation (27,44). The greatest concern is that protection in statute rarely provides protection in practice: even the small MNP's in the Inner Seychelles are affected by poaching and other anthropogenic activities.

A survey of the shell and coral trade was completed by CNP in 1995 (35). Although Seychelles was a signatory to the Convention for International Trade in Endangered Species (CITES) it was recognized that some CITES species continue to be collected from reefs and sold in local markets, predominantly to tourists who are often not aware that they are purchasing CITES species. The blue coral *Heliopora coerulea*, red organ pipe coral *Tubipora musica* and many *Acropora* species have been seen on sale (35). It is notable that

Table 13.3. Organisations concerned with research, management or conservation on Seychelles reefs.

Organisation	Role
Government Organisations	
Division of Environment	Environmental education, pollution control, environmental assessment, conservation
Conservation and National Parks, CNP (1991-1996)	Management of Marine National Parks (MNP) Reef monitoring
Marine Parks Authority (1996 on)	Management of MNP Reef monitoring, park patrols, removal of illegal fishing gear, demarcation buoy maintenance, park access and ticketing
Ministry of Foreign Affairs, Planning and Environment (MFAPE)	Coordination of overseas consultancies and training of Seychellois in reef monitoring and management Creation and maintenance of Ste. Anne MNP underwater nature trail
Ministry of Education (MoE)	Education of Seychellois in marine conservation Management of National Audio Visual Centre (educational conservation programmes)
Ministry of Industry (Seychelles Bureau of Standards, SBS)	Monitoring of air and water quality Provision of export permits for marine life
Seychelles Fishing Authority (SFA)	Control and Development of Fisheries Fish stock assessment, resource management and aquaculture
Ministry of Tourism & Transport	Control of ship discharges in harbours and EEZ Cleaning of beaches
Ministry of Defence	Placement (not management) of demarcation and mooring buoys Jetty construct and hydrographic survey
Ministry of Community Development	Assesses planning applications including those for reclamation
Seychelles Based NGO's and related	
Enviro Consultants	Representation and NGO project co-ordination
Nature Protection Trust (NPT)	Conservation, lobbying and mapping of species distributions
Seychelles Underwater Centre and Ministry of Tourism (SUBIOS)	Promote marine conservation through underwater photography competitions, talks, exhibitions
International NGO's and related	
International Union for the Conservation of Nature (IUCN)	Preparation of management plans for MNP's Co-ordinate Biodiversity and Conservation Areas Programme (1995)
Seychelles Islands Foundation	Management of Aldabra and Vallee de Mai (from 1982)
Royal Geographical Society (RGS), UK	'Shoals of Capricorn' Expedition planned for 1998
BirdLife International	Management of Cousin Island Special Reserve Facilitate and support visiting researchers
Royal Society for Nature Conservation (RSNC), UK	Management of Aride reserve Facilitate and support visiting researchers
International Government Organisations	
Swedish International Development Agency (SIDA)	Training of Seychellois in diving and reef monitoring (1994)
Australian Aid (AusAid)	Review of CNP activities, establishment of reef monitoring in MNP (1996)
Overseas Development Administration (ODA), UK (now DIFD)	Fishery assessment and management
United Nations Development Programme (UNDP)	Remote sensing and mapping of reefs around Mahé, Praslin, La Digue and Aldabra
International Coral Reef Initiative (USAID and French funded)	Develop East African regional reef monitoring programme

Table 13.3 *Continued*

United Nations Environment Programme (UNEP), (Regional Seas Programme Action Plan)	Pollution monitoring Digitising maps and development of Geographical Information System
Commission l'Ocean Indien (COI) (funded European Development Fund, EDF)	Bibliography and diagnostic notes on reefs and MNP's
Advisory Committee on Protection of the Seas (ACOPS)	Promote MNP management and assist with meeting the objectives of International Conventions which relate to the marine environment

Universities and Research Institutes

University of York, UK (with Darwin Initiative Funding, UK)	Effects of pollution on protected areas Reef management plans for Beau Vallon to Baie Ternay (1995-96)
Test Reef Project, Universities of Glasgow, UK and Marseilles, France (EU funded)	Effects of climate change on coral growth (1995 on)
University of Quebec, Canada (PRIMTAFF) (UNDP funded)	Training in use of Geographic Information Systems

attempts to stop the sale of turtle products (all turtles are CITES species) were only effective in the early 1990s, when the World Bank and Seychelles Government funded a program to curb the tourist based demand for turtle shell products and provide artisans with alternative occupations and compensation.

Prior to the creation of the Marine Parks Authority in September 1996 the Government had redirected MNP income away from the then Conservation and National Parks Service (CNP), and within many protected areas, the existing infrastructure was not providing an adequate basis for protection or for the development of full ecotourism potential. The 1990, for example, the total budget of CNP was less than the revenue from entry tickets sold for Ste. Anne MNP. The Marine Parks Authority is starting to act more autonomously and revenue from the MNP's will be used for park management and the promotion of ecotourism.

In order to prevent further degradation of Seychelles reefs there is a recognized need to strengthen the legal basis of marine conservation and to develop national institutional capacity for conservation. Many organizations have interests in the reefs of Seychelles (Table 13.3), but some of their activities may not be effectively coordinated and they may have conflicting responsibilities. One of the greatest problems with MNP management has been that many parks which were identified in statute were not adequately marked. CNP initiated a program in which they placed demarcation buoys to mark park boundaries and provided mooring buoys to prevent further damage to reefs as a result of anchoring. The role of a number of international agencies in helping provide guidance and resources for MNP management has been recognized. Problems common to many MNP's were highlighted during a recent IUCN assessment of Ste. Anne MNP. They recognized a need for longer term monitoring to determine how effectively protection, particularly of corals, is working. Moreover, there are problems enforcing regulations and prosecuting those responsible for the infringements since some poachers continue to threaten park rangers with violence. The IUCN assessment recognized that there was a need to increase the frequency of surveillance until it acted as an adequate deterrent and to educate persistent law breakers through negotiation and conflict resolution. Fines have not been changed for over 20 years and are considered unrealistically low. Since tourist visitors often cause damage to reefs there was also a need to train tourist guides and boat handlers in visitor education and to provide visitors with a code of conduct.

Conclusions and Prospects

While the early history of Seychelles was characterized by unsustainable exploitation and environmental degradation there are signs that public attitudes to the marine environment are beginning to change and that historic precedents can be nullified. The Seychelles government has expressed a desire to move away from the simple concept of 'nature conservation' to develop a broad-based strategy encompassing both environmental protection and the sustainable management of marine ecosystems (1). One of the main reasons for this change is the recognition that the effective management of reef ecosystems can bring long-term socio-economic rewards to the islands. Following recent social and economic reforms, an increasing proportion of Seychellois are in a position to accept management of coral reefs, and, given the importance of tourism, often benefit directly from such management.

The extensive reefs and EEZ in Seychelles, coupled with a relatively small population, allow the Seychellois to address conservation issues which may be insurmountable in countries where exploitation of the marine environment is driven by extreme poverty and rapid population growth. However, it is widely recognized that the diminutive economy and small population of Seychelles also result in a lack of resources and experts to cope with the protection and management of the marine environment and the country remains reliant on international assistance to redress shortages of resources and skilled staff.

References

1. Anon. 1990. *Environmental Management Plan of the Seychelles 1990-2000.* Mahé: Government of Seychelles
2. Anon. 1990. *National Development Plan of the Seychelles.* Mahé: Government of Seychelles
3. Anon. 1992. *Seychelles Artisanal Fisheries Statistics for 1991.* Mahé: Seychelles Fishing Authority
4. Anon. 1993. *Seychelles Artisanal Fisheries Statistics for 1992.* Mahé: Seychelles Fishing Authority
5. Anon. 1994. *Annual Report 1993: Conservation and National Parks.* Mahé: Government of Seychelles
6. Barnes, J., Bellamy, D.J., Jones, D.J., Whitton, B.A., Drew, E.A., Kenyon, L., Lythgoe, J.N., Rosen, B.R. 1971. Morphology and ecology of the reef front at Aldabra. *Symposia of the Zoological Society of London* 28: 87-114
7. Beamish, T. 1970. *Aldabra Alone.* London: Allen and Unwin
8. Bell, P.R.F. 1992. Eutrophication and coral reefs- some examples in the Great Barrier Reef lagoon. *Water Research* 26: 553-568

9.   Braithwaite, C.J.R. 1971. Seychelles reefs: structure and development. *Symposia of the Zoological Society of London* 28: 39-63

10. Braithwaite, C.J.R. 1984. Geology of the Seychelles. In *Biogeography and Ecology of the Seychelles Islands*. ed. Stoddart D.R. pp. 17-38. The Hague: Dr W Junk

11. Braithwaite, C.J.R., Taylor, J.D., Kennedy, W.J. 1973. The evolution of an atoll: the depositional and erosional history of Aldabra. *Philosophical Transactions of the Royal Society* B226: 307-340

12. Brown, B.E. 1997. Disturbances to reefs in recent times. In *Life and Death of Coral Reefs*. ed. Birkeland, C. pp. 354-377. New York: Chapman and Hall

13. Bruce, A.J. 1984. Marine caridean shrimps of the Seychelles. In *Biogeography and Ecology of the Seychelles Islands*. ed. Stoddart D.R. pp. 141-169. The Hague: Dr W Junk

14. Clark, A.M. 1984. Echinodermata of the Seychelles. In *Biogeography and Ecology of the Seychelles Islands*. ed. Stoddart D.R. pp. 83-102. The Hague: Dr W Junk

15. Coppejans, E.G.G., Kooistra, W.H.C.F., Audiffred, P.A.J. 1994. Preliminary report on the research on macroalgae. In *Oceanic Reefs of the Seychelles*. ed. Land, J. pp.157-178. Leiden: Netherlands Indian Ocean Programme

16. Dustan, P. 1992. Estimates of Indian Ocean productivity using natural fluorescence. *Atoll Research Bulletin* 378: 1-13

17. Fransen, C.H.J.M. 1994. Marine palaemonoid shrimps of the Netherlands Seychelles Expedition 1992-1993. *Zoologische Verhandelingen* 297: 85-152

18. Frazier, J. 1984. Marine turtles in the Seychelles and adjacent regions. In *Biogeography and Ecology of the Seychelles Islands*. ed. Stoddart D.R. pp. 417-468. The Hague: Dr W Junk

19. Gabrie C., Richard G. 1989. *Etude des Matieres Premieres d'Origine Marine Utilisables pour le Developpement de L'Artisanat*. Mahé: Agence de Cooperation Culturelle et Technique

20. Gardiner, J.S., Cooper, C.F. 1907. Description of the expedition. II. Mauritius to Seychelles. *Transactions of the Linnaean Society* 12: 111-175

21. Garth, J.S. 1984. Brachyuran decapod crustaceans of coral reef communities of the Seychelles and Amirante Islands. In *Biogeography and Ecology of the Seychelles Islands*. ed. Stoddart, D.R. pp. 103-122. The Hague: Dr W Junk

22. Hartog, J.C. 1994. Sea anemones of the Seychelles. In *Oceanic Reefs of the Seychelles*. ed. Land, J. pp. 75-80. Leiden: Netherlands Indian Ocean Programme

23. Hoeksema, B.W. 1994. Species diversity of stony corals and mushroom coral sizes. In *Oceanic Reefs of the Seychelles*. ed. Land J. pp. 133-138. Leiden: Netherlands Indian Ocean Programme

24. Hoeksema, B.W., Borel-Best, M. 1994. Stony Reef Corals. In *Oceanic Reefs of the Seychelles*. ed. Land J. pp. 81-92. Leiden: Netherlands Indian Ocean Programme

25. Jennings, S., Boullé, D.B., Polunin, N.V.C. 1996. Habitat correlates of the distribution and biomass of Seychelles' reef fishes. *Environmental Biology of Fishes* 46: 15-25

26. Jennings, S., Grandcourt, E.M., Polunin, N.V.C. 1995. The effects of fishing on the diversity, biomass and trophic structure of Seychelles' reef fish communities. *Coral Reefs* 14: 225-235

27. Jennings, S., Marshall, S.S. 1995. Seeking sustainability in the Seychelles. *Biologist* 42: 197-202

28. Jennings, S., Marshall, S.S., Polunin, N.V.C. 1996. Seychelles' marine protected areas: comparative structure and status of reef fish communities. *Biological Conservation* 75: 201-209

29. Kalugina-Gutnik, A.A., Perestenko, L.P., Titlyanova, T.V. 1992. Species composition, distribution and abundance of algae and seagrasses of the Seychelles Islands. *Atoll Research Bulletin* 369

30. Land, J. 1994. The 'Oceanic Reefs' expedition to the Seychelles (1992-1993). *Zoologische Verhanddelingen* 297: 5-36

31. Lewis, M.S. 1968. The morphology of the fringing coral reefs along the east coast of Mahé. *Journal of Geology* 76: 140-153

32. Lewis, M.S. 1969. Sedimentary environments and unconsolidated carbonate sediments of the fringing coral reefs of Mahé, Seychelles. *Marine Geology* 7: 95-127

33. Littler, M.M., Littler, D.S., Titlyanov, E.A. 1991. Comparisons of N- and P-limited productivity between high granitic islands versus low carbonate atolls in the Seychelles Archipelago: a test of the relative-dominance paradigm. *Coral Reefs* 10: 199-209

34. Marshall, S.S. 1994. Proposed management strategy for Seychelles Marine National Parks. Mahé: Division of Environment, Government of Seychelles

35. Marshall, S.S. 1995. *Coral and Shell Trade Survey*. Mahé: Conservation and National Parks

36. Mees, C.C. 1990. *The Fishermen of Seychelles: Results of a Socioeconomic Study of the Seychelles Fishing Community*. Mahé: Seychelles Fishing Authority

37. Mees, C.C. 1990. *Seychelles Schooner Fishery: An Analysis of Data Collected During the Period January 1985 to July 1990*. Mahé: Seychelles Fishing Authority

38. Polunin, N.V.C. 1984. Marine fishes of the Seychelles. In *Biogeography and Ecology of the Seychelles Islands*. ed. Stoddart D.R. pp. 171-191. The Hague: Dr W Junk

39. Polunin, N.V.C., Lubbock, R. 1977. Prawn associated gobies (Teleostei: Gobiidae) from the Seychelles, Western Indian Ocean. *Journal of Zoology* 183: 63-101

40. Randall, J.E., van Egmond, J. 1994. Marine fishes from the Seychelles: 108 new records. *Zoologische Verhandelingen* 297: 43-83

41. Rosen, B.R. 1971. Principal features of reef coral ecology in shallow water environments of Mahe, Seychelles. *Symposia of the Zoological Society of London* 28: 163-183

42. Rosen, B.R. 1979. Check list of recent coral records for Aldabra (Indian Ocean). *Atoll Research Bulletin* 233: 1-24

43. Selin, N.I., Latypov, Y.Y., Malyutin, A.N., Bolshakova, L.N. 1992. Species composition and abundance of corals and other invertebrates on the reefs of the Seychelles Islands. *Atoll Research Bulletin* 368

44. Shah, N.J. 1995. Managing coastal areas in the Seychelles. *Nature and Resources* 31: 16-33

45. Smith, J.L.B., Smith, M.M. 1968. *The Fishes of Seychelles.* Grahamstown: Rhodes University

46. Stoddart, D.R. 1971. Scientific studies at Aldabra and neighbouring islands. *Philosophical Transactions of the Royal Society* B260: 5-29

47. Stoddart, D.R. 1971. Settlement, development and conservation of Aldabra. *Philosophical Transactions of the Royal Society* B260: 611-662

48. Stoddart, D.R. 1984. *Biogeography and Ecology of the Seychelles Islands.* The Hague: Dr W Junk

49. Stoddart, D.R. 1984. Coral reefs of Seychelles and adjacent regions. In *Biogeography and Ecology of the Seychelles Islands.* ed. Stoddart, D.R. pp. 63-81. The Hague: Dr W Junk

50. Taylor, J.D. 1968. Coral reef and associated invertebrate communities (mainly molluscan) around Mahé, Seychelles. *Philosophical Transactions of the Royal Society* B254: 129-206

51. Titlyanov, E.A., Littler, L.M., Littler, D.S. 1992. Introduction to the Soviet-American expedition to the Seychelles Islands. *Atoll Research Bulletin* 365

52. van Soest, R.W.M. 1994. Sponges of the Seychelles. In *Oceanic Reefs of the Seychelles.* ed. Land, J. pp. 65-74. Leiden: Netherlands Indian Ocean Programme

53. Walsh, R.P.D. 1984. Climate of the Seychelles. In *Biogeography and Ecology of the Seychelles Islands.* ed. Stoddart, D.R. pp. 41-62. The Hague: Dr W Junk

Chapter 14

The Coral Reefs of Madagascar

C. Gabrié, P. Vasseur, H. Randriamiarana, J. Maharavo & E. Mara

Madagascar is one of the largest islands in the world with a coastline of about 6000 km. In 1993 the human population was 12 million or 20.6 individuals per km². This is relatively few, but the distribution of the population is heterogeneous with the eastern coastal zones being densely populated while the western coast is less inhabited, with the exception of cities such as Toliara and Mahajanga. The mean annual increase in population is about 3% per year and migrations to and along the coast intensify pressures on coastal resources.

A great asymmetry exists between the island's two coasts. On the east coast, the continental shelf is very narrow (the 100 m depth contour lies 5 to 8 km from shore) and coral reefs and mangroves are poorly developed. The west coast, with a broader continental shelf (between 50 and 100 km) and high tidal range, has the majority of the country's reef formations and mangroves. The west coast also has the main part of the fisheries and coastal tourist activities of the country.

Malagasy coastal ecosystems are rich and diverse and include coral reefs, seagrass beds, mangroves and other habitats, such as those along the Pangalanes Canal which extends on the east coast (Fig. 14.1). Coral reefs cover an area of 2000 km², or more than 20% of the 1400 km malagasy coastline. On the west coast, they extend from the mouth of the Linta River in the south, to the Antsiranana region in the north. On the east coast they are mainly restricted to the north and mid-east portions of coastline. Seagrass beds are also most extensive along the west coast. More than 425 000 ha of tidal marshes (mangrove forests and 'tannes' or salt marshes or salt swamps) are also present, of which 320 000 ha are mangroves. Over 99% of Malagasy mangroves are situated on the west coast (19), representing one of the most important area of mangroves in the western Indian Ocean.

Past and Present Scientific Research

The knowledge of the coral reefs of Madagascar is very fragmentary and, at the national level, most coral reefs are still poorly known. Extensive work

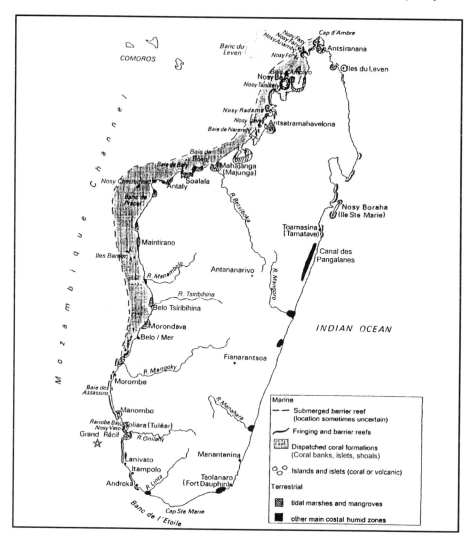

Figure 14.1. Coral reefs and other coastal ecosystems of Madagascar (50, modified from 9,30,13,15).

has,however, been done on the reefs of the south-west coast (Toliara region) and these are the best-known reefs of Madagascar. The reefs of the northwest coast, from Cap d'Ambre to Cap St. André, but mainly reefs around the island of Nosy-Be, have also been studied. More recently some short-term investigations on the Masoala peninsula reefs on the east coast have been completed. Apart from these three regions, the other reefs remain unknown and much of the Malagasy coast has never been scientifically explored. Pollution and destruction of the reefs are very poorly documented but often described as a problem by reef investigators.

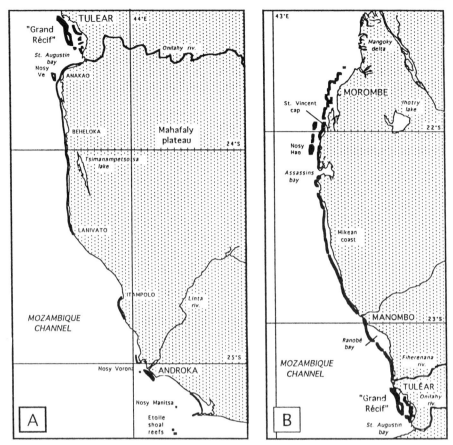

Figure 14.2. South-west reefs: A: from Androka to the Onilahy River; B: from the Onilahy River to the Mangoky delta (based on 30),

There are two main research centers that study coral reefs. In 1954, the French Office for Overseas Scientific and Technical Research created the first marine research center of Nosy-Be, that became, in 1977, the National Center for Oceanographic Research (CNRO). It comprises three departments: 1) Biological Oceanography, 2) Fisheries, and 3) Physical and Chemical Oceanography staffed by about 10 researchers. It also houses an oceanographic museum and an important bibliographic center, which is part of the western Indian Ocean scientific information network RECOSCIX-WIO. CNRO concentrates its investigations around Nosy-Be and, today, these are focused on traditional fisheries.

The reefs adjacent to the Marine Station were also studied intensively from 1961 to 1972 producing about 400 scientific reports largely on the taxonomy of the flora and fauna, of which more than 6000 species were identified. In addition, there are a number of publications on the hydrology, geomorphology, sedimentology, plankton and benthic ecology, and ichthyology of these reefs (54). Hence, these works represent the basic knowledge of the 'Grand Récif' and of the Toliara Bay. For years, this knowledge, has been used worldwide for the study of reef formations.

The station was closed after 10 years and is now the Institute of Saltwater Resources and Marine Sciences (IHSM), of the University of Toliara, for research, training and development, and is staffed by about 40 researchers. Since 1984 at least 100 reports of restricted distribution have been published, on traditional and artisanal fisheries, fish aggregation devices (FADs), mangrove fishery, sea cucumbers, aquaculture (algae, *Artemia*), and on the value of marine resources. The institute also has an oceanographic museum.

Coral Reef Distribution

The South-West Coast

Coral formation extend from Androka, in the south, to an area just south of Morondava. The reefs can be classified into three categories (Table 14.1, Figs. 14.2, 14.3, see 30), namely 1) fringing reefs, 2) barrier reefs, and 3) reefs with sand cays (see the Toliara section for a description of the reefs). Seagrass beds are also well developed in this region. From the north, between the Mangoky delta to Belo-sur-Mer, at about 10 to 15 km from the coast, and extending from 50 km, is a succession of coral shoals, coral banks, and reefs with sand cays (Fig. 14.1). A submerged barrier reef begins about 10 to 15 km from the coast. This ancient barrier reef, now submerged and represented by coral banks, extends offshore to around 600 km, up the north of the island.

The Mid-West Coast

Between Morondava and Mahajanga, the coral formations are poorly known, and there may be no real formations along the coast. Isolated coral formations are found on the continental shelf and these can be divided into two large groups, 1) the Barren Islands in the south and 2) Pracel Shoal in the north. The Barren Islands extend over 50 km,with most of the islands and shoals or cays emerging at low tide. The Pracel Shoal is also a series of scattered shallows where only Nosy Vao and Chesterfield Islands are permanently above water (30). The submerged barrier reef is present offshore, with shoals and sand cays in the south. In the region of Mahajanga, the coral reefs are not well developed near the coast, because of the large amount of terrigenous sediments discharged from the rivers. Numerous banks extend offshore such as Grenouille, Thetys and Turquoise Banks.

The North-West Coast

This region extends from the Baie de Narendy to Anstiranana. The ancient submerged barrier reef still extends to the open sea, at 10 to 60 km from the shore, interrupted in front of the great river deltas. It consists of a series of great elongated coral banks such as Banc de l'Entrée, Banc des Cinq-Mètres, Banc

Table 14.1. Reefs on the southwest coast from Androka to Belo-sur-Mer (30).

Location	Reef description
Androka	Two fringing reefs, 11 and 7 km long
Itampolo	Fringing reef, 10 km long
From Lanivato to Onilahy River	Long fringing reef, 100 km long by 500 m to 3.5 km width
Nosy Ve, Nosy Vorona, Nosy Manitsa..	Sand cay reefs
From the Onilahy River to the Manombo River	Barrier Reefs with the main coral habitats, including lagoon reefs and coral banks
From the Manombo River to the Baie des Assassins	Fringing reefs 2 to 3.5 km wide extending for almost 80 km
From the Baie des Assassins to the Mangoky Delta	Fragmented reefs from barrier reefs, sand cays reefs and coral banks to fringing reefs

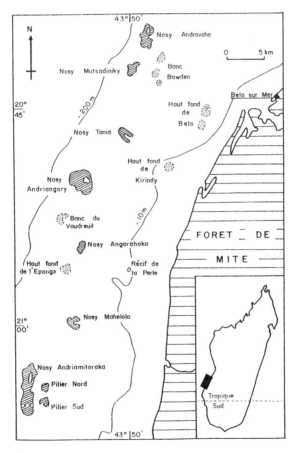

Figure 14.3. Location of Belo-sur-Mer coral reefs (based on 46).

des Gorgones, Banc Eloïse, Banc du Serpent, Banc du Castor, and others. Situated at 5 to 15 m depth on the southern part, it emerges above the sea to the north to form the numerous coral islands near Cap d'Ambre (such as Nosy Faly and Nosy Anambo). On the outer slope of this barrier reef off shore, coral cover often reaches 100% largely attributable to plate coral *Pachyseris speciosa* (21).

Fringing reefs lie along the coast, except near estuaries and bays where terrigenous sedimentation is high, and around all the numerous non-coral islands and archipelagos (the Radama and the Mitsio archipelagoes). Reefs built along this coast display the zonation typical of fringing reefs having an *Acropora*-dominated fore reef and a *Porites*-dominated back reef and with extensive seagrass beds in the lagoons. Spurs in the south-west reefs are covered by calcareous red algae (*Melobesiae*), but corals are dominant in the northwest reefs. Fringing reefs on the wave-exposed northwest side, around the large non-coral islands such as in Nosy-Be, have typical fringing reef structures with spur and groove structures and associated species on the fore reef, and typical lagoonal structures and species on the sheltered side (30). The fringing reefs are not well developed in the very northwest coast because of the large input of terrestrial sediments in this region. In the non-muddy bays, coral patches and pinnacle formations are present (30).

Most of the coral reefs of the northwest region are in good ecological condition and mostly undisturbed by humans because the islands are difficult to access. Reefs around Nosy-Be Island are less pristine, attributable to human activities such as the discharge of sugar industry waste in Dzamandjar, urbanization in Mahatsinjo, and unregulated tourism in Nosy Tanikely (21).

The East Coast

The coral reefs are not well known, except for recent work on the Masoala reefs (23). In the northeast section, around Antsiranana (Diego-Suarez) the coast is fringed by an ancient aerial reef. The ancient reef formations are bordered at the edge of the sea by a discontinuous fringe of living coral. The fringing reefs present along the Masoala peninsula show a high dominance of *Acropora* and an abundance of secondary colonizing species, which is an indication of low to moderate human influence on the corals (23). Fringing reefs are also present around Mananara and Ste-Marie Island, near Toamasina (Tamatave - Bain des Dames) and Foulpointe. Further south, along the sand bar forming the shore for several hundred kilometers, the reef formations disappear completely. Few islets of coral life, very isolated, are present. A submerged fragmented barrier reef is described at Toamasina (30).

Coral Reef Diversity

The total species diversity of the Malagasy marine fauna and flora is still poorly known (Box 14.1). The older taxonomic publications, mainly based on the Toliara reefs (between 1961 and 1973), describe more than 6000 species. Although no synthetic work on the total marine biological diversity has been completed a rich diversity would seem reasonable. An inventory of species diversity of the northwest coast is still in preparation (Laboute, unpublished data). An inventory of the Malagasy marine biodiversity, based on bibliographical search was recently conducted, but it is incomplete with only 2000 species found (49). There is a need to synthesize the available

Table 14.2. Known marine species richness in Madagascar. Key: * skiophilous = shade loving, photophilous = light loving.

	Max. # species recorded	Region	Community	Sources
Flora				
Algae	108	Toliara	photophilous* sessile	31
Phanerogamia	12	Madagascar		30
Fauna : Invertebrates				
Cnidaria				
Hydroids	65	Toliara	skiophilous* sessile	53
Hydrocorals	8	Toliara	skiophilous sessile	53
Octocorals				
Gorgonians	40	Nosy-Be		Laboute (in preparation)
Alcyonarians	71	Toliara	photophilous sessile	31
Scleractinians	130	Toliara	photophilous sessile	31
	200	Madagascar	estimate (Pichon, unpublished)	
Bryozoans	99	Toliara	skiophilous sessile	53
Ascidians	182	Toliara	skiophilous sessile	53
Sponges	280	Toliara	skiophilous sessile	51
Worms	121	Toliara	mobile cryptofauna	26
Echinoderms				
Crinoids	3	Toliara	photophilous sessile	31
Holothurians	28	Toliara		
Ophiurids	19	Toliara	photophilous sessile	31
Echinoids	14	Toliara	photophilous sessile	31
Asteroids	15	Toliara	photophilous sessile	31
Mollusks	1158	Toliara	coral/sand bottom	48
Crustaceans	779	Toliara	coral/sand bottom	48
Fauna : Vertebrates				
Fishes	552	Toliara	Great Reef	11
	700	Toliara		22
	1500	Madagascar	estimate (Harmelin-Vivien, personal communication)	
Turtles	5	Madagascar		
Mammals				
Cetacea	32			
Sirenia	1			
Total	4761	Madagascar	estimated > 6000 sp.	56

information on species diversity, even though this information will only give partial view of the richness as many parts of the coast have not yet been studied. A more complete study of the diversity is underway by the Global Environmental Fund/UNDP (see below). The works on Toliara reveal the following estimates of species richness (Table 14.2):

- about 200 species in 53 genera of corals (Pichon, M. personal communication)
- about 1500 species of fishes (Harmelin-Vivien, M. personal communication)
- at least 280 species of sponges (53)
- at least 227 species of echinoderms (48)
- at least 1158 species of mollusks (48) and
- at least 779 species of crustaceans (48).

It is very difficult to compare the biodiversity of the different parts of Madagascar (Toliara, Nosy-Be and Masoala) because of great differences in the

Box 14.1. First Official Capture of a Coelacanth in Madagascar

Photo. Coelecanth caught by artisanal fishermen.at Grande Comore (photo: Stevens).

On August 5, 1995 a coelacanth *Latimeria chalumnae* (Smith 1939) was caught south of Toliara (SW coast of Madagascar, 1). The first capture of this fish, a real 'living fossil', was made near the canyon of the Saint-Augustin Bay. The species is the only survivor of the crosspterygians, a zoological group that appeared 400 million years ago. This group is probably at the origin of the first terrestrial tetrapod. The Toliara specimen measured 133 cm total length and weighed 32 kg. It was caught by young fishers off the coast at a depth of 140 to 150 m on the precipitous slope of the fringing reef situated between the fishing villages of Soalara and Anakao. The coelacanth was transferred to the museum of Toliara where it was fixed in 10% formalin. Unfortunately the specimen was unsuitable for mitochondrial DNA analysis and, therefore, could not reveal if it was a refugee off the Comoros or a member of a Malagasy coelacanth population (3). A second coelacanth of 130 kg has just been caught, at the beginning of 1998, in Toliara (Plante, R. personal communication).

At the Comoros, especially at Grande Comore, the coelacanth has been caught for many years. Because the coelacanth lives deeper than 100 m, little is known on its biology. Only since 1986, owing to diving with a small submersible, was the coelacanth observed in its natural habitat by H. Fricke and

R. Plante (1,2). Coelacanths are active during the night at depths of 200 to 300 m and aggregate during the day to take shelter in caves at depths between 150 and 200 m. Still caught incidentally by the fishers on the narrow shelf of the Grande Comore (about 10 specimens per year), the coelacanth population that was initially estimated at 300 to 600 individuals may now be less than 200 individuals, according to a report made by R. Plante in December 1995. Today, it is threatened by extinction. Consequently, a plan to protect it is proposed in form of a 'coelacanth park', to be situated in a portion of the coast where fishing with bottom lines will be prohibited (3) and replaced by fishing on Fish Aggregation Devices (FADs) that will be established at intermediate water depths.

H.D. Rabesandratana & P. Vasseur

References

1. Heemstra P.C., Freeman A.L.J., Yan Wong H., Hensley D.A., Rabesandratana H.D. 1996. First authentic capture of the coelacanth, *Latimeria chalumnae* (Pisces: Latimeridae), off Madagascar. *South Africa Journal of Sciences* 92:160-151
2. Plante R. 1992. Coelacanthes: les géants bleus des Comores. *Océanorama* 19: 26-28
3. Plante R. 1997. Un fossile vivant en sursis? *Océanorama* 27: 16-18

sampling effort of studies. The extensive work done in Toliara (more than 10 years of studies) in all the habitats will evidently give a higher diversity in all groups, than in Nosy-Be and Masoala where the surveys were more rapid (about 10 days of survey at Masoala).

Seagrass beds in the region are generally composed of mixture of species (mainly *Thalassia hemprichii, Syringodium isoetifolium, Cymodocea serrulata, C. rotundata, Halodule uninervis* and *Thalassodendron ciliatum*. Turtles are represented by five species: *Eretmochelys imbricata, Chelonia mydas and Caretta caretta, Dermochelys coriacea, Lepidochelys olivacea,* of which four species are known to nest in Madagascar. Marine mammals are well represented by 32 species, as Saint-Augustin Bay, Nosy-Be and Antongil Bay are in the path of marine mammal migration routes (49). For example, humpback whales (*Megaptera novaeangliae*) migrate every year, during the austral winter, from the sub-Antarctic regions to the breeding and birth sites located mainly around Antongil Bay and Ste-Marie Island (58). *Dugong dugon* is also present in Madagascar, mainly on the south-west coast. They are very rare now, although no comprehensive study has been done on their populations.

Socio-economic Importance of Reefs and Related Ecosystems

The coastal zone supports the three main sources of foreign exchange, fisheries, aquaculture and tourism. In 1994 fisheries and aquaculture supplied 24

264 tons of export products which represented US $80 million of which 8000 tons were shrimp (US $58 million). In the same year, 65 000 tourists visited Madagascar providing an income of US $37.2 million.

Fisheries and aquaculture provide protein for a large part of the population as well as foreign currency. Production and export (about 20% of the total production) have been rapidly increasing during the past 10 years; between 1986 and 1989 production nearly doubled. In 1994, the production of marine products was estimated at 117 500 tons of which 55% was captured by the small-scale artisanal and traditional fishery.

The traditional coastal fishery involves approximately 50 000 people using 22 000 pirogues (without engines) and living in 1250 villages. Fishing is mainly focused on reef formations, and reef-associated species account for 43% of the total production (6,38, and Tables 14.3, 14.4). The two main ethnic fishing groups are the *Sakalava* people in the northwest and the Vezo subgroup in the southwest, while in the Menabe region, in the midwest coast near Morondava, both groups are present. The traditional customs and *fady* (taboo) of fishing are more or less still observed. They are, however, being abandoned because of human migration leading to an increase in the number of fishers entering the fishery with no prior fishing tradition. For example, in Ambaro Bay migrants are the majority in most villages (36).

The Fishery and Aquaculture Master Plan predicts an increase in total production to around 190 000 tons in 2001, so that the fish consumption per person will be 8.5 kg/y (world level = 13.6 kg/y). The Plan also projects a 100% increase since 1990 in foreign income from the export of fish (7). The main strategy is the diversification of marine products, particularly the promotion of shrimp aquaculture, and an increase in the export of crabs, lobsters, seaweeds, and sea-cucumbers (trepang). Since 1986, the Malagasy government has developed a large shrimp aquaculture program. Studies have estimated the potential mangrove sites to be 55 000 ha and the potential production to be about 50 000 tons/y, more than 10 times the present production from the sea. Two projects are currently in place and many more are being requested. The effect of this development has still not been well studied. Fish caught as bycatch (30 000 tons/y) in shrimp nets, that could supply the local finfish market, are poorly exploited and frequently discarded into the sea (14).

Tourism has turned toward the sea, with five main development regions: Nosy-Be, Ste-Marie, Toliara (Toliara), Tolanaro (Fort-Dauphin) and Antsiranana (Diego-Suarez). Of the 65 000 foreign tourists that came to Madagascar in 1994 at least 50% are estimated to have visited the coast. Ecotourism and marine ecotourism have a high potential in Madagascar considering the many near-pristine coral reefs and other possibilities such as whale, shark and turtle watching.

The Threats

At a national scale the marine environment of Madagascar can be regarded as relatively well preserved, as large parts of the coast are uninhabited, particularly in the west. But in the more densely populated places, problems of pollution, degradation and over exploitation of marine resources are commonly observed. These problems are the consequence of high human populations in

Table 14.3. Data on Madagascar fisheries, reported in 1992 (6).

Region	Number of fishing villages	Number of fishers	Number of boats
Antsiranana	370	7 244	4104
Fianarantsoa	71	3 460	1278
Mahajanga	346	11 593	4784
Toamasina	200	4 990	2932
Toliara	263	15 269	8357
Total	1250	42 556	21 455

Table 14.4. Traditional fishing production (6,38).

Resources	Production (tons) in 1994
Shrimps	3000
Crabs	1300
Lobsters	390
Fishes	50 200
Mollusks	187
Algae	702
Others	9311
Total	65 090

some parts of the coast, a very heterogeneous distribution of this population, a lack of proper urban coastal planning, inappropriate traditional methods of agriculture, and a centralized system of production that does not favor responsibility by local communities in managing their resources. The main problems and their locations are known despite the lack of quantitative field studies (Fig. 14.4).

Coastal Erosion and Sand Accretion

One of the most serious threats to Malagasy coral reefs is the large amount of sediment arising from poor land-use practices. For example, deforestation by burning leaves the land devoid of woody vegetation. After burning, the land is susceptible to large-scale soil erosion which presently affects nearly 80% of the total area of the island (25). The threats of soil erosion are greatest in the northwest coast, up to Belo-Tsiribihina, and along most of the east coast. Siltation from rivers is rapid and occurs mainly in the coral reefs and mangroves of the west coast. In contrast, some parts of the coast, including some villages, mainly in the south-west, are silted up by sand because of the movement of sand dunes. In addition, harbors have been filled with silt, as in Mahajanga, which is particularly troublesome for the country's economy (see special section on Toliara). The problems of coastal erosion are very acute in some regions where infrastructure has been destroyed and fallen into the sea, as in the town of Morondava (37). The effects of natural phenomena are increased as the sedimentation often modifies the hydrodynamics of river deltas, leading to unexpected changes in river flow.

Pollution

The main pollution problems are present in the largest towns such as Toamasina, Mahajanga, Toliara, and Antsiranana. Effluent from urban

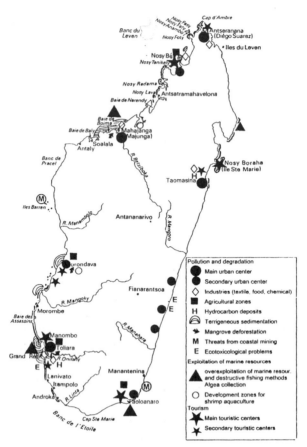

Figure 14.4. Sources of pollution, degradation and overexploitation of Malagasy coral reefs (many data incomplete).

waste treatment is frequently discharged directly into the sea while chemical pollution from chemical, textile, and the food and sugar industries is locally a problem. Studies near the sugar industry of Nosy-Be have found seawater with high acidity (pHs between 3 and 4) that have lead to coral mortality (21). Additionally, pollurion control systems such as waste-water treatment facilities are often bypassed because of rapid development of some towns. Madagascar still does not have regulations or legal standards for the disposal and treatment of urban and industrial pollutants, nor are there any standards for water quality. Agricultural pollution probably comes from large plantations (such as cotton, sisal, and sugar cane), but no water-chemistry data are available. Local nutrification of coastal waters and beaches also occurs due to the discharge of the shrimp fishery by catch.

Risks of pollution resulting from shipping are high, as Madagascar is on the path of the big oil tankers and of ships carrying toxic chemicals. Accidents or deliberate beachings have already happened, mainly in the south and in the ports. Accidents occur because harbor and coastal maps are old and inexact and because the coastal morphology has changed since the map's production, often because of high sedimentation in harbors such as in Mahajanga. As an example, one boat transporting 30 000 tons of manganese recently ran aground at Fort-Dauphin.

Mining industries are not highly developed adjacent to the sea but a project is underway, in the south near Tolanaro (Fort-Dauphin) to extract heavy mineral sands containing titanium dioxide. Additionally, a project is proposed for the mining of phosphates in the Barren Islands (14) and kaolin at Androka.

Overfishing and Destructive Fishing

In 17 years, the number of Malagasy fishers and boats has increased by a factor of five (6). It is difficult, however, to determine the influence of this growth because of the paucity of data on fish stocks. The Ministry of Fisheries estimates that most of the resources are under or optimally exploited with the exception of sea-cucumbers which they consider to be over exploited (6,7 and see Box 14.2.). Overexploitation problems are mainly local such as near urban centers (Toliara, Mahajanga) where uncontrolled exploitation of marine resources has led to diminishing stocks, decreases in the size and weight of catches, and the deterioration of fish habitats. In contrast to the Fishery Service view, nearly all traditional fishers report decreasing catches. For example, surveys in the northwest (Ambaro Bay), mid-west, Menabe region (36), and Masoala reefs on the east coast have shown that almost all resources, fishes, turtles, sharks, sea-cucumbers, octopus, lobsters, crabs, mammals (*Dugong*), oysters and mollusks were estimated, by the fishers, to have decreased over a 10-year period (24). The results also indicated a strong decrease in catch per unit of fishing effort and in average body sizes. A survey of marine snails in Masoala found that the most common snail was the coral-eating snail (*Drupella cornus*) whose high abundance may reflect overfishing of predatory fishes (23).

Destructive fishing practices include industrial trawling within the two mile prohibited zone adjacent to the coast, fishing while walking on the reefs, the use of small-meshed gillnets, the use, in the south, of poisons extracted from *Euphorbia* plants, the destruction of coral habitats with crowbars. The use of harpoons and spear guns seems to locally decrease the number of some species of groupers and parrotfishes.

The threats to marine diversity are poorly studied. It is known, however, that dugongs and some turtles are threatened mainly by hunting and the prawn fisheries which catch them in their nets. In the case of turtles the adults are sold for their meat and shell, and the eggs are eaten. Artisanal exploitation of corals and shells exists, but there is no data on the state of the stocks. The only marine species to be registered on the CITES list for Madagascar are : *Dugong dugon,* all the turtle species, whales (Annex I) and the coelacanth *Latimeria chalumnae* (Annex II). No corals or mollusks are registered.

Tourism

Tourism and associated uncontrolled development is said to be an increasingly important factor in marine degradation, but no studies have been completed. The proliferation of tourist hotels and coastal land speculation, largely for tourist development, is leading to the privatization of coastal land, excluding beaches. This often limits space available for fisher populations such as in Nosy-Be. Construction on or near beaches threatens the equilibrium of the beaches, which increases or reinforces the risks of beach erosion. Additionally, few hotels are equipped with waste-treatment facilities and they therefore discharge their wastes into septic tanks or directly into the sea. Potential problems with tourist activities include fishing, collecting ornaments, anchoring on the reefs, poor diving practices, or conflicts between fishers and tourist activities.

Management

Integrated Management

The Institutional Framework. There is, at the moment, no specific national institution or institutional mechanism with the sole responsibility of integrating the management of coastal areas. Responsibilities are presently shared among different government departments. This is mainly the Ministry of Aquaculture and Fishery Resources, whose primary mandate is to manage and develop marine and coastal living resources, and which has, from very recently, the responsibility to oversee marine diversity. The Ministry of Waters and Forests has the ultimate responsibility for managing all forests, including mangroves, and of all protected areas, even marine areas. The other ministries involved less directly include the Ministries of Environment, Tourism, Agriculture, Management of Land and Urban Planning, Energy and Mining, and Transport.

Two other government services important for the marine environment include the National Office for Environment (ONE), which has the responsibility of coordinating and managing the National Environmental Action Plan (NEAP, see below), and the National Association for the Management of Protected Areas (ANGAP). Most of the government services are located in the capital, Antananarivo, but there are plans to distribute these services among other regions.

The National Environmental Action Plan. The National Environmental Policy, described in the Charte de l'Environnement, is being implemented through the National Environmental Action Plan and its specific five-year application programs (Environment Program PEI, PEII and PEIII). PEI, undertaken between 1991 and 1996, has developed the institutional framework with the creation of ONE and ANGAP. Their primary focus has been on concrete actions to preserve terrestrial biodiversity, to protect forests, and to limit soil erosion. Direct actions to protect the marine environment were largely absent during this first phase.

The need to integrate the marine environment into NEAP has rapidly arisen because of the economic and ecological importance of marine resources, the rapid degradation of some parts of the coast and the reefs, and the absence of data and knowledge on the status of these ecosystems. Consequently, for the PEII (1996 to 2001) a marine and coastal component (EMC) was developed (8). This National Integrated Coastal Zone Management Program is funded by GEF (Global Environmental Fund), UNDP, and the World Bank. In order to avoid overlap among the marine and coastal projects in the country, understandings have been reached between the national and other programs (such as the Indian Ocean Commission and WWF) to insure that all the parties will coordinate their activities.

The general goal of EMC are to ensure the sustainable development of coastal and marine areas. Specifically, this includes ensuring the sustainability of the exploitation of marine resources (fishes, mollusks, echinoderms, and crustaceans) and coastal resources (mainly wood), to ameliorate the livelihood of coastal communities and their ability to participate in the economic development of the country, to prevent coastal pollution, erosion, and degradation, and to maintain marine and coastal biological diversity and ecological function of coastal ecosystems. This five-year action plan will acquire better knowledge of the ecosystems and their threats and will conduct actions at three administrative levels, national, regional, and local.

At the national level, the program will provide a national framework for the protection and the sustainable use of coastal and marine resources and activities. It will favor integration over sectoral policies to ensure the harmonization of the different coastal economic sectors. The actions will be to 1) develop a policy and a strategic plan for integrated coastal zone management, and 2) to develop coastal legislation to support the coastal zone master plan. This plan will establish zones, mainly spatial, for the development of activities (tourism, ports, mining, and others), the exploitation of resources, and for protecting the most ecologically important marine and coastal sites. This zoning plan will be accompanied by thematic action plans for 1) the establishment of a national network of protected areas, 2) for the prevention of coastal pollution, terrigenous sedimentation, and coastal erosion, and 3) for the sustainable development of marine and coastal resources. An institutional framework for integrated coastal zone management will also be organized.

At the regional level, the administrative regions will be given the legal authority to implement the regional zoning plan. At the local level, depending on the local problems, the objectives are to implement concrete actions that will include local zoning plans, specific actions against pollution or erosion, creation of protected areas in the most sensitive zones, and concrete management actions relying on local communities. Recent legislation permits transfer of the responsibility for managing the common renewable natural resources to local communities. After an initial rapid study of the ecological value, gravity of the problems, and willingness of the participants it was decided that these actions will first be focused in the Toliara and the Nosy-Be regions, and in the Menabe region, for the Indian Ocean Commission Program.

For the realization of this program, a coastal coordination team, located in ONE facilities, has been set up to coordinate the program. An interministerial commission will provide the intersectoral integration at a political level. A pilot committee will provide administrative and scientific expertise to orient the program. Finally, a transectoral working group, subdivided as necessary, into thematic commissions such as protected areas, development of tourism, and management of marine and coastal resources will oversee the specific actions.

Protected Areas. There are 40 national parks and reserves, all under the responsibility of the ANGAP, but very few marine protected areas (Fig. 14.5). One marine park, The National Marine Park of Nosy Antafana, is part of

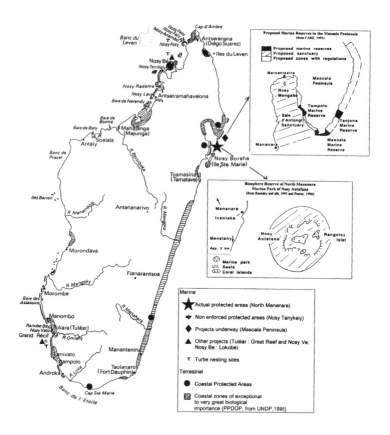

Figure 14.5. Marine protected areas and other coastal zones of ecological importance.

the Mananara-Nord Biosphere Reserve managed by UNESCO (40,32). Created in 1989, the marine park is 1000 ha, surrounded by a circular buffer zone with a 2 km radius. The Park consists of small coral banks and three small coral islands, the largest being Nosy Antafana, surrounded by coral reefs which are partly emerged at low tide. The biology, ecology, and conservation status of these reefs remain unknown. In this region, fishing by the Betsimaraka population is a secondary economic activity after agriculture. Finfishes, lobsters, sea cucumbers, and octopus are the main resources. Fishing used to be authorized only on Tuesday, Thursday, and Sunday, but this tradition has declined and presently some fishers fish any time. Fishing is the main environmental threat to the Park as crowbars are often used to extract hidden invertebrates, and nets with small mesh sizes are also used.

The management plan of the Park has tried to limit fishing pressures. Management includes limiting the number of authorized fishers to those coming from the four villages opposite the park, limiting the number of fishing days as traditionally observed (Tuesday, Thursday, and Sunday), limiting the time of fishing (between 6:00 to 17:00 hours), prohibiting the extraction of juvenile fishes, octopus and squids, establishing a minimum mesh size of 5 cm and

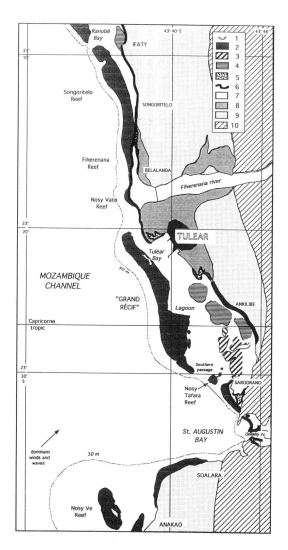

Figure 14.6. Map of the coral reefs in the vicinity of Toliara (SW of Madagascar) (modifiedafter 3). 1. Limit of the continental shelf, 2. barrier reefs and fringing reefs, 3. lagoon reefs, 4. coral banks, 5. mangroves, 6. sandy and muddy sand beaches, 7. recent alluvial deposits, 8. modern alluvial deposits, and 9. quaternary coastal plain.

prohibiting the use of hoop nets with small meshes. In addition, compensatory activities such as aquaculture of sea-cucumbers, fish aggregation devices (FADs), the introduction of new types of pirogues with balancing poles that allow fishers to travel further, and a fishers association are or will be developed by the managers.

The second set of marine protected areas will be part of the Masoala National Park of Masoala, in the Masoala Peninsula, on the east coast, which was recently approved in 1997. Three marine parks and reserves have been selected on coral reefs that fringe the Masoala peninsula and include Tampolo (8 x 3 km), Cape Masoala (12 x 5.3 km), and Tanjona (103 x 0.25 km). Zoning is currently underway to define core protected areas and multiple use zones. Furthermore, all the other coastal marine waters of the peninsula are recommended for some form of integrated coastal zone management. For example, Antongil Bay is being proposed as a sanctuary for marine mammals and turtles. Masoala Park will be managed by ANGAP in collaboration with the Wildlife Conservation Society (WCS) and the non-governmental organization CARE International.

Other areas under consideration for marine protected are in Lokobe and Nosy Tanykely, near Nosy-Be (1). Here there is a strong will from tour operators to develop parks. Additionally, a national marine park near Toliara has been proposed many times, even as a Biosphere Reserve, but with no subsequent action. A study of Nosy-Ve, near the Institute of Marine Science (IHSM), is underway with the intention of making a reserve (Fig. 14.6.). The turtle nesting sites, such as Nosy-Anambo (Anstiranana), Nosy-Iranja (Nosy-Be), Chesterfield (Pracel Shoal), Nosy-Trozona and Nosy-Ve (Toliara), are protected under a colonial decree of 1923, but, in reality, these turtle reserves are not managed. In view of the economic and ecological importance of coral reefs and related ecosystems, there is a need for more conservation and marine protected areas. There is hope that further efforts will be developed during the second phase of the National Environmental Action Plan.

Other Programs. Apart from regional programs or initiatives such as UNEP (Regional Sea Program) or the SEACAM program (Secretariat for Eastern African Coastal Area Management, in Maputo), several programs and projects are underway on the coastal environments that pay special attention to coral reefs. The Malagasy component of the Regional Environmental Program of the Indian Ocean Commission, titled "Assistance to the Environmental Projects to the Members States of the Indian Ocean Commission", is funded by the European Commission (4). This program is mainly focused on integrated coastal zone management. After a first phase of environmental diagnosis (5) a pilot study is underway in the Menabe region (mid-west coast). Programs on fisheries and aquaculture which are part of programs on integrated development of the traditional fishery of the Toliara region are being undertaken with UNDP/FAO funding. A study on the traditional fishery has been conducted on the Nosy-Be and Morondava regions by the CNRO and the Canadian International Development Agency. World Wildlife Fund (WWF) projects are mainly focused on the conservation of biological diversity, particularly turtles and dugongs, which will soon be part of the marine component of the National Environment Program. The main program for the management of coral reefs and coastal environment is, however, the marine and coastal component of the National Environmental Action Plan (NEAP).

Coral Reefs of Toliara: A Case Study

Geography

The reef formations of the Toliara region are geographically limited by the Manombo Estuary in the north (latitude 22°38' S) and Onilahy Estuary in

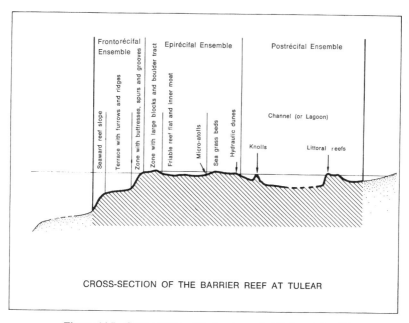

Figure 14.7. Cross-section of the barrier reef at Toliara (after 30).

the south (latitude 23°35' S, 3). They are divided into three areas (Fig. 14.6): 1) the reefs of Ranobé Bay, in the north, 2) the shore reefs from Ifaty to the Fiherenana River, in the center and 3) the reefs of the Toliara Bay in the south. The southern Toliara reefs also contain three reef sectors: 1) the Grand Récif of Toliara, an 18 km long barrier reef completely separated from the shore with a width between 1100 to 2900 m, 2) the inner or lagoon reefs in the south of the bay which are separated from the shore by a 2 km wide channel of 2 m depth, and 3) the coral banks located north of the inner reefs.

The Grand Récif is divided into three large 'assemblages', or 'ensembles' which share common geomorphological and ecological features. They are from offshore to the coast (Fig. 14.7):

1) The outer slope and the reef front which are characterized by alternating spur and groove formations. *Echinophyllia*, Agariciids, and Pectinids occur between 30 and 40 m deep (31). The flora is represented by a diversity of red algae. The most common faunal groups are sponges, alcyonarians, and gorgonians.
2) The reef flat which emerges at low tide is characterized by an outer and inner reef flat. On the outer flat, the upper platform is created by coralline algae (*Porolithon*), living hard corals (mainly *Acropora, Pocillopora, Favia, Favites, Goniastrea, Galaxea*), some soft corals (*Lobophytum*), and rarely *Palythoa* (zoanthids, 31). The inner reef flat, behind the boulder tract, is characterized by coral-built formations including successively: a compact reef flat, a reef flat and sandy channels, and a reef flat with microatolls (3). From

Table 14.5. Description of the hard-ground communities of Toliara. *The 'very skiophilous animal dominated' category can be divided according to environmental factors (water movements, temperature, sedimentation) into six distinct aspects as on the reef flat (see Fig. 14.8).

Sub-communities	Distribution	Main features
Photophilous sessile (dominated by corals - Pichon, 1978)		More than 650 species
Reef	Outer slope, reef flat, lagoon	Scleractinians, coralline algae
Hemiskiophilous deep reef	Outer platform below -30m	Soft algae, hydroids, big sponges, gorgonians, antipatharians and corals, dominated by Agaricidae
Skiophilous sessile (shade loving - Vasseur, 1977, 1981)		
Algal dominated	More or less shadowed subhorizontal surfaces (light: 8.7 to 3.5% of the initial surface radiance)	Corallinacea, squamariacea soft algae, epiphitic hydroids
* Very skiophilous animal dominated	Tunnels, overhangs, very shadowed cavities (light : 3.5 to less than 1%)	Sessile foraminifera, sponges, hydrocorallia, octocorallia, ahermatypic corals
Very high skiophilous, exclusively animal	Galleries, dark cavities (light < 0,01%) of the reef front and slope	Sponges mostly cave-dwelling or of bathial affinity (lithistids, pharetronids, sclerosponges)
Borers of the reef flat buildings (Peyrot-Clausade and Brunel, 1990)		
	Mainly in the residual ponds of the boulder tracts	31 species, mainly sipunculids
Mobile Cryptofauna of hard grounds (Peyrot-Clausade, 1977)		
		784 species
Reef	Whole cryptic habitats of the reef flat	Cryptofaunal biomass dominated by polychaetes.
	Spurs-and-grooves	Crustacean community (brachiourians, anomourans)
Deep Reef	Lower sloping platform (< 30m)	Crustaceans (brachiourians, anomourans) different from the one of spurs-and-grooves zone

there extend sandy bottoms colonized by seagrass beds (*Syringodium, Halodule, Thalassodendron, Cymodocea, Thalassia,* and *Halophila*).

3) The inner slope and lagoon are composed of hard substrates (pinnacles and coral patches), seagrass beds, and soft bottoms of coarse coral sands or mud.

Diversity and Principal Communities

Investigations in the vicinity of Toliara led to a detailed analysis of the ecology of the reef and littoral communities (12). Three large types of reef communities have been studied and include: 1) hard-ground communities, 2) soft bottom communities and 3) fish communities. Depending on environmental factors the three communities can be further divided into sub-communities.

Hard-ground Communities. The four hard-ground communities have been classified into 1) photophilous sessile community, dominated by anthozoans (31), 2) the skiophilous (= shade-loving) sessile community which is extraordinarily rich and diverse housing around 1000 species of plants and

Table 14.6. Species richness in Toliara reef communities.

Taxa	Communities			
	Photophilous sessile (31)	Skiophilous sessile (53)	Mobile cryptofauna (26)	Coral sand bottom (48)
Algae	108	84		62
Sea-grasses				11
Sponges		306		43
Cnidaria	280	163		95
Hydroids	23	65		
Hydrocorals	8	6		
Octocorals				
Gorgonians	27	35		
Alcyonarians	71	29		
Hexacorals				
Actininians	4			
Scleractinians	130	15		
Zoantharians	9	5		
Antipatharians	8	8		
Worms	4	20	121	39
Picnogonids			13	
Crustaceans	9		361	779
Mollusks	37	6	208	1158
Bryozoans		99		34
Echinoderms	68		57	227
Fishes			24	111
Total	**506**	**860**	**784**	**2559**

animals of which 77 species were described for the first time (Fig. 14.8 and Tables 14.5, 14.6, 52,53), 3) the borer community (28) of the reef flat buildings, and 4) the mobile cryptofauna of hard grounds (26,27). This last community is suggested to have three additional formations depending on the three physical factors of aerial exposure, water movement, and temperature. With the exception of the mobile cryptofauna on the lower slopping platform, 784 species have been identified (Table 14.6).

Coral Sand Communities.
Fauna living in coral sediments are distributed according to hydrodynamic and sedimentary gradients. In each of the communities, species are arranged along a gradient of sediment erosion to sediment accumulation. The comparative study of all the soft-bottom assemblages, as well as coralline and littoral habitats showed the existence of a deep-water community (an assemblage associated with detrital shelf bottoms) and three communities that have been identified in the subtidal zone of the outer slope, reef flat, and lagoon. During this study 73 plant species and 2569 animal species were recorded, including 159 species new to science (48).

Coral Fish Communities.
On the reef flat and on the inner and outer reef slope to water depths of 60 m, three communities were distinguished differing in species and importance (11). These include: 1) a deep reef community of the lower sloping platform between 20 and 60 m, 2) a typical shallow-water reef community, which can be further subdivided into outer and inner slope communities, with the highest species richness and abundance in the spur and groove zone (-6 to -18 m), and 3) communities of the reef flat which display

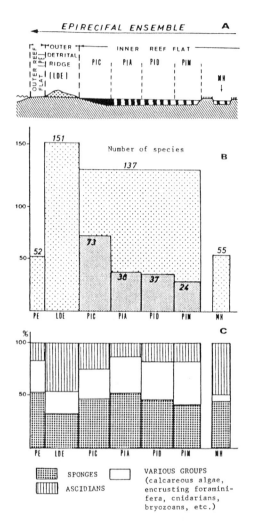

Figure 14.8. Distribution of the number of skiophilous species (B) and importance of the various groups (C) across a transect of the reef flat (A), (Grand Récif, Toliara) (52). Legend of abbreviations: PIC (stopping-up and filling-up reef flat or compact reef flat), PIA (reef flat with transverse stripes), PID (reef flat with irregular coral growths), PIM (reef flat with microatolls), and MH (sea grass bed hollows).

faunal differences according to environmental conditions. Finally, there is also a seagrass bed community. The fish fauna of the spur and groove zone of the outer slope is the richest with greater than 200 species while fish populations of the lower sloping platform is poorer with 109 species (10).

   In addition to species distributional studies, the trophic relationship of fishes was studied by Harmelin-Vivien (11). She studied the diurnal and nocturnal diets of 100 fish species from 26 families by using qualitative and quantitative analysis (number and weight) of their stomach contents. She found, for instance, that the stomach contents of species in the Holocentridae and Apogonidae, living on the reef flat, showed a high dominance of polychaetes. This dominance was related to the high polychaete biomass in the reef-flat cryptofauna. For the whole area around Toliara, Maugé (22) counted more than 700 fish species but the actual number of species is probably twice this figure.

Coral Reef Status

The Grand Récif of Toliara is very degraded although some small areas, such as the outer reef slopes, are less degraded. Ten years ago the state of the coastal and reef zones had been studied (56,57) and this analysis showed that the principal causes of reef degradation were 1) the necrosis or mortality of a number of corals, 2) the proliferation of brown algae (*Sargassum*) during the summer, 3) sea urchin infestations (especially Diadematidae), and 4) reduced water clarity in the reef lagoon. These factors appeared to reduce the species richness, population density, and size of the coral fish populations. Since then, the sources of degradation and human influence have further increased.

Since this study the following problems of the Grand Récif can be added (55): 1) localized coral bleaching; substitution of 90% of the branching corals of the outer reef flat by *Palythoa* (zoanthids) and alcyonarians, 2) the proliferation of green algae changing to brown algae during winter, 3) a reduction in depth of the oxygenated zone of coral sands, probably the consequence of an excess of organic matter, 4) large modification of the hydrodynamic conditions on the reef flat, creating a reduction in the height of the boulder tracts, and 5) the scattering of coral debris, behind these boulder tracts, over a long distance.

Recently, changes in sediments have been analyzed (39). The analyses showed that the average sizes of the epirecifal sediments were bigger than previously measured (59). In the middle part of the Grand Récif the fine sands and gravel changed to medium sands and rubbles indicating that the speed of tidal currents on the reef flat has increased. In addition, the Grand Récif seems to play less of a role as a barrier to offshore waves. Previously, the boulder tracts had a summit 1.5 m above datum which corresponded, at high tide, to the extreme limit of breaking waves. According to P. Vasseur (personal observation, 1995), waves now reach further inshore and break in the inner reef flat zone, which was previously sheltered.

Hence the ecological state of the Grand Récif is critical at present. The whole of Toliara Bay can be considered as a sensitive area due to terrigenous inputs, pollution, and the long-term overexploitation of the marine environment. Perhaps degradation of the reefs could explain the presently high incidence of ciguatera in Toliara, as shown by samples collected in October 1995 (Berland, B. and Thomassin, B.A. personal communication).

Sources of Degradation

Coastal and reef zone management and protection in the vicinity of Toliara are concerned with some preoccupying problems. The town of Toliara increased from 40 000 inhabitants in 1970 to more than 140 000 at the present time. The principal sources of pollution and degradation are related to human activities

(21,34,56,55) which include agriculture based on burning to clear natural vegetation, tree cutting for fire wood and charcoal production, urban and harbor pollution, and overexploitation of marine resources. The major consequence of the loss of vegetation cover is soil erosion while urban pollution is dangerous for public health. Overfishing is due to continued human population growth whose rate of increase is about 3.5% per year in the Toliara region.

Terrigenous Sedimentation. Wood cutting is harmful to the fragile soils of this semi-arid zone. For the town of Toliara, the consumption of wood and charcoal was, respectively, 14 000 and 5000 tons/y. This corresponds to 5000 ha of forest destroyed per year, resulting in abundant soil erosion. In the vicinity of Toliara a large volume of silt and sand is carried by the Fiherenana and Onilahy Rivers, during the rainy season. Over time sedimentation increases in the coastal habitats and, particularly, in reef lagoons. Sedimentation became serious for the Grand Récif since the main arm of the Fiherenana River (a delta) changed its location in 1989 to the level of the reef of Nosy Vato (see Fig. 14.6). Since then, the turbid waters have been transported in the direction of the Passe Nord and the Toliara Bay (Lebigre, J.M. and Vasseur, P. personal observation). South of Toliara, terrigenous sediments of the Onilahy River have drowned the coastal reef of Sarodrano (see Fig. 14.6). All the microatolls of *Porites* and the seagrass beds, flourishing 25 years ago, are now covered with mud (55). North of Toliara, the reef flat of the fringing reef of Songoritelo, slowly disappeared under muddy and sandy banks from the sediments of the Fiherenana River (21,34,55).

Pollution. The sources of pollution of Toliara Bay include sewage, domestic garbage, and human and animal excrement. No sanitation system exists in Toliara. The beach and the sandy-muddy tidal flats in front of the town and harbor area are noticeably odorous and polluted when uncovered at low tide. Organic pollution is further augmented by hydrocarbons (gasoline, kerosene, fuel-oil, and lubricants) from petroleum tanks in the harbor, and by accidental leaks of the pipeline which follows the wharf for 1.5 km. In addition, there are harmful effects of harbor traffic, particularly in the ship's mooring area situated 1 to 2 km behind the Grand Récif. Little information exists on the dumping of industrial effluents from the oil mill, soap factory, brewery, power plant, and other industries located at the periphery of Toliara. Usually the effluents from these enterprises are carried to sewage farms where some water evaporates and the rest penetrates into the ground water. Finally, large farming areas (Miary Plain on the lower Fiherenana River, plains of the lower Onilahy River) situated around Toliara agricultural chemical pollutants such as fertilizers, insecticides, fungicides, herbicides and specifically, DDT and aldrine, which are toxic to the marine environment (56,57).

Uses of Marine Resources

The coral reefs of the SW coast of Madagascar, and particularly those between Ranobe Bay and Toliara Bay, representing a coastline of about 50 km, are subjected to intense exploitation by fishers of the Vezo ethnic group. These people practice intertidal gathering and fishing with pirogues.

Table 14.7. Exportation of shells (in tons) from Toliara (42,43,56). Values for multiple years given as mean per year.

Shellfish	Years	Export (tons/y)
Turbo marmoratus	1976 to 1979	70.0
	1980 to 1983	30.15
	1984 to 1988	26.3
	1989	54.2
	1990	48.0
	1991 to 1993	14.7
Cypraeacassis rufa	1987	22.9
	1988	10.0
	1989	10..0
	1990	27.6
	1991	10.0
	1992	23.4
	1993	10.0
Ornamental shells	1981	68.3
	1982	139.3
	1983	102.6
	1993	108.1

Gathering Fishery. The coral reef flats attract, at low tide, a large number of fishers (men, women and children) who collect for food and sale (33,34,55,56,57). The following is a description of the major groups gathered.

Algae - naturally occurring *Eucheuma* stocks have been collected north of Toliara since 1992 and south of Toliara since 1994. This area includes more than a 200 km stretch of reef. About ten fishing villages are occupied with *Eucheuma* collection. In 1994, the production reached 540 tons of dry algae. The algae are exported via Tamatave harbor to France for the extraction of carageenans.

Corals - formerly, massive colonies of *Porites somaliensis* had been used for house building. *P. somaliensis* is removed for coral blocks, and sold to building contractors at less than US $3/m^3 (56). The quantity of corals extracted fluctuated between 100 and 200 m^3/y but sometimes reached 500 m^3/y. The porous skeleton of *P. somaliensis* is used as a filter in the sunken drains and septic tanks of houses. Branching corals (*Acropora* and *Stylophora*) are only lightly exploited, but are regularly collected by a few fishers who sell them to tourists. Export of branching corals is poorly documented, but has been reported at 1.3 tons in 1979, 4.1 tons in 1981 (33) and about 10 tons in 1987 (56,57).

Shellfish - Many shellfish species are eaten by the coastal populations of Toliara. The main groups are the gastropods which principally include species in the families Turbinidae (*Turbo*), Fasciolaridae, Muricidae, and the bivalves in the family Arcidae (especially *Anadara antiquata*). The collection of *Anadara* represents today almost 19% of the weight of the total capture of various marine resources (45). The flesh of this bivalve is consumed or sold in the fish market of Toliara at a very modest price, of about US $0.05 for a small heap (34,45).

Shells for industrial use are collected intensively, and shipped to Europe (UK, France, Italy, and Spain), mainly *Turbo marmoratus* exploited for nacre, and the red helmet (*Cypraecassis rufa*), *Murex ramosus*, and *Fasciolaria*

Box 14.2. Sea Cucumbers in the SW of Madagascar: Problems of the Fishery and Sustainable Management

Sea cucumbers have long been exploited in Madagascar for the export of trepang (gutted and dried sea cucumber) to China. For example, the Bulletin économique de Madagascar (1921) refers to exports of 11 metric tons of trepang to China and Mauritius, and statistics for the 1920 to 1928 period varied from 50 to 140 tons (5). Export data for Madagascar from 1987 to 1995 presented below show a considerable increase in recent times. The 539 tons recorded in 1994 placed dried sea cucumber in fifth place on the list of national exports in terms of value (2% of the total, 3). This resource has great social and economic importance for coastal villages where it is often exploited as a family activity.

In the south-western region of Toliara this fishery is very active. There are, however, various indications that this fishery, as many others world-wide, is experiencing difficulties (1,2). Although data are incomplete, studies currently under way at the Toliara Fisheries and Marine Science Institute (IHSM, 4) will eventually provide more precise data on the status of this resource. It already appears, however, that 1) the fishers are staying near their traditional fishing grounds in this region, contrary to the migrations observed in other regions from Madagascar, 2) collectors are forced to go much farther, to get enough products, as the catches from individual fishers have decreased, 3) the sizes of specimens, fresh or dried, are diminishing for the collected species, and 4) all species, regardless of their commercial value, are being collected. Processing techniques should be improved as the processed product often fails to meet quality criteria (6).

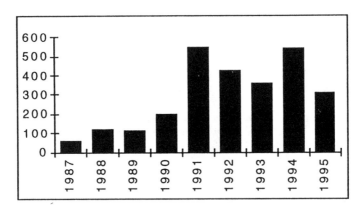

Figure. Sea cucumbers export data (tons/y) from Madagascar (1987 to 1995).

The Indian Ocean Commission (COI) is currently conducting a regional program on integrated coastal zone management. Madagascar has, therefore, resolved that the sustainable management of its resources, and in particular sea cucumbers, is an objective to be achieved through coordination and integration of government and private sectors. The Madagascar National Trepang Traders Groupe (ONET) was set up in Antananarivo on 25 September 1996. The group's

Photo. Sea cucumbers following drying in a processor, with IHSM scientists, near Toliara. (photo: Conand).

objectives are to 1) manage trepang quality, 2) train traders and fishers in resource management, and 3) work closely with the government administration in the management and exploitation of trepang.

C. Conand & E. Mara

References

1. Conand C. 1997. Are holothurian fisheries for export sustainable? *Proceedings of the 8th International Coral Reef Symposium*, Panama 2: 2021-2026
2. Conand C., Byrne M. 1994. A review of recent developments in the world sea cucumber fisheries. *Marine Fishery Review* 55:1-13
3. Conand C., Galet-Lalande N., Randriamiarana H., Razafintseheno G., de San, M. 1997. Sea cucumbers in Madagascar: difficulties in the fishery and sustainable management. *Beche-de-mer Information Bulletin*, S.P.C., 9: 4-5
4. IHSM. 1996. *Etude de la Pêcherie aux Holothuries et Projet d'aménagement.* Rapport projet BM/ONE/IHSM
5. Petit G. 1930. L'industrie des pêches à Madagascar. Bibl. Faune Colonies Franç./Société d'Edition Géographique, Mar. et Coloniales-Paris
6. S.P.C. 1994. *Sea Cucumbers and Beche-de-mer of the Tropical Pacific. A Handbook for Fishers.* SPC 18, Nouméa, Nouvelle-Calédonie

trapezium (42,43,56 and Table 14.7). No management plan has been established for *T. marmoratus* or *C. rufa* fisheries. The exported tonnage of *T. marmoratus* shows that the collection of this big gastropod is excessive. The periodic crashes in the capture of this species during the last ten years may signify a progressive stock depletion of this important commercial species.

The collections of a large variety of ornamental shells for export or for the local tourist market is also intensive but poorly documented (Table 14.7). These ornamental shells mainly include cowries, cone shells, olive shells, auger shells, trumpet shells, strombs, mitre shells, and harp shells, among others. The total shell export from Toliara harbor between 1976 and 1993 was 1810 tons. During the first seven years, 942 tons were collected with a mean annual production of 135 tons/y. Already, in 1987, many juvenile or immature specimens were collected (56). To this is added the additional traffic of rare or endemic species (55). These shells are shipped to Europe, but also to countries of the Indian Ocean region, for instance to tourist destinations such as Mauritius and the Seychelles, which have better conservation practices for their own malacological fauna.

Octopus - on the SW coast of Madagascar, the traditional fishery of octopus *Octopus cyanea* is also an important activity, generally carried out on the inner reef coral formations. Women dominate this gathering activity, but at times the proportion of children and men can be high. Octopus are consumed by the fishers, but there is also a local and international trade to Mauritius and France.

In 1985 and 1986 the production reached more than 16 tons between Toliara and Morombé (200 km north, 56). A preliminary study of this fishery was carried out in front of two fishing villages, 60 km north of Toliara (17), and the production was estimated at 2.1 tons/km^2/y. A more recent study, on the reef flat of the Grand Récif of Toliara, showed that octopus represented 11.8% (by wet weight) of the total of various marine resources captured (45). This total represents 18.9 tons/km^2/y, which is greater than the capture of fish by the fishery with pirogues.

The edible sea urchin *Tripneustes gratilla*. Vezo fishers consume or sell the gonads of *T. gratilla* on the local market. This sea-urchin has always been abundant on the reef flats of the SW Malagasy coast. During spring tide low waters women and children collect these urchins and remove the gonads. The yield of this collection is about 3 kg of gonads per fisher per 3 to 4 hour fishing trip (56). Although the collection of gonads is traditional, it is very active and even intensive. For example, during a field trip to the northern part of the Grand Récif in 1995, 27 fishers (8 women and 19 children) collected 90 kg of gonads which required opening about 32 000 sea-urchins (55). Maharavo (20) observed, for three fishing villages around Toliara, that during the warm season the capture of this species was around 1 000 000 specimens per village. In a study of the gathering fishery, the gonads of edible sea-urchins represented 22.9% of the total weight of the collections and 28.2 % of all fishers were exclusively collecting this sea urchin (45).

Fishing with Pirogues. For the Vezo fishers, the capture of fish in the reef lagoon has always been the main form of subsistence. Today, this has changed as traditional fishing has developed into an artisanal and commercial fishery

Figure 14.9. Coral-built formations of the inner reef flat (Grand Récif of Toliara) showing the presence of three fishers turning and breaking several blocks with heavy wooden wedges in order to catch cryptic species (photo:Vasseur).

associated with the significant population increase along the coast and the country as a whole. In the principal fishing villages along the SW Malagasy coast the total number of fishers has doubled or tripled. In 1990 they had reached 15 300 people (35), representing 35% of all Malagasy inshore and offshore fishers. For example, in Ankilibé village south of Toliara, the number of fishers increased from 60 in 1972 to 170 twenty years later (41) while 1560 professional fishers were recorded between the Ranobé Bay and Toliara Bay and 1330 fishers in Toliara (18). In addition, a relatively high percentage of young fishers (between 10 and 19 years) was observed. In order to maintain their fishing effort, the fishers have progressively given up traditional techniques in favor of destructive methods and fishing is now often practiced both day and night (56).

In 1986, the local consumption of fish in Toliara reached 559 tons which was almost twice the reported consumption in 1983 (56,57). For the whole SW Malagasy coast, the quantity of fish caught exceeded 3100 tons in 1986, not including local consumption estimated at 3 to 4 kg per day per fishing family. According to Rafalimanana (35), the 15 300 fishers of the southwest would catch about 15 000 tons of fish per year. In 1991, the yield of the artisanal fishery was estimated at 12 tons/km^2/y for reefs around Toliara town (16). This corresponds to reported yields of overexploited reef lagoons in Mauritius and the Philippines. Consequently, the pressure of the pirogue fishery on the fish stocks is of concern because of the degradation of many reefs, such as the Grand Récif, and the reported reduction in the weight and size of captured fish (16).

Fishing Influences on the Reefs. Fishing effects are manifold and are composed of both direct and indirect effects. For example, fishing seems to change the trophic structure of the ichthyofauna (56). In 1972, carnivorous fishes were the dominant group in the Toliara reefs in terms of the number of species (74%) and individuals (63%, 11). Today, however, groupers (Serranidae) represent only 2.5% of captured fish and the two dominant trophic groups (29% of all captures) are constituted by herbivorous and detritivorous fishes (18).

More direct impacts include trampling of the reef by fishers collecting algae and invertebrates on the reef flats. For example, in the SW coast of Madagascar, about 150 000 persons collect *Eucheuma* to which fishers collecting shellfish, edible sea-urchins, holothurians, and other groups must be added. The gathering fishery has become as important as or more important than fishing with pirogues. It affects all the reefs of the Toliara Bay and many reef complexes to the north and south (44,45,55). The gathering fishers collect all the edible or ornamental marine products they find and many of these fishers are young (15 to 19 years old) and not educated in traditional fishing methods and associated restrictions. The destruction by collectors can also include turning over coral heads or breaking corals with long iron bars or with heavy wooden wedges (Fig. 14.9) to catch the animals sheltered in the reef crevices (34,55). Some sectors of the Grand Récif have become cemeteries of turned coral blocs. In one year, in a given sector, the surface of the inner coral reef flat destroyed by the fishers (12.5 trips per month) can reach 22 to 36% of the surface area (39). In this study, more than 36 gathering fishers per km^2 of reef per activity day were counted. In 150 activity days per year, 1 km^2 of the Grand Récif can be trampled by 5400 fishers.

The major effects of the pirogue fishery are the use of destructive techniques, like nylon gillnets and beach seines with small meshes and the use of a vegetable poison called 'laro' (extracted from the latex of *Euphorbia laro*) (56,21,34). Beach seines also cause damage to reef-associated seagrass beds in the vicinity of Toliara (Vasseur, P. personal observation). Despite the fishing pressure and these different human effects, almost no management or preservation plan for the marine living resources in the vicinity of Toliara exists, but, nonetheless, the zone has been designated as a high priority site for the recent integrated coastal zone management program.

References

1. ANGAP. 1995. *Etude de Faisabilité de la Composante Aires Protégées et Ecotourisme. Plan d'Action Environnemental.* Unpublished Report
2. Battistini R., 1964. Les récifs coralliens: 448-483. In *Etude géomorphologique de l'extrême Sud de Madagascar.* Paris: Cujas
3. Clausade M., Gravier N., Picard J., Pichon M., Roman M.-L., Thomassin B., Vasseur P., Vivien M., Weydert P. 1971. Morphologie des récifs coralliens de la région de Tuléar (Madagascar): Eléments de terminologie récifale. *Téthys,* suppl. 2 : 74 p.
4. COI. 1995. *Projet PRE-COI : Appui aux programmes environnementaux dans les pays membres de la COI.* Programme Général 1995-2000
5. COI. 1996. *Projet PRE-COI: Premiers résultats du Pré-audit. Document de travail intermédiaire.*
6. DRH/FAO. 1992. *Pêche et aquaculture à Madagascar.* Rapport DRH/UNDP/ FAO

7. DRH/FAO. 1993. *Pêche et aquaculture à Madagascar:* Plan Directeur. Rapport DRH/UNDP/FAO

8. Gabrié C., Randriamiarana H. 1996. *Gestion Intégrée des Zones Côtières à Madagascar: la Composante Marine et Côtière du Plan National d'Action Environnemental.* Rapport de l'Atelier sur la Gestion Intégrée des Zones Côtières, Nosy-Be, Novembre 1996

9. Guilcher A. 1958. Mise au Point sur la Géomorphologie des Récifs Coralliens de Madagascar et Dépendances. *Mémoire de l'Institut des Sciences de. Madagascar.*, Séries F 2: 89-115

10. Harmelin-Vivien M.-L. 1977. Ecological distribution of fishes on the outer slope of Tuléar reef (Madagascar). *Proceedings of the 3rd International Coral Reef Symposium*, Miami 1: 289-295

11. Harmelin-Vivien M.-L. 1979. *Ichtyofaune de Récifs Coralliens de Tuléar (Madagascar). Ecologie et Relations Trophiques.* Thèse Doctorat d'Etat-ès-Sciences, Universite Aix-Marseille

12. Harmelin-Vivien M.-L., Peyrot-Clausade M., Thomassin B.A., Vasseur P. 1982. Biocénoses des récifs coralliens de la région de Tuléar (S. W. de Madagascar). Résultats synthétiques. *Comptes rendus de l'Académie des Sciences-Paris*, Séries 3, 295: 791-796

13. Hoeblich J. 1988. Mise au point sur la répartition géographique des récifs coralliens de Madagascar. *The Journal of Nature* 1: 27-36

14. Jain M. 1995. *Inventory of Coastal Resources and Activities. Proposal for a Strategy in Madagascar.* Rapport KEPEM n° 20

15. Kiener A. 1972. Ecologie, biologie et possibilités de mise en valeur des mangroves malgaches. *Bulletin de Madagascar* 308: 49-84

16. Laroche J., Ramananarivo N.V. 1995. A preliminary survey of the artisanal fishery on coral reefs of the Tuléar region (Southwest Madagascar). *Coral Reefs* 14: 193-200

17. Laroche J., Vasseur P., Toany in press a. Aspects of the biology and artisanal fishery for *Octopus cyanea* off the coral reefs of southwest Madagascar: 15 p. dactyl., 10 Fig., 1 tab.

18. Laroche J., Razanoelisoa, Fauroux E., Rabenevanana M.W. in press b. The reef fisheries surrounding the Southwest coastal cities of Madagascar: 15 p. dactyl., 4 Fig., 5 tabl.

19. Lebigre J.M. 1990. *Les Marais Maritimes du Gabon et de Madagascar.* Thèse Univ. Bordeaux III. Institut de Géographie

20. Maharavo J. 1990. *Contribution à l'étude Biologique d'une Espèce d'oursin Comestible: Tripneustes gratilla (L. 1758) sur le Récif Frangant de Songoritelo, Région de Tuléar (Sud-Ouest de Madagascar).* Diplôme de DEA en Océanologie Appliquée, Station Marine/Université de Tuléar (Madagascar) et Université d'Aix-Marseille

21. Maharavo J. 1996. *Les Récifs Coralliens de Madagascar: Nature et Localisation, Ressources, Menaces et état de Santé.* Madagascar. Rapport de l'Atelier sur la gestion intégrée de la zone côtière, Nosy-Be, Novembre 1996: 41-55

22. Maugé L.A., 1967. Contribution préliminaire à l'inventaire ichtyologique de la région de Tuléar. *Rec. Trav. Sta. mar. Endoume*, Marseille, fasc. hors sér., suppl. 7: 101-132

23. McClanahan, T.R., Jaomanana, Kamukuru, A.T., Kiambo, R., Obura D. 1997. *Survey of the Shallow Waters Corals and Marine Snails of the*

Masoala Peninsula. Madagascar. The Wildlife Conservation Society, Unpublished Report

24. Odendaal F.J., Kroese M., Jaomanana 1995. *Plan Stratégique Pour la Gestion des Zones Côtières de la Péninsule de Masoala*. Unpublished report n°4

25. ONE, 1994. *L'état de l'Environnement à Madagascar*. Rapport ONE

26. Peyrot-Clausade M. 1977. *Faune Cavitaire Mobile des Platiers Coralliens de la Région de Tuléar (Madagascar)*. Thèse Doctorat d'Etat-ès-Sciences, Universite Aix-Marseille

27. Peyrot-Clausade M. 1981. Mobile cryptofauna of Tuléar Great Reef outer slope: Brachyura and Anomura distribution. *Proceedings 4th International Coral Reef Symposium* 2: 745-754

28. Peyrot-Clausade M., Brunel J.F. 1990. Distributional patterns of macro-boring organisms on Tuléar reef flats (S.W. of Madagascar). *Marine Ecology Progress Series* 61: 133-144

29. Pichon M. 1971. Comparative study of the main features of some coral reefs of Madagascar, La Réunion and Mauritius. *Symposium Zoological Society London* 28: 185-216

30. Pichon M. 1972. The coral reefs of Madagascar. In *Biogeography and Ecology of Madagascar*. eds. Richard-Vindard G., Battistini R. pp. 367-410. Monography Biology, 21, The Hague: Junk

31. Pichon M. 1978. Recherches sur les peuplements à dominance d'Anthozoaires dans les récifs coralliens de Tuléar (Madagascar). *Atoll Research Bulletin* 222: 1-447

32. Poirier A. 1996. *Contribution à la Recherche d'indicateurs de Durabilité. Application au Parc Marin de Nosy Antafana (Madagascar)*. Mémoire de DEA. CIRAD-GREEN

33. Rabesandratana H.D. 1985. Sur quelques utilisations récifales à Madagascar. *Proceedings 5th International Coral Reef Congress*, Tahiti 2: 661-668

34. Rabesandratana H.D. 1996. *Etat des Récifs Coralliens des Zones Côtières de Madagascar*. Madagascar-Rapport de l'Atelier sur la gestion intégrée de la zone côtière : 12-18

35. Rafalimanana T. 1991. *Estimation des Captures de la Pêche Traditionnelle Malgache en 1990*. Ministère de la Production Animale, Eaux et Forêts. Direction de la Pêche et de l'Aquaculture. UNDP, projet MAG/85/014

36. Rakotoarinjanahary H., Randriambololona C., Rasolofo V., Razafindrainibe H., Razakafoniaina N.T., Roby D. 1996. *La Pêche Traditionnelle et Maritime à Madagascar*. Rapport du Projet PATMAD

37. Ranaivoson J. 1996. Coastal erosion in the Morondava region, Madagascar. *Tropical Coast* 3: 13-14

38. Randriamiarana H. 1996. *Etat de la Pêche et de l'Aquaculture à Madagascar*. Rapport de l'Atelier sur la Gestion Intégrée des Zones Côtières, Nosy-Be, 1996: 113-127

39. Randriamanantsoa B.J. 1997. *Modifications de la Morphologie et des Sédiments du Grand Récif de Tuléar (Comparaisons 1969/1970-1995/1996). Impacts sur la Pêche et les Ressources Vivantes.* Diplôme de DEA d'Océanologie Appliquée, IH.SM/Université de Tuléar (Madagascar)

40. Raondry N., Klein M., Rakotorinina V.S. 1995. *La Réserve de la Biosphère de Mananara-nord 1987-1994.* Bilan et perspectives. Documents de travail UNESCO n°6 : 72p.

41. Rarivoson S. 1992. *Les Activités Halieutiques Nocturnes dans la Baie de Tulear.* Exemple d'un village de pêcheurs: Ankilibé. Diplôme d'Ingénieur Halieutique, I.H.S.M/Université de Tuléar

42. Ravelo C. 1994. *Bioécologie de* Turbo marmoratus *L. 1758 (Gastéropode Marin) du Récif Frangeant de Songoritelo (Tulear, Sud-Ouest de Madagacar).* Diplôme de DEA en Océanologie Appliquée, IH.SM/Université de Tuléar

43. Ravelo I. 1994. *Bioécologie de* Cypraeacassis rufa *L., 1758 (Gastéropode Marin) du Récif Frangeant de Songoritelo (Tulear, Sud-Ouest de Madagascar).* Diplôme de DEA en Océanologie Appliquée, IH.SM/Université de Tulear

44. Rosa J.-C. 1997. *Etude de la Pêche-collecte à pied sur les Platiers des récifs Frangeants entre les villages de Maromena , Befasy et Beheloka (Sud-Ouest de Madagascar).* Diplôme de DEA d'Océanologie Appliquée, IH.SM/Université de Tuléar

45. Salimo, 1997. *Etude de la Pêche -collecte à Pied sur les Platiers du Grand Récif de Tuléar (Sud-Ouest de Madagascar).* Diplôme de DEA d'Océanologie Appliquée, IH.SM/Université de Tuléar

46. Salomon J.N. 1980. Les récifs coralliens de Belo-sur-Mer: étude géomorphologique (Sud-Ouest de Madagascar). *Madagascar - Revue de Géographie* 37: 87-109

47. Salomon J. N. 1987. *Le Sud-Ouest de Madagascar.* Université d'Aix-Marseille

48. Thomassin B.A. 1978. *Peuplements des Sédiments Coralliens de la région de Tuléar (S.W. de Madagascar) et Leur Insertion dans le Contexte Côtier Indo-Pacifique.* Thèse Doct. d'Etat-ès-Sciences, Univ. Aix-Marseille

49. UNDP. 1996. *Monographie sur la Biodiversité à Madagascar: la Biodiversité Aquatique, Continentale, Côtière et Marine.* UNDP

50. UNEP/IUCN. 1988. *Coral Reefs of the World.* Vol 2. Gland: Switzerland IUCN/UNEP

51. Vacelet J., Vasseur P. 1977. Sponge distribution in coral reefs and related areas in the vicinity of Tuléar (Madagascar). *Proceedings 3rd International Coral Reef Symposium* , Brisbane 1: 113-117

52. Vasseur P. 1977. Cryptic sessile communities in various coral formations on reef flats in the vicinity of Tuléar (Madagascar). *Proceedings 3rd International Coral Reef Symposium*, Brisbane 1: 95-100

53. Vasseur P. 1981. *Recherches sur les Peuplements Sciaphiles des Récifs Coralliens de la Région de Tuléar (S.W. de Madagascar).* Thèse Doct. d'Etat-ès-Sciences, Univ. Aix-Marseille

54. Vasseur P. 1994. Further news on coral reef research in Madagascar. *Reef Encounter* 15: 22-23

55. Vasseur P. 1997. Ecosystèmes côtiers en danger dans la région de Tuléar. Analyse des agressions humaines et problèmes de gestion. *Milieux "naturels" et sociétés dans le Sud-Ouest de Madagascar (Coll. Iles et Archipels), Université Bordeaux* 3(3): 97-120

56. Vasseur P., Gabrié C., Harmelin-Vivien M. 1988. *Tuléar (S.W. de Madagascar): gestion rationnelle des récifs coralliens et des mangroves dont des mises en réserve. Rapport définitif.* Rapp. EPHE/Centre de Biologie et Ecologie Tropicale et Méditerranéenne/Université de Perpignan, n° RL 31

57. Vasseur P., Gabrié C., Harmelin-Vivien M. 1988. State of coral reefs and mangroves of the Tuléar region (SW Madagascar) : assessement of human activities and suggestions for management. *Proceedings 6th International Coral Reef Symposium*, Townsville 2 : 421-426

58. Vely M. 1995. *Première Mission sur les Mégaptères (Megaptera novaeangliae) et autres Cétacés de la Baie d'Antongil et de la Côte Orientale de la Presqu'île de Masoala.* Madagascar 15 Septembre - 17 Octobre 1995. Tropical Ocean Mammals Service, Madagascar

59. Weydert P. 1971. Etude sédimentologique et hydrodynamique d'une coupe de la partie médiane du Grand Récif de Tuléar (SW. de Madagascar). *Téthys*, suppl. 1: 237-280

Chapter 15

The Chagos Archipelago

Charles R.C. Sheppard

The Chagos Archipelago lies at the southern end of the Laccadive-Chagos ridge, in the geographical center of the tropical Indian Ocean. Politically it is a UK Dependent Territory, known as the British Indian Ocean Territory, administered from the Foreign and Commonwealth Office, London (23). The group has five islanded atolls, and several others which are awash or completely submerged (Fig. 15.1). Its central feature is the 200 by 100 km Great Chagos Bank, the Earth's largest atoll in terms of area. This is mostly submerged, but there are eight islands on its western and northern rim. This is surrounded by the smaller atolls: Peros Bañhos and Salomon to the north, Egmont (on some charts called the Six Islands) to the southwest, and Diego Garcia to the south. Among these lie many submerged reefs, the whole complex covering about 250 by 400 km. These submerged structures are one of the most notable features of the central Indian Ocean.

It would be surprising if the widespread seafaring civilizations of 500 to 2000 years ago never discovered Chagos, but records of this are apparently absent. In this respect it is different from the relatively nearby Maldives. The islands' first documented discovery was by the Portuguese in the 16th Century (2) and they were not inhabited for the next 200 years until, in the late 18th Century, the larger ones were farmed for coconuts or copra. The dominance of copra, which exceeded about 0.5 million liters annually in the 19th Century (21), caused the atolls to be known as the Oil Islands. In the 1970s when copra ceased to be an important global crop, all the copra plantations were abandoned. Today all atolls except Diego Garcia are currently uninhabited, the latter supporting a communications, naval and air facility of a few thousand personnel.

The atolls and reefs of Chagos attracted some distinguished early attention. All its reefs were mapped in detail in 1837 by Moresby (21), which permitted Darwin (10) to incorporate them extensively in his exposition of coral reef formation, though Darwin did not land there. Bourne (8) visited its islands and interpreted its rock strata as evidence against reef formation by subsidence. Gardiner (16) described several parts of Chagos which he visited in 1901. Afterwards, few visits by reef scientists were undertaken until Stoddart and Taylor (45) visited Diego Garcia and made collections of species for several groups of organisms from the island and reef flat. The first detailed, deeper reef

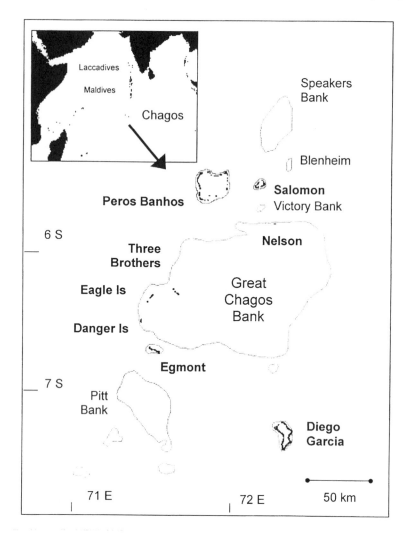

Figure 15.1. Map of Chagos Archipelago. Grey lines are 100 meter contour.

surveys were carried out in the 1970s when several submerged banks were examined (5,6,40). No more scientific visits occurred for a further 18 years, until a visit in 1996 of about 12 island and reef ecologists. Much of the work of the 1970s was published and subsequently summarized (43), while the varied work of the 1996 program is likewise being published, much of it in a single Proceedings (34). This chapter summarises the ecological work of the 1970s (and earlier where not superseded) with the very recent work.

From these studies it is clear that Chagos contains the largest expanse of totally unimpacted reef in the Indian Ocean as well as some of the biologically richest. With the exception of part of Diego Garcia, Chagos' reefs have been undisturbed for at least 30 years and have never been subjected to major human interference. An absence of many forms of human interference may be claimed for some other areas of the ocean such as the large swath of limestone banks running between Seychelles and Mauritius, but the latter are heavily fished. Chagos is subjected to some fishing through licenses issued by the UK authorities (though some illegal fishing occurs), but the fishing is limited and the reefs continue to support very rich fish stocks.

Geological, Geographical and Physical Background

Chagos is the southernmost and oldest part of the Chagos - Laccadive ridge, formed when the Indian tectonic plate migrated northwards towards Asia. The entire chain was created by hot-spot activity since the late Cretaceous, and the trace of this can be followed from the Deccan traps in western India and from there southwards down the chains of atolls to Chagos (18). Located just south of the equator, Chagos covers an area of about 60 000 km². The archipelago is a limestone cap a few hundred meters to a few kilometers thick, resting on volcanic rock (15).

Structure and Form

Most of the present islands are those of typical atolls, located on the atoll rim with elevations of no more than two or three meters (Fig. 15.2). Two areas in Chagos have raised reefs; these are found in southern Peros Bañhos and the adjacent, northwestern part of the Great Chagos Bank, both sites containing islands with small, uplifted and vertical cliffs to over six meters above the high tide level (Fig 15.2). One of the main features of the Chagos reefs is the number of submerged banks and 'drowned' atolls (Table 15.1), the latter mostly exhibiting typical atoll-like cross sections including a 'lagoon' and passes cut through the submerged atoll rim. Most of the Great Chagos Bank itself is 'drowned' in that its rim currently lies between three and 20 m deep in all parts except the west where shallow reef flats and islands exist. In Figure 15.3, enhancements from SPOT satellite are shown for several atolls, including Salomon, a classical islanded atoll, Blenheim, an atoll of similar size but which is awash at low tide and totally submerged at high tide, and Victory, an atoll which is submerged by at least 5 m. These three atolls are all located within a few kilometers of each other. In Figure 15.3, white color indicates water deeper than 15 m; both Victory and Salomon have lagoons deeper than this while Blenheim has a shallower lagoon.

All reefs visited in Chagos, including the apparently drowned atolls, have profusely growing corals, so the reason why some have islands, some are awash and others are drowned to 5 m or more is not known. Blenheim reef, for example, is a typical atoll in most respects except for a lack of islands. Its depth/frequency profile is compared with that of Salomon, an atoll whose rim is over 50% islanded (Fig. 15.4). Blenheim shows abundant shallow substrate, and indeed its wave-resistant algal ridges are the best developed in the Archipelago and possibly in the entire ocean (see later). It is the same size as the islanded Salomon and Egmont atolls, so its small size has probably not precluded the emergence or development of islands. Indeed, some of the largest atoll-shaped structures in Chagos, more properly called banks, have no islands (Table 15.1).

Figure 15.2. (Top) part of the atoll rim of Peros Bañhos showing typical structure of reef flat, lagoonal reef (foreground), island of no greater than 2 meter elevation and seaward reef flat. (Bottom) the raised reef part of the Great Chagos Bank on western side. The limestone cliffs are over 5 m high.

Diego Garcia

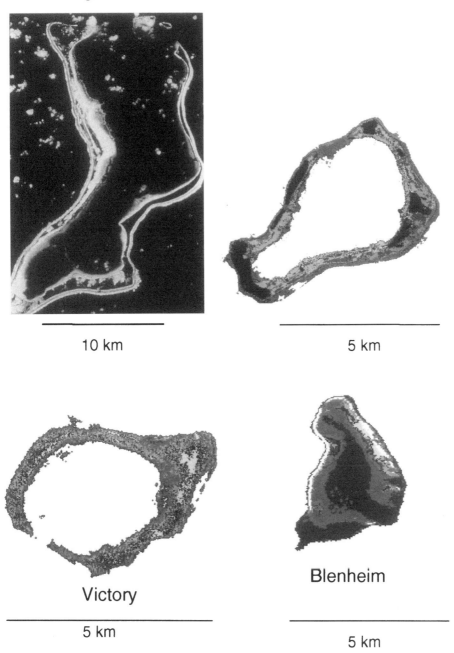

Figure 15.3. Selection of atolls and submerged banks in Chagos. The Diego Garcia photograph was taken from a space shuttle. Others are enhanced digital images from SPOT satellite In these diagrams, the white color within the atolls indicates water over 15 m deep. Blenheim reef is awash at low tide with a shallow lagoon; Victory bank has a rim 5 m deep; Salomon atoll is islanded.

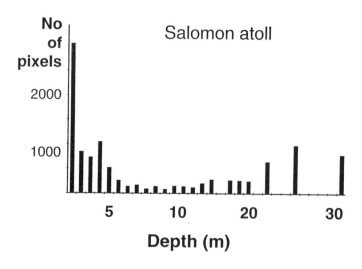

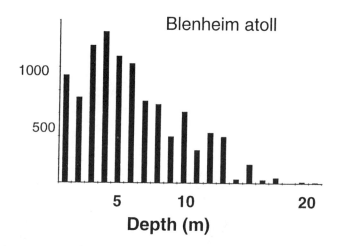

Figure 15.4. Histogram showing the amount of benthic substrate at each depth at Salomon atoll and Blenheim reef. The horizontal axis represents depth in 1 m intervals, while the heights of each bar is the number of 20 m x 20 m pixels at each depth (from SPOT satellite). Note the different scales on the vertical axes.

Other reefs are crescent shaped (such as Benares, Colvocoresses, not discussed further) which may represent fragments of older atolls, though bathymetric maps do not give enough resolution to give more than a hint of an atoll shape in these cases. On some large deeper reefs, such as Speakers Bank, corals and seagrasses are profuse, indicating high benthic productivity. On the largest system of all, the Great Chagos Bank, complex patterns of reefs exist showing several ring shaped structures within the main atoll rim, which attest to a complex past history of growth and erosion. Nowhere in Chagos are lagoonal

Table 15.1. Physical characteristics of the major atolls and banks. Several small banks with atoll cross sections also exist, whose shallowest rim sections are <10m, but have not been studied.

Atoll	Atoll area (km²)	Land area (ha)	Number of islands	Lagoon greatest depth (m)	Lagoon mean depth (m)	Shallow-est depth (if no islands)	% Rim enclosure by islands or reef flats
Atolls							
Diego Garcia	<200	2733	4	31	10	-	95
Solomon	38	311	11	33	25	-	85
Peros Bañhos	463	920	24	80	38	-	60
Great Chagos Bank	18 000	445	8	84	50	-	<5
Egmont	40	~300	6	26	12	-	35
Submerged atolls							
Blenheim Reef	40	0	0	17	8	awash	60
Victory Bank	16	0	0	33	25	5	_
Speakers Bank	680	0	0	35	44	7	-
Pitt Bank	1200	0	0	44	35	<10	-

faros seen, although these structures are typical of the Maldives immediately to the north. Depths of over 1 km separate each atoll or reef.

Seismology, Sea Level and Ages

The Chagos Bank is affected by frequent but generally low intensity seismic tremors, though one measuring 7.7 on the Richter scale was recorded in 1983 (48). Since measuring began in 1965, 123 tremors have been recorded, 70 being in one year (47) though tidal waves of no more than 0.5 m have been recorded. Historically, a notable tremor remarked on by Darwin (10) concerned an island in Peros Bañhos which was destroyed by an earthquake, the noteworthy consequence to the inhabitants being the loss of productive copra plantation. Indeed, that reef in 1979 was seen to have been greatly fragmented to 30 m deep, and lacked the classical profile of reef flat and reef slope. Evidence of the importance of seismic activity comes from occasional raised reefs noted earlier in Peros Bañhos atoll and the Great Chagos Bank, structures of limited area which are elevated 3 to 5 meters above the surrounding reef flats (18). Apart from seismic activity found on conventional plate boundaries, Chagos is possibly the most intense source of oceanic seismicity today, and it appears likely that there is a diffuse boundary between the Indo-Arabian and Australian plates extending from the Central Indian Ridge through the Chagos area to the Ninety East Ridge and Sumatra Trench.

The general sea level profiles of the Pleistocene and Holocene have been confirmed by recent work in Chagos (18). In the lowest sea level stand of about 12 000 years BP, it is likely that about 13 000 km² more land was emerged than is the case today. It is also likely that sea level was about 1 to 2 m higher than present in the more recent past. Some corals collected from their positions of growth in reefs currently elevated on the islands have been dated by Uranium/Thorium methods to ages of 830 years, 2300 to 3000 years and 5200 years before present. This, and other dating results from fossil corals taken from emerged beach rock, suggests that the islands themselves are relatively recent (18).

Climate, Tides, and Nutrients

Chagos is located between about 5° and 7° S, so is not regularly subject to cyclonic strength winds, although severe storms from the edges of cyclones are sometimes experienced, especially in Diego Garcia in the south. From October to April, winds are light or moderate and generally from the north-west. For the rest of the year, the southeast trades blow strongly. Rainfall has a strong seasonal pattern (44), with most falling between October and April and much less falling during the southeast trades. Total annual rainfall averages about 2500 mm or more in the southern atoll of Diego Garcia, but reaches 4000 mm in the northern atolls, making Chagos the wettest group of atolls in the Indian Ocean. December to February is the wettest time, when the Inter-Tropical Convergence Zone is over or just south of Chagos. The low latitude of Chagos means that developing tropical cyclones are weak, the maximum wind speed recorded being a peak gust of 120 km/hr in 1984. On average, about 11 tropical storms or cyclones develop each year in the region. These build up to the east or southeast of Chagos but then track away from the archipelago to the southwest.

Spring tidal ranges are about 1.2 m with neap ranges of about 0.2 m (27,28). Low spring tides usually occur at 9:00 and 21:00 hours. Several times each year, however, low water lasts until nearly noon, causing the reef flats to be emerged to 30 cm during periods of strong sun (Fig. 15.5). This is the supposed reason why the reef flats of Chagos are particularly poor in coral cover. Since other reefs in the Indian Ocean experience similar tidal conditions yet support rich reef flat corals and other fauna, the paucity on Chagos is also attributable to greater absolute elevation of the atolls.

Tidal-water exchange has a stabilizing effect on the thermal characteristics of the lagoons. Even though there are marked differences in lagoon depths between atolls, temperature rise in lagoonal water is of the order of 2°C, varying with tidal height more than with lagoon depth. In both the open, large lagoon of Peros Bañhos and the relatively small and enclosed Salomon lagoon water is pumped by wave action on both the rising and falling tides over the reef flats into the lagoon. This water becomes increasingly oxygenated during transit over the flats, from photosynthesis as well as from aeration in the breaker zone. The water also progressively accumulates nitrogen, presumably mainly from nitrogen-fixing blue-green algae (29). The implication of enhanced nitrogen in the lagoons, particularly Salomon, is that primary production should also be raised, and indeed carbon fixation was two to 10 times greater in the lagoon than is the case for the open ocean (29). Phosphate levels varied much less, suggesting fast recycling of this element. Dissolved phosphate was also found to rise after heavy rain with no parallel increase in nitrogen, suggesting run-off from the guano produced by numerous nesting birds on many of the islands.

Figure 15.5. Section of seaward reef flat on Chagos, showing exposed platform at low Spring Tide. Horizontal extent of this section is about 400 meters perpendicular to islands, and this section, in southwest Peros Bañhos extends for over 10 kilometers.

Reef Ecology

The distinction of reef scientists, such as Darwin and Gardiner, did not guarantee their accuracy when commenting on the richness of Chagos' reefs. Darwin reported that Chagos had 'scarcely any live coral', that the rim consisted of 'sand with a very little live coral' although some patches in the lagoons had 'luxuriantly growing coral'. Darwin never visited the archipelago but relied on conversations with Moresby, but Gardiner (16) generally agreed with Darwin even after his own visit, quoting Darwin at length. These views were presumably based on observations on reef flats, which was the only part easily accessible to the early naturalists, and on the results of a little dredging and examination of what stuck to tallow coated weights. There are some deeper and richer reef flats, so the older views of coral paucity can only be explained by inadequate viewing and, of course, an inability to see the reef slopes at all. All atolls and submerged banks appear to be actively growing reefs (43).

Reef Flats, Coralline Algal Ridges, Spur and Groove Systems

Reef flats on Chagos dry and thus are depauperate compared to many others in the Indian Ocean, partly due to the occasional coincidence of low spring tides with solar noon (27). Drying areas with little biota lie nearest to shore, while seaward is a boulder zone with storm-tossed reef fragments colonized by the surge-resistant cup sponge *Phylospongia* and the alga *Turbinaria*, followed by an algal ridge at the extreme outer edge of the reef flat. Where the distance from seaward shores to reef slope is <100 m the entire reef flat has the appearance of a boulder zone. There is a marked contrast to this pattern in some parts of the lagoons where reef flats may be 1 m deep, and where *Acropora* stands may provide 50% cover over small areas, and where *Porites* and several faviid corals develop into micro-atolls.

Algal ridges and associated spur and groove systems occur on the seaward edges of most Chagos seaward reef flats. Those of Chagos atolls appear to be the largest and best developed in the Indian Ocean. These structures occur where water movement and aeration are strong (11) and are crucial in enabling reefs to resist abrasion. Formed by coralline red algae, in the Indo Pacific the main genus is *Porolithon* which has great mechanical strength and thrives in the shallowest, surf washed areas at the edge of the reef flat. Other very large spur and groove structures, such as those of southern Madagascar, are likely to be created more by erosion than construction (25).

In Chagos, different stages of spur development occur (Fig. 15.6), related to prevailing degrees of exposure (41). Firstly, and most unusually, the large atoll of Peros Bañhos has a lagoon which is open and exposed enough to support the development of rudimentary spurs. Spurs develop along over 1 km of reef flat, each spur being blocks or ridges with sides 0.4 to 1.0 m, separated by gaps of equal dimension. Lagoonal spurs (Fig. 15.6 top) are located at the extreme edge of the lagoon reef flat, and are completely emerged at low spring tides. Where exposure is greater, the rudimentary spurs become connected laterally at their landward ends. This can develop into a rudimentary algal ridge, connecting a dozen or more of the spurs, which still, however, are generally small.

On concave or otherwise more sheltered parts of seaward reefs, individual spurs may have a cross section of 1 m by 1 m, but extend for up to 20 m perpendicular to shore. These features are entirely constructional; the groove floors being continuous with the reef flat and reef slope.

The most developed spurs are seen on exposed seaward reefs (Fig. 15.6 bottom). Spurs are connected laterally by a ridge of *Porolithon* extending around the rim of the atoll for several kilmeters. These ridges are up to 20 m wide and are elevated 0.5 m above low springs. Seaward of the ridge, spurs extend for 20 to 75 m to a depth of 5 to 8 m. Typically they taper towards the seaward end. They are a rich pink due to the *Porolithon*. One penetration of the ridge to 0.5 m showed that construction appeared consistently to be a mix of *Porolithon* infilled with particulate matter. Occasionally a groove penetrates through the ridge to the reef flat. Seaward of all spurs, projections of richer coral growth continue on from each algal spur for an additional 75 m. It is conjectured that the enhanced coral growth is a result of the same factors that induce development of algal spurs.

Figure 15.6. Spur and algal ridge systems in Chagos. The top series is found in Peros Bañhos lagoon, consisting of small (1 m x 1 m) detached cubes of *Porolithon* grading to cubes attached laterally at their landward end. Bottom photograph is a typical, large algal ridge, looking seaward to algal spurs. These are exposed at low Spring Tides. In this example, the ridge is 20 m broad, and spurs extend 75 m to seaward from the ridge.

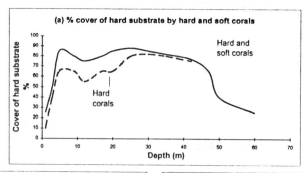

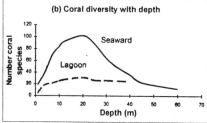

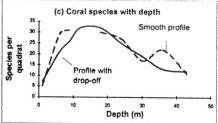

Figure 15.7. (a) percent cover of hard substrate (excluding sand) by stony corals (broken line) and by stony corals plus soft corals combined (solid line), with depth. Average of several transects around two northern atolls of Peros Banhos and Salomon (38). (b) coral diversity on reef slopes. Solid line is seaward reef slopes, broken line is lagoonal reef slopes. In excess of 20 transects on each were pooled for each series (38). (c) coral diversity on reef slopes. Solid line is diversity pattern on a typical reef slope with a 'drop-off': 20° slope to 15 m followed by 45° slope to 60 m. Broken line is diversity pattern on a reef slope of 20° throughout (38).

One almost certain consequence of the spur and ridge system is a greatly increased resistance to erosion from waves. Oceanic swell is substantial in Chagos, even in periods of relative calm. No appreciable coral growth occurs on the spurs' tops or ridges, and only *Porolithon* appears able to survive. Indeed, it thrives in, and may even require, such conditions.

Biological Patterns on the Reef Slope

A common premise of reef ecology is that competition by benthic biota for space on reef slopes is intense. This appears to be the case on Chagos' reefs.

On both seaward and lagoonal reef slopes, coral cover on hard substrate is between 50 and 80% to at least 40 m deep, with the stony corals providing most of this cover (Fig. 15.7a). One exception occurs in southeastern Salomon, where soft coral cover exceeds stony coral cover to 20 m deep, a condition which has persisted in that site for at least the past 20 years. Below 40 m, coral cover dropped, but was still 25% at 60 m deep, and soft corals provided a diminishing proportion of this cover (though gorgonians increased visibly). Encrusting red algal cover increased with increasing depth, covering up to 75% of the hard substrate at 50 to 60 m depths.

Coral diversity increases rapidly with increasing depth until 20 m deep (38), after which point it declines (Fig. 15.7b). This is an unusually deep peak, contrasting with depth values of 5 to 10 m in many other regions such as the Red Sea. Possible reasons for the peak being this deep include the exceptionally clear water, oceanic swell, and reef profile. The reef profile on seaward slopes is typically a gentle slope descending from the reef crest or algal ridge, followed by a rapid drop-off between 10 to 20 m deep. The steep slope descends to undetermined depths or to a second shelf at 40 m or deeper. The highest diversity is thus on or just deeper than the drop-off. The drop-off itself, however, is not the cause of the pattern. One example found where there was no drop-off showed a similar profile of diversity (Fig. 15.7c).

Coral zones are generally named after dominant or conspicuous species. Chagos reefs exhibit clear coral zones. In shallow, turbulent water immediately below the algal ridge and spurs, the stoutly branching *Acropora palifera* defines a zone, while below this, tabular forms of *Acropora* may dominate (38). There is high cover of the blue coral *Heliopora coerulea* in some shallow, turbulent reef slopes, while *Galaxea astreata* dominates deep lagoon floors, possibly because of its high aggression (36). The commonest coral, in terms of numbers of colonies, on most Chagos reef slopes was the generally inconspicuous *Pavona varians*. Deeper down, the dominant forms are foliaceous forms such as *Pachyseris speciosa*, *Echinopora lamellosa* and/or *Leptoseris* spp. which provide high cover between 25 and 45 m, and this is followed by a clear zone of *Craterastrea levis* which provides up to 20% cover down to at least 60 m deep (38) on several seaward reef slopes.

Soft corals are still an under-sampled group, in Chagos and the ocean as a whole. In a brief survey in 1996, about 70 octocoral species were found, including two new genera and five new species (30).

Macromolluscs have also been examined to a depth of 40 m (35). Using data collected earlier and applying consistent synonyms, 384 benthic molluscan species were found. Cluster analyses of the presence-absence data show that on hard substrate mollusks had a clear zonation along with depth (Fig. 15.8), and to a lesser extent with seaward or lagoonal position. As with corals, total mollusk diversity rises with depth to 10 to 20 m on all the atoll reefs, and then declines to 40 m. Shallow water of <2 m contained <1% of the total species present, while the region of the reef drop-off contained up to 40% of the total.

Sand-dwelling mollusks, which contained 28% of all species recorded, showed no zonation with depth. In sand, the nature of the substrate alone was important, though it should be noted that sandy habitat was only encountered in significant amounts in the lagoons and not on seaward slopes. Molluscan diversity in Chagos compares favorably with those of the Seychelles, Cocos Keeling, the Maldives and even the Red Sea.

Information on the ecology of reef fishes is limited at present, but total numbers of species documented is presently about 773 species (20). Community structure of reef fishes as described through species accumulation and species abundance curves, are typical of many other complex and diverse ecosystems (20). The community structure of reef fish appears to vary little across distances of up to 150 km. This apparent homogeneity can be linked to the oceanic location, the lack of terrigenous inputs and the very low influence of man on these reefs.

Biogeographical aspects of the Indian Ocean and the position of Chagos in this respect are examined in Chapter 1 of this volume. It is clear that the

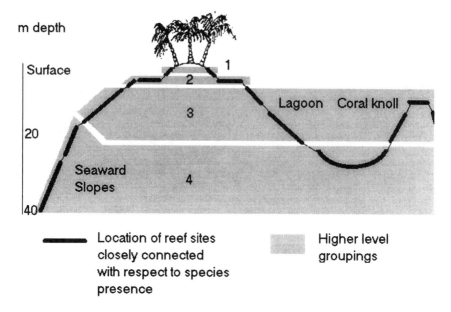

Figure 15.8. Groupings of mollusks in Chagos as determined from cluster analysis, performed on species lists from several authors (35).

central location of Chagos gives it a considerable importance in the Indian Ocean. From the point of view of the corals, analysis shows (Box 15.1) that Chagos provides a strong connecting link in an east-west direction, and has a lesser connection with the chain of atolls extending to the north. With reef fishes, however, Chagos shows close affinities with the Maldives to the north, possibly greater than its affinities with both eastern and western reefs, a contrasting pattern which has no explanation at present. With terrestrial flora and insects, Chagos shows stronger affinities with the Indonesian region than with Africa. Clearly dispersal rates and mechanisms may, therefore, differ for marine and terrestrial groups.

Changes Over 20 Years

Few Indian Ocean reefs sites afford the opportunity for comparisons over a 20 year time span, and two sets of measurements were made to compare studies taken in 1978 with similar studies in 1996.

Changes in Reef Corals

Data on reef coral cover from vertical tape transects from 1978 and 1996 were compared (42). Problems occurred in relocating each transect, and exact relocation probably did not occur. However, since each section of reef slope on

Box 15.1. Biogeographic Position of Chagos in the Indian Ocean

Chagos is the most diverse coral site in the Indian Ocean, with 220 species in 58 genera of zooxanthellate corals. Its geographical position suggests that it may provide an important stepping stone in the spread of corals westwards from the southeast Asian high diversity center. This was tested with GIS (1). Similarities in coral species composition between Chagos and 25 other well sampled sites in the Indian Ocean were computed (2), and a digital map of the Indian Ocean was resampled by replacing geographical distances with 'biological' distances. Biological distances were derived from species dissimilarity, and resampled maps were 'anchored' on Chagos using a method known as 'rubber sheeting'. Using second order then third order polynomial resampling methods, the map of the Indian Ocean is increasingly 'warped', pulling the extreme east and western sides of the Ocean towards Chagos and towards each other, while sites around the northwestern, northern and southwestern rims of the ocean are 'pushed' further away (Figure). The 'biological map' is thus greatly elongated north-south, and contracted east-west compared with a geographical map. This supports the suggestion that Chagos is

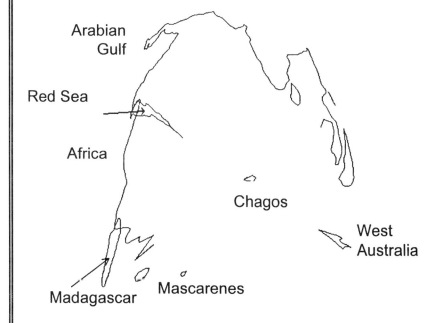

Figure. Map of Indian Ocean after resampling ("rubber sheeting") using a cubic, or third order polynomial procedure, in the GIS software Idrisi. This map amounts to a more or less complete replacement of geographical distances by biological distances. The 'inversion' of the Red Sea reflects greater similarity of the northern Red Sea to Chagos than the southern Red Sea. Madagascar to the West and the Nicobar-Andaman chain to the East are pushed further away from Chagos than the continental coast near which they are located.

an important site or stepping stone in an east-west flow of coral species. Taking this further with multi-dimensional scaling which does not 'anchor' Chagos but allows it to 'float' freely with other sites, confirmed the closeness of Chagos to eastern and western sites (1) further suggesting Chagos is an important east west stepping stone. The atolls of the Maldives, Seychelles and Red Sea are also connected biologically.

Charles R.C. Sheppard

References

1.   Sheppard, C.R.C. in press. Corals of Chagos, and the role of Chagos reefs in the Indian Ocean. In *The Chagos Archipelago*. eds. Seaward, M., Sheppard, C.R.C. Special issue of Linnean Society of London
2.   Sheppard, C.R.C. in press. Biodiversity patterns in Indian Ocean corals, and effects of taxonomic error in data. *Biodiversity and Conservation*

which each transect was measured was relatively homogeneous, and given the method used, whereby a large number of data points were recorded under line transects on each reef on each occasion, it was likely that errors from incorrect relocation were minor. The method measured gross characters on seven seaward reef slopes around both of the two northern atolls of Salomon and Peros Bañhos, each slope being divided into three depth spans: to 10 m deep, 10 to 20 m deep and 20 to 30 m deep.

Changes to reef cover had occurred in the later sampling period, despite visual impressions of totally unimpacted and vibrant reefs on both occasions (Table 15.2, top). In 1996, total coral cover of all sites pooled had fallen from 59% to 36%, and sand, leafy and encrusting red algae, and soft corals, had all increased slightly. These changes occurred mainly in the shallowest zone, that to 10 m deep, and the main cause of the decline in cover is a loss of two species of *Acropora* (Table 15.2, bottom). Replacing these two species of corals is a near doubling of apparently unoccupied substrate, and to a lesser extent by increased red algae. *A. palifera*, the most dominant of the two *Acropora* species, is a coral which thrives in turbulent, shallow areas. It had high cover in 1978 particularly on the western sides of atolls, with very low cover on the eastern sides (Fig. 15.9).

The areas which had high cover in 1978 are exposed to the generally moderate northwest trades, while the eastern and southern quadrants, which were very low in *Acropora palifera* cover, are exposed to the much more severe southeasterlies. Reasons for this change are elusive and still being investigated, but possible factors include changes in weather patterns. Disease of the corals, and bleaching, were not seen in any of the living *A. palifera*, which still is far from being a rare coral in shallow reef areas. While episodes of bleaching may have occurred a number of years ago, these causes of coral decline, so prevalent elsewhere in the world, may be difficult to determine in the case of Chagos.

Table 15.2. Main changes in a) all 42 sites, and b) shallowest sites, between 1978 and 1996. Values are percent cover of substrate, ± standard error. Depth spans are: shallowest, down to 10 m, middle, 10 to 20 m deep, deepest 20 to 30 m deep.

Category	1978	1996
a) All sites combined		
(7 reefs x 3 depth spans x 2 years)		
coral (all species)	59 ±2.9	36.4 ± 2.5
sand	1.6 ±1.0	7.8 ±1.7
sponge	<1 ± 0.2	3 ± 1.1
red algae	6.7 ± 1.2	12.5 ± 1.4
green algae	~0 ± 0	0.5 ± 0.3
soft corals (all species)	11.9 ± 1.8	16.3 ± 2.1
unoccupied substrate	19 ± 1.8	20 ± 2.1
b) Shallowest sites		
(7 reefs x 1 shallow span x 2 years)		
coral (all species)	70.6 ± 4.3	40.6 ± 3.3
Acropora palifera	17.2 ± 4.5	2.7 ± 0.7
Acropora hyacinthus	8.4 ± 3.2	4 ± 2.0
sand	0.1 ± 0.1	2.6 ± 0.8
sponge	<1 ± 0	3 ± 1.0
red algae	4.3 ± 0.9	11.8 ± 1.7
green algae	~0 ± 0	~0 ± 0
soft corals	9.6 ± 3.4	13.3 ±3.4
unoccupied substrate	15.1 ± 2.5	27 ± 3.6

Shark Densities

Another major change between the two sampling periods was a major drop in numbers of sharks (1). Two sets of diver records taken in 1975 and 1978/9 showed high numbers of five species, averaging 4.2 sharks per dive (Table 15.3). These results also agree with anecdotal observations from an even earlier period in 1972. All three sets of observations in the 1970s were taken in the same months of February and March. In February and March 1996, shark numbers were also counted and seen to be greatly reduced, to about 14% of the earlier numbers. Average numbers were only 0.6 sharks per dive which is significantly reduced (p<0.05). The total length of observing time spent underwater in 1996 was 127 hours, and this was considerably greater, though not quantified, in the periods in the 1970s. In general, numbers in the later period are still greater than may be seen in reefs in many other areas of the Indian Ocean, but, nevertheless, there undoubtedly has been a major decrease over 20 years in Chagos.

This is probably a general Indian Ocean phenomenon, not limited to Chagos. Recorded shark fishing throughout the Indian Ocean shows a catch of over 50 000 tons per year for most of the past decade at least (14). Actual landings and mortality are likely to be considerably greater than these recorded landings. While shark fishing is not permitted in Chagos waters (later section) several arrested vessels filled with large quantities of shark attest to the activity and the continuing use of the area for shark fishing.

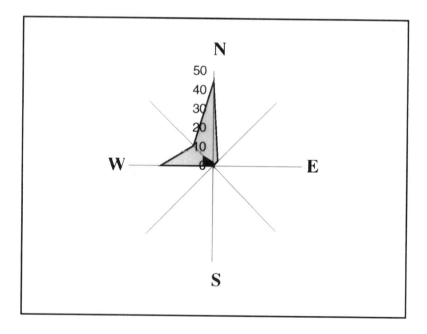

Figure 15.9. 'Radar' plot of cover by *Acropora palifera* (example of the species shown above) on transects around two northern atolls of Salomon and Peros Bañhos. Light shading is cover in shallow water in 1978, dark shading is cover in same areas in 1996. For the NW transect, values of 45% (Salomon) and 15% (Peros Bañhos) for 1978 are combined to a single average value of 30%.

Table 15.3. Summary of shark sightings by divers in Chagos, 1975 to 1979 and 1996. Source (1).

	1975 - 79	1996	Species seen in 1996 (number seen)
Number of dives	207	113	
Number of sharks seen	874	66	*Nebrius ferrugineus* (16)
			Carcharhinus albimarginatus (4)
			C. amblyrhynchos (38)
			C. melanopterus (7)
			Triaenodon obesus (1)
Number sharks per dive	4.2 ± 0.3	0.6 ± 0.1	

One other change since the 1970s with consequences to the coral reefs is the increasing use of the northern atolls by yachts. In the 1970s, two or three yachts might be observed taking shelter, while in 1996 and 1997, up to 36 may be seen at any one time, all at anchor in Salomon lagoon, most of whose shallow lagoon floor supports over 90% coral cover. The damage done to lagoon corals in such areas is considerable but unmeasured (Sheppard, C.R.C. personal observation). The lagoon of Salomon is very sheltered, and has conditions not replicated in any of the other atolls of Chagos outside Diego Garcia. Yacht owners also have developed an encampment on the islands around Salomon, though the effects of this are not likely to be significant unless new species are inadvertently introduced.

Island Ecology

Plants

Vegetation on all the larger islands in the group has been disturbed by the copra industry and nearly all the larger islands are dominated by coconut trees, though most are still fringed by the shrubs *Tournifortia* and *Scaevola* Some islands are dominated by *Casuarina* instead. These have replaced the hardwood trees which were once abundant enough to "furnish good timber" (21) and which included tatomacca and guiac. Other soft wooded trees were also abundant. Many smaller islands have, however, remained unplanted and thus remain relatively undisturbed, supporting stands of the original hardwoods and other native vegetation. About 250 higher plants including ferns have been recorded in 1997 (47,49) but none are endemic. It is thought that the original native flora numbered about 45 species (49), maybe more (31), the rest being introduced by man, mainly during 30 years of military development in Diego Garcia (Fig. 15.10). Diego Garcia is by far the largest atoll, providing about half the total land area. For these atolls, all plants and native plant numbers bear a clear relationship with island size, and there are distinct vegetation zones and plant communities (49). The number of higher plants has now probably stabilized.

There is a poor correlation between island size and diversity of lower plants (lichens, mosses, hepatics, fungi, terrestrial cyanobacteria and algae). In this case, *Cocos* is such an important substratum for lower plants that its high presence on islands of all sizes provides similar numbers of different lower plant species (33). The overall diversity of lower plants is low, as would be expected for islands of such remoteness, young age and small size.

Higher plant species in Diego Garcia

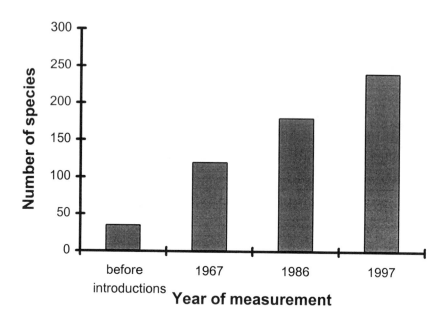

Figure 15.10. Numbers of higher plant species in Diego Garcia. The first bar represents the number of plants which probably were indigenous to the Chagos before introductions.

There is a notable lack of mangroves and groves of the screw pine *Pandanus* (31). Indigenous plant species are mostly of pantropical or Indo-Pacific distribution and numbers are limited because of the relatively low range of habitat available on small, low coralline islands, as well as by the difficulties of dispersion. Their diversity is fairly similar to that found on other Indian Ocean islands of a similar nature such as Cocos Keeling and several of the Seychelles islands.

Birds

Earlier accounts of birds on Chagos showed a high diversity (5,9,19). The main seabird nesting areas in Chagos are the islands of the Great Chagos Bank and several islands of Peros Bañhos atoll. In 1996, a total of 181 000 pairs of 16 breeding species were censused (46). A total of over 50 species have been sighted (5). Notable among the breeding birds are some such as the red-foot booby *Sula sula*, masked booby *Sula dactylatra* and lesser noddy *Anous tenuirostris* which are rapidly declining in other parts of the Indian Ocean.

The large numbers of birds transfer significant quantities of nutrients from the sea to the islands. Calculations show that they consume annually about 30 000 tons of food, of which 62% are fish and 38% are cephalopods. Through the production of guano, approximately 236 tons of free ammonia and 373 tons of phosphates are returned annually to the nearshore water and terrestrial habitats, providing a continuous replenishment of nutrients to underpin the rich vegetation. The presence of porous, limestone soils and high rainfall suggests a high degree of leaching from islands to the water, suggesting that the birds form an important link in the nutrient chain. There are several indications that birds are steadily recovering from past impacts, but nevertheless, continuing infestation by rats on the majority of islands have continued to prevent full recovery of bird populations.

Turtles

The islands are important breeding grounds for green and hawksbill turtles (4) and support the largest hawksbills so far recorded (12). Greens, *Chelonia mydas*, nest in at least four of the atolls, coming ashore in June to September during the southeast trade winds. Hawksbills, *Eretmochelys imbricata*, also nest in the northern atolls, and this species tends to breed more during the northwest monsoon between December and March. Large numbers are seen in Diego Garcia lagoon.

Human Influences

Gross Impacts, Trace Metal and Organic Contaminants

Broad scale assessment of beaches shows that Chagos is not immune to the problem of trans-oceanic floating debris. Debris, mostly plastics, but including bottles and metal containers were seen on all beaches, even forced into piles on some sand spits by currents and tides (26). Oil contamination was detected by chemical means at 38% of sites, though mostly this was at barely discernible levels and no evidence of large slicks was seen. Analytical work confirmed the lack of oil inputs into water, sediments and tissues.

Organochlorine compounds were generally at limits of analytical detection, indicating a pristine environment, and the presence of more volatile poly-chlorinated biphenyls (PCBs) and lindane indicate atmospheric transport rather than marine transport as their major route of entry. Heavy metals in tissues and sediments were exceptionally low (13), an exception being nickel in some biota from Salomon atoll; nickel is a constituent of fungicides and may have originated from use of such chemicals in previous times of copra farming. Cadmium levels, even in bird livers and eggs where bio-concentration would be expected, were extremely low and similar to those generally detected in invertebrate fauna from remote open ocean areas. PCBs and chlorinated biphenyl congeners levels were generally below quantifiable levels in sediments, though some organochlorine pesticides could be detected in bird livers and eggs at levels of 12 to 300 ng/g lipid.

On the basis of chemical contamination and aside from the global problem of floating debris, Chagos can be considered to be among the least contaminated of all reefal sites in the Indian Ocean and even in the world (13). The copra farming ended in the early 1970s, before widespread use of modern pesticides, and because of this none of the usual pesticides commonly found around the world, in elevated levels, appear in the Chagos biota.

In Diego Garcia, human occupation has increased considerably since the 1970s due to the development of a military facility, in contrast to the trend of population and nature of activity in the rest of Chagos. On the island, introductions of numerous plants has continued as already noted, together with several species of fauna. For example, the toad *Bufo* sp. is now common in Diego Garcia although no earlier records of it exist (4). Construction of accommodation has resulted in the loss of the protective ring of *Scaevola* in some places with the resultant inevitable erosion which is now countered by concrete sea walls. Almost nothing is known about the seaward reefs of this atoll, except for the fact that considerable quantities of reef-flat material were excavated for purposes of construction in the early phases of building the military facility. In the lagoon, brief work in the late 1970s showed little damage outside the immediate port area, despite dredging. No observations from the greater port construction work in the past 18 years have been published.

Fishing

Fishing is licensed by the British authorities resulting in a number of vessels being permitted to catch tuna in territorial waters of Chagos. Undoubtedly shark and other large pelagics are caught also. Unlicensed vessels are confiscated when seen and caught, though there is no data on the efficiency of detection. A limited amount of fishing near reefs is permitted for some Mauritian vessels, but fishing inside the lagoons (even entry of the vessels) is not permitted. There is some recreational fishing in Diego Garcia, but the quantities and identity of the species caught are not recorded (22).

Conservation

The UK/USA 1966 Treaty Agreement (3231 of 30 December 1966) specifically states that the whole of the Chagos Archipelago shall be available for defense purposes. In fact, the remoteness of all the atolls and banks apart from the part of Diego Garcia used as a military base probably safeguards them in the most effective way. Nevertheless, several conservation provisions exist, and: "As far as possible the activities of the defense and its personnel shall not interfere with the flora and fauna of Diego Garcia" (7). Wildlife in the British Indian Ocean Territory (BIOT) is protected under the Wildlife Protection Ordinance of 1970 and Wildlife Protection Regulations of 1984. The latter states that all marine and island wildlife of Chagos except vermin risking public health, and fish taken lawfully under existing licenses, are protected. Heavy penalties apply for infringement of the regulations, and various specific measures include prohibition of nets and spear-guns for fishing, taking of shells or corals, damage to bird and turtle nests. Controls are also applied to the importation of plant species.

BIOT is included in the UK's ratification of CITES and the Convention on the Conservation of Migratory Species of Wild Animals (Bonn Convention). Several other conservation and pollution conventions also apply. BIOT is not associated with the UK ratification of the World Heritage Convention due to the UK/US defense agreement. However, it has long been the case that the islands are treated with similar strict regard for natural heritage considerations that apply to designated sites. BIOT has now asked the UK to arrange to have the provisions of the RAMSAR Convention applied to it, and will propose possible sites for listing under RAMSAR (7). It intends also to designate Strict Nature Reserves as defined by the IUCN classification system, and to consider designating Marine Protected Areas. BIOT imposed a 200-mile Fisheries Conservation Zone around the Territory, and contracts fisheries consultants to manage the fishery including issue of licenses for tuna and inshore fishing. No fishing is permitted inside lagoons. On Diego Garcia itself, access outside the area reserved for the military facility is carefully controlled, and the authorities are co-operating with the US on a Natural Resources Management Plan.

Conclusions

Recent studies on the reefs of Chagos over a 20-year period have shown, on the one hand, that some changes have occurred including substantial reductions of some top predators and of the previously dominant shallow-water coral. On the other hand, the condition of the reefs is still among the least impacted and least disturbed of any in the Indian Ocean and possibly the world.

The causes of the decline of *Acropora palifera* are unknown; no known widespread human activity occurs on the seaward reefs slopes of the Chagos atolls to cause the decline. The shark decline is likely to be important, but whether this is due only to local and illegal catches, or whether this in some way reflects an ocean-wide collapse of sharks, is also not known. On the reefs, there is no indication of past crown-of-thorns infestation, though this species exists in low numbers throughout, and in 1996 there was no indication of coral disease, bleaching or physical damage by any of the usual and now widely-quoted causes of coral reef impact such as sedimentation or eutrophication (with the exception of the localized effects in Salomon of yacht anchoring and of port construction in Diego Garcia). The two large changes noted certainly require monitoring, but even after this decline has occurred, the numbers of sharks, and the present measures of coral 'health' (32) still suggest that these reefs are in better condition than any other. A recent report stating that Chagos has been badly damaged by Sri Lankans is baseless (24).

As far as terrestrial biota are concerned, the islands' tiny size and relatively recent emergence between about 1000 to 3000 years ago, makes them important for only a few groups. They are not of great importance in a botanical sense. Measures to encourage the survival of indigenous species of hardwood into areas where coconut trees were cleared in the 1970s appear to be succeeding, though this recovery may have taken place anyway, if more slowly. One island, Eagle on the Great Chagos Bank, is among very few tropical low islands to support a small peat deposit. Unfortunately its young age and small size has meant that its peat has not been able to preserve pollen - a useful tool for investigating pre-human vegetation. Of great importance is the fact that islands without rats and with a variety of vegetation types support globally important bird populations, which is also something which could be further encouraged, though it is notable that red-foot booby and other bird populations are increasing rapidly in Diego Garcia even where rats are present.

This archipelago is one of the very few where most management concerns are absent, simply because in most of it, people, industry, development and (for the last 20 years) agriculture are absent. There has been some controversy and claim over ownership of the islands, but a fortuitous environmental result of its present political status has been the survival of the most pristine set of reefs in the Indian Ocean. Ownership may change over the centuries, so guarantees of this condition and its exceptionally low human use may not remain certain.

New measures to include Chagos under stronger international conventions, as noted above, may help to insure that, for example, heavier fishing never takes place. The islands are too small for economically viable 'ecotourism' and diving tourism (17) to take place without causing rapid and marked damage. It may be argued that every ocean should have at least one set of reefs where no run-off, no dredging, no pesticides and no nutrient enrichment takes place. Indeed every ocean may need one. For the Indian Ocean, the reefs of Chagos are the prime candidate.

References

1. Anderson, C., Sheppard, C.R.C., Spalding, M., Crosby, R. 1998. Shortage of sharks at Chagos. *Shark News* 10:1-3
2. Anon. 1979. *Under Two Flags*. Ministry of Defence, London. pp. 100
3. Anon. 1997. *The British Indian Ocean Territories Conservation Policy*, October 1997. British Indian Ocean Territories Office, London: Foreign & Commonwealth Office
4. Barnett, L.K., Emms, C. 1997. Herpetological observations in the Chagos Archipelago, British Indian Ocean Territory. *British Herpetological Society Bulletin.* 59: 6-12
5. Bellamy, D.J. 1979. *Half of Paradise*. London: Cassell
6. Bellamy, D.J., Hirons M.J., Sheppard, C.R.C. 1975. *Scientific Report of Reef Research*. In *Joint Services Expedition to Danger Island*. ed. Baldwin, E.A. London: MOD Publication
7. BIOT 1997. *The British Indian Ocean Territory Conservation Policy*. London: Foreign and Commonwealth Office
8. Bourne, G.C. 1888. The atoll of Diego Garcia and the coral formations of the Indian Ocean. *Proceedings of the Royal Society* 43:4 40-461
9. Bourne, W.R.P. 1971. The birds of the Chagos group, Indian Ocean. *Atoll Research Bulletin* 149: 175-207
10. Darwin, C.R. 1842. *The Structure and Distribution of Coral Reefs*. London: Smith Elder and Co.
11. Doty, M.S. 1974. Coral reef roles played by free living algae. *Proceedings of Second International Coral Reef Symposium* 1: 27-33
12. Dutton, R.A. 1980. The herpetology of the Chagos Archipelago. *British Journal of Herpetology* 6: 133-134
13. Everaarts, J.M., Nieuwenhuzie, J., Maas, Y.E.M., Booij, K., Fisher, C.V. 1997. Assessment of the environmental health of the Chagos Archipelago (Indian Ocean). Abstract: *Ecology of the Chagos Archipelago, British Indian Ocean Territory*. Linnean Society of London
14. FAO 1992. *Yearbook: Fishery Statistics, Catches and Landings*. Vol 74. Rome: FAO

15. Francis, T.J., Shor, G.G. 1966. Seismic refraction measurements in the northwest Indian Ocean. *Journal of Geophysical Research* 71: 427-449

16. Gardiner, J.S. 1936. The reefs of the western Indian Ocean. I. Chagos Archipelago. II The Mascarene Region. *Transactions of Linnean Society, London* (2) 19: 393-436

17. Hawkins, J., Roberts, C. 1992. Effects of recreational SCUBA diving on fore-reef slope communities of coral reefs. *Biological Conservation* 62: 171-178

18. Heiss, G., Eisenhauer, A. 1997. Geology of the Chagos. Abstract: *Ecology of the Chagos Archipelago, British Indian Ocean Territory.* Linnean Society of London

19. Loustau-Lalanne, P. 1962. The birds of the Chagos Archipelago. *Ibis* 104: 67-73

20. McGlade, J., Spalding, M. 1997. Reef fishes of the Chagos. Abstract: *Ecology of the Chagos Archipelago, British Indian Ocean Territory.* Linnean Society of London

21. Moresby, Commander Indian Navy 1884. Untitled. *Transactions of the Bombay Geographical Society* 1: 307-310

22. Naughton, J., Tribble, G. 1994. Diego Garcia Fisheries survey. Manuscript report to BIOT, London

23. Oldfield, S., Sheppard, C.R.C. 1997. Conservation of biodiversity and research needs in the UK Dependent Territories. *Journal of Applied Ecology* 34: 1111-1121

24. Pearce, F. 1997. Paradise lost to Pirates. *New Scientist* 156: 15.

25. Pichon, M. 1978. Recherches sur les peuplements a dominance d'anthozoaires dans les recifs coralliens de Tulear (Madagasgar) *Atoll Research Bulletin* 222: pp. 477

26. Price, A.R.G., Jolliffe, A., Readman, J.W., Bartocci, J., Tolosa, C., Cattini, C., Horvat, M. 1997. Broadscale assessment and use of molecular organic markers to characterise the coastal environment of the Chagos Archipelago. Abstract: *Ecology of the Chagos Archipelago, British Indian Ocean Territory.* Linnean Society of London

27. Pugh, D.T., Rayner, R.F. 1981. The tidal regimes of three Indian Ocean atolls and some ecological implications. *Estuarine Coastal and Shelf Science* 13: 389-407

28. Rayner, R.F. 1982. The circulation and water exchange properties of Salomon Atoll (Chagos Archipelago). Proceedings of Sixth International Scientific Symposium, World Underwater Federation, London

29. Rayner, R.F., Drew, E.A. 1984. Nutrient concentrations and phytoplankton productivity in two Chagos Archipelago atolls. *Estuarine Coastal and Shelf Science* 18: 121-132

30. Reinicke, G.B., Van Ofwegen, L.P. 1997. Soft corals (Octocorallia, Alcyonacea) from the Chagos Archipelago (Indian Ocean) - species assemblages and distribution. In *The Chagos Archipelago.* eds. Seaward, M,. Sheppard, C.R.C. Special Issue of Linnean Society of London

31. Renvoize, S.A. 1979. The origins of Indian Ocean Island floras. In *Plants and Islands.* ed. Bramwell, D. pp 107-129. London: Academic Press

32. Roberts, C. 1993. Coral Reefs: Health, Hazards and History. *Trends in Ecology and Evolution* 8: 425-427
33. Seaward, M.R.D. 1997. Cryptogamic flora of the Chagos Archipelago. Abstract: *Ecology of the Chagos Archipelago, British Indian Ocean Territory*. Linnean Society of London
34. Seaward, M.R.D., Sheppard, C.R.C. eds. 1998. *Ecology of the Chagos Archipelago, British Indian Ocean Territory*. Linnean Society of London
35. Sheppard, A.L.S. 1984. The molluscan fauna of Chagos (Indian Ocean) and an analysis of its broad distribution patterns. *Coral Reefs* 3: 43-50
36. Sheppard, C.R.C. 1979. Interspecific aggression between reef corals with reference to their distribution. *Marine Ecology Progress Series* 1:237-247
38. Sheppard, C.R.C. 1980. Coral cover, zonation and diversity on reef slopes of Chagos atolls, and population structures of the major species. *Marine Ecology Progress Series* 2: 193-205
39. Sheppard, C.R.C. 1980. The coral fauna of Diego Garcia lagoon, following harbour construction. *Marine Pollution Bulletin* 11: 227-230
40. Sheppard, C.R.C. ed. 1981. Report on Scientific work completed on Joint Services Chagos Research Expedition 1978/9. In *Chagos: The 1978/79 Expedition*. ed Griffiths J.D. pp 1-52. London: MOD Publication
41. Sheppard, C.R.C. 1981. The groove and spur structures of Chagos atolls and their coral zonation. *Estuarine Coastal and Shelf Science* 12: 549-560
42. Sheppard, C.R.C. in press. Changes in corals over 18 years. In *The Chagos Archipelago*. eds. Seaward, M,. Sheppard, C.R.C. Special issue of Linnean Society of London
43. Sheppard, C.R.C., Wells, S.M. 1988. *Coral Reefs of the World. Volume 2: Indian Ocean, Red Sea and Gulf.* UNEP Regional Seas Directories and Bibliographies. IUCN, Gland, Switzerland and UNEP Nairobi
44. Stoddart, D.R. 1971. Rainfall on Indian Ocean Coral Islands. *Atoll Research Bulletin* 147:1-21
45. Stoddart, D.R., Taylor, J. 1971. Geology and ecology of Diego Garcia atoll, Chagos Archipelago. *Atoll Research Bulletin* 149: 1-237
46. Symens, P. 1997. Ecological importance and conservation needs of breeding seabirds in the Chagos Archipelago. Abstract: *Ecology of the Chagos Archipelago, British Indian Ocean Territory*. Linnean Society of London
47. Topp, J.M.W. 1988. An annotated check list of the flora of Diego Garcia, British Indian Ocean Territory. *Atoll Research Bulletin* 313
48. Topp, J.M.W. 1997. Geography and climate of Chagos. Abstract: *Ecology of the Chagos Archipelago, British Indian Ocean Territory*. Linnean Society of London
49. Topp, J.M.W. 1997. Higher plants of the Chagos. Abstract: *Ecology of the Chagos Archipelago, British Indian Ocean Territory*. Linnean Society of London

Section III:

Management

Chapter 16

Management Status and Case Studies

Nyawira Muthiga, Sibylle Riedmiller, Eleanor Carter, Rudy van der Elst, Judy Mann-Lang, Chris Horrill & Timothy R. McClanahan*

*Authorship by sequential order of contribution

This chapter describes four case studies of management of coral reefs and associated fisheries. The first two case studies cover management of Marine Protected Areas (MPAs): the national government programs of Kenya, and a private MPA in Zanzibar. The second two case studies cover different approaches to fisheries resource management: at the national level in South Africa and at the community level, supported by donor aid, in northern Tanzania. The case studies describe the origin of their specific management problems, trace the history, justification and objectives of management, and give recommendations for future programs.

National Marine Protected Area Management

Kenya's National Programs for Marine Protected Areas

The Marine Protected Areas (MPAs) of Kenya fall under the responsibility of the Kenya Wildlife Service (KWS) under the Wildlife Conservation and Management Act of 1989. Kenya Wildlife Service is a government parastatal organisation under the Ministry of Natural Resources, mandated with the management of Kenya's 52 marine and terrestrial protected areas, with the following objectives (13):
1) To ensure the conservation of Kenya's biological diversity and functioning of ecological processes.
2) To ensure viable populations of selected endangered species.
3) To enhance environmental quality, such as the protection of catchment areas and reduction of soil erosion.
4) To enhance educational and scientific value by maintaining near natural ecosystems.

Table 16.1. Tourist based activities within Kenya's marine protected areas.

ACTIVITY	REMARKS
1. Glass bottom boat tours	Tourists and local residents hire boats to the coral garden, often goggling is involved. A daily park fee is charged.
2. SCUBA diving	Tourists and locals are taken to the reef edge, wrecks and caves for SCUBA usually by companies affiliated with hotels. This activity requires a daily park fee.
3. Snorkeling.	Visitors who swim from shore to the reef using mask and snorkel are charged a daily fee.
4. Sailing	Modern and traditional sailboats including dhows and ngalawas ply the waters of MPAs either for tourist or transit purposes in parks, and fishing in reserves. Sailing does not require a fee.
5. Windsurfing	Tourists and locals can windsurf in MPAs without paying a fee.
6. Jet skiing	Several hotels have watersport desks that hire out jet skis. MPA managers by legal notice restrict the area and time for this activity.

5) To provide for development and diversification of recreation and tourism.

6) To contribute to the economic and environmental well being of Kenya.

7) To protect and preserve selected areas of scenic beauty or special interest

The MPAs of Kenya include four Marine National Parksand six Marine National ReservesChapter 7, Table 7.4) and 2 of the reserves (Watamu and Kiunga) also designated as Biosphere Reserves under the UNESCO Man and the Biosphere Program. No form of extractive utilization is allowed within marine parks but traditional forms of fishing are allowed within marine reserves. The MPAs of Kenya include coral reefs, mangrove forests, and seagrass beds (see Chapter 7, 31).

Management and Activities within MPAs

The daily management of individual MPAs falls under the administration of a Park Warden, assisted by a cadre of staff including rangers with paramilitary training. Rangers provide security, collect revenue and interact with visitors. Research and monitoring activities are carried out by research staff based at the coast regional headquarters, assisted by rangers, and by scientists from other national and international universities and institutions. Community education and extension work is carried out by community officers.

Several tourist activities are allowed within Kenya's MPAs (Table 16.1). Tours to the coral reefs in glass bottom boats are currently the most popular activity, frequently also involving snorkeling and SCUBA diving. Wind surfing, jet skiing, sailing and dolphin watching in traditional and modern craft are also common. In most parks daily entry fees and annual boat fees are collected, except in the Mombasa park and reserve where a new system of management based on bed-nights in adjacent hotels is being experimented with (Box 16.1, 28).

Role of Coastal Communities in MPAs

Artisanal fisherfolk living adjacent to or close to marine reserves fish in the reserves using a variety of gear types, including traps, hook and line, beach seines and gill nets. Dugout canoes are the main types of fishing vessel, but

---

Box 16.1. The Beach Management Program: An Experiment in MPA Management

The Beach Management Program (BMP) is a joint agreement between beach operators, hotel owners and the Kenya Wildlife Service (KWS) working in or near the Mombasa MPA. This program was developed after a stakeholders workshop in 1992 that identified ways to reduce conflicts between these groups. The agreement is voluntary and hotels, upon membership, charge their guests $ 0.5 per bed night and remit these funds to KWS. Visitors staying at these hotels are allowed unlimited daily entry to the Mombasa MPA during their stay. In return KWS maintains security on the beach, assists beach users with information, and cleans beaches of non-biodegradable materials. The boat operators benefit through greater assistance to the Mombasa Boat Operators Association (MBOA), which maintains a local monopoly over glass bottom and sailing boats using the Mombasa MPA. MBOA has also benefited from donations of boat equipment and maintenance materials, improved business, since boat operators market only the boat and tour charges and not the park fee, reduced annual boat fees, and through a safer and more aesthetically pleasing environment. Hoteliers benefit through improved security and less harassment of their guests, lowered park fees for their guests, and cleaner beaches. KWS benefits through a timely and less cumbersome collection of revenue which allows it to concentrate on their primary business of protecting biological diversity. The daily management of this program falls under the responsibility of the park manager. A BMP Advisory Committee composed of hotel managers, KWS, various local tourism associations and local government administration, such as the local District Officer meets monthly to coordinate the BMP. Despite teething problems, such as delays in payment of BMP dues by some hotels, the Mombasa MPA has recorded high visitor satisfaction especially in relation to visitor safety and beach cleanliness.

N.A. Muthiga

---

sailing canoes with outriggers, called *ngalawas*, are also used. Currently the Fisheries Department licenses all fishing activities in Kenya including the fishing area and type of gear. MPA managers can, however, limit the type of gear and the area of fishing by posting legal notices. Currently only fishing using traditional and non-destructive gears and techniques is allowed in marine reserves. Many local fisherfolk are not licensed, however, and the Fisheries Department lacks basic information on their numbers. Additionally, transient fishers often use an area on a seasonal basis, usually for a specific resource, such as lobsters or sea cucumbers. Consequently MPA managers lack reliable information about the levels of fishing in their MPAs (29,30).

Local people also own glass bottom boats and *ngalawas* for sailing. In the Mombasa MNP, boats traditionally used for fishing have been converted for sailing trips and tours. Along the beaches of most MPAs there are also curio and handicraft businesses, tour sales, and camel rides (in reserves only) licensed by the Tourism Department. KWS does not have any control over the

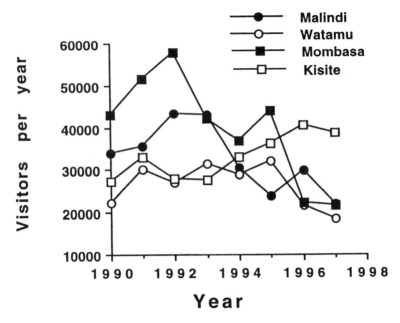

Figure 16.1. Annual number of visitors to Kenya's marine parks. Pie chart inset represents the percentage of park visitors who reside in Kenya (25%) versus those from outside Kenya (75%).

numbers and types of activities on the beach but has some influence through membership in the Tourism Licenses Processing Committee. Many of the beach operators do not originate from communities living adjacent to MPAs, causing resentment in local enterprises.

Tourism Support for MPAs

The link between KWS and the tourist sector is strong as much of the tourist industry in Kenya is based on wildlife, and KWS funds its entire recurrent budget from tourist revenue (Fig. 16.1). Additionally 70% of tourists that come to Kenya travel to the coast and account for 75% of visitors to the MPAs (34). Over the last few years, the tourism sector has been a major force in the drive to increase the number of conservation areas, leading to establishment of the Mombasa Marine Park and Reserve and to the Diani-Chale Marine Reserve. The beach management program of Mombasa marine park is a good example of a mechanism that has allowed close collaboration between KWS and the private sector (Box 16.1). Additionally individual hotels support awareness programs, including the annual marine environment day and the Kenya sea turtle committee (KESCOM), among others.

National Perspectives on Collaborative Management in Kenya

Benefits of Collaborative Management. In the past, biodiversity conservation in Kenya tended to emphasize the international and scientific values and benefits of biodiversity. Many Kenyans depend largely on biological resources at the subsistence level, including agriculture, livestock, fisheries and logging, making these resources vulnerable to overuse. Given this overwhelming dependence on biological resources, it has become increasingly clear that new strategies that incorporate local and national interests must be developed. At the national level, there is a new awareness that sustainable economic development and biodiversity are intricately linked and, as a signatory to the Convention on Biological Diversity (CBD), the government of Kenya has shown its commitment to biodiversity conservation. Within institutions mandated to manage natural resources, such as KWS, Fisheries and Forestry Department, more and more emphasis is being put on integration of communities and other stakeholders in management. All these institutions are in the process of developing new policies in line with requirements of the CBD. The framework within which collaborative management (especially inter-institutional collaboration) can work at the national level is, however, lacking.

Framework for Collaborative Management. The evolution of KWS in the late 1990s developed because of the need for a more participatory form of management that involves many stakeholders including local communities, regional and national government authorities, scientists, the private sector and NGOs (27). Currently, several instruments to enhance collaboration between different government sectors exist including Memorandums of Understanding or Agreement (MOUs and MOAs) between KWS and Coast Development Authority (1994), Kenya Marine and Fisheries Research Institute (1995), Forestry Department (1994), Fisheries Department (pending) and the National Museums of Kenya (pending).

KWS has also formed partnerships with NGOs and local and international universities and organizations to enhance collaboration in monitoring and other scientific studies, such as with the Wildlife Conservation Society's Coral Reef Conservation Project, Birdlife International and WWF. In terrestrial protected areas local associations and landowners have been encouraged to manage wildlife in collaboration with KWS. Additionally, joint projects such as the Tana Delta GEF project, and the GTZ integrated forest management project in the Shimba Hills emphasize integration of stakeholders. These kinds of arrangements are beginning to be developed for marine protected areas, such as the beach management program of the Mombasa MPA (Box 16.1), and a joint project with WWF to develop a participatory management plan for the Kiunga Marine Reserve.

Constraints, Conflicts and Their Resolution. The constraints to collaborative management can be divided into those that occur within KWS (internal) and those that occur nationally or globally (external). Internal constraints include the lack of adequate skills in collaborative management, inadequate resources, a wildlife policy which has not yet been endorsed by the Kenyan Parliament, lack of clear enforcement of policies, and managers that adhere to outdated management methods. External constraints include the inequality in resources, variation in skills, and lack of trust among partners, lack of recognition of key players, political interference, and overlapping mandates.

In order to facilitate collaborative management in Kenya's MPAs, the following issues must be tackled. Adequate resources must be provided for management. KWS is responsible for all wildlife in Kenya, but daily operations depend mainly on revenue collected from a few very popular terrestrial parks. It has become difficult over the years to maintain normal operations in all protected areas without donor support. It is important, therefore, that the Kenya government allocate money for some costs, especially in areas where benefits are shared, such as for security and antipoaching activities.

The lack of a clear understanding of the issues and conflicts and threats to biodiversity in protected areas is also a hindrance to resolving conflicts. Serious effort must be put into identification and sensitization of key players in the needs and benefits of biodiversity conservation. The Diani-Chale Marine National Reserve has met with resistance from the local fishing communities mainly because the communities were not sufficiently involved in the planning process (Chapter 7). Additionally, in Kenya, local leaders and authorities including village elders, chiefs and local councilors interact closely with communities and organizations at the grass-roots level., and must be included as important mediators in resolving conflicts (29).

Unfortunately, none of the MPAs of Kenya have integrated management plans that recognize the inter-multi-disciplinary nature of coastal resource use issues, and outline mechanisms for resolution of these issues(11,14). Their development will be an important step forward,m currently being supported by the KWS/Netherlands Wetlands conservation and training program.

Many conflicts in MPAs arise from the need for ever-shrinking resources by an increasing population. Recent surveys have indicated decreases in fisheries catches in some marine reserves (29,30). Alternative resources would greatly reduce the pressure on MPAs, for example seaweed farming, aquaculture of blacklip pearl oysters or sea cucumbers. High value marine products that do not damage the environment have yet to be exploited in Kenya. The Fisheries Department, Kenya Marine and Fisheries Research Institute and KWS should work together to study the feasibility of such developments.

A lack of awareness of the true benefits of MPAs and coastal resource issues among communities, local government authorities, and other MPA stakeholders often leads to problems in resolving conflicts. The KWS has carried out some awareness programs under the auspices of the Integrated Coastal Area Management Committee. These programs target many sectors including schools, hotels, MPA users, and fishing communities. The sustainability of such programs over the long term is, however, in question as most programs are temporarily funded by donors.

MPAs, Tourism and Fisheries

The Kenya Wildlife Service is a government parastatal body that has been exempted by the Kenya Government from the state corporations Act. This allows for the collection and retention of revenue, but KWS does not receive any funds from the Kenya government. There are 52 protected areas in Kenya but very few generate a net revenue and, therefore, many programs depend on donor funds. Some, but not all MPAs, collect entry fees and, although tourism and fisheries are the main activities within MPAs, KWS does not issue associated licenses, therefore is missing these sources of income and the ability to control the number of licenses. Despite the hope and prediction that KWS could become self-sufficient and generate enough revenue to cover recurrent and development costs, a slump in tourism prevented this possibility (Fig. 16.1). Consequently, KWS requested financial support from the Kenya government to cover key operation areas and, especially, security. This would enhance the ability of KWS to provide adequate services and security to visitors as well as fund activities for biodiversity conservation.

Even with government intervention, there is still a need to develop ways to improve and increase the management of MPAs. The beach management program is one method that benefits KWS, boat operators and hotels, but is troubled by delays in payments by members with no legal instruments to enforce payment (Box 16.1). In Mpunguti marine reserve a project funded by USAID has provided motorized boats and fishing gears to assist local fisherfolk to fish further offshore. In principle this should reduce fishing pressure in the Reserve. The development of other alternatives including aquaculture, reef restoration and artificial reefs are also being explored.

A Private Marine Protected Area: Chumbe Island Coral Park of Zanzibar

A recent survey commissioned by the World Conservation Monitoring Center (WCMC) in selected African countries has reviewed private initiatives where wildlife conservation is a primary activity (54). The study found that more than half of all protected areas in South Africa are under private ownership and management, while Namibia, Botswana and Kenya also have a considerable number of private protected areas. Generally, countries which have had free-market economies for a long time and in which the purchase of freehold property is permitted, have attracted private individuals and corporate bodies to invest in conservation-oriented initiatives (54).

The study concluded that 'the private sector makes an invaluable contribution to biodiversity conservation', and that 'private protected areas provide a variety of important conservation and other services'. The overall conclusion was that 'there is much to learn from the private sector, particularly with respect to the economies of managing protected areas through sustainable use of wildlife resources, ecotourism and other enterprises' (54).

Though endowed with a wealth of natural resources that have a high conservation value, Tanzania has so far not attracted private investment in conservation. Two decades of socialist policies and large-scale expropriations of land resulted in a weak economy, and made the country highly dependent on donor funding. This was compounded by the fact that, until recently, tourism was not encouraged and, therefore, the revenue potential of conservation areas could not be realized. Tanzania traditionally has a well-established system of world-renowned terrestrial protected areas, while the several marine parks designated along the coast in the early 1970s remained only on paper. The result is that rampant dynamite fishing and other destructive fishing methods have severely damaged many coral reefs (Chapters 5 and 6, 45).

Geography and Biology

Chumbe Island is a small coral island of around 16 ha situatted eight miles southwest of Zanzibar town and close to the shipping channel between Zanzibar and Dar es Salaam. The island was not included in any previous proposed MPAs (36) and it is unlikely that it would have been made a conservation area without private initiative. A company was created in 1992, Chumbe Island Coral Park Ltd. (CHICOP), for the establishment and management of the MPA. Chumbe Reef Sanctuary was gazetted in December 1994 under provisions of the Zanzibar Fisheries Act of 1988, and is now a fully managed conservation area.

Chumbe is bordered on its western shore by a fringing reef of exceptional diversity and beauty. Scleractinian coral cover and species diversity are among the highest in the region, and the reef contains more than 90% of the coral species recorded from East Africa (Veron, J. personal communication). Over 370 species of fish, belonging to 50 families, have been recorded, including giant groupers *Epinephelus lanceolatus* and 16 species of butterflyfish, a group thought to be good indicators of coral quality and diversity (32).

Most of Chumbe island is covered by an undisturbed coral rag forest, an ecosystem of potentially high conservation value which is little researched and rapidly diminishing elsewhere in Zanzibar and Tanzania (6). The island is a refuge for the rare and threatened coconut crab, *Birgus latro,* which elsewhere is widely eaten and used as bait in fish traps. In cooperation with the Zanzibar Commission of Natural Resources, CHICOP started a sanctuary for the endangered and endemic Ader's duiker (*Cephalophus adersi*) to protect it from poaching.

Institutional Structure of Reserve Management

The Government of Zanzibar approved the project as a tourism investment based on the provisions of the Zanzibar Investment Protection Act (1986), and gave CHICOP the lease of the project site on Chumbe Island. CHICOP was also given management contracts for the whole of the island and the reef sanctuary. An Advisory Committee was established with the assistance of the Institute of Marine Sciences (IMS) of the University of Dar es Salaam, Ministry of Agriculture and Natural Resources, the Department of Environment (DOE), and village leaders of neighboring fishing villages. Several joint programs have been conducted with government departments including a rat eradication program and school environmental club excursions.

Ongoing and planned research programs, with the Institute of Marine Sciences, are focusing on coral recruitment, coral transplantation, measurements of temperature and tidal currents, coral reef monitoring, and fish population dynamics. Priority is given to research essential for reef and forest conservation and only non-destructive and non-extractive methods are allowed.

Management Plan and Operations

Management of Chumbe Island has followed the common practice of donor-funded conservation projects. A management plan was produced which was endorsed by the Advisory Committee and is now the basis for project operations. The following program components were implemented between 1992 and 1997:

(1) Baseline surveys and species lists on the island's flora and fauna.

(2) Negotiations to gazette the Chumbe Reef Sanctuary.

(3) Production of the Management Plan.

(4) Employment and training of park rangers.

(5) Establishment of forest and marine nature trails.

(6) Procurement and production of educational materials.

(7) Rat eradication.

(8) Establishment of a sanctuary for Ader's duiker.

(9) Rehabilitation of the lighthouse keeper's house for use as headquarters and visitor center.

(10) Construction of visitor 'eco-bungalows'.

Many of the above projects were completed with some donor support, but others were privately funded. The Chumbe Island Nature Reserve is now registered with the World Conservation Monitoring Center in Cambridge (UK) as a recognized private conservation area. CHICOP was also chosen as an innovative conservation project implementing Agenda 21 and exhibited at EXPO 2000.

Management Experiences

In 1991, Chumbe was uninhabited and seemed to face little immediate threat. Similar to other historic sites in Zanzibar it appeared an abandoned place with signs of past glory, such as an old lighthouse built during colonial rule in 1904, and other ruined historical buildings. A lighthouse keeper was still on the payroll of the Harbors' Authority but had not been residing on the island for decades. Fishing was traditionally not allowed on its western side, as small boats would have obstructed vessels plying the shipping channel to Dar es Salaam, and also because the whole area surrounding the island was a military area where the army routinely conducted exercises from the adjacent Chukwani coast. In addition, few boatmen could then afford an outboard engine to go to this most distant of the islets surrounding Zanzibar town. Therefore, conditions appeared quite favorable for the establishment of a protected area at Chumbe, as no traditional users were displaced or had to be incorporated or compensated.

Resource Users. With the advent of economic liberalization, beginning in the early 1990s, conditions in Zanzibar changed rapidly. The expanding tourism industry took possession of the most attractive sites and also created a rapidly growing market for marine products. High prices made fishing an attractive occupation for urban youths and destructive fishing methods, such as dynamite and *kigumi* increased (Chapter 7, 21,23). Although the sanctuary had been gazetted by the Government of Zanzibar, enforcement was left to rangers employed, trained and equipped by CHICOP. Protecting the Park from fisherfolk turned out, however, to be a minor challenge compared with the demands and bureaucratic requirements posed by government departments.

Former fisherfolk from adjacent villages were employed and trained as park rangers and stationed on the island. When patrolling, rangers first inform encroaching fisherfolk of the protected status of the Chumbe Reef Sanctuary. Many fishermen unaware of this information will obligingly and immediately exit from the protected zone. The majority of fisherfolk are, however, already aware of Chumbe's status. Consequently, the rangers explain the importance of

CHICOP, MPAs and coral reefs. CHICOP rangers carry no weapons and have limited powers of enforcement. They can only try to verbally convince fisherfolk to leave. The names of frequent offenders are turned over to the police. Fisherfolk experiencing problems at sea are assisted by the rangers which has contributed to the success of the project. Over 110 vessels and approximately 500 people in four years have been assisted by Chumbe rangers. including helping to fix broken sails, leaks, and engines, providing food and water, and offering radio use and refuge from bad weather. Consequently, good relationships have developed between rangers and most fisherfolk.

There has been a clear decline in the total number of incidents over time, particularly from 1995 (Fig. 16.2). This suggests that the rangers' methods have been successful although the decline was slow. The distinctive peaks in 1994 to 1995 coincide with the months of Ramadhan or fasting when fishing pressure increased as fisherfolk prepared for the fast and to increase their earnings to buy quality food, clothes and gifts. Others used the protected area for anchorage in the evening to prepare their food and break their fast. Rangers noted that there was also a greater number of attempts to fish at night during these years.

It was also possible to crudely gauge the changes in attitude over time (Fig. 16.2 bottom). The reactions of people who were annoyed and verbally abusive to threatening violence if stopped from anchoring reached a high of 49% in 1994. The vast majority of aggrieved people originated from near Zanzibar town but were not necessarily fisherfolk. On a few occasions the rangers' lives were threatened, but no physical attacks were ever recorded. Sometimes as many as 15 boats simultaneously dropped anchor in the protected area and buoys were cut. These incidents suggest an organized attempt to challenge the status of the park. There is also evidence of political motivation as after the general elections in late 1995, infringements from category (c) reduced to 14%.

Management and Bureaucracy. Much investment had to be spent in patiently exploring legal possibilities for the protection of the island and campaigning for changes in the legal framework. Zanzibar had no policy or legal framework for conservation areas until 1997 and has not yet established a government body to manage protected areas. Before 1995, there was also no legal way to establish non-governmental organizations. Therefore, the project had to be presented as an investment in a permanent tourism facility. This had important financial implications as official Zanzibar investment policy favors high investments in large tourism projects. The present minimum for foreign investors is US $4 million, which encourages multinational hotel chains. Palm thatched roofs preferred by smaller hotel projects are discouraged and tented camps are also not approved in Zanzibar. Chumbe Island project, therefore, became a challenge for a moderate investor to create and manage a low-impact conservation area. Altogether seven different government departments with ambiguous and sometimes divergent policies were involved in the process over several years. A clause of the Zanzibar Fisheries Act of 1988 provided the legal justification.

Difficulties in Developing an Eco-Island

The very substantial bureaucratic delays tripled implementation time from two to seven years and quadrupled costs from an original estimate of US $250 000 to

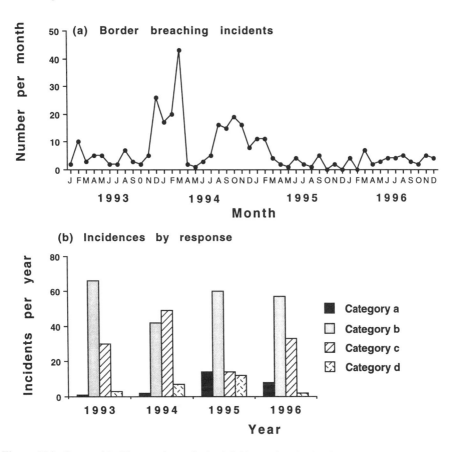

Figure 16.2. Reported incidences of unauthorized fishing and anchoring in Chumbe Island Marine Park as (top) total number of monthly incidents and (b) by the different categories of response to the rangers' requests. Rangers categorized their encounters with fisherfolk as (a) those who did not know Chumbe was a MPA and who left without argument when informed, (b) those that knew the status but still tried to anchor and fish, (c) those aware of the status but were angry about being unable to anchor or fish, and (d) those that were aware but thought they were outside the boundaries.

US $1 million. Some government departments still regard CHICOP as just another tourism venture. Conservation activities are only beginning to receive official local recognition and support. CHICOP has no favored tax status or exemption from ever-increasing costs of land rent, licenses, permit fees and taxation. In 1998 this reached a minimum fixed amount of US $10 000 per year or about one third of operating costs.

Tapping the ecotourism market was considered critical for revenue generation. Revenue expectations were originally high but had to be reduced as ecotourism is only a small portion of the tourism market. Few visitors make it out to Chumbe. Many other conservation activities in Zanzibar are donor-funded and little or none of the management costs are passed on to visitors. As a consequence, most local nature destinations can be visited at low costs while a private offshore island attracts a smaller and, perhaps, more elite, ecologically-minded or adventurous visitor.

The tourism market is split between backpackers coming to the country individually, and an increasing number of up-market tourists brought by international tour operators through prepaid package programs. Backpackers opt for low-cost destinations. Up-market tourists are also taken to unmanaged areas, or areas managed by donor-funded projects, at little cost to the operator. From 1997, CHICOP has offered day excursions that include boat travel, guidance through the marine and forest trails, hire of snorkeling gear and a meal. Few travel agents have, however, shown interest because it is more profitable to organize local islands trips than earn the modest commissions from CHICOP. They can even organize trips to unmanaged offshore islands, with no park management costs, more profitably. CHICOP is, therefore, facing uneven competition from unmanaged nature destinations and donor-funded projects that subsidize conservation. CHICOP management has learned that local marketing has a limited potential for generating the income to professionally manage the reserve and subsidize local environmental education.

Advice and Future Needs

The Chumbe experience suggests that private management of marine protected areas is technically feasible and efficient even when the enforcement machinery of the national government is not available or ineffective. The costs of private management are probably considerably lower and the incentives to struggle for commercial survival much stronger, than would have been the case with a donor-funded project. Experiences also suggest that the commercial viability of private conservation projects is at risk when cumbersome and expensive bureaucratic requirements increase the costs of investment and innovative project designs. Overseas marketing is, therefore, seen as one way to access wealthier markets directly.

More fundamental issues in Tanzania, and probably many other African countries, are the lack of long-term security and supportive legal and politico-administrative environments. For example, land tenure in Tanzania and Zanzibar is only available on leasehold, in contrast to other African countries, such as South Africa, Namibia, Botswana and Kenya, which attract considerable private investment in protected areas (54). The Environmental Management Act (1996) allows for management by private bodies but still requires that income be passed on to the government management authority. This will not encourage a private commitment to conservation.

Secondary constraints to private investment include corruption, immigration and worker protection laws, and the instability of tourism. Cumbersome bureaucratic procedures and the wide discretionary powers of civil servants encourages corruption and increases costs of investment. Investors who may wish to retire in the country of their project need to renew their permits every year at a considerable cost. Labor legislation makes it difficult to dismiss employees even when they are found breaking the law. Finally, capital recovery from investment is entirely dependent on tourism which is particularly volatile and sensitive to political turmoil associated with elections, bad weather and perceived or real security and health risks such as cholera and malaria epidemics.

In a recent analysis of the investment climate in African countries, Rauth (39) concluded that, in spite of major policy reforms towards economic liberalization, many African countries still use control-oriented approaches that have resulted in rule-driven bureaucracies with little service mentality. Institutional practice assume that a guilty private sector threatens a benign public sector, producing cumbersome procedures and regulations that give government officials wide discretionary powers. The combination of ambiguous environment and high taxes creates a hothouse for corruption where business people need to pay bribes to survive and remain competitive while the corrupt practices of business people further leads the government to erect more stringent controls. As a result, a vicious circle of increasing delays and corruption is maintained (39).

There is much to be changed before countries like Tanzania and Zanzibar become more attractive for private investment in general and private commmitment in particular. It is extremely encouraging, however, that Chumbe's park rangers, or those who directly felt the increasing degradation of their environment and had no access to donor money, are now the staunchest conservationists on Chumbe. They proudly and competently show visitors the reef and the forest while vigilantly protecting it. Without the rangers' enthusiasm and commitment Chumbe Island would not have succeeded, the investor would have been demoralized, and ended the project before completion.

National Fisheries Resource Management

South Africa's National Fisheries Programs

South Africa is bounded by both Indian and Atlantic Oceans, providing a range of habitats, physical features and considerable biological diversity (Chapter 3). The East Coast, from the Mozambique border to the Eastern Cape is a relatively high energy coastline and remarkably straight, with few bays or capes (42,43). The continental shelf is narrow, between 3 and 11 km, especially in KwaZulu-Natal. The shelf edge is generally so close to shore that the total shelf area is small. There are many minor, and a number of medium sized, rivers that open into the sea and opposite these, centuries of silt deposition has created shallow muddy banks which extend outward from the coast (15). Nonetheless, the total shallow-water area available for harvesting fish with non-industrial gear is limited.

South Africa's major commercial fish resources are located along the south and west coasts, where large demersal and pelagic fisheries can yield up to 1 million tons per year (35). Towards the east, there is a greater diversity of species and more individual fishing operations, but the fisheries are of a smaller scale and the total catch is more modest (46). Here, fisheries, such as the reef-associated line fish, squid and prawn, are managed by input controls, especially effort limitations.

History of the Reef Fishery

The development of the reef fishery along the East Coast can be broken up into distinct sequential historical phases, not unlike many other fisheries, with exploration, development, consolidation and overexploitation as the series of phases. The separate stages are discussed here to demonstrate the various research and management responses and actions implemented during each of these phases.

Initial Exploration and Development. The rich and untapped fish resources of South Africa's East Coast reefs were discovered by colonist fishers who, around the turn of the century, commenced the harvesting of the most sizable and valuable species. Initially this was conducted from steam powered vessels operating out of Durban HarborAs geographic fishing range increased some ventured into Mozambique and Eastern Cape waters, distances of more than 500 km. The primary gear used was hook and line, usually attached to a stout rod with a non-geared reel, to permit operating in depths of 100 m or more. The number of vessels fluctuated considerably from year to year but reached a total of 20 around 1930.

For many years this fishery flourished, targeting primarily four species of very large endemic sparid reef fish, the red steenbras *Petrus rupestris*, the seventyfour *Polysteganus undulosus*, the Scotsman *Polysteganus praeorbitalis* and the poenskop *Cymatoceps nasutus*. Some of these fish could attain individual weights of 40 kg and most were in excess of 7 kg. For close to a century there was no management of this reef fishery except for the issuing of permits. Initial capital costs and limited port facilities did, however, provide some limits to the total effort. Fisheries officers in Durban maintained excellent records and these indicated an erratic and apparently declining trend in reef fish landings at that time (7). Scientific research was, however, limited to museum collections, and descriptions of economically important and scientifically curious species. Most applied research was devoted to locating new fishing grounds.

Primary Species Collapse. For many years the reef fishery prospered, with reef fish becoming an increasingly popular commodity on South African fresh fish markets and in restaurants. Most plentiful of these species was the seventyfour, a gregarious sparid fish that undergoes massive spawning aggregations at a few select sites during spring and summer. These aggregations formed the basis of the fishery and contributed to the enormously high initial catch rates. Inevitably, catches declined and this prompted fisherfolk to call on the government for assistance and to introduce protective measures. The State, however, did not consider this fishery important at this time and failed to react. Fishers continued fishing the seventyfour for several more years until in the early 1960s a spectacular drop, by up to 85%, caused economic extinction of this fishery. This was later shown to have occurred when the stock reached 25% of the virgin spawner biomass (10,47,51, Fig. 16.3). Management measures were introduced many years later in 1986 but no detectable stock rebuilding has occurred.

During the last few years of the seventyfour fishery, the Oceanographic Research Institute (ORI) in Durban initiated a study on this species (1). Although it proved to be a post-mortem, the data collected was of immense value in launching stock rebuilding initiatives in later years. More importantly, the biological and age determination material collected in the 1960s is simply no longer available today due to the overexploited status of seventyfour.

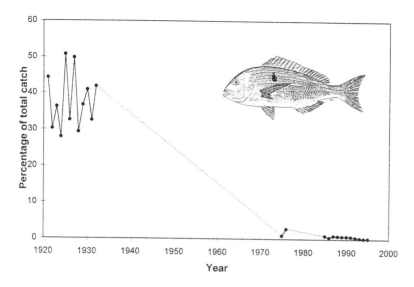

Figure 16.3. Changes in abundance of the seventy-four (*Polysteganus undulosus*) as reflected by their historical proportion of the total linefish catch.

Recreational Fishery Development.

Recreational interests can be traced back to the 1920s when day-charters were offered to anglers. Around 1950, however, pioneering and innovative fisherfolk built small plywood outboard engine boats and joined the reef fishery. The recreational skiboats are highly versatile and launch from any of the 50 or more recognized skiboat launching sites along the coast. This means that the boats can be launched in areas where fish are known to congregate. This fishery grew spectacularly and in the late 1990s there was an estimated 45 000 trips per year (Fig. 16.4). Domestic tourism from inland regions significantly supplemented the fishing effort from coastal communities, and this gave rise to considerable seasonal variation associated with peak vacation periods. There is, however, also evidence of inter-annual fluctuations. For example, lower effort in the 1970s is attributable to high fuel prices, while after 1985, a suite of management measures caused a reduction in recreational fishing effort.

For many years the recreational fishery targeted reef fish. Rapid improvements in technology made it easier to locate reefs and soon there was growing competition between commercial and recreational operators. Although the steadily declining reef fish stocks resulted in many recreational fishers turning to pelagic gamefish species, the pressure on reef fish stocks continued to increase as total fishing effort escalated. To date there has been no attempt to limit entry to the reef fishery by recreational users. Some control over launching sites exists, but this is primarily directed at safety and seaworthiness rather than resource management.

Changed Gear Efficiency.

In common with many fisheries, the reef fishery underwent significant changes in gear, including new technology such as

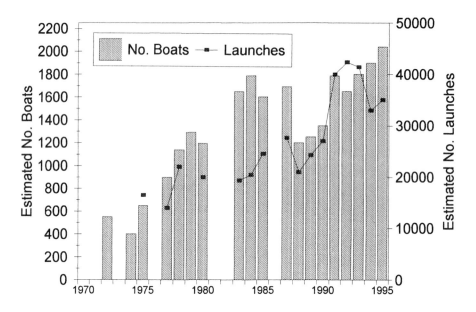

Figure 16.4. Annual growth in recreational skiboat fishing in KwaZulu -Natal as reflected by the number of boats and total number of yearly launchings.

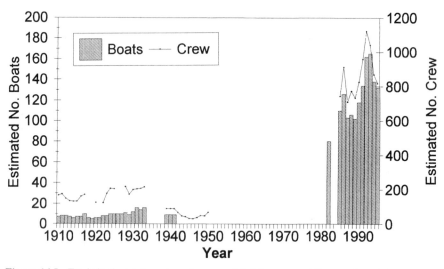

Figure 16.5. Tends in the total number of commercial fishermen and licenses issued for KwaZulu-Natal from 1910 to 1995.

echo sounders, radar and later GPS navigation systems. The most significant change, however, was that the harbor-based commercial lineboats were progressively being replaced by the smaller but more versatile skiboats. Thus, while about 15 boats were operational in the 1920s, the commercial skiboat numbers reached 150 in the 1990s (Fig. 16.5). Greater versatility of the recreational fishery resulted in major changes in the distribution of fishing effort (Fig. 16.6). Gear changes contributed to improving fishing efficiency and effective fishing effort, hence altering the catch rate and the bio-economic equilibrium. Improved technology maintained or improved catch rates but the overall effect was to lower fish stocks.

Serial Overfishing.

Serial Overfishing. Following the early collapse of the seventyfour, several of the other large endemics displayed signs of collapse. With the growth in effort, the fishery was forced to switch to less desirable fishes. Thus, species previously discarded were now gaining favor, resulting in a clear succession of serial overfishing. In the late 1990s the seventyfour and red steenbras together were less than 1% of the catch by weight. Effectively, the endemic reef fish fauna has been depleted and reached economic extinction (47,50). Consequently, commercial fishing has slowed and the recreational sector has increasingly turned to the more migratory pelagic species such as king mackerel, kingfishes, jacks and tunas.

The poor state of the fishery motivated descriptive and biological research into the biology of reef fish. Official government support was still not forthcoming except for the State's Department of Sport and Recreation which along with self-funding from the ORI (an NGO) revealed that many of the reef fish were protogynous and hence had inherently vulnerable lifestyles (16,17). The lack of quantitative information was a critical shortcoming that was recognized by ORI. A concerted effort was made to address this problem and included the establishment of a large-scale fishery monitoring program known as the National Marine Linefish System (NMLS, 52). This initiative began a countrywide collection of catch and effort statistics from all sectors of the line fishery. Now approaching its 20th year, there are at least 1 000 000 annual fisher outings documented. The NMLS provides one of the finest long-term fishery data sets in Africa. Other projects included the introduction of a large-scale tagging study (49) and an age determination and growth modeling facility at ORI (20). Greater attention was devoted to coordinating reef fish research at the national government level, and this considerably reduced the costs of research.

Much of the research was conducted as part of the South African Network for Coastal and Oceanic Research's (SANCOR) line fish initiative, which produced five-yearly reviews and plans for managing line fish problems in the future. Initially, in 1978, five major areas of research activity were identified by the SANCOR program (40). These were:

(1) To investigate the biology and reproductive characteristics of the main species concerned.
(2) To develop and implement a long-term monitoring strategy involving catch and effort.
(3) To investigate the dynamics of larval distribution and recruitment.
(4) To collect basic biological information and track fish migrations through a tag and recapture program.
(5) To conduct age and growth determinations of key species of reef fish.

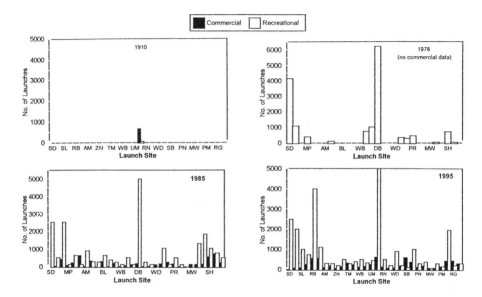

Figure 16.6. Expansion of fishing effort from 1910 to 1995 in KwaZulu-Natal. Data expressed as number of commercial and recreational boat launchings at various sites along the coast of KwaZulu-Natal ranging from Sodwana Bay (SD) in the north to Ramsgate (RG) near the Eastern Cape border, in the south. Durban is shown as DB.

These objectives were funded, undertaken and completed by five research institutions within one decade (53).

Management

Initial Management. Recognizing that the reef fishery was in decline, proposals to manage the fishery were not difficult to motivate. In 1984, ORI drafted a management plan that would accommodate the fish's biology. Management plans were created such that future fishing would progressively shift away from slow-growing endemics towards less vulnerable pelagics (51). Growing public concern for the declining fisheries assisted the creation of participatory forums and interest groups. In particular, the formation of the South African Marine Linefish Management Association (SAMLMA), as an advisory interest group to the Minister, proved to be of great value.

The first plan of SAMLMA was to categorize all species into groups depending on their biology. Fish were, therefore, grouped into the following categories:
(1) Open - fish species not under serious threat and, therefore, open to exploitation.
(2) Regulated - species not considered inherently vulnerable but in need of controlled harvesting.

(3) Protected - heavily exploited fish in need of stock rebuilding and stricter harvesting controls.
(4) Critical - stocks of fish species that have collapsed, especially aggregating spawners in need of protection while spawning.

A legal size limit was established, as the size at which 50% attainment of sexual maturity of individual species occurred. In addition, fisherfolk were categorized as commercial, semi-commercial and recreational, and each was given different levels of access. Commercial and semi-commercial categories were subjected to permit control and the total number of permits was fixed. Entry of recreational users was not limited but daily bag limits were imposed. This plan caused considerable public debate and was eventually accepted and incorporated into national and provincial legislation.

Follow-up Management. For about six years the fishery operated under the initial Plan. Much of the research and monitoring during this time was directed at detecting changes in abundance, evidence of stock rebuilding and general recovery of the fishery. A notable product was the improved information, its synthesis and increased availability to management (48). Research went through an important developmental phase where greater emphasis was placed on quantitative and predictive aspects of fisheries science. Models were developed and modified for local conditions and accommodated such features as sex change, slow growth and longevity important for sparid and serranid species.

Commercial fishing effort was slowing while recreational effort continued to increase. Additionally, there was evidence that the fishery was shifting away from the reef fish towards the less vulnerable pelagics. While population declines may have been halted there was no evidence for the return of the overexploited endemics. The lack of a positive trend for these species heralded a revision of the original Plan. Furthermore, more robust data on stock status was at hand and thus Plan 1 was considerably revised. The categories of fish were altered and described as follows in Plan 2:

(1) Bait - small and abundant species primarily used for bait.
(2) Recreational - fish of greater value to recreational users than commercial fishers.
(3) Exploitable - species that underpin the commercial sector and which can be demonstrated as being sustainably harvested.
(4) Restricted- species that have vulnerable life styles and reduced abundance, usually showing a 50% catch-rate decline.
(5) Critical - species proven to be grossly overexploited.

The distinction of fishers remained the same. Plan 2, however, tried to further separate the species used by recreational and commercial users. This reduced some user-conflict and gave greater responsibility to specific user groups to protect specific species for their own sustainable use.

Stock Rebuilding Strategies and New Policies. There is no good evidence that the endemic reef fish stocks have recovered. This is not altogether surprising for two reasons. First, it is known that most of these species are slow growing such that the interval between spawning and subsequent maturity is measured in decades rather than years. Furthermore, it seems increasingly likely that other species have occupied niches vacated by the endemic species. Visual underwater surveys on some overfished reefs indicate an abundance of reef fish, such as parrotfishes, fingerfins and wrasses, but none of the type that freely takes bait.

Despite reasonably well structured management forums and legislative mechanisms, the potential to introduce protective legislation remains problematic. In particular, the continuous indecision, ad-hoc nature of actions and demands for absolute scientific proof has led to calls for major changes. These concerns first arose when South Africa was developing a new fisheries policy and the issues of sustainability were being discussed. Final policy proposals presented to parliament recommended an entirely new Fisheries Act known as the Living Marine Resources Bill which has now been introduced. Among the recommendations is the adoption of a concept known as the Operational Management Procedure- OMP (8). An OMP is a management plan that has a series of pre-determined and pre-negotiated actions that come into force once certain identifiable indicators or target reference points have been reached. These indicators are biological or fishery reference points, most already well known (9). Limit or threshold reference points indicate the lowest tolerable level of stocks. Once this point is reached a stock rebuilding strategy is introduced.

The present effort in reef fishery management includes collecting available information to develop OMPs for all the major fisheries species. This information on OMPs will be used to rebuild stocks and simplify management. A further significant development has been the study of Marine Protected Areas as refugia and possible management alternatives for reef fish. Though MPAs have been in existence for many years, none were created specifically for the protection of fish. It is only recently, following innovative studies (4) that their potential for stock enhancement is being recognized. The new fisheries legislation developed in September 1998 includes a number of positive steps to promote the rebuilding of stocks. This includes the creation of a new category of protection the "Specially Protected Species" which are not permitted to be taken or killed by any person or activity. The seriously threatened seventy-four is included in this category which will serve to contribute to the long term recovery of this species as well as provide 'experimental opportunities' to determine whether slow growing reef fishes can in fact recover after serious stock depletion.

Advice and Future Needs

From the above information it is apparent that the reef fishery along the east coast of South Africa, having passed through several phases (Fig. 16.6), is now largely overexploited, with several endemic species having reached levels of economic extinction. Most of the research and management actions were post-mortem, with management plans only being implemented after the event. It is also clear that original concerns of fisherfolk were ignored and consequently government must accept a major part of the blame. Such delays compromised the possibility of developing co-management options, as subsequent regulations were necessarily harsh and unavoidably not popular. It is increasingly apparent that the rebuilding of the reef fish stocks will only be achieved with a considerable temporary sacrifice by fishers and through the determination of all groups, especially the State.

A further factor of concern has been the multiple use of the reef fish resources, especially by recreational fishers who have no limitation placed on their numbers. Moreover, recreational fishing does not conform to the conventional bio-economic fishery model (12), as profits need not exceed costs. This means that recreational fishing can continue long after extracting the resource is unprofitable. OMPs hold great promise as no fishing group will be exempted and the establishment of clear thresholds probably represent the most workable management arrangement for a diverse reef fishery (37). There is a need to involve user participation in the OMP process and there are several forums and interest groups that are active in making recommendations. Too much grass roots debate is, however, not always useful as it can dilute actions to the lowest common denominator at a time when focused leadership and strong action is of greater importance. The South African experience suggests that the following ingredients of an OMP are essential to its success:

(1) A major reduction in fishing effort.
(2) Establishment of reef fish reserves.
(3) A commitment to support research, monitoring and implementation.
(4) An efficient monitoring program to detect and track changes in the fishery.
(5) Determination, refinement and publication of key fishery indicators and reference points.

There is much more at stake than salvaging a few fisheries as the biological diversity of the marine environment is also threatened by the regional overexploitation of reef fish. Options to reverse this trend are waning and immediate coordinated action on a regional scale is needed. The establishment of strategically designed and managed marine protected areas is also one action likely to hold promise (2). Several South African fisheries scientists have used tag and recapture studies to developed models that can assist in determining the optimal size of MPA's for different species of reef fish (3,4). Such initiatives need to be developed on a regional scale for maximum effect.

Community-Based Resource Management

Tanga Region, Tanzania.

Tanga Region is the most northern coastal region of Tanzania and includes the three coastal Districts of Muheza, Pangani and Tanga Municipality. The Region extends 180 km south from the Kenyan border and supports a number of ecologically important and diverse habitats including coral reefs (see Chapter 6), mangrove forests, seagrass beds and coastal forests. It is also important as a turtle feeding and nesting area and provides feeding grounds for over 1% of the world's population of crab plovers (*Dromas ardolea*).

There is little formal employment in this region and, therefore, these natural resources largely support the people in Tanga's 86 coastal villages and two towns. Fishing is, by far, the most important economic activity, being ranked first in all villages and employing between 25% and 80% of the working population (19). Farming is the second most important activity with trading (fish mongering, restaurants, small shops, clothes), small scale livestock rearing, wood cutting, seaweed farming and salt boiling also being significant sources of income. Larger scale commercial users of coastal resources include trawlers, traders and exporters of fish and other marine products, saw millers and traders of timber products, the sisal industry, the tourist industry, and solar salt producers.

Prior to the program described below, natural resource management was the sole responsibility of government agencies. However, this type of management coupled with the lack of resources, both human and financial, resulted in inaction of government and communities to deal with management problems leading to the emergence of six key issues. These were declining fish catches, coastal erosion, deforestation, low agricultural production, beach pollution and lack of basic social and financial services in most villages (19).

Institutional Framework

The failure of sectoral, directive management by government agencies resulted in government willingness to try a collaborative, integrated approach to the management of coastal resources. This is now being developed under the auspices of the Tanga Coastal Zone Conservation and Development Program which is funded by Irish Aid with technical support from the World Conservation Union (IUCN). The Program started in 1994 and is an integrated conservation and development initiative implemented in a number of three-year phases. The overall goal of the Program is the sustainable use of coastal resources in Tanga Region for the benefit of present and future generations of residents, as well as other people and programs in Tanzania and East Africa.

To achieve this goal, the Program works with key government sectors of the three coastal administrative Districts within Tanga Region and a number of village communities. A small number of priority issues in localized areas is identified using an IUCN project cycle (38). The cycle starts with identification of stakeholders and their management needs. Management options are tried on a small scale before successful ones are incorporated into everyday practice. Monitoring and evaluation are an integral part of the cycle, allowing for an adaptive and evolutionary approach to the development of management strategies. This strategy allowed the program to address the priority issues of two of the larger fishing communities, Kigombe and Kipumbwi, whose fishing grounds cover 25% of the coastline.

Collaborative Management

The formation of a management partnership between local communities and government to manage common property fisheries was undertaken in three stages. The process was initiated with the training of key government and village personnel and the conducting of participatory socio-economic and resource assessment surveys (listening phase). The second stage started with the selection of two pilot villages where a rapport between government personnel and villagers had been established through the participatory surveys. Village-based resource users determined their priority issue and then formed management committees to deal with the issue. The government officers and villagers involved in the survey made the information arising from the meetings available to all users in the region. Information included reef status, fish population status, coral diversity, identifying villages that use the reef, importance of the reef for different fisheries, fishing gears and fish species.

After discussions the users gave the committees the mandate to develop management proposals on condition that the proposals were subsequently discussed and agreed on with all fishers and fish traders. The third stage was one of negotiation and implementation of management actions. In this stage the committees developed the principles of management, overall management objective, purpose of the action plan, results and indicators. Users then defined the areas for management, who would be involved, and their activities. Activities included reef closures, special rules for closed areas, general rules for the larger management area, and auxiliary activities required to support management. The latter included trials of fish aggregating devices, exchange of beach seine nets, and the identification of future activities to control trawlers.

The committees defined how rules will be enforced, who will do what, the penalties, and the training required for effective enforcement. Committees also developed a program for monitoring and review of management based on verifiable indicators and presented their management objectives, results and actions in village meetings. Draft plans arising from these meetings were submitted to the district and central governments for approval. In the village meetings attendance, minutes and support for the actions were recorded. Overall attendance was high, as was support for the action plans (18).

The Management Plans

Management plans addressed declining income from fisheries and, the overall objective of increasing income through higher fish catches, reflected this objective. The objective is to be achieved through a series of conservation measures including the reduction of fishing pressure, diversification of fishing activities, and reductions of the numbers of fishers. Key results were:

(1) the reduction of illegal fishing (enforcement of existing regulations).
(2) a reduction of legal but destructive techniques.
(3) closure of reefs to extractive resource use.
(4) trials of fish aggregating devices.
(5) reduction in fishing pressure through controlling the number of visiting fishers.

These management action plans represent the agreed strategy of both Districts and users and are now supported by village by-laws and by the central government's Fisheries Regulations of 1994.

Effectiveness of Management

The first activity to be initiated as part of the management plans was the provision of patrol boats manned by villagers and marine police to provide stricter law enforcement and control illegal fishing, especially the use of

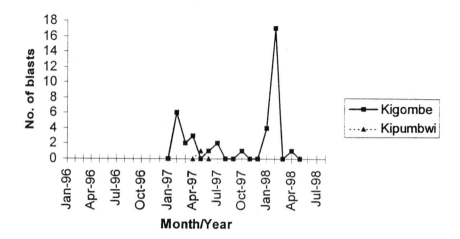

Figure 16.7. Number of dynamite blasts recorded within the management areas of Kipumbwi and Kigombe since January 1996. Incidences of dynamite fishing were recorded in logbooks by village committee members and fishers. Logbooks also recorded action taken by the patrol unit and the outcome of that action.

dynamite. Unfortunately, before the advent of management there was no data on how many dynamite blasts there were within the management areas. Anecdotal reports suggest, however, that there were approximately two blasts per day at Kipumbwi and three to five per day at Kigombe. These figures were given for spring tides when dynamite fishing is most intense.

Patrols initiated toward the end of 1995 initially controlled dynamite fishing (Fig. 16.7). However, dynamiting resumed in February 1997 because of the ineffectiveness of the marine police and village militias to deal with threats of violence used by the dynamiters. It was eventually brought back under control in March 1998 with the assistance of Navy personnel. The use of the Navy to support the patrols was enabled by the signing of an agreement between the Navy, District government and village governments. There has been only one blast since March 1998 and the perpetrators were arrested and their boat impounded.

There has also been a significant increase in the successful sentencing of fishers convicted of dynamite fishing. Previously, convicted fishers were given fines between US $3 and 7.50, but recent convictions have resulted in fines of US $500 and/or imprisonment for two years. This improvement resulted directly from a greater awareness among prosecutors and magistrates of the damage caused by dynamite fishing, achieved through workshops. Stricter enforcement has also led to an increase in the number of fishers who have valid fishing licenses. This, in turn, has led to raised revenue for district governments with Tanga Municipality receiving the unexpected income of US $11 700 from license fees.

Once enforcement was established other management actions could be implemented. This included the closure of three reefs to extractive use, two in Kigombe and one in Kipumbwi. These reefs include one example of each of the reef types found in Tanga region, a coastal reef, an inner patch reef and an outer patch reef (see Chapter 6). Although the closure of these reefs had

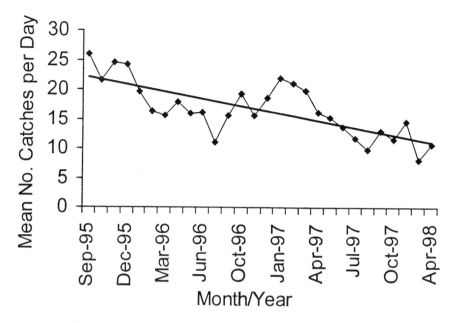

Figure 16.8. Mean number of fish landings per day at Kigombe fish receiving station.

been agreed on by the majority of users, the maintenance of their status was made possible by improved patrols and law enforcement. Initially there were a number of infringements reported from the closed areas but the fishers were arrested and fined by the village government and subsequently there were no reported incidents.

Monitoring systems for fish catches established prior to and during plan implementation have shown a trend towards reduced numbers of landed catches (Fig. 16.8). This may be due to a reduced number of visiting vessels or fishers avoiding taxation by landing catches at other sites. To determine the cause of this decline, the number of fishing boats leaving was being recorded (5), but insufficient data preclude firm conclusions. Over the period of reduced dynamite fishing and reef closure, effort, total catch and catch per gear showed a slight decline for traps, handlines and gillnets (Fig. 16.9a,b,c). Declines were not as severe as expected and have not produced complaints. In fact villager perceptions' are of rising fish catches. This may arise from catches not being recorded or from the observed rise in catch per gear from beach seines associated with reduced fishing effort (Fig. 16.9d). An additional reason is that these seine nets are now taking fish that would otherwise have been removed by dynamite fishers. Since dynamite and beach seines are both unselective and because beach seines catch small fish (Chapter 2) they may be the first to benefit from reduced effort and dynamite fishing. Alternatively beach seines maybe outcompeting other gear types.

One problem in implementation was the delays in dealing with destructive but legal fishing techniques such as trawling and beach seine nets. Trawling is undertaken by private, joint-venture (Tanzanian and foreign partners) companies based in Dar es Salaam. Management plans and Fisheries

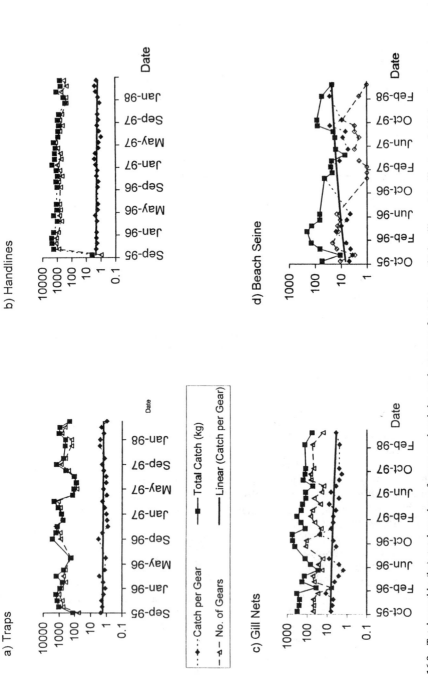

Figure 16.9. Total monthly (kg), total number of gears used and the catch per gear for (a) traps, (b) handlines, (c) gillnets and (d) beach seine nets recorded at Kigombe fish receiving station.

Regulations make trawling, within the management areas, illegal. This has reduced but not eliminated trawling, because there is no clear policy or guideline from the central Division of Fisheries for restricting trawling. Patrol boats have stopped and boarded trawlers but captains insist that the patrol boats have no jurisdiction over trawlers and are only answerable to authorities in Dar es Salaam. Further action is not taken by patrols as they are under instruction from Dar es Salaam to only report this type of incident. Each time an incident occurs it is reported to the central Division of Fisheries but no reply is received. To break this seeming impasse, the Districts and Regional authorities have now proposed that all the reefs in Tanga Region be included in an artisanal fishing zone which will be legislated with its own regulations and enforcement procedures.

Beach seine nets are used extensively throughout Tanga and have probably caused coral destruction on a number of reef flats (24). Added to their direct destructive effect on the benthos is their very small mesh size, of about one centimeter, and, in many cases, the cod end is lined with a fine weave plastic or gunny sacks which releases only water and not small fish (Chapter 6). To counter small mesh sizes and the use of liners, village bylaws were passed that stated that beach seine mesh sizes should be greater than 2.5 inches, and that liners should not be used. Enforcement of the bylaws against liners has been successful, but enforcement of the regulations for mesh size has been difficult. The reason is that many net owners are influential members of the village and government communities. Negotiations to exchange and ban beach seines are underway, but this remains a problem.

Financial Sustainability of Management

The assumption made by most conservation initiatives is that sustainable use can be achieved and management can also be economically sustained through the profits from well-managed resource extraction. Key to this is the building of institutions that have sufficient financial resources. Management costs are likely to be those associated with enforcement, provision of technical assistance, training, and monitoring and evaluation. The cost of running one patrol unit, including equipment depreciation, per year is about US $5000 (25) and the other costs are likely to double, if not treble, this total. Thus, it could cost a minimum of US $10 000 per year to finance one village management unit. Given that there will be around nine such units, or three in each district, then the annual cost of management per district will be around US $30 000.

Despite abundant natural resources, Tanzania is a poor country dependent on donor assistance. Development of the private sector, including local communities, is often hampered by heavy taxation (see above). It is, therefore , difficult to raise finances for management costs through increasing the tax burden, finance has to come from existing revenues. Revenue in the fisheries sector in Tanzania is raised through export royalties, licensing fees and a fish catch levy. Export royalties are collected by the central government whereas licensing fees and one half of the fish catch levy is paid to the district government. The other half of the catch levy is paid to the village government. Typically the fish catch levy is between 10% and 15% of the total value of the catch and is paid by the seller to the local fisheries officer. Larger villages or fisheries centers such as Kigombe have an estimated annual fish catch of around US $60 000 giving an estimated revenue of US $3000 to the district and the same amount to the village government (26).

Muheza District and Tanga Municipality have three large fishery centers and so could theoretically collect US $9000 per year from levies. It is estimated that Pangani District revenue will, however, be lower at US $6000 because there are only two large fisheries stations, Pangani town and Kipumbwi. When estimates of revenues from licenses are included, fisheries revenue for Tanga Municipality could be in the region of US $20 000, Muheza District US $14 000 and Pangani District US $12 000. These figures are far short of the estimated needs for effective management. It is clear that cost sharing mechanisms must be found to ensure the long-term sustainability of management. Other partners being considered are the central government, retention of export royalties, village governments, Tanzania Revenue Authority and the private sector. Proposals for central Government support and for the use of export royalty retention have already been submitted.

Advice and Future Needs

The Tanga experience of using a collaborative approach to management of reef and reef fisheries resources has given noticeable results within two years and has shown that villagers are prepared to deal with issues and implement solutions. Progress was largely attributable to the support of users and by focusing on a small number of priorities and the critical actions required to rectify the problems. This was reflected in the setting of clear objectives and receiving consensus for the village action plans. Additionally, participatory resource assessments were another important tool in changing attitudes and building better relationships between villagers and government officers. These assessments were the start of participatory dialogues.

The assessments showed that knowledge of reef and fisheries resources of the villagers was high and exceeded that of some government officers. Resource users displayed considerable knowledge and awareness of the state of health of their coastal resources. There were, however, differences between villagers' perceptions and independent observations. Consequently, it is important that perceptions are tested independently during assessments. Thus, ongoing monitoring and regular evaluations, such as every six months, are needed to check how well anticipated changes match field measurements. These meetings were also very useful in the community learning process. The process of reaching agreement is, however, lengthy and requires many meetings with good leadership and well defined agendas.

Villagers are more effective in controlling offenders from their own than from other villages. Moreover, the expectations of villagers for government officers can be too high and unrealistic given the government's inadequate resources. Villagers also do not readily recognize limits to the use of firearms and detainment of offenders without solid evidence. Additionally, as in the case of trawlers, it is often the lack of clear policies and shared implementation that hampers conservation. Government support is critical to the success of collaborative management as government personnel are needed to provide good, timely technical and policy advice and to objectively monitor progress. Government staff do, however, require substantial technical support at times, as they are inexperienced in dealing with many of the diverse management issues.

For example, both government staff and villagers required technical training in site assessment, participatory methods, fisheries management techniques and the implementation of monitoring and evaluation. Transparency in decision making, at all levels, is also essential so that stakeholders are aware of the current status of decisions.

Success requires the development of economically sustainable institutions, strong inter-institutional arrangements and mechanisms for financing management. Reliable and simple monitoring systems that evaluate the effectiveness of management are also required. Work on developing these mechanisms is ongoing and will largely depend on effective support from the central government and the continuing commitment of local government and villagers.

Conclusions

Historical accounts of the four different management activities above show that much of the conservation initiatives have arisen from a perceived crisis in the protection of marine species or ecosystems. These crises stimulated different responses in each situation, but conservation and management often took the form of protected areas or restrictions on resource users. Kenya's MPAs were created to stop unregulated overfishing and associated habitat destruction with the recognition that MPAs could make money from burgeoning beach tourism. MPAs were unsuccessful in Tanzania because of an impoverished government and the lack of sufficient beach or marine tourism. Consequently, a private MPA, reorganization of the countries marine and fisheries regulations, and local collaborative community efforts were responses to these limitations. The wealthier central government in South Africa did not, however, take great interest in their reef-related fisheries until the crises of their lost endemics was made clear by fisherfolk and an active NGO. Over time, however, the interaction between NGOs, resource users and the central government has been instrumental in developing MPAs and sophisticated fisheries restrictions that should improve the conditions for preventing further fishery collapses.

All the case studies above suggest that people are aware of the condition of their natural environment and that they will make a variety of efforts, depending on local limitations, to conserve dwindling resources. Individuals, communities, and even central governments each play important roles but also have limitations, and partnership problems that make it difficult for any single sector to competently conserve resources. All of these cases show that conservation is difficult, particularly financially, but possible if there is a broad-based societal support for conservation efforts and viable mechanism for sharing the responsibilities of conservation. In some cases, such as the South African sparid fishery, the first battle is often over before conservation initiatives are begun, but here there is also hope that the institutions and human organization formed around this crisis will be better prepared to respond to future environmental problems (44). In many cases, key institutions or people are the backbone of conservation efforts and they require auxiliary support from other institutions and society to achieve their goals. Scientists, fisherfolk or other observers of nature play the important role of informing society and managers of potential problems and actions and can, therefore, structure the policy debate's required for management plans and actions (22). Management, regardless of its form or history, needs to work on the elements of establishing key players, cooperative partnerships, collection of information and communication to improve the chances of success.

References

1. Ahrens, R.L. 1964. *A Preliminary Report on the Biology of the Seventy-four Polysteganus undulosus (Regan) in Natal Waters.* MSc Thesis, University of Natal, Durban
2. Attwood, C.G. 1997. Towards a New Policy on Marine Protected Areas for South Africa. *South African Network for Coastal and Oceanic Research.* Occasional Report No 2
3. Attwood, C.G., Bennett, B.A. 1994. Variation in dispersal of Galjoen (*Coracinus capensis*) (Teleosti: Coracinidae) from a marine reserve. *Canadian Journal of Fisheries and Aquatic Science* 51: 1247-1257
4. Attwood, C. G., Bennett, B. A. 1995. Modeling the effects of marine reserves on the recreational fishery of the South-Western Cape, South Africa. *African Journal of Marine Science* 16: 227-240
5. Beckley, L.E., Govender, A., Mann, B.Q., van der Elst, R.P. 1997. *Artisanal Fisheries Management Consultancy Report.* Oceanographic Research Institute: Durban
6. Beentje, H.J. 1990. *A Reconnaissance Survey of Zanzibar Forests and Coastal Thicket.* FINNIDA-COLE, Zanzibar
7. Bell-Marley. 1925. *Report of the Natal Fisheries Department. Administrators Office Pietermaritzburg, Province of Natal.*
8. Butterworth, D.S., Bergh, M.O. 1993. The development of a management procedure for the South African anchovy resource. *Special Publication in Fishery Aquatic Science* 120: 83-99
9. Caddy, J.F., Mahon, R. 1995. *Reference Points for Fisheries Management.* FAO Fisheries Technical Paper No 347
10. Chale-Matsau. J.R. 1996. *Age and Growth of the Queen Mackerel (Scomberomorus plurilineatus) and Seventy-four (Polysreganus undulosus) off KwaZulu-Natal..* MSc Thesis, University of Natal, Durban
11. Chebures, B. 1989. *Mombasa Marine National Park and Reserve Management Plan.* Kenya Wildlife Service: Nairobi
12. Clark, C.W. 1985. *Bioeconomic Modeling and Fisheries Management.* John Wiley: New York
13. Consultant. 1991. *Kenya Wildlife Services: A Policy Framework and Development Program 1991-1996.* Kenya Wildlife Service, Nairobi
14. Erftemeijer, P., Mwakoyo, D. 1995. *Information and Management Review of Kisite-Mpunguti Marine National Park and Reserve.* Kenya Wildlife Service, Nairobi
15. Flemming, B.W., Hay, E.R. 1988. Sediment distribution and dynamics on the Natal continental shelf. In *Coastal Ocean Studies off Natal, South Africa: Lecture Notes on Coastal and Estuarine Studies*, ed. Schumann, E. H.

16. Garratt, P.A. 1986. Protogynous hermaphroditism in the Slinge, *Chrysoblephus puniceus* (Gilchrist and Thompson, 1908) (Teleostei: Sparidae). *Journal of Fisheries Biology* 28:297-306

17. Garratt, P.A. 1995. *The Offshore Linefishery of Natal. II. Reproductive Biology of the Sparids Chrysoblephus puniceus and Cheimerus nufar.* Report Oceanographic Research Institute: Durban No. 63

18. Gorman, M., Urono, G., Semtaga, S., Mfuko, A., Kabamba, J., Mfuko, M., Challenge, L., Mosha, R., Kwalloh, H., Mahanyu, M., Seumbe, A. 1996. *Assessment of Participation and Support for Pilot Village Environmental Committees.* Tanga Coastal Zone Conservation and Development Program: Tanga

19. Gorman, M. 1995. *Report on Socio-Economic Study / Participatory Rural Appraisal.* Tanga Coastal Zone Conservation and Development Program: Tanga

20. Govender, A. 1994. Growth of the king mackerel (*Scomberomorus commerson*) off the coast of Natal, South Africa form length and age data. *Journal of Fisheries Research* 20: 63-79

21. Guard, M. 1997. *Dynamite Fishing in Southern Tanzania.* Wildlife Conservation Society of Tanzania, Dar es Salaam

22. Hass, P.M. 1997. *Scientific Communities and Multiple Paths to Environmental Management. In Saving the Seas,* eds. Brooks, L.A., VanDeveer, S. D. pp.193-228. College Park, Maryland: A Maryland Sea Grant Book.

23. Horrill, J.C. 1992. *Status and Issues Affecting the Marine Resources around Fumba Peninsula.* COLE-Zanzibar Environmental Study Series

24. Horrill, J.C. 1996. *Coral Reef Survey: Summary Report.* Tanga Coastal Zone Conservation and Development Program, Tanga

25. Horrill, J.C. 1997. *An Evaluation of the Enforcement Trials.* Tanga Coastal Zone Conservation and Development Program: Tanga

26. Horrill, J.C., Kalombo, H., Karia, W. 1998. *District Revenues from Fisheries Taxation.* Tanga Coastal Zone Conservation and Development Program, Tanga

27. Idwasi, E., Rotich, N., ole Somoire, D., Kathurima, C., Taiti, S. 1994. *Wildlife Human Conflicts in Kenya: A Five Person Review.* Kenya Wildlife Service: Nairobi

28. Kavu, B. 1993. *Report on the Mombasa Boat Operators Association Financial Management Seminar.* Kenya Wildlife Service, Nairobi

29. McClanahan, T.R., Glaesel, H., Rubens, J., Kiambo, R. 1997. The effects of traditional fisheries management on fisheries yields and the coral-reef ecosystems of southern Kenya. *Environmental Conservation* 24: 1-16

30. McClanahan, T. R., Muthiga, N. 1988. Changes in Kenyan coral reef community structure due to exploitation. *Hydrobiologia* 166:269-276

31. McClanahan, T. R., Obura, D. 1995. Status of Kenyan coral reefs. *Coastal Management* 23: 57-76

32. Mildner-Fiebig, S. 1995. *Fish Species List and Management Report on the Chumbe Reef Sanctuary.* CHICOP, Zanzibar

33. Muthiga, N. A. 1996. *Report of the KWS Strategic Planning Workshops : Coast Region.* Kenya Wildlife Service, Nairobi

34. Muthiga, N. A., McClanahan, T. R. 1997. The effects of visitor use on the hard coral community of the Kisite marine park, Kenya. *Proceedings of the 8th International Coral Reef Symposium* 2: 1879 - 1882
35. Mutsambiwa, M., van der Elst, R. P. 1996. *Management of Living Aquatic Resources. In Water in Southern Africa.* SARDC. pp. 99-124. Harare
36. Ngoile, M.A. K. 1989. *Development of National Marine Park Systems in Zanzibar Islands.* Institute of Marine Sciences, Zanzibar
37. Penney, A.J., Griffiths, M.H., Attwood, C.G. 1997. *Management and Monitoring of the South African Marine Linefishery.* South African Network for Coastal and Oceanic Research, Occasional Report No 3
38. Piccotto, R., Weaving, R. 1994. *A New Project Cycle for the World Bank? Finance and Development.* World Bank, Washington
39. Rauth, R. 1997. *Bureaucracy killing business in Africa.* Financial times, Dar es Salaam
40. SANCOR. 1979. *Marine Line Fish Research Program.* South African National Scientific Programs Report No. 37
41. Scheinman, D., Mabrook, A. 1996. *The Traditional Management of Coastal Resources.* Tanga Coastal Zone Conservation and Development Program, Tanga
42. Shannon, V. 1989. *The Physical Environment. In Oceans of Life Off Southern Africa.* ed. Payne, A.I.L., Crawford, R.J.M. pp. 12-27. Vlaeberg: Cape Town
43. Shillington, F.A. 1993. East Coast Oceanography. *Proceedings of the Second South African Marine Linefish Symposium* 2: 7-13
44. Thomson, M., Trisoglio, A. 1997. *Managing the Unmanageable. In Saving the Seas,* eds. L.A. Brooks., VanDeveer, S.D. pp. 107-127. College Park, Maryland: A Maryland Sea Grant Book
45. Pearson, M. 1989. *Coastal and Marine Environmental Problems in the United Republic of Tanzania.* UNEP Regional Seas Reports and Studies No. 106
46. van der Elst, R.P. 1988. *Shelf Ichthyofauna of Natal. In Coastal Ocean studies Off Natal, South Africa,* ed. Schumann, E.H. pp. 209-225. Springer Verlag: New York
47. van der Elst, R.P. 1989. *Marine Recreational Angling in South Africa. In Oceans of Life Off Southern Africa.* ed. Payne, A.I.L., Crawford, R.J.M. pp. 164-176. Vlaeberg: Cape Town
48. van der Elst, R.P., Adkin, F. 1991. *Marine Linefish: Priority Species and Research Objectives in Southern Africa. Special Publications of the Oceanographic Research Institute of South Africa* Report No. 1
49. van der Elst, R.P., Bullen, E. 1993. The ORI-Sedgwicks Marine Linefish Tagging Project Yields results. *Proceedings of the Second South African Marine Linefish Symposium* 2: 64-67
50. van der Elst, R.P., Freitas, A.J. 1987. Long-term Trends in Natal Marine Fisheries. In *Long Term Data Series Relating to Southern Africans Renewable Natural Resources: Report of South African National Scientific Programs.* eds. MacDonald, I.A.W., Crawford, R.J.M. pp. 76-84
51. van der Elst, R.P., Garratt, P.A. 1984. *Draft Management Proposals for the Natal Deep Reef Linefishery.* Oceanographic Research Institute Report No. 36

52. van der Elst, R.P., Penney, A. 1995. Strategies for Data Collection in Marine Recreational and Commercial Linefisheries of South Africa. In Recreational Fishing: What is the Catch? *Australian Society for Fish Biology Workshop Proceedings*, ed. Hancock, D.A. pp. 31-41. Australian Society for Fish Biology: Canberra
53. Wallace, J. H., van der Elst, R.P. 1983. *Marine Linefish Program Priority Species List*. Report for South African National Scientific Programs No. 70
54. Watkins, C.W., Barrett, M., Paine, J.R. 1996. *Private Protected Areas: A Preliminary Study of Private Initiatives to Conserve Biodiversity in Selected African Countries*. World Conservation and Monitoring Center (WCMC), Cambridge

Concluding Remarks

This book summarizes most of the existing knowledge on coral reefs in the western Indian Ocean region, but much remains in the specialized papers, theses and reports which formed the basis for this review. The quoted literature will form a basis for advanced students to explore. Clearly, there is an impressive amount of information and most of it has accumulated since the descriptive reviews of the geology, and coral and fish fauna in the 1970s [1,2]. Much of the recent research has been driven by a desire to understand the factors that degrade reefs, and to search for ways to manage reefs. So, although much remains to be learned, these later studies provide a basis for determining the general status and threats to reefs and guidelines for their management.

State of Knowledge

Investigations in much of the region are still restricted to descriptive field studies of the flora and fauna in different regions and reef locations. Despite a fair number of descriptive studies (Chapter 1) further exploration and surprises await as shown by recent descriptions of flourishing reefs in areas previously thought to be poor in coral reefs, such as northern Somalia (Box 9.1) and the deep-water banks of Chagos (Chapter 15). Despite the recognition that the regional species pool is fairly similar (Chapter 1) there has been insufficient effort to classify the species composition of reefs by the ecological factors that affect them. There is, however, an increasing focus on the factors or processes that affect species diversity patterns and these combined with more descriptive studies will, hopefully, form a basis for this needed ecological or species composition classification. For instance, investigations on the nutrified reefs of Reunion or sedimented reefs of Kenya have taken the descriptive approach and applied it to the study of environmental and human influences. Further, studies on Kenyan reefs suggest that fishing is dominating species and functional-group composition (Chapter 7). Given the recognition of the extent of over or destructive fishing reflected in these chapters, reefs can now be ecologically classified as much on management status as physico-chemical and geographic or geophysical influences. More studies that take advantage of human-induced or natural gradients of environmental influence are needed to clarify the role of the natural and human environment on reef ecology.

Major Threats

Nearly all of the regions studied, even the remote Chagos, report changes in reefs that are likely to have some human cause ranging from overfishing to global warming. The most frequently repeated human-induced threats to reefs in this region are overfishing, nutrification and sedimentation and they appear to exist nearly region wide, albeit on different scales. For instance, large predatory sharks appear to have been overfished in the Chagos during the last 20 years (Chapter 15), while even small reef fishes are showing signs of overfishing in East Africa (Chapters 5, 6, 7). Recognition of these threats and their extent in the different countries should provide the basis for actions that will reduce the detrimental influences on reef ecology. Unfortunately, even if the regions' people manage to organize themselves to reduce these local influences, the threat of global warming remains ominous as there are close links between warming, coral bleaching and the death of corals. In 1998, one year after the International Year of the Reef, reefs throughout the region were devastated by warm water El Niño conditions and lost over half their coral cover (Box 2.3). If this warm water is part of the global warming signal, it remains to be seen what the sum effect will be on coral reefs and their recovery from this loss, but further investigations are greatly needed.

Interaction with other Ecosystems and Species

Coral reefs are only one of a number of marine ecosystems found in this region (Chapter 1) and they interact strongly with seagrass, plankton, mangrove and other ecosystems. Changes in any of these neighboring ecosystems are likely to influence coral reef ecology and management of all ecosystems is needed to insure that they all flourish. Additionally, a number of species including turtles, sharks, and many fishes and invertebrates move among these ecosystems. Their survival may depend on this movement and they may influence each of these ecosystems in important and different ways. The book's focus on coral reefs does not negate the importance of other important marine species and ecosystems but attempts to show their degree of importance with respect to coral reefs, for comparison with other published works.

Resource Use and Human Population Issues

The chapter reviews remind us that people have explored and exploited reefs in this region for decades and even centuries, therefore many reefs cannot, presently, be seen independently from this human influence. The region's human population and poverty continue to rise and efforts are being made to extract more from reefs and the marine environment in the face of true ecological and thermodynamic limits. We are entering a new era where the hope for sustaining or, perhaps, increasing these resources is closely tied to conservation efforts that protect species and their ecosystems. Increased efforts are needed to recognize the limits of exploitation and human population increases. Further efforts are also required to find and maintain an ecological balance that sufficiently supports people and their culture, rather than one that is a result of poverty and associated lack of planning and management.

The Future

We hope this book will stimulate further efforts to understand and manage coral reefs in the region and that it will form a basis for identifying critical scientific and management problems. Beyond the ecological investigations mentioned above, efforts are needed to try and test various management approaches, such as different harvesting restrictions, and alternative methods of resource production, such as aquaculture and brick making. Clearly much remains to be known and done and we hope this book will stimulate the next round of scientific and management questions and projects.

References

1. Endean, R., Jones, O.A. 1976. *Biology and Geology of Coral Reefs: The Indian Ocean.* London: Academic Press
2. Zoological Society of London. 1971. Reports of the Indian Ocean Expedition. *Symposium of the Zoological Society of London*, vol. 28

Index